Africa—ANGRY
YOUNG GIANT

Africa—ANGRY YOUNG GIANT

Smith Hempstone

FREDERICK A. PRAEGER, *Publisher*

New York

BOOKS THAT MATTER

Published in the United States of America in 1961
by Frederick A. Praeger, Inc., Publisher
64 University Place, New York 3, N.Y.

© Smith Hempstone 1961

Library of Congress Catalog Card Number: 61-15893

Printed in the United States of America

For
W S R
who made it possible
and
KITTY
who made it fun

CONTENTS

CONTENTS

MAPS

11

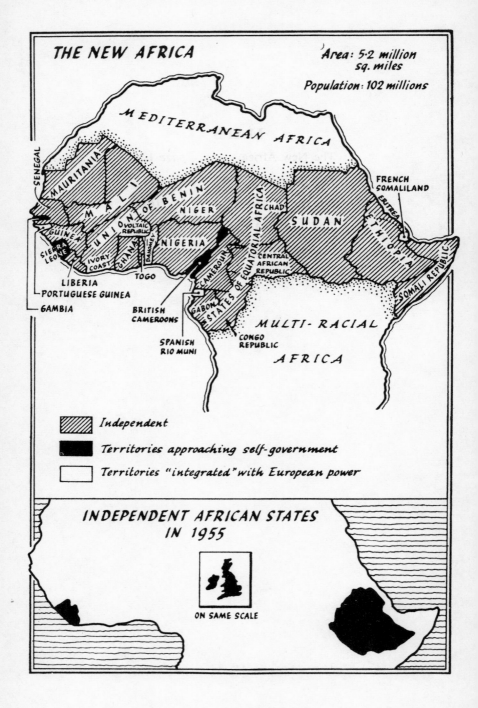

THE NEW AFRICA

Area: 5·2 million sq. miles

Population: 102 millions

MEDITERRANEAN AFRICA

SENEGAL

MAURITANIA

MALI

UNION OF BENIN

NIGER

CHAD

SUDAN

FRENCH SOMALILAND

ERITREA

ETHIOPIA

GUINEA

VOLTAIC REPUBLIC

NIGERIA

STATES OF EQUATORIAL AFRICA

CENTRAL AFRICAN REPUBLIC

SOMALI REPUBLIC

SIERRA LEONE

IVORY COAST

GHANA

DAHOMEY

TOGO

CAMEROUN

GABON

LIBERIA

PORTUGUESE GUINEA

GAMBIA

BRITISH CAMEROONS

SPANISH RIO MUNI

CONGO REPUBLIC

MULTI-RACIAL

AFRICA

///// Independent

■■ Territories approaching self-government

☐ Territories "integrated" with European power

INDEPENDENT AFRICAN STATES IN 1955

ON SAME SCALE

INTRODUCTION

In the autumn of 1956, through the generosity of a donor who wishes to remain anonymous, it became possible for me to take a leave of absence from my paper, the Washington *Evening Star*, and to journey to Africa. It was my intention to live for two and a half years south of the Sahara, to listen, to travel, to learn as much as I could and then, if I felt I had anything to say, to write about it all.

I came to Africa equipped with the usual prejudices and perhaps a few unusual ones. My mind, however, was reasonably uncluttered with misinformation, facts or ideas about the continent. It presented a clean slate for Africa to write upon.

In the course of our thirty months in Africa, my wife (who not only typed the manuscript but changed many a tyre and handled the tedious administrative details of living which often become so irritating to the white man in the tropics) and I travelled some 70,000 miles through forty nations and dependencies. Since I was determined to avoid the distortions which necessarily arise when one's knowledge is limited to visits to the big cities with perspective-foreshortening plane flights in between, we covered all but a few miles of this distance in a light lorry which came spanking new off the quay at Massawa and did yeoman service until we abandoned it in the Gambia. It is now in the possession of a Bathurst Syrian who plays the organ and is a renowned weight-lifter. May he treat it kindly for it served us well.

Before we were through, I had interviewed more than 1,000 labour leaders, priests, agricultural officers, teachers, black nationalists, white settlers, merchants, miners, bums, physicians, housewives, chiefs and witch-doctors, and had quenched my thirst—and Africa produces some monumental ones—with twice that number.

Such is the essential ego of all writers that, when we clambered aboard the jaunty little French mail boat which was to take us from Dakar back to Europe, I felt I did have something worth saying. The question was what to say and how to say it.

The books about Africa which I read had, for the most part, been aimed either at the specialist or at the travelogue audience. I had

13

no wish to ignore the specialists because I believed that I had new information which would be of value to them. On the other hand, I believed (and still do) so firmly in the present and future importance of Africa that it seemed to me that the continent should no longer be their exclusive preserve, that it had become imperative that the intelligent layman should have a working knowledge of the great forces which have been unleashed on this ancient and ageless continent. There were those who told me that such an audience does not exist. I prefer to believe that it does and, if it does not, to attempt to create it.

Having decided to whom I was writing, I next had to define in my own mind the scope of the book. At first I had thought to cover the whole of Africa south of the Sahara. But I soon realized that, to treat the material as seriously as it deserved, I would have to confine myself to a smaller area. In addition, as we travelled around Africa, it became increasingly obvious that the political and economic problems of the continent were sharply divided depending upon the extent and permanency of white settlement in the area observed.

So this book deals only with the emergent African states south of the Sahara and north of the Congo, an area which I have chosen to call the New Africa because it produces new nations in litters. At least seventeen new flags will go up this year and all of these nations are either on their own or will be within five years. Here is taking place the great experiment of African freedom. I hope in a succeeding book to trace the threads of conflict between the races which temper the lives of all those Africans, black, white and brown, who live south of the Congo.

The canvas which I have chosen is far from cramped: the New Africa consists of twenty-six countries with an area two-thirds again the size of the continental U.S. with a population greater than that of South America, a great land of snow-capped mountains and burning deserts, a reservoir of minerals, hydro-electric power, human resources and space, a dark and untouched treasure trove which an over-populated and under-fed world needs more desperately than it knows.

The people of Africa, who are as different from each other as Swedes are from Japanese, were extraordinarily and almost invariably kind to us, whatever their shade of pigmentation or degree of civilization. They shared what they had with us, whether it was a meal of rat and cassava or a dinner at Government House, and through their hospitality we learned much not only about them but about ourselves. They have our thanks.

This book has not been footnoted because it is not a document of record but a means of communication and footnoting, I feel, destroys the flow of a narrative. There are many excellent books about Africa and those to which I owe most are listed at the end of this volume. I hope that reading this book will lead at least a few to cultivate an interest in what to me is the most fascinating of all continents.

There is this about Africa: it is an out-sized continent filled to such an extent with cruelty and kindness, with joy and sadness, with monumental sins and great compassion, that it seems to inspire in the stranger either loathing or a curious passion and fascination. Nowhere are there greater opportunities for good or for evil, for the recognition of one's essential character. After only six months away from here, we found the pull of Africa intolerable.

And now we are back and I am content.

Timau, Kenya   S.H.
March 1960

I

THE HORN

Chapter 1

————————————*————————————

HALFWAY HOUSE

The engines changed their pitch, the Dutch airliner dropped her flaps, banked over the Nile of the Caesars and the Ptolemys, and went into the approach run. Beneath us, smudge pots burst into flame as shadowy figures flitted back and forth along the edge of the main runway. We came in too fast, bumped hard once, the brakes screaming, and shuddered to a stop.

And so thirty months in Africa had their beginning. As the door was flung open, the pale stars of dawn began to fade into the heat of a new day. Here was Khartoum, the capital of the Sudan, a nation which is a bridge between Africa and Asia, Islam and Christianity, an ideological halfway house.

Of all the nations of this new and independent Africa, which stretches almost 5,000 miles from the Indian to the Atlantic Ocean, the Sudan is among the most vibrant, interesting and puzzling. It is a tremendous land, the largest independent nation in Africa and bigger than all the NATO countries of Europe combined. Put another way, the Sudan, if superimposed upon a map of the United States, would stretch from Bangor, Maine, to Miami, Florida, from the Atlantic Ocean to the Mississippi River. Although the British ruled the Sudan—with the assistance of the Egyptians—for fifty-seven years, the Sudan was never a British colony and is not now a member of the Commonwealth. It was ruled instead as a condominium under the Foreign Office, a unique arrangement of which we shall hear more later.

This vast country, two-thirds of which is very difficult or impossible to develop because of lack of water and desperate climatic conditions, is bounded on the north by Egypt and Libya, on the west by the independent French African republics of Chad and Central Africa, on the south by the ex-Belgian Congo and the British dependencies of Uganda and Kenya, and on the east is the Red Sea coast which gives the Sudan access to the world through Port Sudan, and Ethiopia.

Although the Sudan was born in a *götterdämmerung* of blood and fire, the British never needed more than one battalion of troops to garrison the Sudan's one million square miles. Credit for this must go largely to the Sudan Political Service, an *élite* corps of British administrators never numbering more than a hundred and fifty men. This little group of lonely men, often serving as doctor, administrator, judge, social worker, policeman and priest among wild and unruly people, in fifty-seven years made it possible for the Sudanese nation to be born. No written examination was required for the Sudan Political Service for the very good reason that only honours graduates of the best British universities, most of them top athletes, were even considered.

The Sudan is a shimmeringly hot country and temperatures as high as 126·5 degrees have been registered. In June an oven-hot wind called the *haboob* pelts the cities and scorched fields with desert dust as black as ashes, tempers grow short, and the muezzin's wail comes flat and sorrowful from the minaret of the mosque. What saves the Sudan from becoming a desolation and makes it viable as a nation is the Nile, a great life-giving artery which winds through the country from south to north. From the 6,000-foot-high fastness of the Ethiopian mountains, the Blue Nile tumbles from Lake Tana, a bouncing, turbulent stream which supplies 84 per cent of the flow of the main Nile. When in its August spate the Blue Nile's rate of discharge is forty times as great as at low water. It roars down from the highlands bearing thousands of tons of Ethiopian top-soil, floods its banks when it reaches the plains of the Sudan and races on to Khartoum, where its boisterous flow backs up the more placid White Nile, which rises in Uganda's Lake Victoria. The White Nile loses much of its thrust and a distressingly high percentage of its water by evaporation in the bogs of the southern Sudan. In contrast to the Blue Nile, at spate its rate of discharge is only six times greater than at low water. The Nile is navigable on a year-round basis for more than 1,000 miles from Juba, in the deep south, to Khartoum. North of Khartoum, one 200-mile stretch is navigable but the rest is broken by cataracts, a transportation bottleneck but also an untapped source of hydro-electric power. In its entire course through the Sudan, which as the athletically-inclined crow would fly is about as far as from Nova Scotia to Mexico, the Nile is bridged exactly four times, all in or near Khartoum. The Nile breathes life into the baking Sudan and gives it an economy which, although supplementary to some extent to that of Egypt, its northern neighbour, is also competitive. The struggle for the waters of this great river, as we shall see, contains all the elements necessary to provoke a clash between the two countries.

Black porters wearing brown burlap smocks and green turbans

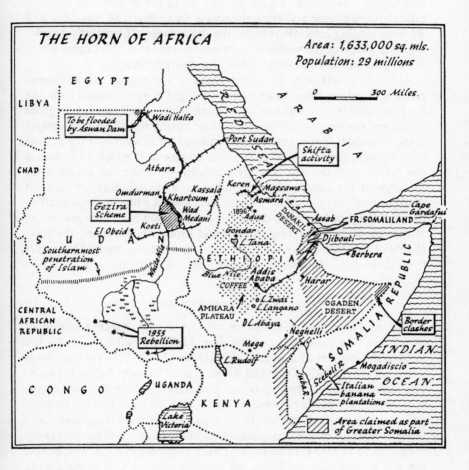

THE HORN OF AFRICA

Area: 1,633,000 sq. mls.
Population: 29 millions

0   300 Miles.

EGYPT

LIBYA

CHAD

To be flooded
by Aswan Dam

Wadi Halfa

Atbara

Port Sudan

ARABIA

Shifta
activity

Keren   Massawa
Kassala   Asmara
Omdurman   Khartoum
Gezira   Wad   1896   Adua   DANAKIL   Cape
Scheme   Medani   DESERT   Gardafui
El Obeid   Kosti   Assab   FR. SOMALILAND

SUDAN

Southernmost
penetration
of Islam

Gondar
•L.Tana

Djibouti
•Berbera

ETHIOPIA

Blue Nile•Addis
Ababa
COFFEE

Harar

CENTRAL
AFRICAN
REPUBLIC

AMHARA
PLATEAU

•L.Zwai
•L.Langano

OGADEN
DESERT

1955
Rebellion

•L.Abaya

Neghelli

Border
clashes

Mega

•L.Rudolf

INDIAN

CONGO   UGANDA

KENYA

Lake
Victoria

SOMALIA REPUBLIC

Scebeli R   Mogadiscio   OCEAN

Juba R.   Italian
banana
plantations

Area claimed as part
of Greater Somalia

shuffled sleepily out of the gloom of the unlit air terminal on horny bare feet. In their wake came Arab officials trim in flared British shorts and brown knee-socks. Lights blinked on in the terminal as customs officials were roused and the bar opened. In an hour, all was done and we were rattling into Khartoum—the name means 'Elephant's Trunk', after the shape of the wedge of land between the two Niles upon which the city stands—in a venerable bus of unknown vintage.

Although it was only six o'clock, the city was awake: tall Sudanese, ranging in colour from darkest ebony to light brown nomads from the northern desert, clad alike in shin-length white robes, orange or green skull-caps perched on the backs of their heads, rolled up their prayer mats, stretched, spat expressively, wandered off in search of the minute cups of thick, sweet Turkish coffee without several of which no Sudanese can get through the day. The great golden eye of the sun peeped over the edge of the desert, giving promise of a blistering day. Pint-sized donkeys and shaggy, saddle-worn camels loaded with firewood shuffled through the powdery white dust of winter; a radio blared Arabic music at a raucous decibel rating. Syrian and Greek shopkeepers, the merchants of the Nile valley for generations past, threw back the shutters from their store windows and glanced unlovingly at the sun.

PROGRESS AND PARADOX

You soon learn that this Muslim country is very much a nation of paradoxes. The big holiday of the year, Mulid en-Nabi, celebrates the birth of the Prophet Mohammed on October 17, A.D. 571. Yet Christmas is also an official day of rest and 40 per cent of the population is pagan. The Sudan considers itself to be an Arab nation, yet, in the last census, only 39 per cent of the population was so classified and half the Sudan's people speak no Arabic at all. There are 115 indigenous languages. Only three of the twenty-six professors at the country's lone university (which has a 56,000-volume library) were Sudanese in 1958. The British put £40 million into the Sudan for development projects in the decade before independence and the Sudanese have spent an equal amount since independence, yet the Sudan remains one of Africa's more primitive countries. There are more domestic animals than people (6·9 million cattle, an equal number of sheep, 5·8 million goats, 1·4 million camels, 500,000 donkeys and 100,000 horses, worth together £183 million) and the Sudan is an ornithologist's delight with its 871 species of birds. Although there are no paved roads to run them over, the Sudan has seventeen mobile cinema vans, a valuable educational weapon in a nation where illiteracy is rampant. Although the Sudan has produced more than forty lawyers since the first attorney passed the bar in 1938 and has a progressive legal code modelled after that of the British, the Mohammedan personal law, the *sharia*, is an integral part of the civil law of the country. Despite the fact that twenty-five women attend the University of Khartoum, many Sudanese tribes still practise pharaonic circumcision on their girls. Although the Sudan is ringed with twenty-one airfields and outdoor movie theatres dot the country-side, there is no all-weather road from north to south and as late as 1945 many tribesmen paid their taxes in cattle.

Radio Omdurman, the official Sudanese station, is heard as far afield as Sweden or the United States and eleven daily newspapers flourish in Khartoum, yet nine out of every ten Sudanese can neither read nor write. A force of 170 Sudanese doctors staffing 400 hospitals and clinics have all but eliminated smallpox, typhus, yellow fever, cholera, yaws, relapsing fever and cerebro-spinal meningitis and a fully-equipped hospital ship noses into the remote southern swamps to treat recalcitrant tribesmen. But no one has figured out how to rid the country of the *nimitti*, swarms of midges which make life along the river unpleasant for most of the winter. The northern Sudanese is one of the world's natural gentlemen, yet his customary way of addressing a southern countryman is *abid*, slave. The country is ruled by a conservative military junta, yet the Sudan's well-developed trade union movement is 70 per cent controlled by Communists. And lastly, the Sudanese Army, more efficient and driven by a greater *esprit de corps* than any other fighting force in the Muslim world, with the possible exception of Jordan's Arab Legion, has less than a dozen southern officers, all subalterns. This is a complex and devious land still in search of a definition of itself, one in which sweeping generalities have a habit of boomeranging.

The Three Cities—Khartoum, the government centre, Omdurman, the great native city, and Khartoum North, the industrial area—are the heart of the Sudan as the desert is its soul. Omdurman, which stands across the White Nile from Khartoum, is the biggest of the three with a population of more than 150,000. Omdurman, which boasts no less than fifty mosques, is a city of red-mud houses, many of them ringed with Madras thorn, which the Sudanese call *Tamr al-Hindi*, through which run sandy streets. It is throbbing with life, timeless, hospitable, surprisingly clean, smelling of coffee, onions, sacking, sandalwood and spices, vibrant with the sound of a thousand radios blaring at top volume. To the American ear, no matter how dull the subject under discussion, the announcer's voice always seems to reach an hysterical pitch. The streets are crowded with people, rich and poor alike wearing the flowing white *ghalabia* and turban, surely the most democratic costume in the world.

Khartoum (population 85,000), which a holy man established as a village in 1691 and the Egyptians made the capital in 1825, is sedate and orderly and has a governmental air which reeks of dossiers and development plans, budgets and bureaucracy. Streetcars rattle down paved, well-shaded streets whose names are posted both in English and Arabic. It is a flat city, ideally suited for rickshaws. These were introduced in 1904 but flopped because the proud Sudanese reckoned that they were not draught animals. The shops are porticoed against the blinding sun and each block boasts several coffee shops gay with the clatter of *tric-trac*, a vigorous sort of backgammon which is the Sudanese national game.

The fifty-eight-year-old Grand Hotel, which ranks with Cairo's Shepheard's (burned by an Egyptian mob in 1952) and Singapore's Raffles as one of the great colonial British hostelries, is the centre of the city's social life. Here waiters in white *ghalabias* and wide green sashes scurry among the tables on the terrace to slake Khartoum's thirst, while enormous ceiling fans hum from the lobby. It is all very *pukka sahib* but the *ancien régime* note is quelled by the sight of a team of burly Bulgarian wrestlers, bound for the People's Republic of China, working out in sweatshirts on the river front and registering prim Marxian disapproval. Near the hotel is the old Governor-General's palace and its Kitchener Tree. This is one of a thousand gummeiza cuttings planted by the conqueror of the Sudan. White ants, which have consumed so much of what the white man has tried to create in Africa, ate the other nine hundred and ninety-nine.

Although Khartoum is a city of clubs—there are more than one hundred and fifty in the Three Cities—the Sudan Cultural Centre, which used to be a British Junior Officers' Club, is the only real rival of the Grand Hotel's terrace as a meeting place for Khartoum's *élite*. There the tone is more intellectual, for the Centre boasts a library of 7,500 volumes in English and Arabic, and more than 1,000 members of eight nationalities. Much of the international air of Khartoum is provided by the city's 3,000 Greeks, 550 Armenians and 350 Jews. But Islam's force is felt here, too, and although alcohol is served, Tuesday is Ladies' Day at the swimming pool. Khartoum North, which has a population of 50,000, contains the Three Cities' brewery, match factory and other light industry and is no rival as far as either interest or beauty go, to the other two.

A WORD ABOUT HISTORY

Man has lived in the Sudan for at least one million years and the valley of the Nile, which wanders more than 4,000 miles from the lakes of central Africa to the Mediterranean, may well be the cradle of civilization, rather than the Euphrates. About four centuries before Christ the *sagia*, the ox-driven water-wheel which still plays a vital role in the country's economy, was introduced to the Sudan. At the same time came camels, brought with them by the Persians when Cambysses invaded Egypt in 525 B.C. Homer knew of the Sudan and his countrymen came here, as they still do, to barter cloth, wine and trinkets for gum arabic, spices and slaves. Nero sent a reconnaissance expedition far up the river but the commander's experience with the *Sudd* (Arabic for 'obstruction'), a vast and impenetrable papyrus swamp in the southern Sudan, dissuaded the emperor from any thoughts of conquest. During the reign of Justinian, many Sudanese kingdoms were converted to Christianity and churches dotted the great sweep of the Nile until the spread of militant Islam in the sixteenth century.

Modern Sudanese history, oddly enough, owes much to Napoleon. It was the Corsican's victory in 1797 at the Battle of the Pyramids which shook the power of the Mamelukes, the Caucasian ruling class of Egypt, and paved the way for the rise to power of the Albanian soldier-of-fortune, Mohammed Ali. Although he owed nominal allegiance to the Sultan of Turkey, whose *khedive* or lieutenant he was, Mohammed Ali was the founder of modern Egypt. After smashing victories in Arabia, Syria and Greece, he turned his eyes to the South, dreaming of a great Egyptian empire stretching from the Mediterranean to the lakes. Farouk and Nasser have had the same vision.

Mohammed Ali sent his third son Ismail at the head of 10,000 men across the desert and, by 1821, all of north and central Sudan was his. For the first time, the Sudan—the name means 'Land of Blacks' and was once applied to most of Africa—began to take shape as a political entity. Mohammed Ali's grandson, who became khedive as Lee's regiments began their dusty march to Gettysburg, extended the borders of his southern satrapies through the efforts of a band of European

25

mercenaries, explorers and administrators which included 'Chinese' Gordon, Sir Samuel Baker, and the Austrian adventurers, Emin Pasha and Rudolph Slatin.

Egyptian control, where it existed, was often corrupt and avaricious; where it did nŏt, small private armies led by the hard-cases of the world ravaged the land in search of slaves and gold. The government itself launched slave-catching expeditions against the Nuba in the West, drove the Negroes of the South deep into the swamps in search of sanctuary. The political chickens hatched from the warmth of burning southern villages are coming home to roost today.

Purification was to come, as it has since the world was young, from the desert. Mohammed Ahmed, the son of an unremarkable Dongola boat-builder, was born in 1844. The boy, who bore the three small cuts on each cheek which are the tribal marks of the Danagla, grew into a man of medium height, almost black in colour. This soft-spoken young tribesman with the projecting forehead and the bright, piercing eyes soon demonstrated a marked mystic bent and, as a young man, retired to Aba Island, 150 miles south of Khartoum, to live the life of a religious recluse. Soon word of his asceticism and piety spread far. In 1881, Mohammed Ahmed, who even at the height of his temporal power never owned more than a single garment, proclaimed himself to be the Mahdi, the second great prophet, come to the salvation of his people. At his side was one Abdallahi, a strong, ruthless man, who believed it was his destiny to achieve fame in the service of a great reformer.

Embittered by years of oppression and misrule, the tribes of the west rallied to the Mahdi's call for a war against the infidels and despots. In battle after battle his white-robed hosts routed their Egyptian over-lords and fanned a flame of fanaticism which was to crackle down the Nile like a wind-blown bush fire and engulf the entire Sudan, cause the death of millions, topple a British government, and lay the foundations of the modern Sudan. By early 1884, the Mahdi was master of all Sudan save Khartoum, the capital.

SIEGE OF KHARTOUM

Britain, who meanwhile had moved into Egypt, resolved that the Sudan could not be held and sent General Charles Gordon, a former Governor-General of the Sudan under the Khedive, to evacuate Khartoum. No man could have been more ill-fitted for such a routine and humiliating job. Gordon was an impetuous mystic, of the stamp of

Stonewall Jackson and Orde Wingate, and in his character he combined a curious mixture of faith in himself and Calvinistic fatalism. Gordon, who had served brilliantly in many parts of the world and earned the nickname 'Chinese' for his bravery in that country, evacuated many civilians and continued to hold Khartoum after it was cut off and besieged by the Mahdi's *Ansar*, which is Arabic for 'helpers'. As more and more white-robed *Ansar* trekked in from outlying districts to join in the siege, the little Scot shored up the flimsy fortifications of Khartoum with his rag-tail army of 7,000, kept the city's 30,000 civilians calm, and dispatched riders across the desert asking for help.

As the hot summer days burned out, disease and starvation began to take their toll and it became obvious that help would not come in time. The garrison, which had long since devoured all the camels, cattle, horses, donkeys and dogs in the city, was reduced to eating unripe grain, mice, crickets and cockroaches. There was no money to pay the troops. This the General remedied by issuing scrip bearing his own promise to pay. Gordon refused all surrender offers but allowed all those who wished to do so to leave the city and make their peace with the Mahdi. It is an index of Gordon's dynamism and strength of character that he, a Christian, was able to keep his Muslim subjects at his side when death could be the only outcome. A British expedition was making its way leisurely across the desert. But one of its senior officers had an attack of boils and the column was forced to slow its pace because of his discomfort.

As the result, after a siege of 317 days, the Mahdi's dervish hordes breached the defences, speared Gordon to death on the steps of the Governor-General's palace, put the garrison to the sword and razed Khartoum. Two days later, the British relief force arrived to find the city a smoking, vulture-covered wreck. The column returned to Egypt and the Sudan was left to thirteen years of horror and misery which were to surpass even the worst phases of the Khedive's administration.

Five months after the fall of Khartoum, the Mahdi died of typhus, asking those about him to lay him on the ground for 'only on the earth would I meet my God', and was succeeded by the Khalifa (lieutenant) Abdallahi. Scarcely had the Khalifa, a giant of a man, light-skinned, big-voiced and lacking in the Mahdi's spiritual qualities, come to power when the Sudan was embroiled in a series of civil wars. On the heels of this came famine and a plague of locusts. In outlying areas where the Khalifa's writ bore little authority, free-lance slavers began large-scale operations. Fields lay waste, trade was at a standstill, the administrative system broken down, fire and pestilence ravaged the land. In all, it is estimated that five million of the Sudan's 8·5 million people died or were killed during the period of Mahdist rule.

Forces were at work now, however, to end this rule. In 1895, a wind-broken and footsore camel bearing a wreck of a man dressed in Arab clothes staggered into southern Egypt. This was Rudolph Slatin, one of Gordon's lieutenants, who was escaping across the desert after ten years as a Mahdist captive. Slatin's story, which received wide publicity, stirred British pride. Perhaps a more potent factor was the fact that now the scramble for Africa was on and French patrols, pushing in from the Senegal, had reached Lake Chad and were approaching the Nile Valley. To avenge an old defeat and to forestall French occupation of the upper reaches of the Nile, Britain determined to reconquer the Sudan.

General Herbert Kitchener launched a drive up the Nile which was to culminate in one of the most one-sided victories in the annals of warfare. Kitchener took his time, built a railway (which has since vanished, its rails and sleepers used as building material by the villagers), hauled much of his army up the Nile by boat. By September 1898 he had assembled a force of 26,000 men, 3,500 camels and 2,500 horses, and 40 guns outside the walls of Omdurman, the new Sudanese city built across the Nile from Khartoum. The Khalifa had 60,000 fanatical *Ansar* under his banner. As Kitchener's guns smashed the Mahdi's tomb into rubble, the Khalifa ordered the attack.

Across an open plain outside Omdurman came the Mahdist horde in a great dense mass of white which measured five miles from flank to flank. The modern weapons of the Anglo-Egyptian force mowed them down like wheat but still, as the sun rose higher in the sky, screaming *Ansar* waving battle flags hurled themselves against the wall of steel. The gunboats on the Nile opened up and the cavalry, which included a young lieutenant named Winston S. Churchill, made spirited charges into the swirling mass of bloodstained robes. In four hours the battle was over and the Khalifa a fugitive. *Ansar* losses were 10,800 killed and 16,000 wounded. The British lost 48 killed and 382 wounded.

Kitchener entered Omdurman as a conqueror. The Khalifa, who wore boots to conceal a lame leg, fled into the desert where he was killed in action two months later. Britain and Egypt signed a condominium agreement to jointly administer the Sudan on January 19, 1899. Thus ended the agony of the Sudan.

Kitchener, after checkmating a French expedition which had reached the Nile at Fashoda after a march of terrible privation from the West Coast, took stock of the Sudan. There were no schools, law courts or hospitals worthy of the name. Trade was precarious and travel dangerous. The country was still seething against the 'Turks'—as Sudanese to this day term any foreigner—pestilence and poverty stalked the land. Kitchener reacted in a spirit which has since characterized Anglo-Sudanese relations: he launched a successful appeal for funds to build Gordon College, now a part of the University of Khartoum, a fully-accredited co-educational institution granting its own degrees in a wide range of studies including law, medicine and engineering, and enjoying a mutually profitable exchange programme with North-western University. Three years after the battle of Omdurman, Gordon College had 149 students and primary schools were springing up like thorn bushes from the desert soil.

After twelve years of peaceful British administration, the Sudan's revenue had increased seventeenfold, its expenditures tripled, and its budget reached a balanced state which was to be maintained until 1958.

In theory, Britain and Egypt jointly ruled the Sudan for the fifty-seven years after the fall of Omdurman until the country's declaration of independence on January 1, 1956. In fact, the Sudan has been a British show. Although the Governor-General, always a Briton, was appointed by the Khedive on the recommendation of the British Government, policy decisions not made in Khartoum came from London. In the first half of the condominium, Egypt supplied minor civil servants and troops, made a contribution to the Sudanese budget and bore the major part of the cost of the military occupation of the country.

Mounting Egyptian nationalism in the period after the First World War, the slogan of which was then as it is now, 'Unity of the Nile Valley', culminated in 1924 in the assassination in the streets of Cairo of Sir Lee Stack, Governor-General of the Sudan and Commander-in-Chief of the Egyptian army. Egyptian agents succeeded in stirring up a revolt of one Sudanese battalion in Khartoum and the reaction of the British was to expel all Egyptian officials from the Sudan. After the Anglo-Egyptian *entente* of 1936, a few Egyptians were allowed to return to the country in minor posts.

INDEPENDENCE

The signing of the 1936 agreement stimulated Sudanese nationalists who objected both to the return of the Egyptians and to the fact that

29

other nations were deciding their destiny. Expression of this feeling was seen in the formation, under the leadership of Ismail al-Azhari, of the Graduates' Congress, membership in which was open to those Sudanese with more than an elementary school education. The outbreak of World War II, in which Sudanese troops served with distinction, froze the nationalist movement until the 1940s.

By 1945, two political parties were in the field. The National Unionist Party, led by al-Azhari, a stocky bull of a man who wears glasses and sports a bristling moustache, demanded union of the Sudan and Egypt under the Egyptian crown. Al-Azhari, a school teacher educated at Gordon College and the American University of Beirut, had the support of Sayed Sir Ali el Mirghani, leader of a powerful religious sect of which we will hear more later. The Umma ('People's') Party, backed by the late Sayed Sir Abdel Rahman el Mahdi, a posthumous son of the founder of the *Ansar*, demanded independence and no links with Egypt.

These two religious leaders, known respectively in the Sudan as SAM and SAR, were bitter enemies. It was felt in some quarters that the Mahdi hoped to make himself king of an independent Sudan and this, rather than any love of Egypt, was what drove SAM to support al-Azhari.

After Naguib and Nasser ousted Farouk in 1952, Egypt agreed to the election of a Sudanese parliament which would decide within three years whether the Sudan was to become independent or to join Egypt. Naguib and Nasser obviously had a vested interest in which party won the election. Sudanese estimate that Egypt poured £4.3 million into the Sudan to ensure al-Azhari's election. A bargain rate at which to buy a country four times the size of Texas. As the date for the Sudan's first national election approached, campaigning reached a fever pitch. Egyptian Major Salah Salem arrived on a 'good will mission' and danced a frenzied fandango in his undershorts to woo tribal voters for the pro-Egyptian National Unionist Party. Election officials in the interior faced problems seldom encountered in America, even west of the Appalachians: nomads had to be tracked to the water-holes to obtain their ballots, officials in Nuba country tore their hair over the tribe's custom of naming all eldest sons 'Cuckoo', while in the east the practice of new names for everybody after the annual wrestling matches somewhat complicated voter identification. As things worked out, al-Azhari's N.U.P. came to power and Cairo shouted its joy.

But al-Azhari, the Prime Minister, saw things in a different light from al-Azhari, the campaigner and two-time server of jail sentences for sedition. As Nasser replaced Naguib, who is half Sudanese and popular south of the border, the Sudan's enthusiasm for union cooled. At the same time, Sudanese intellectuals found the vision of nationhood increasingly attractive. Al-Azhari startled the world by demanding and receiving independence on January 1, 1956.

Al-Azhari, although he is the son of a religious leader, rallied to his banner most of the young educated Sudanese whose exposure to Western ideas had impelled them to reject the ties of traditionalism and secularism. This led to disenchantment on SAM's part, he withdrew his support shortly after independence, formed his own People's Democratic Party, and brought down the government. SAM and SAR, the old enemies, joined forces to create an Umma-P.D.P. coalition which promptly destroyed the Sudan's first currency issue because the notes bore al-Azhari's signature and they feared circulation of the bills might make propaganda for their political foe. With some support from the Southern Liberals, the third political grouping, this coalition ruled the Sudan from July 1956 to November 1958.

THE COUP

There followed one of the most tragic events of modern Africa's political history: the first—and probably not the last—collapse of a democratic government. In the early hours of November 17, trucks loaded with crack units of the Sudanese army rolled out of their barracks near the city and sped through the darkened streets. As the wind sighed softly in the banyan trees which line the Nile, contingents seized the radio station, the telephone exchange and the airport. Armoured cars prowled through the city's streets, designed with imperial self-confidence by Kitchener in the form of a Union Jack, special squads were posted at key intersections. At 5 a.m., the pro-Western Premier Abdullah Khalil and his Cabinet Ministers were roused, presented with letters stating that their services were no longer required, and advised to consider themselves under house arrest (Khalil and al-Azhari later were awarded £100 per month pensions by the revolutionary régime). At dawn, to the tune of martial music, General Ibrahim Abboud, Commander-in-Chief of the Sudanese army, announced over the radio that he was assuming power and would rule through a thirteen-member army junta. He padlocked all newspapers, banned political parties and forbade meetings or demonstrations. General Abboud, a chubby, congenial man with a reputation for toughness when the situation

31

demands it, declared that democracy in the Sudan was being suspended in the name of 'honesty and integrity'. He asserted that he would try to resolve 'artificially contrived tensions' between Egypt and the Sudan. The U.A.R., which had dubbed the coup an imperialistic plot, quickly changed its line and was the first nation to send congratulations and offer recognition to the new government.

What happened? Why had a country which had had the benefit of what was probably the best colonial administration in all Africa come to this pass? Why had a people long known for its good sense and feeling for fair play had to resort to guns to solve its political problems? Why had a nation with one of the finest African civil services on the continent let democracy die without a complaint?

For there were no complaints. The tough troopers of the Sudanese army had not to fire a shot to end representative government. What little reaction that could be seen in Khartoum was one of relief and approval. Sayed Siddik el Mahdi, president of the Umma Party and son of the religious patriarch who died last year, stated in Rome, where presumably he could speak freely, that he was 'completely confident that anything General Abboud has done is in the interest of the country'. Dr. Ibrahim Anis, then the Sudan's ambassador in Washington, added that 'the government of my country was changed because partisan strife between political parties threatened to bring about a demoralization of our people'. Democracy was dead and none seemed to mourn its passing.

There were a number of reasons why General Khalil's coalition government was in trouble. The first of these was economic. High-grade long-staple cotton accounts for more than half of the Sudan's revenues, 80 per cent of its exports, and almost all of its foreign exchange earnings. Half of the country's eleven million people earn their living from cotton. This appeared to be no bad thing: long-staple cotton prices have been going up steadily for the last twenty years. But, in 1956, the Sudan Gezira Board (we shall hear more of this remarkable agricultural scheme) set the price of its cotton at an artificially high level on the premise that, with the Suez crisis, Egypt's traditional customers would take their cotton where they could find it and would pay high prices. It didn't work that way. The Lancashire mills bought in South America and the United States while France went on purchasing Egyptian cotton. The United States made an incredible political blunder by picking this moment to dump large quantities of surplus American cotton on the world market at bargain-basement prices.

General Khalil, now 72, fired Mekki Abbas, the able ex-Rhodes Scholar who headed the Gezira Board, and cut prices. But the damage was done. At the time the coup took place, 20 per cent of the Sudan's 1957 cotton crop was still unsold, 45 per cent of the 1958 crop was crammed into bulging storehouses, and no buyers were in sight for a bumper 1959 crop. Despite Khalil's imposition of drastic import controls, gold and foreign currency reserves tumbled from £63·5 million to £28·5 million. For the first time in more than forty years, the Sudan was unable to balance its budget. Most of the country's ambitious £133 million five-year development plan had to be junked, unemployment rose, prices and rents spiralled. Ismail al-Azhari's opposition National Unionist Party was not slow to hang the blame for the financial crisis on General Khalil's coalition government.

In addition to his fiscal difficulties, Khalil, whose father was Egyptian, was under heavy fire from the Left for being too pro-Western. His recent negotiation, despite strong protest from the N.U.P., of an £11 million American aid programme coupled with his acceptance of a British arms gift led al-Azhari to predict that Khalil would suffer 'the fate of Nuri as-Said', the murdered Iraqi strong man. Despite pressure from the Sudan's Communist-infiltrated trade unions, Khalil staunchly refused to barter Sudanese cotton with Russia. When United States Marines went into Lebanon, the hard-boiled veteran of thirty-four years in the army declared that he was 'overjoyed', and moved quickly to block an Egyptian attempt to seize a contested border area. When Egypt refused to allow the Sudan to take more than the 8 per cent of the water of the Nile allocated to it by a 1929 Anglo-Egyptian agreement, which the Sudan did not recognize since it was not party to the treaty, Khalil took the water anyway. Not all of Khalil's cabinet was loyal to him. He is an *Ansar*, a follower of the Mahdi, and members of the rival *Khatmia* sect, who were members of his coalition, were inclined to be more pro-Egyptian. At the time when the coup took place, opposition politicians were conducting private negotiations with Nasser which would have weakened Khalil's position for effecting a new division of the Nile's waters.

And, as General Abboud charged when he took power, corruption and inefficiency were not unknown in the Sudan. Corruption is a problem with which every emergent African nation is faced. In part it stems from the fact that the people of this vast band of free Black Africa, stretching from the Eastern Horn to the Bight of Benin, have not fully accepted the Western code of values. For generations, the way to get things done in Africa has been to make a 'present' to the appropriate tribal or clan official. This demonstrates your respect for the official and is an indication that you are a 'solid citizen'. Old practices die slowly. Also, in a poor country where official salaries are comparatively low, honesty is sometimes a luxury which only the very rich can afford. Under circumstances less understandable, we have had our deep-freezes, our minks, our vicuna coats. The charge of inefficiency is also true and stems from the fact that almost all British officials were forced to leave the country before adequate Sudanese replacements were available. Many older Sudanese officials were competent to take over top jobs but there weren't enough of them and their simultaneous promotion left too many weak spots in the lower echelons. The Sudanese Government recognized this and began rehiring Britons and other foreigners—at contract salaries much higher than the original stipends—but it was too late: the machinery of government groaned, wheezed and threatened to come to a standstill.

It became obvious to the two grand old men of Sudanese politics, the late Sayed Abdel Rahman el Mahdi, leader of the *Ansar*, and Sayed Ali el Mirghani, leader of the *Khatmia*, as well as to General Khalil himself, that Khalil's coalition government must fall. To be replaced by what? The only alternatives seemed to be al-Azhari's anti-Western National Unionist Party, the sworn foe of the sects and a party without sufficient support to bring stable government to the Sudan; or worse still, a radical coup led by Leftist army elements and the trade unions which might well signal the end of the Sudanese nation. To forestall either of these unpleasant possibilities, the two religious leaders with General Khalil's prior knowledge apparently arranged the bloodless moderate coup which was to bring General Abboud to power on November 17, 1958.

WHO RUNS THE SUDAN?

Who is really in charge, then? The kingpin of Sudanese politics, Sayed Sir Abdel Rahman el Mahdi, died within a few months of the coup. But no story of the Sudan would be complete without a word about this remarkable man. SAR, who was born in 1885, was a posthumous son of the great mystic who expelled the British and Egyptians from the Sudan and from him he is believed by his followers, who pay him an annual tribute known as *zeka*, to have inherited certain qualities of *baraka*, or divine grace. In the early years of his life, the British, who wanted to be sure that no new Mahdist revolt broke out, kept him under surveillance and granted him the munificent pension of £7 a month. Needless to say, the Mahdi lived quietly and without pretensions. When Turkey entered the First World War at Germany's side, Britain sought to counteract Turkish influence in the Sudan by recognizing SAR's religious and political position. He secured the support of the *Ansar* for the Allied cause and from that day on he grew in stature, wealth and power. Although he never held a public office, he was the master of those who did. He was the power behind the Umma Party and his keen business acumen made him the wealthiest man in the Sudan. He never veered from his goal of independence for his country and when the great day came, the grizzled old man wept for joy, then fainted, overcome by emotion as the Sudanese flag went up for the first time. He was consistently anti-Egyptian—many said he would be king—and ever a staunch friend of Britain and the West. At the hour of his death on March 24, 1959, there was a partial eclipse of the moon, an event which in no way detracted from the belief held by his followers that this was no ordinary man. An estimated 100,000 of these saw him to his final resting-place beside his father's bones at Omdurman. The big question now is whether his forty-nine-year-old son, Sayed Siddik el Mahdi, can command the allegiance of the two million *Ansar* as totally as did his father and, if so, in what direction he will lead them.

SAR was tall, erect, dignified and wore a clipped grey beard going white. He had the bright, piercing eyes and projecting forehead of his father and, like him, spoke in a quiet, determined voice which was seldom raised in anger. His counterpart and lifetime foe, Sayed Sir Ali el Mirghani, head of the *Khatmia*, is physically less imposing but every bit as able as the late Mahdi. SAM is the head of orthodox Islam in the Sudan. The *Ansar* are something close to Muslim heretics to SAM because they believe that the Mahdi is the physical embodiment of an Islamic second-coming.

SAM, who is small and has the liquid eyes of the Levant, was born at Dongola in 1879 and, at the outbreak of the Mahdist rebellion, was taken to Cairo by his pro-British father to study Mohammedan law and doctrine. When Kitchener recaptured Khartoum, SAM was in his train as a captain in the Egyptian army. On the death of his father he became head of the *Khatmia* and, for at least twenty years, was considered the Sudan's unofficial leader. As SAR rose to power, so did SAM's prestige decline and his bitterness against the British grow. To block the Mahdi, SAM threw the support of his two million *Khatmia* to

Ismail al-Azhari, a move which almost cost the Sudan its independence. When al-Azhari started kicking up his secular heels with too much abandon, SAM dumped him and joined with SAR to create the coalition government which ruled the Sudan until the coup. The fact that General Abboud is *Khatmia* indicates that SAM played more than a passive role in engineering the power play which ended representative government in the Sudan. Now that SAR is dead and the new Mahdi's power untested, Sayed Ali el Mirghani is unquestionably the most powerful individual in the Sudan.

Mahdist leaders have a firm grip on the people of the three central provinces of Darfur, Kordofan and Blue Nile; the *Khatmia* are supreme in the three northern provinces of Kassala, Northern and Khartoum. But throughout these six provinces, particularly in the provincial centres and in Khartoum, the bad boy of Sudanese politics musters considerable support.

He is Ismail al-Azhari, a pudgy, ebullient man, the Sudan's voice of tomorrow. Although he is the grandson of a former Grand Mufti of the Sudan, al-Azhari stands against everything which the *Ansar* and the *Khatmia* hold dear. Fifty-eight years old and a former mathematics teacher, he was the first to raise the voice of nationalism in the Sudan when he formed the Graduates' Congress in 1936 and he has always made it quite plain that he sees the Sudan as a secular state. He came to power on a platform of unity with Egypt and it is said that al-Azhari still looks north for ideological support and campaign funds. Despite this, his is the glory of having led the Sudan to independence. An elusive and ambiguous man, yet destined to play a major role in the development of the Sudan.

There is one more northern Sudanese whom we must mention in passing if only because he is one of the most influential anti-Western individuals in the country. This is fifty-five-year-old Mohammed Ahmad Maghub, Foreign Minister of the Sudan from 1956 until the coup. Maghub, who studied both engineering and law at the University of Khartoum, is a member of Umma, although he is far left of the party's leadership. He is also legal adviser to the Mahdi's family. Maghub, who has been known to complain that the United States' policy toward 'Popular China' is 'stupid' and that the Sudan has behind it '6,000 years of culture' while Americans are 'barbarians', was responsible for keeping the Sudan out of the Western camp. He played a prominent part in the 1958 Accra Conference, brought the Sudan into the Arab League, and was that group's candidate for the presidency of the General Assembly of the United Nations. This strange, bitter man skilfully guided his country's foreign affairs but there are those who maintain that he created more tensions than he resolved. He will be heard from in the years to come.

So much for the northern two-thirds of the country. What about the southern Sudan, the black people of the *Sudd* and the far mountains? Who speaks for three million primitive tribesmen? This is hard to say. For reasons which we will come to later, the southern Sudan, which is African while the North is Middle Eastern, is the retarded child of this ninth largest nation in the world. Education and representative government came late to the South and there is no common language, culture or religion to bind the people in a single political bloc. In the days before the coup, however, the South was able to exert considerable pressure on political events if only because no coalition was possible without some southern support. Southerners from the three up-Nile provinces—Bahr el Ghazal, Upper Nile and Equatoria—amalgamated to form the Southern Liberal Party which demanded a federal government in the Sudan, with the North and South on an equal basis, and a greater share of the country's development programme. No single leader emerged who clearly could be said to speak for the South. In fact, there was a collective Southern leadership shared by Father Saturnino Lahore (a Roman Catholic priest), Benjamin Lwoki (a minister in Khalil's government), and Stanislaus Pysama.

For the moment, these political leaders are off the stage, although it would be incorrect to assume that they no longer exert any influence on the course of events. Running the show now but still sensitive to pressure from all quarters is sixty-year-old Kaid ('commander-in-chief') Ibrahim Abboud. Born at Suakin, a small Red Sea village, Abboud is a member of the fierce Hadendowa tribe, the 'Fuzzy Wuzzies' immortalized by Kipling because of their penchant for breaking the British square. After studying engineering at Gordon College, he graduated from what is today the Sudanese West Point in Khartoum. Like his old boss and the man he replaced as chief of state, Abboud served with distinction during World War II in Eritrea, Ethiopia and Libya. After tours as leader of the Camel Corps, chief of the Service Corps, and Deputy Commander of the Army, Abboud became *Kaid* in 1956. Two years later he led the junta which seized power in the Sudan.

Like Khalil, Abboud is a gregarious person but not one to suffer fools or rascals. He has a reputation for being a good administrator and is said to be personally incorruptible. Although not as outspokenly pro-Western as his predecessor, General Abboud can be counted upon to steer a moderate course representative of the wishes of most Sudanese. The Sudan is not going to join the Baghdad Pact under Abboud; neither is it going to go Communist or barter its sovereignty to Egypt for a few more gallons of Nile water.

Chapter 2

*

RIVER AND DESERT

So much for soldiers and statesmen, cabbages and kings. They come and go and are forgotten with their dust. But the land and the people remain, at once changing and changeless, the two not separate but one, a part of each other in the endless cycle of birth, life, re-creation and death, which alters the substance but does not destroy it, the timeless rhythm which nothing can change and which creates the essence of any people. If you seek this, you must look for it in the country.

So it was that at 3.30 of an eyeball-searing afternoon we found ourselves at the Khartoum bus station. A crowd of white-robed Sudanese was grouped at the rear of the bus where, with the benefit of advice from many mouths, a character clad in khaki shorts and a dirty undershirt was binding the baggage to the roof. Up went a series of tin suitcases made of old petrol cans. Up went a bed-frame and several mattresses. Up went a host of wicker baskets—two containing chickens who obviously had mental reservations about the trip—and clay jugs. The jumble was topped with an old automobile tyre destined for some venerable vehicle in the South. The advice became a torrent of abuse as some family heirloom was strapped down inadequately. A second man climbed on to the roof to remedy the situation. The dust from the shuffling of two score bare feet rose like a morning fog around the bus. Goats bleated, donkeys brayed, roosters crowed, beggars whined and men swore. Out of the confused mass appeared one who could be nothing but the driver: he wore the traditional white gown but purple socks adorned his ankles above his yellow shoes, his face was splendid with reflecting sun-glasses and an arrogantly tilted cigarette. There was a mad scramble for the bus, the driver vaulted into his seat, gave a single blast to his musical horn, and we roared off leaving at least half our passengers protesting in the dust. We were headed for the Gezira—Arabic for 'island'—the million-acre cotton bowl which is the economic heart of the Sudan.

The bus was a new Italian model and a sign over the driver's head

39

advised us that it was *vietato fumare*. Not being Italian, we felt free to smoke, as did the Sudanese. The afternoon sun turned Khartoum's square mud houses to a dull bronze. Our driver threaded his way with cheerful abandon through frantic herds of sheep, disdainful camels and complaining pedestrians, all to a cacophony of horn blowing. Finally free of the city, we sped out along the paved road past the airport and bounced off the macadam and on to the sand track which would take us a hundred and fifty miles south to Wad Medani, the commercial centre of the Gezira. Ahead the country opened up, parched, dry and flat as an abandoned tennis court, whipped by a hot wind from the desert. There was no horizon; in a vast semicircular sweep the great plain melted almost imperceptibly into the metallic sky. For a moment there was a feeling of immensity and loneliness. And then it ended with the cheerful chatter of the Sudanese, who unwound their turbans for the trip, leaving their heads covered by orange, turquoise or white skull-caps. The more sophisticated unfolded single-sheet Arabic newspapers like so many commuters on their way home from the city. Others talked, munched kola nuts, polished their already glistening teeth with chewing sticks, or simply sat alone with their thoughts.

The track was almost invisible except in the occasional hollow where huge ruts had been cut by some adventurous soul, perhaps the first to drive from Wad Medani to Khartoum at the end of the last rains. But this is a land of shifting sands and such signs do not last long. The abrasive sand and whipping winds soon obscure or grind anything to powder: abandoned vehicles, bones, human hopes. Where the track was visible, it split off, looped, turned back on itself, marking the trail of an individualist who felt the going was better in the scrub. Our driver, whose face was beautifully scarified in the manner of one of the Western tribes, stuck to what he apparently considered to be the main road.

Fastened to the windshield at eye-level was a small glass vase and in it was a single pale desert flower. Our blaring horn stampeded little herds of thin-shanked hump-backed cattle, scattered flocks of swollen-uddered goats and sheep with tails like five-pound bolognas. The sinking sun hung for a moment like a great bloody eye in the colourless face of the sky and then it was gone and darkness blew in on the desert wind with no twilight to slow its course. Our world shrank to the inside of the bus and the few yards ahead of us that were stolen from the night by the headlights. Every few miles a figure in white, walking or riding a donkey, his heels bouncing on the earth, would whirl into our vision only to fade away before the last notes of our clamorous horn had died. A jackal cried at the pale stars and another answered from a distant hillock. A frantically waving figure standing in the road was nailed in light against the wall of the night and we slithered through the sand to a stop. Behind him now an old car could be seen. He had a flat tyre and no spare. He climbed aboard to go to the next village for help. We ate an orange, the juice running in tart rivulets through the coating of dust in our mouths. At the next village several people got off and the man across the aisle from us removed his sandals, curled up across two seats and was soon asleep.

In five hours we clattered into Wad Medani, a town of 65,000 and cotton capital of the Sudan, and checked into the box-like Gezira Hotel, a two-storey adobe structure generously endowed with bats. Dinner appeared in the form of a mutton chop rising like Gibraltar from a Mediterranean of grease. Also chocolate pudding and German beer in quart bottles with silver paper wrapped around the necks. In the morning, having breakfasted on eggs fried in peanut oil and fatty sheep's liver, we emerged into a Wad Medani already bustling with life: labourers were climbing into trucks bound for the cotton fields, a loudspeaker blared Arabic music, and countless donkeys clucked on by their white-robed riders surged through the dust towards the *suk*, the market-place, where their masters would exchange a few eggs and a small pile of beans for tobacco, matches or coffee.

Later, as we drove through the flat, white-puffed fields of cotton, an earnest young Sudanese who had taken his agricultural degree in Britain explained the £18 million Gezira scheme to us. The first man to plant cotton in this once-parched triangle between the Blue and White Niles, oddly enough, was an American named Leigh Hunt. Other private planters worked the area with increasing success until, in 1925, the Government built the two-mile-long Sennar Dam on the Blue Nile. The Sudanese (British) Government bought or rented at the highest pre-irrigation prices five million acres, reallotted the land—often to the original owners—in 40-acre plots. The Gezira Board, a public corporation, maintains the dam, its 57-square-mile reservoir, 80 sluices, 112 spillways and more than 3,000 miles of irrigation canals. Water goes to the tenants free and selected seed is theirs at cost. The Board advances money to the farmers, processes and markets the cotton crop, and conducts scientific research programmes.

For his part, the farmer agrees to plant only a quarter of his 40 acres in cotton each year. The rest either lies fallow or is planted in *dura*, a millet which is the staple food of the Sudan, or *lubia*, which anyone from south of the Mason-Dixon Line will recognize as black-eyed peas. These crops belong to the farmer. Of the proceeds from the sale of the cotton crop, 44 per cent is kept by the farmer, 4 per cent goes for the schools, clinics and other social services at his disposal, 10 per cent to the Gezira Board for research and capital reserves, and 42 per cent to the Government. Peasants who are landowners may sell their holdings but only to local inhabitants or to the Government. This scheme, which the Sudanese are the first to admit is a legacy of British imperialism, has given the 30,000 peasants who participate in it the highest standard of living of any smallholders in Africa or Asia. Over the last ten years, the annual income per farmer has been as high as £860 and never lower than £180. This gives the Gezira farmer enough ready cash to hire a few Nigerians to help him with his harvest. These are Muslim pilgrims from that great West African state making the arduous trip to Mecca. Thousands come and many stay in the Gezira for two or three seasons to earn enough money to continue their pilgrimage. The road is long and hard for a poor man—the rich can fly by chartered Stratocruiser from Kano—and many never make it. Still they keep coming. Has it not been written that he who dies on *hejira* shall go straight away to Heaven? Oddly enough, although most of the Gezira tenants are illiterate and wouldn't know Karl Marx from Groucho, many say that they are Communists.

A word should be said here about the Communist movement in the Sudan if only because the term has lost much of its meaning in recent years through over-use or misuse. In Africa, for instance, there is a considerable difference between a white South African Communist, who is usually just that, and a West African trade unionist who mouths Marxist phrases mostly because they have a nice ring and usually succeed in annoying his white boss. First it should be said that Sudanese law prohibits any association practising or promoting Communism or its goals. This has not prevented a small but efficient band of Sudanese Communists from exerting considerable influence through 'front' organizations, particularly in urban areas. University and high school students have been their principal target but they have not forgotten the leaders of the Sudan's emergent feminist movement, the trade unions or the peasants.

Although they had no legal standing, there were at least two Marxist political parties before General Abboud's coup. These were the Sudan Communist Party and the National Assembly, a Trotskyite splinter group. Although neither party could legally enter candidates, the Sudan Communist Party, under the label of 'The Anti-Imperialist Front', was able to get one candidate elected to parliament. It has also been extremely effective among the Sudan's 157 registered trade unions and an estimated 70 per cent of the total trade union membership of 100,000 (half of the country's non-agricultural workers) belongs to Red-run unions. The Communists, through their emphasis on social and economic reform, have also made important gains among the Gezira tenants. To back up the locals, in one recent year, the heavily-staffed Russian Embassy in Khartoum provided free trips to the U.S.S.R. for four hundred Sudanese. In the same year, four Sudanese went to America on United States government grants. Enough said.

A scheme smaller than the Gezira but equally important in many ways is under way in Zandeland near the Congo border. About 180,000 Zande were scattered over a remote area of 20,000 square miles. They had no cattle and only a primitive form of agriculture. The Government spent over £1 million to resettle the entire tribe in neat 50-family villages, each family being allotted 40 acres of cotton land. The Government built a mill which gins, spins and weaves this cotton into three million yards of cloth for the local inhabitants and for distribution in other parts of the country. A sugar factory is in production and cotton-seed oil is processed for food or soap manufacturing. Schools, clinics and roads are an integral part of the scheme, as they are in the Gezira, and, in a matter of less than fifteen years, the Zande have developed from a primitive and shy forest people into farmers and factory workers with full bellies and, incidentally, enough cash to pay their taxes.

Our young agriculturalist led us through a colourful and well-watered garden to the comfortable bungalow which is the home of Mahi al-Din Hadar, one of the Gezira's nine block inspectors, master of Wad Attya, a 13,000-acre cotton kingdom farmed by 525 tenants. With the ubiquitous courtesy which is so much a part of the Sudanese national character, Hadar pumped us full of Kitti Kola, a sweetly foul soft drink dear to the hearts of non-imbibing Muslims. Having refreshed us against the heat, Hadar took us to the farm of one Abdullah Sheik, a gap-toothed gentleman in his late sixties, who has only one wife but ten living children. How did the crop look for this year? Abdullah Sheik said that 'the cotton is doing its best' but added that he was worried about the sales. Things had been bad for the last two years and he had many mouths to feed. One son was due to go to high school but there was the matter of the school fees. Was he a Communist? The old man shook his head and smiled. 'The Communists tell us that we should get more money for our cotton. I would like to get more money, or at least pay the Government less. Perhaps I am a Communist.'

We left Abdullah Sheik pondering the intricacies of political science and returned to Hadar's bungalow to have a look at a map of the entire Gezira. Currently under irrigation are more than one million acres producing 800,000 bales of cotton, 80,000 tons of seed and 65,000 tons of grain worth about £36 million each year. The 800,000-acre Managil extension, which will provide farms for 52,000 tenants and probably support a population of 200,000, is well under way and is scheduled for completion in 1961. When it is finished at a cost of £35 million (£5·6 million or 41 per cent of the nation's 1959 development budget was devoted to the scheme), over one hundred villages equipped with elementary schools, sewerage systems, community centres, clinics, orchards and sports grounds will spring up where before there was only desert. Construction of the proposed £31 million Roseires Dam on the Blue Nile will bring another 1·4 million acres (the Kinana Scheme) into production. Here is a real social and economic revolution. People whose fathers before them for generations have had no means of earning a living other than following their flocks from water-hole to water-hole, at the mercy of the sun and the wind, are being transformed in a single generation into a prosperous yeomanry with pride in their holdings and hope for a better life for their children. This is the real battle in Africa, the fight against disease and ignorance and poverty, and it is far from won in this underfed nation where only 2·3 million of 8·5 million potentially arable acres are under cultivation. One Gezira scheme holds more hope for this continent than a thousand Accra conferences.

Water has been the principal problem in the past. The 1929 Anglo-Egyptian Nile Waters Agreement allocated to Egypt 92 per cent of the Nile's flow, leaving the Sudan only 8 per cent, and gave both nations a veto over proposed dams in the other country. In effect, this meant that the Sudan could pump as much water as it wanted from July to December, in the Nile's period of spate. During these months, one-third of the river's annual flow is lost, washed into the Mediterranean with tons of fertile silt. Another 15 per cent evaporates in the papyrus swamps of the southern Sudan. During the dry season, when the water was needed most urgently, the Sudan was forbidden to pump more than 2 per cent of the Nile's waters, the rest being allocated to Egypt.

Ever since the Sudan gained its independence four years ago both countries have been anxious to negotiate a new agreement. The Sudan needed a more generous allocation to enable it to proceed with extension of the Gezira; Egypt had to have Sudanese approval to get on with the Aswan High Dam, which will submerge the Sudanese market town and railhead of Wadi Halfa (population: 11,000), cover countless Nubian archaeological treasures, flood out 55,000 other villagers and wipe the Second Cataract off the map. International financiers made it plain to both parties that no financial aid for either project would be available unless and until a new Nile Waters Agreement was reached.

Negotiations broke down time and again as both countries attempted to use their veto power as a political weapon. Differences arose, too, on the question of compensation for the flooding of Wadi Halfa and on what the apportionment of the flow should be and where the water should be stored. The Sudan favoured a Nile Valley Authority including the other riparian states, Ethiopia, Kenya, Uganda and the Congo. Sudanese spokesmen maintained that a series of small up-stream dams could increase the amount of water available to both countries from 52 billion cubic metres each year to 81 billion cubic metres; of this, it said it should have one-third.

Egypt, on the other hand, maintained that a series of small dams would not conserve as much water as the Sudanese thought, felt its Aswan High Dam would be more efficient, and took the line that the Sudan could get along on 13 billion cubic metres rather than the 27 billion cubic metres which it sought. As far as compensation was concerned, Egypt was prepared to pay £9 million while the Sudan was asking £36 million.

With each collapse of negotiations, relations between the two countries worsened and trade virtually came to a standstill. One of the factors bearing on General Khalil's removal was that many Sudanese felt his staunchly pro-Western and anti-Egyptian position would prevent him from obtaining the best terms possible from Nasser when the time came to divide the waters.

On taking power, General Abboud stated that one of the first tasks of his government would be to negotiate a new agreement and to restore good relations with Egypt. Nasser, anxious to get on with the Aswan High Dam and aware that further deterioration of his prestige in the Sudan could be fatal to his ambitions as a Pan-Arab leader, already compromised by political shifts in Iraq, Jordan and the Mahgreb, quickly recognized the revolutionary régime and ordered Interior Minister Zakaria Mohieddin to reach an agreement as quickly as possible. The result was the signing of a new Nile Pact in Cairo on November 8, 1959.

Under the new agreement, the Sudan gave its assent to the construction of the Aswan High Dam. From the time that the dam begins to store water (about 1964) the Sudan will be entitled to 25 per cent of the total annual flow. The dam is expected to store 22 billion metres of extra water and the new nation's quota will be increased from 4 billion to 18·5 billion cubic metres. Egypt's share will rise from 48 billion to 55·5 billion cubic metres. The total flow of the river is estimated at 84 billion cubic metres but 10 billion cubic metres will be lost from the High Dam by evaporation. Egypt further agreed to share the cost of works on the Upper Nile which could add another 10 billion cubic metres, these waters to be divided between the two countries. Since it is unlikely that the Sudan will be able to use her full allocation until completion of the Roseires Dam, she will lend Egypt 1·5 billion cubic metres annually, to be repaid over a ten-year period dating from the completion of the irrigation schemes.

On the matter of compensation, the Sudan made a considerable compromise by accepting an Egyptian offer of £15 million which will be used to find new homes for those inundated by the waters, which will stretch back at least 400 miles behind the High Dam. To top things off, the two countries signed a trade agreement for the exchange of £11 million of goods annually and agreed to study the requirements of the other riparian states and to adopt a unified policy in regard to them. The new treaty is valid for one hundred years provided the Nile's flow remains constant although it is probable that there will be periodic reviews of the situation.

The question of the division of the waters of the Nile has been a matter not only of prosperity-or-poverty but of life-or-death to the peoples of this valley for thousands of years. Although the Nile remains, as it always has, at once the rope which binds together the peoples of the Sudan and Egypt and the wedge which drives them apart, the new agreement seems an equitable one and credit is due both to Nasser and Abboud. The signing of the agreement is the one great accomplishment of the revolutionary régime.

RIVER AND DESERT

ABA ISLAND

Most trains in the Sudan begin their journey at night to take advantage of the cool hours and it was nearly midnight when we clambered into the midget-sized sleeper at a Wad Medani siding. The fawn-coloured Sudanese trains with their huge windows tinted blue against the glare of the desert sun are among the best in Africa. The sleeping cars are divided into compartments with two bunks perpendicular to each other on different levels. Although the railways and river boats which annually haul 1·7 million tons of freight and 3·3 million passengers over 3,000 miles of track and 1,500 miles of navigable water (while Sudan Airways annually carries 35,000 passengers and 700,000 tons of freight) are Government-owned and the service is reminiscent of the Indian Railways in their pre-independence salad days, transportation employees are grouped into a 25,000-member union which is the strongest in the Sudan and has been led by militant Communists since 1958. It should be said for the Sudan Railway Workers Union that, whatever the political persuasion of its leaders, they have obtained for it a higher wage-scale than that enjoyed by any similar union on the continent, including the wealthy Union of South Africa. One of the last acts of General Khalil's government was the procurement of a twenty-year £14 million World Bank loan to modernize the Sudan's vital transportation system.

We awoke at dawn to find the train crawling across a dun-coloured plain broken by thorn bushes. Occasionally there was a small village—round mud houses with thatched roofs or square adobe ones with tin roofs, depending on the wealth of the community—where the train stopped and hordes of small boys scurried out from the shade of the trees to sell kola nuts and cups of water. An hour later and we were at Rabak, the nearest station to Aba Island, the Mahdi's 30,000 acre stronghold and the most holy spot in the Sudan, for here it was that the Guided One emerged from his cave in the bank of the White Nile to proclaim his messianic mission. Sayed Yahia el Mahdi, the natty-dressing younger brother of the new spiritual head of the *Ansar*, had arranged our visit and one of his men was to meet us in Rabak. This personage failed to materialize and we beat a strategic retreat, both from the sun and the Arab merchants who kept insisting that I would look well in a Sudanese robe, to the adobe home of the leader of the Rabak *Ansar*. Here we were plied with thimble-sized cups of coffee, sweet and thick, and bottles of Kitti

47

Kola. Scrawny chickens scratched without enthusiasm in the dust of the yard and the great burning oval of the sun climbed higher in the sky.

Three hours and countless Kitti Kolas later, a Volkswagen bus spreading a plume of dust roared into the yard and disgorged two sockless but otherwise impeccably dressed characters in sun helmets who announced themselves to be the Mahdi's envoys and apologized profusely for the delay. The car had broken down. An hour's drive through dry, desolate country inhabited by only a few skittish goats brought us to a dirt causeway through a swamp which boasted patches of wild rice and clumps of white water-lilies. A startled flock of egrets rose in a great chalky cloud and Negro women, topped with immense loads of firewood, urged the stunted cattle which they drove before them off the road and fetlock-deep into the mud of the swamp. These are the Mahdi's people—more than 100,000 of them—and here his word is law. They are his vassals and he their liege lord and this relationship implies rights and responsibilities for both parties, as did the European feudalism of another age. This relationship between the 'big men' and the peasant class is one which we will find almost without exception all the way across Black Africa. In some places it comes close to being slavery. But before we condemn this we should understand that it is an old and well-understood relationship deeply engrained in the African character in the course of thousands of years. Social habit and mental attitude are not changed by fifty years of European administration. Only the fuzziest thinkers among those Americans and Britons who interest themselves in African affairs can still equate the granting of political freedom to small groups of vociferous African nationalists with the extension of social and personal freedom to the masses of this tortured and ancient continent.

We rattled across the causeway and through a clean village of adobe houses fronted with doors made from flattened petrol tins. Women washing their husbands' gowns, beating the cloth against stones in a timeless rhythm, looked up without missing a beat, stared and continued with their work. Small naked children ran out to wave. From the middle of a garden, in which a donkey browsed undisturbed, rose the palace of the Mahdi, two double-storey buildings with balustrades around each floor, the second storey supported by silver-lacquered columns. Between these two wings, on a terrace reached by ten wide steps, stood a one-storey building. The gate to the garden was surmounted by the Mahdi's totem, a spearhead rising from a ball and crescent.

After a light breakfast of grapefruit, fish, oatmeal, goat's liver, tomatoes, eggs, toast with English marmalade, and more fruit washed down with tea, the Mahdi's foreman took us on a tour of the vast estate. He was especially proud of the orchards, heavy with the perfume of mangoes, guavas, grapefruit, oranges, limes and bananas, something which the Gezira Board is only now going into on a large scale. But cotton here, as at the Gezira, is the big thing and the Mahdi's people work the fields on roughly the same basis as the tenants at the Government scheme: 60 per cent for the Mahdi, 40 per cent for the tenants. The big difference in the two schemes is that the Mahdi has to pump his water from the White Nile while the Gezira is irrigated by the slope from the Blue Nile.

A young, blond German engineer, clad only in a pair of khaki shorts and covered with grease, emerged from the pit where he was supervising the mounting of a boiler to show us the new ginning factory built by the Mahdi. Here, as elsewhere in Black Africa, West Germany is doing a land-office business of selling and installing heavy machinery, contracts which could go to American businessmen. Why? The Germans accept payment in local currency, leave engineers on the spot not only to supervise installation but to train local maintenance men and make sure that no kinks show up in the initial phases of operation. In short, they give better value for less money. A vast new market is being lost to America on a continent which has an almost pathological desire for industrialization.

Here on the Mahdi's estate exists a complete society: two primary schools chock-full of bright-eyed children in khaki shorts or gingham dresses, scribbling on slates and darting to their feet to answer the teachers' questions, a jail (empty), a tidy but not spotless clinic, local council building, and the Mahdi's much-loved stable of English racing horses. Downing spice cake and drinking tea on the terrace in the afternoon, while the Mahdi's uniformed marching band, complete with bagpiper, played 'Marching Through Georgia' and 'Way Down Upon the Swanee River' from the garden below, it was hard to realize that this was the twentieth century, not the nineteenth. And yet the Mahdi's estate rivals the modern, state-run Gezira project. More than once in Africa we will find this curious mixture of yesterday, today and an unsure tomorrow. Perhaps this is what Dr. Nkrumah means when he speaks of an African personality.

PROBLEMS

A short ride took us to Kosti, a big trading centre on the White Nile. There we sank into wicker armchairs at an outdoor movie theatre—so eminently practical in a country where you know for certain that it won't rain for the next six months—to share with the Sudanese their enthusiasm for Miss Rita Hayworth, then doing her stuff in a jazzed-up version of *Rain*. Having paid tribute to Miss Hayworth, we boarded with some difficulty the river steamer that was to take us north to Khartoum. There was plenty of room—in fact, there were no other applicants for first or second class passage—but such a thing was unheard of and almost an insult to Sudanese national pride: there was a train which would have us in Khartoum within five hours so why take a three-day boat trip? It was unthinkable. Pleas and threats finally prevailed and the stationmaster grudgingly issued our tickets. In due time, with appropriate hooting of the whistle, the steamer and the barges attached to either side and to her bow, churned into midstream, were caught by the current and whirled downstream towards Khartoum like a chip thrown into a forest stream by a boy.

As the miles slipped by with the low banks echoing to the even throb of the engines and the minutes turned to hours and the hours to days, all the life of this great emerald snake which rises in the game-filled forests of central Africa to flow 4,000 lonely miles to the sea is revealed: the endless and backbreaking task of tilling the flat fields on to which the life-giving Nile will burst in time of flood, the steady rhythm of the *sagia* and the man-powered *shaduf* during low water, the constant battle against sun and wind and heat to coax from the sullen earth a bale of cotton, a bowl of peanuts, a handful of beans. By dint of extraordinary effort and a none-too-demanding standard of living, the Sudan is able to feed itself, although it must import coffee, tea and sugar (as well as cotton piece goods, machinery, base metals, petroleum products and vehicles). But the country's light rainfall—six inches or less north of Khartoum—is not sufficient to allow for much expansion of cash crops, and since the Sudan has yet to reveal substantial mineral deposits, the Government's revenues, until more land can be irrigated, are frozen at about £47·4 million per year. Industrial development (the Sudan annually produces 100,000 tons of cement, 15,000 tons of soap, seven million bottles of beer and 160 million cigarettes) is hindered by lack of capital, cheap power and skilled labour. So cotton and gum arabic it is. Britain is the Sudan's best customer, buying about

30 per cent of her £43 million worth of exports, and most important supplier, providing 32 per cent of her £59 million worth of imports. India, West Germany and Egypt are also important while the United States is a long way down the list, buying only 3 per cent of the Sudan's products and providing about the same percentage of her imports. Annual trade with Russia, a new factor since Abboud's assumption of power, amounts to £3 million, while another £4 million worth of cotton is bartered for satellite (and Red Chinese) textiles, chemicals, tyres, sugar, iron, steel and machinery.

But these riparian farmers who grow the cotton for export, although they are the economic heart of the Sudan, are only a part of its people. On either bank of the river, in the distance dimly seen because of the swimming mist of heat, wander the fierce desert tribes, wolves who since time had its beginning have come on the soft 'shif-shif' of their camels' pads to raid these placid river sheep, to burn, to rape, to plunder and then to fade away again into their desert home, leaving the river dwellers to rebuild and await the next raid. Out in the desert, where the wind blows hot and harsh in the midday sun, there is little trade and less cultivation. There live the stately Kababish, who feel naked without long camel-whips tied to their wrists, and the Kawahla, with their great herds of camels, each beast capable of carrying a 360-pound load for ten dry days before slaking its thirst with a fifteen-gallon drink. Also in the West roam the Baggara, stocky cattle people and devout Mahdists, renowned for the beauty of their women. On the slopes of the rocky mountains which spring from the western plain live the bull-riding Nuba, big, black, muscular people once prized as slaves. Near them are the Hamar, settled villagers who store water against the dry season in the enormous hollow trunks of the *tebeldi* trees, each of which is named and listed, a prized treasure in this thirsty land. The Hamar, hard-working, fanatical Mahdists of West African appearance, cultivate melons and tap the acacia thorn for the 50,000 tons of gum arabic which the Sudan sells to more than sixty nations of the world. This versatile substance, which is used in the manufacture of postage stamps, matches, sweets, cough drops and paper products, is a bad second to cotton among the country's money-earners. Although the Sudan supplies 90 per cent of the world's demand for gum arabic, it drops only £6·4 million per year into the country's coffers.

The nomads, people with faces which the harsh desert wind has carved into strong lines, lead a life indistinguishable from that of their fathers and forefathers, except that tribal warfare is now forbidden them. There is the never-ending slow, lunging walk of the camels, the same battle for survival against a desperate environment, the same endless seeking after water and grazing for their flocks. And yet there are cold desert nights when the stars shine hard and clear over the ocean of moon-bathed sand when one can understand why to settle a nomad is to kill not only him but something which burns, however dimly, in all men. Like their fathers, they can neither read nor write and, despite the fact that 13 per cent of the Sudan's budget is devoted to educating 230,000 students in 1,800 schools, 90 per cent of all adults above the age of 15 are illiterate and only one out of every seven school-age children goes to school.

In the South, where telephone lines must be strung seventeen feet above the ground or be torn down by high-stepping giraffes, the people are even more primitive. Here live some four million black tribesmen split into small groups speaking thirty-two different languages and more than 250 dialects. Most of these non-Arabic-speaking peoples are pagan but about 250,000 are Christian. Since 1902, this area south of the 12th Parallel, great plains merging into rain forest and swamp, has been the stepchild of the Sudan. Entry of Northern Sudanese, who for centuries had used the South as a hunting ground for slaves, was strictly controlled; Christian missionaries were admitted and did valuable work. In the early days of the South there was no question of progress. The job was simply to establish law and order and confidence among a people strange to these concepts. That this job was neither easy nor without danger was recognized by the government, which gave added weight to service south of the 12th Parallel for pension purposes. Young district commissioners, 'Bog Barons' who single-handedly administered vast tracts of forest and swamp the size of Scotland, gradually and often at cost of their lives brought a degree of order to the country. But the South lagged far behind the North—in 1946 exactly seven out of 139,899 Nuer tribesmen in one district could speak English—and independence caught them in a still primitive condition.

The Nuer, and the two other great southern tribes, the Dinka and the Shilluk, are fine physical specimens who traditionally go naked because they see no reason for a man, unless he is deformed, to hide the body which God gave him. These proud men, bearing the six parallel scars on the forehead which are their tribal signature, stand well over six feet, are never to be found without a spear, and stuff the bowls of their out-sized pipes with a none-too-fragrant mixture of tobacco and cow dung. His stock is everything to a Nuer and he knows each one by name and trains their horns like those of ancient Egyptian cattle. These children of the swamps stand for hours on one leg, like storks, but if he is a chief, he would sooner give up a fat young wife than part with his deck chair, the traditional status symbol here as an umbrella is on the West Coast. The long-standing disparity between the social development of the North and the South, their different racial and religious backgrounds, and the far-from-forgotten slaving expeditions launched by Northern Arabs into the deep South combined to produce a feeling of superiority on the one hand and of mistrust on the other.

This erupted in late 1955 when Southern troops in Equatoria and Bahr el Ghazal provinces mutinied, killed their Northern officers and 300 Northern traders—while scrupulously leaving foreigners alone— and radioed an appeal for *British* help. An odd action for people on the verge of having the yoke of oppressive colonialism raised from their necks after fifty-seven years! The British told the mutineers they neither could nor would assist them and advised them to lay down their arms. As the blue, green and yellow flag of the Sudan fluttered to the tops of Khartoum's flagpoles on the day of independence, to the wild jubilation of the Arab North, much of the Southern third of the country, a land of neck-high elephant grass sprinkled with the yellow blossoms of *talh* trees, was still seething from the abortive rebellion. When the mutineers found that no help could be expected, hundreds doffed their uniforms and fled into the neighbouring British colony of Uganda. Months later, in Uganda, we were to talk with some of these refugees. One, a Christian, came up to me in the little town of Moyo. 'You know what is happening across the border,' he said. 'Will America or the United Nations help us?' I explained as best I could that there was nothing we could do. He nodded his head slowly, not understanding, and said: 'Then only God can help us.'

Order was slowly restored, at least 300 Southerners were condemned to death and 1,500 others sentenced to prison terms. The Sudanese Government, which feels that British administrators and missionaries emphasized the North-South cleavage by making a 'human zoo' of the South, has sought to ease the tension by improving the calibre of Northern civil servants there and by imposing restrictions on the Christian missions with the ultimate goal of eliminating the Southern problem by imposing Islam and the Arabic language on the population. The government has taken over, in most cases without compensation, all mission schools in the South, including the far-flung 274-school Roman Catholic system. Northern principals have been appointed, a government syllabus imposed, and the Christian religion is now offered only as an elective. As in other Sudanese schools, Arabic will be the language of instruction until the student reaches one of the nation's seventeen high schools where the switch is made to English. In short, a colonial situation exists with the Arabs in the role once played by the British.

The South is in for some rough years. But there are many practical reasons why a policy of assimilation must be pressed. The South is bound by the Nile to the North and is not economically viable by itself. The North has the money, which the missions did not have, to establish a solid school system and to provide for the economic development of the area. Despite our personal religious convictions, Christianity may well be less suited to these people than Islam. Lastly, the South has nowhere else to go. It may for a time be dominated by the North but that may be preferable to neglect. In every way, the South's future seems to lie with a united Sudan and her virile people in time are destined to play a major role in the country's destiny. This problem of uneven development of differing peoples within the same political unit is one which we will see throughout Africa. It may come as a surprise to some well-meaning people of liberal persuasion to learn that the primitive tribes often prefer the overlordship of a white district commissioner to the less gentle rule of their more advanced countrymen. Although the African has many charms, he is inclined neither to be tolerant of those whose *mores* are at variance with his own nor fair towards those who lack the power to strike back.

The explosive factor in the situation is this: under the parliamentary régime, the South had a means of expressing its grievances; under that of General Abboud, it does not. There are few Southern army officers, and administrators in the South, with a few exceptions, are Northerners. Even mention of the South's dream of a federal form of government (although 90 per cent of the funds expended in the three up-Nile provinces are contributed by the rest of the country) is forbidden. The old Equatoria Corps, which consisted of Southerners, has been disbanded and army units sent to the area are invariably composed almost entirely of Northerners. Southerners are suspicious of government plans to lease land in the South to Arab businessmen. Northern merchants have been encouraged to settle in Southern villages and hundreds of mosques have been opened while Christian mission activity has been sharply curtailed. Unrest has been added to by a serious famine which struck the South during the summer of 1959.

Troubled by real and imagined grievances and denied the constitutional means of making these grievances known, there is a real danger that exiled Southerners may appeal to the increasing number of independent non-Islamic African nations for financial and military aid. Unless the Sudan is able to provide a national vision with which all its peoples can identify themselves, the South could become a black Algeria.

As we glided slowly downstream, these worrisome thoughts lost themselves in the slow rhythm of the great river. It soon became apparent that each meal was to consist of fish, mutton and orange pudding. There was no bar, since this is a Muslim country, but an ice-box is provided and you can bring your own. From time to time the steamer would blast on her whistle and swing into the bank to tie up at a village. And out would pour a stream of villagers, like great black ants after a discarded sandwich.

The river's flow decreased and slowly the waters fanned out into a great sheet. We were approaching the Jebel Aulia Dam, a vast reservoir holding two billion tons of water and irrigating 40,000 acres of cotton. This great 5,000-yard-long hunk of masonry, another legacy from colonial days, slows the turgid White Nile's flow to such an extent that the effect of the dam can be felt four hundred miles upstream. Barefooted men in *ghalabias* opened the locks, we untied our barges and slipped through piecemeal, stopping on the other side of the dam to load cotton and peanuts and take on a few third-class passengers. Among these were two English-speaking teen-age schoolgirls, on their way to Khartoum accompanied by their mothers, with whom Kitty soon made friends. They were captivated by her sun-backed cotton dress which they could not believe was ready-made, were solicitous of her fair skin being in the sun and frankly mystified by an item which apparently has yet to reach the Sudan: the strapless bra!

RETURN TO KHARTOUM

We were anxious to get back into the over-sized rooms of the government-run Grand Hotel after three nights on the boat so it was not good news to hear that the hotel was full. Our sense of well-being was not enhanced when we discovered that 'the annexe' to which travellers are sent under such circumstances consists of three steamers moored to the wharf in front of the hotel. Since it was low water, the view from our cabin consisted of several square feet of muddy river bank. But it is impossible to be grumpy in Khartoum: there is too much to do and too many Sudanese to help you do it. There followed an orgy of breakfast parties, and motor-car races on an abandoned airfield built by Americans during World War II, near the monument to the forgotten charge of the 21st Lancers at the bloody battle of Omdurman. There was horse racing, with long-legged Sudanese jockeys, their heels almost scuffing the ground, riding the Mahdi's prized English mounts against wiry little Arab ponies, the Islamic clientèle of the course faithfully leaving the grandstand between races to make their obeisance to Mecca. There were cool evenings at the Sudanese Cultural Centre, where the young educated set gathers to talk of the rights or wrongs of the coup, or on the terrace of the Grand, drinking away the night with Westernized Muslims while Arab traders hawked their ebony and ivory figurines under the arcade. There was the heady night when the Greek community gathered at the St. James cabaret to hear an itinerant chanteuse from the motherland sing the sad old songs of the Hellenes . . . and demonstrated its devotion to her by smashing every glass in the place at her feet. There were visits to the little Church Missionary Society bookshop, where one can buy a two-month-old copy of *The Tatler* or pick up the latest P. G. Wodehouse epic. And there were quiet Fridays, while the town celebrated the Muslim sabbath, and Sundays at All Saints Cathedral, where Englishmen in shorts and knee-socks sang hymns in voices whose edges had been honed by years of sand and whisky. There were visits to the zoo, where the gazelles and the great hornbills are allowed to run free, to the cool depths of Morhig's store where, wonder of wonders, you can buy an ice-cream soda.

Finally, there was that early evening when the sun glanced over the silver egg-cup of the Mahdi's tomb and fell in dying rays on the lateen sails of the feluccas crossing from Tuti Island, and we knew that it was time to go. There was sadness that the Sudan had tried democracy, found it wanting, and let it go. But not despair. The Sudan has too many assets on its books for that.

The first and greatest of these lies in its eleven million people, many of them backward but most of them industrious, proud and freedom-loving. The Sudan has, as we have said before, an excellent civil service. It has a fine university, with almost a thousand students, which will continue to turn out the men and women to build the new Sudan. It has the great, life-giving river. It has a government which, if not democratic, at least seems to be able and willing to fulfil the needs and satisfy the aspirations of most of the people. The ability of any people with a long and autocratic history to become democratic by fiat in one generation is, at the least, disputable. The problem here is one which is inherent in any government which seizes power by non-democratic means: where do we go from here? General Abboud has promised to 'broaden' his government in the future. For the moment this means, at most, the appointment of an advisory council of civilians, probably including most of the political leaders we have met. Whether the General will ever relinquish army control and allow a completely free election is another matter. In other times, other countries, a coup has only been replaced by another coup.

During its two years in power, Abboud's junta has had to suppress at least three coups. At least five army officers have been executed and about thirty others, including two brigadiers who held ministerial rank, sentenced to long prison terms. The staff of the University of Khartoum has been placed under political surveillance and press censorship has been imposed. Trade unions and workers' associations have been banned and twenty-four allegedly Communist union leaders confined to remote camps in the south. More than a dozen Christian missionaries have been expelled from the country. All of these measures may well have been necessary to maintain order; but the point is that Abboud has had to tighten his grip on the tiger's tail. The longer he holds on, the more difficult it becomes to let go with any degree of safety.

Shortly after the coup, Abboud stated his principal goal: 'We want stability to prevail in the Sudan: political stability to enable the Government to do their duty, economic stability that would grant the people the chance to lead decent lives and enable us to increase production, and moral stability to enable the citizen to attend to his work.' This goal to a large extent has not been realized.

The junta has had a little more success in the economic and social field than it has in the political. Through a vigorous austerity programme (including reduction of cabinet ministers' salaries by £200) which has meant quadrupling import taxes to 40 per cent, the budget has been balanced, the country's tiny sterling reserves increased from £3 million to £9 million and a favourable balance of trade created. A £5 million development loan has been negotiated with Yugoslavia (to add to £47·2 million obtained by Khalil from the United States, United Kingdom, West Germany and World Bank) and an American textile firm has been induced to build a £6 million mill in Khartoum which will go into production next year and is expected to give employment to 3,000 Sudanese and produce 75 million yards of cloth a year. Barter agreements, necessary if the Sudan was ever to be rid of vast stores of surplus cotton, have been concluded with Czechoslovakia, Hungary, Rumania, Bulgaria, Poland, Yugoslavia and Red China. Restrictions laid by Parliament on the productive uses of American aid have been lifted. A £4·5 million contract has been let to an international consortium for the construction of two power stations and transmission lines, the project to be completed by 1962.

Civil servants have been forbidden to engage in private business ventures and stiff penalties instituted against profiteering and hoarding of consumer goods. Rents have been reduced by 20 per cent and office hours have been increased for government physicians who are now forbidden to practise privately. Facilities have been made available to transport unemployed to areas where they can obtain work.

But much remains to be done. The Sudan desperately needs to develop hydro-electric power to make good her lack of coal and oil. She needs more water for her thirsty fields and new crops such as rice, sugar, tobacco and coffee to relieve her dangerous reliance on a cotton economy. She must erase the internal frictions between Northerner and Southerner. She must develop a strong trade union movement free of Communist influence. In foreign affairs, she must steer a line close enough to Egypt to allow for amicable relations between the two countries but independent enough to preserve her sovereignty. It is in the nature of things that the Sudan's policies must be geared to Egypt's as much as Finland's are to Russia's or Mexico's to those of the United States. The United States cannot hope for alliance here but we can hope for friendship.

There are two events which give a key to the Sudanese character and should be appreciated. Within twenty-four hours of the coup, the deposed political leaders were released from house arrest and newspapers were allowed—within limits—to resume publication. Lacking were the burnings, lynchings and public trials which have characterized so many Middle Eastern revolutions and others closer to home. Said Abboud: 'I am through with the past. I am starting fresh. Anything that is past, let it go.' Only when the government's leniency was mistaken for weakness was it necessary to introduce more stringent security measures.

The second incident involved the dismantling of the statues of General Gordon and Lord Kitchener from their Khartoum pedestals in December 1958. It was perhaps inevitable that these emblems of imperialism should disappear. What was remarkable in a world in which gentlemen are at a discount was the manner of their going. It would have been an easy and perhaps a natural thing to make political capital out of the removal of the statues. They could have been dynamited—as was the statue of de Lesseps in Egypt—and the occasion used to mouth about the evils of imperialism before a howling mob. When the time came for the statues to go, a sunset ceremony was held at which time tribute was paid to the role played by both men in the founding of the Sudan. Taps was blown and the statues were covered. After nightfall they were carefully removed and taken to a museum to await shipment to Britain.

This is an honourable people. One can only wish them well in their search for economic prosperity and national integrity.

Chapter 3

*

BLACK TIBET

To the south-east of the Sudan, rising in great forested terraces to stark, snow-capped peaks, lies Ethiopia, the once legendary Land of Prester John, sought after by Christian princes, an unmapped, twilight land whose inhabitants, as everybody knew, ate raw dragons' flesh and washed their clothes in liquid fire.

If you happen to have been re-reading your Septuagint recently, you will, of course, remember that the name of Cush, son of Ham and grandson of Noah, is rendered 'Ethiops' in the Greek, which means 'he of the burnt face'. The Ethiopians prefer this derivation of their country's name to Abyssinia, which has an Arabic connotation and means 'mixed'.

Ethiopia is a little smaller than France and Spain combined or twenty-five times as large as Denmark and it has a population of about 17 million. To put it another way, Ethiopia would blanket Texas, Oklahoma and Kansas. To the north lies the vassal state of Eritrea, the small enclave of French Somaliland, and the deserts of ex-British Somaliland. On the east is ex-Italian Somalia, which received its independence last year. To the south is Kenya and the Sudan is to the west. On three sides the approaches to Ethiopia are barred by waterless deserts while the fourth is blocked by high mountains and lush jungle. There are no rivers navigable for any appreciable distance. The internal topography of the country is almost as fearsome as its wild frontiers. Although the area around Addis Ababa, the capital, is volcanic plain as flat as a billiard-table, much of the rest of the country is a tortured mass of steep mountains and deep gorges which make communications almost impossible, put sixty-two turns in one seven-mile stretch of road near Addis Ababa, and provide some of the most spectacular mountain scenery in the world.

Well-travelled Ethiopians like to think of their country as an African Switzerland. But in many ways, as we shall see, it more closely resembles a Black Tibet.

The people of Ethiopia are patriotic, proud, high-spirited, conservative, curious, quick and intelligent, lazy, polite, indulgent and kind but given to outbreaks of barbarism. They are fond of dramatics and goateed third-formers have been known to stage seventeen-act morality plays lasting six hours. Many Ethiopian damsels (*sans* dulcimers) like to tie their hair with ribbons of bright silk; others plait it in the bowels of oxen. Not so many years ago, courtiers approached the emperor by crawling across the ground stripped to the waist; the new protocol is stiffly Swedish. The army is an efficient outfit equipped with light tanks but warriors of the interior still wear collars of lions' manes, carry rhinoceros-skin shields and bound about the country emasculating each other. There is an Ethiopian navy but the fishermen of Lake Tana still use a papyrus boat which Moses would recognize.

Ethiopia is fanatically devoted to what is the only indigenous church in Africa. But a few emperors have been Roman Catholics. In the backwoods some tribesmen still obey an ancient imperial edict that requires them to wear an amulet on their forehead reading 'I belong to the Father, Son and Holy Ghost', one armlet inscribed 'I deny the devil in Christ the God', and another stating, 'I am the servant of Mary, Mother of the Creator of the World'. A Venetian artist named Niccola Brancaleone reached Ethiopia in the fifteenth century and caused the death of hundreds by painting the Child on Mary's left arm, which is less honourable in this part of the world than the right. The Ethiopians believe that they are of Jewish origin and reckon that they became a doubly-blessed people when the Hebrews rejected Christ. There are towns named Nazareth, Magdala and Bethlehem, and the Ethiopians have a flat, Byzantine-like religious art in which black warriors are depicted performing prodigious feats of valour and fuzzy-headed saints mortify themselves to heaven. Their Christmas comes on January 7, New Year's Day is September 11, and hailstones as big as golf balls fall in December and January.

Although Christianity is the state religion, two out of every five Ethiopians are Muslims and one out of five is pagan. Muslims have their own courts and their rights are respected as long as they remain loyal to the state and make no effort to interfere with the Church.

Christian Ethiopians wear jodhpurs, cloaks, shade themselves with straw umbrellas and carry fly-whisks made of horse tails which are useful as well as decorative. Over the shoulders goes a length of white gauze with a woven border of bright colours. This is called a *shamma* and, although he may be dressed to the teeth, an Ethiopian is regarded as naked unless he wears one.

Ethiopians consider themselves white and us pink. Young bloods like to drink scotch, turn the lights down low, and listen to the jazz of Wilbur de Paris. The Ethiopian dollar, worth 2s. 9d. and hard enough to escape devaluation in 1949, is the country's currency but Austrian Maria Theresa thalers have been used as a medium of exchange since 1780 and are still obtainable at the State Bank of Ethiopia. So were bars of salt, of which the Bank's supply is less adequate.

Ethiopia did a thriving trade in *chat*, a stimulant popular among the Muslim people of the Red Sea, until 1957 when Britain, which was finding the tribesmen of southern Arabia obstreperous enough in their natural state, banned its import into Aden (the ban has since been lifted).

Ethiopia has three times as many livestock as people. Coffee grows wild and 3 per cent of your breakfast cup comes from Ethiopia. Castor and ginger also grow naturally and abundantly and other spices found include saffron, cardamom, tamarind, sage, mustard and caraway. Also available are sixty-foot pythons and two game animals which live only in Ethiopia, the Mountain Nyala and the Walia Ibex.

The Blue Nile rises in Ethiopia and gives the country a diplomatic weapon over Egypt. In 1093 when the Nile failed to rise the Caliph of Egypt sent the Patriarch of Alexandria loaded with gifts to the Emperor of Ethiopia and the river went up twenty feet in a single day. Three hundred years later, another emperor stayed a persecution of his Egyptian co-religionists by warning the Caliph that he would turn Egypt into a desert if Christian blood was shed. Haile Selassie has also toyed with the idea of damming the river.

In the old days, bodies of traitors were thrown into the streets to rot and could not be buried. Although the Italians killed an estimated 30,000 people in a single purge, most Ethiopians bear no grudge against individual Italians. In the wild days immediately after liberation, many Italians were hidden from mobs by their Ethiopian friends. The Ethiopians call all foreigners *Ferengi*, or Franks, and enjoy a bit of cattle rustling or slave raiding. As recently as 1957, Christian Ethiopians shouting 'Mariam! Mariam!' clashed with British-led Kenya troops crying equally positively that there is no God but Allah.

Ethiopia belongs to a host of international organizations but, when last heard from on the subject, the nation was promising the president of a British anti-slavery society to end slavery by *1952*. There were no schools in Ethiopia until 1908 and the country had no written constitution until 1931. There are three agricultural colleges but only one out of twenty children goes to school. In some remote areas, creditors still chain themselves to their debtors and the plaintiff must provide food for the accused and his guards. A case may be judged on the spot by a passer-by. Ethiopians enjoy a feast of raw meat almost as much as a Stork Club habitué does his steak *tartare*. Movement outside the capital often requires written authorization and passes permitting the bearer to be on the streets after midnight are sold at the desks of Addis Ababa hotels for 1s. 3d. Ethiopia joined the League of Nations in 1923 and is a charter member of the United Nations but the gold mines of Adola are still worked by convicts who, until recent years, were not fed unless they brought in gold from the placers.

Although Ethiopia has a modern tele-communications net, many areas of the interior still depend on the mule trains loaded with salt, the one commodity which men must have or die, to bring them news of the outside world. Gondar, which was the capital at various times during the last century, is ringed with imposing stone castles built by the Portuguese for a seventeenth-century Negus. But ninety-nine out of a hundred Ethiopians live in mud huts whose design hasn't changed since before Christ. Ethiopia now has an elected assembly but the time-honoured way to gain the Emperor's ear is to throw yourself in front of his car or lob a note into the window as he drives past. In the old days, crowds gathered outside the palace to shout for justice. They did this even if the emperor was a gentle ruler, so that he wouldn't get lonely in his royal seclusion. Ethiopian pilots fly fighters and commercial aircraft but many areas of Ethiopia are still innocent of the wheel. The Emperor Menelik had a telephone in his palace by 1903 but less than 1 per cent of the country's homes have electricity today.

Foreign advisers have served in Ethiopia since the fourteenth century but dead children are still hung in trees by some Galla clans. There is one hospital bed for every 4,000 Ethiopians and one doctor for every 250,000 people. Most educated Ethiopians know Paris, London or Washington considerably better than they know Harar, Jigjiga or Jimma.

Although Ethiopia now enjoys an enviable degree of political stability (malcontents staged a bloody but remarkably unsuccessful coup last year), there were no less than twenty-three emperors in one turbulent fifty-eight-year period. The main reason that she has progressed as far as she has is that two of the country's three great emperors—Theodore, Menelik II and Haile Selassie—have come back-to-back.

A visit to Ethiopia is a journey in time as well as space. Although the country is going through an economic face-lifting, Ethiopia still has much in common with Medieval Europe. The church and the nobles are great forces. Both own huge tracts of land, exert powerful political influence. The threat of excommunication can still bring a recalcitrant war-lord to heel. The people cultivate the soil with tools that were old-fashioned before Columbus made his New World landfall. And Haile Selassie, the little Emperor, although he is an advanced political thinker, rules his country with as much self-assurance in his divine right as any Stuart prince. In the end, you can never really understand Ethiopia, you only sense it.

What makes Ethiopia physically distinctive are her towering, jagged mountains. Some of these are shaped like truncated cones, flat on the top with almost sheer sides. These are called *ambas* and they form almost impregnable fortresses, accessible by only a few paths and with enough fields and grazing on top to provide food for a garrison.

These *ambas* have played a major role in Ethiopian history. They have been the strongholds of rebel tribes defying imperial authority, the refuge of bandits, and centres of resistance to foreign invaders. One emperor went so far as to confine to an *amba* every male of the royal blood with the exception of himself and his eldest son in an attempt to ensure tranquillity. They still provide excellent sites for the rustication of troublesome politicians or ambitious *rases*, as Ethiopian war-lords are termed.

For most of her history Ethiopia has been sealed off by mountain, desert and ignorance from the rest of the world, and the different peoples living within her present boundaries have had little contact with each other. Her hardy mountaineers, conservative and suspicious of strangers, have been quick to lock themselves into their mountain fastness, the men of the desert have been secure in their waterless wastelands.

The people, like the various parts of the country which they inhabit, vary enormously. There is no Ethiopian just as there is no American. A Somali camelman from Harar has about as much in common with a fuzzy-headed Wallega from Lekempti as has a Swede with a Chinaman. The first and greatest of the tribes, if only because they have subjected the others to their rule, are the Christian Amharas (a word of Arabic derivation meaning 'mountain people') who live on the high central plateau. They are a rather short people but are long-legged, straight-nosed, and have Caucasian features with skin brown to mahogany, and curly, sometimes kinky hair. Their women swathe themselves in yards of gauze-like cloth, go unveiled, and sometimes wear their hair in floppy pompadours. Upper-class Amharas are too proud to work with their hands, a factor which still inhibits Ethiopia's development. They are an intelligent and hospitable people who, although not lacking in courage, have a taste for intrigue and litigation. They were Semitic conquerors who invaded Ethiopia from Arabia thousands of years ago, seized the highland kingdoms of Shoa and Gojjam and have since inter-bred considerably with the Hamites who were the original inhabitants. They evolved one of Africa's few written languages, a formidable tongue with its own script and 276 characters. Most of its literature is religious. Amhara genealogies are difficult to follow because the father's Christian name becomes the son's surname.

The Amharas are almost surrounded by the Gallas, the most numerous group of the country (they are divided into many tribes). The Gallas, a Nilotic people, occupy both the mountains to the south-west of Addis Ababa and the scrub plains to the south-east. They are tall, flat-nosed, fuzzy-haired, fierce, good horsemen, humorous, treacherous and generally more industrious than their Amhara over-lords.

The Somalis, who are mostly nomadic, roam over the great eastern barrens from Harar to Neghelli and over to Ferfer. They are Muslims, mixed in blood but with a strong injection of the Semite, tall, austere but fond of bright colours, mentally quick, politically minded, prone to talk at length on important subjects such as war, women, religion, water, grass and politics, and are good men with camels. Their cousins, the Dankalis, who live along Ethiopia's north-eastern border, are similar to them in many ways but much more primitive and fierce.

NEW FLOWER

Addis Ababa, which sits 7,800 feet above sea level in an evergreen-wooded mountain valley flecked with wild flowers, was founded by Menelik II, one of the greatest of Ethiopia's emperors, and is only about sixty years old. Before that the Negus Negasti (King of Kings) ruled from a great shifting city of tents, which despite its impermanence was laid out in a regular plan. The tents of the king were flanked by two tent-churches, called St. Mary and Holy Cross, and there was a special bakery for making the Communion bread. When the king went out, he rode a mule and was covered by a great red canopy. He was always accompanied by four lions. He once lived in almost complete seclusion but it became a practice to show himself to the people thrice a year (Christmas, Easter and Holy Cross Day) so that his subjects could know that he had not been poisoned by his courtiers.

When Menelik II finally came to roost at Addis Ababa—which means 'New Flower'—he decreed that each of the city's inhabitants should plant a eucalyptus tree and today the city is bathed in the aromatic smoke of the wood fires.

The streets are jammed with flocks of sheep and goats coming to market, burros carrying firewood, pith-helmeted members of the Imperial Guard and bereted army and police, black-robed Coptic priests, wearing white turbans and followed by entourages of servants, guiding their mules beside the open sewers, sports cars roaring up and down at breakneck speed, threading their way among huge potholes and between the motor-cycle taxis. German businessmen and Point IV technicians jostle each other on the dirt pavements. Posters and signboards exhort the wanderer in three languages to use Socony Vacuum petrol, Michelin tyres and Ipana toothpaste. Mud huts behind fences of sharpened stakes lean against modern office buildings and oversized pancakes of cow dung fuel bake in the sun beside the elegant compounds of embassies and ministries, guarded by ragged, rifle-carrying watchmen called *zabanias*. There are Cadillacs on the streets during the day, hyenas at night.

The business centre of the town, Haile Selassie Square, which everyone still calls the Piazza, boasts a real indication of progress, a monumental *pissoir*. Concrete benches made of imitation logs line the sides of the Piazza and here are two of the town's three bookshops. In these one can buy the latest Italian, French, Swedish and British, Russian and Arabic magazines as well as dog-eared copies of *Confidential* and *See*. From the windows of the United States Information Service library, which serves as a film auditorium for free showings of Americana ('President Eisenhower's Inauguration', 'How to Write a Police Report'), one can see barelegged boys gazing in the windows of the Soviet Information Centre at a picture display captioned in English and Amharic depicting the glories of life in Russia. Jutting into the Piazza is the King George Bar, where down-at-the-heel expatriates of a dozen countries sit moodily behind piles of saucers sipping a lager named after Ethiopia's patron saint, St. George.

Addis Ababa has a dial telephone system, an opera house with banjo-sized seats which has never shown an opera, three movie theatres, hundreds of brothels, and some of the riper beggars in East Africa. The locals bow when passing a church, stare in awe at the monumental equestrian statue of Menelik II, and are frankly fascinated by the traffic lights which are regarded as decorative rather than functional. In the market you can buy a hand-written Bible bound in wood, a specific to cure warts or an elephant hair bracelet which will make you brave in battle.

Down Churchill Road (there are streets named after King George, Queen Elizabeth, Roosevelt, Smuts and other luminaries, intersections and squares for Matthew, Mark, Luke, John, and the Father, Son and Holy Ghost) is the Ras Hotel, partially owned by the Empress Menen, as are said to be a goodly proportion of the *tej* houses which line the road. *Tej* is a yeasty brew made of fermented honey and is Ethiopia's national drink. In the bad old days, the buyer of a glass of *tej* also purchased rights to the girl who served it. Nowadays, an additional cash outlay is required.

At the Ras you get a room with tiled bath and the barman builds a noteworthy dry martini. But flashlight batteries and shoe-laces fill the lobby showcases and the people from miles around still flock to the Ras to observe the wonders of Ethiopia's only revolving door. Addis Ababa's nattily dressed and well-perfumed rakes gather at the Ras on Friday nights with their proud, fine-featured ladies to dance to the somewhat inhibited melodies of the Imperial Band (available for hire during off-duty hours) and eat *enjira-wat*, a highly spiced meat stew poured over paper-thin slices of grey bread.

Across a hill the base of which serves as a rubbish dump, sits the Emperor's new Jubilee Palace and the plush Ghion Hotel, also owned by the Empress. There, for £5 6s. a day, the visitor gets a murky swimming pool, tennis courts, a telephone in his room, three bars and a fighting chance of escaping amoebic dysentery.

Twelve-foot fences shield sensitive eyes from the sight of the native slums near the modernistic Legislative Assembly and Haile Selassie Cathedral, built, logically enough, by Haile Selassie. Near one of the monoliths built to commemorate the liberation of Ethiopia from the Italians is a large circular cage which contains the Emperor's lions. He used to give them to favoured visitors but now seems to concentrate more on autographed photos. It is legally permissible but actually forbidden to take pictures of street scenes on grounds that photographs might show some of the backward aspects of Ethiopian life.

The social life of the capital is stiff, brittle and exhausting. Ethiopians have a habit of accepting, refusing or ignoring invitations and then doing the opposite thing. In defence, many dinners are planned buffet.

Although Addis Ababa, which has a population of about 350,000, boasts three Amharic, two French and one English newspaper, press censorship is strict. The name of the Emperor and names of the royal family must appear before those of anyone else, no matter what their news relevance, and all imperial adjectives and pronouns must be capitalized. Group pictures in which any of the individuals shown are dead are *verboten*.

Addis Ababa is as international as New York, with substantial colonies of Americans (North and South), Russians (Red and White), Germans (Jews and *staatlos* Nazis), Swedes, Britons, French, Yugoslavs, Italians, Syrians, Jews, Dutch, Indians, Pakistanis, Austrians, Czechs and Danes. These build roads, staff hospitals, fly the planes of state-owned Ethiopian Air Lines, train the army, supervise the telephone system, teach school, bore for water and oil, practise medicine, serve in most departments of the administration, run the railway, engage in trade and generally make Ethiopia tick.

Most numerous are the Greeks, Americans, Italians, Armenians and Indians. The Greeks are active in the textile trade, Italians predominate in lumber and construction, Armenians have the shoe business almost to themselves, the Indians are general merchants and the Americans are to be found in most government departments. Russian interest in Ethiopia dates from the days of the czars when the Dejazmatch Baltcha hospital was established. In general, Russian influence in Addis Ababa has been exaggerated. Their diplomatic staff, although high-powered, is considerably smaller than that of the American Embassy. Their information centre has a small budget but does a good job because they go in for pictures rather than books in a country where most people are illiterate. The hospital is excellent and many an imperialist warmonger goes there to have his appendix out because it's cheaper than at the Seventh Day Adventist Zauditu Memorial Hospital. Both hospitals have their hands full dealing with a bewildering array of ailments which include malaria, typhus, relapsing fever, amoebic dysentery, tuberculosis, sleeping sickness, leprosy and strangulated hernias. There are about 125 White Russians.

In some ways the saddest group of expatriates is the clutch of American Negroes. In the 1920s Ethiopia was something of a Black

Zion to the coloured people of the world, who saw in it the redemption of their racial pride. A handful made their way to Addis Ababa only to find that the Amharas looked on all Negroes as inferior people. Most of them stayed on because they had nowhere else to go. They speak Coolidge-era slang, have curiously dated ideas about America, and eke out their lives in minor government posts.

With the exception of the Italian occupation (1936–1941), Ethiopia has been free since the dim beginnings of time, although it did not achieve political unity until a few years before the turn of the century. Homer and Herodotus mentioned Ethiopia, the 'furthest of all mankind'. The structure of the society and the life of the land has a flavour appropriately Biblical, since it is an article of faith with every Ethiopian that his rulers are descended from Old Testament kings.

It all started when Solomon began sub-contracting for the building of the temple. An Ethiopian merchant delivered a consignment of wood, gold and sapphires and returned with vivid tales of the Jewish court. Makeda, Queen of Ethiopia, who the locals say was the Queen of Sheba, decided that this she had to see and forthwith she departed with 797 camels and mules laden with gifts. Solomon converted Makeda to Judaism and tricked her on to the royal couch. In due time, she gave birth to a son called Menelik.

When Menelik started asking embarrassing questions about his father, Makeda told him her story and presented him with a ring which Solomon had given her. Menelik set forth post-haste for Jerusalem. There he was received with joy by Solomon who urged him unsuccessfully to stay and rule over Judah. When Menelik would not agree to this, Solomon ordained that none but Menelik and his line should ever be kings in Ethiopia and commanded that the first-born sons of all his nobles should accompany the lad back to Ethiopia to help him rule over the land. Menelik begged a piece of the fringe of the covering of the Ark of the Covenant to take back with him and Solomon granted his request. But Menelik's new-found Israeli comrades, who were not overjoyed at the prospect of being exiled to a backwater like Ethiopia, spitefully stole the entire Ark. When the word got out, Solomon tore his hair, but the dynasty was founded and if you don't believe that Haile Selassie is Solomon's seed you are a blasphemer.

Historians and archaeologists are generally agreed that the whole story is a complete fabrication. But there are many Judaic tints to Ethiopian life and legends such as this, firmly believed by the mass of the population, do not spring from nothing. An amateur going against the word of all the established authorities used a similar legend to establish the location of Troy where the academics said it could not be.

The first white visitors to Ethiopia were the Greek admirals sent out by the Ptolemys in the third century B.C. to capture African elephants. Ethiopia is mentioned in a first-century Greek sailors' handbook called the *Periplus of the Erythraean Sea* and an Alexandrian merchant visited the country in the sixth century. Greek writers of that time maintained that the Ethiopians were the descendants of Syrian colonists established there by Alexander the Great and knew that the King of Axum wore a golden collar, draped himself in a single garment studded with gold and pearls, and rode around on a four-wheeled chariot pulled by elephants.

The second great event in Ethiopia's history—the first, of course, being the high-jinks between Solomon and Makeda—was the introduction of Christianity. The Ethiopians maintain that they followed the Hebrew faith from ancient times until the fourth century. Scholars say that both faiths were introduced about the same time from the Arabian peninsula in the fifth, sixth or seventh century.

According to the Ethiopian version, the Church was founded in A.D. 330 by a shipwrecked Syrian youth named Frumentius and his younger brother, Aedesius. They were spared in the slaughter of the survivors and brought to the court of the Negus. The two boys were kept at court for several years, served as tutors to the king's children, and roused the ruler's interest in Christianity. Eventually he freed them and commanded them to go and bring back bishops to instruct his people.

Aedesius went home and considered himself well out of a bad business. But Frumentius, who was 'sagacious and prudent', presented himself to the patriarch of Alexandria and told his story. The patriarch was interested enough to consecrate Frumentius on the spot and send him back to Ethiopia as Catholicus ('archbishop'). The Ethiopians referred to him as Abba Salama, which means 'Father of Peace', and to his successors as *abuna* or 'father'. To make sure that the new daughter church kept in line, the Alexandria brethren forged a canon of the Council of Nicea stating that the Ethiopian Catholicus would always be appointed by Alexandria and that he would rank ninth in the order of the princes of the Church.

The heads of the Ethiopian Church for 1,600 years were Egyptian Copts, usually ignorant of Geez, the priestly language, and of the secular tongues, appointed by Alexandria. In modern terms, this would be as if the Pope were always a Swede speaking neither Latin nor Italian. In 1951, after more than twenty years of negotiation, Haile Selassie won the right to appoint an Ethiopian Catholicus, who is confirmed by Alexandria.

The fourth century was a risky time to be a theologian and the next hundred years saw the rise and fall of the Arian, Macedonian, Apollinarian and Nestorian heresies. The Coptic (Egyptian) Church and its Ethiopian daughter were strongholds of the Nicene faith. But they got so irritated with the Nestorians for their belief that Christ wore the Godhead like an overcoat that the Copts fell over to the other side of orthodoxy and maintained the monophysite view that the manhood of Christ was absorbed in His divinity. The Council of Chalcedon (A.D. 451) proclaimed both views to be wrong and asserted that Christ's nature was dual. Their adherence to a doctrine which the rest of the world set aside 1,500 years ago has contributed to the Ethiopians' national sensitivity and the feeling of being a people apart and, of course, superior.

In the fifth century, the liturgy and scriptures were first translated into Geez, the ancient language of the Ethiopians, by a group of Syrian refugees known as the Nine Saints. As the result of their labours, those familiar with Geez can read the Books of Enoch and Jubilees, extant in no other form. We will return to the Church later but let us continue now with the recounting of a few of the fruitier and more important events in Ethiopian history.

THE RISE OF ISLAM

Until the middle of the seventh century, Ethiopia, although remote and barbaric, lay on the fringes of a friendly Christian world to which it was bound by cords of trade and religion. The rise of militant Islam was to slam the door of history in Ethiopia's face and leave her in isolation to develop her own curious culture. Muslim armies occupied Palestine in A.D. 636 and Egypt fell six years later.

For a time, Christian Ethiopia and the Muslim world remained on fairly good terms, if only because the Negus was the only one of all the kings of the world to answer Mohammed when the latter announced his mission (the Negus said 'no'). From time to time hostilities broke out but, in general, Ethiopia was left alone.

In the middle of the twelfth century a letter was published in Europe said to have been written by one Prester John, a Christian monarch who ruled somewhere in the back of beyond over seventy-two kings and twelve archbishops and had a marvellous mirror which enabled him to see all parts of his extensive empire. He went to war, it was said, preceded by thirteen golden crosses and 230,000 warriors and he was keen on marching to Jerusalem and stamping out the infidel. Since Saladin was making hash of the Crusaders about this time, it sounded a good idea.

Nothing came of it, perhaps because Saladin fulfilled the longing of the Ethiopian Church for a monastery in Jerusalem, but men continued to dream of this great Christian prince and, in 1487, King John of Portugal sent Bartholomew Diaz by sea and Peter de Covilham by land in an attempt to establish contact with Prester John. Diaz rounded the Cape of Good Hope, establishing the fact that there was a sea route to India, and Portuguese interest declined for the moment. This was unfortunate for de Covilham, who so delighted the Ethiopian king that he was still there when another Portuguese traveller arrived thirty years later.

In the early years of the sixteenth century, a left-handed Muslim war-lord from the Danakil desert named Mohammed Gran decided that he would set the Ethiopians straight once and for all on this business of religion. Being a practical man, he figured that a couple of hundred Turks armed with blunderbusses would do more towards encouraging piety and conformity than theological tracts. In short order, 90 per cent of the Ethiopians saw the error of their ways, the Negus sent an SOS to the King of Portugal and headed for the high grass. Vasco da Gama's son Christopher showed up with four hundred men in 1541 and set about chastising Mohammed Gran. In the war which resulted, Gran captured da Gama and beheaded him but was killed in a subsequent battle along with most of his Turks. Ethiopia was saved for Christianity and the surviving Portuguese were informed that they were to stay in Ethiopia and serve the King for the rest of their lives. News of the country began to filter back to Europe, perhaps from these lonely mercenaries.

It was said that the Negus never walked except when he went to church and that the streets were cleared then so that none might see him. He never spoke on public occasions and it took ten days for the camel train bearing his annual tribute to pass his throne. One king had a palace lined with ivory and Venetian mirrors. Another tried to butcher all of his subjects named George because a soothsayer had warned that one of that name not related to him would follow him on the throne.

The Jesuits got interested in Ethiopia and sent out a series of priests who were to build some first-rate palaces for the kings of Ethiopia and create considerable ill-will. The Ethiopians reckoned that they had been Christians for more than a thousand years and they took serious umbrage when informed that all their priests were suspended and the entire population would have to be rebaptized and the churches reconsecrated. Although more than one Negus became Catholic, the public outcry was so great that the Jesuits were sold into slavery and three Capuchins who picked a bad time to show up were flayed alive. So aroused were the Ethiopians that the only white man allowed to live in the country for fifty years thereafter was a Scottish Presbyterian who was able truthfully to say that he hated the Catholics as much as they did.

By 1800, Ethiopia had virtually collapsed as a result of its struggles against Islam and internecine quarrels. There were at least six claimants to the throne. Order was restored by a man so poor that his widowed mother had been reduced to selling *kosso*, a tapeworm remedy. Theodore, as he came to be known, had nowhere to go but up. He started life as a highwayman and parlayed the personal loyalty of his hard-bitten gang of cut-throats and an amazing talent for intrigue into the kingship. He was a terrible-tempered man of considerable administrative ability. One by one he subdued the recalcitrant chiefs, converted the Muslim tribes to Christianity or expelled them from their lands. At his right hand were two English adventurers and, when one of them was mistakenly murdered, Theodore apologized to Queen Victoria and added that he hoped the punishment he had imposed would be considered sufficient. He had put to death *1,500* people.

But as Theodore grew older, he began to lose hold on himself and on his people. He drank himself into a wild rage every night, rose at dawn to howl the Psalms, took Muslim women to his bed. When his subjects objected, he burned thousands alive. As the result of an unanswered letter to Queen Victoria, Theodore imprisoned the British representative at his court and brought about his own downfall.

NAPIER'S EXPEDITION

Nowadays almost any tin-horn country apparently can imprison Britons (or Americans) with impunity. But in 1867 the British bulldog had teeth in his jaws and Sir Robert Napier landed near Massawa with 3,400 men, some Indian elephants, and a Welsh bastard named Henry Morton Stanley who had just finished tours of duty in the Confederate *and* Union armies, was to make a name for himself by rescuing people who had no desire to be rescued, develop into one of Africa's greatest explorers, and finally, loaded with years and honours, die a member of the British Parliament.

Napier's army met Theodore at Arogee and it was the story which was to be repeated at Omdurman thirty years later: the Ethiopians charged with reckless bravery, were mown down by modern weapons and, although the army was completely eliminated as a fighting force, retired shouting their defiance. 'I had intended,' mourned Theodore, 'if God had so decreed, to conquer the whole world.' He shot himself on Easter Monday as Napier's troops marched into his capital. It is tempting to think how Ethiopia's history might have changed if the British had stayed and established a colony in the healthy highlands. But Britain was busy elsewhere and Napier freed the European prisoners and withdrew, carrying with him the crowns of the Abuna and of Theodore, and the royal copy of *Kebra Negast* (Glory of Kings), the Ethiopian chronicles. The *Kebra Negast* was returned to Theodore's successor who pleaded that his subjects would not obey him without it, and Theodore's crown was brought back by Haile Selassie in 1925.

Ethiopia fell into a disorder from which it was only to be rescued by a great emperor, Menelik II. Menelik was a king of Shoa who, with assistance from the poet Rimbaud, who was doing a little gun-running and dabbling in the slave trade, was able to procure French arms at only eight times their actual value. In short order Menelik added Harar, Kaffa (the home of coffee) and the Galla countries to Shoa, and married his infant daughter Zauditu to the son of the Negus Negasti. Menelik then forced the ageing Emperor to conclude a treaty recognizing him as his heir. When Menelik ascended the throne in 1889, most of what is today Ethiopia was for the first time ruled by one man.

Seven years later Ethiopia was to put this new-found unity to good use. Italy had seized Eritrea and Somalia and was anxious to link the two by acquiring Ethiopia. The Italians remembered Napier's expedition and did not expect too much resistance. But they overlooked two factors: the Ethiopia conquered by Napier was a divided kingdom ruled by a hated and half-mad monarch; and Menelik had received, in addition to his French arms, a gift of 28 cannon and 38,000 rifles from King Umberto of *Italy*.

Hoping to surprise Menelik's army at church in Adowa on a feast day, the Italians attacked on Sunday, March 1, 1896. They were hopelessly routed. Menelik killed 8,000 Italians and 4,000 of their Eritrean *askaris* and captured 1,865 others. Only 635 of the invaders escaped to the coast. Italy recognized Ethiopian sovereignty and agreed to pay reparations to obtain the release of the prisoners. Thirty Italians had been mutilated against Menelik's orders. The Eritreans fared not so well: Menelik, to show his contempt for them as traitors to their race, ordered that 406 of them should have their right hand and left foot amputated.

This major victory, the first and last to be achieved by a native chief against a modern European power, put Ethiopia on the map and the Powers sent their representatives scuttling to Addis Ababa, Menelik's new capital, to establish relations with Ethiopia. Adowa earned for Ethiopia thirty-nine years of peace, years which Menelik, as progressive in peace as he was fierce in war, was to put to good use.

He granted the French—under the urging of a Swiss engineer named Ilg whose frock coat and top hat were one of the sights of Addis Ababa—the concession to build a railway from their Red Sea port of Djibouti to Addis Ababa. He took steps to suppress the slave trade, softened Ethiopia's harsh legal code, and established a semblance of civil administration. He introduced the telephone, telegraph and postage stamp to the country, built Ethiopia's first schools and hospitals, and established a rudimentary cabinet system to replace the old personal rule of the Negus. He anticipated Haile Selassie's international military co-operation during the Korean War by sending Ethiopian units in 1900 and 1904 to aid the British against Mohammed Abdullah, the Mad Mullah of Somaliland. Under Menelik, the Ethiopians who Gibbon said had 'slept a thousand years, forgetful of the world, by whom they were forgotten', finally woke up. Menelik established order, turned the face of Ethiopia from the past to the present, and brought in foreign advisers to smooth the path of progress.

The story of Haile Selassie's rise to power will be told when we consider that remarkable man's career. He came to the throne in 1930 only to be forced into exile six years later when Italy revenged herself for Adowa and occupied Ethiopia. On May 1, 1941, five years to the day after leaving his capital, Haile Selassie returned in triumph to Addis Ababa at the head of a British army supported by Ethiopian irregulars. Much has been accomplished in the post-war years but the structure of Ethiopian society remains much the same.

THE CHURCH

The Church, although Haile Selassie in 1951 separated it from Egypt and successfully asserted his right to appoint the Catholicus, retains much of its original colour and flavour. The Ethiopians have a talent for mortification of the flesh and are prone to religiosity without being essentially spiritual. Sitting all night up to the neck in a tank of icy water is considered to ease the path to heaven and one Ethiopian was canonized for standing on one foot for thirty years. Penitents who domicile themselves in open graves are also highly regarded. The liturgy of St. Mark is followed, more than 200 fast days are observed, Lent is fifty-six days long and the godly do not sit down, and eat only bread and water during this period (making it a favourite time for Muslim attack, since most of the Christian population is in a state of near-starvation), ritual bathing takes place at Epiphany, and the Ethiopian calendar dates from the Era of Martyrs, which means that it is eight years behind ours. There are twelve months of thirty days and a thirteenth month of five or six days to make the year come out even.

Many practices of the Ethiopian Orthodox Church have an Hebraic ring: Ethiopians observe the Mosaic distinction between clean and unclean meat, they regard those who have had sexual intercourse as impure on the following day, and they celebrate the Sabbath as well as Sunday. The Amharic renderings of religious words such as Hell, idol, Easter and purification are obviously of Hebrew origin. An ox, a ewe and a she-goat are sacrificed at the dedication of churches. Practices such as the dancing of the priests, the beating of drums during the liturgy, and the lunar celebration of certain feasts are probably hang-overs from pagan days.

Ethiopian churches, of which there are about 18,000, are usually octagonal in form with a central sanctuary. Most churches have no seats and segregation of the sexes is practised. Divorce is easy and the keeping of concubines is an accepted practice. Few sins are mortal and they mainly concern breaches of ritual, such as wearing shoes in church. Excommunication frequently follows failure to observe fasts and it has been estimated that as much as a third of the Christian population is excommunicated at any given time. Those who are excommunicated or who do not consider themselves saved attend services but stand outside in the church courtyard while only the pure go in.

Services are conducted in Geez, the forgotten tongue of Ethiopia, which most priests can read but do not understand. The Bible was not translated into Amharic, the everyday language of the Ethiopian Christians, until 1934. The first edition was printed in London during the war but most of it was destroyed in the blitz. The clergy is immense, an estimated one out of every six adult Christians being a member of the cloth. Children are ordained as deacons and become priests at the age of twelve or fourteen. Although the Emperor has taken steps to educate the clergy, most are still illiterate. As many as two thousand have been ordained in a single mass ceremony. Monasteries flourish and the monks often spend their days in disputations of the how-many-angels-on-the-head-of-a-pin variety. When the monks of Debra Libanos came up with the wrong answer, one old emperor put the whole bunch to the sword. The Ethiopians of old hewed huge churches out of solid stone. Priests may marry but monks are celibate and those of the monasteries on Lake Tana, where the kings of Ethiopia are buried, are so pious that not even female animals, wild or domestic, are permitted on the islands.

The Old Testament character of the country is enhanced by the presence of the *Falasha* ('exiles'). These live north of Lake Tana (which abounds with huge pythons) and are black Jews. They have the same physical appearance as the local people and they know no Hebrew, neither do they possess the Mishna nor the Talmud. Their brand of Judaism is curiously archaic and they do not celebrate the dedication or the destruction of the second temple. They have a monastic system and believe themselves to be the descendants of the first-born Israelites who stole the Ark from Solomon and accompanied his son, Menelik, back to Ethiopia.

The *Falasha*, who number about 70,000, are a shy and introverted people and will not enter their homes after talking with a Christian without washing and changing their clothes. They are blacksmiths and workers with iron which, as everybody knows, gives them the ability to change themselves into hyenas at night.

The Ethiopian Church has evolved into its present somewhat curious form as the result of the national history of its people. Cut off for centuries from the rest of Christendom, it was not unnatural that it borrowed from its Judaic and pagan past and emphasized the literal interpretation of such gospels as it possessed. Most observers like to refer to the Ethiopians as quotation mark Christians and to scorn their practices, perhaps forgetting that these do little harm and are intended only to glorify God. The Ethiopians naturally are proud of the fact that they have maintained their Christianity for centuries against a hostile infidel world and they resent today the attempts of white missionaries to proselytize among the Copts as much as they did when the Spanish Jesuits tried it for the first time four hundred years ago.

The Ethiopian Church has played a major role in the past as a defender of learning and civilization and today it acts as a great bond which ties Ethiopia together and to its half-divine monarchs.

THE NOBLES

The nobles, the second great historic power group in Ethiopia, have not always played a unifying role. The nature of the country is such that, in the past, a strong noble has been able to rule his vast holdings with the same contempt for the imperial authority as the dukes of Burgundy once showed for the kings of France. They owned (and still do) vast estates and maintained private armies. Many of the old emperors sought to keep the loyalty of the great dukes by contracting plural marriages with their daughters. This practice worked fairly well although a generation of ruinous warfare was touched off by the refusal of the Emperor Lebna Dengel to marry the daughter of the King of Hadya because the lady in question had buck teeth. As the result of wedding and bedding, almost every person of noble blood is related to the rest of the nobility and almost all can boast a touch of royal blood. This has complicated the political history of the country as it has always been all too easy to find a noble with as good or better a blood claim to the throne of the King of Kings than the occupant could boast. And these pretenders, of course, have served as rallying points for those dissatisfied with the man of the moment.

As the Wars of the Roses eradicated the flower of the British nobility and made possible the rise of democracy and pickle barons, so the Italian war and the occupation which followed broke the power of the Ethiopian nobility. Ethiopian intrigues and jealousies gave way, as they always have, under the threat of an invader and the nobles rallied to meet the common foe. As the natural leaders of the country, thousands were mown down by Mussolini's machine-guns in two years of campaigning. Of those that survived, the more dangerous ones were executed and the remainder were almost exterminated by the Italians in 1937 as retribution for an assassination attempt on the life of Marshal Graziani, Mussolini's viceroy in Ethiopia.

Since the war, Haile Selassie has created no new *rases*. These were never strictly hereditary titles and, as a result, the nobility is much less numerous than it was once. The powers of those who remain have been curbed and the provinces, which once were ruled as personal fiefs, are now tightly controlled by the central administration. Many of the vast estates have been broken up and the hold of the nobles over the peasants has been weakened by the abolition (on paper) of feudal taxes, and the *watarane*, the two months labour owed by each serf to his lord. Although one cannot help but mourn the passing of these warlike men who were, after all, the best which their country could produce, they tended to be reactionary and it is difficult to see how the Emperor could achieve the mild degree of democratization which he has, had their position of power remained unchanged.

THE ARMY

The Imperial Army, along with the Church and the nobles, has been the third traditional source of power in Ethiopia. The Emperor has counterbalanced the army by the creation of an *élite* 5,000-man Imperial Guard, many of whom are Muslims or pagans who were presumed to be personally devoted to him. One battalion of the Guard fought beside the U.S. 7th Division in Korea for many months and never had a man captured. Oddly enough, it was the Imperial Guard which formed the core of the revolt against Haile Selassie in last year's disorder.

The army has been completely re-equipped with American arms and trained by U.S. instructors since World War II and is an efficient 25,000-man fighting force. In the old days, emperors retained the loyalty of their armies by allowing them periodic holidays of rapine and looting among the defenceless tribes. This sort of thing is out of fashion now and Haile Selassie, like the Roman emperors and the U.S. Congress, courts favour by giving land to veterans and granting them special privileges. One of Haile Selassie's best recommendations for high office, as we will see, was the loyalty of one wing of the army. That loyalty still exists, although severely shaken by the trends of last December.

New additions to the Ethiopian armoury are a navy and an air force, and these are the apples of the Emperor's eye. His Swedish-trained fliers pilot a dozen or so propeller-driven fighters and Ethiopians who a decade ago considered the poky Djibouti railway as the last thing in modern transport are eager to obtain jets. The Norwegian-trained navy was officially launched in 1957 with the presentation by the

United States of a submarine-chaser. The navy is based at Massawa and Haile Selassie is determined that his country, with its newly-acquired Eritrean ports, shall once again become a Red Sea naval power.

And now let us see how Ethiopia obtained Eritrea and what she is doing with it.

Chapter 4

*

LOST PROVINCE

North of Ethiopia, between that country and the Red Sea, lies the former Italian colony of Eritrea, an 'autonomous unit' (to use the United Nations phraseology) the size of Greece, now federated with Ethiopia. Eritrea, which has a 650-mile coastline, is shaped like a funnel, with the spout to the south-east bordering on French Somaliland and the widest part of the country lying up against the Sudan. Its people vary from the wild and primitive Muslim tribes who eke out a bare existence in the Danakil desert of the spout, one of the hottest lands in the world and a region which no white man crossed until 1928, to settled agriculturalists—differing little from their cousins across the Ethiopian border—who farm cool highland meadows. The country's 1·2 million people are about equally divided between the Christian and Muslim faiths and their enthusiasm for Eritrea's federal relationship with Ethiopia is largely conditioned by the faith to which they adhere. In general, the Christian population favours the merger while the Muslims resent it.

For reasons which we will explore a little later, the Eritrean population as a whole tends to be more advanced than that of Ethiopia. Many Eritreans fought against Ethiopia during the Italian invasion and the Eritreans, like the Poles, have a strong separatist tradition which they have been too weak to fulfil at most stages of their history. The Semitic strain is stronger in Eritrea than it is in Ethiopia and the people tend to be lighter in colour. Although many Eritreans can speak one or more of the Ethiopian languages, their tongue is quite different from Amharic. These political, religious and ethnic differences combine with a grinding poverty and a sense of better times past to make Eritrea a rather unhappy place.

Eritrea has no university, a tiny handful of college graduates and only four high schools. Eighty per cent of the population is illiterate and about 10 per cent of the children go to school. There are only 250 miles of paved roads and Eritrea is so poor that she has to import a good deal of her food. She exports hides and skins, fish, salt, buttons and

81

ceramics, mostly to Italy. Eritreans are small-boned people with finely-chiselled faces and they tend to be excitable, perhaps as the result of their long association with the Italians. The Eritrean police (the country is garrisoned by the Ethiopian army) wear ten-gallon hats pinned up on one side in the Anzac fashion, starched khaki shorts and puttees pipe-clayed to a gleaming whiteness. As in northern Italy, the trunks of the sycamore and wild olive trees which line the roads are whitewashed from ground to eye-level.

Asmara, the capital, is a pleasant, poplar-lined city which was to have been the gem of Il Duce's ill-fated East African empire. The Italians built it from scratch at the turn of the century, they built well, and Addis Ababa suffers in the comparison. The wide streets are paved, the buildings are solid, the sewerage system works. But it was a European city and the Eritrean who ventured on to the pavement was likely to be assisted off it with the business end of a boot. The Italians built high schools for their own people but an Eritrean could go no further than primary school. After 1934, Asmara, which has a millionaire's climate, boomed as the principal base for Mussolini's jump-off into Ethiopia.

Bearded Italian friars, wearing brown robes and sandals, pedal bicycles up the town's gentle hills and venerable Fiats driven by white cabbies vie with camel trains lurching into town loaded with salt. The European market offers *pasta* in a dozen shapes, olive oil in green, half-gallon tins, bright-red tomatoes and sickly celery. In the twisting maze of the native market you can buy anything from a thimbleful of frankincense to a complete dinner service hammered out of old beer cans. Asmara's ladies of the night do a thriving business and, for the celibate, there is a threadbare night club which cannot be the best on the Red Sea belly-dancing circuit.

In its hey-day, Asmara had a population of more than 30,000 Italians. Today the European population has dropped to about 10,000 and every day the shutters clang down on another shop whose owner has given up and applied for repatriation to Italy. Some small businessmen leave for political reasons, more because taxes are too high and trade bad. Most of the big firms—including an ultra-modern textile factory, the brewery, a ceramics house and a primitive match factory where nimble-fingered girls make the boxes by hand for 50 cents a day and *tout confort* (a hard roll and tea at noon)—have managed to hang on.

But the Italian flavour remains. The Avenue Haile Selassie, which has been the Viale Mussolini, is called by most people by its old name,

Corso Italia. There are *espresso* shops where you can buy *pizza*-take-away and restaurants with check tablecloths, white waiters, breadsticks and chianti. The bougainvillaea still climbs around pastel-coloured villas from which the paint is beginning to peel.

Asmara is perched at 7,765 feet and nights are cold when the fog whips up from Massawa, its port, a sweltering place, old and run-down, full of Maugham characters eating spaghetti in their undershirts. The two cities are connected by part of Eritrea's 190 miles of railway and by a beautifully-engineered Italian-built road. There is also an aerial ropeway which carried freight between the two cities in boom days. Hard times have closed it and the iron carts swing on their rusting cables.

CONQUERORS (ASSORTED)

Of the early history of Eritrea little is known. This forlorn and thorny coast and the mountains which edge it have been fought for and conquered countless times by people from both shores of the Red Sea. The Axumite kingdom, one of the forerunners of the Ethiopian Empire, ruled both coasts and one of its kings boasted that he held sway from Somaliland to Egypt. Axum traded with the Greeks and its early kings spoke the language of the Hellenes and worshipped Zeus, Ares and Poseidon. This civilization, which has left a legacy of gigantic and puzzling columns of solid granite, lasted from the third to the ninth century, when it was overrun, probably by Semites from what is today Yemen. There followed seven centuries of disorder. The fierce Dankali tribesmen, who roam the desert today in the same fashion as did their forefathers and like to give their girl-friends the genitalia of fallen foes as corsages, were never conquered by anyone. The Muslim tribes of the West asserted their freedom whenever they could. Various quasi-independent Ethiopian *rases* from time to time extended their control from the highlands to the coast. But it was an age in which a man owned only what he could defend and the extent of political control depended entirely on the ferocity of the local war-lord and his fealty to the Negus Negasti. Still, it was upon this period that Ethiopia was to base her successful bid to include Eritrea in her empire at the end of World War II.

In 1557 the Turks seized the ports of the Eritrean coast and held them for three hundred years before leasing them to Egypt. The Khedive, who was busy sending Baker, Gordon, Emin and Slatin to spread his domain to the Great Lakes, next turned his attention to Eritrea. The Swiss adventurer, Baron Munsinger, with assistance from some American Civil War veterans, was placed in command of a force which pacified much of Eritrea and then attempted to invade Ethiopia. In 1876 the Ethiopian Emperor John met and defeated Munsinger and the Egyptians withdrew to their ports. The Mahdi's rise to power in the Sudan checked any further Egyptian expansionism and, at the same time, rocked Christian Ethiopia: a dervish expedition triumphantly bore the head of the Emperor John to the Khalifa's tent.

As far as Europe was concerned, Eritrea was a worthless backwater. This situation was radically altered with the opening in 1869 of the Suez Canal. Italy, busy with her own problems of unification at home, came late to the African banquet but was quick to grab what she could. An Italian trading company bought the port of Assab and its oasis from the local sheikh in 1869. The Italian government took over the concession and, in 1885, occupied Massawa. Italian columns fanned out into the interior and, within ten years, modern Eritrea—named after the Latin designation of the Red Sea—took shape.

We have already seen how Italy was humbled at Adowa by Menelik II. For forty years she was to have to content herself with Eritrea, Somaliland and Libya. She held Eritrea for fifty-one years from the Treaty of Ucciali to the fall of Asmara on April 1, 1941. It is not wise to say anything good about European imperialism in present-day Africa, the more so when the nation concerned happens to have been fascist. It is true that the Italians did little for the Eritreans and put down revolts with harshness. It is also true that they brought order and an administrative system to a people who had known only inter-necine war before. They introduced Eritrea to a money economy and gave it a higher standard of living than Ethiopia had ever known. They built the railways and roads which are the economic backbone of the country. And it should be said that the majority of Italians, like the Portuguese, whatever their politics, get along better with Africans than do most Anglo-Saxons. There is little difference between an Umbrian peasant and an Eritrean farmer, a point which many Italians demonstrated in the age-old fashion by marrying Eritreans, living happily and raising squads of beige bambini. If few Eritreans were afforded the opportunity of going beyond primary school, they were no worse off than most Neapolitans. These may be minimal achievements but they deserve to be stated.

LOST PROVINCE

THE BRITISH ARRIVE

A series of brilliant feints on the part of the Sudan Defence Force kept the Italians locked up in Eritrea during the early months of the war. Wavell's victory at Sidi Barrani freed the Fourth Indian Division in 1940 and General Platt was able to patch together an army made up of everything from crack regiments like the Cameron Highlanders to cooks-and-bottlewashers for the campaign to seize Eritrea and thus safeguard the Red Sea supply line to the Middle East. The Anglo-Indian-Sudanese force gained quick victories at Kassala and Agordat, pushed on to Keren where they were momentarily held by Marshal Lorenzini, the 'Lion of the Sahara'. Lorenzini fought well for six weeks at Keren and left his bones as proof of his valour. After his death, Italian resistance crumbled and Asmara fell like an over-ripe tomato to the advancing British. Thus began the ten-year British occupation of Eritrea.

Although the British administration was military in character, it was far freer than anything Eritreans had known. Health, agriculture and veterinary officers were posted to each of the six divisions into which the country was divided. Native councils were established in Asmara and Massawa and four towns received full municipal status. The same British Labour government which set in motion the Sudanese trade union movement saw to it that Eritrean unions were established. Local industries were encouraged, the production of food crops was doubled and a free press took root. Additional years were added to the primary syllabus and more schools, including Eritrea's first girls' school, were provided. Water-holes were dug and the transportation system maintained. Eritrea took a giant step forward.

THE PAWN

But the little country's future was not unclouded. Yet to be decided was the problem of its ultimate status. Ethiopia claimed Eritrea as her *Bahr Negash*, her lost coastal province. Italy asked for a United Nations trusteeship over her former colony. Britain, on behalf of the Sudan, pointed out the racial and religious affinities of the people of the Condominium and those of western Eritrea. Russia, most Arab nations and many of the South American states, favoured an independent Eritrea.

The Eritreans themselves were divided. Most Christian highlanders favoured unity with Ethiopia. Most of the Muslims of the western plains, where the sun beats down with an almost animate fury, favoured annexation to the Sudan. Some from both camps wanted independence, a solution which appeared to be economically unfeasible. The United States, which has an interest in Eritrea of which we will hear more later, was rumoured to be under consideration as a U.N. trustee for the country.

In 1949 came the Bevin-Sforza plan. This had much to recommend it. The Muslim northern half of Eritrea, which contains about a third of the total population, was to go to the Sudan. The remainder, including the ports which Ethiopia so desired, were to go to her. The Bevin-Sforza plan would have wiped Eritrea off the map but, in so doing, it would have destroyed nothing which had enjoyed a political personality sixty years ago. As it was, the plan passed through two committees successfully but failed by one vote to get the necessary two-thirds majority in the General Assembly.

No other solution presented itself and, in 1950, the General Assembly voted to federate Eritrea with Ethiopia. Eritrea was to have local autonomy with defence, foreign affairs, currency and finance, foreign and inter-state commerce, and communications coming under Addis Ababa. Little was to be left to Eritrea in form and even less in substance.

The United Nations sent Eduardo Mateinzo to Eritrea to explain the new deal to the local citizenry, arrange for the transfer of power and draw up a constitution. Mateinzo dutifully tramped over the countryside, lectured recalcitrant Muslim tribesmen who had no idea what a ballot box was but had strong opinions on the desirability of having an Ethiopian overlord, then withdrew to Europe to draw up a constitution which one wag was to call 'a Bolivian concept of a Swiss federation for use by an African absolute monarchy'.

The constitution guarantees free elections, universal male suffrage and the existence of an Eritrean flag, seal and coat of arms. It establishes Arabic and Tigrinya, the two local tongues, as official languages and outlaws the use of torture, not unknown in this part of the world, as a political weapon. It guarantees freedom of movement, religion, speech and assembly. It extends to Eritreans, most of whom live at a sub-subsistence level, the right to regular holidays with pay. In short, it is a political scientist's dream which has little bearing on the society for which it was supposedly drawn up and does less towards solving the age-old problems of a warrior people divided both by race and religious affinity.

Here we have the problem of the southern Sudan in reverse. There a primitive Christian-pagan people fear domination from the more advanced Arabs; here the Muslim population objects to the overlordship of what it considers to be a backward Christian power. As was true in the Sudan, independence was no real solution. With Haile Selassie's Ethiopia developing rapidly, the disparity between the two regions will, in time, disappear. Economic advance in Ethiopia will eventually mean a greater degree of prosperity for Eritrea. But this means little to the restive Muslims of the West and partition would have been a better solution from their point of view.

FEDERATION HANGOVER

Federation between these unequal partners has worked out about as well as might have been expected. The Emperor is politically the most advanced man in Ethiopia but he is not used to having his will frustrated. His Ethiopian subordinates take an even dimmer view of any Eritrean intransigence to the imperial pleasure. To demonstrate the importance with which he viewed the federation, Haile Selassie sent his son-in-law, the Bitwoded ('Dearly Beloved') Andargachaw Masai, to be his Eritrean viceroy.

The first Eritrean assembly, elected in 1952, was a fairly representative one. By law, half of its sixty-eight members must be Christian, half Muslim. In the assembly were many Muslims and not a few Christians who dared to be critical of the federal administration. This distressed the Ethiopians and, by dint of methods not unknown in Kansas City or Memphis, the legislators elected in 1956 proved better-mannered. It soon became apparent that a docile assemblyman was a prosperous assemblyman. Those too dumb or honest to see the light occasionally found that a trip to Addis Ababa could remedy the situation. Sometimes retirement from public life was indicated.

Of the new assembly—dominated by the Coptic priest, Meleche Selam—only two out of the sixty-eight proved to be any problem. One of these, a young Muslim named Mohammed Omar Akhito from the port of Assab, had his election invalidated on the shakiest of charges. The other, a tough Christian named Fessala Uoldermariam, who has survived seven assassination attempts, was jailed without charge when he announced his candidacy, released on habeas corpus proceedings instituted by a Scottish judge twenty-four hours before the election, and still won easily over the Ethiopian-backed candidate.

There are plenty of signs of the decline of political freedom. In the early days of federation, the flag, seal and coat of arms of Eritrea were occasionally seen. In 1959 Eritrea did away with its flag and 'adopted' that of Ethiopia. The following year the Eritrean Assembly unanimously ruled that the Eritrean Government should no longer be known by that name (it is now the Eritrean Administration) and that the Chief Executive of Eritrea should be known as the Chief of the Administration. The Ethiopian lion insignia is now used for administrative purposes and the Eritrean seal has been modified to bear the inscription 'Eritrean Administration under Haile Selassie, Emperor of Ethiopia'. Press censorship is effective. There are no political parties. Uniformed police are stationed outside the homes of political recalcitrants, who, if they are businessmen, find it hard to get necessary licences. The secret police and a web of informers are active and effective.

On the economic side, federation has brought depression to Eritrea's 50,000 square miles as more and more Italians pull out. The white population is down from an immediate post-war 60,000 to about 12,000 and they are still going. Although the Ethiopians have acted with as much restraint here towards their former foes as they have in Ethiopia, the imposition of heavy corporate taxes has made it difficult for most Italian firms to stay in business. They are, in addition, particularly vulnerable to blackmail on the part of unscrupulous politicians and administrators. Several coffee and cotton plantations have gone by the board as have innumerable smaller businesses. The departure of some makes it more difficult for those who remain, particularly the small firms which depend on a European clientele.

Hardest hit, of course, are the Eritreans who have entered the money economy, become detribalized and are dependent upon Italian entrepreneurs for their livelihoods. At a conservative guess, the departure of 48,000 Italians must have cost 150,000 Eritreans their jobs. It is estimated that 40 per cent of Asmara's population is unemployed and the town is thick with beggars. There is some reason to believe that the Emperor is not sorry to see the Italians go and has directed policy to that end. Although he bears individual Italians no rancour, he is an eminently practical man and a political realist. He knows that Eritrea is in an unsettled state and the presence there of a large alien population which has had imperialistic dreams before and may have them again cannot be a source of satisfaction to him.

The economic and political restiveness of Eritrea is well illustrated by the bands of *shifta* which roam its craggy highlands. Banditry is no new phenomenon in this part of the world. It is in the time-honoured tradition of the Red Sea to take by force what one cannot earn by sweat or obtain by guile. But the dimensions of the *shifta* problem indicate that the trouble is more deep-seated than just boyish playfulness.

The *shifta* movement, unlike the Mau Mau terror in Kenya, has no anti-white connotations. It is pure and simple armed banditry, born of poverty and hopelessness, nurtured on tribal and religious differences, and matured with the dissatisfaction stemming from the act of federation. *Shifta* attacks are concentrated on the main roads around Asmara. They usually take place after dark, road blocks are used, and the bandits, armed with Italian carbines, British Enfield ·303s and a smattering of American Garand M-1s, often wear uniforms stolen or otherwise obtained from the police. Money, clothes and arms are the principal targets and blood is seldom shed unless resistance is encountered; Ethiopians and Italians seem to fare worse than Americans or Eritreans. In one recent year, the Eritrean police and Ethiopian army inflicted 503 casualties on the *shifta*, captured thousands of rounds of ammunition and a variety of arms which included machine-guns and hand-grenades. Most of these weapons were issued to guerrilla bands of tribesmen by the British during the fascist occupation to keep the Italians too busy to invade the Sudan.

There is no indication that they receive any substantial amount of arms from outside sources although some observers maintain that the better-organized *shifta* bands, which may have from a dozen to a couple of hundred members, play a prominent role in two old and well-established Red Sea professions: gun-running and the shipment of slaves to Saudi Arabia. Although the Ethiopian government has done its best to wipe out this traffic, there is nothing to indicate that it has been completely successful.

The official Ethiopian line in regard to the *shifta* problem is to deny that it exists. '*Shifta*,' said Colonel Tedla Ogbit, chief of the Eritrean police, 'is finished now; it was only in the British time when the people were agitating for union with Ethiopia.' The next day ten cars were stopped on the Massawa road, their passengers stripped and robbed. Most towns have road barricades up at night and, where traffic after dark is allowed, it is often unwise. At the time of federation there may have been as many as 10,000 *shifta* roaming the country. As the result of some tough campaigning, a series of public hangings, collective fines against villages thought to be harbouring *shifta*, and an amnesty offer, the number is undoubtedly far less today.

But it should be said again that the *shifta* are in arms as much or more because they are hungry as because of political dissatisfaction. Eritrea is an agricultural country which can barely feed itself. Rainfall is light—less than twenty inches in most of the country—and a bad year means not just tight belts but starvation. There are no minerals and the departure of the Italians has presented hundreds of people with the choice of banditry or death. Whatever the causes of the situation, the *shifta* by their presence contribute to the political unrest even as they are a partial manifestation of it.

AMERICAN INFLUENCE

American influence in this restive country is profound. It all started in 1942. The British found Asmara's Radio Marina, the Italian military net, in good condition and a small group of U.S. Army Signal Corps technicians were called in to make the station operative. Renamed Kagnew (an Ethiopian word meaning 'that which brings order out of chaos'), the American base grew like Topsy. Asmara's altitude and weather conditions are excellent for reception, relay and transmission and Kagnew handled most of the Pentagon–Japan radio traffic during the Korean War. In addition, its value as a Middle Eastern monitoring station is obvious. A twenty-five-year lease was signed with Ethiopia in 1952 and the new Centia base, which includes everything from bowling alleys to a dry-cleaning plant, was established in 1957.

Camp commandants in the past have done their best to keep their men on the base and out of Asmara. There are, of course, good reasons for this. The Eritrean population, like that of most of Africa, is riddled with V.D. and boys will be boys. Americans also seem to be a bit too frank and playful for the Ethiopians: one soldier was dutifully court martialled when an informer reported to Ethiopian officials that the G.I., after a few beers in a local bar, had suggested that Haile Selassie had bugs in his beard! White-helmeted military police prowl the streets in jeeps and, sometimes forgetful of the fact that they are in Asmara, not Fort Bragg, attempt to impose curfew restrictions on American civilians.

To make its 'Little America' policy palatable, the army has installed a closed-circuit TV net (which Asmara *espresso* shop-owners have tied into, to the delight of the barefooted 'drugstore cowboys'), the 'best chocolate milk-shakes south of Rome' (the Emperor has admired their consistency), four-shilling T-bone steaks flown in from the United States and dispensed at three army clubs, a burgeoning sports pro-gramme, Boy Scouts, University of Maryland extension courses, hunting and educational tours, and a complete kindergarten-through-secondary school system. As a result, the American invasion from the political point of view has hit Asmara with the impact of a wet noodle. There is little contact between Americans and the local citizenry and at least one army officer was unaware that Eritrea is not a province of Ethiopia.

But if there is little interchange of ideas, the base has not been without effect on Asmara. A Yuletide beggar is more likely to approach you with a snappy 'Merry Christmas' than a *'Buon Natale'*. The restaurants, for the benefit of those bored and desperate individuals who manage to evade the Khaki Curtain, feature separate (and more expensive) menus in English. Asmara's fine-featured street-walkers have a sliding price scale with tariffs rising from Eritrean customers up through Ethiopians and Italians to Americans. Ragged boys under the impression that Americans exist exclusively on Wrigley's chewing gum are a traffic hazard and Asmara's 'flaming youth' twirl long key-chains, wear drape coats and slouch hats *à la* Harlem.

The £3·5 million base is important to Eritrea if only because the lease provides the country's largest source of dollars. In addition, the 1,200 Americans employ about twice that number of Eritreans and American spending amounts to about £36,000 per month.

In addition, the United States has given the Eritrean government a small but well-rounded library. The usefulness of this is somewhat compromised by the fact that all books are in English, a language which few Eritreans can read. Still, it is well patronized and may have a long-range effect. In the main, Asmara seems to prefer Presley to Parkman, bubble gum to Bernard DeVoto. The stark poverty of the Eritreans, the arrogant pride of the Ethiopians, and the 'Little America' policy drive a sharp gulf between black and white. The Americans stick to their softball, square-dancing and barbecues and far more than the beggar-strewn walk to the base separates Centia's G.I.s from Asmara's 100,000 men and women.

THE HORN

Threads of fog were whipping through the poplars on a frosty January morning as we gulped our coffee and caught a *gharri*, an Ethiopian one-horse shay driven by a grizzled little Eritrean who almost disappeared into the depths of his ragged G.I. overcoat, to take us to Asmara's railway station. It was *Timcat*, the Coptic Epiphany, and the *littorina*, the single-car diesel which plies thrice weekly to Agordat, the western railhead, was jammed with people homeward-bound for the holiday. Many carried spears or knobby throwing sticks. We settled on to a pile of hides stacked in the rear of the car and the *littorina* lurched off. Christian villages, each with its round Coptic church, gave way as we dropped off the plateau to the open Muslim country, grazing lands dotted here and there by low ovals of piled stone from which flew tattered white flags. Each enclosure had an opening facing Mecca and the East, for these were Muslim graves.

Keren is a beautiful little flower-drenched town of 13,000 people, once the centre of a prosperous Italian agricultural community. It still has its Albergo Sicilia and its Ristorante da Baffone, where one may restore the tissues with a spot of *fetuccini* washed down with *Melotti*, the excellent Eritrean beer, but all but two hundred whites have left and Keren is in decline. Life goes on in the native town, as it always has and always will, whatever the fate of conquerors. A drunken Beja warrior, a wooden lice-comb and a sprig of lavender bougainvillaea jammed in his woolly mop, the masticated goat fat with which he dresses his hair dripping down his face, lurches from a native tavern with a hand on his broad-bladed knife. The women wear brightly coloured cheap rayon cloth which they have bought from the Greek trader at the corner, their noses are ringed in gold and their wrists and ankles jingle with the low-grade silver which is mined nearby. The bleat of goats being dragged to market by their ears is deafening and the high babble of children reciting the Koran hangs in the hot air.

In the war cemetery it is cool. On the left are the graves of six hundred Italians, on the right are those of an equal number of their *askaris*, segregated even in death. Metal plates giving the man's name and regiment mark each grave. A few—and you can imagine the artillery barrage in which they died—say *ignoto*, unknown. A lonely place for an unknown son of Italy to lie. Nearby is the British cemetery and here again proper social distinctions are made. First come the graves of the British (Cameron Highlanders, Yorkshire Light Infantry, West

Hampshire Fusiliers), then the Indians (First Sikhs) and the black
askaris (Sudan Defence Force). Each grave marker is topped by a
cross, a Star of David or a crescent. In the distance are the ridges where
they fell: Camerons' Peak, named after the Scots who stormed it a
dozen times but could not hold it; Peake's Peak, named after the
British commander who died there; Fort Dologordoc, the toughest
nut of all and the place where Lorenzini fell. This compelling, burned-
out continent has eaten the dust of a hundred armies and its earth is
red with the blood of every nation. Phoenicians and Greeks, Chinese
and Egyptians, Turks and Italians, British and French—all have sought
its secrets and left their bones. And Africa remains unsmiling and
unchanged.

In Keren we were met by Pastor Olle Andersson Hagner, a conqueror
of another sort. Hagner, a plump, balding man in his sixties, is as
Swedish as meat loaf and his countrymen have been evangelizing in
western Eritrea for close on a century. The first Swedish missionaries
rode into Kunama country by mule from Massawa when it was held
by the Egyptians. In four years, eight of the eleven pastors were dead
and the others returned to Sweden for reinforcements. They have been
coming ever since and eighteen Swedish Lutherans now work in
Eritrea.

Hagner rode in on a mule in 1923 and began a love affair with the
primitive Kunama people which lasts to this day. His comfortable wife
joined him three years later and has borne him four children in the bush.

'In some ways,' he recalled, 'it was better in the old days when we
travelled by mule. There was time to stop and talk with the people, to
enjoy a view or watch a colourful bird, time to get to know the tribesmen and the country. Still, we must keep up with the times.' He said
it with an edge of doubt in his voice, as if unsure that change inevitably
equals progress.

Unlike so many missionaries Hagner is a realist who accepts the fact
that Islam in many ways is more suitable to the tribal African than is
Christianity: 'In their society, a man cannot sleep with his wife from
the time she conceives until the baby is weaned, more than three years
later. Is it worse for a man to be polygamous than to bed with
prostitutes?'

During the last years of the Italian occupation, Hagner was the only
Protestant missionary allowed to remain. Although individual Italians
were kind to him he was not allowed to work, because the fascist
government had signed a concordat with the Vatican making Eritrea

a Catholic preserve. Hagner's job was to supervise the disposition of the property of the Protestant missions. He dragged this out so successfully that he was on hand to cheer the Cameron Highlanders as they marched into Keren.

His hard feelings—if he is capable of any—are reserved for the people of the American pentecostal mission who, in a country starved for doctors and teachers, have recently established themselves across from his Keren mission. Here, as elsewhere in Africa, American missionaries have more funds at their disposal and discipline is less severe. Pastor Hagner was losing converts to the American mission, which the Africans call the People-of-the-Deaf-God, since they shout so loudly when they call upon Him, and the good Swede's sense of Christian charity was under a considerable stress.

The Pastor took us to Keren's button factory. The buttons are slices of the nut of the *dom* palm and, although they are very hard, will dissolve in a glass of water. The factory is primitive and production is low. Competition with plastics, so the manager said, is getting tougher all the time.

We left the Pastor to catch the *littorina* to Agordat, promising to meet him in a few days' time in his beloved Kunama country. From Keren the train goes down again into the flat plains which merge finally into the Sudan. This is nomad country and many of our fellow-passengers were proud, fine-featured Valentino-types clad in the white robes of the desert and carrying long swords with handles of beaten silver. The hotel in Agordat is not difficult to find: it and the old Italian *residenza* are the only double-storeyed buildings in this town of 10,000. The hotel's six rooms are open and without glass in the windows. This saves money, catches each possible breath of air and provides excellent lodging for the pigeons of Agordat. On a clothesline outside our room hung the headless carcass of an antelope which the cook was draining preparatory to passing it off as veal *scallopini*.

In the morning there was the usual frenzied battle to board the bus for Barentu. Spear-carrying Bejas threw bundles through the windows in an attempt to claim the seats upon which they fell. These were as quickly thrown out of the windows on the other side of the bus by equally well-armed tribesmen already established within. We, slow to jab with elbows or use the knees and hips to best advantage, found ourselves standing. All the successful claimants, however, were not going anywhere. Many board the bus, procure a seat, sell it to a tardy arrival and then get off with their profit. One such entrepreneur willingly surrendered the two seats across which he was stretched for a small consideration.

Here a tawny gazelle, there a tiny dik-dik, or more often a moth-eaten camel, bolted in terror as our bus wheezed over the low hills and painfully climbed the scarp upon which Barentu sits, the last hill town for two thousand miles. The heavy heat of noon lay on Barentu like a thick wool blanket and it was good to be in the coolness of the arcade which fronts on the shimmering square and laces the hot dust with pools of shade.

A Kunama warrior, stocky, dark and Nilotic in feature, strode through the blazing light of the square, a live sheep thrown over his shoulders, his other hand clasping the double-pointed spear. The Kunama and their cousins, the Baria, have had to be tough to survive. They differ in race and religion from both the Coptic highlanders and the Muslims of the far plains. As a pagan people they have been as fair game for the spears of the Negus as for the Khalifa's hordes. Only their poverty and their ferocity have protected them from extinction, and this pocket of 25,000 Kunama lives today in the Iron Age.

Hagner showed up in his battered panama hat and off we went through the bush in the ubiquitous Volkswagen microbus. The track took us past a well where bare-breasted Kunama maidens, their *coiffures* tastefully built around a cow dung base, were loading goatskin water-bags on to a donkey. They cried out in mock alarm and skittered off into the bush, leaving the donkey standing by the well. A thousand yards further and Hagner braked to a stop beside a pile of rocks surmounted by a concrete slab. On the slab was the inscription, 'J. Vanberg—1869'. 'One of our first missionaries,' said the Pastor. The inscription was hard to read. Originally it had been spelled out in iron letters and figures. But the metal-hungry Kunama had torn them off to forge into spear-heads. Death is too close to everyday life in Africa for the dead to have much prestige, particularly when something like an iron spear-head, which may mean to a hunter the difference between a dead gazelle and an empty stomach, is at stake. Ahead, stuck high against the mountains like a white postage stamp on a manila envelope, perched *Ausa Kunama*, the ancient Swedish mission station. In the 1930s Hagner took the revolutionary step of admitting a few Kunama girls to his school. The tribal elders warned that this would mean war, since the girls would inevitably become sterile through their association with 'Franks'. This rumour was scotched within a matter of months when one of the girls produced a bouncing male child. 'Today we would consider that a discipline problem,' quipped Hagner, 'but in those days we were extremely grateful to the young lady. The boy she bore is now one of our evangelists.' In addition to his normal educational and pastoral duties—the Swedes have made 5,000 converts among the Kunama in a century of evangelism—Hagner has opened a school for the deaf and dumb, the third of its kind in Africa, and found time to give the Kunama a written language.

Swedish influence in Eritrea is not splashy. Only a little progress has been made but the gains achieved are solid. Eritrea, racked by poverty and torn by political strife, needs every bit of help it can get.

ETHIOPIA'S CASE

In this chapter some unpleasant things have been said about a country which has always sided with the West and whose ruler is a good friend of America. It does no good to ignore the situation. By the same token, it would be unrealistic as well as unfair to ignore Ethiopia's point of view. Her position has its roots deep in the Ethiopian character and history. As is the case with all nations, and particularly with these emergent states of the new Africa which have been subjected to so many stresses and influences in so short a time, we have to take into account what happened yesterday to understand why they act the way they do today. For this reason we find ourselves stating at some length the historical forces which have shaped the political personalities of these states.

In Ethiopia's case, her national history has been characterized by two conditions: internal disorders and aggression from the outside. We would do well to remember that, until the advent of Haile Selassie, Ethiopia was continually torn by civil wars which frequently threatened her national existence. Even in times of peace, a strong *ras* was often able to defy the power of the central government. An historic seat of unrest has been Tigre, the area which straddles the Eritrean-Ethiopian border. From Tigre came the war-lords who most often threatened the political supremacy of the Negus Negasti. Eritrean troops played a major role in the conquest of Ethiopia. With this in mind, it is perhaps a little simpler to see why Haile Selassie or any Ethiopian with a sense of history looks with disfavour on the growth of the slightest form of Eritrean nationalism. This is an old story to them and they have their own ideas as to how the problem should be solved.

Secondly, Ethiopia has had to fight for centuries to keep her sea coast free of foreign invaders: Arabs from Yemen, Turks, Egyptians, Italians, French and British have all sought to seal her into the interior. Ethiopia's psychological yearning for a Red Sea port has been just as impelling as Poland's drive for the Danzig corridor or Russia's search for a warm-water outlet to the world. Her ships once ravaged the coast of the Arabian peninsula and Haile Selassie is determined that Ethiopia shall once more be a Red Sea naval power. He came close to losing Eritrea during the post-war bickering and one can hardly blame him now for wanting to cement his hold there.

Thirdly, Ethiopia's Amhara ruling class has an almost psychotic fear of Islam. Again, this is understandable in the light of the nation's history. Christianity has been at once Ethiopia's most prized spiritual possession and the backbone of her political system. For most of her history she has been cut off by Islam from the rest of Christendom, more than once she has been overrun by fanatical Muslim armies, and she has had to fight a holy war against her own Muslims as recently as 1921. With the Muslim Sudan to the west, the fanatical Somalis to the east and her own Islamic population restive as the result of the vituperative blasts of Radio Cairo, Ethiopia feels that she cannot afford— and she may well be right—to give much rein to Eritrea's Muslims.

Lastly, there is this: anyone who thinks the Eritreans can be dealt with as if they were Scandinavian burghers is just deceiving himself. Democracy is a rather peculiar institution which evolved out of a given set of circumstances to fit the needs and aspirations of a part of humanity at a certain stage in its political and economic development. It was not imposed by well-wishing, alien political theorists to fit their personal and national predilections. The Eritreans are a wild and woolly bunch who, through fifty-one years of Italian occupation and ten years of British administration, had some of their rough edges polished off. But they certainly have no deep understanding of or dedication to democratic political theory. As elsewhere in Africa, you either rule or you get out. Ethiopia intends to stay. Nobody would be happier than Haile Selassie to see the conditions for the evolution of true democracy develop both in Eritrea and in his own country. He is doing everything possible to bring such a system into existence in Ethiopia. But he is too much of a realist to let political theory interfere with Ethiopia's evident self-interest.

The Imperial Government has very real problems to contend with in Ethiopia. It needs no advice from South American statesmen, no matter how well-intentioned, to tell it how it can and must rule Eritrea

THE HORN

It was not so long ago that unruly subjects of the Negus had their noses cut off as a lesson in etiquette. The padlocking of newspapers, suppression of trade unions and gagging of politicians is a definite improvement on that.

Chapter 5

*

LION OF JUDAH

Haile Selassie I, Elect of God, Conquering Lion of the Tribe of Judah, King of Kings, 225th in the line of Ethiopian emperors who trace their ancestry back to Solomon's couch, is remembered with a vague twinge of conscience by most Americans as the kindly little man who pleaded his country's case against fascist aggression before the League of Nations with an eloquent lack of success.

He is thought of as a gentle little man with a beard and a rather comic pith helmet who wears cloaks, believes in collective security and likes to give schools to his country's children. There is that Haile Selassie. But behind the Emperor's benign smile is one of the most ruthless, dedicated, energetic and intelligent rulers in the world.

Haile Selassie, as the world sometimes forgets, is not the son of the old emperor. He reached the throne by force in a brilliant *coup d'état*. In June of 1908, Menelik II, the victor of Adowa, the warrior-statesman who unified modern Ethiopia, lay paralysed by a stroke in his Addis Ababa palace. To his side he called his twelve-year-old grandson, Lij Yasu, the Catholicus of the Ethiopian Church and all his principal chiefs. In a whisper barely audible to his vassals, Menelik named Yasu to be his successor, warning that 'cursed shall be he who shall refuse to obey him, and he shall have a black dog for a son'.

Lij Yasu had a good part of the pack stacked against him to start with. The Empress Taitu, who despite her vast bulk and advancing years had personally led a regiment against the Tigre rebels in 1902, was scheming against him. This bizarre but able personality, a veteran of five marriages, all with great *rases*, wanted to place on the throne Zauditu, Menelik's daughter by an earlier marriage (Menelik was something of an Ethiopian Henry VIII: he married at least four times).

The ageing Minister of War, Fituari Hapta Giorgis, also had some ideas on the succession as did twenty-one-year-old Ras Tafari, governor of Harar and son of Makonnen, Menelik's great general and diplomat.

Tafari, despite his youth, was an able and experienced administrator and no greenhorn at intrigue himself. He was educated at a French mission school in Harar, caught Menelik's eye and, with a push from his father, became governor of a town in Harar at the age of *fourteen*. Before he needed a shave Tafari was ruling a part of Shoa. Statecraft he learned at the court of Menelik, his great-uncle, and the cost of trying to move too fast was brought home to him when he fell out of favour and was exiled for a short time to Kaffa. When the dying Menelik named Yasu as his successor, Tafari was back at Harar, this time as governor of the province. He laid his plans. And waited.

Yasu, who took nominal control in 1911 at the age of fifteen, proved to be a clever but unstable youth. With a small bodyguard he wandered off into the remote country near the Sudan border where he offended the Amhara nobles by dallying with Islam and contracted a series of temporary 'marriages' with the daughters of Muslim chiefs.

Four years later Yasu made an extraordinary announcement: he was descended from Mohammed, not Solomon. He put away his coronet and *shamma* and donned the turban and scimitar of a Muslim, disposed of his Christian wife, and proclaimed Ethiopia subject to the religious rule of Turkey. This was received with approximately the same degree of enthusiasm as would a proclamation by the head of the Mormon Church that everybody in Utah was to consider himself a Roman Catholic. Nor were the French and English, now influential in Ethiopia, delighted at the prospect: they were at war with Turkey and feared the spread to Egypt and the Middle East of the *jihad* which inevitably must follow Yasu's proclamation.

The Shoan chiefs, encouraged by the foreign legations, massed their forces in Addis Ababa, and asked the Abuna to release them from their oath of allegiance to Yasu, proclaiming Zauditu as Empress in his stead with Ras Tafari as regent and heir. The Abuna complied, saying that all who supported Yasu would incur 'the wrath of the Father, Son and Holy Ghost, of the Twelve Apostles and of the 318 Fathers of the Council of Nicaea, the curse of Arius, and the approbation of Judas'. This was serious and Yasu fled into the Danakil desert to raise the Muslim tribes.

Ethiopia was in turmoil for six years until Yasu fell into the hands of the Empress Zauditu. Since it was forbidden to shed the blood of an heir of Solomon, he was fettered in chains of gold, as befitted his rank, and stored away for safe keeping. There followed a three-cornered struggle for power among the Empress, old Hapta Giorgus and Ras

Tafari which ended with the deaths of the first two and the latter's coronation as Negus Negasti in 1930. Tafari took the throne name Haile Selassie, meaning 'Power of the Holy Trinity' (other colourful throne names enjoyed by Ethiopian monarchs have included 'Seed of Jacob', 'By the Hand of Mary', 'Incense of the Virgin' and just plain 'Jesus').

Haile Selassie was barely settled on the throne when the Italians invaded. The Emperor's troops fought well but in May of 1936 he was forced to flee the country to escape capture. Lij Yasu was not to play a Quisling's role; nobody knows how Yasu died but it is said that he was drowned, so that no royal blood was shed. Haile Selassie went first to Jerusalem, where the Ethiopian Church has a monastery, and then to England where he was to live in exile at Bath's Villa Fairfield (since given by the Emperor to the people of Britain for use as an old people's home) for almost five years. The tough old war-lords like Ras Kassa and Ras Desta fought on for several months but, in the end, were overwhelmed.

MODERN ETHIOPIA

On a clear May morning in 1941, the booming of cannon, the chanting of Coptic Christian priests to the rhythm of throbbing drums and jangling silver rattles, the cries of an excited people greeted the return to Ethiopia of Haile Selassie at the head of a liberating British army.

The homecoming of the pocket-sized, bearded monarch to the eucalyptus-clad hills of his Addis Ababa capital ended the five-year occupation of Ethiopia by fascist Italy and was seen by many as the beginning of a new era of progress.

Stuffed in the little Emperor's briefcase were plans which, if they could be put into effect, would haul Ethiopia by its bootlaces into the twentieth century. Yet when the last bearded priest dropped exhausted, when the drumbeats faded and died, when the last champagne toast was drunk in the palace, the real Ethiopia remained: feudal, primitive, suspicious of change, exhausted by war, her economy shattered, a nation of black illiterates still living in the Middle Ages. The reality seemed stronger than the dream.

Haile Selassie, who is now sixty-eight, knew full well that practically the whole fabric of Ethiopian life would have to be rewoven. He also realized that his first problem was to reach his people: without an adequate communications net he could never hope to modernize

Ethiopia's agriculture, revitalize education or institute public health programmes.

Ethiopia's 450,000 square miles had less than 500 miles of railway and a war-damaged, flood-menaced 2,900-mile road net built by the Italians. A 200-mile trip almost anywhere in the country came under the heading of high adventure, consumed weeks in good weather and was impossible during the rains.

Haile Selassie, who made his first aeroplane trip in 1923, decided to skip the rail age and vault from ox-carts directly to multi-engined aircraft. But Ethiopia lacked both money and know-how.

Know-how arrived in the person of an ex-Marine Corps fighter pilot named 'Swede' Golien. Golien, who flew the Atlantic some thirty times during the war for the Air Transport Command, headed a cadre of Trans-World Airlines personnel. His job: to build Ethiopian Air Lines, owned by Ethiopia and operated by T.W.A. on a contract basis, from scratch into an efficient international airline.

E.A.L.'s first American pilots blanched when they saw the terrain over which they would be flying: most of the twenty-six Ethiopian cities which Golien and the Emperor wanted to link were cradled in mountains rising to 8,000 feet. The runways were pockmarked with shell craters, overgrown with bush, often teeming with game or dotted with nomadic tribesmen herding their flocks.

Golien's ground crews, often against the opposition of tribesmen who objected to losing their pasture lands, cleared the airstrips and filled in the craters. An £8·5 million loan from the Export-Import Bank financed the building of the fields and the purchase of six surplus American Air Force C-47s.

By 1948 E.A.L. was flying 5·6 million revenue-passenger miles. This year its volume will be at least 800 per cent over the 1948 figure.

Riding E.A.L. still provides some excitement for Americans used to the more prosaic United States lines: you may sit next to a leopard-skin clad native chief who has never been in a car or ridden in a train or share a magazine with a Muslim sheikh on pilgrimage to Mecca. If there are few passengers aboard you may find a load of hides or a crate of chickens dumped in the aisle. The landings and take-offs from the mountain airstrips will scare you silly. Yet in eleven years of flying over country that would turn any barnstormer grey, E.A.L. has never had a fatal accident.

Although the creation of a commercial air service eased the task of administering outlying areas, it was no solution to the problem of transporting Ethiopia's bulky agricultural products. A road-building programme was obviously called for. Again, money and technicians were lacking.

But Ethiopia's credit was good and a loan of £1·8 million came from the International Bank for Reconstruction and Development, the first loan made by the World Bank in Africa. Ethiopia put up £7 million and the U.S. Bureau of Public Roads contributed top management and engineering services.

Remarked one American engineer: 'It wasn't all smooth sailing: we'd build a culvert to carry off the heavy rains and the tribesmen would fill it up again so that the road, while it lasted, served as a very nice dam for their flocks.'

But, despite torrential rainfall and occasional harassment by bandits, the roads went through. The existing roads were rebuilt, tapping the country's richest agricultural areas and providing an all-weather route to the port of Assab. Encouraged by the resulting jump in exports, a 50 per cent increase in highway traffic and a sharp drop in freight rates, Ethiopia in 1957 signed up for a second highway loan from the World Bank, this one for £6 million repayable in twenty years. In addition to the loan, the Ethiopian Government will spend another £8 million on road development, for a total of £20 million since 1950. Today, Ethiopians who had never navigated anything more complex than a camel are mastering the intricacies of power steering.

With its communications needs met by a serviceable road network and a dependable airline, Ethiopia next turned to the problem of improving crop yields to pay for the progress so desperately wanted.

Coffee historically has been Ethiopia's principal export crop and, with cereals, hides and skins, it accounts for nearly 75 per cent of the country's exports by value. Coffee grows wild in many parts of the country, which some say is the original home of the bean. Unfortunately Ethiopia's coffee crop was badly picked and cured. Much of it rotted before it could reach the sea because of the creaking transportation system.

With transport improved, the principal problem became to increase yields and quality, train native agricultural officers (up from five in 1954 to sixty-nine in 1958) to see that any gains made were permanent. International help came in the form of the United States' Point Four programme.

Oklahoma Agricultural and Mechanical College extension officers journeyed into the most remote portions of the empire to bring the gospel of modern farming methods to primitive tribesmen who had never seen a plough or a pair of shoes. 'It was fantastic,' recalled one A. & M. professor: 'We found the people scratching at the soil with implements that were considered obsolete in fourteenth-century Europe.'

Old customs die hard: ignorance was as great an enemy of progress as the broken mountain trails. Ethiopian farmers had dried their coffee on the ground for generations. They found it hard to believe that the fact that animals walked over it cut their profits. It was only after long study that the Point Four experts discovered that the coffee, brought to market on burros, was absorbing the sweat of the animals, thus earning lower prices because of the impurities.

Improved methods of production coupled with the road programme soon paid off: within the past decade, coffee exports have trebled in volume and quintupled in value. Exports of oil seeds, another big earner, have increased seventy-fold by value. Over a ten-year period total exports have climbed 600 per cent and the annual national budget has trebled to about £20 million.

In contrast to much of Africa, Ethiopia has no land shortage and the soil over much of the country is bursting with nutrients. In addition to export crops, Ethiopia grows enough millet, wheat, barley, sugar, yams, coffee and tobacco for her own use. One of the one hundred and thirty Point Four technicians in the country told me that Ethiopia could add £8 million to her coffers by curing all her coffee properly, save another £6 million on textile imports by going in for cotton on a large scale, a crop eminently suited to the hot eastern lowlands. Less than 60 per cent of the country's arable land is farmed and Ethiopia could easily grow enough food to support three times her present population.

As improved communications spurred agricultural production, so they also made it easier and cheaper to bring in the heavy machinery which is the bone and sinew of progress. Higher foreign exchange earnings have made it possible for Ethiopia to quintuple the value of rubber and petroleum imports since 1946. Imports of machinery are up more than sixty-five-fold and the value of motor vehicles and parts imported annually has rocketed in the post-war period from £143,000 to about £2·3 million.

As economic progress raised the national income it became financially possible for Ethiopia to turn its attention to other problems. One of the most pressing of these was public health.

Of Ethiopia's 17 million inhabitants, one American doctor estimates that more than a third suffer from malaria. Tuberculosis and eye diseases are also prevalent and medical attention in the past has usually been limited to the ministrations of *hakims*, native witch doctors. As recently as 1956, there were no qualified Ethiopian doctors. Foreign physicians bring the doctor-population ratio in rural areas to about one to 400,000. Today one out of every four Ethiopian college students abroad is studying medicine. To fill the gap until these doctors start coming down the pipe—many Ethiopians are studying public health overseas under Point Four's auspices—the Ethiopian government, with the assistance of the United States, the World Health Organization and U.N.I.C.E.F., established the country's first training centre for health officers and nurses. Ten nationalities staff the Gondar centre.

If Ethiopia's battle to vault from feudalism to frigidaires taught her anything, it was that progress, to be lasting, must be based on education. One Ethiopian student recently returned from the United States put it this way: 'It does us no good to have tractors if we don't know how to clean the plugs.'

American Point Four instructors, backed financially by 50 per cent of the more than £10 million in non-military aid which the United States has poured into Ethiopia in recent years, arrived ready to teach everything from algebra to shop mechanics. They found tremendous enthusiasm . . . but little else.

Six years of war and foreign occupation had all but destroyed Ethiopia's school system. There were almost no educated Ethiopians. Worst of all, there were no texts.

'We arrived ready to teach and found there were no books,' recalled one American instructor. 'So we printed the books.' With the enthusiastic support of Haile Selassie, who acts as his own Minister of Education and devotes 17 per cent of the national budget to schools, Point Four produced more than half a million textbooks and 300,000 teachers' manuals, set up trade schools, teacher-training institutes and agricultural colleges.

In 1955 the eight shilling per term fee in Government elementary schools was abolished and enrolments have increased from practically nil to about 250,000 within fifteen years. The annual education budget of £3 million, small as it is, represents a tremendous effort on Ethiopia's part. Enrolment in teacher training colleges at present is more than ten times greater than it was in 1952. University College of Addis Ababa has survived a ludicrous start and now, staffed largely by mufti-clad (because of Ethiopian religious sensibilities) French-Canadian Jesuits, can boast a Faculty of Science, a School of Law, a Department of Commerce and an Extension School. It produced its first graduates in 1954 and today students from all over Africa (fifty of them on Ethiopian government scholarships) are in residence. In addition, more than three hundred young Ethiopians are studying abroad, about a third of them in the United States.

But Ethiopia is still woefully short of teachers and 350 instructors of seventeen nationalities have been brought in. The attrition rate is alarmingly high: of 30,000 first graders who started school in 1953, 23,000 had dropped out by 1956. The jump from a grass-roofed *tukal* to a chemistry lab is just too much for most students.

Improvements in the school system such as the use of English as the language of instruction on the intermediate and high school level have made it possible for industry to find reasonably competent local employees, although most have an overblown impression of their own abilities. In the old days, Ethiopian 'industry' was limited to the extraction of musk from civet cats for use in making perfume. Today the Government runs airlines, banks, hotels, power plants and cigarette factories. Currency reform and at least theoretically favourable conditions for foreign investment have resulted in the establishment of thirty private firms producing everything from soap to beer and employing 20,000 workers on a £1·6 million annual payroll. One of the most successful ventures has been the establishment of a sugar factory by Dutch industrialists. The company, in the original agreement signed in 1951 and through an option right, obtained 12,500 acres in the Wonji plain south of the Awash River. It undertook to reach an annual production figure of 8,000 tons within five years. In 1954, the last year before the factory came into production, Ethiopian sugar imports totalled 21,000 tons. In 1954 the Wonji factory produced 15,000 tons, a figure which has since risen to 35,000 tons. This meets all Ethiopia's requirements and a second factory, now under construction, will produce a surplus for export.

Cultivation of rice along the Awash began in 1957; five factories producing forty-two varieties of wheat paste varying from macaroni to vermicelli have been set up to cater for eating habits conditioned by the Italian occupation, and rapid expansion of the meat and livestock industries has reached the point where soon they will challenge coffee's position as Ethiopia's most important source of foreign exchange (coffee annually brings in about £18 million). The livestock population is estimated at 20 million head of cattle, a similar number of sheep and about 9 million goats.

In an effort to trigger investment in Ethiopia Haile Selassie in 1957 launched a five-year development plan which envisioned the expenditure of £96·9 million, 69 per cent mobilized from domestic sources and the remainder from external loans and foreign private investment. About two-thirds of this was to be devoted to communications, power, education and health services.

One deterrent to development in the past has been the almost total absence of electricity. In part this will be remedied by £5·9 million paid to Ethiopia by Italy for reparations. The major portion of this has been applied to the construction of the £4·3 million Koka hydro-electric scheme on the Awash River ninety miles from Addis Ababa (Italy will also return historic relics taken to Rome during the occupation, build five 400,000-spindle cotton mills, and provide ships and marine equipment). Completion of the Koka scheme is expected to raise Ethiopia's production of power from 62·6 million kilowatts in 1957 to 110 million kilowatts in 1961.

But foreign investors are still plagued with a bewildering amount of red tape and often faced with the necessity of bribing the appropriate officials if anything is to be accomplished. This is to be the pattern all across an Africa which fails to realize that capital is in short supply and will go where it can get the best terms.

A great deal still remains to be done here: Ethiopia is known to have considerable deposits of a spectrum of minerals ranging from platinum to mica, none of which have been properly exploited. There may be oil, although Sinclair has given up exploratory work in the Ogaden Desert after ten dry years. Above all, Ethiopia has its rich soil and a tremendous hydro-electric potential at the source of the Blue Nile.

Africa, in itself a relentless and powerful foe, has yet to be beaten. Drought and famine are no strangers to this part of the world. A large percentage of the people still cling to the ancient, unproductive ways of their ancestors.

HAILE SELASSIE

It is no exaggeration to say that almost all of Ethiopia's progress has its source in the five-foot-one frame of Haile Selassie. Nowhere else in the world is there a rule so personal. The Emperor will scrutinize the contract of a palace cook with the same intensity with which he settles the fate of thousands. He will officiate at the opening of a new handicraft school, then dash back to the palace in his green Rolls-Royce through streets lined with prostrate tribesmen and bowing Europeans to receive a foreign dignitary. His gnome-like shadow falls across every aspect of life and he rules 17 million wild mountaineers and fierce nomads with a gentle smile and a fist of iron. No power is delegated, no responsibility is shunned. In comparison to him, the Adenauers, Changs and De Gaulles of the world look rather wishy-washy. This is no halfpenny dictator, no comic opera emperor. This is a strong ruler whose mind encompasses the subtleties of the Orient, a king of the stamp of the Mings and the Tudors.

The Emperor, whose mother died when he was only three months old, is a modernist in every way. His father visited Europe as early as 1889 and Haile Selassie, in addition to his visit to the United States, has seen most of Europe as well as Russia, India and Japan. Although the Emperor is a respecter of tradition, he will break one he feels is un-important: he was the first of the Solomonic rulers not to be crowned in Axum—his coronation took place in Addis Ababa—and he was the first Emperor to visit the outside world.

In addition to being a very inquisitive and well-travelled man, the Emperor is also a very rich one. No one knows exactly how wealthy he is, since the state funds and his personal fortune are closely inter-twined. But one-third of Ethiopia's gold production is his by right which alone, at the current rate of production, gives him a tidy £250,000 a year. He and other members of the royal family also own vast estates. But the Emperor lives on a modest scale, and likes nothing better than building schools and clinics out of his personal fortune.

His Imperial Majesty, to give him his correct title, is a deeply religious man who starts each day with devotions, attends church regularly, and observes the frequent and strict fast-days of his faith. He rises early, downs a mammoth breakfast, reads for a short time and then devotes the rest of the morning to cabinet sessions. Since he not only rules but reigns, much of his afternoons are filled with ceremonial functions.

Haile Selassie, who is a great-grandfather, is a health faddist and eats very lightly at both lunch and dinner. He is a great film fan and, after dinner with the Empress and any of the royal children who happen to be in town, there is usually a private showing at the palace. On weekends he tries to get away to one of his many country estates for a bit of horseback riding or boating.

There are those who say that the Emperor holds too tight a grip on

Ethiopia, that his sort of rule precludes honest criticism and inhibits the development of initiative among the subordinates who will one day have to run Ethiopia. All this is true. Any decision to have force must come 'from the Palace', thus much is left undone. But before being over-critical we should remember where we are. Ethiopia as we know it was created only sixty-five years ago. As recently as 1915 it looked as if the empire would disintegrate. Haile Selassie is the first emperor of a new dynasty ruling over a wild people. He must either wield power or step down.

It should also be noted that he gave the country a modern written constitution in 1955 and, three years later, called Ethiopia's first general election. The new constitution, however, involves no lessening of the Emperor's powers. The 210-member lower house is elected but the Emperor appoints all members of the 100-seat Senate. He may accept legislation approved by one house, initiate legislation himself and any bill which he vetoes may be discussed no further. He may convene and dissolve the legislature at will and, when it is not in session, may legislate by proclamation. The Emperor appoints, promotes, transfers, suspends and dismisses all officials of the government and cabinet ministers. Only he may declare war, state of siege, martial law or national emergency; only he may conclude peace. He retains the right to organize and command the armed forces and he exercises control of foreign affairs. He alone may confer titles and has the authority to print money. He appoints all judges and Star Chamber sittings are not infrequent, particularly in cases involving political offenders. The constitution states that the Emperor's person is 'sacred', his dignity 'inviolable' and his power 'indisputable'. And that rather clearly states the position.

But such democracy as there is exists because of Haile Selassie and despite the opposition of important segments of society. If the Emperor has not made the people of Ethiopia into Swiss democrats, he has at least made it possible for public sentiment to be expressed through constitutional channels.

In this time and in this place, Haile Selassie has brought about as much democracy to Ethiopia as could be hoped for.

THOSE AROUND THE EMPEROR

Because of the very personal nature of his rule, it is difficult to identify other powerful figures in Ethiopian politics (the term is used advisedly: there are, of course, no political parties in Ethiopia).

The Empress Menen, a grand-daughter of King Michael of Wollo, a massive, powerful woman who has been in ill-health in recent years, is an impassive, uncommunicative woman with a keen business mind. Like most Ethiopian empresses, she is religious, intent upon maintaining the continuity of the new dynasty and somewhat reactionary.

Crown Prince Asfa Wosen, now forty-four, has much of his mother in him and is something of a question mark. He was educated in Ethiopia and Britain, has been married twice and has a son named Jacob to ensure the succession. He has had some administrative experience as a governor of a province. Haile Selassie's other son, twenty-nine-year-old Sahle Selassie, was educated at Cambridge and likes jazz, fast sports-cars and flying his own plane. The able Duke of Harar, another son, was killed in a motor-car accident in 1957. Two of the Emperor's three daughters are dead and the surviving one, the widow of Ras Desta, is married, as we have seen, to Andargachaw Masai, Viceroy of Eritrea.

The Abuna is no longer the power in the land which he once was since he is appointed by the Emperor, who has a firm grip on church finances. Several foreign advisers have influence with the Emperor but he has so far succeeded in playing off one against the other and thus preventing any from gaining real ascendancy either over him or with the court. In the end, you come back to the fact that Haile Selassie is the real as well as the apparent power in the land and, after that, little more can be said.

THE EMPEROR'S GOALS

Before discussing Haile Selassie's objectives we would do well to remember that Ethiopia is just emerging from feudalism into the Atomic Age. Fifty years ago, Ethiopians believed that all the world beyond their steep mountain passes was desert. Their maps claimed half the continent as Ethiopian territory. As late as 1930, the British complained that Ethiopians were raiding into Kenya for slaves and the Italians claimed that they liberated 420,000 slaves when they occupied the country. Domestic slavery still exists in Ethiopia and it will for some time to come. Although the Emperor has set his face against the institution by proclaiming that slaves must be freed on the death of their master and that children of slaves are free, he is the first to realize that abolition would fall most heavily on the slaves, many of whom could not fend for themselves. Forty different languages are spoken, secular education is little more than fifty years old and the soil of the land, although rich, is cultivated with appallingly primitive methods. Almost 99 per cent of the adult population is illiterate and only 10 per cent of the children go to school. Ethiopia is still short of everything except pride.

This dainty, tenacious and dignified ruler is determined to bring Ethiopia into the twentieth century, by the scruff of the neck if necessary. He wants schools, bridges, roads, airports, clinics, hydro-electric projects, telephones, sewers, railways, jet aircraft, trucks, agricultural tools, factories. Most of all, he wants an enlightened population capable of using all this. His enemies are the reactionary nobles, the ignorance of the peasantry and, to a lesser extent, the Church. His trump cards are the near-divinity with which the mass of the population regards him, the devotion of the younger generation, a sizeable coffee crop, a good credit rating and reasonable political stability.

The new agreement with the Coptic Patriarch in Alexandria gives the Emperor ultimate control over the Catholicus through his appointive power. The strength of the nobles has been sharply reduced through programmes of land reform and administrative reorganization. Prior to 1942 the aristocracy kept private armies and levied taxes within their fiefs to meet administrative expenses. Haile Selassie has replaced these feudal holdings (at least in theory) with a pyramid of administrative units ranging upward from 1,122 sub-districts, 360 districts and 74 sub-provinces to the 12 provinces, each under an appointed officer. The private armies have been declared illegal (although there is little doubt that several could still be called into existence overnight) and the old system of levies in land and in kind, as we have seen, has been replaced by a uniform cash tax payable to the Ministry of Finance.

Haile Selassie would like to see Ethiopia emerge as a democratic state but not if it means the loss of his throne or the sacrifice of his economic and educational programmes. The Emperor understands his people and knows that he could lose everything by trying to do too much too fast.

I met the Emperor at the new Jubilee Palace. He stood rigidly erect as I manœuvred through the three required bows necessary to reach the Louis Quinze desk on which lay an ivory letter-opener, a leather desk set and some sharpened pencils. He wore a khaki uniform with crimson lapel tabs and a rainbow of decorations. Behind the desk was a mural map of East Africa and beneath it dozed two fluffy dogs. The Minister

111

of the Pen, Tafara Worq, acted as interpreter (although the Emperor understands English) and I asked Haile Selassie to explain his goals.

The light-skinned, hook-nosed little man, who looks like nothing so much as an Old Testament patriarch, replied that he regarded dedication to a system of collective security, although it had failed him in 1935, as the foundation of his foreign policy. This is no extraordinary statement but it should be remembered that for thousands of years Ethiopia's policy was one of isolation.

The Emperor has a soft spot in his heart for America which, like Russia (but unlike Britain and France), never recognized the Italian occupation of his country. He considers good relations with the United States, which he visited in 1954, as essential. The Emperor once flirted briefly with Bandung neutralism, then placed himself firmly in the Western camp. In recent months, however, Ethiopia's diplomatic posture has changed and not to our advantage.

Haile Selassie always appreciated such American aid as he received—he said he realized it meant a sacrifice on the part of every United States taxpayer—but it just was not enough to accomplish what he wanted to do. Time and again government officials of the New Africa brought up the same point: 'You give India, who frequently opposes you in the United Nations, £123 million a year; we support you and get less than £2 million; obviously you are more generous to your enemies than to your friends.' And the Emperor has always suspected that, while Britain was the prime mover behind the Greater Somalia concept (which we will discuss in a moment), the United States has given its blessing to the scheme.

Convinced that he was getting less than his diplomatic and financial due from the Western powers, Haile Selassie in June of 1959 embarked upon a six-week tour of Egypt, Russia, Czechoslovakia and Yugoslavia (he also paid brief visits to Belgium, France and Portugal). Two weeks of his sojourn abroad were spent in the Soviet Union where he steered a river-boat on the Volga, attended the Bolshoi Theatre, was awarded an honorary degree by Moscow State University, was decorated by Khrushchev, and visited the tombs of Lenin and Stalin. He also toured the Ural Mountains, Stalingrad and Sochi, the Black Sea resort. The Russians gave him the full treatment: thousands of peasants were trucked in from surrounding districts to line his route through Moscow, Red banners with Amharic inscriptions touting Soviet-Ethiopian friendship adorned every street, and both Khrushchev and Voroshilov saw him off at the airport.

There is no doubt but that Haile Selassie was impressed and delighted with his reception. He came away with a low-interest long-term £35 million loan to develop industry and agriculture, a trade pact (Russian machinery and ferrous products for Ethiopian hides, peanuts and oil seeds), a two-year treaty of cultural co-operation, and the gifts of an Ilyushin-14 aircraft for himself and a 1,000-student technical school for his people. Khrushchev (as well as Nasser) agreed to make a return visit to Ethiopia. On his return to Ethiopia, the Emperor expressed his thanks for the loan 'so generously offered by the great and friendly Union of Soviet Socialist Republics' and announced that part of the funds would be devoted to constructing a refinery at Assab to refine Russian crude oil to be supplied at half the price of Western petroleum. He urged the West to accept Russia's disarmament proposals.

Russia has undertaken an extensive geological survey of Ethiopia and is constructing gold mining and processing installations. And the Soviets lost little time in initiating construction on the school at Bahr Dar, in Gojjam province on the banks of the Blue Nile, which will be Russian-staffed. It was later announced that the Ethiopian Church and the Russian Orthodox Church are considering a merger, a possibility first raised in Czarist days. All this indicates that Ethiopia is virtually in the neutralist camp and we have no one to blame but ourselves.

More East-West sparring can be expected when the Emperor, who has the smallest hands and feet I have ever seen, starts his pet project, a Blue Nile hydro-electric scheme. Haile Selassie has long dreamed of harnessing the Nile at its Lake Tana source and he was angered at not being consulted during negotiations between the Sudan and Egypt. Ethiopian rivers contribute about 84 per cent of the total amount of water which reaches the mouth of the Nile, and the seasonal run-off from Ethiopia's high plateaux, which slope to the north-west, is the greatest single factor in the annual floods which have governed life on the Nile for thousands of years.

The source of the Blue Nile is Lake Tana, with a surface of 11,000 square miles, which is located about 200 miles north-west of Addis Ababa. The lake is 6,000 feet above sea level and the Blue Nile drops 719 feet in the first twenty-seven miles after it leaves the lake. What the Emperor would like to do is to build a series of a dozen turbines in this distance to pump water for irrigation and to provide power to attract industry. These dams would help both the Sudan and Egypt because they would store much of the 'untimely' water which rushes through a 2,000-foot gorge when the river is in spate. The project has been surveyed (with American funds) and there is evidence that the Russians will be strong bidders for the dam contract.

If he can get the necessary power, Haile Selassie would also like to build a new capital city at Bahr Dar, where the Russian school is located. The city would be on the banks of the lake, where the Blue Nile begins its long journey to the Mediterranean. Lake Tana, he explains, has 'a strong mystic pull' for him because his ancestors, 'the kings of Ethiopia', are buried there.

In the past, Ethiopia has played little part in the Pan-African movement sweeping this continent from the Congo to the Sahara. In part this is due to Ethiopian race consciousness: the worst thing that you can call an Ethiopian, even if he is the colour of tar, is a *shankalla*, a black. Ethiopians have regarded black nationalism as no concern of theirs. In addition, Ethiopian emperors have been unwilling to rock the British and French boats, both because of the *entente* which existed among these three nations and the fear that interference in the affairs of the colonial powers might cost Ethiopia her own independence. Of late, however, the Ethiopian position has been altered and the country is taking a more active role in African affairs. The Emperor's second son, Prince Sahle Selassie, represented his country and his father at the Accra Conference of independent states. And the Emperor has visited the Sudan. Haile Selassie is obviously intent on having Africa and the world know that he, not Nasser, speaks for the Eastern Horn of Africa. If the Ethiopian despises the black man, he fears the militant Islam of the Middle East. Also, it is natural that this oldest independent nation south of the Sahara should play an important role in African affairs.

It is this fear of Islam which remains the mainspring of Ethiopian foreign policy. It sparked Haile Selassie's desire to procure Eritrea and it is at the source of his hostility to the concept of a Greater Somalia. Ex-Italian Somaliland obtained its independence on July 1, 1960. Britain retained administration of the Haud area of Ethiopia for several years after World War II and relinquished control only when Somalis from the British protectorate were guaranteed the right to graze and water their flocks at certain seasons on the Ethiopian side of the frontier. In addition, there is a large indigenous Somali population in the province of Harar and some of the political leaders of ex-Italian Somaliland would like to include 40,000 square miles of Ethiopian territory in a Greater Somalia, a concept first suggested by the British immediately after World War II. At the urging of the inhabitants of British Somaliland, the United Kingdom on June 26, 1960, granted independence to the protectorate so that it could merge the following week with an independent Somalia. The Somalis had hoped that the French would follow suit but, now that French Somaliland has become a department of France, this would seem to be out of the question.

Haile Selassie is unalterably opposed to the Greater Somalia concept for the simple reason that it would shatter his empire. This deceptively mild little imperialist instead would like an *anschluss* with the Somali Republic, perhaps on the same federal basis as Eritrea enjoys. He has made repeated speeches promising the Somalis schools, hospitals and wells if they join him. The Emperor's position is strengthened by the fact that the Somali Republic's two life-giving rivers rise in Ethiopia and the best grazing is on his side of the border. The least he could or would accept is an independent Somali Republic within its present boundaries and a cessation of Greater Somalia propaganda from Mogadiscio.

At the crux of the question is the border dispute. Ethiopia asserts that it is willing to accept the border established in 1908 and claims that Italy, negotiating on Somalia's behalf, has attempted to open the whole question to revision and is 'encouraging and supporting the dismemberment of Ethiopia'. Trygve Lie, former Secretary-General of the United Nations, has been appointed neutral arbiter of the question, which has been further complicated by reports of oil in the contested area. As we shall see in Chapter VII there is another side to the story.

Ethiopia's future looks bright. She has rich soil, ample rainfall, access to the sea, an improving administration and a strategic position guarding the southern approach to the Suez Canal which ensures her of an important role in the global strategy of the West. In time, she can become the granary of the Middle East.

We had seen Ethiopia and now it was time to move on to Somalia. But there was the problem of how to get there.

Chapter 6

*

OUT OF ETHIOPIA

'BORDER CLOSES MARCH 15,' read the cable, 'YOU MUST REACH MOYALE NOT LATER THAN MARCH 12 AND YOU MUST TRAVEL IN CONVOY.'

It was signed by the Provincial Commissioner of Kenya's desolate Northern Frontier Province, one of the last demi-gods of the British Empire, ruling a kingdom larger than England, Scotland and Wales, a man from whose decisions there is no appeal except to God. And in Northern Kenya some doubt His jurisdiction.

'Fine chap,' said Ronnie Peale, director of the British Information Service in Addis Ababa, between munches on his cold pipe. 'I should get cracking towards the border immediately, if I were you.' It was then March 7.

'Go by way of Neghelli,' Ronnie said as we bade him farewell. 'It's a bit rougher and longer than the direct route through Dilla but at least you're sure to make it that way. If the rains catch you on the Dilla road, you'll never get through.'

We thanked him and dashed off to do our last-minute outfitting for what we knew would be a brutal trip over a road which few trucks, let alone passenger cars, will attempt. Our purchases included five five-gallon jerry cans for petrol, a shovel, a tow-rope, tyre repair kit, wash basin and canned goods.

After an eleventh-hour audience with the Emperor the following morning, scattering forwarding addresses around town, and liberating the soap and toilet paper from our hotel room, we shoved off to the south, the corners of our mouths turned down scornfully at the libertines of Addis Ababa who had never, like us, braved the unknown.

The unknown turned out to be not half bad. The day was bright and glistening after an all-night shower, the air fresh and bracing. Herds of fat mares and frolicsome colts grazed the flower-strewn meadows between groves of stately cedars in country which could have been the Blue Grass around Lexington. With firm jaws and bold hearts, we crossed the Awash and lurched into the crater-lake country.

116

Any connection between this area and any other lake district in the world is purely coincidental. Lakes Zwai, Langano, Hora Abyata, Shala and Awasa, apart from being unpronounceable, are inexcusable. They sit flat and waveless, their oily surfaces merging into the soda flats, surrounded by mile after mile of baking bush and scrub thorn. They give pleasure only to the bilharzia and the crocodiles which inhabit them. But the road was not bad, the weather, although getting hotter all the time, not impossible, and we passed without incident through the country of the fierce Arussi Gallas, skipped through the great cities of Shashemenne and Yrgalem, and came to rest as the light was fading and the rain falling, at the Sudan Interior Mission in Wondo, a hill town on the edge of the forest.

The missionary, a Canadian with a Joe Palooka physique—he turned out to be a reformed hockey star—took us in, fed us, regaled us with stories of his recent home leave (after he had given a lecture at a church in Georgia, a red-necked farmer got up and said, 'Thank you so much, Brother and Sister Middleton, for giving us such a fine description of your mission work in Utopia'), produced natives to tell us about witchcraft which Middleton, like every other missionary who has been in Africa for a few years, takes quite seriously. After a hearty breakfast the next morning he accepted my baseball and mitt in return for his hospitality (I always carry them; it pays to be prepared) and pointed us in the general direction of Neghelli. There was a Norwegian mission and petrol for sale there, he said. We would be there that night.

We threaded our way carefully through Wondo at 10 m.p.h. Ethiopian law makes little distinction between manslaughter and murder. Each is an offence against the clan of the victim and retribution must be paid either in blood or money. One's equanimity is not increased by the people's practice of waiting until a car is almost abreast of them and then dashing across the road. The priests have told them that the devil is always following them and the pious attempt in this fashion to give the devil a good jolt with the motorist's bumper.

As we turned to the south-east, the road dipped lower and lower into a tropical jungle filled with screaming birds and long-haired colobus monkeys with black bodies and white-tufted tails. The road was dirt and the surface was good. In the morning we passed two villages. At each there was a road-block. One has been well brought up and led to believe that courtesy will always be reciprocated. This is not the case when dealing with minor officials of the Ethiopian Government. Such behaviour in Ethiopia is interpreted as a sign either of guilt or weakness.

Instead, highly recommended is this procedure: hold breath until suitably apoplectic tinge is obtained, jump out of car, curse colourfully and shake fistful of letters bearing Imperial seal in official's face. Since most rural officials cannot read, these letters need not be relevant; a dog licence will do. In nine out of ten cases, the official will yield. In each of these instances it worked.

We passed an Imperial Highway Authority camp—the advance guard of the construction crews—and the road, which had been good, deteriorated immediately into a boggy trail pocked with huge holes filled with water. Each mile we went on, the road narrowed, the jungle closing in, compressing it between huge green hands. As the road got narrower, the holes got wider and deeper. At some, we cut branches and filled them with stones and dirt; at others, we put the car in second and blasted on through.

At noon, I blasted when I should have shovelled. We were hopelessly mired in a three-foot bog, the water lapping over the running-board. Always a gentleman, I put the blame on Kitty, thoughtfully showed her how to put stones under the wheels without getting wet above the knees, and walked back down the road for help. After a quarter of a mile I met a spear-carrying citizen with filed teeth clothed in a loin cloth. I explained our difficulty. He smiled and shook his spear. I smiled and patted the revolver in my belt. We were soul-mates. We walked back to the car together.

On the way we were joined by a scabby gentleman in a ripe goatskin who had no teeth at all and carried only a stick, no spear. Soul-mate explained the situation to him and he clucked understandingly. I suggested that he find himself a new dentist and he nodded in a friendly fashion.

Soul-mate whistled softly when he saw the car sunk in above its hub-caps. He said something to Ripe Goatskin and the old man slipped off into the jungle. Soul-mate sat down. I sat down. Kitty, who was beginning to look as if she wished she had married anybody but me, leaned against the car.

Within a few minutes Ripe Goatskin reappeared with a baker's dozen of his fellow lodge members. There was a decent amount of soft whistling at the height of the water and a certain amount of spear-shaking. Then we began to push. Nothing happened. We filled with dirt and rocks and pushed. Nothing happened. A gentleman clad in loin cloth and pinstripe vest and coat arrived on the scene. He was very good at shouting and gesturing but not much good at pushing. After he had managed to get everything thoroughly disorganized, I told him that I would handle all the shouting and gesturing but that it would be perfectly all right for him to push. His feelings were hurt and it started to rain so he went home. A genius in the crowd cut a channel from the bog off into the jungle and the water started to pour out. I noticed that the channel was smooth with use. Being known for my quick perception, I realized after half an hour that the villagers had made this bog themselves by blocking the ditch, either to water their cattle or to make money by getting people out. After unloading the car in the rain, draining the bog, filling with stones and dry dirt, cutting down the edge of the incline, putting steel mats under the wheels, and pushing and prying with saplings my assistants had cut, we got the car free. We reloaded, passed out some coins with bonuses for Soul-mate and Ripe Goatskin, shook hands all round and expressed the hope that we might see them all some day in Washington. And off we went.

A few miles up the road a half-caste, clad in khaki drill and topi, stopped us and asked in Italian if he could have a ride to Adolla, the town twenty miles up the line.

We had several other narrow escapes with bogs. I asked our friend how the road was to Neghelli. 'Strada buona, buona,' he said. It was an answer we were to get many times in the next two weeks. Neghelli, he said, was twenty miles beyond Adolla. We let him off at Adolla and headed into a country of black cotton soil and steep, low hills. We picked up a country squire who indicated that he was in the market for a ride. The next few hours found the Squire more than earning his way—he chopped out road to give us clearance, pried the car out of ditches with tree limbs and pushed up hills. We gave him some gumdrops when we dropped him off.

We began to hit more streams. Everybody else builds bridges by putting two supports across the stream and covering them with logs laid parallel to the stream bed. Ethiopians simply fell a number of logs across a stream and push them together. Then they sit around and wait for a car to slip off the logs. It brings a certain amount of excitement into otherwise dull lives. We negotiated five or six of these bridges.

The seventh was a murderous-looking thing bridging one arm of a swamp which crawled through a patch of jungle choking the gorge between two abrupt hills. We came on it almost at dark. Halfway across, one of the logs gave way. We came down on the gear-box with a resounding smash, the right rear wheel suspended and spinning slowly over the swamp. We jacked, filled, inflated the tyres to the bursting point to try to raise the car off the gear-box. It was dark, it was raining, and we could hear a leopard coughing at the bottom of the ravine. We got back in the car and broke out our last bottle of Scotch.

While the mud with which we were caked from head to foot dried a bit, we had a drink to Ronnie Peale. Then we had one to the Imperial Highway Department. Then we had one to Their Imperial Majesties and to the leopard in the ravine. By mutual consent we skipped dinner, crawled on to the soaking mattress in the back of the car and went to sleep.

We hopped out of bed to a dank and misty dawn, bubbling with the high spirits of constipated water-buffaloes. The car wouldn't budge. We had three choices: we could stay with the car and wait for somebody to come along to help us get out, we could walk back five miles to the last village for help, or we could walk to Neghelli, less than twenty miles up the line. I hadn't walked twenty miles since I parted company with the Marine Corps. Kitty had never walked that far. Man's memory, fortunately, soon forgets the unpleasant things. The vote was 2–0 for walking to Neghelli.

Taking a can of fruit juice, a can of peaches and my revolver, and with a Rhodesian set to our jaws, we trudged down the road.

This was life, adventure, a return to the basic verities. After five hours of walking through gullies choked with jungle growth, over rocky ridges and across uninhabited flats, it was no longer life, adventure, or a return to the basic verities. It was blistered feet and a pain in the posterior.

We passed two people in the morning. One was a jolly Muslim type who responded to our Amharic greeting by squinting around his nose and expectorating noisily. The other, apparently on his way to get a job as a spear-carrier in Aida, was a more agreeable person. We found that we had brought a great deal of joy into his life when we told him we were walking to Neghelli. He whistled, smiled, laughed, hopped around on one foot and otherwise indicated that he thought we were crazy. We agreed and kept walking. There were scattered showers all day, the jungle steaming in the bright sun that appeared between them. We ate our peaches in the early afternoon and polished off the tomato juice. Around three o'clock we came on some native cattle and their Gudje herdsmen, frizzy-headed gentlemen clad in skins, each carrying a spear, wearing bone murder rings around their upper arms to which were tastefully attached, as a sort of jungle costume jewellery, the genitalia of the men they had killed (the Gudje, like the Dankali, must kill a man before they can marry). The Gudjes took one look at us and bolted off into the bush. The cattle were as wild as foxes and began to make threatening noises and motions in our direction. When staring them down proved unsuccessful, we skirted the herd with a couple of passes that would have done credit to Juan Belmonte and exhorted our mushy feet to greater efforts.

Still no sign of Neghelli. As dark was coming on, we climbed the highest mountain of the day and began to see signs of human habitation: an occasional path leading off into the jungle, a log which had been chopped down, a bundle of juniper saplings bound with vines, a deserted hut swarming with baboons. A little further on we came to a village. It was not Neghelli by a long shot. There were about fifty huts. We asked for the police and were taken to a compound fenced with banana leaves. We sat down on the ground. A number of police in various approximations of uniform came out of the hut accompanied by a big Amhara mama. I showed them all my letters. One of them could read a little, a couple could speak a few words of Italian.

'Maquina roto,' I informed them, just so they wouldn't think we were out on a bird-watching hike. 'Dormir. Domani retorner con tutti gente a maquina. Andaremos a Neghelli domani.' If the reader knows Italian, he will see that this is sort of a cross between Italian, Spanish, Latin, baby-talk and Urdu. Accompanied by a suitable amount of gesticulating, grimacing, nodding and delivered at hi-fi volume, it usually produces a reaction if not understanding.

The sergeant in charge, after shooing away the children, led us to the village night-spot. We sat down on wooden benches against the mud wall. The Muslim owner came forward and produced a couple of fly-specked glasses and a jar of boiling hot, sweet tea and a couple of hunks of bread. Visions of diphtheria, typhoid, venereal disease and internal parasites danced in our heads. The immediate condition of our throats and stomachs was considerably more real than our future health. We dived in. It was delicious. By this time most of the population of the village—Wadere, we were told, was its name—had poured into the tavern. They were all talking at once, in several dialects, and mostly to us. This was accompanied by considerable cross-consultation between those who thought I was Marshal Graziano and those convinced they had Wilbur de Paris as their guest.

After more tea and shouting, I felt I had conveyed these basic thoughts to the assembled populace: we were Americans, not Italians; we had walked a long way, were tired and would spend the night in

Wadere; our car was stuck, not broken, eight or nine hours' walk from here; in the morning, if they would provide me with a mule and six men, we would get the car out and then we would go on to Neghelli; I would pay for all this. The sergeant and the village fathers seemed satisfied with my analysis of the situation. The sergeant motioned to us to follow him. We walked through the village, stopping to exhaust our Arabic vocabulary with a genial Muslim shopkeeper who wanted to be of assistance, to the police post on the other side of town. This was a compound of five or six round huts and a central building, square and also of mud, surrounded by a fence of saplings. We went in and sat down and the police clerk began writing his report. Periodically the sergeant got up to shoo little brown faces from the glassless windows.

In a few minutes we were finished and the sergeant led us away. We would stay with him, he indicated. His house was a square, two-room affair with a dirt floor. The mud of the walls was whitewashed and the roof was of tin, not thatch. There were two other thatched huts on the compound which was surrounded by a paling fence.

The big Amhara mama proved to be the sergeant's wife. She made us sit down and sent a boy to bring hot water. The boy washed Kitty's feet and then went to work on my aching dogs. Big Mama lit a lantern and had the cot upon which she and the sergeant slept brought into the front room, otherwise innocent of furniture. Big Mama's Italian was as bad as mine. We understood each other perfectly.

She asked if we would like coffee or tea and food. She produced some *pasta* to indicate that she had European food as well as *enjira wat* to offer us. We said we would like coffee but were too tired to eat. Big Mama was not too happy about that but finally let us have our way. She got a fire going on the floor and produced a shallow wooden bowl with coffee beans lining the bottom. These she ground with a pestle. When the water she had heated was boiling, she threw in the ground beans and sugar. In a few minutes it was ready . . . hot, strong and rejuvenating.

The sergeant took his rifle, an old Hungarian model, and made his rounds of the village. When he came back, he was accompanied by a big pock-marked man with a penchant for spitting in the corners of the room and smoking my cigarettes. He was mayor of the village, Big Mama's brother, and spoke really atrocious Italian with a disagreeable flamboyancy.

'Tutti Amhara, tutti Galla, tutti gente de Wadere,' he announced, would go back with me tomorrow to get the car. Good. Could he scare up a mule for me? He would see. Could we leave at one o'clock (the Ethiopians figure time from dawn; one o'clock is 7 a.m.)? He thought so and how about a cigarette? I gave him one.

Big Mama, after refilling our glasses of coffee, told us that Haile Selassie would weep if he could see our feet, he was so kind and gentle. He had given the sergeant the land for this house, many blankets and money. He would weep.

We agreed. Nobody showed any signs of going home so we said we were very tired and would go to bed if they didn't mind. They didn't. I crawled under the blankets and took off my clothes. Kitty had a bit more trouble in wiggling out of hers as Big Mama had insisted that she change from her filthy shorts and shirt to a large print dress and a *shamma*. But she made it and, despite the smoke and the muted conversation, we were soon asleep.

By morning we were stiff as boards from our long walk and the cold night. We gulped tea and I said good-bye to Kitty and went to investigate the progress of my expedition. Nothing had been accomplished. A mule, at a rental of $1·50 Ethiopian (four shillings) was finally produced, as were a corporal, a private, a citizen clad in skins and two small boys. I assumed the other men from the village had started earlier. Off we lurched, the men with their arms draped over their rifles which they held behind their necks, the citizen swinging a machete and the boys flinging stones at the baboons. The mule and I soon established an *entente cordiale*: I let him have his head and kicked him in the stomach only when he tried to rake me through thorn bushes.

After four hours of fast walking, my escort was a bit disgruntled and my dignity shattered by a broken saddle girth. It seems that they had been told that the car was only two or three hours away. We were able to cut off a couple of miles by following the trails through the bush instead of the 'highway'. After another hour, one of the small boys dropped out and was left behind. My colleagues stopped a gentleman strolling through the forest and relieved him of some maize which they ate in its powdered form. Finally, we reached the car. We unloaded it completely, jacked and filled with stones, and with the three men pushing were able to get clear. The Citizen who was to ride the mule back to Wadere wanted his money. I told him that I hadn't brought any but would leave his with the corporal. He apparently not only didn't think I had an honest face but had some doubts about the corporal. I could see his point as concerned the corporal. The latter was delighted with the prospect of acting as trustee for the Citizen's funds. Citizen continued to complain but finally agreed to the arrangement after the corporal had planted his rifle butt firmly on his bare toes a couple of times. Off we went again. It was raining.

After negotiating several miles of bog and rock outcroppings with the skill of a master teamster, we came to a great soft mud-hole in the road. I tried to pass it through the bush, but slipped off into the bog. We were stuck again in fender-high water. Three hours of pushing, digging, filling and draining followed with little progress. Finally, I talked them into using the strips of steel matting which I had bought in the Asmara flea market for traction purposes. They didn't believe in the mats, but when nothing else worked, agreed to try them. In gradual stages we worked the car free. Two hours later, as night fell, we were back in Wadere. I paid off the boys and, surrounded by the usual retinue of children, walked back to the sergeant's house.

Kitty had had herself quite a day. After seeing us off in the morning, she had gone back to bed, and awoke several hours later to find the room full of local types guzzling *tej*. It seemed that Big Mama made her pin-money by running a *tej* house. The local clientele was pretty well in its cups by 10 a.m. This group was soon joined by the wild Gudjes who had come into the market to sell a few scraggy chickens and get drunk. They asked her for cigarettes, money, if she would care to dance, and one chap, who got himself a clout on the head from Big Mama for his troubles, went so far as to suggest a liaison. Kitty retreated to the market. Most of the children had never seen a white man, let alone a white woman. They conducted a series of investigations to determine whether she was constructed in the same way as their mothers. Her underwear was of particular interest. At some sacrifice to her modesty, she had made fast friends with one and all of the small fry by the time I got back.

Big Mama had boiled some potatoes for us. We ate them and washed them down with more tea while the sergeant made his rounds. The sergeant, she said, had killed six men. There was a big band of *shifta* in the area. But we were safe in the village and should have no trouble on the way to Neghelli. We had walked through the worst area.

When the sergeant got back, he showed me his rifle and I handed him my ·38 pistol. Did I have another like it? I was sorry, it was the only one I had. But in a few years all Ethiopian army and police were to have American weapons. That would be good, he said.

I didn't want to insult our hosts by giving them money. So to the sergeant I gave a German knife. Big Mama got half a dozen plastic spoons from our 'K' ration packs. To top it off, we made a present to the house of a picture of the Emperor with Mayor Wagner in New York. Big Mama kissed the picture. The sergeant kissed the picture. All our visitors that evening admired the gifts and kissed the picture. A couple of little girls, having satisfied themselves as to Kitty's anatomy, came round to check me out. They were delighted with the hair on my arms and belly and asked me to take them to Kenya. It was a thoroughly successful evening and I feel sure Kitty could run for mayor of Wadere and win in a walkaway.

Having enshrined Mayor Wagner and Friend on the wall of the sergeant's hut, been presented with a bunch of Big Mama's bananas and taken on a policeman's wife who wanted to go to Neghelli—which turned out to be more than seventy miles further down the road—we said our farewells in the pre-dawn darkness and chugged out of town. The hills flattened out and the dawn came in faint and ghostly over our left shoulders. First the clouds looked black, edged with pink and then with scarlet. Finally the clouds themselves turned to crimson and the rock faces of the mountains still on our right began to glow. And then the clouds were gold and it was day and there were jackals racing for the cover of the hills. The evergreens gave way to flat-topped acacias, some of which contained the tubular straw containers placed there by the natives in the hope that the bees will swarm and there will be honey for *tej*.

We reached Neghelli, a fine town set on a low hill rising from the baking plain, with nothing more untoward than a flat tyre although it became increasingly obvious that the damaged drive shaft, which cut our speed to a pelvis-shattering 20 m.p.h., was not going to last much longer. With a sense of timing brought to a fine art by years of free-loading, we arrived at the Norwegian mission just as a lunch of thick stew, potatoes, boiled cabbage, preserved beets and tinned butter was going on the table. We were coaxed into staying.

The missionary was a doctor and he commented on how much of his time was taken up with treating venereal disease. 'But syphilis,' he added, 'is lazy and will not climb a mountain. In the far hills you find entire villages without a single case.' Was there any social stigma attached to having V.D.? The missionary laughed. 'Last week I asked a man if he had ever had it and his answer was "No, but I hope to get it soon." Having syphilis is like owning a pair of sun-glasses: it's a sign of sophistication.'

There was no mechanic in town. The police mechanic had gone to

Addis Ababa for a few days with the Major. His apprentice said he thought he could fix the drive-shaft. The missionary advised against it. He said he was afraid the apprentice would break the shaft while trying to fix it. Then we would be stuck for weeks. The flat was something of a problem because it was the first tubeless tyre seen in Neghelli. It was impossible, the mechanic assured me, for a tyre to inflate without a tube. I explained that a quick rush of air would seal the bead. He looked doubtful but pumped manfully. There wasn't enough pressure to seal it. The missionary came up with the brilliant idea of putting a rope tourniquet around the circumference of the tyre, using a jack handle to force the tyre on to the rim. It worked perfectly, much to the astonishment of all concerned. We decided to try to make it without attempting to repair the shaft. Then we dug up the Somali trader who sells petrol in Neghelli. It is the last place in Ethiopia where petrol can be bought and the fact had not escaped this entrepreneur. He charged us almost two shillings a quart.

We could reach Mega in ten hours, the missionary said. We thanked him for lunch and got on our way.

Neghelli was intended by the Italians to be their big trading and administrative centre in south-eastern Ethiopia and a tarmac road had been built part of the way to Mogadiscio. We travelled on this for five miles, then turned south over a desert track towards Mega. This was really desert, burning red sand, stunted thorn bushes, gazelle and ostrich. After making another ten miles, we ploughed through a sand drift and the car stopped. Just stopped. The starter and ignition were working but nothing was happening.

By now we had things down to a system. We put on our walking shoes, dug out our hats, grabbed a bottle of water, a can of fruit and the revolver, and started walking. The missionary had been about to go out in the bush for a couple of weeks with a mule and camel train to preach to the nomads. We were sure that we would catch him if we reached a certain point where his trail crossed ours. Nobody was in sight when we reached the crossing except a Somali driving a camel whose flanks were covered with blood. As we approached he chased the camel off the track into the bush and we saw two skinny legs protruding from the blood. She was giving birth and the Somali, who carried an out-sized spear and had a curved knife in his belt, apparently was intent on getting her back to his hut before she had the baby so that the young camel would not have to spend his first night in the bush with hungry cats.

We knew we could save a couple of miles by cutting through the bush rather than going all the way back to the road. The trail through the bush was fairly plain. We followed it. On the way we passed several Somali camel trains on their way out from market; the herdsmen tittered and giggled at finding two Europeans on their caravan trail miles from town, and the fact that both of us, one with long hair, one with short hair, wore shorts amused them. When night fell, Neghelli was nowhere to be seen. We followed the trail as best we could, cheered on by a chorus of hyenas. We came to several shepherds' campfires but each was deserted. In this country, when a man hears a stranger coming, he gets out of the firelight and into the shadows. He lives longer that way.

After more than an hour of walking in the dark—we had expected to reach Neghelli by dusk—all hands were feeling a bit low. Some even suggested that being in Washington was an improvement over this. Such seditious statements were dealt with severely. We almost stubbed our toes on the mission wall. There are no electric lights in Neghelli, of course, and, as the moon had not risen, we were on the town almost before we knew it. Old Leatherstocking and his sturdy mate had walked twelve miles, the last three in the dark, and made a dead reckoning landfall.

Our missionary friends were somewhat surprised to see us. The preacher had delayed his start to the bush for one day and that was why we had missed him. We borrowed the one car in town and, after breaking my tow rope six times, got the car back into town and fell into bed.

All the next day we worked on the car with the assistance of the police mechanic's apprentice and the engineer from the waterworks. They managed to bang out the drive shaft a bit and to fix whatever had been the matter with the engine. We were roadworthy again by late afternoon.

We decided to have dinner and then drive straight through after dark when we would have the advantage of the cool night air. I was short of funds after paying off the mechanic and the missionary cashed a small cheque for me. He had an account in Chicago, he said, for buying books.

It was then March 13 and time was short. We pushed off. The desert lasted for two hours. Then we started to climb a series of low rocky hills, the sky filled with green dwarf parrots and glossy blue starlings. The road in many places was simply a stream bed. The bottoms of the hills were steep, narrow gulleys where the rear fender of the car, sometimes the gear-box, scraped ominously as we crept down one side and up the other. Three hours out of Neghelli, we found ourselves wedged at the bottom of one of these gulleys. We could neither go forward nor backward. We went to sleep.

By dint of a lot of chopping away of one side of the ravine and filling of the other, we were able to get the car free the next morning. With hearts high, we churned off. One mile further, a portion of the road near a deep wash collapsed under the weight of the car. A piece of road as big as a piano was gone and would have to be filled with rock. Our jack was broken and the car would have to be pried out. This would take more and stronger backs than ours. We unloaded the car, set up camp in a tiny patch of shade, and got out the book bag. I was reading Kenneth Roberts' *Arundel* and found it hard to sympathize with men struggling knee-deep through the icy waters of Maine's Chaudiere River while the locusts here were singing their heat song and we were on rationed water.

Late in the morning a policeman walked up. He was commuting twenty miles to work at the next police post. He stopped and the two of us tried to fill the gaping hole. It was no good. I gave him a dollar and a note to his sergeant asking him to send me ten men. I wrote the note in English, lavishly illustrated. He left and we went back to our reading, having stripped down to our underwear in an effort to catch the slightest breeze. By mid-afternoon our friend and five policemen had returned. More pushing, pulling, prying and filling and we were out. We got stuck in gulleys three more times but made the police post by 7 p.m.

The sergeant gave us tea and two cots to sleep on in the open. I asked him if he would give me three men to go as far as the next post. He said he couldn't send them all the way as it would take them three days to walk back and the country was full of 'leones' and, he wagged his arm in front of his nose to indicate a trunk, elephants. He would give me three men to go halfway.

Two hours from the post the next day we ran into the British consul from Mega on his way to Addis Ababa. He was roughing it in a Land Rover accompanied by a five-ton truck full of kit and native police. We should be in Mega in five hours. Would we call on his wife? We would. And visions of a bath and ice water leapt to mind.

After nothing more than the normal filling and pushing and re-building a plank bridge over the first real river we had seen, a roaring torrent of brown rain water, we reached the halfway point. All hands went down to the river for a wash, a long drink and a refill of water-bottles. The water smelled like the lion cage at the zoo and was the colour of coffee. We drank deeply.

Here, our three police friends said, they would have to leave us. I asked them if they wouldn't go on. It was impossible. It was three days' walk back to their post and there were many lions and elephants (we never saw any). I appealed to their patriotism, their sense of duty, and devotion to the brotherhood of man. Then I said I would pay $5 Ethiopian (fourteen shillings) plus cigarettes to any man who would come. A policeman makes £6 a month. The little corporal threw his canteen and rifle into the car and said he would come. The others complained for a while and finally climbed in.

We reached the Wachelli police post, a forlorn stockade in a stark white soda plain at 4 p.m. The lieutenant couldn't give us any water because theirs was all salty from the soda and would make us sick. He would give us two men to go with us to Mega. We said good-bye to our other three friends—they were still kissing and hugging their seldom-seen chums at Wachelli and were obviously delighted that we had led them astray—tucked the money into their canteen cups so the lieutenant wouldn't see it, and climbed back into the car, visions of iced beer supplanting earlier thoughts of Mega.

Five miles from the post the car stopped. And wouldn't start. Being well-versed in things mechanical, I checked the oil, water, petrol, and tyre pressure and clucked wisely over the engine. Our two friends were suitably impressed that there was nothing more to be done. I told the police that they could go back to the post if they wanted. We would stay with the car until a truck with a mechanic came along. One of our friends suggested that this was not such a good idea since it had been more than a month since the last truck came through. He, he said, would walk back to the post and inform the lieutenant. The other trooper would stay with us.

The trooper walked back to the post and returned to our car after dark. The lieutenant was coming the following morning, he said. We turned in, the two of us in the back of the car, one trooper sleeping on the front seat, the other watching by the fire.

That morning we sighted a large female kudu crossing the road ahead of us and nothing would do but that I should shoot the beast. Stalking her with the careful cunning and the cat-like silence of a splay-footed mastodon, I jumped the doe in a thorn thicket just off the road. From the angle at which she faced I would have given her a rather painful hysterectomy if I'd fired, provided I'd hit her, which was extremely unlikely as I hadn't shot a rifle in six years.

'Too close,' I said deprecatingly as the doe bounded away. 'I never shoot 'em at less than five hundred yards.' The two police seemed a trifle disappointed and just a shade cynical about Old Natty Bumpo. I recovered their confidence in my woodlore by showing them how I could light a fire with the aid of a gallon of petrol and a match.

We were just brushing the ashes of what had once been eyebrows from our faces when the lieutenant and a column of about twenty men, about evenly divided between police and local citizenry, came marching down the road. I checked the water again to show them that everything mechanically possible had been done to rectify the situation. The lieutenant was satisfied. He said his men would push the car into town. Since it was five miles through sand drifts, I marvelled at the civic spirit of the non-military types who had volunteered for such a job. My faith in their community spirit was somewhat dampened by the fact that every time the lieutenant looked the other way, a couple of our friends slipped off into the bush. Our labour supply was replenished, however, by those locals unfortunate enough to have picked this day to go in to market.

With lots of cheering, pounding on drums and more grunting than anything else, we were pushed into the police stockade. The lieutenant took us to a small dirt-floored *tukal* which was to be our quarters and produced a prisoner to sweep it out. We moved in and set up house.

The lieutenant, who was bashful about his English and spoke no Italian, returned a few minutes later with a Somali interpreter to add further blocks to communication.

We went through the 'Haile-Selassie-would-weep' routine again with suitable ramifications and expansions including the fact that this was bad country with many animals and bad people and no European rations and that is why he (the lieutenant) had come to bring us back.

'Wherefore,' said the interpreter, 'you and Sister [I was Mister so it was quite logical that Kitty should be Sister] stay here in hut; everything safe; no kit stolen; have water to wash and for to drink; wherefore, mechanic sometime come and fix lorry; wherefore you go to Mega.'

We were in complete agreement on all basic principles. We expressed our thanks and accepted an invitation to coffee at the lieutenant's hut for later that night.

The first day passed pleasantly enough. It was good just to know that we didn't have to try to drive. In the evening a policeman came to give us three small eggs. He refused payment but cast covetous eyes on two empty tin cans, much in demand in the bush for use as dinner service. These we parted with to the joy of our benefactor.

The high-domed mud-and-wattle hut was cool enough during the day but the constant wind, unimpeded by the barricade which I constructed of a car seat and blankets, blasted sand devils in on us. Our water gave out but we found the local stuff—too saline for drinking but good enough for coffee or tea—available at 3d. the two-gallon *debbi*. We read and typed and dug the worms from under our toe-nails with penknives.

We learned the lieutenant's life history—he was from Addis Ababa, had spent six years in the bush during the Italian occupation, was a consumptive, had a wife and three children in Addis—and listened to the chief clerk's wireless.

'If no truck come,' the lieutenant told us through the interpreter, 'Mister and Sister leave lorry here, go by camel to Mega; rains come soon, no rations for Europeans.' I knew with what relish the lieutenant would greet the fact that our car would be left with him. He was fascinated by the horn. I determined to stay in our hut through the three-month rains, if necessary.

But the truck did come three days later and the driver was able to fix the car. We said good-bye to our Wachelli friends and, hopefully, set out again for Mega. This time our luck was good. The track was across flat desert studded with moon-landscape anthills twenty feet high and we had to drive through the bush most of the time because the road was too deeply rutted. But we made it. At the Mega police post, where we had to stop to check in and have passport numbers recorded, one tyre gave a sigh and went flat. The Norwegian missionary in town was a good sort and produced a jack and some very welcome assistance. I gave him the mail I had brought from Neghelli, and Kitty and I drove up the mountain to the British Consulate.

There the wife of the absent consul gave us a gin and tonic (real ice), sandwiches, an invitation to stay a week or so, and, when we declined, a packet of mail to take to Barry McDermott, an official of the Kenya government.

'You'll like Barry,' she assured us, 'he's a dear.' Since it was then March 18, three days after the official closing of the frontier, we were glad to hear that Barry was a dear. It lessened the chances of our being turned back at the border.

The run to Moyale was a piece of cake. We cleared Ethiopian customs with no difficulty and, our mouths dry in anticipation of Barry McDermott's hospitality, passed from Ethiopia through no-man's-land to the barrier of British Moyale.

The barrier was slammed in our faces. The District Commissioner, indicated the trooper, was on safari. So was the police officer. At this juncture up galloped a wild-eyed young man followed by a couple of mounted *askaris*.

This was Barry McDermott. He was not happy to see us. The border was closed. We would not be admitted. I could come and see him about it in the morning if I wished. No, I could not come inside the compound. I would have to go back to Ethiopian Moyale. Thanks awfully for bringing down the mail, old chap. Barry McDermott, Empire Builder, cantered off in a cloud of dust.

To emphasize his ultimatum, a trooper appeared from the administrative compound with a three-foot length of iron cable with which he proceeded to tie up and lock the barrier. Obviously we were the type who would try to run the border after dark.

We spent the night by the barrier. The Empire Builder cantered up in the morning and told us again that we wouldn't be admitted. There was a German journalist named Lutz Herold in the same position. Both of us would have to go back to Addis.

Kitty and I decided that the best course of action was to try to get in touch with Herold so that we could present a united front to the Empire Builder. We found him in the *dukka* of Mr. Keren, an Indian who runs the finest establishment in British Moyale. In the cool shade of his shop, its walls lined with rusting tins of sardines, generators, cheap cotton cloth and flashlight batteries, all Moyale comes to trade. Lutz Herold was no exception.

He was short and blond, an ex-fighter pilot. We formed the German-American Press Club of Moyale on the spot, initiated ourselves with steaming tea provided by Mr. Keren, who accepted an honorary membership, and laid horrid plans to bring about the downfall of the Empire Builder.

Our plan was laid on a single premise: McDermott's principal delight was in dashing around on his blooded stallion with his two cossacks behind him. The best way to force him to let us go on to Wajir was to threaten to stay with him through the three-month rainy season. Two white men in town would be more than he could stand. If the worst came to the worst we could always hire mules and a couple of ragamuffins to follow us and canter around town ourselves. This would be stealing his thunder, there would be unrest in the hills, and he would be more than anxious to send us along. Thus we reasoned. And then we were summoned to appear before the mighty man.

'Sorry, but you chaps will have to go back to Addis,' he said. 'Roads are closed.' We pointed out that although he certainly had the right to refuse us permission to continue if the roads were washed out by rain, he had no right to refuse us entry to Moyale, since our Kenya visas were in order. We pointed out that our Ethiopian exit visas had expired and that we would not be allowed to re-enter that country. We pointed out that we had brought him his mail and would be happy to spend the rainy season with him. At this he noticeably quivered. But true to the spirit of the Thin Red Line, refused to let us pass.

In that case, we said, we wished to inform him that we were wiring our respective consuls to file a formal protest and added that we would shoot ourselves (and him, too) before going back to Addis. We threw in the clincher by adding that we rather enjoyed horseback riding and intended to do a good deal if we had to stay in Moyale.

At 7 p.m. the Empire Builder gave us permission to pass. Jung had prevailed over Rhodes.

Lutz and his fiancée, travelling in a tiny, decrepit Lloyd, led the way. He didn't like driving at night, so we drove five miles outside Moyale and camped.

The next day was spent in crawling across baking flats at low speed. The Lloyd had very little clearance, its guts had been torn out on the road down from Addis (he'd had to load it on a truck at one point), and the starter was broken. His fiancée couldn't drive, so she had to push the car to get it started every time they stopped.

He got stuck a couple of times that morning and we both broke down once. But we discovered what had been causing all my engine trouble. Sand was getting into the distributor and blocking the electrical contact. By taking it apart and brushing it with a toothbrush, all was made right again.

The afternoon was even worse. Lutz kept getting stuck, his fiancée had sunstroke, and his car almost collapsed. We camped to hold council. The next morning, he discovered that his entire electrical system was burned out. We would go on to Wajir, send back water and insulated wire, and, if possible, wait for him there.

The D.C. at Wajir, a whitewashed Beau Geste fort, greeted us with a certain lack of enthusiasm. No doubt we would be leaving for Isiolo immediately, say within half an hour? No doubt. He assigned his assistant to see that we were able to refill our water cans and leave his town.

This gentleman had only been in the N.F.D. for two months and had not yet become an Empire Builder. He gave us coffee, promised to look after Lutz, and did his bit towards repairing our personal and rather threadbare Atlantic Alliance.

'Dreadful place, Wajir,' he said. 'Thought I'd joined the Foreign Legion when I first saw this fort and these soldiers dashing around on camels with neck-cloths on their caps. Sorry you chaps have to go but don't blame the D.C. too much. He had twelve people on his hands through the last rains when the roads washed out. Cheerio!'

All that day we bulled our way through deep sand drifts across a plain shimmering in heat waves. That night we camped fifty miles from Isiolo, on the edge of the White Highlands, and the centre of Metro-Goldwyn-Mayer Africa, with giraffes and gazelle and zebras cavorting about our camping spot. The clutch was worn out and the car wouldn't go into first.

But we really didn't care. We had covered 1,600 miles in fifteen days and we were home free.

Chapter 7

*

REGIO AROMATICA

An hour and a half out of Nairobi the serpentine green miracle of the Juba River relieves the harshness of the desert and you know you're over the Somali Republic. By craning your neck, you can see the jade of the Indian Ocean breaking against the unfriendly reefs which ring the spice coast. Mile after mile your plane chases its shadow across dun-coloured bush. There is nothing. Not a bushman's hut or a herd of goats.

This country, which the ancients called the aromatic kingdom because they knew it as the source of frankincense and myrrh, is one of the most malevolent lands in the world. Most of it is desert and, until you reach the far north, the highest 'mountain' is about 900 feet. You can't get to Mogadiscio, the capital, by road from Kenya during much of the year, mostly because there isn't one.

Somalia originally consisted only of the Spain-sized ex-Italian colony; after the briefest of negotiations, Britain granted independence to British Somaliland on June 26, 1960, and, a week later, the protectorate (which is twice the size of Austria) joined ex-Italian Somalia to form a single unitary republic. The new state made up of the two territories is bounded on the north by the Gulf of Aden, on the east by the Indian Ocean, on the south by Kenya and on the west by Ethiopia.

Its soil, less than 2 per cent of which is suitable for agriculture, is so poor that there are fewer people in the ex-Italian section than there are in Detroit or Barcelona. Seven out of ten Somalis spend their lives in groups of as few as half a dozen men and women, wandering with their flocks from water-hole to water-hole under the wide and pitiless sky. Others follow the sea and there are Somali communities in most of the world's ports.

The Somalis enjoy camel rustling, fighting for water or grazing lands and castrating Ethiopians with sharpened sticks. They disapprove of taxes, central government, foreigners, white men and Christians. One out of every two Somali children dies before his first birthday, 50 per cent of the population has been exposed to tuberculosis, illiteracy is

135

general. In the former Italian colony there are two thousand hospital beds, sixty-two foreign doctors and six pharmacists. One World Health Organization physician estimates that the only way to rid the republic of syphilis would be to shoot the entire population full of penicillin for a two-year period.

Every Somali man, woman and child owns an average of one camel, one cow and four goats. Bananas, grown in the two river valleys by the Italians, are the land's only important cash crop. Midjurtein nomads in the far north, which was recently parched by a *ten-year* drought which killed 90 per cent of the livestock and more than a few of the population, barter incense for an equal weight of grain. The somalo, worth one shilling, is the unit of currency but most of the people still pay for their wives with cattle.

The Somalis, who are Hamites with perhaps a small injection of Semitic blood, are divided into one hundred and twenty tribes wandering across four countries. But they all speak the same language and are one of the largest ethnic groups south of the Sahara. The basic social organism is not the individual or the family but the *rer*, a clan which sometimes looks to a common ancestor and assumes collective responsibility for each of its members, paying or receiving blood-money called *dia* for injuries inflicted or wrongs suffered. Somalis store their grain in holes, weave a striking cotton cloth in long colourful strips called *futa Benadir*, and have no paramount chiefs. Low-caste people called Midjan and Tumal do ironwork and tanning, which are despised occupations, and there is a priestly clan called Yebir. Bantu-speaking negroid people, who were once the slaves of the Somalis and today are little more, farm little plots at the river mouths, a job too menial for the Somalis. Most Somalis live in tents of skins or, if they are more settled, huts made of cow dung, mud and sticks. Each year several thousand of the inhabitants of one region, in gratitude for the rains, get together and beat the stuffing out of each other with staves.

Although the Somalis are fanatic Muslims whose lives have changed little since the days of the pharaohs, many oppose polygamy, allow their women to accept employment, permit male doctors to treat their wives and vote for a government which is as progressive as any in Africa.

The rainy season is appropriately dubbed the *Gu*. Most of the country gets less than twelve inches of rain a year and it often falls in belts only three or four miles wide. The nomads chart their courses by these damp spots and, when they can, water their stock at ponds called *desheks* formed when the rivers overflow their banks. There are no lakes. After the *Gu* comes the *Hagai*, the planting time. Then, if Allah is kind, there is a second rain called the *Der* followed by the bitter *Gilal*, or dry season. Total crop failures are frequent and famine is no stranger to this land.

This nation of two million has yet to graduate its first doctor, engineer or lawyer. Until recent years, Somalia had almost no schools and few of the cabinet members who charted the ex-Italian sector's march to independence and ably represented it before the United Nations have had more than four years of formal schooling. Somali schoolchildren have to master three languages and two alphabets.

In sixty years of European administration, ex-Italian Somalia has never been able to make ends meet. Administrative salaries absorb more than 50 per cent of the country's revenues and more is spent on maintaining the 4,000-man police force than on education and public health combined. Ex-Italian Somalia has 3,500 motor vehicles and 400 miles of paved roads, which is high for Africa, but half of these are being abandoned because the country is too poor to maintain them. Men of seventeen nationalities help to administer the republic but only eight years ago was the executive of the former U.N. trust territory separated from the judiciary.

One reason that the Somali Republic is so poor is that the people refuse to pay taxes. Somali sensibilities were so affronted by an attempt to impose a hut tax in 1957 that eight were killed and scores injured. After this the government conceded that it might be 'a wise policy' to educate the people to their responsibilities and ordered tax collectors 'not to force the issue'. Might be worth trying at home.

Somali women are among the most voluptuous in the world; the men are hard-bitten, austere and dangerous. Many are as black as midnight but ethnically and culturally they belong to the Middle East, not Africa. There is no middle ground about Somalis: you either like them or you don't. Some British, who deal with a considerable Somali population in Kenya, fought against Italian-led Somalis in World War II, and administered Somalia until it became a U.N. trust under Italy in 1950, regard the Somalis as deceitful and treacherous. But other Britons swear by them and Somalis make up a large percentage of the non-commissioned officers in British East African regiments. There is this about the Somalis: unlike many Africans, they are sensitive people capable of great love or tremendous hate. If you earn the respect and friendship of a Somali, he will lay down his life for you; and for the sake of a real or imagined wrong, either to himself or to a kinsman, he will wait ten years for the chance to put a knife between your shoulder-blades.

MOGADISCIO

A piece of glass or a bit of whitewashed wall catches the sun and throws back the light at the plane like a dart. The flashes become more frequent. And before you realize it, there is Mogadiscio, stark, pitiful and bright, a pile of glaring stucco tempered by the brown huts of the Somali villages which hang on its flanks like bloated ticks on a dog, a city crushed between the red desert and the unbelievable blue of the sea. The fascist monuments under that wide sky seem pitiful rather than impressive and then your plane's wheels are bumping down the runway.

A blast of hot air comes in with the sanitary inspector and his bug bomb. It seems unlikely that we have brought him anything from Kenya that the Somali Republic does not have in a more refined state. The customs shed is in an uproar. But it's a jolly Italian sort of uproar and an expressive shrug of the shoulders seems to cover any discrepancies in your papers. There is no Ethiopian formality here: officials wear shorts, short-sleeved shirts, leather sandals and sunglasses. And incredibly enough, they seem more interested in getting the job done than in raising obstacles or demonstrating their importance. Somebody presses a cold beer into your hand, offers you a ride to the hotel, and already you are violently pro-Somali—if it is possible to be violent about anything in a heat which would make Cerberus sweat.

You are really a free man here. You can spell Mogadiscio any of seven ways (other versions: Mogadisho, Mukdisha, Magadisho, Mukdishu, Mogadaxo or Mogadischo) and nobody will criticize. It gives you a wonderful feeling of lightheadedness. There are other things which make you either laugh or cry: the first time you brush your teeth at the Croce del Sud, Mogadiscio's finest hotel (until last year it was the only one), and discover that there is only salt water in the pipes, the signs in your bathroom respectfully requesting that *i Sigg. Clienti* uses the shower only for the purpose for which it was designed(?), finding out that a bottle of water costs you more than a cup of coffee.

In the end it is best to grab your swimming trunks and head for the beach. If it is afternoon few people will be on the streets and the shops are shut until 5.30. A clamouring of brass from the great pile of the cathedral, its steps exactly aligned with those of Government House to indicate the relationship of Church and State under the Italians, drives the swallows from the belfry in protesting clouds of grace. The streets of Mog, as the British call it, are narrow, studded with musty cafés and bazaars heavy with the odour of incense and musk, lined with sightless beggars crooning in the shade, surrounded by naked pot-bellied children and half-starved cats. The houses of the crumbling, stinking, beautiful Arab section lean against each other for support, like waspish dowagers who have known better days.

As you walk down the Via Regina Elena, the sun dancing inside the back of your head, history comes rushing at you. Many of the buildings, bleached by sea and sun, their doors ornately carved, seem to have been here since the Arabs founded Mogadiscio in the eighth century, or at least since 1892 when the Sultan of Zanzibar, who did not own the place but came as close as anybody else, sold Somalia to Italy. North of the harbour you can find a piece of beach over which no one seems to exercise suzerainty and soon you are paddling happily in the Indian Ocean, slowly drifting (by courtesy of the monsoon) towards Muscat, Oman and the Hadramaut. There may be a small freighter tossing on the swell outside the harbour, trans-shipping to lighters and making heavy weather of it. Most ocean-going ships cannot get across the reef and passengers coming ashore are lowered to launches in baskets. Fun, but not recommended for the faint of heart.

As the sun drops to the horizon, the streets come to life again. Groups of Somalis driving strings of camels tied nose-to-tail glide by on big splay feet. The men are wrapped in red and white checked cloths needing only the corn sticks and the chianti to look like an Italian restaurant in motion. A black boy, clad in a loin cloth, trots down the street balancing a freshly-caught ifty-pound tuna on his head. And then an Italian girl—there are still three thousand Italians in this ex-colony—minces past you in a tight skirt and gay blouse and you think you should be munching almonds on the Via Veneto instead of strolling up the Horn of Africa.

But here, for once, the Italian girls are far excelled by the local product, the long-limbed, fine-featured Somali women who have been the joy and despair of sailormen since the first *dhow* warped its way across Mogadiscio's reef. They walk with a grace that can only be bred, not taught, clothed in long shawls of riotous colour. Each seems to have her secret and to find life a quaint, attractive thing, made for laughter and banter. And many bear within them a bacillus which merely chuckles when confronted with a million units of penicillin.

Mogadiscio, which is home for 75 per cent of the country's Italians, has a sprightly newspaper called the *Corriere della Somalia*. It is the country's only paper and, as one U.N. commission primly observed, it lacks a 'children's corner'. This in a country where a child is doing well to survive, let alone read the comic strips.

The Somali Republic is not everybody's dish of tea. But there is that moment when the sun has sunk behind the old Arab fort, turning the sea to brass, that sometime instant between day and night, when it is good to be in Mogadiscio with the whores combing their hair on the roofs of houses which have forgotten time and the muezzin's cry shredding the dying light.

A BIT OF HISTORY

Nobody knows exactly when the present inhabitants moved into the land. There are still more than 100,000 Negroes in the river valleys who are probably the descendants of the original people. The Somalis are thought to have come in small waves of invaders during the twelfth century. Arabs, Indians and possibly Chinese have coasted these shores for centuries on the winds of the monsoon, which blow the high-pooped *dhows* south to Zanzibar in the winter and north to fabled Ophir in the summer. The season between monsoons is known as *Tangambile*—'two sails'—because then a careful navigator can sail either way. The lateen-rigged Arab craft brought with them Islam, cloth and weapons and returned laden with slaves, spices, incense and sweet-smelling wood.

Small settlements of Arabs were established on the coast and their descendants—30,000 of them—live here today, lonely, white-robed figures walking in pairs, holding hands and sighing for the age when their great-grandfathers ruled in wealth and splendour. The Sultan of Oman once exercised nominal suzerainty over the entire coast as far south as Zanzibar. But each city was vassal only in proportion to the fewness of its cannon or the timidity of the local sheikh. This hold became perhaps a little stronger when the Sultan of Oman moved his palace and capital to Zanzibar but was soon shaken when the Portuguese appeared off these coasts on their way to India in the fifteenth century. The Portuguese warred against all these coastal towns but none gave them more trouble than Mogadiscio. In the end, the Portuguese contented themselves with Zanzibar, Mombasa, Malindi and India, and the Somalis were left in freedom behind their unfriendly reefs.

In 1885, His Italian Majesty's ship *Barbarigo* rounded Cape Gardafui to explore the mouth of the Juba River and rushed to Zanzibar to join the British and the Germans in the seizure of the continental holdings of the Sultan of Zanzibar. Germany grabbed Tanganyika, Britain occupied the Kenya coast, and Italy had to be content with a commercial treaty permitting her to trade in Somalia. The trouble was that the Sultan of Zanzibar's hold on Somalia was somewhat less than tenuous. Three years later the Italians made the first of a series of treaties with Somali chiefs which were necessary before they could move in. By 1891, the Italian flag flew from most of the landing stages from the Juba River to Cape Gardafui and, the following year, the Sultan of Zanzibar ceded his rights to the country in return for an annual payment. The government, as was the practice in those days, turned the management of Somalia over to a series of three private companies, each of which soon demonstrated its total inability to control the wild tribesmen of the desert. In the early years of this century, Italy found herself in the anomalous situation of having a war in which she had no part fought over northern Somalia, ostensibly her territory, by the British, Ethiopians and the warriors of the 'Mad Mullah'. She revoked the company's charter and, in 1905, Somalia became an Italian colony.

But the Italian writ was never very strong far from the coast. The tribes of the interior lived and fought as they always had and, when an Italian patrol put in an appearance, either chopped it to pieces or drifted away into the waterless desert where no white man could follow. As late as 1927, Italy was campaigning in the Midjurtein in an attempt to pacify the wild tribes of the north. She was never able to de-limit Somalia's western boundary with Ethiopia and, as we shall see, blood may still be let over this thorny problem.

The boundary question became academic in 1935 when Italy conquered Ethiopia, linking it with Eritrea and Somalia into Italian East Africa. The British invaded Somalia in 1941.

SAME STORY, NEW ENDING

The same situation developed here as in Eritrea: the Italians wanted Somalia back, the Ethiopians claimed it, the British, who were still administering it nine years after they arrived, would have been content to have it, and the Somalis wanted to rule themselves. Here, however, there were a couple of important factors not obtaining in Eritrea. In the case of that country, Ethiopia did have a valid if not decisive historical claim. In the past she had been hard put to control the Somalis of the Ogaden desert and could make no real claim at all to Somalia itself. Almost half of the population of Eritrea is tied to Ethiopia by blood and religion while the Somalis are different people who worship another god. Both countries were just as ill-prepared to govern themselves; each wanted to do so. In neither was there a hope for economic solvency; both were willing to try.

In the end, as we have seen, Eritrea was federated with Ethiopia. Somalia was made a U.N. trust under Italy with the condition that the country was to become fully independent by December 2, 1960, the only case in which the United Nations has imposed a time-limit for self-government on any of the territories under its jurisdiction.

As was the case with Eritrea, trade unions, newspapers and politics flourished under the British administration. It should be said now that the Italians exercised their ten-year trusteeship in the most exemplary fashion. There were a couple of riots staged by extremists for the benefit of visiting U.N. commissions, and the late Sylvia Pankhurst, silvery-haired English propagandist for Ethiopia, charged oppression on several occasions. The facts are that, as early as 1956, more than 80 per cent of the civil service and almost all of the military forces were 'somalized'. The U.N., which maintained a permanent commission in the country, stated that elections were held 'freely and secretly'. The Italian Administrator never vetoed an act of the Somali legislature. When Italy discharged her trust on July 1, 1960, she could do so with a clear conscience.

THE S.Y.L.

A vigorous political party known as the Somali Youth League runs ex-Italian Somalia. The S.Y.L. was formed in 1943 during the British administration of the country and was at one time believed to be Communist-infiltrated. Nothing could be further from the truth. The S.Y.L. is an ultra-nationalistic group whose principal article of faith is that Somalis, whether they live in the former Italian colony, in French Somaliland, in Ethiopia or Kenya, are one nation united by blood and by religion. The S.Y.L. seeks to reunite these people into a Greater Somalia, to destroy the tribal social structure, and to formulate a far-reaching educational and social programme. Amazingly enough in a Muslim country, the S.Y.L. is committed to enfranchisement of women at the earliest possible date.

The S.Y.L. is far from the only political party in Somalia. A rash of parties, mostly headed by men too late to climb aboard the S.Y.L. bandwagon or unacceptable for other reasons, sprang up in the late 1940s. These groups aimed for goals as diverse as the retention of Italian colonialism and the maintenance of every aspect of the tribal system.

The first test of strength came in 1954 when urban voters went to the polls to elect candidates for 281 municipal council seats throughout ex-Italian Somalia. The S.Y.L. polled 47 per cent of the 38,000 votes cast and won 141 seats, the rest being divided among the twenty other parties, including the Hisbia Dighil Mirifle, the Somalia African Union, the Progressive League of Somalia, the Benadir Youth Union, the Liberal Party and the Somali Democratic Party. S.Y.L. predominance was confirmed in 1956 when it won forty-three of the sixty seats allotted to Somalis in the national assembly of the U.N. trust territory. The ten delegates of the Gruppo Misto representing the Italian, Arab, Indian and Pakistani communities also support the S.Y.L. In lonely and not terribly effective opposition are the thirteen members of the Hisbia Dighil Mirifle, a regional party which defends the tribal interests of the sedentary people of middle Somalia.

Once having gained the initiative, the S.Y.L. has never relinquished it. After the 1956 elections, Hisbia leaders asked the S.Y.L. to be allowed to participate in the government, arguing that until independence was achieved all Somali political parties should act in consort. The S.Y.L. rejected this thesis, although representatives of all groups meet at irregular intervals in what is called the National Front to discuss questions of pressing national importance, such as the border problem with Ethiopia or the reunification of all Somali people.

The secret of the S.Y.L.'s success seems to be that it gained prestige by fighting for independence from the beginning, stole a march on the other parties by getting organized first, skimmed the cream off the top of Somali leadership, formulated a positive and popular programme and went to the people to sell it. There have been complaints from opposition leaders that the S.Y.L. is not above using bribery and strong-arm methods to achieve its ends. The U.N. found no evidence of this. S.Y.L. leaders feel, with some degree of justification, that they are the only party interested in the emergence of a modern, democratic state. As elsewhere in Africa, there seems room for only one political interpretation of 'the national interest' and those who do not agree come close to being regarded as enemies of the people. This sort of thinking, of course, at best leads to abuses and at worst prophesies the end of real democracy. It is debatable, however, if the average Somali needs the ideals of political democracy as much as food to eat, reasonably good health, work to do, a home where he can raise his children, to associate with his friends and to worship his god without intrusion.

The S.Y.L. draws its principal support from two of Somalia's three great nomadic tribes, the Darot and the Hawiya. Most ministerial posts are held by Hawiya, who fear domination by the more warlike Darot, who would outnumber them if all Somali-speaking people were ever united. The Hisbia Dighil Mirifle represents the more settled people who live between the Juba and Uebi Scebili rivers. They would like the republic to have a federal constitution giving them virtual internal autonomy.

This land lives and breathes politics and tempers often flare, as they did in 1957 when a young Somali stepped up to the Egyptian member of the three-man U.N. advisory commission and, with consummate skill and a six-inch knife, let enough daylight through that gentleman to precipitate an international incident. When they aren't knifing people, Somalis like to sit in the shade of the Croce del Sud's arcade, sip cups of Turkish coffee and talk politics in voices ranging from the low tones of subversion to the excited yelps of the political 'ins'.

But the S.Y.L. is the only party with a real programme. When asked in what ways his party differed from the S.Y.L., the leader of the Hisbia said, 'They are in power.' What plans did his party have to make a more successful appeal to the voters? 'I think,' he said, 'that we may change the name of the party.'

MEN BEHIND THE S.Y.L.

At any Young Republicans meeting one encounters 'youngsters' who will never see forty-five again, overfed gentlemen whose jowls are shaded with five-o'clock shadow by mid-morning. With the exception of the few old hands who have guided the party since its inception and still hold the top jobs, the membership of the nineteen-member central committee which runs the S.Y.L. is decidedly youthful. Unlike the Sudan, Somalia has no powerful religious leaders to dominate politics. In contrast to Ethiopia, there is no established monarchy. As a result, young men of ability have come rapidly to the top and many a member of the Somali cabinet has yet to see thirty.

Two of the most powerful and able men in Somalia are Abdullahi Issa, Aden Abdullah Osman and Haji Farar ali Omar.

Abdullahi Issa is Somalia's handsome, ebony-coloured foreign minister. He was born thirty-nine years ago at Afgoi, a one-street town twenty-five miles from Mogadiscio. His father died a few months after Issa's birth and his mother brought him to Mogadiscio where he attended the Italian government primary school and received some Koranic education. Like most Somali leaders, Issa worked for the Italians if only because the colonial government was the sole occupation open to a smart young Somali. At sixteen he became a postal clerk at the port of Merca, later was sent back to Mogadiscio to work in the Department of Economic Affairs. When the British took over he found himself out of a job. He went into business, helped to create the S.Y.L. in 1944 and, four years later, was elected to the powerful central committee. He served as general secretary of the party, was elected to the national assembly in 1956 and named prime minister. When Somalia became independent last year, Issa stepped down in favour of little-known Abdi Rashid Ali Shermarke, 41, who became the first prime minister of an independent Somali Republic. But Issa's control of the foreign ministry indicates that he is still a potential political force.

Issa, who has appeared before the United Nations, speaks and writes English and Italian. Although of only medium height, he strikes you as tall because he carries himself well. He plasters his speech with political clichés and is a master of the evasive answer. Issa is moderately pro-Western (he has asked for and received American aid) but, like most Somalis, is so devoted to his own country's cause that he has little room in his make-up for outside loyalties, ideological or otherwise.

A less complicated and in some ways more appealing person is Aden Abdullah Osman, president of the S.Y.L. This slight, greying father of eight children was born at Belet Uen, near the Ethiopian border, in 1912. His family were refugees from the raids of the 'Mad Mullah' and they brought the boy to Mogadiscio at the age of eight. When he was twenty he joined the colonial government as a health assistant.

Like most Somalis, young Aden Abdullah had a compelling thirst for education. He finished grammar school, the highest facilities available to Somalis, at the age of twenty-three and applied to the Italians for further schooling. 'They told me,' he recalls with a chuckle, 'that if I wanted more education, I could go through grammar school again.'

He served in the Italian administration until the British arrived and, with Abdullahi Issa, was one of the founders of the S.Y.L. He served as party president from 1953 to 1956, when he was elected to the ial assembly. In 1958 Abdullahi Issa and Aden Abdullah crushed internal party revolt led by Haji Muhammad Hussein, a firebrand iucated in Egypt, who the year before had become president of the S.Y.L. Haji Muhammad, who broadcast for Radio Cairo during his five-year sojourn in Egypt, was ousted from the party by a majority of forty-two votes to thirty-eight and Aden Abdullah again became S.Y.L.'s president. In 1960, he became first president of the independent Somali Republic.

Aden Abdullah, who speaks and writes English, has a habit of placing the tips of his fingers together and cocking his head to one side while speaking. He has a shy smile and that rare quality in an African, the ability to laugh at himself. Aden Abdullah is frank, open and realistic and goes after the heart of a question like a terrier worrying a rat. He is his country's most experienced politician. He knows its problems, is a reformer without illusions. Aden Abdullah Osman approves of U.S. economic assistance to Somalia, favours U.S. mediation of the border dispute with Ethiopia, and feels that American naval and air bases, if these are desired, 'might be acceptable but will take some education of the people'. This astute man is one of the best friends we have in this new galaxy of African states.

THE ECONOMICS OF DESPAIR

Bananas, which are grown by Italians in the valleys of the Juba and Uebi Scebelli rivers, account for 75 per cent of the republic's £4 million worth of exports (imports are valued at £5·1 million). In the Sudan we have seen the dangers of a one-crop economy forcibly illustrated when a single bad year did much to overthrow Prime Minister Khalil and end representative government in that country. Here the problem is compounded: not only is the republic a one-crop producer but the entire banana crop is sold in one country, Italy, at subsidized prices considerably above those prevailing on the world market.

Even given the favourable conditions of a guaranteed and high-priced market, Somalia has not been able to make ends meet. The 'colonial oppressors'—who offered Somalia 'anticipated independence' before 1960 and were refused—have got nothing out of Somalia. In the first half of her ten-year trusteeship, Italy put £26·4 million into Somalia. Despite improvements in the quality and quantity of Somalia's other exports—spices, hides and skins, and a little long-staple cotton—it is extremely doubtful if the republic will have enough money to pay *operating* expenses now that independence has come, without thinking about capital improvements such as schools, clinics, roads and harbours. Foreign loans are of little assistance. The Somali Republic needs outright grants of at least £2·5 million per year, probably for about twenty years.

The country's problem is simple: it is poor in everything. There is not a mile of railway. Her harbours are blocked by reefs and the sea is too rough for fishing for at least a third of the year. Most of the land is almost waterless, whipped by wind and scourged by the sun. There are only two rivers and neither of them has suitable dam sites. Only one, the Juba, can be counted on to flow all the year round. Little of the land is suitable for agriculture. Although the Institute of Somali Credit performs a valuable service by accepting grain as security for small loans to farmers and storing it against times of famine, banking services could hardly be termed adequate. There are no minerals, but some chance of oil. The population is too small, poor and nomadic to provide a market for most industries. Capital is unavailable, raw materials scarce, skilled labour non-existent, power expensive and transport costs prohibitive.

The republic grows almost enough sorghum, millet, corn, sugar cane, rice, oil seeds, peanuts and bananas to feed herself at a very low level of consumption. Even so, she must import dates, coffee and tea. Food production has fallen since the war and exports have risen, which means a tighter belt for every Somali. In the days of Italian colonialism, 150,000 tons of salt a year were sold as far away as Japan: now the nation exports not a pound of salt although she has almost half a million tons stockpiled. Still in existence are a sugar refinery, the cotton mill, a tannery, a soap factory and a couple of canneries.

Italy and the Somalis have made heroic efforts to achieve something near solvency. Italy still buys all the country's bananas, most of her cotton and a third of her hides and skins and supplies the East African nation with most of her imports. Revenues more than doubled during the Italian trusteeship, exports were tripled and imports doubled. But the republic's £4 million annual budget is still less than some cities spend on snow removal and, if it is to be balanced, revenues must be tripled. Somalia's trade deficit now amounts to 50 per cent of the total value of her exports.

It is problematical if Italy will maintain the banana subsidy, although she is giving technical assistance. This uncertainty coupled with the nervousness which accompanies the granting of independence to any

African state has been driving the Italians home for the last several years. A few years ago there were 8,000 Italians in Somalia; now there are about 3,000. As in Eritrea, the departure of one Italian means unemployment for five natives. In a country where the difference between life and death is a marginal thing, this can have tragic consequences. Equally important is the loss of investment capital and technical knowledge at the very time that the new nation needs both most.

The Somalis are not to be blamed for the departure of the Italians. Italian colonial rule was sometimes heavy-handed and the Somalis have shown the same reasonable attitude towards their former masters as have the Ethiopians. Italian trusteeship rule was just and positive and there were few troubles between the two races. None of this, however, obviates the fact that few of the Italian settlers have faith in the economic or political future of the country. It does no good to ignore this.

If the £1·4 million annual banana subsidy is dropped the crop will be unable to compete with bananas from the Cameroons and the Canaries, which produce larger fruit closer to the European market. There seems to be no other crop suitable for expatriate production.

The republic has got to find an alternative crop to replace bananas. Cotton could become important if the Somalis accept the discipline imposed by this exacting crop, and cultivate on a big scale and in an organized scheme such as the Gezira. Since the republic has yet to produce a university-trained agriculturalist, this possibility seems remote. In addition to its export value, cotton is needed to fill the looms of one of Somalia's few industries, its textile factory which today produces 1·5 million yards of cloth each year, a third of the country's requirements. But the principal scope for development lies in livestock. There is already plenty of it. The problem is quality and availability.

Somalia's 1·2 million cattle, a similar number of camels, and four million goats and sheep are far too many for the land to carry. Perpetually short of water and grazing, prone to disease and dwarfed by constant trekking, a Somali cow is often smaller than a donkey.

A man's social status as well as his wealth is determined by the number of cattle he owns, not their quality. Cattle are used as a lever to obtain political power, to purchase wives, to pay for blood claims against the clan. Tell a nomad to get rid of his sick and stunted cattle and he'll laugh in your face. You'd laugh just as hard if someone told you to tear up half the notes in your wallet because they were dirty.

The problem goes far deeper than education. The entire life of the nomad must be changed before the nomad himself can be altered. In other words, the causes of nomadism have to be eradicated. Lack of water is the most important of these and the United States has spent almost £1 million over the past six years to help Somalia finance a programme which has sunk more than 600 wells providing water for 330,000 cattle. But there is more to it than that: additional wells shorten the distances which the nomads have to trek but more water does not change their hearts. In all men is the realization that it is more honourable to be a herdsman than a dirt farmer. The Somalis have held this view for thousands of years and a few more wells cannot change this attitude in a generation. Water is needed but time is also required. And in Africa, the timeless continent which God forgot, time has suddenly become desperately short.

The search for oil by two American companies, now eight years old, cannot be depended upon. It failed across the border in Ethiopia and, even if it is successful here, it will be years before the royalties begin. The Somali Republic needs help now, this year. She has only two commodities to offer in exchange for such help: gratitude and her strategic position. The support of an uncommitted Islamic state in the United Nations would not be unwelcome. Neither would an air-naval base guarding the southern approaches to the Suez Canal and the oil-rich Persian Gulf and providing an Indian Ocean staging area. Perhaps these considerations coupled with the desire to see democracy take root on the Eastern Horn and stability assured in a new nation will inspire the United States to give the Somalis the assistance which they need.

EGYPTIAN INFLUENCE

There are others interested, for their own reasons, in assisting the Somalis. At the beginning of 1957, there were 169 Somalis studying in Italy, most of them at Rome's government-run Centre for Somaliland Studies. Many of these have been contacted by the Italian Communist Party and several have had Red-carpet tours behind the Iron Curtain. The Soviets have two goals in the Somali Republic: to forestall American influence in this strategically vital area and to keep the Horn of Africa, including pro-Western Ethiopia, in political ferment. So far Communist gains have been negligible. But the danger is far from past.

Egyptian influence is apparent. Pictures of Nasser adorn the walls of many shops. Radio Cairo's Somali language broadcasts come in loud and clear, stressing Islamic unity and calling upon the Somalis to 'push the white dogs into the sea'. In 1957, 170 Somalis were studying in Egypt and the number at Cairo's El Azhar university is said to be even greater now. In Somalia itself, sixty-five Egyptian teachers are lecturing in every major village.

Egyptian interest is no new thing. The sailors of the pharaohs came to the land of the Somalis to trade for spices and it was Farouk who initiated the Egyptian scholarship programme. What was once a purely cultural connection has now assumed political dimensions. This was forcibly demonstrated in 1958 when Haji Muhammad Hussein, while in his last term of a four-year course at El Azhar, was elected president of the Somali Youth League. On his return to Somalia he adopted a radical posture and sought to seize control of the S.Y.L. central committee and make himself the virtual dictator of Somalia. Only prompt action by Abdullahi Issa and Aden Abdullah Osman, who expelled him from the party, blocked the rise of this East Coast Nasser. Haji Muhammad has since formed his own Greater Somalia League—a strange mixture of pro-Egyptians, pro-Britishers, extreme nationalists and political malcontents—and more will be heard from this volatile young man in the future.

Some observers have seen all this and assumed that the Somali Republic inevitably will become an Egyptian puppet. Nothing could be further from the truth. As an Islamic state, the new nation is bound to Egypt by culture and religion. And she appreciates the scholarship help given by Egypt: in the same year that 170 Somalis were studying in Egypt, exactly three had scholarships in the United States. If allowed to continue, this situation eventually is bound to produce a generation of Nasser-orientated Somali statesmen. But as Abdullahi Issa and Aden Abdullah have shown by squelching Haji Muhammad, Somalis resent Egyptian political meddling as much as they do the same sort of thing from the West. It should not be forgotten that the Somalis, although they are Muslims, are not Arabs. It is just as fallacious to assume that the two countries are inevitably bound together as it would be to say that Ireland's objectives coincide with Brazil's because both are Roman Catholic nations.

EDUCATION AND THE LANGUAGE FLAP

No African people have a greater thirst for education than the Somalis. When the British took over in 1941, they found not a single Somali university graduate. Things were not much better when the Italians came back nine years later: Somalia had no university, no high schools, and only thirty schools of any description with a total enrolment of 3,000. There were not more than a few hundred Somalis equipped to enter high school. At least 90 per cent of the population was illiterate.

Ten years later, ex-Italian Somalia has a School of Politics and Administration with junior college standing, an agricultural college, a maritime school, a commercial institute, a school for aeronautical specialists, an Islamic instruction centre, and a string of technical schools turning out everything from midwives to laboratory technicians. Fifty thousand children study in 204 schools, 14 per cent of the budget (£450,000) goes for education, and there are almost a hundred university students studying abroad. Primary education is free and, unlike some Muslims, Somali parents have no objection to their children going to school, although they do not like the Italian schools because Arabic is not taught. There are more than 385 qualified Somali teachers in the ex-Italian territory alone.

The language problem is one of the roughest anywhere in Africa. The language of the Somalis, which like the Berber and Galla tongues belongs to the Hamitic group, has yet to find an acceptable written form. Italian, Arabic and English (in the two of the new state's eight provinces which once constituted the protectorate of British Somaliland) are used as the official languages of instruction but Somali is also employed. The easiest and perhaps most natural texts to use are those in Italian. The content of these, however, leans heavily on the lives of the saints, the Blessed Sacraments, confession and original sin, subjects which can be of only passing interest to Somali Muslims. Nor would it seem necessary that their vocabularies should contain words like polygon, rhombus and parabola.

Somalis like to deceive themselves into thinking that Arabic is their natural language. The majority of the Muslim world, the Somali Republic included, does not know Arabic except for the few *suras* (verses) of the Koran necessary for prayer. These are learned by rote but seldom understood. Although a Somali may be able to recite or even write portions of the Koran from memory, he cannot understand what he has written, read a newspaper or enjoy an Egyptian film because he knows no grammar. The same situation obtains as if a Spaniard claimed that he could read and write Latin through a knowledge of his own language. Although the new nation undoubtedly needs a few Arabic ars to interpret the Koran for her, it is difficult to see how four of Arabic can help the average boy or girl.

erhaps in realization of this, a Somali named Osman Kenedid in 1922 set himself to the task of creating an alphabet. Unfortunately, Kenedid was enough of a nationalist to feel that his country needed its own alphabet, unrelated to either the roman or arabic systems. Today nationalist extremists are pushing to have Kenedid's 'Osmania' accepted as the republic's official language and alphabet. What the country, which already has enough troubles, fails to realize is that to adopt a unique alphabet for nationalistic reasons is to create commercial difficulties, intellectual isolation and educational expense. Too few linguists have had the guts to tell the Somalis that the roman alphabet is pre-Christian, has no religious significance and is best suited for commercial reasons.

GREATER SOMALIA

Dominating Somali political thinking is a question which may well keep the Horn of Africa in ferment for generations to come: the creation of a Greater Somalia.

No borders in the world have less justification than those which cut across the 2·5 million Somali-speaking peoples of East Africa, splitting them into four fragments. These borders make no sense from the ethnical, religious, linguistic or geographical point of view. And there is little reason that they should: they were drawn up arbitrarily for administrative purposes by foreign powers who had little knowledge of and less interest in the people inhabiting the land. This cavalier cartography has caused the deaths of thousands and it will continue to do so.

Little more than half of the Somali people (1·3 million) live in ex-Italian Somalia while another 700,000 inhabit what was once the protectorate of British Somaliland. On July 1, these two countries achieved a part of their national destiny through their union in a single republic. Now they seek *anschluss* with the other 760,000 Somalis scattered across French Somaliland, the Ogaden desert of Ethiopia, and northern Kenya. And the Somalis of these areas share to a greater or lesser degree this same aspiration.

The two provinces of the new state which lie north of the Ogaden and between French Somaliland and Somalia were known until June 1960 as British Somaliland. It was the Labour Foreign Secretary Ernest Bevin who sparked the drive for a Greater Somalia by suggesting in 1946 the 'lumping' together of all Somalis to give the nomads 'a real chance of a decent economic life'.

In 1875, the Khedive of Egypt claimed most of the Somali coast of the Gulf of Aden and his troops occupied the principal ports; but ten years later, during the Mahdist rebellion in the Sudan, the Egyptian garrisons were withdrawn and the British moved in. The protectorate established was first administered from Aden as a dependency of the Government of India. But in 1898 it was transferred to Foreign Office control and, seven years later, to the Colonial Office.

For two decades, from 1901 until 1921, the peace of British Somaliland was destroyed by the activities of the so-called 'Mad Mullah', Mohammed bin Abdullah Hassan, a fanatical Somali politico-religious leader who preached Holy War against the white man. This brilliant leader rallied thousands of dervishes to his standard and displayed such a degree of military genius that the better-armed British were forced in 1910 to give up all of the interior, retaining only the coastal settlements which lay under the guns of their warships. There followed a three-year period which must have been reminiscent of the early days after the Roman withdrawal from Britain: the British, before retreating to the coast, armed those tribes of the interior which had remained loyal so that they could defend themselves from the 'Mad Mullah'. Chaos ensued. Old tribal feuds were reopened among the loyal tribes and the dervishes attacked. Trade was disrupted and the seasonal migrations of the herds were blocked to such an extent that large areas of the protectorate became over-grazed and eroded, never to recover. In the orgy of killing, it is estimated that 33 per cent of the male population died.

Two events led the British to undertake again the pacification of the interior: the slaying of Richard Corfield, Somaliland's 'Lawrence of Arabia', with half his Camel Constabulary, and a 1914 night raid by the 'Mad Mullah' on Berbera, the coastal stronghold of the British. Although Mohammed bin Abdullah Hassan was slowly forced back, he further demonstrated his military genius by building at Taleh a formidable stone fort and by constructing other fortifications at Medishe around a fertile valley where he established gardens which are cultivated to this day. Only the use of aeroplanes spelled his doom: bombed out of Taleh (which was later demolished by the engineers) he fled into Ethiopia where he died of influenza in 1921. Contemporary Somali nationalists quite rightly are proud of this vigorous warrior and the ruined fort today is a national monument.

The next nineteen years were, for British Somaliland, relatively quiet. In the summer of 1940, strong Italian forces invaded from Ethiopia and, after a brief and bitter struggle, the British withdrew to Aden. They returned seven months later to oust the Italians from both Somaliland and Ethiopia and, for eight years, the Protectorate remained under military administration. Throughout this period and on until 1954, a total of thirteen years, the so-called Haud and Reserved areas, Ethiopian grazing lands in the triangle between that country, British Somaliland and Somalia, were under British military administration. These lands, ceded to Ethiopia by Britain in 1897, contain wells and fodder vital to the welfare of the Somalis of the Protectorate and of Somalia. Under British rule nomads of both countries were allowed to migrate into the Haud and Reserved areas. The Ethiopians, however, sometimes on complaint of the Somalis established in the region, sometimes as a political weapon to force the Somalis to drop their dream of a Greater Somalia and sometimes out of sheer perversity, have on occasions closed the border. Britain attempted without success to lease the Haud, exchange it for other territory or obtain an extension of the status quo. The issue remains a troublesome one.

Ex-British Somaliland cannot have changed much since the 'Mad Mullah's' day. The region, which enjoyed a week of separate independence before uniting with Somalia on July 1, 1960, has no labour department, hotels, trade unions, railways, public debt, income tax, industries, newspapers, rivers, missionaries, dry cleaners or university (the Protectorate did not produce a secondary school graduate until 1957). There are exactly fourteen miles of paved road, one commercial cinema, two cities with piped water, three secondary schools, 780 hospital beds (85 per cent of the population over twenty years of age has tuberculosis), 1,177 motor vehicles, 330 telephones and eight post offices in a country twice the size of Austria with a population estimated at 700,000 (no census has ever been taken). There was no school at all for girls until 1953 and only this year will the territory's crack military regiment, the Somali Scouts, receive its first two Sandhurst-trained Somali officers. A colourful 900-man para-military organization called the 'Illalos' (a Somali word meaning 'protection'), which comes under the six district commissioners, combines with the Somaliland Police to keep the peace among this turbulent people.

The country, which has a 450-mile coastline, is marked by three principal physical features: a coastal lowland belt, known as the Guban, meaning 'burnt' (temperatures here vary between 70 and 108 degrees); an escarpment called the Golis, which reaches heights of 7,000 feet and runs from west to east parallel with the coast; and a plateau, the Ogo, which drops gently to the south. For the most part, the country is hot, dry, barren and waterless, although water accumulates during the rains in shallow depressions called 'ballehs'. Rainfall varies from a reasonable twenty-five inches at some spots in the mountains to two inches, little more than a Scotch mist, at Berbera (population: 7,500), the principal port. Most of ex-British Somaliland's four hundred whites live in Hargeisha, the hill capital of 40,000 population, where it is cold enough for a fire in December and January. One of the more shunned settlements is the town of Las Anod, where a strong wind blows all day long from June to September and everyone is quite mad. In the west there is a series of eighteen ruined towns in which fragments of Chinese porcelain of the period of the Emperor Kiang Hsi have been found and strange, pre-Islamic graves formed of rocks piled in conical mounds, often to the height of ten feet, dot the mountain country.

Ex-British Somaliland is so poor that relatives of long-term prisoners are transported at government expense to visit their incarcerated kinsmen. Although a bit of beryl, mica, columbite and tin is exported, and three companies are prospecting for oil, the mass of the people are dependent upon their flocks (6 million sheep, 4 million camels, 2 million goats and 250,000 cattle) for their livelihoods. Only about three hundred square miles are suitable for farming and on this sorghum is cultivated. Exports, almost entirely limited to livestock and hides and skins (others: frankincense, guano), are worth only £1·4 million while ex-British Somaliland's imports cost her about £4 million. To scrape together funds for a pitiable annual budget of £2·1 million, the Protectorate received an outright grant from Britain of 40 per cent of this sum. And this did not include maintenance of the Somali Scouts (£1·5 million from 1950 to 1958) or schemes financed by the Colonial Development and Welfare Acts (£3·3 million between 1945 and 1960).

This grinding poverty, the nomadic life of the people and the distrust of Islam (the former Protectorate is, of course, solidly Muslim) for Western educational methods have combined to make ex-British Somaliland one of Africa's scholastic backwaters. In 1941 exactly £500 was allocated to the Education Department. Conditions have improved and now there are about 5,000 children attending 50 primary, 11 intermediate and 3 secondary schools (there are another 4,000 students attending 245 Koranic schools, half of them government-aided). And more than 115 Somalis are now studying everything from law to nursing in the United Kingdom.

Political activity, as is so often the case in the New Africa, has been more intense than economic or social development. Shortly after World War II the Protectorate Advisory Council was established and municipal councils were founded in five of the six principal towns. In 1957 a fifteen-member Legislative Council with six unofficial (but appointed, not elected) members was established. Two years later, as Somalia's impending independence gave impetus to political activity in the protectorate, the Council was expanded to thirty-three members, thirteen of them elected. In these elections the moderate, pro-Commonwealth National Union Front, led by Ahmed Hassan and Michael Mariano, won seven of the thirteen elective seats. The N.U.F., which is the mouthpiece of the chiefs and traditional leaders, did well in country areas where election was by a system of tribal 'acclamation' while the more radical and pan-Somalist Somali National League, which took its cue from Mogadiscio and has close ties with Cairo, scored in urban constituencies. Both parties demanded self-government by 1960 and the right to join independent Somalia if they so desired, a principle conceded by Britain in 1956 'if political and economic conditions were propitious and proposals were both well conceived and favoured by Somalis concerned'.

In February of 1960 Britain agreed to hold new elections and increase the number of elective seats from thirteen to thirty-three, creating an unofficial majority and virtual internal autonomy. With a broadened franchise as an enticement, camel-riding nomads flocked down the *tugs* (dry river beds) to polling places and town-dwellers emerged from their *aqal*, skin-covered beehive huts, to cast their ballots. In an astounding *volte face*, perhaps produced by Britain's inability to solve the problem of the Haud, the more radical S.N.L., under the leadership of Mohamed Ibrahim Egal, increased the number of its seats from six to twenty while Mariano's N.U.F. fell from seven to one. The other twelve seats went to the United Somali Party, a new group whose platform varies only slightly from that of the S.N.L. Egal became Leader of Government Business ('prime minister in training') and Minister of Local Government. The new Legislative Council immediately passed a motion calling for independence and union with Somalia, and talks were held in Mogadiscio between representatives of Somalia and of Egal's government. It was resolved that the two territories should merge 'under one flag, one Parliament and one government' when Somalia achieved independence.

In May 1960 a four-man delegation led by Egal, who is thirty-two, visited London for discussions with Colonial Secretary Iain Macleod. In an imaginative move which met the desires of the Somalis if it had little to recommend it from an economist's point of view, Britain quickly agreed to grant independence to British Somaliland on June 26, with the understanding that the protectorate would unite with an independent Somalia on July 1. It was also agreed that Britain would give the former Protectorate £1·5 million in aid during its first year of independence (aid may or may not be continued and, in any case, will be subjected to an annual review), that a U.K. Aid Mission would be established for six months, that British personnel would continue to serve with the Somaliland Scouts for the same period, and that the B.B.C. relay station at Berbera would continue in operation.

On July 1 the two states merged, the Legislative Council of Somaliland and the Legislative Assembly of Somalia were combined into a single National Assembly, and Mogadiscio became the national capital. Former British Somaliland became nothing more than two of the eight provinces of the republic. Egal has been named Minister of Defence of the new country.

The British are far less accommodating in regard to the 80,000 Somalis who wander over the northern quarter of Kenya. While they encouraged Somali nationalism in Somaliland, the British have banned agitation in Kenya. To a statement by the colony's Somali chiefs in 1960 that they want to join Somalia when Kenya becomes independent, Governor Sir Patrick Renison replied that there would be no border changes while Britain was responsible for Kenya and that any such readjustment at a later date would have to be a matter of agreement between the two nations. At the same time, Britain reneged on the Greater Somalia concept when Mr. Macmillan stated, in answer to a question in Parliament, that Britain would not 'encourage or support any claim affecting the territorial integrity of French Somaliland, Kenya or Ethiopia' without the agreement of the governments concerned.

French Somaliland amounts to only a small enclave the size of Haiti around the port of Djibouti, the railhead town which acts as the gateway to Ethiopia. French Somaliland, as most historians have forgotten, has the distinction of being the point at which Russia first attempted to penetrate Africa. In 1888, a party of 175 men, women and children—

including Ukranian peasants, craftsmen, monks and four ex-officers of the Imperial Engineers—sailed from Odessa and seized an abandoned Egyptian fort near Djibouti. They dispatched emissaries to the Ethiopian emperor but the French, whose presence on the coast dated from 1856, forestalled any colonization attempt by shelling the fort from the sea and packing the whole bunch back to Russia.

The population of French Somaliland is 63,000, of which slightly less than half are Somalis. The remainder, apart from a few Europeans, are Arabs and Dankalis, a tribe related and traditionally hostile to the Somalis. After the constitutional reforms of 1957, thirty-nine-year-old Mahmoud Harbi, a rabid Somali nationalist who won the *croix de guerre* fighting for France in World War II, became Premier. When de Gaulle in 1958 gave France's African territories the choice between independence or membership in the French Community, Harbi urged his Republican Union party, a Dankali-Somali coalition backed by Arab traders, to break with France and seek union with Somalia. He failed and, after being felled by a stone in a street fight and arrested by the police, was ousted from office. He was killed in an aeroplane crash late last year. French Somaliland voted 75 per cent for further association with France, and de Gaulle, when he visited the enclave in 1959, stated that France would not abdicate its responsibilities towards the Somalis 'no matter what others may do'. Although the Somali Youth League is clandestinely active, it appears likely that the rivalry between Somali and Dankali coupled with France's intense desire to remain a Red Sea power will block any chance of the territory's union with Somalia.

Ethiopia, of course, is unalterably opposed to the Greater Somalia idea for the simple reason that it would deprive her of a third of her territory and destroy the imperial unity which Menelik and Haile Selassie fought so hard to achieve. The S.Y.L., like all political parties, is banned in Ethiopia and Eritrea, although several Somalis sit in the Ethiopian parliament and a score hold administrative posts in the Ogaden. Ethiopia is perfectly willing to see her 450,000 Somalis united with their brethren . . . under the Solomonic throne.

Addressing Ethiopian Somalis in 1956, Haile Selassie promised his Muslim subjects schools, hospitals and wells, urged them to combat any attempt to 'break Ethiopian unity and violate her freedom'. The Emperor claimed that 'we are united by race, colour and economics', scoffed at the idea of a Greater Somalia and warned that an independent Somalia cannot 'stand alone from Ethiopia'. If Somalia, he continued, were to join Ethiopia as Eritrea had done, hydro-electric projects of value to all Somalis could then be undertaken on the Juba and Uebi Scebeli rivers, both of which rise in Ethiopia. The Somali national assembly immediately went on record as refuting each of the tenets of the Emperor's speech.

Ethiopia now seems willing to tolerate an independent Somali Republic although she does not enjoy having another independent Muslin state on her frontiers. But she will not permit Somali expansionism. This is a situation which could well lead to war.

Even if the Greater Somalia dream were realized, it is hard to see how greater prosperity or political stability would be achieved. The Somali Republic, although she has a 50 per cent deficit in her balance of payments and in her budget, has the most viable economy of the four Somali regions. French Somaliland receives a substantial subsidy and the Somali regions of Ethiopia and Kenya are worthless.

But the nationalism of the Somalis is no more rational or less potent than that of any other people.

THE BORDER QUESTION

An additional irritant to this already ticklish situation arises from the fact that the border between the Somali Republic and Ethiopia has never been clearly de-limited. The Italians were unable to get together with Menelik on a question which became irrelevant after Italy conquered Ethiopia. The question was not brought up during the British administration of Somalia. When Somalia became a trust territory, the United Nations ordered Italy to negotiate the question with Ethiopia on behalf of Somalia. There could not have been a more unfortunate choice. Although Ethiopians in general bear no animosity towards individual Italians, they are still very suspicious of Italy. Italy went to the conference table with the ghost of fascism hovering over her shoulder, and, as might have been expected, there have been ten years of fruitless negotiations.

Border incidents continue and at any given time there are likely to be several hundred nomads shooting up Ethiopian frontier posts in an effort to force their way through to the water and grass of the Haud. The Somali Republic realizes she could not win a war against Ethiopia and officially her claims to the Ogaden have been dropped. But this means little to the nomads and their claim to live has not been altered. Somalis feel that Ethiopia, faced with unrest on both sides of her eastern frontier, may use the border incidents as a pretext for a little preventive imperialism involving the conquest of the Somali Republic. The Somali Republic, of course, is doing her best to obtain the arms necessary to defend her freedom. The tragedy of the situation is that the new nation, which so desperately needs schools and hospitals, has to spend more than 20 per cent of her budget on military expenses.

It is still too early to determine the Somali Republic's fate or to trace more than the vague outlines of her political profile. Here we have one of the most intelligent peoples of the new Africa coming to independence with the deck stacked against it in almost every way. The Somalis are a proud and individualistic people who, with a modicum of supervision, have come close to making democracy work. But the ancient traditional social order of the feudal nomads remains very much in the background. Whether democracy can survive the impending economic crisis which independence brought coupled with the threat of military disaster has yet to be seen. In times of trouble, England and America have found it convenient to short-circuit the democratic process in the interest of the national good. Whether democracy on the Eastern Horn of Africa has roots deep enough in the Somali Republic's sandy soil to bloom again if once it withers is doubtful.

And now we leave East Africa, cross three thousand miles to the Atlantic and that great river, the Congo, upon whose banks a different, darker people are moving towards an even more exotic brand of democracy.

II

THE GALLIC GIANT

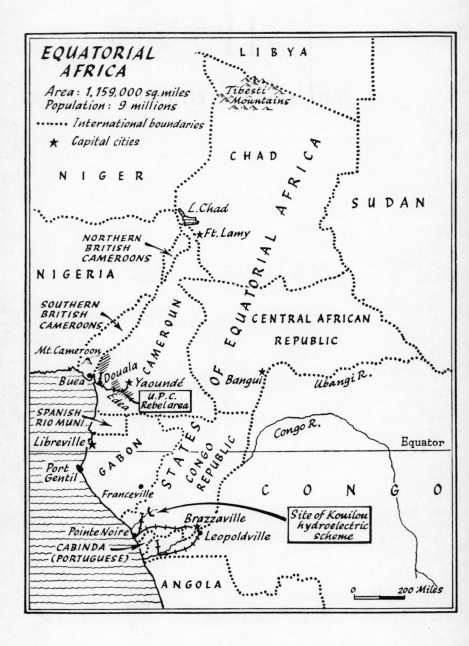

EQUATORIAL
AFRICA

Area: 1,159,000 sq. miles
Population: 9 millions
······· International boundaries
★ Capital cities

LIBYA

Tibesti
Mountains

CHAD

SUDAN

NIGER

L. Chad

★ Ft. Lamy

NORTHERN
BRITISH
CAMEROONS

NIGERIA

SOUTHERN
BRITISH
CAMEROONS

Mt. Cameroon

Buea

CENTRAL AFRICAN

REPUBLIC

OF EQUATORIAL AFRICA

Douala

CAMEROUN

★ Bangui

Ubangi R.

Edéa

Yaoundé

U.P.C.
Rebel area

SPANISH
RIO MUNI

Libreville ★

Congo R.

Equator

Port
Gentil

GABON

STATES

CONGO
REPUBLIC

CONGO

Franceville

Brazzaville

Site of Kouilou
hydroelectric
scheme

Pointe Noire

Leopoldville

CABINDA
(PORTUGUESE)

ANGOLA

0   200 Miles

Chapter 8

HEART OF DARKNESS

In Leopoldville we waited two weeks for our visas for what used to be known as French Equatorial Africa. The rain drummed down in a bitter tattoo and the roads changed from foot-deep dust to bottomless quagmires. Finally, as we were beginning to give up hope, French bureaucracy, by dint of a tremendous effort of will, produced the authorizations.

Within the hour we drove to *Le Beach*, the dock where the ferries call on their twenty-minute run across the four-mile-wide Stanley Pool which separates Leopoldville and ex-Belgian Congo from Brazzaville, once capital of the now-defunct French Equatorial Africa. While we waited for the ferry to take us across the turgid, chocolate-coloured sweep of the Congo, Muslim money-changers in flapping white robes surrounded the car waving fistfuls of pastel French colonial franc notes, suitably embellished with bare-breasted African beauties. So well developed is this kerb exchange that the Leopoldville banks have no French francs to sell.

After the ten-minute haggle over the rate which is not so much a means to an end as a delicious pleasure not to be denied the seller of banknotes, we wandered down to the dock, had our exit visas stamped by a well-starched official, and bought our tickets from a sleepy African in a booth. Brazzaville is the showplace of Equatorial Africa and there are no customs or immigration formalities for those wishing to cross the river for the day. This is convenient for the bloods of Leopoldville who, like Washingtonians escaping to Baltimore for a dirty weekend and Baltimoreans trooping to Washington for the same purpose, like to leave their block-long American cars, their pudgy wives and bustling, charmless city, for an evening of only slightly scandalous gambolling with the dusky beauties of Brazzaville.

After scraping one fender, I was able to squeeze the truck on to the four-car ferry through a throng of brightly-clad mammies making the return trip, their ample bosoms well padded with contraband Belgian cigarettes and Dutch wax print cloths. Going the other way, they bring cognac and French perfume and, presumably, everybody is happy.

Under a damp blanket of humid heat, the ferry's engine coughed tentatively, caught, and we swung out into the broad Congo, pointing upstream in the parabolic course necessitated by the strength of the current. A sixty-five-foot dug-out heavily laden with anonymous freight over which a tattered tarpaulin was thrown, fought against the will of the great river, its mighty strength eloquently expressed by the knotting muscles of sixteen bare and glistening backs. 'Oho, Congo! Oho!' the boatmen chanted as their churning paddles whipped the river to froth. Over the chug of the straining engine could be heard to the south the roar of the Livingstone Falls, that bubbling cauldron of white water and huge black rocks which almost killed Stanley and effectively blocked for years European penetration of these equatorial forests. To the north, beyond the 272-square-mile Stanley Pool, stretches the great brown-scaled snake of the Congo slithering for 2,900 miles into the green and living flesh of the jungle, pressing, as Joseph Conrad said, 'through the joyless sunshine to the heart of darkness'.

THE JOKE

Ex-French Equatorial Africa, which stretches 2,000 miles from the shifting sands of the Libyan desert to the mangrove-choked shores of the south Atlantic, is one of the most disconcerting 'countries' in Africa, a geographer's joke. It is not essentially French, totally Equatorial nor wholly African: the old federation, formed by France in 1910, disintegrated in 1958 into four black republics (three of which are linked by a loose union) French only in the sense that India is British; although the two southern republics, Gabon and Congo, are equatorial enough to suit the fancy of any Edgar Rice Burroughs devotee, those to the north—the Central African Republic and the Republic of Chad—shrug off the dripping cloak of the jungle to become flat savannah merging into waterless desert; most of the people of the south are appropriately negroid but, as you travel north between the watersheds of the Ubangi and the Shari, noses become more prominent, lips thinner, hair straighter, and skin fairer until, at the last, you meet wandering tribes of bedouins with eyes grey enough and hair sufficiently nordic to dupe the membership committee of any American country club.

There are 4·5 people to the square mile (409·7 in Connecticut),

84 per cent of the population ekes a living from the soil (only 7 per cent are salaried), half are animists and the remainder are divided more or less equally between Islam and Christianity, two-thirds of the latter being Roman Catholics. There are 200 Protestant missionaries, of which more than half are Americans, and the first American Protestant missionary arrived in 1842, two years before the first French Catholic priest.

Equatorial Africa's Congo-Ocean railway, which was begun in 1922 and took fourteen years to build, annually hauls more than 85 million ton-miles of freight and 25 million passenger-miles. Three ports handle about 1·5 million tons of freight per year and there is a 38,000-mile road network although in 1956 less than 2,700 miles of this was passable year-round to Equatoria's 20,000 motor vehicles. Supporting this man-made communications net are 2,900 miles of navigable but unconnected waterways.

The main agricultural export is 115,000 tons of cotton-seed grown by 550,000 peasant farmers in the two northern republics. But in 1957 lumber accounted for 42 per cent of the value of all exports, a percentage rapidly diminishing as the region's mineral wealth is tapped. For their own consumption the people annually produce 2 million tons of manioc, 1 million tons of millet, a little rice, a few peanuts and a bit of corn.

Equatoria contains twenty ethnic groups and has 250,000 square miles of desert and 173,000 square miles of rain-forest. Rainfall varies from a bone-dry half-inch per year at Largeau, in Chad, to 145 inches at Gabon's soggy Cocobeach. There are 143 post offices.

Witness at once to the terrors of the early white occupation and to the benefits accruing to the African from the European administration which ended tribal warfare, eliminated famines and introduced modern medicine, is the fact that 37 per cent of the population is under fourteen years of age. There are only 179 doctors, 50 midwives and 2,000 nurses to combat the health hazards of Equatoria (malaria, yellow fever, amoebic dysentery, sleeping sickness) and 75 per cent of the population was treated an average of more than three times in one recent year. Equatoria has 150,000 lepers, 12 hospitals and 300 dispensaries with a total of 9,000 beds. The number of vaccinations is up from 400,000 in 1947 to 2·5 million and each year 20,000 operations are performed. Brazzaville has a Pasteur Institute which does invaluable research and played an instrumental role in the successful war against sleeping sickness.

Free but not compulsory education is skimpy but improving: attendance of school-age children, which stood at 5 per cent in 1946, is now about 30 per cent. In the two southern republics the figure is 65 per cent, falling away to 45 per cent in the Central African Republic and 9 per cent in Muslim Chad. There are about 1,200 primary schools with 200,000 pupils and 20 secondary schools with an enrolment of 3,600. There are 5,000 technical students. More than 200 Equatorial Africans are studying at French universities and in 1959 Brazzaville took its first tentative steps towards the creation of a university. Less than half of 1 per cent of the population is white and Deep South racial supremacists would turn in their graves if they could see African boys sharing their desks with white girls in the schools, all of which are integrated.

Equatorial Africa's black-shirted zoot-suiters are called *zazous*; prisoners (guarded only by an African with a stick) are tastefully garbed in red and white smocks with crimson tams, and each of the green tiles in the roof of Brazzaville's Cathedral of St. Anne of the Congo costs 3s. 6d. This remarkable church, designed by a Protestant architect, is built of brick and without steel. Its doors and vaults resemble hands clasped in prayer, or the bamboo arcade which arches above a jungle track. There is to be a ninety-foot steeple but, for the moment, there is no money.

Equatoria has an area of almost one million square miles and is four and a half times the size of France, its diminutive foster-mother. Put another way, if Equatorial Africa—which has a population equal to that of Venezuela—were laid sideways on a map of the United States, its borders would stretch from Connecticut to Idaho and from the Canadian border to Texas. The four republics have the shape of a jackboot, with the toe touching the Atlantic and the top on Libya's southern border, or a Notre Dame gargoyle turned upside down. Although a new prosperity may be just around the corner, F.E.A. has always been the 'Cinderella Colony', the poor daughter of a France which in at least one stage of Equatorial Africa's history has been well-cast in the role of the wicked stepmother. There is little relationship among the economies of these four calabash republics except for the fact that all are too poor to afford their inhabitants sufficient education, ample social services or a reasonable standard of living.

If ex-French Equatorial Africa has little political, geographical, ethnic or economic homogeneity, the social disparity which exists among its infinitely various peoples is equally obvious: while some are polished *boulevardiers* more at home in the drawing-rooms of St. Germain than in the mud huts of Ubangi-Shari, pleasing to the palates of others (piquantly dubbed Fangs) is *homme* rather than *homard*; some ebony courtesans tint their mouths with the latest shade of lipstick while others embellish them by inserting bone discs; their men may wear Savile Row tweeds or penis-sheaths of grass with equal aplomb.

Scattered over this vast area are five million people, more than half gathered in the great basin of the huge inland sea of which Lake Chad, still forty-two times the size of Lake Geneva, is but a pitiful vestige. Lost in this great human sea of black are twenty thousand white traders, missionaries and administrators, gathered around lonely storm lanterns smothered in charred insects, living reminders that French Equatorial Africa was born of a political idea which began with the concept of one France, unitary and indivisible, a new Rome guided by a divinely-inspired civilizing mission. Although two World Wars, the decline of Christianity and the rise of Black Nationalism have shaken and altered this grandiose vision, the French language, revolutionary spirit and culture—call it Gallicism, if you like—remain the bonds tying together the peoples of French Equatorial Africa to each other and all to France. France exported more than cotton goods and sunglasses to Africa.

FATHER OF SLAVES

Most of the French colonial effort before the middle of the nineteenth century was concentrated upon the Senegal and it was not until the anti-slavery pronouncements of the Congress of Vienna (1850) that France established naval stations on the coast of Gabon. Libreville, the port-capital of Gabon, was founded as a refuge for freed slaves and French cruisers vied with British frigates from the Congo to the Senegal in the curiously ambivalent role of abolitionists and conquerors.

But French control, where it existed, was confined to the coast; the limitless interior stretched away in its enormity and shapelessness into infinity, a riddle awaiting the advent of a man big enough to unlock its secrets.

That man was Pierre Savorgnan de Brazza, a lean, hollow-cheeked Venetian nobleman with the sad, dark eyes of a poet, an adopted son of France, 'innocent of human blood', as his epitaph in the cemetery of Algiers reads, who was to give his fortune and his life to Africa and live to see his work dishonoured by the lesser men who followed in his wake.

De Brazza, who was the seventh son of a papal count, looked rather like Gregory Peck with a beard or Fidel Castro without his Sten gun. You can take your pick as to his birthplace: some say that he was born in 1852 in the harbour of Rio de Janeiro, others say Rome. These were the days before Gallic anti-clericalism, and the Italian nobility felt stronger ties to France than to Garibaldi's revolutionary Italy. De Brazza obtained an appointment to the French Naval Academy and became a citizen of France. He was commissioned and served in the North Sea and the Mediterranean before, at the age of twenty-three, submitting a plan for the exploration of Dr. Schweitzer's Ogooue River which, he argued, would open up the interior of Africa to France.

This vision-haunted, tattered aristocrat led (and partially financed) three expeditions which, within ten years and without firing a shot, added half a million square miles to the French empire. De Brazza, a thoroughbred all the way, went bare-foot and tattered through savage tribes with a dignity impossible and incomprehensible to the parvenu Welsh bastard, Henry Stanley, who was shooting his way down the opposite bank of the Congo. The Venetian, who sometimes dressed as an Arab, was courtly, courageous and patient, human as well as humane, loving the Africans as he found them. They called him 'the Father of Slaves' because in his steps freedom grew.

His explorations concluded, the thin and hairy wanderer stayed on in Equatorial Africa as governor until his gentle rule became intolerable to the men of lesser character, the fat and greasy parasites who have always followed the idealists and deformed that which they created, who saw in Africa only a land from which fortunes could be wrung. They forced him out and French Equatorial Africa—or the French Congo, as it was then called—was cut up and handed to forty concessionaires who wrote a story of excesses no more fragrant than that of Leopold's agents south of the river.

The concession companies, which had obtained complete rights over the land and its people, imposed taxes which the natives were unable to pay unless they went to work on the plantations. By extorting high taxes and forcing the Africans to buy cheap goods at dear prices, the companies assured themselves of a permanent labour force. The French government gave them a free hand in return for 15 per cent of the profits and the concessionaires ravished the land and the people, returning virtually nothing to the economy of the country.

Finally the stench became too great even for the French public and de Brazza was sent back in 1905 to investigate and make recommendations. He left his bones in Africa after writing his report. It must have been a sizzler because, although it was never published, the concessions were curtailed and the worst features of the system eradicated.

With several magnificent exceptions, French Equatorial Africa has scraped the bottom of the barrel of Frenchmen anxious to serve overseas: the bright went to the Barbary states, the cultured to Indo-China. To what they called 'the country of the damned' came the 'hard cases' willing to spend a season in Hell in the hope of monetary gain, younger sons lacking sufficient connections to obtain a better post and demon-haunted men looking for a living grave. But Equatoria has a spell: to eat the millet and curdled milk of Ubangi-Shari, to drink the waters of the sludgy Ogooue is to put native blood in your veins; they call it Congomania and few (these usually die) can resist its call.

After de Brazza's report there followed a period of economic and political stagnation. This has been the typical pattern in Africa: trade at the coast, exploration and annexation of the interior, exploitation in the worst sense of the word, a cry of protest from missionaries and humanitarians followed by a period of somnolence to last until World War II set Africa aflame with nationalism. This lack of African progress common in all colonial territories between the turn of the century and World War II was less a case of wanting to keep the African back than lack of sufficient resources and personnel to bring him forward. The Colonial Powers scrambled for Africa mainly for political and strategic reasons, to prevent their rivals from obtaining territory and to guard the sea-routes between Europe and the wealth of Asia. When the continent had been divided up, the Powers found themselves over-extended with neither the money nor the technicians necessary for development. If these had been available they might not have been used, for the Colonial Powers saw in Africa only a source of raw materials and a market for the manufactured goods of Europe. That each country might some day become an independent political and economic entity was to the theorists of this classical age of colonialism not only unthinkable but blasphemous. In Equatorial Africa, de Brazza had seen to it that the French would rule, if not justly, with a gentle yoke; France lacked the means or the desire to do more.

BLACK DEFENDER

If de Brazza was the father of Equatorial Africa, Felix Eboué was midwife to the land. This thickset Negro from a South American pepper port (Cayenne, French Guiana) was born in 1884, a descendant of slaves. He did well in school and was sent to France to study in the school of colonial administration. Eboué served in the French Sudan and Guadalupe, worked himself patiently up through the colonial hierarchy to become governor of Chad, the northernmost of French Equatorial Africa's four territories.

As Nazi Germany forced France to her knees, Eboué, who risked not only his career but his head in so doing, led Chad and two other Equatorial African territories into the Allied camp, blocked Rommel out of central Africa, provided Britain with the only feasible overland supply route to Suez when Hitler's bombers closed the Mediterranean to Allied shipping, and gave homeless Charles de Gaulle real estate upon which to mount his Cross of Lorraine. Overnight, Eboué became a symbol both of Free France and of a renascent Africa, worthy of honour and capable of action. The words 'This is Radio Brazzaville calling . . .' for five long years spelled self-respect and hope to millions in Occupied France. Although Eboué's fame has been overshadowed by that of his military colleague, in history he will share with de Gaulle the role of saviour of France's honour in her darkest hour. The people of Little Rock, Algiers and Notting Hill would do well to remember that they owe much to this black man.

But Eboué was very much more than a brave Frenchman. He was an accomplished musician who could play with equal facility the most intricate sonata or pound out a message on the piano understandable to the players of Africa's talking-drums. He was a perceptive anthropologist and a wise administrator who urged France to treat the African 'as a human being capable of progress in his own environment and, in all likelihood, lost if he is taken from it'. Few wiser words have been written about Africa and Eboué well deserves his resting-place in the Panthéon in Paris.

His last act was just as important as his defiance of Vichy: in reward for and recognition of Africa's contribution to the cause of freedom, a conference was held in Brazzaville with Eboué as host in January 1944. Filled with the spirit of the Resistance and warmed by the knowledge of the coming Liberation, de Gaulle met with Eboué and other African leaders to blueprint the economic and political structure of a greater Franco-African community.

Although the men of Brazzaville specifically ruled out any definition of French Africa without France, they guaranteed to Africans the right to participate in the drawing up of the new constitution and to be represented in all the assemblies of the French Union. In Africa itself there was to be a decentralization of administrative control, the election of territorial assemblies by universal suffrage wherever possible, land reform, extension of the French labour code to Africa, a vast programme of economic development in which the needs of the African territories would receive equal recognition with those of France and the abolition both of forced labour and of the *indigenat* (the legal differentiation between French citizens and French subjects). Taking a leaf from the book of Caracalla, emperor of third-century Rome, full French citizenship was to be conferred upon all those living within the boundaries of France's empire.

Eboué died a few months later and de Gaulle retired from public life. As a consequence, the spirit of the Liberation and of Brazzaville was diluted and smaller-minded men of the it-can't-be-done stamp came to power. But if not all of the hopes of Brazzaville were immediately realized, substantial gains were won: France's feet were set upon the path from which there is no turning. Even the watered-down caricature of the spirit of Revolutionary France acknowledged that, henceforward, Africans were to have a major say in shaping their own destiny.

Brazzaville was followed by a decade of jockeying and indecision as a France fearful of Communist agitation in her closed colonial preserve, angered at the outbreak of warfare in Algeria and Indo-China, fearful of aggressive American capitalism and mistrustful of Black nationalism, hesitated between liberalism and reaction.

Lacking was not only the will but the means. The architects of the New Africa, in the main, had only one qualification: they were free of the taint of Vichy. The planning of the economic phase of African reconstruction was hasty and faulty, there was insufficient money even to launch the plan or to buy abroad the equipment needed for its consummation, and almost nothing in French Africa around which to build the industrial society so much desired by black theorists.

Despite all this, France has poured £110 million into Equatorial Africa since the end of the war, more than half in outright grants, the remainder in long-term low-interest loans which, in all probability, will never be repaid. Educational facilities have multiplied and public works burgeoned. Most important of all, while British Africans were agitating for self-determination, French Africans were sitting in Paris debating not only their own laws but those of *France*. Nothing points out more forcibly the different theories behind British and French colonialism. The British ideal is one of association, of equal autonomy for each component of the Commonwealth. The French now and always have stressed identification, the theory that Africans are to become not the equals of the French but black *Frenchmen*. To those gentle readers of the 'If-you-eat-with-'em-you've-got-to-sleep-with-'em' school, one can only say that this is not a prospect totally displeasing to many a Gaul.

In 1956, the new Socialist premier, Guy Mollet, took two Africans into his cabinet and tabled before the French Assembly the so-called *loi cadre* (enabling law) which was to revive the spirit of Brazzaville and even extend the promises of that conference. Black Africa was not yet actively restive but events in Indo-China and Algeria indicated to the jittery statesmen that the pressure of events might soon leave France with no alternative south of the Sahara.

If carried to its logical conclusion, Overseas France would have 248 deputies in a 520-member French Assembly. This, of course, was and is politically impossible and unrealistic for many sound reasons. But the *loi cadre* did increase African representation in the Metropolitan assemblies, establish universal suffrage throughout the Union, create a single electoral college for blacks and whites, reorganize the civil service, enhance the powers of the local assemblies and elevate the top Africans in each territorial assembly to local cabinet rank.

This did much to satisfy Equatorial Africa's political aspirations but little to solve her pressing economic problems: then as now, she imports £3 worth of goods for every £2 she sells and two-thirds of her exports by value consist of two products prone to price-shimmering, wood and cotton. Neither French liberalism nor the often fuzzier brand peddled by the United Nations can do much about the fact that three out of every four inhabitants of F.E.A. live more than six hundred miles from the sea in areas without easily navigable rivers or the possibility of railway construction. Nor can merely wishing it so make the Muslim population any less suspicious of Western education. Belgian administrators were able to say with some truth that, if *their* blacks lacked the political freedom afforded by the *loi cadre*, they at least had full bellies and shoes on their feet. But even more startling political developments were in store for the Gallic giant.

DE GAULLE'S RETURN

Wearied of the political merry-go-round which had given each French government for thirteen years an average life-span of six months, fearful of the neo-fascist threat posed by Algeria's colons and rightist factions within the army, France turned in the summer of 1958 to her war-time saviour, Charles de Gaulle, to restore her stability and her honour.

It was characteristic of de Gaulle, as a man of Brazzaville, that he dared to present French Africans with the choice between independence and closer identification with France and, having dared, won. De Gaulle made only one whirlwind trip through Africa a month before the September 28 referendum in an attempt to rally Africa to his proposed French Community. The General offered the African territories political independence (with an end to French financial aid) or autonomy within the French Community and continued economic assistance. Where, the African politicians wondered, would the money come from to fulfil their promises of more schools, roads and dams, a better standard of living for their people? Perhaps more important, who would pay the politicians' fat salaries, provide them with free mansions, cars, servants and four round-trip air tickets to Paris each year? The African, ever a materialist, got the message.

De Gaulle promised that an affirmative vote would not bind a territory to France indefinitely. Implicit but unsaid was the future formation of a French Community resembling the British Commonwealth of Nations. For the moment, however, the Community, dominated by France, was to retain control of foreign affairs, defence, currency matters, over-all economic planning and higher education.

'In effect,' said a Frenchman in Gabon, 'de Gaulle said "take our money as long as you need it; if you ever want complete independence, just drop me a postcard".'

Despite the scope and generosity of this offer, it appeared at election time that de Gaulle might well go down in history as the man who lost France her African empire in one throw of the dice. Thirty-five days before the election, Reuters stated that 'French-African leaders are presuming that Madagascar and at least nine of twelve territories of French West and Equatorial Africa will vote for independence'. In the event, de Gaulle rolled up an affirmative vote in these territories. Only Guinea exercised the right to opt for independence.

The British pundits erred (it is always easy to be wise after the fact) by under-estimating the force of four things: the economic factor, racial goodwill created over the years by the policy of identification, the appeal of de Gaulle's personality to the average African and the confidence of the African leaders that, at a later date, they would be able to obtain a more liberal revision of the Community's ground-rules.

This revisionist movement was led by the politicians of Mali and Madagascar, who persuaded the General to grant their countries full independence in 1960 while still retaining loose links with France. Their success inspired the remainder of the French African states to follow their example and all did so before the year was out. But back to the 1958 referendum:

In Brazzaville, de Gaulle walked to pray at the Church of St. Anne of the Congo, a memorial to Africans who fought in the Resistance, flanked by Eboué's son (a colonel in the *French* air force) and by the late Barthelemy Boganda, President of the Federal Assembly of French Equatorial Africa, Premier of Ubangi-Shari and son of a cannibal. After a mass sung to tom-toms and accompanied by a choir of two hundred and fifty, de Gaulle stood once more before Africa as the man of Brazzaville. As the natives chanted and sang the General's fame, the perspiring mayor of the city pushed his way through the throng and presented de Gaulle with a golden key to the town and a stuffed crocodile.

Gaullism, particularly within the four territories of French Equatorial Africa, is literally a cult. Fetishist tribes sacrifice chickens to images of the General encased in bottles. Neo-Christian sects include de Gaulle in their Trinity with the Father and the Son. Even those less spiritually inclined who have never heard of Louis XIV, Napoleon, Rousseau or Foch smile with pleasure at the mention of the General's name.

In part this adulation is based on de Gaulle's war record. But de Gaulle's magic speaks even to those Africans—and there are more than a few—who are unaware that there was a world war. The General is everything that the African seems to like and respect in a leader: tall, hefty, imperious, calm and at the same time flamboyant, a speaker in parables and a wearer of braid and feathers. It is highly unlikely that the able Pierre Mendès-France could have sold the same programme with an equal degree of success: physically and emotionally, he just doesn't coincide with the African image of a leader.

Just to reinforce the General's magnetism, in the days when the outcome of the referendum seemed in doubt, the French army and officialdom launched a well-organized propaganda drive in his behalf. Colourful posters slapped indiscriminately on city skyscrapers and bush huts informed such of the electorate as were literate that a vote for de Gaulle was, among other things, a vote for equality, liberty, fraternity, prosperity, community, Africa and France. All of this turned out to be as necessary as a Democratic doorbell-ringing campaign in Georgia during an election year. There was no anti-Gaullist propaganda in Equatorial Africa and one government publicist, worried about how this would look to the outside world, pleaded (unsuccessfully) for a little government money to 'print and scatter around a few *Non!* posters'.

As far as the political leaders of Equatorial Africa were concerned, the structure of de Gaulle's Community offered much, denied little. As Boganda put it, 'the choice was between being allowed to drive your own battered Chevrolet with a nearly empty tank or being chauffeured by a white driver in a new Cadillac as far as you like. And, in the end, one has always a chance of acquiring title to the Cadillac.'

On the day of the referendum bare-breasted Bakongo women and Ubangi damsels with plates in their lips jostled with pale Arab bedouins, Frenchmen with existentialist beards and sallow mulattos from Libreville to cast their votes. When the tally was finished, the dimensions of the Gaullist vote were totally surprising to most and reached proportions almost embarrassing to some. Metropolitan France had voted four to one for de Gaulle; Eboueland (Middle Congo, Ubangi-Shari and Chad) gave him a 99 per cent *oui* vote; even in Gabon, the fourth territory of Equatorial Africa and the one that stuck longest with Vichy, the General received a majority of 92 per cent. In the event, the black political leaders of Equatorial Africa had opted for the Cadillac rather than the Chevrolet.

Having assented to belong to the French Community, Equatorial Africa had then to decide whether it would become a large unitary state, a federation of states, a department of France, or four autonomous republics each with an individual relationship to France and none to each other. After considerable jockeying, the same centrifugal forces which nearly wrecked the United States within months of Yorktown smashed Equatorial African unity. F.E.A., which had never been more than an administrative reality, dissolved into four political entities. But events outside Equatoria were at least partially to re-create this unity: the independence of Mali (the republics of Senegal and Soudan) coupled with the sudden Belgian granting of freedom to the Congo drastically altered the concept of the Community and strengthened the hand of the pro-independence elements in Equatoria. After prolonged negotiations, three of the four territories of Equatoria—Congo, Central African Republic and Chad—joined together to form a customs union within which many consumer services are shared. Gabon, which has both a history of separatism and a stronger economy, remained outside the union. And now let us consider each of these four republics.

GABON

This republic, the size of Yugoslavia, is bordered on the west by the Atlantic Ocean, on the south and east by her sister equatorial Republic of the Congo, and on the north by the Spanish enclave of Rio Muni and by newly-independent Cameroun, a former United Nations trust under France. Gabon, which boasts a population the size of that of Louisville, has terrific tarpon fishing, gorillas, the rare bongo antelope, more okoume trees than any other place in the world, a satisfactory supply of elephants and buffaloes, and the most promising economic situation of the four republics. Thirty white families still own a vast 200,000-acre tract of Gabon and labour is in such short supply that entire families of Nigerians are imported to work in the fields. Census-takers are somewhat frustrated by the fact that names are secret and may be pronounced only by the initiated at special times and under certain conditions. There is also Dr. Schweitzer.

Although we had the pleasure of visiting that craggy old philosopher and humanitarian at his Lambaréné hospital, those who do not know his story must seek it elsewhere: the unquestioned good work of the Doctor is by no means unique in Africa and he bears no relationship to political developments on the continent. Schweitzer has never been two hundred miles from Lambaréné, has no contact with or interest in either African nationalism or black leaders. His is an act of personal contrition which could have been performed equally effectively in any part of the world and bears no reflection on events in Gabon or elsewhere in Africa.

Gabon, as we have seen, was the scene of initial French settlement in Equatorial Africa and its capital, Libreville, was built—as its name implies—as a sanctuary for slaves snatched from the Middle Passage by French men-of-war. The Ogooue, which bisects the country, was de Brazza's highway to the interior and is today its great hope for economic progress. Here it was that Paul du Chaillu, an explorer with a penchant for purple prose, became the first white man to see a gorilla. Gorillas, despite the *New Yorker*, do not impose their horrid wills on naked white women. Those who know them maintain that these primates have extremely affectionate dispositions, which is more than you can say for Paul du Chaillu, who shot the gorilla. Other fauna of Gabon include a species of monkey with a pale blue scrotum nicely set off by a rose penis, a sect which dances on twelve-foot stilts, and the cannibalistic Fangs.

Mary Kingsley, history's one great female explorer, who danced 'many a wild waltz' with the Ogooue and died of fever during the Boer War, recounts finding in a Fang hut a bag containing 'a human hand, three big toes, four eyes, two ears, and other portions of the human frame'. Miss Kingsley, who had the joyful ability to write factual material in a light fashion, recounts that 'the hand was fresh, the others only so-so'.

Our route north took us through the Fang country during the rains, a nightmare trip of one hundred and sixty miles which took seven days of axle-cracking, up-to-the-hub-caps ploughing in greasy mud. We saw no severed human hands, fresh or otherwise, although the filed teeth of the Fangs did nothing to contribute to my sense of well-being. The water poured down upon the soaking creepers which wound around the great trees, sometimes joining together to shut out the sky. The villages were small and miserable and the people listless. Cannibalism is a forest phenomenon, mostly because—contrary to what people may think— there is little game in the jungle. The few animals are so scattered and well-concealed that the craving for meat becomes an obsession which the native can satisfy only by dining on his colleagues.

Miss Kingsley reports that the Fangs ate their relatives 'yet they like to keep a little something belonging to them as a memento (the hands, toes, eyes and ears)'. This is all out-of-date, of course. The modern Fang, while liking live meat when he can get it, has adapted himself to cadavers (the African palate prefers its meat and fish a bit 'high') and he now refuses to eat the corpse of a relative, preferring to exchange his late uncle for a deceased of equal tenderness from a neighbouring village.

Premier Leon M'Ba, the pudgy, balding mayor of Libreville and head of the Gabonese government, has never eaten a soul. His city, built on a series of small hills around the estuary of the river from which the republic takes its name, is a bustling port through which pours 300,000 tons of wood for the sawmills of Europe each year. Libreville contains a statue of Captain N'tchorere, a black officer shot by the Germans in France during World War II when he refused to be humiliated by them. Gabon, with a population of about 400,000 (8 per cent of Equatorial Africa's total), accounts for 40 per cent of the exports by value from all four republics combined. It has a trade deficit of only 25 per cent, remarkably low for this impoverished region.

Gabon contains almost all of Equatorial Africa's valuable timber, the most magnificent stands of mahogany, limba, okoume (false mahogany) in the world. It also has the rare striped zebrawood. Forest products in one recent year were worth nearly £9 million, or 85 per cent of total exports, and production is going up all the time. As yet Gabon has only scratched the surface of her logging resources, 20 per cent of her territory being immediately exploitable. Less than a tenth of this has come under the axe. In the old days, a stand of timber in Gabon was useless unless it was within a few hundred yards of a river. The trees, many of them twenty feet in diameter, were cut by hand and humped down to the rivers by natives, there to begin a journey which frequently took two years before the logs reached the sea. Modern lumbering equipment coupled with intelligent reafforestation could make Gabon into an African Scandinavia.

In addition to hardwoods, Gabon shares with the Congo Republic the great oil palm groves of Equatorial Africa. But Gabon's palms are three hundred miles closer to the sea, a heavy factor in the country's favour in an area where transportation costs are high. In an average year, Gabon's palm products bring in £700,000 and she earns £350,000 each from diamonds (a 149-carat rock was found in 1955), gold and lead.

But gold and lead are only the beginnings of Gabon's mineral wealth, a vast treasure trove which has yet to be fully exploited. A fifteen-year search for petroleum ended with a strike of a small but easily exploitable pool near Port Gentil in 1956. Production reached 500,000 tons by 1958, 20 per cent of the value of total exports. By the end of this year shipments should amount to one million tons annually and Socony Mobil Oil in 1959 agreed to invest £16 million in prospecting and drilling over a six-year period in Gabon and the Congo Republic.

At Mekambo in northern Gabon vast deposits of iron ore, said to exceed one *billion* tons, have been discovered. The ore is high grade (up to 69 per cent) and, although the deposits are three hundred miles inland, no more inaccessible than the great iron fields of Labrador and Venezuela. Exploitation involves the construction of 440 miles of railway and the creation of a new port near Owendo. The concession company, in which Bethlehem Steel has a 50 per cent interest, will invest £100 million over an eight-year period at the end of which

production is expected to amount to 10 million tons per y
smaller deposit (150 million tons), capable of producing 3 million
per year, will be exploited at Tchibanga, twenty-five miles from th
sea.

An even more ambitious project is the exploitation of the Franceville manganese deposits which total at least 150 million tons, one of the world's largest lodes. Pre-production costs, which will include the building of forty-five miles of cableway and one hundred and eighty miles of railway to tie in with the Congo-Ocean line (work began in 1958), will exceed £32 million. The World Bank is helping to finance the project with a £12·5 million loan. The loan is for fifteen years at 6 per cent and is the twenty-sixth made to eleven African countries by the Bank, whose lines of credit to Africa in mid-1959 exceeded £221 million. The United States Steel Corporation holds a 49 per cent interest in the company which will exploit the manganese, which lies on the upper reaches of the Ogooue River, near the Congo border. The French Government owns 22 per cent and private French investors hold the balance. First shipments will be made in 1962, with initial production reaching an annual figure of 500,000 tons. It is anticipated that manganese will bring in £5·7 million, increasing the value of Gabon's exports by 40 per cent. With the construction of a ferro-manganese plant at Franceville, powered by the vast Kouilou hydro-electric scheme across the border in the Congo Republic, Gabon hopes to be exporting 200,000 tons of ferro-manganese and one million tons of manganese by 1965. Also planned is the exploitation of sizable uranium deposits near Franceville and the electrification of the Ogooue valley to provide power for cellulose and salt industries.

French aid to Gabon between 1947 and 1957 has amounted to £17·7 million and intensive effort is being made to develop the cultivation of coffee and cacao, both good hard-currency earners. Gabon's two good ports, Libreville and Port Gentil (which boasts the world's largest plywood factory under one roof, producing 1·3 million cubic feet per year), and a diversified economy based on hardwoods, palm products, coffee cacao, diamonds, gold, manganese and iron afford her people the highest *per capita* income in Equatorial Africa. Because of her comparative wealth and small population, Premier M'Ba knew that Gabon would have to bear most of the cost of the unification of Equatorial Africa while having virtually no say in the political fortunes of the state. In a proportional allocation of seats in an eighteen-member assembly, for instance, dirt-poor Chad would have ten seats and the

Republic (Ubangi-Shari) would have four, while
...ngo Republic, which is also relatively rich, would
...1. Despite all the talk about Pan-Africanism, M'Ba
...are Gabon's wealth with her poorer sister republics
...ental in seeing to it that his country, at least for the
...outside the union of the other three equatorial
... With a relatively stable government and a burgeoning economy, Gabon gives promise of becoming one of the most prosperous black republics of the French Community.

THE CONGO REPUBLIC

The Congo Republic (formerly French Middle Congo and not to be
confused with its giant neighbour south of the river, the ex-Belgian
Congo), is a little smaller than Finland and has a population of 800,000.
It shares Equatorial Africa's coastline with Gabon, contains the old
federal capital of Brazzaville and the 320-mile Congo-Ocean railway
which huffs across ninety-two bridges and through twelve tunnels to
connect Brazzaville with Pointe-Noire, and ranks next to Gabon in
economic and educational progress.

In the late 1930s, the Lari people of the Middle Congo produced a
prophet-chief known as Matswa (his real name was André Grenard).
Matswa, who was opposed to taxes, identity cards and peanuts, filled
the Laris with a blend of religious hokum and anti-white nationalism,
assuming himself the dual role of spiritual messiah and political leader.
The former army sergeant went to Paris where he founded the Congo
Friends' Society, whose funds he promptly appropriated to his own use,
was charged with fraud, convicted and jailed. He died in prison in 1940
but the Lari people refused to accept his death and they elected him to
represent them in Paris in 1946.

His successor, the forty-two-year-old Abbé Fulbert Youlou—a
Bakongo chief whose name means 'reflection'—is no less colourful a
personality. Youlou, a smoothly plump man who hails from a small
village a hundred miles west of Brazzaville, captured the loyalty of the
Matswaists and swept to power with a slender one-vote majority in
1956. The Congo Friends' Society is now known as the Fulbert's
Friends Society (although many Matswaists now are violently opposed
to Youlou) and the bespectacled Abbé, who speaks French with a
compound fracture, is doing very well indeed politically.

The Abbé Fulbert is not above blessing the ballpoint pens of primary students, thus guaranteeing them a pass in their examinations. He is mayor of Brazzaville and likes to wear the tri-coloured sash of office over his white cassock topped off with a homburg and to distribute five-franc notes to enthusiastic supporters as his blue-green Pontiac takes him to work in the morning. At the time of our visit, his white secretary was the wife of the manager of the whites-only swimming pool, the last redoubt of racial exclusiveness in Equatorial Africa.

Although the Abbé Fulbert is a good-natured fellow who listens without complaint every morning to the troubles of his constituents, who jam his office and clamour to kiss his bishop-sized ring, he is not very keen on political opposition. When Jacques Opangault, former premier and leader of the twenty-two-member Opposition in the Congo Republic's forty-five-delegate National Assembly, rose in early 1959 to suggest that since Youlou's *Union Démocratique de Défense des Interêts Africaines* (UDDIA) had a majority which could hardly be termed overwhelming, it might be a good idea to have new elections to determine whether the Congo would join a union of French African states or go it alone, pandemonium broke out. Opangault, one of the milder African politicians, knocked the Speaker out with his own microphone and events reached such rollicking proportions that police had to clear the chamber with tear gas. Youlou's weeping supporters used their one-vote majority to ram through a motion for autonomy and another to delay elections until 1962, at which time Opangault's red-eyed cohorts walked out in protest.

The smiling Abbé, who is given to using colourful turns of phrase, such as 'the thirst for a better state itches us', then ordered the capital of the country switched from the Opangault-dominated Pointe-Noire to his Brazzaville stronghold. Fearful that his outraged opponent might stage a coup, Youlou loaded his entire parliamentary caucus, their women and a few gentry who happened to be lounging around the platform into coaches, commandeered a locomotive and, with a hand-car loaded with troops to clear the way, blasted through to Brazzaville where he was met by 5,000 trigger-happy supporters sporting headgear ranging from parachutists' berets to Davy Crockett caps. As his gnarled mother shuffled through a dance of joy and fell on her knees at his feet, her exultant son told the cheering throng that he would rule the Congo Republic for ever. Opangault's Brazzaville followers, to whom this was not an enticing prospect, took to their war drums and in the ensuing riots 124 were killed, 186 wounded and more than

500 jailed. French-led African soldiers confiscated hundreds of shot-guns and three *tons* of spears and knives wielded by enthusiastic partisans of both leaders.

Opangault persisted in being a bad loser and continued to assert that Youlou was not acting according to Erskine May. To show that every-thing was above-board, the Abbé called for new elections in June 1959. As insurance, he jailed Opangault (and five hundred M'Bouchi tribes-men who are among the opposition leader's most fervent supporters) and did such a good job of gerrymandering that his party won 50 of 61 seats, thus increasing his parliamentary majority from 1 to 39, although UDDIA polled less than 64 per cent of the popular vote. With the election safely in the bag, Youlou released Opangault, who now has joined the Abbé's coalition government. Europeans, who customarily stood as candidates under various party labels, have deemed it prudent to withdraw from politics as the pace becomes more exuberant and Youlou has dispensed with the services of his white cabinet ministers. Although he may win no plaudits from the Better Government League, it would seem that UDDIA and the Abbé Fulbert Youlou are in the political saddle for the foreseeable future.

The Congo Republic, which is bounded on the west by Gabon and the Atlantic, on the east and south by the ex-Belgian Congo and on the north by the Cameroun and the Central African Republic, is richer on a *per capita* basis than her northern neighbours, but that isn't saying much. Coffee, timber, tobacco, zinc, peanuts and palm products bring in only £5·4 million annually while she must import more than £10·8 million worth of goods. Apart from a few light industries in Brazzaville, which handles 200,000 tons of river freight per year, that's about all the Congo Republic has in the way of resources. During the decade ending in 1957, France primed the economy with £32·5 million worth of development grants. A major effort has been made to turn the Niari valley, in the south of the republic, into an equatorial bread-basket. The valley contains 740,000 exceptionally fertile acres and, by setting up research stations and introducing mechanization, it is hoped that the Congo Republic one day will be a major producer of crops both for internal consumption and for export.

But the Abbé Fulbert Youlou is pinning his immediate economic hopes on a hydro-electric scheme now being developed on the Kouilou River at Sounda. By blocking a narrow gorge between two mountains of granite, Kouilou will generate 9 billion kilowatts a year of a

Norwegian cheapness. A ready market is available for 700 million kilowatts at the Franceville manganese fields, many times this figure if Gabon carries through on its plans for an aluminium plant. The remainder of the power will be used to develop a general industrial area producing cement, magnesium, phosphate fertilizers and cellulose.

On the shores of the lake which will be created—three times the size of Lake Geneva—bananas, rice, sugar and jute will be cultivated. In a word, all the Congo's hopes depend on Kouilou.

The Congo Republic has two other advantages which should be noted: she has, in Brazzaville, the finest city of Equatorial Africa, and for the entire length of her southern and eastern boundaries flow the Congo and the Ubangi rivers, providing a ready-made highway down which to float her goods.

If it could be harnessed, the Congo—which is innocent of bridges—could produce 150 million kilowatts. This magnificent stream, the fifth longest in the world, is second only to the Amazon in volume of discharge: at high-water, 75,000 cubic metres *per second* pour into the sea from this outsized tap.

Across the river from Brazzaville is Leopoldville, and the two cities, as different as two sisters, react upon each other. Leopoldville is modern, bustling, and wealthy. Brazzaville, dedicated more to the enjoyment of life than to its conquest, has a lighter modernity, a bougainvillaea-perfumed grace, at once languid and effervescent. The French city is smaller (Leo: 250,000; Brazza: 100,000) but L'Aiglon, its upper-class suburb, is just as smart as anything across the river. Brazzaville was the first capital of Free France and its name became a household word for millions who didn't know Lake Chad from Lake Pontchatrain. The more glamorous days of Radio Brazzaville are over now, but music spun by its African disc jockeys from a collection of 25,000 records can be heard as far away as Japan, and the station receives three hundred letters a month from the United States. Brazzaville, which was founded by one of the explorer's companions and was known as M'Fa, has a magnificent 750-bed hospital (12,000 beds in all Equatoria), the ultra-modern Savorgnan de Brazza high school of 500 pupils (20 per cent of the republic's budget is allocated to education), and Maya-Maya, one of the finest international airports in Africa. The second city and old capital of the Congo Republic, Pointe-Noire, is a masterpiece of city planning: the city is laid out in the shape of a fan and the gaily painted huts of the new Tie-Tie quarter give this town of 35,000 a constant holiday air. Its bathing beaches, Mondaine and

Sauvage, are right out of a travel brochure and its five-square-mile harbour, used by thirty shipping companies, handles more than 500,000 tons of freight per year and has wine storage tanks capable of holding 130,000 gallons.

Race relations are remarkably good. Any night at the Bal Dou-Dou or the Congo-Ocean, hang-outs of Brazzaville's smart set, you will see Frenchmen dancing with well-turned-out Negro girls. On the terrace of the plush Hotel Relais, mixed couples gather in the soft evenings to watch the lights of Leopoldville go on and catch the stirrings of the evening breeze. This happy situation is the result not so much of French virtue as of mosquitoes, impenetrable forests and the collar-wilting heat of the Congo Republic: these conditions prevented white settlement. Of the 10,000 whites, almost all are shop-owners financially dependent upon an African clientele. In the interior are only missionaries and a few white administrators. The former create no problem and most of the latter, with a few startling exceptions the majority of whom came from Indo-China, are resigned.

THE CENTRAL AFRICAN REPUBLIC

The Central African Republic, formerly the territory of Ubangi-Shari, borders Cameroun on the west, the Congo Republic and the ex-Belgian Congo on the south, the Sudan on the east and Chad on the north. Like the Congo Republic, the life of this republic, the size of California and Kansas put together, is conditioned by its rivers, of which 3,000 miles are navigable for at least part of the year. Its southern boundary is formed by the Ubangi, which connects it to Brazzaville and the sea, and its highway to Chad and the north is the Shari, navigable for 600 miles. The republic possesses not a mile of railway and the 745-mile steamer trip up the river from Brazzaville takes twelve days, if you are lucky enough to miss all the sandbars. It takes thirty days to get a ton of freight from the coast to Bangui.

The Central African Republic has 1·2 million people and is a veritable anthropologist's paradise. In the north live the Sara people, whose women insert huge discs into their lips. This is the southernmost point of Arab conquest and it is said that, to save their women from being stolen in slave-raids, these Negroes disfigured their faces to make them unattractive to the Arabs. One would say that they succeeded. Now that the danger of slave-raids is past—although domestic slavery, of course, still exists here as it does all over Africa—the custom is dying out despite the opposition of the older women, who think it scandalous that a circumcised girl should go around with her lips not distended. In a few years, the anthropologist seeking the 'duck-billed women' may well find them painting their lips with rouge from Paris, not stretching them with plates. There is a tribe famed for the ability of its drummers, appropriately named M'Boom, and in the depths of the forest are some twenty thousand Pygmies, a race of aboriginal hunters accompanied by their voiceless yellow dogs. The Pygmies are more mud-coloured than black and the Negroes say that the little people 'come from the root of the world' and are the disinherited fathers of Africa. They live in elliptical-shaped huts seven feet long and three feet high and are generally monogamous, because of a traditional shortage of women. The Pygmies, not yet commercialized like those of the ex-Belgian Congo, live by gathering roots and berries, and by hunting the elephant, 'that great and joyful meat'. In an annual ceremony the Pygmies burn a giant lizard and all members of the clan eat its flesh in ritual communion. The little people are excessively fond of dancing to tunes twanged out on a curious musical instrument called a *sanza*: iron strips drawn across the shell of a tortoise.

The Central African Republic is remote and poor, soil depletion, erosion and deforestation are rampant. It has peanuts, cotton, a few diamonds (2 million carats have been extracted but production now has fallen to 150,000 carats per year) and a little gold. Coffee and cacao plantations are just making a start. From its products, the Central African Republic earns less than £5·4 million annually while imports exceed £7·1 million. A lack of power (cheap or otherwise), shortage of skilled labour, low domestic consumption levels and sparse population all mitigate against industrialization. French aid through 1957 amounted to £18 million and the economic situation might be improved by construction of the proposed 466-mile railway linking Bangui and Berbere, on a navigable section of the Shari, leading to Fort Lamy.

Bangui, the capital and a city of about 70,000, is one of the most charming of Equatorial African towns. Built with taste and a good sense of proportion, it is dominated by a green hill fleshed with giant trees. It has an ultra-modern hotel, a small hydro-electric plant and some light industry. Parts of the interior are cool uplands and the whole country teems with game. But the Central African Republic's economic future appears bleak.

The political leader of the country at the time of our visit was

Barthelemy Boganda, the son of a cannibalistic witch-doctor. This jovial, erudite Negro studied for the Catholic priesthood and was ordained, which meant that he had about six times as much education as anybody else in Ubangi-Shari. In 1946, he ran for and was elected to the French Assembly on a nationalist ticket. His political activities (like all African politicians, he co-operated with the French Communists until 1949) got him into trouble with his bishop, who also took a dim view of the priest's marriage to his French secretary.

Boganda's fall from grace did not worry him too much; throwing himself into political life, the unfrocked priest guided his MESAN (*Mouvement d'évolution sociale en Afrique Noire*) party so well that it soon commanded all fifty seats in the Ubangi-Shari assembly and he became mayor of Bangui. When de Gaulle came to Brazzaville, Boganda, then president of the Federal Assembly of all French Equatorial Africa, threw his considerable influence behind the General.

The fact that Boganda had been educated in Ubangi-Shari, Middle Congo, Cameroun and Belgian Congo—coupled with the impoverished state of his own territory—led him to become the vigorous advocate of a huge state which he hoped would become 'the United States of Latin Africa'. Boganda, who had more than once been accused of enslaving Pygmies to work on his plantations, wanted to join together not only the four states of French Equatorial Africa but portions of Angola, Cameroun and ex-Belgian Congo as well. 'All the peoples of Afro-Latin culture,' he said, 'belong together; we are not responsible for the arbitrary boundaries created by the greed of Europe.'

This prosperous coffee planter was not above using means reminiscent of his witch-doctor father to gain his political ends: he once demonstrated his powers to his terrified followers by announcing, on the verge of a solar eclipse, that he would 'blot out the sun'. Through a combination of bunkum, ability and energy, Boganda, who never denied his followers' belief that he was immortal, established his hold firmly on Ubangi-Shari, gained powerful support in Middle Congo and claimed some adherents in Chad. Leon M'Ba, jealous of Gabon's resources, and the Abbé Fulbert Youlou, who feared that his co-religionist's personal appeal would overshadow his own, combined to defeat Boganda's plans for a great central African empire.

Boganda was still working hard to reverse this trend when, in April 1959, the twin-engined plane carrying him from Berberati to Bangui fell in flames into the jungle. Barthelemy Boganda, ex-priest, ex-Communist and firm friend of France and America, died in the crash at the age of forty-eight, and was succeeded as premier by his cousin, twenty-eight-year-old David Dacko. To the Stone Age people of the Central African Republic, the charred and twisted body of Barthelemy Boganda meant simply that the magic of the Abbé Fulbert Youlou had proved too strong for their black Napoleon.

CHAD

Chad, the largest, most populous and poorest of the four equatorial republics, is bounded on the east by the Sudan, on the north by Libya, on the west by Mali and Cameroun, and on the south by the Central African Republic.

Across the northern wastes wander Senussi nomads who make it a point of honour both to avoid the census and to evade the tax-collector, while the horsemen of the lake district wear quilted armour or chain-mail (reinforced with flattened cigarette tins) whose inspiration must have come from the Crusaders. From the hot flats of the Bahr Azoum to the lofty heights of 11,360-foot Emi Koussi and the lunar lacework of the Tibesti mountains, wander these proud nomads, following their great herds of thin, hunch-backed cattle. On the day of her wedding, a nomad bride is snatched from a richly caparisoned camel covered with cowrie shells, bells, bright enamel pots, feathers and rich cloth, borne away into the desert by her lover in a ceremony whose origins go back into the roots of time.

There is a tribe called the Boo-Boos; some of the people live in huts of curious slates made of mud which look rather like inverted eggshells with scales (or a moulded chocolate jelly), and 91 per cent of the children receive no schooling. It was from Chad's capital, Fort Lamy (population: 20,000), that General Leclerc and his Free French launched their fantastic drive across the Sahara against Rommel. Fort Lamy was a vital stage in the air-ferry route which brought American bombers from the United States to Egypt, and the French—who maintain that he who controls Chad rules Africa—still regard the area as vital to the defence of their community. A section of Fort Lamy, for reasons which escape me, is known as Paris-Congo, and a young Chadian named Idriss Mahamat is the Community's best junior high jumper, having cleared nearly six feet at the age of fourteen.

The country is shaped like a saucer and, millions of years ago, it was a vast inland fresh-water sea. All that remains of this now are the petrified crocodile droppings which dot the desert and the great cattle trough of Lake Chad, as large as Lake Ontario. Chad is equatorial only in the sense that it was grouped in F.E.A. for administrative purposes. Its people are mostly Semitic or Hamitic rather than negroid, Muslim rather than fetishist. Culturally, economically and politically, Chad looks east, west and north to Arab Africa, not south to Negro Equatoria.

This world-without-end, a great pasture twice the size of France (or bigger than California, Texas and New York combined), has a small and backward population. Although the republic's 2·6 million nomads constitute 53 per cent of Equatorial Africa's total population, they are outnumbered four to one by their vast herds of cattle, sheep and goats. It is well that their herds are large, for the soil of Chad is so poor that it will not support even manioc, the starvation crop of Africa. Cotton-seed accounts for £6 million of Chad's £7·5 million worth of annual exports, 40,000 head of cattle, 1,600 tons of meat and a few peanuts making up the balance. The government's annual internal revenue amounts to about £2 million while expenditures are twice that much. French aid since 1947 has been in the neighbourhood of £24 million. The country has 18,504 miles of roads but, as recently as 1956, less than 500 miles of these were described as all-weather. Fort Lamy has a radio station aimed at Muslim listeners in the states of Equatorial Africa and its airfield handles 12,000 tons of freight per year, a total exceeded within the French Community only by Paris' Orly Field.

In the days of King Alfred great kingdoms existed in Chad. Copper-rich Kanem, in the far north, reached the height of its power under the eleventh-century Idris kings (an Idris rules today in Libya). These Muslim potentates, who did not go out in public and spoke only through a curtain, ruled from Kanem to Bornu and from Kotoko to Mousgoum. They conquered the second great Muslim empire, that of Baguirmi, as Columbus made his New World landfall. In the nineteenth century, the bloodthirsty Muslim princes of Oudda made Baguirmi tributary and the half-mad, blind Mohammed-Cherif crushed Bornu.

At the end of the last century, a Soudanese slave named Rabah seized the leadership of Oudda and, driven by the dream of a great Chadic empire, called for a Holy War against the oncoming French. This last great adversary of the European conquest of Africa was killed in 1900. But it was not until 1912 that the French were able to pacify the fierce 'white' nomads of the north. Thus, well within the life-span of living men, Chad has made the full circuit from Muslim empire to

French colony and back again to autonomy. When it comes to politics, the sleeping giant of Africa is the most volatile of all continents.

The dominant figure in Chad's politics for many years was a man in Eboué's image. He is forty-one-year-old Gabriel Lisette, a suave mulatto called by his friends 'the American'. Lisette, who has the stamp of greatness, was born, of all places, in Panama, where his parents had emigrated from Guadalupe. When he was a boy, his parents returned to their island home and he received his education in Guadalupe. It was there that his feet were set upon the track which he has followed. He won an essay contest, the prize for which was a trip with the island's governor. The governor's name: Felix Eboué. Eboué inspired Lisette to enter the colonial service, which he did after winning a scholarship to France, by obtaining admission to C.O.L.O., France's school for colonial administrators. When World War II broke out, Lisette was called up and posted to Morocco, where he remained until the invasion of North Africa. Posted to Brazzaville to work as political assistant to the governor, he was soon in hot water over his radical opinions and—at the moment when Eboué and de Gaulle were creating the shape of a new Africa at Brazzaville—was sent to a punishment post in Chad. Although the smooth-talking West Indian had about as much in common with the average Chadian as an Eskimo does with a Spaniard, Lisette's capabilities were patent and he was asked by the local people to stand as their representative to the French Assembly. Within a matter of weeks after his 'exile', Lisette found himself in Paris. Chad, which had been Eboué's springboard to prominence, had opened the way for another great black Frenchman.

Lisette had associated the Chad Progressive Party, which he founded, with the R.D.A., French Africa's most powerful political bloc, and in Paris he became administrative secretary of the R.D.A.'s parliamentary group. Opposition from the French helped him to lose his seat in the 1951 elections but Lisette stayed on in Paris to work for the realignment of the R.D.A., which meant ending its Communist affiliations, thus winning back French support. He was elected to the territorial assembly in 1952 and, five years later, returned to the French Assembly as president of the R.D.A. group. On the local scene he easily became mayor of Fort Lamy and was selected as premier of Chad. By the sheer force of his personality Lisette ruled his arid adopted country through the *Entente Républicaine*, a hodge-podge of socialists, Gaullists and tribal leaders. But Chad, torn politically in several directions, economically emaciated and racked with tribal feuds, proved too wild a horse to ride: in early 1959, after several reversals in by-elections, a group of tribal delegates withdrew their support from Lisette and he was replaced by an African premier, Sahoulba Gontchome. But Chad soon discovered that if it couldn't live with Lisette, it couldn't exist without him: Gontchome's government fell as did the two which succeeded it within a matter of weeks.

In April of 1959 the R.D.A. swept back to power and Lisette was again invited to become premier. Perhaps because he has his eyes set on bigger targets and realizes that Chad, if only for the sake of its pride, needs an African premier, he declined the post, which went to his deputy, François Tombalbaye. Lisette contented himself with the title of deputy prime minister, with special responsibility for external affairs.

But Lisette remained the power behind the scenes in Chad, which recognized this fact by naming him 'First Citizen of Honour of the Republic of Chad' in 1959. In the same year he was awarded the Legion of Honour for services to the French Community, of which he was one of the architects. As vice-president of the French Africa-wide R.D.A., Lisette's influence extends far beyond Chad's borders and he was instrumental in creating the Equatorial African customs union.

In May of 1959 new elections were held in Chad; Lisette's party won fifty of eighty-five seats, the majority in his own constituency was overwhelming and once more he was offered the premiership. Again he refused. Tombalbaye took over and last year, perhaps fearing for his own political future, stripped Lisette of his honours and barred him from Chad. De Gaulle, recognizing his abilities, last October gave firm evidence of his respect for the West Indian by naming him one of the four *Ministres-Conseillers* from Africa, with special responsibilities for economic and social affairs for the entire community. Gabriel Lisette, assisted by his talented French wife, seems destined to play an important role in the future of both France and Africa.

But it takes more than a man to alter the fact that Chad has no good route to the sea, no railway (although a branch of the Nigerian system is being extended towards Lake Chad, and, as has been noted, a line may be pushed through from Bangui), no exports except meat and cottonseed, a 100 per cent trade deficit, the lowest *per capita* income in Equatorial Africa and few schools.

HEART OF DARKNESS

A SHORTAGE OF DEMONS

Before leaving Gabon and the Union of Central African Republics, we must take a look at something which we never saw in the Sudan, Ethiopia or Somalia: a living, indigenous art. European art patrons, painters and sculptors of the second quarter of this century have so idealized African art that one expects to find a continent bursting with creativity. One finds, instead, only work that is for the most part shabby and imitative.

The great African art of the past—and it was truly great—was a religious art glorifying (and hoping to propitiate) a pantheon of animistic deities. The spiritual world of the African was a universe of demons and terror and it was in the portrayal of the demonic that the priest-artist excelled. When sunglasses, crepe-soled shoes, bicycles, missionaries, Harvester tractors and Western administration routed this empire of fear, the art form died with it.

Within twenty years of the arrival of the Europeans, there was no painting, no good sculpture, little weaving and only a bit of crude pottery. The people, once they were able to buy an enamel basin, were unwilling to decorate an all too perishable calabash.

It should be pointed out, however, that many forms of Negro art were already forgotten *before* the white man reached Africa. Is Africa, then, a primitive or a degenerate society? Is it on the way up or is it a civilization in decline? These are questions which have political as well as artistic relevance.

People interested in African art—and it should be noted that these are almost entirely whites, not Negroes—are doing their best to preserve what is left of it and to help the African towards new forms of expression. 'The Plains' of Brazzaville (the lower part of town as opposed to the upper, called 'The Plateau') is the focal point of this movement and boasts two art centres.

Pierre Lods, a young French artist-photographer with a thin fringe of a beard, nervous hands and a mincing walk, came to Brazzaville for a visit in 1949, saw a painting done by his houseboy in imitation of his own work and was impressed by the natural rhythm and form of the untrained African's work. He stayed on to open an art centre in two thatched huts.

Lods' 'students' vary in number from day to day. An African walks in, perhaps from hundreds of miles away in the bush, and says he wants to paint. Lods, who receives financial assistance from the government, gives him brushes, paints, paper and leaves him to it. He offers no advice unless asked but accepts for exhibition and sale only about a tenth of what each artist produces. Some Africans stay with him only a few days, learn enough basic techniques to paint the crude stuff to be sold to airline pilots at a shilling a throw and resold in New York for £3 10s. as 'an African original'.

Of those who stay on with Lods at Poto-Poto (a suburb of Brazzaville; the name means, in a word, 'mud'), some produce works both beautiful and grotesque, fantasy-worlds peopled with almost-men and strange animals writhing and bending, flashing in colours unimagined by the European eye. All our verbal and written knowledge of the African mind is conditioned by the fact that the African is expressing himself in a foreign language, be it English, French or Portuguese; it is like looking through a pane of faulty glass. With no language barrier to contend with, the best of Lods' students bring the white man, for a moment, into a world which he never knew existed because he views it with a different eye.

Not all Poto-Poto art, of course, reaches this standard. But most of it conveys a remarkable sense of rhythm—everything the African does, from fornicating to digging a ditch, exudes this quality—and the form and composition are interesting. Although Lods has been able to prevent his students from becoming derivative in regard to European art, he has no means of preventing them from adopting a symbiotic relationship to each other. As a result, after ten years of existence, most Poto-Poto art has tended to become highly stylized and a little flat. The demonic has gone out of it or, if it remains, has become merely funny. But the best of Poto-Poto is still very good indeed.

At Brazzaville's other art centre, the *Ecole des Arts et Artisans*, also government-supported, young Africans produce paintings, ceramics, sculpture and bookbinding of a high degree of competence and with occasional flashes of genius. This centre, however, is geared to production of art of commercial value and the African falls all too easily into aping what has gone before rather than seeking a new fount of creativity within himself.

This generation of African artists, with a few exceptions, has shaken off the old demonic spirit, the artistry of malevolent fear, and is now in the process of absorbing the techniques of Western art without understanding its substance. In the best works coming out of Brazzaville one senses that, although the demons are gone, they are not always completely forgotten. When another century has diluted the

Western influence, these exceptions to the rule raise the possibility of an African artistic rebirth, either in the old tradition or something entirely new. For the moment, the shortage of demons is to be lamented.

Chapter 9

---
*

HOUSE DIVIDED

Wedged between the Nigerian giant and what used to be French Equatorial Africa, is newly-independent Cameroun, a country the size of California with fewer people than Chicago. Cameroun—the name comes from the Portuguese word for prawns, a suitable number of which inhabit the offshore waters—has red orchids fifteen feet tall, a giant frog with feet as big as a man's fist, and a galaxy of bugs, mostly of belligerent disposition.

Cameroun, which has been under three flags (German, French and British), unfurled its own red, yellow and green tricolour on January 1, 1960, its day of independence, to become Africa's eleventh nation and the eighty-third member of the U.N. It has an official motto ('Peace, Work, Country'), a national anthem, 12,000 citizens with postal savings accounts and considerably more with V.D.

The new nation is bordered on the south by the Spanish enclave of Rio Muni, Gabon and the Congo Republic, on the east and north by the Central African Republic and Chad, on the west by Nigeria and the Atlantic Ocean. The country is shaped like an amply-proportioned matron seated looking towards Khartoum, or a pistol with the barrel pressed against the head of Lake Chad. The rains are so torrential and the heat so muggy that French settlers and civil servants—of whom there are still about 10,000—refer to Cameroun as 'Africa's arm-pit', a crude but accurate metaphor.

Cameroun lies just north of the Equator and its people range from light Semites in the savannahs of the North to coal-black Bantus in the forested South. So diverse is the population—the 3·2 million Camerounians are split up into nearly 200 tribes—that this has been called the racial crossroads of Africa. In the arid North live the cattle people, 700,000 pagans ruled over by half as many light-skinned Muslim Fulanis headed by emirs or lamidos. As throughout the west coast of the New Africa, these tribes of the interior are primitive, conservative, economically retarded and opposed to Western-style education.

The South, stream-creased and shamrock-green, contains the capital city of Yaounde, the country's humming industrial centre of Edea, Douala, the principal port, and matches the North in population. Most Southerners are Catholics or animists with a sprinkling of Protestants, and socially they range from the most polished of gentlemen to depraved corpse-eaters. One tribe has developed seven varieties of millet but none bothered to invent the wheel.

The West, which amounts to only about 3 per cent of the area of Cameroun, is densely populated by the Bamileke people, a progressive tribe (650,000-strong) now racked by civil war, which once tilled its highlands like Swiss peasants and grew rich on coffee and cacao. Here Protestants are in the majority.

To pay for its newly-won independence, Cameroun each year exports 320,000 tons of produce worth £28·4 million. Two-thirds of this is accounted for by five crops: cacao (56,000 tons), coffee (15,000 tons), bananas (85,000 tons), wood and cotton. She also exports aluminium, some tobacco, rubber and palm products. In come 360,000 tons of trucks, cement, petrol, wine (of which the Camerounians are inordinately fond), cotton cloth and other manufactured articles worth about £32·4 million. Before independence Cameroun had such a huge trade deficit that France had to subsidize directly 50 per cent of the £19 million national budget. Through an austerity programme geared to slash expenses, and by retaining a loose association with France which enables it to receive substantial French financial assistance, Cameroun somehow manages to make ends meet.

Food crops grown in the South include cassava, yams, corn and plantains while the North lives on rice, millet and peanuts. An estimated 600,000 head of cattle roam the North but the social structure and lack of processing facilities or cheap transport retard the development of meat production. All cacao production is in black hands and one Yaounde chief has a plantation of 18,000 trees (another owns 26,000 rubber trees).

Hopeful aspects of Cameroun's economic picture include the Edea aluminium factory and the presence of considerable mineral reserves. The Edea dam across the Sanaga River, completed in 1957, has the third largest power plant in the French Community with its installed capacity of two million kilowatt hours. The £6 million plant produces 1,200 million kilowatt hours per year to light the port of Douala and run the ALUCAM (*Compagnie Camerounaise d'Aluminium*) factory. ALUCAM, which is 10 per cent owned by the Camerounian government, went into operation in late 1957 and now produces 45,000 tons of aluminium per year. Edea is the largest aluminium plant in Africa and yet another dam may be built up-stream to double its capacity. Alumina is imported from *France*, processed and exported to the Metropole in the form of aluminium ingots, a startling reversal of the classical colonial situation in which Africa was expected to export raw materials and absorb the manufactured articles of Europe. Only now are economists beginning to realize that Africa is poor in agricultural produce but potentially rich in minerals and hydro-electric power. In time, the continent may well become an *importer* of food, an exporter of manufactured goods.

Cameroun is banking heavily on exploitation of the recently-discovered Nkongsamba bauxite deposits. These have only a 45 per cent alumina content but are close to the railhead, and the presence of large quantities of natural gas near Douala would facilitate the first processing stage necessary before the ore could be treated at Edea, thus completing a very profitable manufacturing cycle. Large deposits of iron ore have also been found and, although these are low grade (40 per cent), they are only seven miles from the sea, hence exploitation and transport would not be difficult. There are also vast deposits of rutile, a strategic mineral from which titanium is made, and a complex of light industries has been established in Douala and Yaounde. To put Cameroun on its economic feet (and to demonstrate the advantages of membership in the French Community), France sank £100 million in the country between 1947 and 1959, most of it in outright grants and the rest in long-term loans.

Highways were improved—the country has 400 miles of paved roads —and the 300-mile rail network built by the Germans, which links Douala with Yaounde and taps the once-rich Bamileke country, was modernized. Plans are afoot to extend the railway all the way to Lake Chad. The port of Douala has been modernized and a magnificent 1·5 mile bridge constructed across the Cameroun River. Whatever her colonial sins may be, French aid to under-developed areas has been exceeded only by U.S. contributions (when national incomes are compared, France proportionately spends three times as much as the United States) and 10 per cent of France's tax revenues over recent years has been devoted to the economic development of the Gallic giant.

Yaounde, which has 3,800 white residents, is in the centre of the country and has little to recommend it, although our memories may be warped by the difficulties we had in reaching the town. It was

November and the roads from the Ogooue to Yaounde were just that. For days we lurched through the jungle, got stuck in quagmires and either dug ourselves out or were providentially extricated by the arrival of a forestry officer or a game warden in a Land Rover. At one point we reached a gorge to find the bridge completely out and the water rising fast. A fistful of francs and the good offices of a local Frenchman produced fifty Africans who, in a few hours, built a log bridge which looked as if it might just hold the weight of the truck. I sent Kitty across on foot, eased the truck on to the logs, raced the motor and got almost across when part of the bridge collapsed, leaving the left front wheel and me teetering over a fifty-foot drop into the stream. Only the strength of a hundred arms saved the two of us.

Seventy miles south of Yaounde (population: 39,000), a rear-spring coupling broke and the body settled with a thud on to the wheels. I sent Kitty on to Yaounde in a passing African lorry with instructions to seek what aid and comfort the American consulate might be able to offer. By dint of jacking the body off the wheels and tying the broken coupling with my belt I was able to go on at 5 m.p.h. until there appeared a small village which miraculously had a coupling which would fit the Chevrolet. Five hours later, the car and I limped into Yaounde to find Kitty in tears on the steps of the consulate which happened to be closed that afternoon.

It is the saving grace of Gallic Africa that, no matter how bad the day may be, the night always brings a shower, *tournedos provençal*, a bottle of Beaujolais, a cheese-board groaning with Camembert, a cognac and, at the last, a clean bed in a good room (Cameroun boasts twenty-five hotels with 414 rooms). It is among the great crimes of imperial Britain that she failed to introduce the shower to Africa and taught her black minions to cook like the English. It is small wonder that the native *élite* of British Africa is restive under this culinary yoke.

The most distinctive thing about Yaounde is the amount of taxi-riding indulged in at rates far from cheap. Cab drivers are usually accompanied by friends or members of the family and the cash customer must squeeze in amongst these as best he can. Rates are capricious and a white man is charged ten times as much for a trip of equal distance as an African is. Revenge for the Berlin Conference of 1885, I suppose.

Yaounde has a startlingly modernistic cathedral at the base of which are a cluster of petrol stations of dubious artistic merit, a super-market where everything from palm oil in calabashes to £5 nylon slips is sold, a good bookshop, and one stylish dress shop, which is about all the small European population can support. The rest of the commercial town is geared to the African trade. The streets are lined with Greek and Syrian-run shops while 'mammies' peddle huge platters of fried fritters and Muslim merchants hawk kola nuts, sandals and pillows along the streets.

POSTAL IMPERIALISM

On August 7, 1879, King Akwa, who ruled just south of Mount Cameroon, penned a letter to his fellow-monarch, Queen Victoria. This is what he said:

'Dearest Madam—We your servants have join together and thoughts its better to write you a nice loving letter which will tell you about all our wishes. We wish to have your laws in our towns. We want to have every fashion altered, also we will do according to your Consul's word. Plenty wars here in our country. Plenty murder and idol worshippers. Perhaps these lines of our writing will look to you as an idle tale . . . when we heard about Calabar River, how they have all English laws in their towns, and how they have put away all their superstitions, Oh!, we shall be very glad to be like Calabar now.'

The Widow at Windsor apparently was behind on her correspondence because King Akwa—who has a hotel named after him in Douala— never heard from her. Two years later, he and his colleague, King Bell, sent a note to Gladstone ('as we heard here that you are a chief man in the House of Commons') asking that he 'do for mercy sake' take Cameroun under British protection.

Still the British did nothing. Consul Hewett, whose job it was to protect the missionaries and traders scattered along the coast, went home on leave while Lord Granville, the Foreign Minister characterized by one British historian as 'never remarkable for penetration or acumen', twiddled his thumbs.

While perfidious Albion was twiddling, German Chancellor Bismarck who (mistaking cause for effect) believed that Britain was great because she had a colonial empire, was moving to gain for Germany a foothold in West Africa. Like Italy, Germany was slow to come to the African table because of the tardiness of her political unification and indus-trialization. Bismarck called to Berlin Dr. Gustav Nachtigal, an old Africa hand who had wandered all over the Lake Chad-Kordofan area in the 1870's, and told him to start packing. Now these were the days when, if you had the yen to annex a couple of hundred thousand square miles of Africa, it was considered sporting to let the other enthusiasts, the British and French, know about it. Then they could send a gunboat racing for the same spot.

But old 'Blood-and-Iron' had other ideas as to how to play the game. He planted stories in all the German papers saying that Nachtigal was off on a round of visits to German commercial companies on the Gulf of Guinea. This seemed logical enough: German merchants such as the Hamburg firm of Woermann and Co. had been on the West Coast for more than twenty years.

The British finally saw the light and sent a disgruntled Consul Hewett packing back to Cameroun. He arrived on July 19, 1883, to find the German flag unfurled and King Akwa in no mood to write any more 'loving letters'. The monarch's disappointment at not being extended British protection had been well assuaged by Nachtigal's gift of cash and enough rum to keep everybody on Mount Cameroon drunk for a week.

This happy state of affairs did not last very long and, as in their other African possessions, the Germans had to resort to that most persuasive of all implements, the bayonet. They fought no less than twenty-nine campaigns in Cameroun during one twelve-year period. Most of the histories of the European penetration of Africa like to dwell on the horrors of the German administration of Tanganyika, South West Africa, Cameroun and Togo. A more than ample supply there is of stories recounting how the Hun lurched around the countryside skewering piccaninnies like shishkebab and playing poker on the naked bellies of African women. It seems necessary if indelicate to point out that nine out of ten of these histories were written by French or British authors in hot blood after World War I when their countries had a more than casual interest in explaining to the world how much better off the natives of these colonies, which they in their generosity had divided between them, would be under their enlightened care.

The Germans were rough. There's no doubt about that: they killed thousands in Tanganyika during the Maji-Maji rebellion and virtually exterminated the proud Hereros of South West Africa. But there is considerable evidence which suggests that they were just, energetic and efficient. In Cameroun, the Germans respected the integrity of native society in the North and applied themselves vigorously and systemati-cally to the development of tropical agriculture. They have been scored for seizing native lands in Cameroun but at the end of the thirty-three-year German occupation, exactly fifty-six white estates had been established covering 450 square miles, less than one-quarter of one per cent of the area of the colony. The older generation of Africans well remembers the Germans and few speak of them with anger. Said one old Yaounde greybeard: 'German man, he be hard; but he be fair man and by golly native feller have plenty chop in that time.'

BANANA SPLIT

When World War I broke out, the British invaded Cameroun—or Kamerun, as it was then called—from Nigeria while the French marched in from Gabon. The Germans and their African contingents, although heavily outnumbered, fought well and managed to hold out for two years. When their ammunition was all but exhausted, they brushed aside a French column and fought their way into neutral Spanish Rio Muni. They were interned on the island of Fernando Po under guard of a small and sleepy Spanish garrison and remained a constant threat to Nigeria for the rest of the war without lifting a finger.

At Versailles, Cameroun was split between France and Britain as League of Nations mandates. The British took two unconnected slices adjoining the eastern frontier of Nigeria which together have a population of 1·4 million, the fog-wreathed volcano, the old and pleasant German capital of Buea, most of the bananas and an area the size of Hungary. The French, in lieu of bananas, took most of the country (166,800 square miles) including a finger of territory touching the Congo which they had ceded to Germany in 1911 in return for a free hand in Morocco, the two railways, and the port of Douala, which is bigger (118,000) and more lively than Yaounde.

Between the wars the German settlers bought back their banana plantations and when Hitler invaded Poland there were more Germans than British in the British Cameroon and these unlucky farmers again found their estates confiscated and themselves behind barbed wire.

After World War II, both Britain and France converted their portions of Cameroons into trust territories which they administered under the United Nations. Later in this chapter we will consider developments in the British Cameroons. As far as the larger French sector was concerned, the New Deal meant that it shared not only in the political and economic benefits arising out of post-war French liberalism—the Brazzaville conference, FIDES (*Fond d'investissement pour le développement économique et social des territoires d'Outre-mer*), the *loi cadre*—

but that, as 'an associated territory' rather than a colony like Gabon or Chad, it enjoyed a slightly different and more independent position. Ordinances restricting trade, for instance, could not be imposed by Paris without the consent of the Camerounian Assembly. A vigorous trade union movement (membership: 36,000) sprang up and politics, in which tribal associations such as the Ngondo in Douala, the Kolo-Beti in Yaounde and the Kumze among the Bamileke play a major role, became active and radical. Political expression also made itself known through 32 youth movements, 43 cultural associations, 9 women's groups, 232 sporting associations and 68 newspapers and journals. Cameroun, like other French African territories, sent delegates (twelve) to the three representative bodies of France and the French Union.

DESIGN FOR REBELLION

While all this was going on, a squat thirty-three-year-old African was boarding a train in Paris bound for Germany. His name was Ruben Um Nyobe and he was a Bassa tribesman from the broken jungle country between Douala and Yaounde, the district known as Sanaga-Maritime. Now the Bassa are an unusual people. Like Kenya's Kikuyu, they are independent-minded and have no chiefs or traditional headmen. They live in scattered forest villages in the country bisected by the Douala-Yaounde railway and the largest social unit is the clan. Each village is ruled by a council of elders.

From this essentially democratic background Ruben Um Nyobe went to a mission school run by American Presbyterians. There he gained a reputation for being polite, studious and devout, and the missionaries at one time thought he might make a good pastor. Um Nyobe seriously considered it because the Presbyterian Church in Africa fitted in with his political ideals: it was democratically run by Africans, not administered by whites. But he had bigger dreams than preaching in a bush church and Ruben Um Nyobe worked his passage to France.

In Paris he found many friends, both white and black, who shared with him (or said they did) a dream of a reunited and independent Cameroun. It was on their advice that he found himself boarding the train for Stuttgart. There he changed trains and, a day later, he was in Prague. In the People's Republic of Czechoslovakia he learned the mechanics of sedition.

When Ruben Um Nyobe returned to Cameroun in 1950, he was able to get a job as a government clerk. He was active in the Communist-dominated Douala branch of the General Confederation of Labour, kept up with his church work, and with the assistance of a trio who also knew something of Prague-style democracy—'Dr.' Felix Roland Moumie, Ernest Ouandie and Abel Kingue—organized a political party called *l'Union des Populations du Cameroun*. The U.P.C. had three planks to its platform: immediate separation from France, unification of French and British Cameroons, and independence for the combined state. To it and to its sister organizations—the Young Democrats of Cameroun (J.D.C.) and the Democratic Union of Camerounian Women (U.D.D.F.C.)—gravitated the hotheads of the country.

In May 1955 the U.P.C. staged some riots for the benefit of a visiting U.N. mission and the organization and its affiliates found itself proscribed. Moumie, Um Nyobe and other U.P.C. leaders took refuge in British Cameroons and set up a 'government-in-exile'. From its Kumba headquarters the U.P.C. heaped abuse on the *'valets et mercenaires des colonialistes'* and issued a directive to the Camerounian people stating that independence could not be achieved without the formation of an anti-imperialist front, the organization of the workers and an armed revolt. Although the French have never been enthusiastic about complete independence for Black Africa, this was hardly true: universal suffrage had been granted by the *loi cadre* and elections for the Camerounian Assembly were scheduled under this enabling act for December 1956.

It is more likely that U.P.C. leaders and their white Communist advisers reasoned (correctly) that their timing had been off: they had had the field to themselves as the only well-organized political party and now, with elections coming up, they found themselves exiled and their party illegal. It was obvious that others were to snatch the plums of office from the tree which they had shaken.

Since they could not participate in the elections, the U.P.C. leaders determined to wreck them. Ruben Um Nyobe slipped back across the border to organize a revolt along lines remarkably similar to Fidel Castro's. In each administrative region a military organization known as the 'great quarter' was established. Every quarter was divided into sectors and every sector into sections. Um Nyobe knew that he could not stand up to the French in open warfare so in each section he set up guerrilla units of thirty men led by a 'top sergeant'. Each unit was assigned a specific bridge to blow up, village to burn, length of railway to destroy, road-block to build, candidate for the Assembly to terrorize or community from which to extort funds or supplies. Each unit trained secretly and intensively.

The election was set for December 23, 1956. Um Nyobe went into action five days earlier. Within twenty-four hours a locomotive had been derailed, lengths of track torn up, the telegraph between Yaounde and Douala cut, road-blocks established, and tank-traps dug. Non-U.P.C. tribesmen were warned not to participate in the election, candidates were flogged and vehicles belonging to whites were burned. Fortunately for the political stability of Cameroon, the revolt was confined almost completely to Um Nyobe's Bassa people. The proud Muslims of the North—who regarded the Negro as no more than a forest-dwelling eater of dirt, an abomination from Dar el-Harb, the country of the infidels—held themselves aloof. The authoritarian Catholic bishops, who hated Um Nyobe as much for his fundamentalist religious beliefs as for his ardent nationalism, kept their people out of it. The Bulu and Douala tribes, who are related to the Bassa, wavered but thought better of it and stayed at home. The Bamileke people, a vital link in his line of communications to the British Cameroons, were restive but divided.

Even in Bassaland the going got thick: troop trains from Douala chugged slowly towards Yaounde, repairing the track as they went; combat-hardened parachutists fresh from Algeria dropped into Edea and Eseka, industrial centres in the heart of the Bassa country; French and Senegalese troops sortied from Yaounde and smashed several key road-blocks. After election-day terrorism during which two candidates for the Camerounian Assembly were assassinated and polling booths burned, troops supported by tribal levies struck back at the U.P.C. Catholic clans, never averse to having a crack at the Protestant Bassa, hurled themselves against U.P.C. villages. Stores were looted and churches burned. 'If you owed a man money,' recalled a French officer, 'it was an appropriate moment to liquidate your debt with a machete.' Nobody knows how many died on that wild Christmas Eve; government sources say 100, others less sanguine say 2,000.

The revolt was a failure in the sense that it neither ousted the French nor prevented the election, in which 921,000 Camerounians (55 per cent of the electorate) cast their votes. Only in Bassaland were abstentions high. But terrorism continued and, on June 3, 1957, the British ordered the U.P.C. to cease its political activities or leave their sector.

Of the thirteen U.P.C. leaders, all but Ruben Um Nyobe fled to Cairo, leaving their Bassa followers to their fate. Ruben Um Nyobe slipped back into Bassaland to continue the fight. Nothing in his twisted, bloody career became the barrel-chested Presbyterian more than his renunciation of the easy way out, this return to share the fate of those who had followed and believed in him.

With the election completed, the revolution went into a new and more difficult phase: with an African as head of state, Um Nyobe found it difficult to convince the tribesmen that they were fighting for liberation from the French. The tough-talking Roman Catholic Premier, André-Marie M'Bida, threw additional troops against the Protestant Bassa, and offered only limited amnesty to those who gave themselves up. Um Nyobe, no longer able to make a pretence of open military operations, resorted more and more to atrocities to keep his opponents at bay. To prevent the rebels from obtaining recruits, food or information, M'Bida required all Bassa villages to build stockades and watch-towers; any village which could not account for the presence of all its inhabitants was fined.

The pressure built up and, in a single month, 1,600 of Um Nyobe's followers slipped out of the forest and surrendered. With the fall of M'Bida's government, the new premier, Amadou Ahidjo, by obtaining a firm promise of independence in 1960 from France, put the U.P.C. in the uncomfortable position of spilling blood for what had already been won by diplomacy. Um Nyobe knew he was finished but refused to join Moumie in Cairo. On September 13, 1958, a Bassa informer led a French-officered patrol to Um Nyobe's hiding place. As the rebel leader made a dash for freedom, an African sergeant took the top off his head with a ·303 slug. Um Nyobe died the same day and his two remaining lieutenants were captured. The body of the master-terrorist was displayed throughout Bassaland and the rebels, who had believed their leader could not die, flocked in to lay down their arms.

Many Cameroonians, including those who fought against him, regard Ruben Um Nyobe as their country's first patriot and few hate him. He may have been a Communist and terrible atrocities were certainly committed, if not by him, at least in his name. But he was an earnest nationalist, a sound organizer, and a brilliant guerrilla leader. He believed in what he was doing and whom he was doing it with. His methods were wrong but he knew no others. Most important of all, he was too moral an individual to try to escape the fate which he shaped for those who followed him. Moumie, appropriately enough, died in Switzerland in 1960 of an overdose of rat poison administered by person unknown.

BLACK STAR OF BENIN

About the same time that Ruben Um Nyobe was boarding the train which was to take him to Prague and launch him upon his fatal course, a light-skinned Camerounian from the North was getting his army discharge papers, Amadou Ahidjo, thirty-six, was born at Garua, the highest navigable port on the Benue River, a tributary of the great Niger. Nothing about his parentage appears in his official biography but it is said in the North that his father was a Fulani chief and his mother a slave. For this reason, some of the Muslim aristocracy regard him as something of an upstart although, of course, if the story is true, it is all the more to Ahidjo's credit that he has risen to such heights.

Whatever his origin, the little man with the deep-set, intense eyes and the fuzz of a moustache had to make his own way through life. He managed to scrape together the equivalent of an elementary education and obtained an appointment to the Yaounde School of Higher Administration. Despite the high-sounding name, the school is little more than a training centre for technicians and clerks. Ahidjo qualified as a radio operator and served first Vichy and then Free France in that capacity.

Having obtained his discharge, Ahidjo decided to give politics a whirl and, in 1947, was elected to the territorial assembly from his home district of Benue. If the leap from radio operator to Assembly member seems a trifle bizarre, it is only an indication of the paucity of education available to Africans in the past and the brush-fire speed of nationalism in the post-war period. Although there have been several important exceptions, most of the traditional secular and religious African leaders have been unable to adapt themselves to this new tempo and the whirlwind of events has thrown into the political spotlight men of natural ability who would have ended their lives in anonymity a decade ago. Most of the political leaders of the New Africa were driving locomotives, inspecting latrines, teaching primary students or sorting mail during Harry Truman's first term.

Ahidjo had ability and his eight years of formal education made him look like Einstein to the people of a region where even today only one out of every ten children goes to school. In 1955 he was elected to the

Assembly of the French Union and for two years served as one of its secretaries. Paris polished off some of Ahidjo's rough edges and earned him the somewhat pompous title of *l'Etoile Noire du Benin*, his admirers being somewhat weak on their geography, since the Camerounian's bailiwick is something like a thousand miles from the Bight of Benin. At any rate, a new and more confident Ahidjo returned to contest the vital 1956 elections. It will be remembered that at this time Ruben Um Nyobe was making running for office a hazardous occupation. Although he sympathized to some extent with the rebel chief, Ahidjo felt that Cameroun could achieve independence through constitutional means.

He won easily and was elected president of the Camerounian Assembly. As prime minister the French chose the strapping André-Marie M'Bida. The forty-year-old premier looked set for a long and vigorous career: on his forehead was the blue tribal tattoo of the conservative African leader, the French liked him, he had strong support in the progressive southern region and he was not afraid to use strong measures to smash the Red-infiltrated U.P.C. Ahidjo seemed destined for a long career as an also-ran. To conciliate the North, which regards the more advanced southerners with a curious blend of fear and contempt, M'Bida gave Ahidjo the vice-premiership and the portfolio of Minister of the Interior.

After a strong start, M'Bida ran into trouble. Although his vigorous use of French and African troops prevented the spread of the rebellion, his refusal to make the concessions which might have lured the rebels out of the jungle and ended the bloodshed alienated many moderates. As criticism of his régime mounted within and without the Assembly, M'Bida began to use his emergency powers to punish political opponents and journalists who disagreed with his policies. Since political parties (there were eighty-four at the last count) are somewhat informal in Cameroun (candidates stand as individuals, then get together with other deputies with whom they agree on basic policy to form a loose parliamentary group), political discipline is loose and M'Bida began losing deputies to the opposition.

Enter a new French High Commissioner for Camerouns, the lively Jean Ramadier, forty-four-year-old son of the former French Socialist Premier, Paul Ramadier. Ramadier may very well have had nothing to do with it, but M'Bida's coalition government collapsed within a short time of the new High Commissioner's arrival. The Premier flew to Paris, blustered that Ramadier was pushing Cameroun *too quickly* towards independence and playing into the hands of the Communists.

Ramadier was removed but M'Bida was still unable to show a majority in the Assembly and was ousted from office. Ahidjo took over.

But M'Bida's troubles were far from over. His private bodyguards found a Bassa tribesman, whom they assumed (perhaps correctly) to be a U.P.C. assassin, loitering around the ex-premier's house, and beat him so severely that he died. It is something of an index to the exuberance of African politics that the former chief of state of French Somaliland was jailed for street-fighting, a former Equatorial premier pole-axed the Speaker of his Assembly with a microphone and a Ghanaian cabinet minister led a mob to demonstrate outside the American Embassy. These men are not of the cocktail party set.

Proceedings were on the verge of being instituted to strip M'Bida of his parliamentary immunity so that a warrant could be issued for his arrest when he anonymously boarded a plane and flew to Paris. He later joined Moumie, his arch foe, in Conakry.

With his chief political opponent out of the way and the U.P.C. rebellion losing force, the former radio operator announced that he would work for independence, reunification of the French and British sectors of the country, and co-operation with France on a basis of equality. In other words Ahidjo's platform varied not one jot from that of the U.P.C., the difference being that he was able to win by constitutional means that which terrorism had failed to achieve. As architect of his coalition, the orthodox Muslim Ahidjo chose a hulking Roman Catholic, Charles Okala. Okala, who tips the scales at nineteen stone, once studied for the priesthood and has a taste for champagne before noon, had the task of welding a coalition in the seventy-member Assembly from the following diverse groups:

Union Camerounais, Ahidjo's group with twenty-nine members and five allied delegates, mainly conservative northern Muslims.

Democrates Camerounais, the twelve man dissension-ridden remnant of M'Bida's group, now leaderless and bitter, shifting from a strongly pro-French position to demanding immediate independence and no ties with the Metropole.

L'Action Nationale, a tightly-knit circle of eight delegates firmly led by Paul Soppo Priso and Charles Assale, strongly nationalistic and inclined towards conciliation with the U.P.C.

Paysans Independants, seven-member tribal grouping representing the interests of the prosperous Bamileke people, a nationalistic and autocratic splinter led by Daniel Kamajou and M. M. Njine.

In addition to these four parliamentary groups, there were five independent deputies, including Okala himself. There was, of course no reason why Ahidjo—who still likes to drop into a telegraph office and pound out his own cables—had to form a coalition: his northern delegates plus a few independent supporters gave him more than an absolute majority. But he realized that only by building a strong political machine could he assure the political and economic stability which Cameroun needed if she was to earn her independence on January 1, 1960.

In less time than it takes to say Tammany Hall, fun-loving Charles Okala, who at forty-nine is said to owe more money (salary: £5,000) and have more girl friends than any man in Yaounde, had soft-soaped, convinced and coerced everybody but M'Bida's bitter-enders into a coalition which gave Ahidjo a 54–12 majority and guaranteed him the honour of becoming the first prime minister of an independent Cameroun. Okala, who was a formidable sprinter before assuming his present generous proportions, accepted Ahidjo's thanks, the patronage-loaded portfolio of Public Works and an invitation to accompany the premier on a flying visit to America.

If Okala built the coalition, Ahidjo—who carries the portfolios of Information and of Internal Affairs—has·gained tremendous stature through his performance as chief of state. In little more than two years in office, the soft-spoken premier, who is equally at home in flowing Arab gown or dinner jacket, has shown himself to be both a flexible politician and an astute statesman. His retiring nature, self-effacement and air of studious calm are in sharp and refreshing contrast to the bombast of other better-known black nationalists. Ahidjo has shown that he can handle the arrogant feudal lords of the North (no matter how much they may grumble about his pedigree) as well as the evolved Southerners. The fact that he has been able to build a smooth-working cabinet which includes Muslims, Catholics, Protestants and animists on a continent where religious feeling often runs high is tribute both to the good sense of the Camerounian people and to Ahidjo's ability to handle men. He is a solid if not exciting speaker and has a reputation for personal incorruptibility.

THE U.N. FLAP

Having decided that Camerounian independence was inevitable, the French pressed forward with good grace and in all speed to make it so. With an eighteen-year political apprenticeship behind it (during which time it had enjoyed a territorial Assembly), on the first of January 1959 Cameroun got complete internal autonomy. In the spring of that year, France asked the United Nations to certify Camerounian independence for the following year.

There followed a bitter battle which found, of all things, the *African* states opposing an independence resolution proposed by the United States, India and several other states. In thirty-six acrimonious sessions of the Trusteeship Committee, the African bloc demanded new elections and the legalization of the U.P.C. before independence. Ghanaian Ambassador Daniel Chapman accused Cabot Lodge of making 'pious statements' while 'ignoring the reality of the urge for freedom from colonial rule', while conveniently forgetting that it was the United States who was advocating such freedom and his nation which intended to deny it unless it was to be achieved on Ghana's terms. What the African states failed to realize (or did they?) was that legalization of the U.P.C. would condone terrorism and might well lead the conservative North to tear the new nation apart.

Moumie, in his usual dignified and restrained fashion, denounced Ahidjo's government as unrepresentative and accused a recent U.N. Visiting Commission, composed of those old colonial powers, India, New Zealand and Haiti, of being 'biased and ill-informed'. It is obvious now that Moumie, who commuted frequently to Peking and Moscow, pulled the wool over Nkrumah's and Touré's eyes and convinced them that the overthrow of Ahidjo's government should be a priority goal of the Pan-African movement. To those who might still doubt where Moumie's sympathies lay, the French representative earlier had read a letter from the Camerounian (intercepted by the British) to his 'dear comrade' Molotov in which Moumie described the Soviet Union as 'the great champion and defender' of the Rights of Man, termed 'the great party of Lenin and Stalin' to be his 'indefectible ally . . . the bulwark of freedom for all'.

Ahidjo countered by stating that during his administration the number of Camerounians jailed for political crimes had been reduced from 2,303 to 56, all of whom had been convicted of murder. Political exiles, who 'could be counted on the fingers of one hand', would be welcomed back if they renounced violence. He added that he would hold new elections shortly after independence but said his government would not allow the bloodstained U.P.C. to resume operations. On the resolution supporting the position taken by India, the United States, France and Cameroon, there were fifty-six affirmative votes, the Soviet Bloc and sixteen Afro-Asian nations abstaining. Moumie's oath-sworn terrorists reacted by instigating a new wave of violence which resulted in twenty deaths during June 1959.

The new reign of terror, which is far from finished, has assumed even more serious dimensions than the Bassa rebellion. The core of the new revolt is the intelligent and virile Bamileke tribe, which makes up a sixth of the country's total population and tills the rich but over-populated hills along the border of Southern British Cameroons. Land shortage and grievances against their chiefs have played as important a role in persuading the Bamileke to take up arms as has any dissatisfaction with Ahidjo's régime. Many have been forced off their land (40,000 to Douala alone). Their highly organized tribal society, buttressed by French support during the trusteeship period, has failed to modernize itself. Its numerous chiefs have been distinguished primarily for their corruption and autocracy. Many, in contrast to those in other parts of the country, still exercise feudal rights of the most aggravating character, including that of *droit du seigneur*. In this disintegrating tribal society, Moumie found many embittered ears to listen to his rantings, many hands willing to grasp Czech revolvers smuggled over the frontier. Grievances held against the chiefs have easily been extended to include Ahidjo's government and the whites who remain in the country.

The young men of the Bamileke have formed themselves into gangs which intimidate and kill chiefs. The chiefs have replied with counter-terrorism. Feuds on the Sicilian pattern have developed between rival villages, which have formed 'defence groups'. Huts have been burned, women and children butchered. Terrorism in the Bamileke country, which is the republic's most productive agricultural area, has had a strong negative effect on the economic situation. Thousands of tons of bananas have been destroyed, coffee trees have been slashed, villages and plantations put to the torch. The Eseka saw-mill, among the most modern in Africa, has been burned to the ground. Those tribesmen not involved in the terrorism are afraid to till their fields. The more politically militant bands have launched raids outside Bamilekeland with Douala and Yaounde qualifying as the primary targets.

On January 1, 1960, the day of independence, festivities had to be curtailed after the rebels launched attacks on Douala which resulted in more than forty killed. 'As a measure of prudence', the only ceremony in Yaounde was the lowering of the French and U.N. flags and raising of the Cameroun Republic's tricolour. The rebel bands were bold enough to damage Douala's airport control tower, wreck several aeroplanes and assault a police station. The secret of their courage was brought to light through prisoners: the raiders had been drugged with hashish and witch-doctors had made five ceremonial cuts on their chests as protection against bullets. Even Yaounde itself was not safe: on independence night, five taxicab-propelled gangs toured the capital's streets with chattering machine-guns. Rather than see his country collapse into chaos before it was born, Ahidjo, who a few weeks earlier had demanded and received the resignation of Deputy Prime Minister M. M. Njine, a Bamileke, on grounds that he had let the terrorism get out of hand while Ahidjo was touring France, dissolved the National Assembly (in which his majority had shrunk significantly) and imposed martial law in more than half of Cameroun's twenty cantons. Government officials admitted that more than 20 per cent of Bamilekeland was in a state of anarchy.

Even martial law has failed to solve the situation. To combat the terrorists Ahidjo has only the 740-man Cameroon Guard, 690 auxiliary Guards and 635 police, a total of little over 2,000 men. Some assistance comes from the three battalions of French troops still stationed in the republic but both France and Ahidjo are unwilling to heavily engage French forces because it would add substance to charges that the prime minister is a French stooge. In a particularly repulsive raid, terrorists invaded the sprawling town of Dshang and slashed eighty Africans to death, sixty-one of them women and children. In another, a gang of several hundred sacked the Catholic mission and hospital at Bafang, killing two priests (whose heads were taken into the jungle) and seriously wounding an African nun. As the death toll approached 5,000, Moumie proudly took 'credit' for these deeds.

Finally, in the spring of 1960, Ahidjo realized that he needed both to strengthen his constitutional powers and to gain a new mandate if he was to rule with any degree of effectiveness (at least thirty whites and 700 Africans had been killed in the previous six months). He presented a Gaullist constitution providing for a powerful president, a government led by a prime minister appointed by the president, and a 100-member assembly to sit for five years elected on the basis of universal suffrage. The old assembly had 70 members, 28 from Ahidjo's conservative Muslim North and 42 from the South. In the new assembly there are 56 southern seats and 44 in the North, which means that the Muslim vote has been over-weighted. In addition, Ahidjo took the precaution of breaking up some of the larger and more antagonistic constituencies.

Moumie called on his followers to boycott the referendum. Evidence of his declining popularity was furnished when 75 per cent of the electorate went to the polls, 797,498 to vote for the constitution and 531,075 to register their opposition to it. Realizing that there was a split between the terrorists and the more moderate wing of the U.P.C., the latter led by Mayi Matip (one of Um Nyobe's lieutenants), Ahidjo lifted the ban on the U.P.C. and held new elections in April of 1960. Moumie sulked in Conakry (and formed a government-in-exile) but M'Bida, who had once told his constituents that independence before 1970 was an impossibility, came back to lead the opposition campaign with a 'French-get-out' slogan. Ahidjo, however, was returned to power as president and his nominee, Charles Assale, the former Minister of Finance, became premier.

Will Ahidjo, subjected to meddling from the Accra-Conakry axis and troubled by internal difficulties, have enough staying power to give Cameroun the period of relative tranquillity needed in these immediate post-independence years? M'Bida and Njine have strong followings, respectively, among the Catholics and the Bamileke. Now that independence has been achieved, Ahidjo's control over this left wing of his coalition, which figures to pick up support from former U.P.C. adherents, may well weaken in the more normal political climate which exists.

PROBLEMS OF INDEPENDENCE

Welcome as it is, independence has created more problems for the Cameroun Republic than it has resolved. The most pressing of these is economic. Last year's mammoth budget deficit—like those of all previous years—was made up by France. It seems likely that Cameroun, whose legislative salaries are second highest in the world, will need financial assistance merely to meet current expenses for at least the next ten years.

Franco-Camerounian relations have been cordial enough and the new nation's economic situation sufficiently pressing to induce the republic to maintain loose ties with France which permit her to receive financial, military and cultural assistance without prejudice to her political integrity. It is difficult to see how Cameroun could exist without this relationship. Her cash crops receive a higher price in France than could be commanded on the world market and the association, which resembles Commonwealth status, affords the African state a valuable foothold in the European Common Market. Still, it cannot be denied that France's grip on the Camerounian purse-strings places the new republic in a position not wholly consistent with the concept of nationhood. This dependence is a source of irritation to many Camerounians and, inevitably, is a source of political friction.

Another problem facing the new nation is that of finding sufficient African personnel to staff the government's administrative and social services. Last year, less than twelve months before independence, there were exactly four Camerounian lawyers, three university-level professors, one doctor, two architects and six engineers in government service. Again, thanks to the *entente cordiale* which existed between the two races, many French administrators and technicians were willing to stay on and the Camerounians were glad to have most of them. It could be a source of satisfaction to men of neither nationality, however, that as recently as 1959, there were no Camerounian administrators of the country's nineteen provinces, only nine of the fifty-seven subdivisions were headed by Camerounian nationals, little more than half of the judges of first degree tribunals, agricultural officers and mayors were black. One Camerounian cabinet minister estimated that his country would need to employ foreign administrators and technicians for 'at least ten years more'.

At the root of the problem has been the shortage of educational facilities. Before World War II, there were very few schools. Today, education gets the biggest slice of the national budget allocated to any ministry. Over 90 per cent of the boys and 25 per cent of the girls in the South and West receive some education. In the Muslim North, which still has plenty of reservations about Western education and the emancipation of women, the percentage of boys drops to 18 per cent and that of girls to nil.

Ahidjo hopes to be able to make lower primary education, at least in the South, free and compulsory. Cameroun now has eight high schools but no university, although one is planned for the immediate future. At first glance, the idea of a university for such a small country might seem to be an extravagance. But in at least one sense, it is a stark necessity: Camerounians have been attending French universities for years but most prefer to stay on in France, where the lights are brighter and the economic opportunities greater, rather than return to Cameroon. It is hoped that a university at Yaounde, well insulated from the Folies Bergère, might remedy this situation. At present, nearly 1,000 Camerounians—or four times the number of Equatorial

Africans—are studying in France, half on government scholarships. If these young graduates can be lured back and then persuaded to serve in the bush—an educated African looks on any sort of service in rural areas with about as much enthusiasm as Bernard Goldfine might view an enforced sojourn in Saudi Arabia—then the country's personnel problems will be well on their way to being solved. Until then, Cameroun must rely on her former masters to run the government.

Health conditions although improved remain inadequate. In the entire country there are little more than 100 fully-trained physicians, including 28 missionaries and 13 private practitioners. Sixty Dakar-trained 'assistant doctors' are helping to hold the line until the 88 Camerounian medical students now in France complete their studies. There are exactly 12 dentists and 28 pharmacists in the country. Cameroun has 44 hospitals and 'medical centres' (with 10,000 beds, of sorts). So poor is the national health that, in one recent year, 85 per cent of the population saw a doctor every four months.

On the politico-social side there is the rather delicate question common to all emergent African nations of reconciling the position of powerful traditional chiefs with an evolving society which, if not totally democratic, is certainly modern. As we shall see in later chapters, Ghana and Guinea have dealt with this problem by crushing the chiefs; in Nigeria, Cameroun's next-door neighbour, the chiefs have seen the writing on the wall (except in the feudal North) and have declared their political neutrality.

The problem is slightly different and more complex in Cameroun because the Germans with curious ambivalence applied different policies in the same country. In the South they dealt harshly with the chiefs and, as a result, the real leaders went underground and straw-men were set up by the tribes to deal with the Germans. Being human, these false chiefs have attempted to establish their legitimacy. In the resulting hierarchical chaos, the institution of the chieftaincy has lost the respect of the people. In the North the Germans, like most colonial powers, succumbed to Islamania and allowed the proud emirs to retain many of their secular powers. Although the French sat rather more heavily on the necks of the Northern lords, it is here that the chieftaincy continues to enjoy considerable prestige.

Charles Okala, who has a lot to say about policy matters in Ahidjo's government, sees the situation this way: 'If the chiefs behave themselves, they have nothing to fear from us. Where the people want a chief to stay, we will allow it. Where they do not want him, we will heap him with honours and give him a job. We hope also to train the chiefs in administration so that they may play a useful role in the development of the country. In all, it is not so bad for them.'

BRITISH CAMEROONS

The great political problem of the moment is the question of the reunification of French and British Cameroons. British Cameroons is one of the few colonial areas in history which has the choice of joining an independent nation within either the French Community or the British Commonwealth. African politics are so volatile in this year of decision that there is no way of telling whether British Cameroons will become an autonomous region of independent Nigeria, federate or unify with ex-French Cameroun, remain a United Nations trusteeship under Great Britain or become independent. It has chosen trusteeship status, at least for the moment.

The British sector, which is a little larger than Austria and has as many people as Melbourne, is divided into two parts which are not contiguous. The northern sliver, about the size of Denmark, has a primitive population of about 700,000 organized in tribes owing allegiance to the emirs of neighbouring Northern Nigeria. The Northern Cameroons is poor and only 3 per cent of the population is literate. The white population is exactly 104, of which 32 are fundamentalist American Protestant missionaries. It is doubtful if the number of converts exceeds the missionary population. Because of ethnic, religious and administrative ties, Northern Cameroons—which, of course, was part of German Kamerun before the First World War—has always been administered as an integral part of the Northern Region of Nigeria. It has never had its own parliament but in the past sent seven representatives to the Northern Nigerian Assembly and voted for the Northern Nigerian delegates to the federal houses at Lagos. When U.N. missions visited Northern Cameroons, spokesmen for the area always maintained that they wished to stay with Nigeria when she became independent. It came as something of a surprise, then, when the 1959 plebiscite as to the region's future, regarded by all as merely a formality, indicated that the majority of Northern British Cameroons' people wanted not independence as a part of Nigeria but to remain under British trusteeship and to decide their ultimate future at a later date. The region was separated from Nigeria on October 1, 1960, Sir Percy Wyn-Harris has been appointed Administrator, and a plebiscite, in which the people will be given a choice between rejoining Nigeria or associating themselves with the Cameroun Republic, is scheduled to be held not later than March, 1961.

The North has one doctor for every 250,000 people, a population density of 39 to the square mile, not a kilometre of paved road or railway, and no secondary school, university, newspapers or trade unions.

Southern British Cameroons, shown on independence day maps as a part of the Cameroun Republic, is a different kettle of fish. It is a little smaller than the northern region, has a population a little larger (including a considerable group of immigrant Nigerians), is richer and more advanced in every way.

This black Switzerland contains the 700-square-mile bulk of flame-spewing Mount Cameroon, a tribe of whale-hunters called Wovea, a mysterious crater lake of great depth and beauty named Barombi, broad beaches of fine, *purple* sand of volcanic origin, and a wizened little potentate known as the Fon of Bikom who is reputed to have more wives than any other man in the world. The latter is periodically put on display for visiting U.N. missions who presumably fear that he may corner the market in this commodity. Southern Cameroonians, although their country was a part of federal Nigeria from 1954 to 1960, speak of 'going abroad' when they visit Lagos.

What makes Mount Cameroon (at 13,370 feet the highest point in West Africa) so striking and caused startled Carthaginian sailors five hundred years before Christ to term it the 'chariot of the gods' is the fact that this smouldering, Alp-sized peak rises starkly from a region otherwise as hilly as a putting green. A village on its eastern side named Debundscha gets thirty feet of rainfall per year and is the second wettest place in the world (wetter: Chakapunji, India), the *kwifon* or handbell is the chiefly symbol of authority on its slopes, and the local inhabitants insist that this is the mountain where Noah landed his ark.

The modern history of this lush little country began on June 6, 1858, when a British Baptist missionary named Alfred Sacker beached his boat in Ambas Bay near what is today Victoria, a town of 8,000. Sacker, a Kentish engineer and draughtsman employed by the British Admiralty, had gone to the nearby Spanish island of Fernando Po at the age of thirty to preach the gospel. After fourteen years there, he was expelled and sailed with his lone convert to the Cameroons. Sacker gave one of the native languages a written form, translated the Bible, negotiated peace treaties with neighbouring chiefs, named most of the hills around Victoria after his wife and friends, and for sixteen years until his death lobbied unsuccessfully to get the Cameroons taken under British protection.

Two years after Sacker's arrival, a German firm established a trading station on the other side of the mountain. The British Baptists worked around the base of the great volcano (which has erupted twice within the last decade) until the establishment of a German protectorate made the situation uncongenial. The British missionaries sold out, headed for the Congo and German Baptists moved in. Realizing the agricultural potentialities of the mountain, the German Government imported settlers to establish banana plantations.

In 1916, the British got a bit of their own back on behalf of *their* Baptists by expelling the German missionaries and confiscating the banana plantations. In 1922, Teutonic banana-growers and Baptists were readmitted to the British sector but not to the French. During World War II, as we have seen, the German planters and missionaries got the boot for the last time. German Catholics were also active in the territory from 1894 and they shared the spiritual merry-go-round with their fundamentalist countrymen.

If the natives of the Cameroons found it difficult to follow the abrupt changes of nationality of their clergymen in the past, they must find it even more confusing today: 251 missionaries of eleven nationalities are busy peddling five denominations to a total congregation of 162,000 of whom almost half are Catholics. Numerically leading the field in this spiritual sweepstake are the Americans (61 missionaries), closely followed by the Dutch and the Swiss. Far back but leading the second pack are the British (26) and the Irish (22). Perhaps because they got tired of having to buy round-trip tickets, there are no Germans. Christianity is popular in the South among the educated Africans but most of the people are still animists.

The Germans built Buea, the capital of British Cameroons, and they built well. The town, which sits 3,000 feet up the slopes of Mount Cameroon, is something out of the Rhineland (complete with a *schloss* built by a Prussian officer for his mistress) and, although the equator is not far away, roses flourish and open fires are necessary at night through much of the year. Victoria, at the foot of the mountain (which the natives call 'Fako'), still boasts many German buildings, among them the District Officer's house (which has a Prussian cross moulded under each gable), the old Basel Mission Church, the Catering Rest

217

House (formerly the German hospital), and the Nursing Home, once the residence of a German botanist who introduced to the Cameroons most of the crops upon which its financial future rests today. Scattered around the countryside are 'Bismarck' fountains which provide water for many communities. Everything the Germans did in Africa they did methodically and their buildings today are still among the most comfortable and functional in West Africa.

The most striking legacy of the German administration is the Cameroons Development Corporation, formed in 1947 to utilize the sequestered plantations in the general interest of the African population. C.D.C., which has its headquarters at Bota, holds 395 square miles, cultivates about 20,000 acres itself and leases the rest to private investors. The corporation, which is run on business lines but is wholly owned by the British Cameroonian government, has invested more than £7·1 million in its plantations of bananas, palm oil, rubber and tea, provided employment for countless natives (16,000 at any given time), and furnished their families with schools and hospitals. Although C.D.C. has made only small profits in the past to turn over to the government (£16,000 in 1956) and expects no further profits until next year, its contribution through taxes and construction of schools and hospitals has amounted to more than £3·5 million since 1947.

Since 1955 the British government has put £2 million into Southern Cameroons for development. The territory operates on a budget smaller (£1·1 million) than the amount spent for garbage disposal by many American cities. Private foreign investment has been skittish because of political uncertainty and secession from Nigeria means that the territory will have to find another £600,000 in revenue to replace the federal subsidy. Southern British Cameroons has no reserves of its own and no funds for development. Almost all of C.D.C.'s capital is represented by a loan of £1·8 million from the Nigerian government, which will have to be repaid if the trust territory remains outside the federation.

Most Southern Cameroonians, who are divided into sixty tribes with as few as 200 and as many as 58,000 members, devote themselves to raising six of the seven of the country's main export crops: bananas, rubber, cacao, coffee, hides and skins. The seventh—oil palm produce— is grown for export exclusively by the big plantations. Bananas are the big money-earner (£2·5 million) followed by cacao, which brings in nearly £1 million. Apparently there are no mineral resources but the forests which cover the southern part of the country are beginning to yield rich timber, and exports of this commodity have soared from 1,500 tons in 1955 to 72,000 tons in 1958. There are those who say that Southern Cameroons, with a little luck and capital, can become the Ceylon of Africa.

Southern Cameroons has 394 primary schools (of which 363 are run by missionaries) and 50,000 children—or about 25 per cent of the school-age population—get some education. The country has only three high schools and, as recently as 1956, it was impossible for a Cameroonian girl to go beyond primary school in her native land. Educational difficulties are complicated by the fact that there is no native language understood throughout the territory. Consequently pidgin—which contrary to common belief is not merely a corruption of English but a language bearing roughly the same relationship to our tongue as English does to Old Saxon—is richly developed and used almost exclusively on the primary level. Two native languages, Bali and Duala, have been given a written form but if there is a national language it is pidgin, which might better be termed Afro-English. The literacy rate is 10 per cent.

There are 26 doctors and 13 hospitals (the doctor-hospital ratio gives some indication of the size of these institutions) in Southern Cameroons. There is a labour force of 35,000, of which 60 per cent are in unions and most of these work for the Cameroons Development Corporation.

TO BE OR NOT TO BE

As we have seen, the northern sector of the British zone has experienced such constitutional development as it has through the organs of Nigerian Northern Regional government. The story in the South has been slightly but importantly different.

Until 1954, the southern zone was administered as a province of the Eastern Region of Nigeria, the domain of the Ibo leader, Azikiwe. It sent representatives both to the national capital at Lagos and to the Eastern House of Assembly in Enugu. Now the Ibos have certain endearing qualities; they also have an amazing talent for making themselves disliked by 'foreigners'. The Southern Cameroonians kicked up such a fuss about Ibo domination that, in 1954, the zone was made a quasi-autonomous region of federal Nigeria on a par with the Northern, Eastern and Western regions of that country. This meant that while Southern Cameroons retained its six seats in the Federal House of

Representatives, it was given its own Executive Council and House of Assembly; the link with the Eastern Region of Nigeria was cut.

The most ephemeral document in the New Africa is a constitution. Barely had the ink dried on the new document when it was superseded by the constitution of 1958. This enlarged the Cameroonian House of Assembly to twenty-six members, gave it a premier, elevated its Executive Council to cabinet status, created a regional House of Chiefs, increased the number of its seats in the Federal House of Representatives from six to eight and allocated to Cameroons twelve seats in the newly-created Nigerian Senate. For a country with only twenty-nine university students, British Cameroons found itself with a lot of political plums to digest.

The rapid pace of constitutional developments threw up three political parties with distinct ideas about what the future of the country should be. The presence (until their expulsion to Khartoum at the expense of the Federal Nigerian Government) of U.P.C. leaders like Moumie helped to generate support for Ibo-hating groups who saw in unification with French Cameroun a way out of their role as Nigeria's stepchild.

The Kamerun National Congress, led by young and dynamic E. M. L. Endeley, and the Kamerun People's Party (headed by P. M. Kale) both favour independence *within* the Nigerian Federation. The third party, the Kamerun National Democratic Party, led by John Ngu Foncha, a former follower of Dr. Endeley, wants complete separation of British Cameroons from Nigeria and an eventual link with newly-independent ex-French Cameroun. It is significant, however, that all three parties use the German spelling for their party names, since their German past represents the single factor common to both zones.

In 1954, Endeley, one of British Cameroons' first African physicians and a veteran member of the Eastern Nigerian House of Assembly (he also served for two years as a cabinet minister in the *Nigerian* government), forged a political alliance between his own K.N.C. (symbol: banana tree and house) and the K.P.P. which uses the cock as its mascot. The elections gave Endeley's K.N.C.-K.P.P. seven of the thirteen elective seats in the New Cameroonian Assembly and he became the region's first premier. Foncha, backed by five K.N.D.P. delegates and one independent, became leader of the Opposition.

When new elections based for the first time on universal suffrage were called in 1959, Foncha hit the hustings claiming that Endeley, who had preached (and been instrumental in obtaining) separation from Nigeria was now going to 'sell' Cameroons back to Nigeria. The illiterate electorate may be excused for not perceiving that an autonomous Cameroons had nothing to lose through membership in an independent federation of which she was an equal member. Endeley and Kale countered by telling their followers that Foncha was purposely confusing integration and federation, pointed out that Cameroons had been receiving more federal aid *per capita* than any other region of Nigeria.

Most of this passed over the heads of the electorate, enough of whom cast their ballots for the K.N.D.P.'s umbrella symbol to give that party fourteen seats in the enlarged Assembly while the K.N.C.-K.P.P. alliance had to settle for twelve; Endeley, who was re-elected to his Assembly seat, resigned as premier and Foncha, pledged to take Cameroons out of the Nigerian Federation, took over.

Endeley's government fell for several reasons. In the first place, it was laid down in the constitution of his K.N.C. that the party would work for independence and unification with the Cameroon Republic. His switch to support of federation with Nigeria was regarded by many of his supporters as a betrayal. Secondly, many of his supporters who had bitterly fought the K.P.P. were unable to accept the alliance which Endeley forged with that party. Thirdly, in an attempt to modernize the administration of the country, Endeley lost the support of several influential chiefs.

The position now has become even more obscure with the carpet-crossing of a K.N.D.P. member of the House of Assembly. This has precipitated a deadlock in the legislature since both sides now hold thirteen seats, which means that new elections will have to be held. And Endeley's K.N.C. and Kale's K.P.P. have merged to form the Cameroons People's National Congress.

ON THE FENCE

Foncha, who is forty-two, is married and has three children. He was orphaned as a boy and, like Ahidjo, is a self-made man. He is a Bamenda, which means he is from the interior, and received his primary education at government and Catholic schools in Cameroons and in Eastern Nigeria. In 1936 he obtained his teacher's certificate after completing the course at St. Charles College in Onitsha. He became headmaster of a Catholic school in 1940 and, five years later, opened a teacher training institute in Bambui. Foncha, who is short and soft-spoken, made his political start in 1941 by organizing a branch of the Cameroons Youth League in his home district. He later formed the Bamenda Catholic Teachers' Union and followed this with the establishment of a branch of the Nigerian Union of Teachers. He joined the K.N.C. and was one of Dr. Endeley's first supporters, being among those elected to Eastern Nigeria's House of Assembly when Cameroons gained representation in that body. In 1955 he split with Endeley and formed the K.N.D.P.

One of the reasons for Foncha's success is that, although he is a devout Catholic, he recognizes the importance of secret societies among his people, has backed them on several occasions and, so it is said, holds membership in several of the more important groups. Unlike Endeley, who looks as if he had stepped out of a smart tailor's, Foncha prefers to wear colourful native clothes. A thin man with a wide but thin-lipped slash of a mouth and a broad, flat nose, Foncha has two interestingly diverse hobbies: cricket and keeping poultry. He is courageous (he had both collarbones broken in a car crash and waged the 1959 election campaign in an assortment of plaster casts) and humble, preferring to walk to his office rather than use the limousine provided by the government.

It would be premature to infer that his accession to office automatically means that British Cameroons will permanently leave the Federation of Nigeria and join ex-French Cameroun, although that was the major promise of his campaign and Foncha is said to have received substantial financial support from *anschluss* advocates in the new nation. In the first place, the question of the future of the territory has to be decided in 1961 by a U.N.-supervised plebiscite in which the question will not be clouded with other political issues. One is inclined to believe that a considerable number of Foncha's adherents support him more because they do not like Dr. Endeley than through any desire to dissociate themselves from the British Commonwealth, although Southern Cameroonians are not unaware of the rather shabby treatment British Togo received from Ghana after a hard-fought plebiscite resulted in the integration of the former trusteeship territory with that independent black state.

Secondly, Foncha the minority leader and Foncha the premier are two entirely different people. It may be indelicate but accurate to suggest that Foncha's use of this emotional question was dictated more by his desire to get into office than by any real fear that Cameroons would suffer through an association with Nigeria. In this avid and natural desire for office he differs not one jot from any American or British politician.

Evidence that Foncha has not burned all his boats is afforded by the fact that he wants not immediate reunification with his brothers south of the Mungo River but a 'temporary' continuation of the British trusteeship while he negotiates with Ahidjo. There is a chance, of course, that, having found the separation issue to be a successful political cudgel, he might be tempted to use it to such an extent that retreat would be impossible. And there is also the possibility that independent Nigeria, which needs the Cameroons as much as Zsa Zsa Gabor requires a charm course, might refuse to readmit the territory to the Federation. In this case the choice would lie between permanent trusteeship under Britain, which would be politically impossible for both parties, and independence. In the event of the latter eventuality, Southern British Cameroons would be joining the numerically not inconsiderable list of calabash countries unable financially to support the trappings of nationhood.

In many ways reunification makes sense. The two areas were administered as one unit under the Germans from 1883 to 1915 (how odd it is that the forty-five-year-old memory of brief subjugation under a European power which no longer has political interests in Africa should become a source of black irredentism). Economically, geographically and ethnically, Southern British Cameroons has more in common with its neighbour to the south than it does with the hated Ibos of Nigeria. Roads in the area (103 miles paved) are so poor that British Cameroons is cut off from Nigeria for much of the year during the rainy season. Road links with ex-French Cameroun, in contrast, are good. Southern Cameroons finds in nearby Douala a better and more convenient port than any in Nigeria. Douala also furnishes a means of employment for her surplus population. The border between the two sectors neatly divides the large and progressive Bamileke tribe. Most important of all, reunification is the stated and ardent desire of the governments currently in power on both sides of the Mungo.

There are, of course, several factors on the minus side of the ledger. The biggest of these is the language barrier. Although some tribes on either side of the border can understand each other in their native languages, all educated people in British Cameroons speak English and few know any French. Pidgin is spoken along the coast as far as Douala and in all border areas, but French is the language of commerce and politics in the Cameroun Republic. In addition, forty-five years of

British administration has left its mark in Southern Cameroons: everyone from postal clerks to cabinet ministers is accustomed to English form and administrative methods which vary considerably from those established by the French. Trade patterns and tastes for consumer goods have been established and will be more difficult to break than many realize: imagine, for instance, how the people of southern England would regard reunification with Normandy if it meant giving up roast beef for snails!

If she leaves Nigeria permanently, Southern Cameroons will have a tremendous personnel problem. There are as many Nigerians as Cameroonians in the territory's senior civil service and far more British than either. In some departments there are no Cameroonians at all. If Southern Cameroons confirms the decision made this year when she left the Federation in 1960, the Nigerians will have to go home; if she reunifies with ex-French Cameroun, both the Nigerians and the British will leave; in either case Southern Cameroons will find herself in bad shape both for administrators and technicians.

Southern Cameroons, Mr. Foncha included, knows what to expect from Nigeria politically. The powers which she will retain and those which she will delegate to the federal government have been clearly spelled out, as has the amount of federal economic assistance which Southern Cameroons can expect to receive. In contrast, the Cameroun Republic has stated no concrete terms for reunification. If it were to be absorbed into a unitary Camerounian state, Southern Cameroons would find herself culturally and politically swamped. Said one Southern Cameroonian: 'We don't like the Ibos but at least we know them.'

So the political future of this region is well personified by the threatening rumbling of the great volcano which dominates the landscape of this house divided. At this writing it is impossible to state the dimensions, population or constitutional framework of the Cameroonian state. This is what makes cartographers and writers seek comfort in apples; this is what makes the New Africa the seething, changing, ebullient continent that it is.

NOTE

'In February of 1961, plebiscites were held in both sectors of British Cameroons to determine the futures of the two territories. Northern British Cameroons reversed its earlier decision and voted to become once again an integral part of the Northern Region of the Federation of Nigeria. Southern British Cameroons elected to join the Cameroun Republic.'

Chapter 10

---*---

STEPCHILD

Togo is a geographical absurdity artificially inseminated by the scramble for Africa in the 1880's. Bismarck, the 'honest broker' of Berlin, found most of the real estate staked out by the time he sent Nachtigal, whose acquaintance we made in the last chapter, steaming down the west coast. However, the latter was able to spot between British Gold Coast and French Dahomey a thirty-five-mile stretch of palm-fringed beach to which nobody had laid claim. The Germans signed treaties with the coastal tribes and pushed inland from their slender beach-head for nearly 350 miles.

As a result, you can light a cigar at Togo's eastern boundary and still be puffing when you get into Ghana. In contrast, to cross the country from south to north (where the roads are shocking) can take three days.

The new nation has only one newspaper, the four-page *Le Togo Républicain* (a conservative twice-weekly sheet with a circulation of 1,100) and young Togolese politicians bear engaging names such as Theophile Mally, Misre Dzovon, Ditch Ekpegnan and Mama Arouna. There is a bewildering multiplicity of tribes such as (from north to south) the B'mobas, Gourmas, Natchabas, Tchokosis, N'Gan-Gans, Lambas, Konkombas, Kabrais, Cotocolis, Akebos, Anas, Akpossos, Adjas, Ewes, Quatchis and Ahoulans, to name a few. Each has its own language. The coastal groups have a loosely organized social and political structure while those of the interior are more centralized and authoritarian. The decision of an Ewe chief, for instance, can be overruled by the 'stool' elders (the stool is the symbol of authority from Calabar to Conakry) or by the action of the Asaf, the young warriors of the clans. Such a proceeding would be unthinkable among the B'mobas.

Germany's control over her elongated colony was barely effective when World War I erupted. Togo (the word means 'behind-the-sea' in the Ewe tongue), unlike Tanganyika, South West Africa or Kamerun, was too tiny and indefensible a sliver to put up much fight against the Anglo-French invaders and resistance ended within a matter of weeks.

225

The memory of the Germans lingers on in the sleepy port-capital of Lomé, a severely planned township laid out with Teutonic thoroughness in rectangular blocks lined with well-regimented avenues of shady trees. In the middle of the town is a stolid little German Lutheran church, built of stone to last a thousand years, and African boys with long bamboo poles knock juicy mangoes from its orchard laid out many years ago by a nameless Prussian pastor. As was the case in Cameroons, the Germans are not remembered unkindly and there is more than an even chance that Togo, now that it is independent, may seek technical assistance from West Germany.

When the spoils were divided at Versailles, the British took a slab half the size of Eire adjoining the eastern boundary of the Gold Coast. This sector, with its capital at a town with the endearing name of Ho (no exclamation mark) has a population of half a million—the same as Kansas City—and has been since 1956 an integral part of Ghana. Those who tend to think of American interest in Africa as a post-World War II phenomenon should note that U.S. Protestant missionaries have been in Ho since 1847, making it the third oldest mission station south of the Sahara.

France grabbed the port of Lomé (pronounced Low-may), the 266-mile railway, and a chunk of territory twice the size of the Netherlands with a population of just over one million. The division of the country at the peace conference accentuated the disregard shown in the 1880's for ethnic, geographic and economic units. One large and progressive tribe, the Ewes, found itself split into four sections inhabiting Dahomey, French Togo, British Togo and Gold Coast.

The political history of modern Africa is complicated by the fact that the peoples of the continent live in east-to-west groupings while the political framework imposed by the European powers was basically north-to-south. The result has been that tribes historically antagonistic to each other have been linked while homogeneous linguistic and racial units have been cut to pieces. This is one of the principal motivating forces behind the Pan-African movement; it is also an important threat to the success of the same thrust.

Under the terms of the League of Nations agreements, France governed her sector of Togo as a separate unit: its administration was entirely separate from that of neighbouring French Dahomey or French Upper Volta. But the British, as with their slice of Cameroons, were allowed to administer British Togo as an integral part of Gold Coast. The difference appeared slight at the time but was to become of major importance as Gold Coast (Ghana) approached independence: the inhabitants of British Togo were allowed to choose between joining independent Ghana or remaining under British trusteeship. Nkrumah, who was no less of an expansionist in 1956 than he is today, wanted British Togo both for reasons of prestige and to secure the left bank of the Volta River, which would make his proposed Volta hydro-electric scheme an all-Ghana proposition. It is an interesting example of double-think that what was once white imperialism (Bad) has changed clothes to become black Pan-Africanism (Good). In the event, after vigorous pro-union campaigning by Nkrumah's Convention People's Party, 93,095 British Togolanders voted for integration with Ghana and 67,492 voted against it. Thus British Togo, with a death-rattle of bloody rioting, joined Ghana. When we speak of Togo now, we mean only that portion of the old German colony which was administered by France until it gained its independence on April 27, 1960.

In 1945 France converted its League of Nations mandate over Togo into a United Nations trusteeship, as did Britain with her sector. There are several important differences too often overlooked in both the spirit and the mechanics of the mandate scheme as opposed to the trusteeship arrangement. Under the League of Nations set-up, the mandatory powers were required only to rule in an enlightened fashion: they were expected to promote the material, social and moral well-being of the inhabitants of the mandated areas, to abolish slavery and forced labour, to restrict the traffic in drugs and liquor, to guard the integrity of native customs and possessions, and to allow all members of the League free access to and rights in these territories. They were forbidden to create economic monopolies or to utilize the mandates as military or naval bases. Significantly, neither stated nor implied was anything to suggest that the Mandatory Powers had any responsibility for developing political life, introducing democratic theories or leading their charges towards self-determination.

The San Francisco Conference of 1945 made a marked departure from this precedent by declaring that one of the principal objects of the United Nations trusteeship system, which was to assume the obligations of the League, was to set the feet of the trust territories on the path to self-government in the shortest possible time. While the moral and economic obligation remained, the future emphasis clearly was to be political.

Of equal importance has been the altered composition of international commissions established to inspect the trust territories and to hear petitions from their inhabitants. Under the League, *individuals* with personal and exceptional knowledge of Africa were named to such commissions and they performed most of their functions in the detached atmosphere of Geneva. Under the new régime, members of such commissions are representatives of *governments*. The distinction is more than academic: the new 'experts' too frequently have had no knowledge of Africa and represent nations which are as under-developed as the trust territories or have little understanding of the problems of colonial administration. These well-intentioned but not always knowledgeable individuals do much of their work in the trust territories where demonstrations can all too easily be worked up for their benefit by small but vocal groups. They can hardly be blamed if decisions made in this emotion-charged atmosphere often frustrate the spirit if not the word of the mandate-trust ideal.

On the Trusteeship Committee of the United Nations sit nations with the most obvious motives for creating political and economic difficulties for the Colonial Powers and those under their trust. One wonders, for instance, if the Soviet Union (which has a permanent seat on the Committee) is really interested in solving the intricate problems which did and do exist. Russia, of course, is well-qualified in at least one respect: her record as a colonial power in Central Asia and Eastern Europe is far less fragrant than that of any European nation in Africa during the worst era of exploitation, a fact which pro-Russian African nationalists conveniently ignore.

Although Togo has had better luck with its U.N. visiting missions than Ruanda-Urundi or Tanganyika, it has had its share of commissioners, bone-headed or worse. Although the U.N. has been instrumental in winning independence for Cameroun and Togo, it is interesting to note that many French Africans are antagonistic towards the organization which, they say, is dominated by Anglo-American racialism!

RIGHT AND LEFT

In the years immediately following World War II, Togo was allowed to elect a local assembly and to send a total of four deputies to the three representative bodies of France and the French Union. Political leadership was seized by nationalists who were too radical to suit either the French or the conservative Muslim chiefs of the northern part of the territory. With a bit of tinkering extreme nationalists were excluded from every office from dog-catcher up. As premier of Togo, the French tabbed a skilful Francophile mulatto (he is of German descent) with the old African name of Nicolas Grunitzky. Grunitzky's party—which drew heavy support from black civil servants who had everything to gain from maintaining their profitable relationship with France—in 1956 demanded the end of the U.N. trusteeship, self-government and close ties with France. In other words, conservative elements sought to short-circuit nationalist extremists by depriving them of their U.N. forum and, at the same time, ensure that an autonomous Togo would remain within the French Union and continue to receive economic aid from France which, between 1946 and 1955, had amounted to £12 million.

In a large measure, this conservative attitude was based on fear of the other tribes of an Ewe-dominated reunited Togo which would have no ties with France. About 375,000 Ewes (pronounced Eh-vehs) live in Ghana proper, 140,000 in ex-British Togo, 175,000 in Togo and another 5,000 in Dahomey. Ewe agitation for unification dates from 1922 but became most violent at the end of the Second World War. Emphasis at first was upon the creation of an Ewe state; in 1951, Ewe leaders took a new approach to an old problem by advocating not Ewe reunification but the linking of the two Togolands to form a single independent state. Fighting for this was the radical, anti-French and pro-independence *Comité de l'Unité Togolaise* (C.U.T.); equally vehemently opposed to such a solution were the *Parti Togolais du Progrès* (Grunitzky's group) and the *Union des Chefs et des Populations du Nord* (since renamed the *Union Démocratique des Populations Togolaises*), which represents the interests of tradition-bound Northern chiefs.

C.U.T. and Togolese nationalism got a big shot in the arm in 1951 when Sylvanus Olympio assumed leadership of the party. This fifty-eight-year-old Ewe is not a shirtless revolutionary. His father was a prosperous merchant whose ancestors immigrated to Togo from Brazil. Like many other West Coast African families, the Olympios were taken to Brazil as slaves, intermarried with the Portuguese and used their knowledge of the Guinea coast to build a fortune based on the slave trade. Father Olympio did well enough to be able to afford to send his son to England for secondary school and to pay his way through the London School of Economics. Young Olympio returned to Togo in 1926 with a Bachelor of Commerce degree in his baggage, promptly went to work for the United Africa Company, a subsidiary of Lever Brothers.

The slender, chestnut-hued economist, who combines all the astuteness of an old-time Ewe trader with the slick finesse of a Madison Avenue promoter, soon climbed the ladder from clerk to manager of all U.A.C.'s interests in Togo. Under suspicion of harbouring pro-Allied sentiments, Olympio was spirited out of Togo in 1942 and interned in northern Dahomey by the Vichy French. His release coincided with the birth of Togolese political activity. Shortly after the formation of C.U.T. (under the leadership of another Afro-Brazilian named da Souza), Olympio began to take an interest in politics. Realizing that they had a potentially powerful antagonist on their hands, the French brought pressure on the United Africa Co. to transfer Olympio to Paris. Olympio, who was wealthy enough to risk losing his pension, voluntarily quitted his job to become C.U.T.'s full-time boss.

Olympio changed the party's goal from Ewe reunification to union for the two Togos. Convinced that his party could not hope for a fair deal in the 1955 elections, Olympio called a C.U.T. boycott, lobbied in the United Nations until that organization refused to recognize the referendum which had confirmed Grunitzky in power, called for an end to Togo's trusteeship status and advocated further association with France.

Olympio made his point and the French agreed to hold U.N.-supervised elections in April, 1958. The necessary pre-election groundwork revealed the usual African problems which, one suspects, are not fully understood on the Lake Success martini-circuit. Residency qualifications are difficult to establish on this Balkanized sector of the Gulf of Guinea because the population tends to ignore the artificial boundaries imposed by the European conquest. A prosperous Ewe trader born in Lomé may have homes and families in Accra, Ho and Cotonou. Yorubas from Lagos often work in French territory for years while Fulani nomads from Northern Nigeria yearly trek their cattle into Togo to share the grazing lands of their Togolese cousins. Many Africans have as many as eight names which they use on different occasions; others change their name every year and custom forbids them to recognize a dated version. The question of determining who is a minor and who isn't is complicated by the fact that there are no birth certificates in the bush and few Africans have more than a general idea as to their age. The French applied a typically Gallic and eminently practical criterion for determining the eligibility of Togo's female electorate which might or might not receive the enthusiastic endorsement of the Iowa League of Women Voters: the shape and firmness of the breasts, as appraised by critical and presumably expert French officials, determined in borderline cases which girl got the ballot and which did not.

The electoral lists, which United Nations Election Commissioner Max Dorsinville asserted included 'a large number of double registrations, registrations of deceased, absent or unknown persons', eventually closed with 491,000 out of Togo's 1·3 million citizens eligible to vote. As election hour drew near, Lomé was tense. Reports were heard of an impending general strike, of a postponement of the election, of a C.U.T. boycott, of the expulsion of Dorsinville from the country, of truck-loads of pro-government illegal voters coming in from Dahomey. Little was added to the composure of the city by the rumour that C.U.T. toughs and bully-boys from the rival P.T.P. and U.C.P.N. were buying up all available stocks of acid and syringes, presumably to squirt in each other's eyes. In a last-minute attempt to bring off a conservative victory, candidates' deposits (returned if the candidate polls 10 per cent of his constituency's vote) were raised from about £8 to almost £80, ten times more than the average Togolese makes in a year and a sum five times as large as candidates for the French National Assembly are required to post. The French, fearing either a *putsch* or an inundation of ineligible voters, closed the Ghana border. C.U.T. political rallies were curbed by the application of a law promulgated on June 30, 1881, some twenty-five years before France entered Togo. Several nationalists allegedly were beaten for shouting *ablode* (freedom), the party rallying cry. Nigerian traders were selling electoral cards in the market for £1 10s.

As voters trooped to the polls, it looked bad for Olympio and the C.U.T.: the first man on hand at a northern booth loped in wearing nothing but a straw boater and a big smile to cast a pink U.C.P.N. ballot; a centre was discovered by a C.U.T. worker where patriotic voters could have removed the indelible ink which indicated they had exercised the franchise, thus enabling them to perform their civic duty at a host of polling stations; a couple of clashes took place in which batons were applied with perhaps excessive enthusiasm to those advising their neighbours to use the white ballot papers of the C.U.T.

But all in all, the election was as straight as the results were astounding: Olympio's C.U.T. won 19 of 23 seats in the South, showed surprising strength in the North by taking 10 of 23 contests, rolled up a comfortable 60 per cent majority of the popular vote and secured a total of 29 of the 46 seats, more than enough to form a government. The U.C.P.N. took 10 seats, all in the North, and, although Grunitzky was elected to his Atakpame South seat (112 per cent of the electorate in his constituency appeared to have voted), he was joined in the Assembly by only two other P.T.P. candidates. Four seats were won by independents and these soon demonstrated their political astuteness and agility by lining up with Olympio, giving his government 33 seats to the Opposition's 13.

The most ironic aspect of the election was that Olympio had not been permitted to offer himself as a candidate. The nationalist leader had been disqualified and fined £8,000 (which he paid) for contravention of *foreign exchange* regulations: he had failed to tell the French that he had a £5,000 savings account in Accra. The overwhelming victory of the C.U.T. left the French no option but to select as premier the obvious and undisputed leader of that party.

Olympio, who speaks perfect French, German, English and Ewe and a smattering of Portuguese, emerged from his modest *La Hutte* residence, brushed off the white powder dusted on him by his jubilant supporters as a sign of victory, and flew off to Paris and New York to negotiate for Togo's freedom. The French, somewhat to their surprise, found Olympio to be not only a convinced nationalist but a moderate one, a cool hand at political poker with a world view of politics and enough administrative know-how to make his opinions respected, a tough bargainer but one who could be relied upon to keep his word once he had given it.

This reformer without illusions quickly gained full internal autonomy for Togo beginning January 1, 1959, followed this up by obtaining a secret French commitment for independence to come on April 27, 1960. Olympio yielded nothing except a promise (which he kept) to say nothing about the agreement on independence until after the rest of French Africa had voted on de Gaulle's constitution.

Olympio, who retains much of his Big Business manner (he still finds time to manage his own coconut plantation) and bears little resemblance to the more blustery variety of African nationalist, admits that Togo will need French technical and financial assistance for 'some time to come' and he seems unlikely to sacrifice his chances for securing either on the altar of political extremism.

In the months since independence relations between Togo and Ghana have rapidly deteriorated. Again, the bone of contention has been the question of Ewe unification and of *anschluss* between the two

Togos. All Ewes want unification but they differ as to how it should be achieved. Early this year Ghana's president, Kwame Nkrumah, stated publicly that Togo, when it became independent, should be 'totally integrated' with Ghana as his nation's seventh province. Olympio quickly rejected the proposal and said that Togo would enter into no 'master and boy' union with Ghana. Ghana's finance minister, K. A. Gbedemah, who is an Ewe, in March stated that Ghana and Togo would 'definitely be reunified' whether Olympio 'liked it or not'. In its draft republican constitution published the same month, Ghana made provision for the integration 'of peoples who are at present outside Ghana', a direct threat to Togo.

Then, on the eve of Togo's independence, Ghana announced that it had procured what purported to be a copy of a draft constitution for Togo, to be implemented after the French withdrawal, which claimed all of ex-British Togo as a part of the new republic. Ghana's note to the French alleged the existence of a 'conspiracy' the general plan of which 'was to create such a breakdown of law and order in the Volta region as to justify, by the date of Togoland's independence on April 27, 1960, a claim that the administration had broken down and therefore outside Powers should intervene and the frontiers be redemarcated'. The Ghana government said that it had information that preparations were being made to bridge a river to facilitate the passage of insurgents into Ghana, that two training camps for para-military purposes had been established in Togo and that maps showing portions of Ghana incorporated into Togo were being distributed. It added that the 'Underground Army' of the Togoland Congress, an organization in the British sector which bitterly fought the integration of the region with Ghana in 1956, was to spearhead the 'conspiracy'.

Olympio retorted that it was Nkrumah who was planning subversion to secure the forcible incorporation of Togo into Ghana and warned that he would call for United Nations help in the case of any aggression against Togo. Radio Lomé commented that Ghana's charges 'recall the old fable of the wolf and the lamb'. It said that the bridge mentioned in the Ghanaian note was built of logs at the request of both the Togo and Ghanaian communities for whom it was the only means of access to essential markets. To imply that it was built for aggressive purposes, the broadcast added, displayed 'a Boy Scout's conception of military strategy'. The French ambassador in Accra, who examined the alleged 'Togo draft constitution', asserted that the document was not genuine and warned Ghana that it was aware of 'preparations directed against

233

the independence and integrity' of Togo. Nkrumah reacted by moving troops on to the border and arresting twenty-six Ghanaians, including an Opposition M.P. and four chiefs, on grounds that they were implicated in the 'conspiracy'. Two other Opposition leaders fled to Lomé. Relations between the two governments have not improved substantially in recent weeks.

Says Olympio: 'We are the uncomfortable meat in the political sandwich between powerful Nigeria and rich Ghana. I regard the Ghana-Guinea union as rash but would like to see an eventual confederation of states on the Gulf of Benin. Dr. Nkrumah likes to speak of "an African personality"; there is also such a thing as a Togolese personality: we have not fought so long to achieve our national identity to lose it to another state just because it is lucky enough to have cocoa money.'

Olympio, who is married and has five children, is one of the few African leaders who have realized that one of the most significant trends in the world today as far as Africa is concerned is the movement towards European unity. Although there was no political unity in Africa prior to the advent of the European, imperialism emphasized the differences between the Africans rather than their similarities. Olympio believes that the pooling of Europe's resources is the only route to the sound economic integration of Africa which he feels must be achieved before political unity can be anything but a dream. In this he shares to a large extent the thoughts of the Ivory Coast's respected leader, Felix Houphouet-Boigny.

JUVENTO

But if Olympio has given little Togo the sort of far-sighted leadership not always readily in evidence in emergent Africa, this leadership is being strongly challenged at home. His smashing victory at the polls in 1958 left Olympio faced with only a hopelessly demoralized opposition lacking in popular support except in the extreme north. It also underlined the strength of the militant youth wing of the C.U.T. led by forty-seven-year-old Anani Santos.

Santos, a dapper little man who likes to wear metal tips on the heels of his shoes, lived in France for eighteen years, earned a law degree from the University of Paris, returned to Togo in 1946 and has been active in nationalist circles since then. *Le Mouvement de la Jeunesse Togolaise* (JUVENTO), ostensibly C.U.T.'s youth group but in fact a separate and more radical political party which has seen fit to ally itself with Olympio, hired Santos as its legal adviser and he has represented the organization before the U.N. on several occasions.

JUVENTO in the past has presented no candidates under its own label but has had considerable say as to who receives C.U.T. endorsement. As a reward for JUVENTO's role in the election victory, Olympio gave the able, intense lawyer the post of Minister of Justice in his new cabinet. But Santos—who like da Souza and Olympio is probably of Afro-Brazilian origin—soon demonstrated that he wanted to go further and faster than Olympio. Santos is an ardent admirer of Nkrumah and he soon took a page from the Ghanaian's book by gathering around him and building into a personal political machine the young, the poor, the dissatisfied, the half-educated and the vocal. The attorney, who is married to a Ghanaian girl and speaks excellent English, is making it increasingly evident that he sees independence only as a step towards federation with Ghana.

When we talked together in his Lomé office, Santos said that JUVENTO had no other goal at present beyond independence for Togo. But he added that JUVENTO 'differs from C.U.T. on certain basic questions, the nature of which will be revealed at the proper time'. He added that he was a socialist and soon demonstrated that he is one of the few Africans who have any real understanding of the meaning of that over-worked term. It was presumed that Santos and JUVENTO would stick with Olympio's C.U.T. until independence had been won. But Santos, satisfied that his personal political fences were secure, broke with Olympio last summer, gave up his cabinet post (Olympio now holds the Justice Portfolio as well as those of Finance and Foreign Affairs) and threw JUVENTO's hat in the ring. Even before this there had been evidence that all was not well between the two leaders. In January of 1959 the French were informed—it is said that the information came from Ghana Foreign Minister Kojo Botsio, but this seems unlikely—that JUVENTO was about to stage a coup which would include Olympio's imprisonment and a declaration of independence. French paratroopers were flown in from Senegal and Dahomey, and Lomé was encircled. The plot—if there was one— failed to come off and the red-faced French withdrew.

Olympio had this to say about JUVENTO rumblings: 'They are good boys, just immature. The French come to me with tales of palace revolutions. Poouf! I organized JUVENTO and I understand these young men very well: they have not the stomachs for coups.'

Olympio undoubtedly did know the minds of the JUVENTO radicals when he was leader of a party with neither seats in the Assembly nor responsibilities. But the task of ruling has induced a new moderation in the Ewe leader and his apparent policy of further identification with Dahomey and Niger at the expense of Ghana has alienated ardent Togolese Pan-Africanists. A JUVENTO backed by Ghanaian gold and regrouped by party organizers from Nkrumah's C.P.P. figures to become a dangerous antagonist for Sylvanus Olympio and his C.U.T.

PARADISE AND POVERTY

Along its 350-mile south-to-north axis, this shoestring-thin country with a population density of 25 to the square mile is an ethnic and agricultural cross-section of the great continent of which it is such an insignificant part. First there is the thundering, blue-green sea, the broad beaches lined with coconut palms, their trunks bent by the wind in graceful curves no ballerina could duplicate. Behind the dunes is the shining black thread of the thirty-five-mile tarred road which links Togo with Ghana and Dahomey. And then the airy grass huts of the fishing tribes. These fishing villages on the coast of Togo are the closest thing there is in Africa to a black Eden: the broad-backed men slowly pull their nets in to the shore or paddle lazily beyond the reef, nursing their dug-outs to the edge of the surf, then with one great effort and a joyful shout dig their paddles deep in the swell and propel themselves and their foam-spewing craft on to the wide and gentle sands of the beach; the women, naked to the waist or wrapped in a length of eye-rejoicing cloth, laugh around their smoky fires as they split the coconuts, pour out the milk (which will be served a little later as a potent wine) and throw the husks out to dry before they are sold to the Greek copra traders; boys run naked among the piles of rotting fish while for the little girls modesty requires a string of beads around the waist to which, as they grow older, a flap fore and aft will be added. This is a country Gauguin would have loved.

Behind the coastal villages are the people of the lagoons, who live in flimsy, stilt-supported huts raised over tidal sandbars. Here fish are to be had (if you are more skilful than I) by wading through the chest-high water and scooping them up in calabashes or wicker nets and there are great canoe-taxis which chanting boatmen pole from the mouth of the slow-flowing Haho across the lagoon to Togoville.

Behind Lake Togo the soil gets a little less sandy, the coconut palms thin out and are eventually supplanted by oil palms, and corn and manioc can be grown. Here the people, although they are still Ewes, have had less inter-mixture with whites and other coast tribes and their features become slightly more negroid. Further inland the forest becomes thicker and the heat muggier and you are in country scented by the white blooms of the coffee bushes, studded with great groves of trees under which stand the golden-brown cacao shoots, hung with fruit which looks like slightly flattened giant lemons. This in its turn gives way to the hotter and drier plains of the Mono River valley tufted with cotton. Then the cotton can go no further and nothing will grow but peanuts and finally these are not strong enough to suck any nourishment from the arid land and there is the empty open country of the cattle people, Muslim and light-skinned.

Togo is a paradise but it is a poverty-racked Eden which until 1947 could not afford a single high school. The pint-sized nation earns only £9 million per year from her cacao (8,000 tons), coffee (4,800 tons), peanuts, copra and palm oil, half of this being accounted for by the first two exports. She needs all her manioc, corn and meat for internal consumption and still cannot feed herself. Togo's exports under French administration were not large enough to pay for what she imported and the French each year had to make a grant of £714,000 just to balance the books of the country's pitiable £4 million current budget, not counting subsidies for capital improvements such as schools, roads, bridges, airports, hospitals and port facilities.

To the great credit of his administration, Olympio, instead of going begging, has instituted an austerity programme which has resulted in a balanced budget since 1959. Expense accounts of government officials have been subjected to sharp scrutiny, bureaucratic expansion has been opposed, the tax structure has been streamlined to tap new sources of revenue, the value of exports has been increased while import levels have been maintained, thus creating a favourable balance of trade (to set an example, he frequently bicycles to work and carefully turns off the refrigerator before going to bed).

Olympio simply refuses to accept that Togo must collapse from economic debility. He asserts: 'Our country is going to try to live within its means. But we want to improve the living conditions of the people and for this reason you will not hear much from us in international politics. Time and money will be spent on bettering our economic position, not on sending delegates to conference tables. International assistance will be welcomed, but it must fit local realities and serve only to supplement development programmes instituted through our own efforts and our own resources. This is the only route to national self-respect.'

Much remains to be done. Although 200 Togolese are attending French universities and school enrolments top 80,000 (more than 50 per cent of the school-age population), less than 2,000 students attend high school and there are only 355 technical school pupils.

Although the national health is so poor that 24 per cent of Togo's annual budget in one recent year was allocated to this heading, there is still only one decent hospital (Lomé) in the country and eight rural 'medical centres' staffed by about forty doctors, more than half of whom are black. It is this grinding poverty as much as anything else that makes Olympio's political position so shaky.

How much of this poverty is attributable to African shiftlessness? We stopped at a European-owned coconut plantation—one of the few since only 1,400 of 1·5 million acres under cultivation are owned by non-natives—and watched an African slowly hoisting himself up the rough trunk with the aid of a loop of vines used like a telephone lineman's rig. He took his time about getting to the top, lopped off one coconut, watched it smack into the sand below, blew his nose thoughtfully and with satisfaction into his hand, exchanged a joke with a comrade looped to a nearby tree, then slowly sliced the stem of a second nut. The whole process, not including the climbing, had taken about a minute and a half. African women squatted about in the shade of the grove splitting the nuts which naked children collected from beneath the trees. The women set no speed records.

'These people are lazy and there is nothing you can do to make them work,' said a young Frenchman who accompanied us, one of the thousand or so who have stayed on in Togo. 'One native of Indo-China can do the work of three black men,' he added. I asked him if they had ever tried giving incentive bonuses. They had, but discovered that it caused 'palaver' (trouble) among the workers and defeated its own purpose because a man who made double pay one day could see no sense in coming to work at all on the following one.

There are countless examples of African laziness. In part this may be attributed to the nature of the African's diet, which is loaded with starch and very shy of proteins: a tired man is not an efficient worker. But more than this, there is the whole question of the concept of time and differing attitudes towards the question of savings. The African is in no hurry not so much because he is lazy but because he sees no sense in haste. There is this about Africa: it is easy to survive but difficult to prosper. Food of sorts is available in the sea, in the trees, on the bushes and in the roots under the ground. To work hard to improve upon these gifts from the gods is to make the gods jealous: from him who has little, little will be stolen, says an African proverb. And this conditions the African's regard of saving as well as of creating. When there is a food surplus, he sees little sense in storing vast quantities. He has learned from generations of bitter experience that a full granary is an open invitation to a more warlike and less industrious tribe to loot his village and carry away his women. Also there are rats and rain. If you have much food, the African reasons, it is better to eat until you cannot walk and let tomorrow look after itself. Once you have eaten what you have, nobody can take it away from you.

All this is true but it is becoming less so every day as Africans slowly and painfully adjust themselves to a money economy. Postal savings accounts and benefit societies are multiplying and there *are* many Africans who do 'work like blacks'. Perhaps it is no coincidence that most of these work for themselves, not for white planters. And one wonders if we are not so used to our own nervousness that we have made a virtue out of what is little more than an inability to sit still, a sport at which the African is a top-drawer performer.

To bolster his country's emaciated economy, Olympio is banking heavily on a phosphate scheme which got under way early this year and, if all goes well, will produce nearly a million tons a year. The deposits are thirty miles north-east of Lomé and fourteen miles from the sea. Initial costs, including construction of a short rail line, will be about £3·5 million.

There is also a slim chance for oil. But Togo still lacks a good deep-water port and adequate internal transport. The paved road stops abruptly a few miles north of Lomé and the northern half of the country has neither railway nor navigable water to get its products to market. The very shape of the country, which in some places is only thirty miles wide, militates against the development of a sound economy.

The question of a modern port has troubled this stretch of the Guinea coast for years. Either Lomé or Cotonou is equally feasible as a route to the sea for the products of Niger and Upper Volta, the two vast, land-locked republics of the Union of Benin. France, although she has not been ungenerous towards Togo, has been unwilling to sink a lot of money into port facilities for a country whose future membership in the French Community was and is uncertain. Nor have Togo-Dahomey relations been completely amicable: Dahomey, which has the reputation of being 'an intellectual country', has long been jealous of Togo's greater political freedom and fearful that her neighbour to the west might seek (as some Ewe leaders have advocated) to include the Dahomey side of the Mono River delta in an all-Ewe state. For these reasons and because she sees no sense in taking a slice of the pie when she may well get the whole bakery, Dahomey has been unwilling to share a common port with Togo.

Under its special status as a U.N. trust territory, Togo did not vote in de Gaulle's 1958 referendum. Dahomey, of course, did go to the polls and she voted solidly for the General's Fifth Republic. Since preliminary studies began on the improvement of Cotonou's harbour a few months later, it is reasonable to assume that Serou Apithy, premier politician of Dahomey, obtained a French commitment to build the harbour in his country in return for a *oui* vote.

THE DISPOSSESSED

After one of the few bad meals which we had in Gallic Africa, I walked from Lomé's hot, ageing Hotel du Golf past the two-storey, Arab-style Ministry of Justice which is so light and airy that it appears to be built of vanilla icing, into the visitors' gallery of the modernistic National Assembly. It was the closing session and the delegates were fidgeting as they waited for the gavel to fall and the party to begin in an adjoining banquet room.

Olympio, who wore a business suit, was in good form and obviously enjoying an exchange of verbal barbs (in which he was certainly emerging the victor) with an Opposition spokesman, a Northerner who had lost several fingers of his right hand to leprosy. But there was an obvious feeling of restiveness outside in the hot sunlight where young men in sunglasses and patched sports shirts muttered among themselves. They were some of the 7,000 Togolese expelled from Ivory Coast after bloody rioting in Abidjan in the beginning of 1959.

Having little economic opportunity at home, Togolese and Dahomeyans for generations have gone 'abroad', i.e., to other areas of French Africa to seek work. Although Togo is so poor that less than one out of five school-age children receive any education, the Togolese (perhaps inspired by their own poverty) are comparatively hard workers and have a reputation for intelligence exceeded only by Dahomeyans. As soon as one Togolander settles in a job, he sends for a relative and shares

his salary with him until the newcomer is able to get a job. As Togolanders rise in commercial firms and the civil service, other Africans
find it becoming increasingly difficult to get promotion. As a result,
rioting broke out in Abidjan and the entire Togolese community had
to be repatriated. Many of these still have not found jobs and they are
fertile ground for Santos' JUVENTO organizers.

A few weeks later a Frenchman in Abidjan told me that he for one
was glad to see the Togolanders go. 'Why?' I asked. 'They are a bunch
of thieves,' he replied, 'and you can't trust them around a cash box.'
As an afterthought he added: 'Not that they are any worse than the
others, of course.' This is an old cliché which is just true enough to be
deceptive. As a Southerner I was brought up to believe that Negroes
were congenital thieves. In two and a half years in Africa I saw plenty
of evidence of theft in all strata of society. But the question is more a
social problem than a moral one. African society *requires* a man to give
money not only to his close relatives but to his clansmen when they ask
for it. It makes no difference if the clansman is making a reasonable
attempt to earn a living or is spending his days shooting craps. He
has the right to make the demand and his employed kinsman has the
responsibility of complying. To renege on such an obligation is far
worse than stealing. What is reprehensible in our society becomes an
act of virtue in Africa. Who is right, the white man or the black? In
his own society and on his own continent, there can be only one answer:
the African is right. This is the sort of thing that brings a hurt look to
the faces of British and American liberals who, if they had any knowledge of Africa, would have known better in the first place.

Back at the Hotel du Golf we were wrapping ourselves around a
couple of quarts of Heineken's preparatory to facing the next stage of
our journey when a plump little Indian, so dark he could be nothing
but a Madrasi, introduced himself and asked if he could join us. He
was a fidgety man and he kept saying 'Please?' when I asked him what
he was doing and how he liked Togo. He produced a printed calling
card which identified him as a professor at a well-known Indian
university and president of an anti-colonial organization. He liked Togo
and had collected reams of government publications which he intended
to use in his classrooms. He had been head of the African Affairs
Department of his university for several years. 'You have made many
trips to Africa, then?' I asked. It was his first. Did this not make it
rather difficult to lecture on African affairs? He smiled and said he had
plenty of contacts who let him know what was going on. It was **not**

hard to imagine the well-balanced version of events which he received from his African friends. I asked him if the French had given him any trouble. He pursed his lips for a moment and then said slowly:

'No. I wouldn't say that they had given me any trouble. They have provided me with a car, chauffeur and an interpreter, and they are paying my hotel bill. But the man at the publications office appeared aggravated when I told him I'd like to have all my materials air-mailed to Bombay.' He had, of course, made no arrangement about paying for the postage, which must have been considerable.

We finished our beers and said our farewells to the professor and to little Togo, the threadbare stepchild of Gallic Africa, paradise and political volcano.

Chapter 11

*

THE CLAW

The Union of Benin, which superimposed on a map of the United States would stretch from Maine to New Mexico and from Canada to Florida, became something approaching a federation of independent nations almost in spite of itself.

The four states which make up the Union—Ivory Coast, the Voltaic Republic, Niger and Dahomey—under the vigorous leadership of Ivory Coast's Felix Houphouet-Boigny, were the staunchest supporters of the Community as seen by de Gaulle: a grouping of African states with internal autonomy in a direct relationship with France which was to handle their foreign affairs, defence, higher education and economic planning.

It was Houphouet's intention that his republic and those associated with it should become more, not less, French. As a concession to those who wished some form of association in a larger African 'state', he set up the Union of Benin (the name is seldom heard now) after the establishment of the Fifth Republic. But this was to be only an economic union in which the four republics would co-ordinate their policies in certain fields (justice, customs, civil service, labour and public health), have equal access to the port of Abidjan, contribute to a mutual development fund, and send delegations to discuss matters of common concern from time to time.

In a very real sense, de Gaulle (and the trend of history) forced Houphouet into independence. Early last summer, apparently against Houphouet's advice, de Gaulle made it possible for the French African republics to attain independence and still remain within the Community. As republic after republic requested and received independence, Houphouet found himself outflanked and in serious danger of losing political control in his own country. Left with no alternative, he bitterly demanded and received independence for his country.

The Union of Benin is shaped like a claw or a rough human hand. Dahomey, the thumb, separates Nigeria from Togo and touches the Atlantic Ocean. Ivory Coast, which represents the rest of the fingers,

243

also touches the sea. Clasped in the palm of the claw, between Dahomey and Ivory Coast, are Ghana and Togo. To the west of Ivory Coast opposite the fingernails are Liberia and Guinea. The knuckles, pressing into Mali, are the Voltaic Republic. The fourth state, Niger, is in the position of a forearm connected to both Dahomey and the Voltaic Republic by a narrow wrist at its western end. Also to the west is Mali while Algeria and Libya border Niger on the north. On Niger's eastern flank is Chad, and Nigeria is to the south. In all, the boundaries of the Union of Benin touch those of eight independent nations (Libya, Guinea, Liberia, Ghana, Togo, Mali and Nigeria) and France, for Algeria constitutionally is an integral part of the Metropole.

In this vast area (734,000 square miles, a little smaller than the United States east of the Mississippi) live 9·2 million Africans, fewer people than inhabit Pennsylvania. These come in a satisfactory variety of shades ranging from Bilbo-white Tuareg of the north to Robeson-black Baoules in the south. There are fewer 'Europeans' (21,100) than there are in Fond du Lac, Wisconsin. The economies of the four states are as varied as their peoples: Ivory Coast (the well-off member) prospers on coffee, cacao and timber; the Voltaic Republic gets by mostly on army veterans' pensions and remittances from its sons working 'abroad', Niger scrapes along on peanuts and Dahomey keeps the hyena from the door with palm products and the export of clerical personnel.

The Union of Benin (motto: 'Equality and solidarity') has been in business for little more than a year. To understand what and why it is, we must go back for a moment to have a look at the larger political unit of which it was once a part.

Although the merchants of Dieppe had traded on the west coast of Africa and occasionally established temporary trading stations on the shore as early as the fourteenth century, French occupation may be said to date from 1638, the year in which St. Louis (at the mouth of the Senegal River) was colonized. This by no means, however, marks the beginning of the era of French paramountcy: France managed to lose St. Louis to the English three times before, in 1817, she finally secured the town. The French held Assini, on the Ivory Coast, from 1687 to 1705 and established another post further up the same coast in 1787. The island of Goree (across the bay from modern Dakar) was even more of a turntable than St. Louis: the French ousted the Dutch in 1677, lost the post to the English four times before obtaining permanent control in 1817. French attempts to seize the mouth of the Gambia

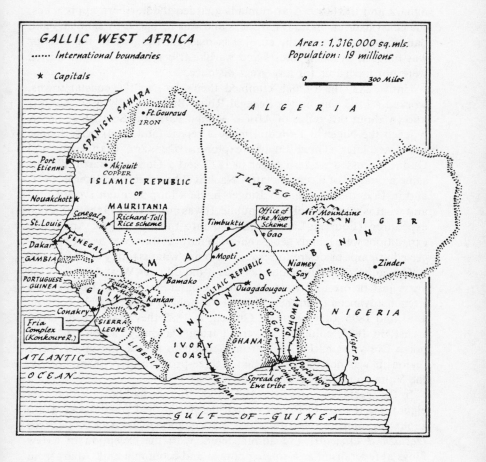

GALLIC WEST AFRICA

...... International boundaries

★ Capitals

Area: 1,316,000 sq. mls.
Population: 19 millions

0   300 Miles

ALGERIA

SPANISH SAHARA

• Ft. Gouraud
IRON

Port
Etienne

• Akjouit
COPPER

ISLAMIC REPUBLIC
OF
MAURITANIA

TUAREG

Nouakchott

Senegal R.

St. Louis

Richard-Toll
Rice scheme

Timbuktu

Office of
the Niger
Scheme

Air Mountains

NIGER

SENEGAL

Dakar

GAMBIA

PORTUGUESE
GUINEA

M   A   L   I

Gao

BENIN

• Mopti

Bamako

Niamey
Say

Zinder

Fouta Djalon

Kankan

VOLTAIC REPUBLIC

Ouagadougou

Conakry

SIERRA
LEONE

GUINEA

UNION

TOGO

OF

DAHOMEY

NIGERIA

Niger R.

Fria
Complex
(Konkoure R.)

LIBERIA

IVORY
COAST

GHANA

Porto Novo

Cotonou

Abidjan

Lome

Spread of
Ewe tribe

ATLANTIC

OCEAN

GULF — OF — GUINEA

from Britain and Bissau from the Portuguese failed during the same period.

Very little was known of the interior. The waterless wastes of the Sahara and the fierce Arab nomads guarded the northern approaches; the coast had few natural harbours and was menaced by sandbars and dangerous tides; once the coast was reached, the way to the interior was blocked by thick forests and warlike tribes; such rivers as existed were not navigable for any great distance.

Until 1883, the French confined themselves to the coastal towns, worked a little way up the Senegal River. But gradually more became known about this bulge of Africa: Mungo Park, the Scottish explorer, reached the Niger in 1796 and made a repeat (and fatal) performance ten years later. Three English explorers (Denham, Clapperton and Oudney) crossed western Niger in 1823 and a German (Barth) did the same a quarter of a century later. Nachtigal hiked across Niger in 1871, and in 1890 the Frenchman Binger made a loop through Ivory Coast and what is now the Voltaic Republic. It was not until 1899 that a French expedition (Foureau-Lamy) ventured into modern Niger. And these expeditions were mainly geographical in nature: there was as yet no concerted attempt or desire to seize or colonize what is today Gallic Africa.

The colonizing drive came here, as it did all over West Africa, in the years just before and after the Berlin Conference (1885). In 1883, the French advanced from their Senegal toe-hold to seize Soudan; between 1887 and 1896, they occupied Guinea; in 1889 they grabbed the Ivory Coast; in 1897, columns converged from Dahomey, which had been taken five years earlier, and from Soudan to invade the upper Volta region; it was not until 1900 that a three-pronged drive from Algeria, the Volta and Chad conquered Niger.

In the seventeen years from 1883–1900, France had occupied an area eight times the size of France or half the size of the United States. Until 1958 this immense territory was to be known as A.O.F. (*Afrique Occidental Français*) and administered, with the exception of a few flings at federalism, as a single political and economic unit. Apart from its vastness, its distinguishing characteristics were a lack of natural divisions, the relative poverty of its soil, the sparseness of its population (four people to the square kilometre, as opposed to twenty-one in the United States, seventy-nine in France), its lack of adequate harbours, navigable rivers, and the multiplicity of languages (126 principal ones and hundreds of dialects) spoken by the 19·2 million people scattered across its 1·8 million square miles.

THE CLAW

Despite these unfavourable factors, the eight territories of A.O.F.—Mauritania, Senegal, Soudan, Guinea, Ivory Coast, Upper Volta, Niger and Dahomey—in 1956 were able to produce for internal consumption: 2·4 million tons of millet, 1·9 million tons of yams, 1·8 million tons of manioc, 600,000 tons of rice, 450,000 tons of plantains and 150,000 tons of meat, with a total value of about £190 million. In the same year, she was able to export £78 million worth of agricultural produce (peanuts, coffee, cacao, palm oil and bananas), £1·4 million worth of meat, £2·8 million worth of timber, and minerals valued at £2·8 million.

There were 2,558 miles of railway (with 335 stations) hauling 365 million ton-miles and 287 million passenger-miles and 50,000 miles of roads, of which 20 per cent were classified as 'highways'. Seven hundred doctors and 500 midwives gave 7·5 million smallpox vaccinations and treated 454,000 people for sleeping sickness. There were 370,000 children in elementary schools, 12,000 in secondary schools and 7,000 in vocational institutes.

The wealth of the area is by no means uniform, however (even within the smaller unit of Benin this is so: two out of every three motor vehicles in the Union are registered in Ivory Coast). The 800,000 tons of peanuts which earn £35·6 million (40 per cent of the total exports by value) come almost entirely from Senegal and Soudan. Most of the coffee (worth £19·3 million) and timber and all of the cacao is grown in Ivory Coast. The bulk of the palm oil comes from Dahomey and Guinea grows the majority of the bananas. Ivory Coast, Guinea, Senegal and Mauritania are more generously supplied with minerals than the other four. Secondary industries are concentrated in Dakar (Senegal) and Abidjan (Ivory Coast). Niger and Volta have very little in the way of any sort of resources. Lacking throughout A.O.F. are coal, oil or adequate hydro-electric power, the indispensables for industrialization. In an attempt to buck up the economy of A.O.F., France poured £193·6 million into capital improvements (mostly transport facilities) between 1947 and 1957.

The year 1957, as we have seen, was a fateful one for Gallic Africa. The *loi cadre*, while it retained the Grand Council of A.O.F., set in motion by giving a greater degree of autonomy to the legislatures of each territory the centrifugal forces which have since balkanized French Africa. The advent of de Gaulle's Fifth Republic the following year abolished the federal framework and left it up to each territory to choose between independence and membership in the Community.

If the latter choice was taken (as it was by seven of the eight A.O.F. territories), each autonomous republic would then determine whether it wished membership in a new federal state of two or more territories, merger with other territories to form a larger unitary republic, or a separatist solution leaving it in a direct relationship with Paris.

We have seen that among the four territories of Equatorial Africa, three of these views found supporters: Chad and Gabon favoured separatism, Middle Congo wanted a federalist state and Ubangi-Shari dreamed of a great unitary republic. The initial outcome was somewhere between the first two solutions: each of the republics became autonomous but three agreed to share certain common services.

Three views were pushed equally vigorously in A.O.F.: Sekou Touré of Guinea and Djibo Bakary of Niger advocated complete independence; Leopold Senghor, Lamine Gueye and Mamadou Dia of Senegal joined with Modibo Keita of Soudan to advocate the creation of a federal state within the Community; Felix Houphouet-Boigny and Auguste Denise of Ivory Coast allied themselves with Daniel Ouezzin-Coulibaly of Volta in calling for separate paths for each republic within the Community. Mokhtar Ould Daddah's Mauritania and Serou Apithy's Dahomey, each faced with special economic and political problems, hung on the fence.

This divergence of opinion had its roots in the events of the last half of the 1940's. Hoping to present a solid African front to France in an attempt to gain political equality within the post-war French Union, Felix Houphouet-Boigny called a meeting of African political leaders at Bamako in October 1946, where he founded the African Democratic Rally (R.D.A.). Houphouet, who used Communist organizational techniques and slogans and allied himself for parliamentary purposes with the French Communist Party, quickly brought under the R.D.A. umbrella many splinter and regional parties and, within two years of the party's founding, was able to boast 700,000 members. But clashes of personal ambition heightened by ideological differences prevented the R.D.A. from reaching a position where it could speak for Gallic Africa in one voice.

The secretary-general of the R.D.A., Gabriel d'Arboussier, who was then closely allied with the Communists, gave the party such a radical slant that the respected Senegal politicians Senghor and Gueye dropped out to form their own more conservative parties which quickly gained control of Senegal and Niger. R.D.A. went into a rapid decline.

Houphouet, who is as astute a politician as ever kissed a baby, quickly realized that the R.D.A.'s early success had been due more to the fact that the party had been an Africa-First group than that it had been far to the Left. He dumped d'Arboussier in 1950, renounced his political pact with the Communists and set about rebuilding his organization, this time with the support of the French who had opposed him before as being too radical.

The R.D.A.'s second rise to power was even more spectacular than its first. By March 1957, Houphouet's party was in power in four of the eight territories (Ivory Coast, Guinea, Soudan and Volta), held a respectable number of seats in Dahomey and Niger. R.D.A. was shut out only in Mauritania, where a strong regional party held sway, and in Senegal, controlled by Senghor and Gueye. Out of a total of 474 seats in the eight assemblies, R.D.A. held 234.

But in many respects this unity was more apparent than real: the R.D.A. was such a big blanket that it warmed many strange bed-fellows. Some regional parties adhered to it only out of respect for Houphouet or to gain access to the R.D.A. money-box and organizational secrets. Although Houphouet by this time had shifted from the far Left to Right of Centre, many branches of the R.D.A. were controlled by radicals. There was less ideological similarity, for instance, between R.D.A. leaders Houphouet and Touré than there is between Democrats Wayne Morse and Harry Byrd. It was this underlying disunity within the R.D.A. which resulted in the differences which showed up when A.O.F. voted on de Gaulle's constitution and, having voted, decided what to do with its new-found autonomy.

First the referendum: Touré (R.D.A.) of Guinea and Bakary (Socialist) of Niger called for complete independence; Houphouet preached his doctrine that French West Africa needs France's economic assistance, that this is the century of regional groupings, not of exclusive nationalism, that freedom is more important than independence and the two are by no means synonymous, that France still has a cultural contribution to make to Africa, as Africa has one to share with the Metropole. The R.D.A. branches of the other territories and leaders of the regional parties of Senegal and Mauritania went along with the Ivory Coast theorist. Guinea followed Touré to independence; Niger rejected Bakary's lead and voted to stay with the Community; the other six territories obeyed their political leaders and also voted *oui*.

That left seven republics which, having chosen the Community, now had to decide if there was to be a big unitary state, a federation or a separate relationship between each republic and France.

Out of the window went questions of communism or socialism: the focus shifted to a battle between those primarily concerned with economic development and those seeking a political solution to French Africa's problems. Houphouet argued that local autonomy had been won and that what was needed was an economic effort to raise standards of living, health and education. This, he maintained, could best be obtained by each territory following its own course. Senghor and Gueye countered that only by federating into a large state would Africans gain the political prestige necessary to negotiate with France on equal terms and implied that the Community was not (as Houphouet proclaimed) an end in itself but merely a step towards complete independence.

On this clearly-stated divergence of opinion, A.O.F. split wide open. Keita and the entire Soudan branch of the party bolted from the R.D.A. to join forces with Senghor, Dia and Gueye. After dissolving their old parties and creating the African Federalist Party (P.F.A.), these leaders called for a meeting at Bamako (now sort of an African Philadelphia *sans* Liberty Bell) of all those who wished to join the Federation of Mali, namesake of an ancient and glorious African empire. Delegations showed up from Senegal, Soudan, Upper Volta and Dahomey, while Mauritania sent observers. Only Niger and Ivory Coast remained aloof and loyal to Houphouet.

On December 29, 1958, Senegal, Soudan, Upper Volta (which changed its name to the Voltaic Republic) and Dahomey agreed to create Mali, a federal state of 696,500 square miles and 11 million people. The assemblies of each state then ratified the Bamako proclamation and designated delegates to meet at Dakar on January 14 (1959) to draw up a federal constitution.

At Dakar, grizzled Lamine Gueye, the grand old man of Afro-French politics, warned the delegates that some would seek to divide them but added that the opponents of federalism 'cannot stop the sea with their bare arms'. Senghor, poet and political theorist, stated that the Federation 'will create one people with one culture, moved by the same faith and with the same goal, which is the realization of its collective personality'. The delegates cheered themselves hoarse, elected Modibo Keita of Soudan as president of Mali, unanimously approved the constitution and pledged themselves to defend their newly-found unity 'to the point of supreme sacrifice'.

Not since 1949 had Houphouet's political fortunes appeared to be at such a low ebb. But things in Africa today are seldom what they seem and—when they are—they may very well not be so tomorrow.

Houphouet, who had won and lost two political fortunes, set to work to build a third by systematically dismembering Mali.

The Ivory Coast leader pointed out to Voltaic premier Maurice Yameogo that the latter's country was tied firmly to Ivory Coast by the Abidjan-Ouagadougou railway while no good means of communications existed between Volta and the western states of Mali or Dahomey, which would be its only outlets to the sea. How, Houphouet asked, did the Voltaic Republic expect to exist if it joined a federation to which Ivory Coast was opposed? To the Moro Naba, emperor of Volta's warlike and numerous Mossi tribesmen, Houphouet (himself a tribal chieftain) stressed the powerless level to which Senegal and Soudan had reduced their traditional chiefs. To other Voltaic leaders, Houphouet pointed out that their republic annually sent thousands of its citizens to work in the Ivory Coast. Did they think that this situation would still obtain if Volta joined Mali?

Everybody got the point. Although the Voltaic Republic had approved the Mali federal constitution, it had not yet drawn up its own organic document. Yameogo wrote a constitution which forbade Volta to participate in the Mali Federation, rammed it through the Assembly, obtained a referendum confirmation, established a new voting system which operated against proponents of the federation, disqualified several pro-federation political leaders and swept to power in a new election.

Dahomey's premier Serou Apithy had never been enthusiastic about federation. His country's economic life depends upon its role as an outlet to the sea for Niger and the eastern region of the Voltaic Republic. Even at the time of the Bamako and Dakar federalist meetings, Apithy had reservations concerning the advisability of joining Mali since Niger refused to do so. When Yameogo led Volta out of Mali, little Dahomey was left in the position of East Pakistan: its natural hinterland was gone, leaving it geographically and economically isolated from the rest of the federation.

Faced with the prospect that all of the produce of Niger and the Voltaic Republic would be shipped out over the Ouagadougou–Abidjan railway, leaving Dahomey to die a not very slow economic death, Apithy resigned from the P.F.A. stating that he could not support Mali at the expense of 'the free growth and economy' of Dahomey. With him went enough of his followers to cause the fall of the government and prevent Dahomey from joining Mali.

In less than thirty days, Houphouet had taken on the 'supreme sacrifice' boys handily, detached two of Mali's four states from the federation, and seen his R.D.A. capture a total of 283 of the 305 assembly seats in the four Benin republics. It is both ironical and a measure of Houphouet's political flexibility that to smash a federation headed by his political rivals he had to establish a similar union headed by himself. As the price for secession from Mali, Houphouet agreed to the creation of the Union of Benin.

Although there was to be no capital and no federal assembly (it was Houphouet's contention that Africa could not afford the multiplicity of political institutions required by federalism), Houphouet agreed that there should be a *Conseil d'Entente* (Council of Understanding) composed of the premiers and representatives of the assemblies of the four republics which would meet periodically to discuss matters of common interest and establish policies which (with the approval of the four assemblies) would become binding on all of the members of the Union. Most important from the point of view of the other three republics, Houphouet approved an arrangement whereby each republic would contribute 10 per cent of its revenues to a common fund. This fund, which could be used for floating international loans for development purposes, would be divided on this basis: each of the other three republics would receive five-sixteenths, Ivory Coast one-sixteenth. Since Ivory Coast not only will receive only 20 per cent as much as each other republic but will contribute four dollars to every one put into the fund by Niger, Dahomey and the Voltaic Republic, Houphouet in effect has agreed to contribute to the support and development of the other three on a permanent basis. Last year Mali's two component states, Senegal and Soudan, quarrelled and dissolved the federation, Mauritania attained independence, and each of the four states of the Union of Benin achieved full sovereignty, while maintaining their economic links with each other.

And now let's have a look at each of the four republics of the Union of Benin.

IVORY COAST

Ivory Coast, the senior member of the Benin Union, is the richest of the eight territories which once constituted A.O.F. Abidjan, its capital, is second only to Dakar for business intensity and graceful living, a chic French city of broad boulevards, endive salads, vintage wines, and arty bookshops (it also has two flower shops—as opposed to outdoor stalls—a sure index of the sophistication of an African city). Ivory Coast's white population of 17,000 is the second largest in French Africa south of the Sahara (larger: Senegal's 50,000) and many of the republic's Africans are among the most Westernized on the continent. This did not deter the Ivory Coast constituents of a Senator of the French Union from eating him in 1953.

Ivory Coast is a country the size of Italy, bounded on the west by the independent republics of Guinea and Liberia and on the east by Nkrumah's Ghana. To the south is the Atlantic and to the north lie Mali (Soudan) and the Voltaic Republic. The republic's geographical position is significant because it separates Guinea, which has a very loose form of union with Ghana, from Dr. Nkrumah's state. Ivory Coast's 2·5 million rich coffee and cocoa farmers contributed more than 50 per cent of A.O.F.'s federal budget before the collapse of that organization in 1958.

Ivory Coast is the only wood-producing republic in Gallic West Africa and it accounts for 42 per cent of the banana exports of the whole bloc. Only Brazil and Columbia grow more coffee than Ivory Coast and the republic ranks fourth in the world (behind Ghana, Brazil and Nigeria) in cacao exports. Coffee accounts for 57 per cent by value of the country's exports, which are worth about £55 million, cacao represents 28 per cent and timber 8 per cent. Her imports in an average year cost £39 million, leaving a substantial favourable balance of trade, much of it in dollars. Revenue and expenditure, which stood at only £15 million in 1956 when Ivory Coast was a heavy contributor to A.O.F., now amount to £33 million. French aid to Ivory Coast in the decade ending in 1947 amounted to £39 million, half of it being devoted to the development of Abidjan. There have been signs recently that Houphouet, who has always been loyal to France and to de Gaulle's conception of the French Community, feels the Metropole is not doing enough for his country.

Thirty per cent of Ivory Coast's children get some education but there are only about 4,000 secondary school students. There are 90,000 known lepers in the country.

Dieppe merchants touched Ivory Coast in 1339 but the French only came to stay more than five centuries later. The numerous Baoule tribe resisted penetration until after World War I (they rightfully refused to pay taxes, which they regarded as a humiliating token of submission) yet the Baoule became so pro-French that one important chief took himself and 200,000 of his people across the border into Gold Coast rather than accept Vichy's peace-with-dishonour. The 750-mile

Abidjan–Ouagadougou railway, begun in 1903, took fifty-one years to complete. Although the country has only 7 per cent of the total area of A.O.F., it has 14 per cent of the population, of which only a handful are Muslims.

Christianity has never successfully opposed Islam in Africa and the only thing that has slowed the advance of the faith of the Prophet is the tsetse fly, the only thing that has stopped it is the rain forest: Islam is a desert faith and it was spread by conquering horsemen. Horses cannot live under the fly and they lose their tactical effectiveness in the forest. Where either of these conditions has existed, Islam has lost its impetus even though traders wandering on foot have brought it as far as the coast. A religious map of Africa would coincide almost completely with one showing the natural features of the land: Islam reigns where the horse can go, in the desert and on the savannahs; Christianity penetrates only so far as the river-boats could take the missionaries; in the inaccessible forest between the two are the pagans. The fly belt cuts across the top of Ivory Coast and one-third of the republic is covered by rain-forest, hence only 6 per cent of the population is Muslim.

Ivory Coast had the first newspaper published in French West Africa (1932) and today it boasts two of the four Benin papers (the other two are published in Dahomey: neither Volta nor Niger have newspapers). The total circulation of all four does not exceed 20,000 but each copy is probably read to dozens of illiterates by their more evolved kinsmen.

The road from Ghana to Abidjan is excellent until you reach the border post at Dormaa, at which point it disintegrates into a sandy (or muddy, depending on the weather) track. This is no coincidence. The French operated on the theory that the less contact their blacks had with British Africans, the better, and they built their road network accordingly. Consequently all the major roads linking their great land empire skirt the British enclaves. This sounds reasonable but one 'enclave' (Nigeria) is bigger than any European country except Russia, so Robin Hood's barn can assume frustrating dimensions. Another only recently remedied instance: to avoid crossing a ten-mile-wide strip of British territory which bisects the 170-mile direct route from Dakar to Zinguinchor, the French built a 450-mile road. Before the Pan-African political movement can make any sort of economic sense, the entire highway and railway system of West Africa will have to be relined. This, however, does not seem to have occurred to either Dr. Nkrumah or Sekou Touré.

THE CLAW

We passed without incident through Ghanaian customs after assuring the officer in charge, who seemed desirous of making something of it, that Ghana was considerably more wonderful than America. His opposite number on the Ivory Coast side welcomed us 'to France' and, after expressing indifference to passports, health cards and car documents, sent us on to the customs post fifteen miles down the road. There a dozen overloaded lorries were lined up: the African inspector, we were informed, was at lunch. He returned in an hour and proceeded to discharge his functions by bullying the passengers of the lorries until a few franc notes found their way into his pocket. After remarking upon the fine quality of my camera and registering considerable disappointment when I didn't present it to him, he sent us on with an *askari* to the office of a gentleman of whose function I am still unsure. He was known as 'the Captain'. This individual was a large mulatto and he was asleep. But he finally awoke of his own accord—his subordinates were horrified at the suggestion that he should be called—and with the minimum amount of delay necessary to demonstrate his authority admitted us to Ivory Coast. It is one of the tragedies of international relations that the customs and immigration officials who create the strong first and last impressions of a country so often are drawn from the most disagreeable and stupid elements of the nation, whether it be Viet Nam or the United States.

We reduced our boiling points with a heaven-sent Amstel at a little thatched hotel in the tongue-twisting town of Agnibilekrou, then drove on to Abengourou where we had one of the few inferior meals and bad rooms we experienced in French Africa. The room lacked a window and the john—one of the Turkish variety where you squat on a couple of footrests teetering precariously over a hole in the floor and take your chances—was located in the middle of the courtyard around which the rooms opened, an arrangement which contributed little to the aromatic atmosphere of the hostelry. The shower was of that classic variety which spits out four thin streams of water no two of which it is possible to get under at the same time. Abengourou is a truck stop and the gentlemen of the road, innocent of the razor and clad in sweat-stained undershirts, were consuming *pastis* at a prodigious rate. They apparently were not the spiritual heirs of Voltaire and Eboué for they slammed their glasses down on the bar and left in a roar of dust when a crowd of noisy but considerably better-dressed Africans arrived to have dinner.

When we had crossed the Comoe River and were well insulated from British radicalism, the road improved considerably and soon became

255

paved. It wound through forested country under whose pale-trunked trees there were dappled groves of cacao, a sure sign that you will sweat because the bush needs constant and high humidity to thrive. Then there were European-owned coffee estates and the spiked sweep of pineapple plantations and the road climbed a short crest and there was Abidjan before us.

It is characteristic of the French African cities that they are more French than African. Abidjan (population: 128,000) is a good example of this. The centre of the town is completely European: whites keep shops, run restaurants, drive trucks (but not taxis), hawk vegetables in little stalls (adjoining those of African market-women) in the central market, sit in the teller's cage at the bank and wait on African women in the super-market, an unthinkable thing in British Africa. In pavement cafés well-dressed Africans swill frothy Alsatian beer, mutter not about freedom but complain, like the whites, of Abidjan's rising cost of living, up in 1959 from a 1947 index of 100 to 359.

But more than this feeling of racial tolerance and the absence of politicians 'of the Hyde Park variety differentiates a British African city from an Afro-Gallic town: the British have brought their suburb mentality with them to Africa while the French have brought their love of city living. As a result, the British work in the centre of town, which is purely commercial, and live in shady villas on the outskirts while the French tend to occupy flats above their shops or in graceful and modernistic apartment houses. Consequently French African towns tend to be busier and gayer than their British counterparts and a French town seems about twice the size of a British town with the same white population.

Native housing in French Africa seems better, more orderly and more attractive than do British developments. And one of the results of the French policy of identification (sort of a cultural 'togetherness' between the races) as opposed to British differentiation (dedication to the ideal of equality before the legal but not the cocktail bar) is that Africans appear to make more of an effort to live up to European standards. This is not to say that there are no urban slums in French Africa: there are plenty but never, as is the case with Lagos and Ibadan, does a whole city take on a slum atmosphere.

Little more than a decade ago, Abidjan was a sleepy hamlet which handled a few thousand tons of freight each year. Today it is the fastest-growing city in Africa south of the Sahara and it owes it mostly to the Vridi canal. As we have seen, almost the entire coast of West Africa is blocked by sandbars and lacking in natural harbours. Abidjan was no exception to this. For years, every ton of freight destined for the interior of Ivory Coast (ivory ceased to be an important export about the time that the slave trade died) had to be unloaded into lighters at the dangerous open roadstead of Grand Bassam, taken through the surf, unloaded, carted across the spit of land which cut Abidjan off from the sea, loaded into lighters again, ferried across the lagoon, unloaded and piled into trucks, taken to the railway station, unloaded and loaded again. By modernizing the railhead and cutting a canal through the spit, Abidjan almost overnight became a major port and today the city handles 1·2 million tons of freight every year, a total exceeded only by Dakar.

As a result both of its strengthened economic skeleton and of the republic's comparative political stability, public and private investment in Ivory Coast has averaged £12·6 million per year for the last decade. Among the most fantastic schemes is one to make cheap electricity by utilizing the difference in temperature between the surface and deep-sea waters two miles from Abidjan. Results have been encouraging and the experiment holds tremendous promise not only for Ivory Coast and Africa but for all under-developed nations of the world. For the moment, however, Abidjan receives its power from the more prosaic but still impressive recently-completed Bia River hydro-electric scheme, which produces 60 million kilowatt hours per year.

We drove across the multi-million dollar bridge which connects Abidjan with the industrial area of Triecherville and on out to the palm-fringed coast which lies between Port Bouet and the old and ramshackle town of Grand Bassam, the initial point of French penetration but now little more than a sleepy fishing village. The great Atlantic rollers smashed upon the coast with the roar of thunder and, as testimony to their strength, a 4,000-ton freighter was breaking up on the beach while an Italian salvage crew cut her to pieces and her cargo of bags of cement moulded into solid piles on the beach. On the way back we stopped at the airport to watch a DC-3 land. It was a special plane bearing the American Ambassador to France, who was on an 'inspection trip'. He deplaned followed by an aide bearing a briefcase in one hand and a hula hoop in the other. 'Cultural imperialism,' Kitty murmured.

In Abidjan there are lovely Indo-Chinese ladies in slit skirts, Hausa traders who will sell you an 'ancient' piece of sculpture which has been buried in the ground for several days to give it an aged appearance, a fine I.F.A.N. (*Institut Français d'Afrique Noire*) museum where you can see the real thing tastefully displayed complete with background music from tapes made of native dancing and drumming, and courts where you can play tennis under yellow fog lights at night, the only time when it is possible to exercise without dissolving. In an odd reversal of form, many African women are chicly turned out in Paris gowns while the French—who do not subscribe to the British theory that a white woman dare not display an inch of flesh above the knee lest she transform the African into a ravening beast lusting after forbidden fruit—mince along in shorts brief enough to sunburn almost everything. It may give some comfort to my fellow-Saxons to know that Africans sipping apéritifs in Abidjan's pavement cafés frequently do lose control of their primitive passions to the extent of registering interest in and (less frequently) approval of the passing parade of *derrières*. In this healthy outdoor sport they are excelled only by the white Gauls, who (like their dark colleagues) seem much more interested in the configuration of the contents of the shorts than their colour. This being the case and since white women in the tropics tend either to get lazy and puffy or uncomfortably emaciated, both the fears and aspirations of the British fair sex would seem to be unfounded. It is an amusing comment upon the ethnocentricity of both cultures that most whites regard blacks of either sex as having greater sexual appetites and capacities than themselves while the Africans attribute the same prowess to us.

'VIVE'

The spirit of Felix Houphouet-Boigny sits heavily on Abidjan as it does over all Ivory Coast, his personal fief for more than fifteen years. This short, fine-featured fifty-five-year-old physician holds or has held more political posts than he can shake a croissant at: Baoule chieftain, mayor of Abidjan, president of the R.D.A., president of the local assembly, minister in half a dozen French cabinets, premier of Ivory Coast. His rise to power began immediately after World War II when he became the idol of his people by giving needy Africans free medical treatment and speaking up against the harsh labour practices of white planters. Since Houphouet himself is a wealthy coffee planter, the French investigated his own labour policies in an attempt to discredit him but could find nothing wrong and, something more unusual in Africa, no African willing to testify against him.

In 1946 Houphouet converted his African Farmers' Union into the African Democratic Rally, used much of his personal fortune to build R.D.A. into the potent political organization it is today.

As we have seen, Houphouet dallied briefly with Communism (he was never a party member), found it ideologically unsatisfying and politically disastrous, rejected Gabriel d'Arboussier and Communism. By 1950 there had germinated in the mind of this Roman Catholic leader a couple of ideas blasphemous in the eyes of most African nationalists. In the first place he rocked African leaders by informing them, at the very moment when nationalism was on the up-swing, that independence was 'illusionary' and nationalism 'out-dated'. He then applied the *coup de grâce* by informing them that it was just as, if not more, important to be French than it was to be black. He summed up his position this way:

'Associated with the people of France in full equality, Africans are sure of finding in the French spirit that sense of humanity, liberty and fraternity that has always been the essence of their aspirations.'

Houphouet thus became a target of hate both for British African nationalists, repelled by his scorn for the only ideal which most of them have proved themselves capable of absorbing, and for intellectuals of both blocs who in a sometimes thinly contrived and exclusive black cultural renaissance were seeking to wipe out the memory of a 300-year-old race inferiority complex. His French enemies of both races called him a black Bao Dai, willing to sacrifice the aspirations of his people for the pleasures of Paris and the honours which France now sought to heap upon him. British African opponents predicted that his 'reactionary' régime would collapse and his head roll. Overnight Houphouet, once a thorn in the side of France, became that nation's last best hope to retain nearly three million square miles of territory and the loyalty of 25 million sub-Saharan Africans.

To Ivory Coasters, this radical change in their leader's political philosophy made little difference: the nickname of 'Vive' which they gave him demonstrated their faith in his vitality and talent for survival; their loyalty to him was shown by their reaction to the Fifth Republic referendum. Houphouet's people, on the instructions of their leader, gave the General such a tumultuous welcome to Abidjan that de Gaulle, who has called Houphouet 'more than a great African, a great Frenchman', raised his arms in triumph, and said quietly: 'So! The Community is made.' When the referendum ballots were counted, Houphouet and de Gaulle had 1,086,890 *ouis*. There were exactly one

259

hundred and fifty-eight negative votes, the most sweeping affirmative vote in the Community and far greater than the negative tally registered by Sekou Touré's well-regimented Guinea electorate. It goes almost without saying that Houphouet's R.D.A. controls all 100 seats in the Ivory Coast assembly and there is no formal opposition to his policies.

But as Houphouet's interest in the larger problems of the Franco-African Community grew more intense, he ran the risk (like Woodrow Wilson and Jan Smuts) of winning the world but losing his country. For several years Houphouet literally ran Ivory Coast and the R.D.A. by long-distance telephone from Paris. Six times a day he was in touch with his loyal and able Ivory Coast viceroy, Auguste Denise. But as federalist forces built up strength on the bulge of Africa and Ivory Coast began to feel the pressure of her geographical and ideological position between Guinea and Ghana, Denise and Houphouet's promising young lieutenants—Philippe Yace, Mene Boka and Louis Diomande (they have an average age of thirty-five)—pressed Houphouet to come home. In August 1959, Houphouet resigned his post as Minister of State in de Gaulle's cabinet and returned to Abidjan to lead Ivory Coast to freedom. De Gaulle and France will miss Houphouet but it seems likely that Africa, in her year of decision, needs him on the spot.

BELLIES AND HEARTS

In contrast to Nkrumah and Touré and, to a lesser extent, Keita & Co. Houphouet does not believe that what the Ghanaian prime minister calls 'the political kingdom' is the open-sesame to the cave of African happiness. (It was de Gaulle, not Houphouet, who reneged on the ideal of an interdependent Franco-African Community.) The Ivory Coast leader felt that French Africa, having achieved the degree of political equality and mutual loyalty which it enjoyed within the Community, needed roads, schools, clinics and improved seed more than it did stirring manifestoes, blustery political conferences and empty slogans. Houphouet, who does not mince words, has refused to attend the Accra Pan-African Conferences, which he describes as festivals of 'idle chatter'. Nkrumah and Touré battle for the mind of Africa; although there is a strong intellectual flavour to Houphouet's posture, it may be said that he is more interested in hearts and bellies.

His policies are paying off for Ivory Coast, as the similar ones of his Equatorial colleague Leon M'Ba are for Gabon. Freed of the necessity of contributing to the maintenance of the costly, bureaucracy-laden A.O.F. federation, Ivory Coast finds itself with something like an additional £7·1 million more each year to devote to its own development. Recognizing the need of republics not so generously endowed with natural resources, Houphouet has, as we have seen, agreed to make a substantial contribution to the development of the other components of the Union of Benin.

Houphouet's country has a solid economy which stands to get better as foreign investors seek the more placid political clime of Ivory Coast. Despite a serious drought in 1958, Ivory Coast produced a bumper crop of 140,000 tons of coffee, 90 per cent of it African-owned. But cacao production fell from a 1957 level of 69,000 tons to 45,000. Banana exports increased from 34,000 to 42,000 tons while timber production zoomed from 254,000 to 333,000 tons. Several new factories were installed including a plant for producing instant coffee, oil exploration continued. Although the decline in cacao revenue hurt, in the first ten months of 1958 exports were worth £42·6 million while imports cost £31 million, leaving a favourable balance of £11·6 million, much of it in dollars, 10 per cent more than the 1957 surplus.

Houphouet plans to devote much of his new revenues to education, and expenditures under this heading increased from £2·8 million in 1958 to £4·6 million the following year. There is still plenty of room for improvement for, despite the fact that education is free and half of the 3,000 West Africans studying in France are Ivory Coasters, only about 18 per cent of the republic's school-age children go to school. And this emphasis on producing doctors and lawyers rather than clerks and mechanics is the sort of thing which provoked the bloody Abidjan riots of late 1958. But if Ivory Coast is imperfect, the future of her peoples seems brighter than those of many neighbouring nations.

THE VOLTAIC REPUBLIC

After an afternoon of asking for road directions in the Voltaic Republic (formerly known as Upper Volta), you find yourself babbling baby-talk: for instance, you reach Tenkodogo from Bobo-Dioulasso by driving to Dedougou, turning right to Koudougou, then going straight to Ouagadougou (Wagadugu, if you prefer). You can imagine what you have to do to get to Fada-N'Gourma or Karagouroula.

Volta borders Mali on the north and west, Ivory Coast, Ghana and Togo on the south, Dahomey and Niger on the east and is the poorest and most densely populated (twenty-nine people to the square mile) of the eight states of Gallic West Africa. There are 3·3 million primitive tribesmen in this Italy-sized republic and the annual *per capita* income is considerably less than £3 10s., about 15 per cent of the Ivory Coast figure. Less than one out of twenty school-age children are in school at any one time and Volta is so poor that a quarter of a million of her young men go every year to Ghana, Ivory Coast and Senegal to work on the railway, build roads or till the fields for wealthier Africans. There is nothing much of any value in Volta and, if there were, there isn't much chance of getting it to market. The western half of the country is served by the Abidjan–Ouagadougou railway but the eastern half is completely cut off from everywhere and there is less than fifty miles of paved road in the entire country.

French aid between 1947 and 1957 amounted to £15·6 million. Volta's exports (mostly shea nuts) are worth only £2 million and her imports cost her twice that amount. The annual budget is about £4 million.

Since there is no employment at home and only so much work available for those willing to go to 'foreign' states as field hands, Volta's Mossi tribesmen have for years been the backbone of France's colonial army. Since nobody had ever heard of Upper Volta (it, in fact, was not then constituted as a separate political unit) and a few people had heard of Senegal, the fierce African troops who did so well in France during the First World War were called Senegalese. They were Mossi from Upper Volta and the same tribe today is doing yeoman work in Algeria for the French, although they still display an understandable aversion to fighting at night when, as everybody knows, the spirits are abroad. The Mossi, who are the exception to the rule among the plains tribes, have vigorously and successfully resisted Islam for centuries (only 14 per cent of Volta's population is Mohammedan) and they welcome any chance they get to have a whack at Muslims of any description. These millet-growers are particularly enthusiastic about service in paratroop outfits. So prodigious has been the military contribution of this small state that Volta's veterans receive twice as much retired pay (£1·4 million per year) as Ivory Coast earns from her exports of bananas.

Two colourful and contrasting Voltaic political personalities are the Moro Naba of the Mossi and Madame Ouezzin-Coulibaly. The former is very untypical of Gallic Africa since it has always been French policy to undermine the authority of the powerful chiefs or even to abolish the royal line, as was done in Dahomey. The Moro Naba (Naba means emperor and Moro is the singular of Mossi) is about the only native ruler left in French Africa who enjoys prestige comparable to that of scores of emirs in Northern Nigeria. Although his temporal powers are circumscribed (there is an elected mayor in his Ouagadougou capital), the Moro Naba's 1·5 million Mossi tribesmen regard him as the incarnate deity and his moral authority and influence are immense.

The present Mossi emperor, a generously proportioned man of twenty-nine who was educated in France, is the forty-seventh of his line and he has been on the throne only since late 1957. His grandfather, one of the grand old men of Africa, was ardently pro-French. He urged his people not to accept the 1940 armistice and, when the Vichy authorities began to close in on him, died by his own hand after making his heir swear to leave the throne vacant 'until the true French come back'. The crown prince (the present Moro Naba's father) was true to his oath and thus earned the deep respect both of his Mossi followers and of the French.

The new emperor is modern and progressive in some ways, reactionary in others. Mossi courtiers are no longer required to crawl into the imperial presence throwing dust on themselves, and one of his wives goes about, to the horror of conservative tribal elders, dressed in the latest Paris frocks. On the other hand, the Moro Naba has not hesitated to call in hundreds of Mossi warriors, who come furiously pedalling bicycles bought with their army pensions and armed to the teeth, to demonstrate outside the Voltaic Assembly whenever a piece of legislation upon which he has strong views is under discussion.

The Moro Naba at first was a strong advocate of Mali since, as he said, 'balkanization will lead us all to such an excess of particularism that our countries will risk losing the benefits that France has brought them'. After a talk with Houphouet and his R.D.A. lieutenant, Maurice Yameogo, the Moro Naba changed his mind and allowed Yameogo to take the Voltaic Republic out of Mali and into the Union of Benin, despite the vigorous protests of the non-Mossi population of western Volta which, of course, resents the Moro Naba's political role.

In an attempt to placate non-Mossi elements, the Moro Naba called for a political truce between the R.D.A. and the federalist party. When this failed, he came out in support of the R.D.A., which instituted separate balloting procedures for Mossi and non-Mossi areas, banned three anti-R.D.A. cabinet ministers from standing for election (including the able and vigorous Ousman Ba, now a Mali minister and one of the coming leaders of Africa), thus easily winning 64 of the 75 seats in the Voltaic Assembly.

The Moro Naba, although he is the spiritual head of his pagan tribe and is (at least officially) himself an animist, has strong ties with Islam, a fact which does not make him any more popular with conservative Mossi. In addition, evolved Voltaians oppose the institution of the chieftaincy and non-Mossi, as we have seen, are bitterly opposed to Moro Naba. But as the head of the royal house which can trace its kingly ancestors back to the twelfth century and as leader of a tribe with seven centuries of military prowess behind it (the Mossi sacked Timbuktu in 1337), this restless, pear-shaped ruler is destined to play a major political role in Gallic Africa for years to come. He would like to be constitutional ruler of the Voltaic Republic and has the best recommendation of all: the biggest battalions.

Quite another dish of tea is Madame Ouezzin-Coulibaly, a handsome little woman whose personal mildness belies her political ferocity. Madame Ouezzin, who is now in her early forties, in 1930 married a brilliant Voltaic teacher named Daniel Ouezzin-Coulibaly. Her husband became a fast friend of Houphouet and the two of them founded the R.D.A. in 1946. Ouezzin rose to be political secretary of the R.D.A., premier of Upper Volta, a deputy in the French National Assembly representing Ivory Coast and a town councillor of Abidjan. A roughly parallel situation would exist if Cabot Lodge, while serving as American ambassador to the United Nations, were vice-chairman of the Republican National Committee, governor of Massachusetts *and* mayor of Chicago.

In 1948, Houphouet and Ouezzin decided that the time was ripe to form a women's wing of the R.D.A. Madame Ouezzin was the obvious choice to lead the movement. Within a matter of months, she had the formidable women of Abidjan so well regimented that within an hour's time she could marshal 5,000 of them to applaud a visiting dignitary or storm a jail. On one occasion she forced the release of a woman political prisoner by depositing thousands of silent women in the prison courtyard and threatening to leave them there until the French gave in. On another, she sprang the entire Grand Bassam R.D.A. policy committee from jail (they were on a hunger strike) by the same methods. In a less belligerent mood, she sent comely Ivory Coast maidens, their bare breasts painted in the colours of the French tricolour, to greet de Gaulle when he came to Abidjan to seek support for the Community.

Madame Ouezzin, like her husband and Houphouet, at one time

played footsy with the Communists. In 1949 she fellow-travelled to Peking to represent the women of Africa at the 'Congress for the Defence of Peace', found herself sentenced to a two-month prison term when she returned to Abidjan. She successfully appealed against the sentence and, since Houphouet and the R.D.A. dumped the Communists, has been politically pure.

A few weeks before de Gaulle's referendum, Ouezzin died suddenly at the age of forty-nine, leaving a serious gap in Upper Volta's political team. Many hoped that Madame Ouezzin would succeed her husband as premier. But in an Africa where women are only beginning to raise themselves from a chattel status, Madame Ouezzin was a bit before her time. Instead, the R.D.A. premier, Maurice Yameogo, named her Minister of Social Welfare and Labour, the first woman in African history to attain cabinet rank.

Madame Ouezzin, whose teen-age daughter Denise is the first licensed black African woman pilot, still controls the women of Abidjan, is head of the female branch of the R.D.A. and serves as a municipal councillor of Abidjan. But this Baoule leader (her father, like Houphouet, was an Ivory Coast chief) is of more use to the R.D.A. in the vacillating Voltaic Republic, which is Ivory Coast's only geographical link with the other members of the Union of Benin, than she is in Abidjan where a foe of Houphouet's stands as much chance for election as Nasser would in North Tel Aviv.

With the Moro Naba on his right hand to control the Mossi and Madame Ouezzin on his left to appeal to the educated class and to non-Mossi, Premier Maurice Yameogo has had little difficulty in keeping the Voltaic Republic in Houphouet's camp. He has achieved this happy state, however, only by dissolving Nazi Boni's Mali-oriented *Parti de la Féderation Africaine* and by banning other groups which oppose (or might oppose) his policies.

Ouagadougou, the capital, is made of mud and for this reason was once called Bancoville (banco is the local name for mud bricks). About half of the 2,600 white inhabitants of the Voltaic Republic live in this town of 36,000, take their meals at Mme Fanny's restaurant and have their hair done at *Chez Josy*, one of the two *coiffeurs* in the country. Ouagadougou also has one dentist and a plumber (it is not true that they trained at the same school) and half of Volta's population sees a doctor an average of four times a year. There are 39,000 primary school students in Volta and 1,500 boys and girls attend high school.

Upper Volta did not come into being until 1919. In 1932 the French decided that it was too poor even to afford its own government, abolished the territory and split the land between Soudan and Ivory Coast. Houphouet's political activities resulted in the territory's rebirth in 1948: at the time, Houphouet was at the peak of his pro-Communist activities; to punish the Ivory Coast leader and to prevent his influence from spreading, the French took part of Soudan and Ivory Coast and gave Upper Volta a separate political personality. In a way, then, the Voltaic Republic is a monument to Houphouet's energies and abilities. Many men can say that a nation was made in spite of them, few can boast that one was born to spite them. Like the rest of the Benin nations, Volta became independent last year.

NIGER

The name Niger conjures up visions of a greasy river flowing turgidly through a rain forest clamorous with the honk of fever-birds, whining with mosquitoes. Nothing could be further from the truth. The Niger River cuts across the extreme south-western portion of the republic fifty miles from its border with Upper Volta and the river waters less than 5 per cent of this great country, the rest stretching away to the north-east in savannah country which soon becomes desert, windswept and waterless. Volta, Dahomey and Nigeria (with which it is sometimes confused) are to the south, Chad to the east, Libya and Algeria to the north, and Mali to the west. Many parts of Niger are nearer to Cairo than to Dakar.

Niger is more than four times larger than Italy and has fewer people than Mexico City, there being less than three people to the square mile. It possesses not a foot of railway and a quart of petrol will take you over every paved road in the republic. Niger exports a little meat and 98,000 tons of groundnuts per year, making it second in this department only to Senegal. Although customs duties discourage legal trade with Nigeria, it is estimated that 1·5 million hides and skins, 80,000 cattle and 600,000 sheep and goats worth £3·9 million are bootlegged over the border every year. In the past Niger's only mineral resources have been a little wolfram and tin exploited in the Air region but there is just a chance that the Saharan oilfields may extend into areas which have been considered worthless.

All Niger's exports are worth £8 million, the French have injected £10 million into development projects since 1947 and the annual budget is a modest £5 million.

Niger's educational performance is the worst in Gallic Africa and only two children out of every hundred go to school. France always had trouble with Niger—it was not considered safe to hand the territory over to civil administrators until 1922—mostly because the French made the mistake of lumping together for administrative purposes the wild 'white' Tuareg of the Libyan region with the sedentary negroid agriculturalists along the Nigerian border. In an odd reversal of form, it is the Tuareg men who go veiled, not the women. Niger is one of the most heavily Islamized territories in this part of the world (85 per cent of the population follow the Prophet) and there are less than 4,000 Christians in the entire country. The river which gives the republic its name is so lazy that it takes nine months for high-water to reach Niamey from the river's source.

Ethnically speaking, Niger should be three countries. The 40 per cent of the republic along the Algerian and Libyan borders is inhabited by 350,000 Tuareg nomads, Saharan people who live around the foothills of the mysterious Air Mountains; in the southern 40 per cent live one million Muslim Hausas and 300,000 Fulanis, closely akin to the people of Northern Nigeria; in the west, along the banks of the Niger, lives the balance of the population, Djermas, Songhais and small pagan tribes. As the result of this variety of peoples, Niger is torn politically three ways: towards Libya, Nigeria and Mali. Ironically, it has solved this dilemma by joining the Union of Benin.

Niamey is the capital of Niger and it is not true that nobody stays there voluntarily more than twenty-four hours: some of the local people have been there all their lives. It is, in fact, an attractive, sprawling town of 17,000 perched above the gently flowing Niger. Niamey has 60 per cent of the republic's total European population of 2,000, a native quarter named after General Leclerc, the country's only hospital and its one high school (317 students in 1958), a Trader-Horn-atmosphere bar mysteriously dubbed 'Petrocokino', an architect named Audibert and a notary public named Diop. Nearby is a little town with the nice name of Say where Barth crossed the Niger, and south of this is Niger's famous 'W' National Park (the river makes a double loop here which, to an imaginative mind, bears some resemblance to a 'W') where you can take a picture of an elephant and dine on roast wild boar.

The country's two commercial centres, Zinder and Maradi, are near the Nigerian border. Zinder, a town of 15,000 inhabitants, was capital of Niger until 1926, when the French decided it was indefensible and moved their headquarters to Niamey. It is a big peanut market and leatherworking centre and has been called 'a lesser Kano'. Maradi is slightly smaller than Zinder, which it very much resembles. There is a very good paved road from Maradi to Kano and the logical route for Niger's exports is over this road and then by rail to Lagos and the sea. In order to follow an all-French route, they are trucked 600 expensive miles to Parakou, then sent by rail to Cotonou, Dahomey's inferior port.

At Agades, on the southern slopes of the Air Mountains, Tuareg silversmiths make curious crosses much favoured by fashionable Parisian Catholics. These are hand-carved from silver, with a swelling central portion, knobs on the ends of three legs of the cross and a symbol like a bumpy doughnut at the top. They do this not from any excess of Christian zeal but because the shape pleases their aesthetic nature. The devout French ladies would get knowing winks from the citizenry of Karachi were they to visit that Pakistani city: Agades 'crosses' are fertility symbols picked up at Mecca from Indian Muslims by Tuareg pilgrims centuries ago.

When Mungo Park and Heinrich Barth reached Niger in the nineteenth century, they found it in an anarchic state. There was unceasing warfare among the Tuareg confederations of Air and Oulliminden, the Djerma kingdoms which had established themselves on the banks of the rivers two centuries before, the resurgent Fulani warriors and the latter's former masters, the Hausa.

The French moved into the area during the last decade of the nineteenth century and had barely quieted the Tuareg when the First World War broke out and agents of Turkey (which, of course, was an ally of Imperial Germany) raised the tribes in a *jihad* against their European conquerors. The Tuareg laid siege to Agades and came within an ace of expelling the French. The Tuareg today remain as free and proud as the wind which whips their desert wastes and it should be said that they are sorry to see the French relinquish control of Niger: they would much prefer to have chucked them out. 'The Tuareg will never change,' said one Frenchman, 'because there is no water: how can you either civilize or corrupt a man who will not and cannot sit down?'

Niger's current political history is just as dynamic as her past. To a great extent this history is the story of two men: Djibo Bakary and Hamani Diori.

THE MAN WHO WOULD BE TOURÉ

If good looks spelled political success, Djibo Bakary would be on the top of the heap in French West Africa. Shortly after the war, Bakary, who is thirty-eight, gave up teaching to devote himself to trade unionism and politics. In the most conservative of West African states he preached the most radical of doctrines: universal suffrage, full rights for women and a reduction in the powers of tribal leaders. Bakary was in on the founding of the R.D.A., with Sekou Touré was considered by Houphouet to be among the most promising of his young lieutenants. But Bakary, even more than Touré, sailed closer to the Communist wind than was pleasing to Houphouet; when Bakary objected to the dismissal of Communist Party ally Gabriel d'Arboussier and charged Houphouet with betraying Africa to the French, the R.D.A. leader gave Bakary his walking papers and the French clapped him in prison.

Although Bakary took a large section of the Niger branch of the R.D.A. with him, Houphouet's other bright young man, Hamani Diori, was able to win the elections in January 1956. Diori, a radical labour leader who had sufficient political intuition to move to the right as Houphouet shifted in that direction, became premier.

As the *loi cadre* elections (March 31, 1957) approached, Bakary tried to get back in Houphouet's good graces by publishing an open letter in which he apologized for having doubted the wisdom of the R.D.A. leader. But Houphouet was satisfied with Diori's leadership, had already granted d'Arboussier a political reprieve, and was in no mood to make any more concessions. He turned down Bakary's plea, whereupon the young radical welded all the political dissidents of Niger into one block, slapped a Socialist Party label on to his rag-tail following, and proceeded to win forty of the sixty seats in the Niger Assembly.

As premier and mayor of Niamey, Bakary shifted further to the left and when de Gaulle eighteen months later made his historic offer of freedom or association, he and Touré (they are close friends as well as political allies) were the only territorial leaders to urge their followers to vote for independence. In so doing, Bakary overlooked several important weaknesses in his political position.

In the first place he had not been in office long enough to consolidate his political power but just long enough to antagonize the chiefs. In the second place Diori's R.D.A. was solidly behind de Gaulle while his own pick-up Socialist Party was internally divided. The fact that he held two-thirds of the seats in the assembly should not have deceived Bakary as to the depth of his popular support: normally only about 20 per cent of the Niger electorate, most of which is more concerned with finding a water-hole or slaying a tribal enemy, bothers to vote. But faced with the prospect of victory for a man who opposed everything they stood for, the important tribal chiefs of Zinder and Djerma urged their people to go to the polls. A record 38 per cent voted and for every vote for Bakary there were four for de Gaulle. Bakary resigned.

'A vote against Bakary,' explained an old Niger hand, 'was not a vote against independence but a ballot for chiefly prerogative and anti-feminism.'

New elections were held in December 1958 and the R.D.A. registered a sweeping victory by winning forty-nine of the sixty seats. Bakary's Socialists—now known as the Sawaba (Freedom) Party—fell from forty to five seats and he was among those not re-elected. Diori, who also lost his seat, became premier. Diori quickly brought Niger into Houphouet's Union of Benin, signed an agreement with France to develop the Saharan region of the country, banned all meetings of Sawaba-controlled trade unions, dissolved the Niamey municipal council of which Bakary had been mayor and expelled from Niger several of the former premier's top aides.

Diori, who is in his forties, comes from a small village near Niamey and was at one time a language instructor at the French School of Colonial Administration. In 1946 he gave up parsing Hausa verbs for politics, joined the R.D.A. and was elected to the French National Assembly. He so impressed Houphouet that the Ivory Coast leader named Diori as one of the three men to tour Gallic Africa on his behalf in 1950 to explain the R.D.A.'s break with the Communists.

With Sawaba's fortunes at a low ebb and Diori firmly in the saddle, Bakary can take consolation in the thought that his own defeat may not be any more permanent than was his period in office. In a country where only 20 per cent of the electorate votes, there is always the hope that a different 20 per cent will show up at the polls next time. Niger's bubbling political pot will bear watching for some time to come.

DAHOMEY

Dahomey is the smallest of France's former West African colonies and one of the most fascinating. Lacking through most of this continent is a sense of history: man was and is very much at the mercy of the elements in Africa and it is the environment rather than men or their institutions which seems to be the only constant factor. But Dahomey has a history and one with a vengeance.

When Europeans came to trade for slaves in the sixteenth century they found two small coastal kingdoms, Whydah (Ouidah) and Jacquin. In the interior behind Whydah, they learned, was the great Fon kingdom of Great Ardra. About 1620, a king of Great Ardra died and was succeeded by his eldest son. The new king's two younger brothers, realizing that they stood a better than average chance of ending up as the main course of a roast pig dinner if they hung around home, set out in search of employment. One founded the kingdom of Little Ardra (Porto Novo), on the coast to the east of Jacquin. The other went inland until he found a likely looking piece of land ruled by a fellow named Dan.

Dan quite naturally objected to an outsider. This altercation was settled to the satisfaction of everyone except Dan, who was decapitated and deposited in the foundations of the new palace. And this is the origin of the name Dahomey, which means 'from the stomach of Dan'. Abomey was its capital but the kings of Dahomey continued to look on Great Ardra as their spiritual home and there they went to be enstooled (crowned).

In the slave trade Dahomey did the dirty work and Whydah, Great Ardra, Jacquin and Porto Novo picked up the middleman's profits. King Agaja of Dahomey, who was in his prime during the War of the Spanish Succession, realized that his take would be larger if he could eliminate the middlemen and wholesale his slaves to the whites. The coast states were not entranced by the prospect of being eliminated and there was a sizable war from which Dahomey emerged victorious in 1730.

Dahomey's aggressiveness involved it in long and bloody conflicts with the Ashanti confederation of the Gold Coast, northern tribes like the Sombas—who still go about naked except for penis sheaths and live in double-storeyed mud huts topped off by miniature straw-thatched turrets—and the Yoruba kingdom of Abeokuta in neighbouring Nigeria (the British occupied Lagos in 1861 ostensibly to check Dahomeyan expansionism). To defend their frontiers and to maintain the slave raids upon which their prosperity was based, the kings of Dahomey created an *élite* force of 2,500 amazons.

Now authenticated amazons are as rare as honesty but these were the real article. They were divided into regiments of musketeers, archers, razor-women (who carried a clasp model with an eighteen-inch blade) and stretcher-bearers. Each regiment had a distinctive uniform and the amazons were proud of their ability to travel in columns more than 1,000 strong in complete silence (a considerable accomplishment for any group of women) and to storm thorn stockades in their bare feet. They were, according to reports, considerably more ferocious than the Dahomeyan males. This may be attributed to the fact that at least theoretically they were kept in a state of sullen celibacy. However, Richard Burton, who visited Dahomey in 1863, estimated that at least 150 were pregnant. There was a death penalty for any male caught corrupting the discipline and reducing the fighting efficiency of the troops, all of whom were considered to be the king's wives.

Burton has left us a colourful picture of life in Dahomey a hundred years ago. The king sat on a throne of earth three feet high covered with gay cotton cloths. If perspiration appeared upon the royal brow it was instantly removed 'with the softest cloth by the gentlest hand'. A gold-plated spittoon was moved within range whenever the king's lips moved and, if he sneezed, his courtiers touched the ground with their foreheads, which I suppose is no sillier than saying *gesundheit*. In short, says Burton, the Dahomeyan king had only to 'condescend to live', all else being done for him. As for the common people, a few were addicted to 'the worst kind of cigars' and all bawled 'Pooo!' ('Take it easy!') when the king took a drink. They sat around in the sun, for the umbrella (of which the king had twenty-four) was an emblem of royalty forbidden to baser folk. The leader of the king's personal guard of amazons (known as 'madwomen' or 'lost children') was 'a huge old porpoise' and Burton reported that once their dancing days were over the fighting-women tended to get hippy. The king kept the bones of three of the forty rulers he had slain in gourds in front of his throne and all his subjects wore crucifixes with the Son of God replaced by a chameleon, a potent ju-ju in this part of the world. The Dahomeyans were obsessed with skulls and, before taking a trophy from a fallen foe, they cut the ramus muscles and tore the lower jaw from their still living victim.

France moved in on Dahomey in the 1870's. At Whydah they found the whitewashed Fort of St. John the Baptist manned by a few Portuguese and Brazilian negroes. The French leader asked the commandant of the fort what land belonged to Portugal and the latter gave an expressive, horizon-embracing sweep of his arm which the new arrivals not over-generously interpreted to mean the eleven acres covered by the fort and its outbuildings. Today the Portuguese flag still flaps bravely above the 280-year-old fort and a descendant of Bartholomew Diaz presides there over the destinies of the world's smallest colony.

But if the Portuguese were unsure of their position, the kings of Dahomey were not. Gelele (1858–89) and Behanzin (1889–93) bitterly protested that the coastal chiefs were their vassals and had no authority to accept French protection.

Gelele, who had danced a vigorous fandango dressed in a white robe and flowered drawers of purple silk on the occasion of Burton's visit, was the head of a powerful and relatively civilized state. His people had learned the art of bronze-casting from Ife (although they did not know how to smelt iron), boasted an intricately organized society which practised crop rotation and dealt with community problems on a co-op basis. In war his legions were invincible and his hut was floored with the skulls of conquered chiefs. He had not feared England, which he assumed to be about the same size as Dahomey, and had treated Burton with consideration only because he hoped by so doing to obtain a coach-and-four, an object very dear to his heart. He knew nothing of France and would concede nothing. It was a situation which could end only in war.

As their excuse for crushing Dahomey the French maintained that they were anxious to wipe out the practice of human sacrifice. At the annual ceremony called the 'king's customs', hundreds of slaves, prisoners and local bad-hats were slaughtered to provide subjects for the spirit-kingdoms of departed Dahomeyan monarchs. And whenever the king wanted to send a message to one of his ancestors, he whispered it in the ear of one of his subjects and then had the messenger decapitated. If the king happened to be a particularly chatty individual, or if his memory was bad enough to require many postscripts, the executioner worked up a pretty good sweat.

When a king died his widows in their hundreds smashed all the royal furniture and then died by their own hands or were sacrificed. Slaves were slaughtered on any public occasion such as the equivalent of the opening of a new super-market or filling station, and a man and woman were decapitated every morning to thank the gods for another day in the king's life. Descriptions of the 'customs' bear a striking resemblance to the *autos-de-fé* which not so very long ago delighted the Christian heart of every good Spaniard: the victims were dressed in knee-length red calico shirts and long white nightcaps trimmed with blue ribbons. They were placed in baskets and carried in them to the walls of the palace. After a suitable speech and a few off-colour jokes from the master of ceremonies, they were chucked from the ramparts. Tho̊se who were killed by the fall were lucky; the rest were butchered by the merrymakers.

The bloody toll was indeed shocking: in some years it even approximated to the number of motorists sacrificed to the Power Steering god over a long Easter weekend. We might do well to remember, as Burton did, that human sacrifice (like slavery) is a stage through which every civilization within the memory of man has passed and that the practice, in Dahomey's case, sprang from the filial piety of an essentially religious people. Keep in mind the public mortal floggings, the quarterings, the hangings and burnings, the notched ears and the brandings in which Western civilization has plunged periodically for the greater glory of God, the political health of the State and the edification and moral well-being of its inhabitants. In 1959 an English widow and mother of two tubercular children drew a jail sentence for failing to report that she was taking in laundry and mending while drawing unemployment compensation. And King Gelele, whatever his shortcomings, would have been appalled by Nazi Germany.

In the end one is forced to the conclusion that Dahomey's position astride the trade routes to the interior made its conquest inevitable rather than any moral revulsion resulting from Dahomeyan social habits. At any rate, the French stormed Abomey in 1893 after heavy fighting against the amazons and, seven years later, Dahomey became a French colony. The French found the kings of Dahomey too troublesome and, by 1911, the stable royal dynasty which had seen only ten kings in more than three centuries was extinguished.

Today little remains of Dahomey's ancient glory except an excellent I.F.A.N. reconstruction of the royal palace at Abomey, a museum at the same place—containing a satisfactory number of skulls and executioners' swords, a Gatling gun presented to one of the kings by the Germans and the royal stools—and Hausa traders on the veranda of Cotonou's hotel who hawk cheap Abomey tapestries depicting appliquéd Dahomey warriors (in red) disembowelling their foes (in black), tossing heads about, and boldly attacking ferocious dragons which have human heads tied to their collars.

THE CLAW

MODERN DAHOMEY

Today no amazons block the road and the drive to Dahomey from hated Abeokuta is easy and pleasant. Porto Novo, the capital of this Cuba-sized republic of 1·6 million souls (2,500 whites), is a ramshackle old town of 30,000 perched on a sandy spit between two lagoons where the slave ships once dropped anchor. Now there are only bamboo fish-traps which look like bird-cages dotting the shallow lagoons, a few fishermen poling themselves along in dug-outs, some waterlogged hulks rotting on the beach.

Porto Novo has no hotel and it is necessary to stay at Cotonou, Dahomey's port twenty miles to the west of the capital. The road is paved but has great sunken depressions in its surface caused by rain washing under the concrete. The effect is rather like driving on a trampoline. As we approached Cotonou, a bare-breasted woman carrying a load of firewood on her head dashed out in front of the car. I swerved, removed the load of wood from her head but left her otherwise unscathed and laughing. She picked the splinters out of her hands and we picked the slivers of glass out of our faces so I suppose it was an even exchange.

Dahomey is poor—although its 300 miles of paved roads put it proportionately ahead of the rest of Benin—and Cotonou handles only about 300 ships a year, loading 300,000 tons of freight and 10,000 passengers. Eighty per cent of the country's 'wealth' (Dahomey's annual budget is a pathetic £4·7 million, of which more than half is a direct subsidy from France) comes from the oil palm, of which there are said to be about 30 million trees. Exports of palm products, in an average year, are worth £11 million, Dahomey imports £3 worth of goods for every £2 she sells, and French assistance since 1947 has amounted to £18 million.

The oil palm is indigenous here and all the trees were the personal property of the kings of Dahomey. The 70,000 tons of palm produce exported by Dahomey make the republic France's principal supplier of this commodity and it is no exaggeration to say that, without the oil palm, there could be no Dahomey: the people cook and light their homes with its oil, drink the wine, sell the kernels for cash, eat the heart of the tree and thatch their homes with its fronds.

Dahomey also sells 10,000 tons of groundnuts, a little shea butter, cotton, tobacco and copra. But far more important to her than these as a source of income is the export of brains. Because of its long-

275

standing enthusiasm for Catholicism, Dahomey has had long and intensive contact with mission schools. Since there is little employment at home for her educated sons, clerks and civil servants of '*ce petit pays intellectuel*' occupy posts of responsibility from Douala to Dakar. Unfortunately, while the Dahomeyans have learned mathematics, they have not gained humility. Their arrogance has earned them an antipathy which they can ill afford, as witnessed by the expulsion of 12,000 Dahomeyans from Ivory Coast after the Abidjan riots of late 1958. Testimony to the general hatred felt for these 'aliens' was the fact that Ivory Coast police stood by laughing while mobs shouting 'Strangers, go home!' liberally applied knives, clubs and broken bottles to the Dahomeyans. Order was only restored by the use of white police.

The success of the mission schools (more Dahomeyans are educated by the Church than by the State) has had more breadth than depth. Although one out of every four children goes to school and 22 per cent of the national budget is devoted to education, there are few really well-educated people in the country. In 1950 the government offered a few scholarships for higher education in France but only a dozen applicants were found who had reasonable qualifications and one of these stated that he wanted the grant to study amateur photography. Of the two youths who were awarded university scholarships, nothing was heard for two years after their arrival in France. They simply disappeared.

And although the Dahomeyans' devotion to Catholicism is striking, it is perhaps unwise to over-emphasize it. All across the continent the African has demonstrated an amazing ability to deform ('adapt' might be a more polite word) both Islam and Christianity until they bear slight resemblance to the orthodox faiths from which they sprang. Dahomey abounds in neo-Christian religious societies which satisfy the African's desire for communal activity, his penchant for impressive titles and his love of flamboyant ceremony. Two of the most revered of these sects in Dahomey are the Eternal Sacred Order of Cherubim and Seraphim and the Organization of Celestial Christians. It is all very reminiscent of another backward area, California.

The economic development of the country is hindered by its shape and location: Dahomey touches Volta and Niger in the north, is wedged between Nigeria and Togo with its southern border buttoned to the Atlantic Ocean by a fifty-mile stretch of coast. Although it is more than 550 miles long, in most places Dahomey is less than 75 miles wide. Its long border with Nigeria makes smuggling of British goods, which are usually cheaper and of better quality than French articles, so easy that Dahomey derives practically no revenue from customs duties. We found that we could buy American cigarettes for less in Porto Novo than we could in New York.

Such bustle as occurs in Dahomey takes place in Cotonou (population: 57,000) and most of it seems to be centred around the Hotel de la Plage, which faces the broad, palm-fringed beach. This idyllic scene is somewhat marred by the fact that families of large and belligerent pigs root with considerable satisfaction among the heaps of litter and refuse which dot the beach and someone is generally to be found relieving himself in stark silhouette against the roaring lacework of the constant surf. Although Dahomey has since obtained £7 million from France to build a modern port (work will be completed in 1963 and will raise Cotonou's freight capacity to 400,000 tons per year), presumably as an enticement to remain within the Community, at the time of our visit the only convenience added since the slaving days was a wharf which reached out beyond the surf. A battered French freighter out of Marseilles was tugging against her chain, her sides rusted and covered with barnacles while zombie-like negroes dusted white by the wheat from her hold unloaded her cargo into lighters which chugged back and forth between the ship and the dock like little waterbugs in a pond scurrying around their mother.

Behind the hotel is an open-air cinema. This fact is of more than passing interest as the sound-track is operated at full volume both to cater to the African's love of noise and in a somewhat futile attempt to be heard above the shouts of encouragement from the Dahomeyan clientele. The redeeming feature of this situation is the fact that if you are lucky enough to have a room on the second floor—the first floor lodgers are just kept awake until after midnight without being able to see anything—you can watch the movie in your underwear without having to pay the four shilling admission charge. Under this arrangement we observed Mr. Stewart Granger and Miss Rita Hayworth doing their stuff in *Salome* (Gelele's descendants loved it when the Baptist's head was produced on a silver salver). Although we found Randolph Scott and Chill Wills expressing themselves in French somewhat unbelievable, the Cotonou film-goers also registered considerable satisfaction with this horse-opera and the audience participation quotient at all the extravaganzas which we were privileged to witness from our balcony would have brought tears of gratitude and pride to the eyes of the late C. B. de Mille.

THE GALLIC GIANT

Randolph Scott's principal problem is to avoid looking his fifty-odd years. The task of Dahomey's two political lights, broad-nosed Serou Apithy and chubby Hubert Maga, is considerably more complex. The ever-present conditioning factor of Dahomeyan politics, no matter who is in power, is the country's poverty: Dahomey cannot afford to follow an independent line, must gear her policies to mesh with those of the larger Afro-French republics where her citizens find work and whose products find their way to the sea through Dahomey. Only slightly less important is Catholicism. Dahomey is the most heavily Christianized territory of Gallic Africa and this has given a conservative cast to the actions of her leaders.

In the 1945 elections, a French priest named Father Aupiais was chosen by black Dahomeyans to represent them in the French Constituent Assembly although he had not been in Dahomey for seventeen years. Serou Mignan Apithy, the favourite son of south Dahomey, an ardent Catholic and a protégé of Father Aupiais, soon gained political supremacy in the post-war years. The forty-seven-year-old politician got started with the R.D.A. but broke with that organization in 1948 when it reached the height of its pro-Communist activities. On the advice of Father Aupiais, he formed his own Dahomey Republican Party (P.R.D.) which he later affiliated with fellow-Catholic Leopold Senghor's Socialist Party.

Apithy soon rose from his job as a notary public in Paris to be a member of the Grand Council of A.O.F., a French Assemblyman and premier of Dahomey. He saw to it that French mission schools in Dahomey received a government subsidy, lobbied hard to persuade France to build his country a modern port. His political control was confirmed in March 1957 when the P.R.D. won thirty-five of sixty seats in the Dahomey Assembly. The other favourite son of Dahomey, forty-four-year-old Hubert Maga, who controls the northern part of the country, led his Dahomey Democratic Rally (R.D.D.) in a drive which procured fourteen seats while the local branch of the R.D.A. led by Justin Ahomadegbe secured the other eleven seats.

All three parties, in 1958, backed the country's participation in the French Community. Having opted for association with France, it would have seemed logical that Dahomey's government party, as a branch of Senghor's Socialists, would follow that leader into the Mali Federation. Dahomey did, in fact, sign the Bamako and Dakar resolutions which made it a part of the federation. But Apithy had long had his reservations concerning the advisability of joining any federation of which Niger was not a part and Upper Volta enthusiastic, since both states constitute its natural hinterland. In addition, his adherence to the Socialist Party was based mostly upon the fact that Senghor was a good Catholic and a Socialist (almost everybody in Africa is too poor to be anything but). As Senghor adopted the role of political theorist and elder statesman and left the leadership of M.S.A., now renamed the African Federalist Party, to Soudanese Muslim Modibo Keita it was perhaps not unnatural that Apithy should turn to Houphouet, his nearer, richer and Catholic neighbour. Apithy resigned from Senghor's party and formed his followers into an independent group. This, of course, delayed and finally killed Dahomey's membership in Mali and required new elections.

Apithy then proceeded to turn in a job of gerrymandering that would have earned him an avuncular pat on the head from any ward-boss. These were the results of the April 1959 elections in Dahomey:

Party	Popular Vote	Seats
P.R.D. (Apithy)	144,038	37
R.D.D. (Maga, in alliance with Apithy)	62,132	22
R.D.A. (Ahomadegbe)	172,139	11

Mr. Ahomadegbe's followers perhaps not unnaturally cried 'foul'. They registered their disapproval of the situation by burning the houses of Apithy's supporters in Cotonou and brawling with troops in several villages. Hundreds were hurt in the disorders and a curfew was imposed throughout the country. Apithy somewhat incongruously said that 'the people have spoken' and would 'be obeyed'. It soon became obvious, however, that unless Dahomey was to dissolve into anarchy, some sort of compromise would have to be reached. Apithy wisely agreed to give nine of his party's seats to the R.D.A. (new strengths: Apithy, 28; Maga, 22; Ahomadegbe, 20) and a coalition government of all three parties was formed with Maga as premier. Both Apithy and Ahomadegbe volunteered to serve as ministers under the northerner. Maga, a former schoolteacher, member of the Grand Council of A.O.F., minister of state in a French government and representative in the French National Assembly from 1951 to 1959, announced that he would reform the status of the chieftaincy, work for federation with Togo, sign trade accords with Mali (while remaining in Benin) and attempt to attract foreign capital to Dahomey. This uneasy coalition broke up in late 1959 when Apithy, reverting to an even more extreme position than that which he had originally held, announced the formation of a 'battle front for the independence of Dahomey'. The front, composed of his P.R.D. and the Dahomey section of the *Parti Fédéraliste Africain*, which takes its cues from Dakar, has no parliamentary representation but contains some influential leaders and militant youth groups, announced its goal as 'independence in 1960'. Maga, who was quickly assured of Ahomadegbe's support, termed the move a 'self-interested manœuvre by irresponsible men', relieved Apithy of his cabinet post and himself led Dahomey to independence last year.

BENIN'S PROSPECTS

The Union of Benin has some rough days ahead of it. At least three forces are working to break it up. Nkrumah sees in Houphouet's insistence upon a Franco-African Community a clear threat to his dreams of Pan-African unity and his government has not hesitated to encourage seditious Ivory Coast leaders such as Amon Ndoffou III, 'King of Sanwi'. Amon Ndoffou, who ruled 45,000 tribesmen near the Ghana border, in 1959 established a separate government and fled to Paris. He was extradited by Houphouet, sent to prison for ten years and condemned to twenty years' banishment and loss of civil rights. In a radio broadcast this year, Houphouet warned Nkrumah not to attempt to annex 'even the smallest piece' of Ivory Coast territory.

Touré regards the Ivory Coast leader, who kicked him out of the R.D.A. in 1958, as a traitor to all that African nationalism has stood for. In addition, by damaging de Gaulle's friend, Touré can hurt France, his avowed enemy. Modibo Keita and the rest of the Mali leaders see Houphouet as the biggest obstacle in their race, more reasoned than Nkrumah's, to achieve Gallic African unity. To fight these formidable opponents, Houphouet—whose emphasis has always been on the economic rather than the political side—has had to become the leader of a federation which shows signs of becoming political as well as economic.

What are Houphouet's chances of survival? It is hard to say. His genius is very great and he has a host of able and loyal lieutenants, friends in both racial camps. The real weakness of the Union of Benin lies in the variety of its components. Look at the Union as a four-member club: one man (Ivory Coast) is a well-educated Catholic banker, one (Volta) is a muscular pagan army veteran, the third (Niger) is an illiterate Muslim shepherd, and the fourth (Dahomey) is a brainy but poor Catholic midget. It would be surprising if they did not quarrel.

Houphouet has said that it is not enough just to be black. The Union of Benin will test his thesis that unity can be built on an Afro-Gallic heritage shared in uneven degrees by its four members.

Chapter 12

*

THE ELEPHANT

W e threaded our way through the dripping hills, the air light and perfumed after the thunderburst, and slithered down a greasy forest track from Ivory Coast into Guinea. The Guinea immigration station was a typical African border post: a log set in two forked sticks did duty as the barrier; next to this was a grass-roofed *barri*, the sideless meeting-house found throughout West Africa; stuck in the thatch of the *barri* was a plastic Guinea flag hanging motionless in the heat; inside was a hammock and in the hammock rested an African official wearing the sweat-stained round hat of a French *gendarme*.

Next to this 'police station' was the long, low timber store of the town's Syrian trader. Piled in front of the shop were baskets of dried fish, a bag of salt and a pan of coffee beans which, with the help of the sun, were blackening. Baking in the morning heat behind the store was the native village of thirty or forty huts, the ground around and between the huts powdered into fine dust by hordes of impossibly thin goats, emaciated chickens and naked children. Each of the last sported an umbilical hernia ranging in size from that of a lemon to a really gorgeous number with the dimensions of a dwarf water-melon. The ubiquitous mammy-wagon, which carries freight, passengers and nationalism from one side of West Africa to the other, was stopped in front of us and amid much chatter the passengers handed down their luggage, wrapped in cloth like so many bundles of laundry, for the inspection of the still horizontal Guinean functionary.

As I was digging the passports and car documents out of the jumble which accompanies the Hempstones on trek, Kitty popped out of the car and began to focus her camera on the mammy-wagon. Out of the hammock came the Guinean official in the closest African approximation to speed, his hand up and his chin at the angle calculated to express official disapproval. The fact that his fly was undone detracted somewhat from his forbidding air.

'Not to take photo!' he exclaimed in fractured French.

282

'Why not to take photo?' I queried in syntax and accent guaranteed to make Malraux blush.

'Because it is forbidden not to take photo,' retorted the outraged official, making a swipe at the camera as Kitty effected a strategic withdrawal to the car.

Changing the subject adroitly, I wished him a good morning. He asked me where I was coming from, where I was going and if I was a German. I told him our route and advised him that we were Americans. Was I a missionary? No, I was a journalist. That seemed to exhaust the conversational possibilities and I stood beaming in my most endearing negrophile fashion. Up sauntered a fellow who may or may not have had some connection with the army, police, customs or post office. He was bareheaded and unshod, wore a pair of dirty khaki shorts and a shirt which looked vaguely military because it had shoulder tabs. But no insignia.

'Take this German missionary to the corporal,' commanded my friend of the first instance. I opened my mouth to clear up the misunderstanding, thought better of it, sighed *merci* and followed my splay-footed guide down a goat path which wound through the village.

'Good morning,' I ventured. Strong silent type. *'L'indépendance c'est bon, n'est-ce pas?'* I queried jollily. 'Not to speak to officer on duty,' retorted my moody companion. I nodded and smiled toothily.

At the end of the path was a large grass hut. My talkative friend stepped aside and indicated that I was to go in. It is difficult for one of my proportions to maintain his dignity while entering an African hut. You can squat on your hams and go in duck-walk fashion, in which case you stand a good chance of fracturing your skull on a beam admirably located for this purpose. You can go in on all fours. Or you can turn around, insert your backside into the entrance and let the rest of you follow as best it can. The last alternative seemed impossible on an official occasion: sort of thing bound to lower standards, cause unrest in the hills and the next thing you know it's the Night of the Long Knives. I apologized for my cracking joints, wormed my way through the door in a duck-walk, mercifully missing the lurking beam.

After being in the bright sunlight, the cool shade of the hut seemed to dance in a murky dimness. I was vaguely conscious of a number of people sitting around the walls and there seemed to be some furniture at the far end. I stumbled into someone and said excuse me. It bleated and ambled over to join another goat. As my vision returned I found that there was a rather large African presiding behind a table made of crates of Perrier water. I slipped him a fast '*bon jour*' and held out my passport. My guide, who had come in behind me, oozed up to the table and said something in Foulah.

The official extended a hand whose fingernails were delicately embellished with 'Shocking Pink' polish and took my passport. 'You are a German missionary,' announced this imposing personage. I was beginning to take a dim view of this conversational line: 'I am not a missionary, neither am I German; I am an American journalist.'

My inquisitor's eyes, already heavily burdened by sleep, narrowed to slits of approved craftiness. 'Are you from West Germany or from the German Democratic Republic?' he queried. I bit my tongue, turned my passport right side up and indicated the page which supplied the appropriate information. The official disregarded this page and began to flip through the passport, squinting slightly and making small whistling noises through pursed lips. The Ethiopian visa, written in Amharic, appeared to be an item of particular interest; he studied it, his lips moving soundlessly, his narrow brow knit into a frown of concentration. He donned his sunglasses, the better to survey this remarkable document. I shifted uncomfortably from foot to foot.

'So!' he announced with triumph in his voice, 'you are not a German missionary at all!' I conceded that it was useless to attempt to deceive a man of his astuteness: I was not a German missionary and I apologized for having misled him in this particular. Why, he asked, had I come to Guinea?

I told him that it was my harsh fate to be required by my war-mongering employers to pass only briefly through sunny Guinea on my way to Sierra Leone which, as everyone knew, was still groaning under the heel of British imperialism. But that I hoped to return as soon as possible to the progressive republic of Guinea to pay my respects to his esteemed leader, Sekou Touré, a man with whom he, as a man well-versed in current affairs, knew I was on the most intimate of terms.

'You have no visa!' he snapped.

I pointed out that the French had stopped issuing visas for Guinea and that it was difficult to get one from the Guinea Foreign Service since such an organization was not yet in existence. In that case, he said, I would have to cable to Conakry for authorization to proceed. Where, I asked, thinking this to be a not unreasonable request, was the cable office?

'There is one in Monrovia,' he said. I asked him if he was aware that Monrovia was 400 miles away and that I would have to travel through Guinea anyway to get there.

He grunted and ordered us to report to the police at Nzerekore, the nearest town. I gave a sigh of relief, made a mental note to avoid the Nzerekore police like the smallpox, and returned to the car to find an harassed but still defiant Kitty protecting our baggage from the sallies of the barricade guard. I expressed to this gentleman the pious hope that he might live a thousand years, his flocks multiply and his wives grow fat and his children as numerous as the birds, and off we lurched into the interior.

Guinea is about the size of New Zealand and has a population of 2·6 million. The republic, which got its independence in late 1958, borders on the Atlantic Ocean, Sierra Leone and Liberia to the west; to the north is the enclave of Portuguese Guinea, Senegal and Mali. To the east is Ivory Coast. Guinea is heavily forested on the Ivory Coast and Liberian borders, then rises into the rugged Fouta Djalon range from which flow both the Niger and the Senegal.

Guinea's golden age was the fourteenth century when it made up a part, one is led to believe by the new school of African historians, of the fabled empire of Mali whose sultans dined on service of solid gold and made Timbuktu a centre of scholarship comparable to the great European universities of the Middle Ages. But just as some white historians have found it impossible to conceive of a highly developed Negro civilization, so many black scholars tend to romanticize the facts or overlook them completely in an effort to provide modern African nationalism with a ready-made mystique tailored to suit its political and psychological needs. When the great French explorer René Caille wandered through Guinea in 1827, finally to reach Timbuktu, he found little evidence of Mali's lost grandeur.

On Caille's heels came adventurers seeking the lode of 'the golden trade of the Moores' and missionaries thirsting for souls. And behind these came the Tricolour of France. The French occupied Conakry in 1887, easily pushed their way inland until, thirty miles from the coast, they struck the mountains which swing in a great crescent to the southeast, locking the British colony of Sierra Leone and the independent republic of Liberia against the Atlantic.

In the Fouta Djalon the French encountered Almamy Samory, the warrior-chief whom Guinean president Sekou Touré (and the rest of the Mandingo tribe) claims as his grandfather. Fantasy has grown thickly and luxuriantly around the real Samory, like a lush bougain-villaea which conceals the lines of a house, and it is difficult today to distinguish the man from the legend. It is not even known to which tribe Samory belonged. He led the Mandingoes but there is a story that he sold himself to them as a slave to buy the release of his mother, and later rose to the chieftaincy.

What is certain is that he was an illiterate and cruel man of con-siderable tactical ability who welded the Mandingoes into a great fighting machine, reigned supreme in his rocky hills, raided as far afield as the Gold Coast for slaves and loot, and successfully defied the combined might of Britain and France from 1870 until his capture and exile in 1898. With Samory out of business, Guinea settled down to half a century of the Pax Gallica. Despite the fact that Guinea's cool highlands are one of the healthiest spots along the West African coast, few whites came to settle. Even with the discovery and exploitation of Guinea's immense reserves of iron and bauxite, the white population, including 2,000 Syrians, never exceeded 12,000. Guinea only became famous for and gave its name to a succulent species of wild hen, a kind of grain and a coin of purest gold struck in the seventeenth century by the English Company of Royal Adventurers Trading to Africa.

Guinea was first called Les Rivières du Sud, from the many small streams which flow from the 5,000-foot high Fouta Djalon plateau into the sea. Its modern name is a European approximation of a Berber phrase meaning 'land of the black men', the equivalent of the Arabic Bilad-es-Sudan, which has given its name to another republic.

The West African state is the world's ninety-fourth nation, the eighty-second member of the United Nations and the twenty-ninth component of the so-called Afro-Asian bloc within that organization. It has 382 miles of paved roads, 7,000 motor vehicles and a population so fecund that it doubles itself every twenty-three years. Guinea possesses one of the finest hotels in the world, ironically named the de France, and half the nation's population sees a doctor every year. The women of one tribe weave their hair into elaborate coiffures shaped like cocks' combs and, when the time comes to move, there is another tribe which simply tips its huts over on their sides and rolls them across the steamy countryside like giant hoops until a new village site is found. Although Guinea has vast reserves of mineral wealth, 95 per cent of the population are peasant farmers or shepherds. The country is predominantly Muslim so offices close on Fridays instead of Sundays and it is not unusual for a politician to stop in mid-sentence during a fiery speech to doff his sandals and bow to Mecca as the sun goes down behind the flamboyant trees.

Guinean women are often startlingly beautiful in their puffy pastel turbans and brightly-coloured, flowing cotton gowns over which a fluff of tulle is thrown, making them look like dark angels in a Christmas pageant. They wander through Conakry's two modern department stores, Monoprix and Printana, buying French scent and rubber pants for their broods, flirting tolerantly with both black and white. They and their menfolk are extremely proud of their country's recent independence and sensitive lest one should think them backward. For this reason the police have 'persuaded' women in bush areas, who usually go naked above the waist, to snatch a filthy rag to their breasts whenever a white person passes. This did not prevent a government-sponsored ballet troupe touring the United States from dancing bare-breasted, an example of the curious African ambivalence.

One of Guinea's odd exports is orange essence. A native armed with a spoon can scrape a quart of this from the skins of 1,200 oranges in a single day, leaving him the problem of what to do with the insides. The education department is one of the busiest in the world because it has the task of rewriting all the history books to make blacks into heroes and whites into villains. If your French is poor, it's better not to employ it: if you use the informal second person singular (reserved for intimate friends, dogs and children) to a native, he can and probably will have you jailed.

Conakry, Guinea's somnolent capital, is a lush, mango-shaded town of 70,000 (2,000 whites) crowded on to the narrow Kaloum peninsula which juts out into the Atlantic. At high tide the beach is crowded with French teen-agers in bikinis listening to *le jazz hot* from a nearby pavilion. At low tide the waters recede leaving an ugly mud flat where gnarled old women carrying sacks search like aquatic scavengers for fish trapped in the tidal pools. A picturesque town of sleepy charm, there is still much that is French about Conakry. You can take your meals at *L'Aiglon*, *Au Père Tranquille*, *Bonne Auberge*, *Le Grillon* or *L'Oasis* (although one sorrowfully must report that the café with the nice name of *Le Rat Palmiste* has closed its door and moved to the more congenial political climate of Abidjan), have your hair done at *Hyzazi*, buy a corsage at *Marjolaine*. Conakry has a taxi company called 'Baby' and, a unique distinction, more *patisseries* (four) than doctors.

Walking in the streets can be a menace because small boys clad in the ubiquitous shirt and shorts of khaki, chattering like magpies, propel stones, sticks and any other projectiles readily available high into the leafy roof of mangoes which covers the streets, bringing a shower of fruit down upon the unwary pedestrian. Conakry gets thirteen *feet* of rain a year and the town's two sights are the war memorial, from which the statues have been removed by rabid black nationalists, and the two crested cranes and the pair of bush-buck which adorn the lawn of the presidential palace. These are much admired by the local citizenry who, like most modern Africans, have never seen a wild animal and would be as much at a loss in the bush as any East Side New Yorker.

Conakry's well-protected harbour can handle 800 ships, 1·6 million tons of freight and 12,000 passengers in a normal year and could do better if the asthmatic old 400-mile railway (completed in 1914) which runs from the capital to Kan-Kan were not in such a decrepit state.

In the northern part of the country, one million aristocratic Peuhls (or Foulahs), descendants of Egyptian shepherds and kinsmen of Nigeria's proud Fulani conquerors, tend their great herds of cattle in the age-old fashion. Half a million Malinkes (Mandingoes) still hold Samory's ghost-haunted hills and lead what the seventeenth-century traveller Richard Jobson described as 'a most idle kinde of life'. On the coast live 225,000 Soussous, great dancers and musicians. The rest of Guinea's 2·6 million blacks—filed-tooth Kissines, cannibalistic Guerzes, dog-eating Tomas, shrewd-trading Nalous, stolid farmers like the Landoumas, expert fishermen like the Bagas and wild Coniaguis who at sixteen show their manhood by beating the stuffings out of their proud mothers—scratch a living and little more from the soil.

Guinea was so poor that French aid between the end of World War II and September 1958, when the territory became independent, totalled £32 million, not counting an annual subsidy of £6 million to balance the budget. Guinea, like the rest of Africa, was shaken awake by this peculiar war which pitted not only white against white but Frenchman against Frenchman. With nationalism on a rising wind in the neighbouring British colonies, French prestige declined in Guinea.

Most restive of all the tribes were the Foulahs, who resented conscription as *tirailleurs*, rightly claiming that they were fighting men, not porters. Nor could the brooding Foulahs forgive France for the destruction of their powerful feudal state, born in holy war and nurtured on the subjugation of the inferior pagan tribes. To the Foulahs there were only two honourable careers: war and shepherding their flocks. The French had forbidden the first and, in search of plantation labour, discouraged the second. As a final insult which at the same time was a terrible economic blow, the French freed the Foulahs' slaves and emancipated their women.

France was able to keep peace in Guinea largely through the efforts of the country's conservative post-war political leader, Yacine Diallo. This quiet-spoken schoolteacher, backed by another pedagogue named Mamba Sano and Maurice Montrat, a Muslim *metis*, gave Guinea eight years of unspectacular but solid political progress. The conservative cast of the government was ensured by the support of French West Africa's most powerful orthodox Muslim leader, the Cherif Fanta Mahdi of Kan-Kan, and by that of Almamy Ibrahima Sory, the potent tribal chief.

Had not two events occurred in 1954 it is unlikely that Guinea would be the neo-Communist state it is today: Yacine Diallo died and the sudden growth of the mining industry overnight created a restless proletariat freed of the restraints of tribal society. It soon became apparent that one who was both a product and a cause of this unrest was destined to seize the political leadership of Guinea.

Broad-shouldered and handsome, Sekou Touré (rhymes with 'hoo-ray') was born in 1922 at the bustling railhead town of Kan-Kan. He was one of seven children and, despite his claim to be the grandson of Samory, his parents were poor peasants. He received a primary education and, at the age of fifteen, was expelled from a trade school shortly after he had enrolled for leading a food strike.

Touré read voraciously and, since he came from a devout and conservative Muslim background, was able to get a job as a post office clerk. His arrogance soon had him in trouble and he was quickly moved to another department. He became interested in trade unionism and his activities took such a radical tinge that the government arranged to have him transferred to the Ivory Coast civil service. Touré refused to accept the transfer and before his twenty-second birthday had parleyed a little education, a good brain and unquenchable energy into the leadership of the Guinea branch of France's Red-tinged *Confédération Générale du Travail*.

In his capacity as a trade unionist, Touré visited France. The Communists saw that the young man in the well-tailored suits who was capable of holding an African audience spellbound for hours with his oratory might be of use to them. They wined him and flattered him, and taught him the secrets of political organization.

Houphouet-Boigny, then being chummy with the Communists,

picked up Touré, made him one of his top political assistants and sent him back to organize the Guinea branch of the R.D.A. At that time the French were doing all that they could to suppress the R.D.A. Since the young Malinke was the obvious leader of the extreme left wing of that organization, he came in for more than his share of persecution.

In the 1954 elections, Touré opposed Barry Diawadou, a conservative former civil servant and Yacine Diallo's political heir. There is little doubt that the election was rigged: after a significant delay, Diawadou was declared the victor although observers at the polls felt that Touré had scored a smashing victory. Diallo's death had removed from the scene the one moderate politician generally acceptable to both camps. As a result, the few white settlers and ultra-conservative Africans adopted a militantly reactionary position; to counteract this threat and to preserve his own political skin, Touré absorbed the Communists and moved with his branch of the R.D.A. far to the Left at a time when Houphouet and the rest of the party was jettisoning its Communists and moving to the Right.

Touré, who although he often begins political meetings with a prayer could hardly be called a strict Muslim, found his new position to be a popular one with Guinea's new and dissatisfied urban proletariat. Nor did he find the role of enemy of France an uncongenial one: Touré has had less formal education and consequently is Gallicized to a much lesser degree than the other French African leaders. He had a history of constant conflict with the authorities, had not had the tempering experience of long service in the French National Assembly. His union contacts with Communist agents had convinced him that France and other colonial nations (and never forget that Africans include the United States in this category) were the real enemies of Africa.

On January 1, 1956, Touré was leader of a party without a single seat in the Guinea assembly. His new doctrine took him to power easily in the elections of that year after bloody rioting in Conakry. Touré made one more attempt to prevent Communist domination of his organization by stringing along with Houphouet's request that twelve Europeans be included among the sixty R.D.A. candidates for the *loi cadre* elections of 1957. Touré was shouted down by the left wing of the party, which agreed to accept only three radical Europeans as candidates, and the R.D.A. won fifty-six out of the sixty seats in the Guinea assembly. Touré, now mayor of Conakry, became vice-president of the executive council and Guinea's top African politician.

To call Touré a Communist, at least at that stage of his career was to misunderstand both him and the political climate of Guinea. Touré was never pro-French, nor was he ever a dedicated Communist. He admired Communist organizational techniques, found Marxism's theoretical brotherhood of man compatible with African communalism and saw in International Communism a tool to use to achieve his own goals. Most important of all, Touré soon realized that Guinea's radicals could either make him or break him. Touré found that to ensure his political fortunes he had to go along with leftist elements of the R.D.A. which were more than willing to light his way to power with the burning homes of his political opponents.

FREEDOM

From his new position of power, Touré set about changing the face of Guinea, a country of 200 university graduates, only 250 primary schools, a 5 per cent literacy rate and an annual *per capita* income of less than £18. He cast off the European affiliation of his far-flung 700,000-member union, re-formed it as a purely African organization called *L'Union Générale des Travailleurs d'Afrique Noire* (UGTAN). He strengthened the party discipline of his branch of the R.D.A. until he (or the radical element) had full control. When Guinea's 270 cantonal chiefs raised their voices against Touré's policies, he summarily abolished the chieftaincy, replaced it with 4,000 village councils elected by universal suffrage but controlled with an iron fist by his lieutenants. To keep his truculent people happy, the premier promised them more schools, better health services and higher family welfare payments. To pay for this he mapped an extensive programme of economic development.

Barely had Touré moved into high gear when he was confronted with a political bombshell: de Gaulle, called to power in May 1958, offered French Africa the choice between independence or internal autonomy within the French Community. There is nothing to indicate that Touré's immediate reaction was to opt for independence. He realized his country's financial dependence on France and recognized the fact that Houphouet, his R.D.A. leader, and even the more radical Senegalese and Soudanese politicians, would stick with de Gaulle. Only Bakary, his close friend and premier of Niger, was committed to independence. To leave the Community would mean political isolation and economic stagnation for Guinea.

As late as August 25, 1958, little more than a month before the referendum, Touré told the Guinean assembly that 'our heart, our reason, even more than our most evident self-interest, make us choose without hesitation interdependence and liberty within this union, rather than a definition of ourselves without France or against France'. Three days later in the presence of a fuming de Gaulle, Touré (wearing not the trim suits or loud sports clothes he often favours but the plain white robe of a peasant which he likes to don when stressing the 'African personality') blustered that 'we prefer poverty with liberty to riches with slavery'. Touré went on to say that Guinea would leave the Community, de Gaulle cancelled a dinner with the Malinke leader and flew to Dakar.

The 64,000-dollar question: what happened between August 25 and August 28 to cause this 180-degree turn? Touré was both naïve and misinformed about de Gaulle's intentions: he apparently did not know ahead of time what de Gaulle would offer, was genuinely disappointed that the General did not propose to give the African territories a greater say in Community affairs.

It is likely that Touré hoped as late as August 25 to remain within the Community and that immediate and intense pressure was brought to bear upon him, as it had been before, by the powerful neo-Communist forces within the Guinean's own party. Numbered among this element was his own brother, Ismael Touré, who could be used to replace him and was able to sing, equally lustily, that old Guinean hit tune, 'I am Samory's Grandson'. This leftist element undoubtedly was able to inform Touré that, if he opted for independence, financial assistance would be forthcoming from the Iron Curtain bloc. Given the premier's own radical tendencies, it would have been surprising had he chosen to campaign for continued association with France.

Touré, convinced that France was relegating Africa to a secondary role and aware that his political career was over if he tried to buck the well-organized and militant extremists, commanded the people of Guinea to vote against de Gaulle's Fifth Republic. They did as they were told (when one political opponent died a few days after Touré attacked him in a speech, primitive natives whispered that their leader could kill a foe with his voice) and never has there been a more striking demonstration of the extent to which Africans can be organized for political action.

In the Dabola district, 19,225 votes were cast against the constitution, eight for it. Only one of 57,071 Gueckedou voters had the temerity to say *oui*. In Faranah there was a complete whitewash: 33,124 voting against the constitution and *none* for it. In only one district (Labe, where 27,440 affirmative ballots were recorded) did Touré encounter any serious opposition and there, as in Guinea's other twenty-five districts, he was victorious. In all, 1·1 million Guineans voted for independence while 57,000 cast their votes for membership within the French Community. In contrast, there were less than 100,000 *nons* in the other eleven territories of French West and Equatorial Africa combined.

The French reacted in a fashion which, if not commendable, is understandable: before the last returns were in, de Gaulle sent a top-level emissary scurrying to Conakry to inform Touré that Guinea was regarded as having seceded from France, that French officials and technicians would be withdrawn forthwith, that although funds already allocated would not be withdrawn, Guinea could expect no further financial aid from France. The courts closed, trade ground to a standstill, Radio Conakry went off the air, shipping bound for Guinea was diverted to Ivory Coast as 5,000 French moved out of the country. With them they took office furniture, files, telephones, air-conditioners, even electrical wiring, everything that could be considered to be the property of France. Some Guinean troops were stripped of their uniforms, most of their arms were collected, and equipment which could not be taken away was in some cases burned.

Comic opera situations developed: as indignant French officials carried household appliances out of the governor's palace and piled them on the lawn to await moving vans, equally annoyed nationalists gathered them up again and threw them back through the palace windows. Strong man Touré, nicknamed 'The Elephant' by his followers, found himself head of a nation with no money in the bank, leader of a government which could barely function. Since all the typewriters were gone as were the secretaries to use them, cabinet ministers scrawled political pronouncements in longhand. With the telephones gone or out of order, runners were the only means of communication. The Minister of Health found himself initialling memos while trying to remove a recalcitrant appendix.

In the bush, the situation was even more unsettled. We arrived in Nzerekore, a town in south-east Guinea, to find the police station in a state of uproar. Under the station's sheet metal roof were crowded Arabs from the north, a group of sullen-looking characters in dirty loin-cloths and African officials in various states of undress. All were talking at once and each seemed to be in the process of bribing the other with fistfuls of crumpled francs. The commandant, I was told, was asleep and the Frenchman who had been in charge had departed with the official seal so nothing could be accomplished anyway.

'Today is not forever,' cryptically shouted a disgruntled Liberian as he stamped out of the station. A Ghanaian visitor stood back aghast from the tumult and, when he saw that I was English-speaking, asked for a ride to Monrovia. 'These chaps,' he said icily, 'are savages.' I repaired to the District Commissioner's office in an attempt to get permission to leave town. The commissioner turned out to be a very nice teen-ager who had been a clerk before the referendum. He listened sympathetically to my problem, experimented with the telephone, gave it up and sent a runner to the police station. The 'runner' negotiated this 600-yard journey in something under an hour, thereby establishing a new Nzerekore speed record.

'You can see the commandant,' the commissioner said, 'in three hours' time. Meanwhile, why not make yourself comfortable at the hotel?' This establishment was a long, low, mud structure covered with a purple splash of bougainvillaea and was about as jolly as a Roman-Briton mead house thirty days after the withdrawal of the legions. The proprietor, a snaggle-toothed little Frenchman fastidiously garbed in sandals, dirty shorts, a three-day beard and an undershirt which had seen better days and at least six recent meals, held forth from behind the bar. Here the true horror of the situation was painted in broad strokes. On the wall behind the bar were shelves with a capacity of at least forty bottles. A bottle containing an inch of Johnny Walker, a jug of *pastis* and two miniature plastic flags of the Republic of Guinea stood lonely sentinel upon these abandoned ramparts. There was beer but the two bottles were otherwise all that remained of our host's cellar.

We bought beer and inquired as to the chances of procuring accommodation for the night since it was obvious that our day's travel was over unless the commandant should suffer from a sudden bout of insomnia. There was no room, said the proprietor, scratching without optimism in one bony armpit: although the white population of Nzerekore had dropped in two weeks from 360 to 45, most of those who remained, perhaps fearing a massacre, had left their homes and moved into the hotel. Still, he would see what could be done. He returned in a few minutes to say that one of the guests had agreed to vacate his room and share a bed with himself. As the proprietor was still scratching moodily, this seemed almost too great a sacrifice on the part of our benefactor. But I protested only mildly. 'My friend,' said our host, 'white men must stick together in times such as these.'

In the evening we routed the *pastis* and put a sizable dent in the beer supply with considerable assistance from a racially mixed crowd which included a Liberian with cowboy boots and a guitar, a couple of hard-faced French businessmen and a bunch of drunk Africans who could have been from either side of the border. As the commandant, having arisen from his nap, polished off the last drink of whisky in the bottle and left without paying, one of the planters sidled over and struck up a conversation. He said that as soon as he had heard the referendum results he had hurried to a nearby *chinchona* (quinine) plantation to see what his neighbour planned to do. He found the lights on in the house, the door open, a half-eaten meal on the table and nothing disturbed. The *chinchona* planter, who received a subsidy from the French government which enabled him to stay in business, had heard the news already, got up from the table without a word to his servants, driven to Monrovia and caught the first planc to Paris.

'I will go as soon as I can get a buyer for my place,' the planter added. He had lost one plantation in Indo-China and was not happy about the situation.

It is an index both of the good nature of the African and of Touré's firm control of the people that there was no real trouble. Slowly the chain-smoking premier got Guinea's administration on its feet, kept the essential services going, reassured jumpy foreign investors and blocked a French move to delay the republic's admission to the United Nations. But Sekou Touré was soon to discover that his problems had only begun with independence.

THE ECONOMICS OF FREEDOM

The economic facts of life cannot be changed by manifestoes or referendums. Touré inherited what a classical economist would call a debtor nation, which is a polite way of saying that Guinea is broke. In 1957, the last full year during which the republic was associated with France, Guinea's exports of bananas, coffee, palm products, iron, bauxite and industrial diamonds were worth £8 million. In the same year her imports cost nearly £14 million which, any way you slice it, leaves her with a heavy trade deficit.

Guinea's business was almost entirely with the West. Her bananas—which with coffee account for almost half of her exports by value—went to France and Italy. These two countries and the United States bought her coffee while the Metropole took 99 per cent of her palm products. France, England, Belgium, West Germany and Canada took all but a minute fraction of her iron ore, bauxite and diamonds, which together account for another quarter of Guinea's exports. Poland, which bought a little iron ore and a few tons of palm products, was the only Communist nation with which Guinea had any commercial contact.

When Guinea woke up on September 30, 1958, to find herself an independent country, she was saddled with a dislocated economy. Touré had no sure buyer in sight for the 75 per cent of Guinea's exports which formerly were sold in the franc zone. The situation in regard to minerals was not too serious: they were handled by big international combines to which the change in the country's political status, although it may have been disquieting, meant little. In any event, they could always be stockpiled. But Touré was faced with the prospect of seeing his more valuable fruit and vegetable crops rot on the ground unless he could swing a quick marketing agreement.

And these crops were most seriously affected by the political situation. Although none of the big firms closed their doors, many of the *petit blancs* who acted as middlemen and buying agents for crops such as coffee and bananas were among the 5,000 French who cleared out of Guinea. In addition, many African growers—who own almost all the coffee and a quarter of the banana plantations—reckoned that independence meant freedom from work and failed to get their crops to market. The withdrawal of French officials clogged the communications system at just the time when Guinea needed it most and threw at least 20,000 Africans out of work, creating a jobless and hungry proletariat which contributed nothing to the political serenity of the country.

In effect, within six months of independence Guinea was about as close to economic collapse as a nation can get. If the country was to survive—Guinea has to import 10,000 tons of rice a year to feed herself—Touré had to act and he had to act fast. An embittered France showed herself to be in no great hurry to conclude trade agreements with her erring daughter, particularly since Guinea's eleven African sister-republics who had chosen to remain within the Community might rightfully regard this as placing a premium on disloyalty. The United States had, of course, made no allocation for aid to Guinea and, in any case, might have been reticent about extending assistance to a nation so close to the Communist line. The other Western democracies, out of respect for French sensibilities and for reasons of their own, made no rush to Guinea's door. Touré soon found that, unlike other African states which had reached independence through a series of planned stages and had had an opportunity to budget for their requirements, Guinea might well founder in the bow wave created by her own impetuous launching.

Well aware of the danger his country was in and pressed to do so by the radical wing of his party, Touré hastily concluded four trade agreements with Iron Curtain countries. Although Guinea also threw in a small sum in francs, the agreements were basically barter deals. She sent iron ore, palm kernels, diamonds and hides to Poland for pharmaceutics, cement, cotton goods, porcelain, rice, beer and machinery. Russian chemicals, drugs, motor fuel and machinery were obtained for coffee, bananas, pineapples, palm oil, citrus oil and diamonds. Iron ore, bananas, orange essence and groundnuts were exchanged for East German sugar, disinfectants, cement, textiles, flour, machinery, rice, ceramics, pharmaceutics and medical equipment. Czechoslovakia took the same general range of products in barter for shoes, sugar, textiles, cement and road-building machinery.

Within a matter of a few months, while the West dawdled and temporized, all of Guinea's bananas, coffee and palm kernels, most of the rest of her fruit production, and a not inconsiderable proportion of her iron ore and industrial diamonds (half of her total exports) were diverted into Communist trade patterns. To frost the cake nicely, the Czechs made their black socialist brethren a free gift of two shiploads of arms, including enough rifles to equip an army four times the size of Guinea's, modern anti-aircraft guns, armoured cars and a complete radio station with a transmitter three times as powerful as that of Radio Cairo—accompanied by the technicians to install it.

In return, Touré established a state trading agency which makes it difficult for firms wishing to export to the West to get the necessary licences and eases the way for those willing to trade with the Communist bloc. By the same means, imports from Iron Curtain countries find it easy to get permits while Western products often do not. Local businessmen, for reasons often remote from politics, are finding it difficult to do business under the new set-up. Said a former president of the Guinea Chamber of Commerce: 'We don't know the specifications, the quality or the fair price of Eastern European merchandise. What about spare parts? How are we to maintain machinery with which we are unfamiliar? We are asked to do business with our eyes closed and that is not so easy.'

But the signing of the trade agreements only partially alleviated

Guinea's pressing economic situation. It provides markets of a sort for most of Guinea's produce but it did nothing to fill the gap left by the withdrawal of French economic aid. Guinea through the trade agreements had ensured her existence but she had not a *sou* for development.

To meet this requirement, Touré pulled off a stunt which was to set humming every foreign office in the world and obscure the West African political picture for months to come. Before Guinea was two months old, her premier flew off to Accra for talks with Prime Minister Kwame Nkrumah of Ghana. After what one correspondent described as 'an expansive evening at Christianborg Castle', the two premiers announced to a startled world that 'inspired by the example of the thirteen American colonies' they had decided to create the 'nucleus of a Union of West African States'. There was to be a union flag and the two governments were to develop the 'closest contacts' in the fields of defence, diplomacy and economic affairs. To top it off, Nkrumah agreed to lend Touré £10 million for development purposes, a sum which represented 10 per cent of Ghana's financial reserves.

Nkrumah, with the African absent-mindedness which comes close to rudeness, had neglected to give the other nations of the British Commonwealth more than five hours' notice of his decision and the immediate reaction in Paris and London was unfavourable. As constitutional lawyers rifled through their files in search of a precedent, London newspapers insinuated that Guinea was trying to sneak into the Commonwealth by the back door, adding acidly that the Commonwealth is 'not a cheap club in which membership is conferred on outsiders by a wink to the doorkeepers'. Paris saw the whole affair as a plot on the part of perfidious Albion to break up the French empire in revenge for the creation of the European Common Market. Accra and Conakry, however, were jubilant, each seeing the so-called merger as an addition to its own territories.

Scarcely had the Union been announced when both Accra and Conakry began to equivocate as to its real nature. Ghanaian Foreign Minister Kojo Botsio admitted that the terms of the merger were 'vague' and the final form of the union might only amount to something like a treaty relationship. Diallo Telli, Guinea's roving ambassador, said that the merger could be likened to an 'engagement rather than a marriage'.

As time passed and little was said or done further to cement the union, it became obvious that too much importance had been attached to the affair, that Western diplomats were going to have to stop expecting an ebulliently self-assertive Africa to act in a cool and reasoned fashion. The 'union' satisfied Touré from three points of view: he got hold of the money necessary to finance his development schemes, twitted the French and demonstrated that he was a man to be reckoned with in any Pan-African scheme. Nkrumah was pleased because it flattered his vanity to play the role of Big Brother to an infant African nation, provided him with a dramatic focal point for the ensuing Accra Pan-African Conference and gave him an ideological beach-head in Gallic Africa. Since Touré came away with the cash, it would seem that he had the best of the bargain.

The premier then set about obtaining admission to the United Nations. In an attempt to mollify France, he asked her to sponsor Guinea's application but was rebuffed. Japan and Iraq agreed to become dual sponsors and, on December 12, 1958, with France abstaining, Guinea was admitted by a unanimous vote. As the red, yellow and green tricolour of the new nation went up outside the U.N. building, members of *Les Ballets Africains*, wearing not only the brassières recommended by the New York censors but thick coats (it was eleven above zero), broke into song and Ismael Touré, who represented his brother, received the congratulations of the world. With Iron Curtain countries scurrying to set up embassies in Conakry (the Bulgars were first), France belatedly recognized Guinea on January 15, 1959. With the usual display of diplomatic finesse, it was not until February 10 that a makeshift American Embassy was established in one room of the Texaco Company's Conakry office, more than four months after Guinea's secession from France. Five more months were to elapse before an American ambassador (the able Negro educator John H. Morrow) was appointed. This slow-footed work was to cost the United States dearly.

Touré had been turned down by the State Department when he made an informal request through President Tubman of Liberia for the arms which he later received from Czechoslovakia and it was not until nine months after her independence that Guinea received a scrap of American assistance, 8,000 tons of grain needed to get her through a hungry period. Since her reception in Washington had hardly been warm, Touré turned to Russia in August of 1959 when he needed more cash for development.

Soviet Premier Nikita Khrushchev, who was on vacation in the Crimea, took the time to see the Guinea delegation led by Saifoulaye Diallo, president of the National Assembly, and to approve a £12·5 million loan. Deputy Soviet Premier Anastas Mikoyan, who negotiated the loan, said that his country 'invariably sympathized with the African peoples' struggles against the shameful system of colonialism', benevolently explained that the twelve-year loan would carry an interest rate of 2½ per cent, admittedly far less than Guinea could have obtained from any other source. What Mikoyan neglected to mention and the Guineans were too naïve to realize is that Guinea must use the money only to buy Soviet equipment, which may well be higher priced and of inferior quality to that available in the West. But the point is that when Guinea needed money she went to Russia; and she got it at an apparently favourable rate. The money, to be spent over a four-year period, is being used to purchase agricultural machinery, improve the railways and Conakry's harbour, establish a technical secondary school, construct new buildings to house parliament and the government ministries, build two hotels and a stadium, create a rice cultivation research centre, and conduct a general geological survey. In contrast, American aid during 1959–60 amounted to £125,000. Africa is beginning to be impressed by Soviet generosity.

In the months between Guinea's admission to the United Nations and the negotiation of the Russian loan, Touré edged away from his 'union' with Nkrumah. The Ghana premier journeyed to Conakry by sea, where he arrived on a muggy April morning to be clasped by Touré in a brotherly embrace. After a three-week tour of the country in the presidential diesel train, and a May Day parade during which Guinean cabinet ministers left the rostrum to pass in review, the two premiers issued a second manifesto. They reaffirmed their decision to establish a union but did little to further define the nature of such an association. They gave the merger a new name—the Union of Independent African States—which clearly implied that nothing more than the loosest form of confederation was intended. They came up with a Union flag—red, gold and green with as many five-pointed black stars as membernations—but asserted that each state would retain its 'individuality and structure'. They devised a motto—'Independence and Unity'—but made no attempt to solve the constitutional problems inherent in Ghana's Commonwealth membership. They stated that there would be a Union anthem (although nobody had found time to write one) but added that each state would have its own foreign representation and seat in the United Nations. There was to be a Union citizenship but no surrender of the national citizenship of inhabitants of the member-states. Although the premiers of the Union's component states were to meet to determine a common defence policy, each nation was to retain its own army. In short, after five months of study, Ghana and Guinea had moved not a step closer to any sort of recognizable union.

Why? It became immediately obvious that Touré was not anxious to commit himself too deeply to any union which might compromise his own dearer ambition to preside over the dissolution of the French Community and, subsequently, to assume the leadership of Gallic Africa. Perhaps also on the Malinke leader's mind was the fact that four West African states with Muslim majorities—Nigeria, Togo, Mali and Cameroon—were due for independence in 1960. As a Muslim, Touré realized that he might well be more appealing as a federal leader than the neo-Christian Nkrumah, who is intensely disliked, particularly in populous Northern Nigeria. By committing himself to play second fiddle to Nkrumah in 1959, Touré realized that he might well lose the chance to lead the whole orchestra in 1960. These were the considerations which led Touré, once he had obtained the £10 million loan from Nkrumah, to shy away from a closer union and to reduce the Ghana-Guinea merger to what it is today: no more than an *entente* such as exists between the United States and Canada.

Having obtained the stop-gap aid necessary to fulfil his minimum development requirements, Touré attacked other problems. In an attempt to have the best of both worlds, he quickly negotiated three agreements with France. These provided for retention of Guinea within the franc zone, the pooling of some foreign exchange, reciprocal trade agreements, the fixing of ceilings on imports from other countries, the use of French technicians on a priority basis in Guinea, the availability of French research teams to study Guinea's development problems, representation of Guinea by France on international bodies to which the former does not belong, the use of French as Guinea's official language, French assistance in the field of higher education and the recognition for pension and seniority purposes of service in the Guinea civil service for French nationals.

In these agreements, Guinea again was the winner. She made no commitment to drop her propaganda campaign against the French Community and she soon violated the economic protocol. Leaving the franc zone would only have accentuated her economic problems and there was obviously no alternative to French as an official language. She gained access to France's foreign exchange pool without surrendering any hard currencies which she herself might obtain through direct negotiations. She obtained equal facilities for her university students, French technical and diplomatic assistance, and a valuable incentive in the form of the pensions and seniority rights to encourage fellow-travelling French nationals to remain in her civil service. France made considerable concessions and received in return only the bare assurance that France would be considered Guinea's 'next friend' in the Western camp, something which the rest of the West would have been willing to concede and a status which Guinea was free to revoke any time she pleased. Once again, Touré had come away from an international conference table with most of the blue chips.

Turning to the domestic scene, Touré—who since independence has had little time for home life with his pretty mulatto second wife—warned Guineans that this was 'no time for dancing', called for a massive 'human investment programme' to take the place of wages which the republic could no longer afford. The Ghanaian and Soviet loans provided barely enough money to supply the materials for the projects which Touré wished to undertake. The people, he said, would have to provide the labour. Individual villages and whole tribes were marshalled to build roads, schools and clinics to save Guinea's precious monetary reserves for the grandiose industrial projects so dear to the heart of every African nationalist. It would be impolite to note that this system resembles the *travail obligatoire* characteristic of the hated early era of French colonialism, the communes of Red China and the communal labour system employed by the Portuguese in Africa against which the delegates to every Accra conference rail. This is just another example of African double-think: a programme designed for the good of the people under a colonial administration is intolerably undemocratic; the same programme inaugurated by a more authoritarian black government is simply an expression of the African personality.

Such a scheme is as questionable, however, on grounds of efficiency as on a moral basis. The first few months of the human investment programme were greeted with enthusiasm but it soon became evident that the people were more interested in building a road or a school than in maintaining it after the first flush of jubilance had worn off. As the days wore on and no manna flowed from the skies, it became increasingly necessary to apply 'persuasion' to get the people out to work.

The authoritarian overtones of Touré's government became more evident as prisoners wearing blue smocks with the inscription 'Enemy of the People' sewn across the backs appeared in greater numbers to work on projects which were once the tasks of free men. One of Touré's cabinet ministers, alarmed at the direction events were taking, fled to exile in France.

To ensure that no opposition arose to his programmes, the thirty-eight-year-old premier made his Democratic Party of Guinea (P.D.G.), which had been expelled from Houphouet's R.D.A. when it voted against the Community, the only legal party in the country. He permanently padlocked the doors of *Guinée-Matin*, the country's only daily newspaper and a foe of his régime, sent mobile film units fanning out over Guinea to indoctrinate conservative villagers with his political theories, dissolved all youth organizations from Boy Scouts to debating societies, absorbed their members into the monolithic youth wing of the P.D.G., and increased his popularity with women by forbidding child marriages and giving them the right to reject unwanted suitors favoured by their families.

Touré established one elective political committee for every 600 inhabitants, arranged for each of these to send delegates to regional committees which have representation on the central politburo controlled by the most radical element in the country. Since the Central Committee, as in Communist states, chooses the candidates for the national assembly, government is effectively in the hands of the political bosses, not the people. If they disapprove of a candidate, they can only stay away from the polls since there are no opposition politicians running for office. But little unnecessary strain has been imposed on this iron-clad set-up: no elections have been held since independence. In effect, the Guinea national assembly has small importance in the political structure of the country. All decisions are made in secret sessions of the Central Committee and are rubber-stamped by the assembly, usually without debate. For the first time one is able to see what some nationalists mean by African-style democracy.

THE ELEPHANT TRUMPETS

Although Touré, who gets by on four hours' sleep a night, has a reputation for accessibility, obtaining an appointment is often difficult. Such requests are channelled through the Guinea Information Service, which is controlled by two French Marxists. Although I had written two months before our arrival in Conakry and checked-in personally two weeks before I wished for an interview, nothing had been arranged by our third visit to Guinea.

Of a morning one would find the earnest young French Marxist—who bears a striking resemblance to that bad old imperialist, Napoleon (one must assume that this does not displease him since he combs his hair forward and cultivates sideburns)—chuckling merrily over a caricature of Herter or Selwyn Lloyd in his airmail edition of that racy newspaper, the German Democratic Republic's *New Germany*. But nothing done about an interview. Finally, after efforts in other directions, I was told to be 'at the palace' at 9 a.m. on the day of our scheduled departure. This arrangement did not appear to have the approval of the palace guards, who waved their new Czech sub-machine-guns around in disconcerting fashion, but at last I gained entrance to a waiting-room crowded with petitioners of every colour and social status, from the new Israeli ambassador to bush natives who looked decidedly uncomfortable hunched up in modern Swedish furniture. After three hours nobody had seen anybody and we were informed that the president had 'go for he chop' (was having his lunch). So I did likewise, returning in the afternoon. After another two-hour wait, I asked to see the guard's commanding officer. I explained to this gentleman that I had had an appointment with the president at 9 a.m. He looked at his watch and said brightly: 'But it's 4 p.m.' I told him that I was aware of that. 'Step down the corridor,' he said, 'and go through the first door on the right.' It was the first time I had ever walked into a president's office unannounced. As I closed the door behind me, I recognized Touré, who was wearing an open-necked sports shirt, sitting behind a desk cluttered with documents which he was initialling. He looked up, motioned me to a chair, did not rise but returned my handshake and offered me a Gauloise.

Touré was about as cordial as the Dean of Men at my university when I once had occasion to return from Christmas vacation two days late. He started off by saying that the most serious problem with which his government had had to contend since independence was the 'disparaging newspaper campaign of the Western press'.

I asked him if he thought that a two-party political system might be possible in Guinea at some future date. He rasped: 'It is not our intention to squander this chance of unity by adopting a system which would only reduce our political strength. What Africa needs is a fundamental revolution. A political system based on two parties would be a certain check on our evolution. The revolutionary dynamism requires no other stimulant than our needs, our aspirations, our hopes.'

He denied that he had ever been a Communist, said that no Communist group 'as such' existed within the P.D.G. and asserted that Guinea had no desire to belong to either world bloc.

Guinea's economic situation, he said with a bass laugh that seemed to fill the room, did not worry him: 'Allowed to develop on their own and not simply to benefit colonial powers, independent African nations such as Guinea will be able both to raise their own standards of living and to make a considerably more substantial contribution to world trade.'

On the subject of investment, Touré said that Guinea desperately needed foreign capital to build up an industrial base. 'But,' he added, 'such schemes must be a part of our political programmes. We will specify what types of investment will be suitable. '

KONKOURE

One type of investment which Touré is intensely interested in attracting involves the construction of the mammoth Konkoure hydro-electric complex. Bauxite prospecting along the Konkoure River valley began as early as 1942. Within six years the area ninety miles from Conakry at Kimbo in central Guinea was determined to contain reserves totalling at least 140 million tons. An international firm known as FRIA (stock division: U.S. firms, 48·5 per cent; French, 26·5 per cent; British, 10 per cent; Swiss, 10 per cent; West German, 5 per cent) agreed to sink £71·1 million into the construction of a railway and a plant to convert the bauxite to alumina (a further and more expensive processing is required to produce aluminium).

Work began in 1957 and Kimbo went into production early this year with a plant which is the largest of its type in Africa or Europe. Kimbo employs 300 whites and 900 Africans, will produce this year 480,000 tons of alumina, a figure which will be raised to 1·2 million tons annually by 1965. The combine holds a twenty-five-year lease with an option to renew for another seventy-five years, at which time the bauxite should be exhausted.

Despite his neo-Communist leanings, Touré has resisted all efforts of the radical branch of the P.D.G. to nationalize FRIA. He fully realizes that if foreign investors are scared out of Guinea, the republic's economic goose will not only be cooked but burned to a frazzle.

Relations between Touré and the international combine have been correct if restrained.

What Touré would like to do is to harness the power of the Konkoure River to provide the power for a newer and larger plant which would convert the alumina to aluminium and give Guinea a far larger slice of the profits than she now receives. FRIA has declared that if Touré can find the money for the dam, it will build the plant.

Touré, of course, hasn't got the money and has had little luck in getting it. What he wants the consortium to do is to build both the plant and the dam, a project that would cost more than £107 million. To get it to agree to this, he has stated that unidentified Communist powers have agreed to finance the scheme in return for a blanket mineral concession over the entire country. The Guinean premier has said that he has rejected the offer pending a decision of the Western consortium. One would almost be inclined to call this blackmail and to wonder if, in fact, such an offer has been made.

In addition to the Kimbo deposits, the Bauxite du Midi Co. (an affiliate of Aluminium Ltd. of Canada) has invested about £40 million to build an alumina plant and an eighty-mile railway from Boke to the left bank of the Rio Nunez where it has constructed a small port. The bauxite deposit at Boke totals 100 million tons and, by 1962, the company expects to be exporting each year one million tons of bauxite and 240,000 tons of alumina worth about £6 million.

Directly across the harbour from Conakry are the Los Islands, known to ancient mariners (who used them as a slaving base) by the more exotic name of Las Islas de los Idolos. Bauxite was discovered on the island of Kassa, one of the group, as early as 1912 but it was not until 1952 that Bauxite du Midi, which also owns this concession, began exporting. Kassa, all nine million tons of it, is almost solid bauxite and the stuff has only to be picked up with a steam-shovel and dumped into the hold of a freighter. Since no European plant can treat the type of ore found on the island, the annual production of 400,000 tons is processed in Canada.

With Kassa, Kimbo and Boke, Guinea is already the premier bauxite producer of Africa; if the Konkoure scheme comes off, she may well become an important world source of aluminium and the £714,000 she earns now from bauxite will look like chicken-feed.

Nor does Guinea's mineral wealth end here. There are immense deposits of iron ore—more than two *billion* tons—literally under Conakry's pavements. The Kaloum peninsula upon which the city stands and much of the surrounding countryside has a 55 per cent iron ore content and each year more than one million tons worth more than £1 million is exported. Diamonds (170,000 carats) add another £357,000 to the republic's coffers and much of the interior is still only imperfectly prospected. So Guinea's economic future is not as uncertain as its present, even though mineral wealth is a wasting asset. The big problem for Guinea is to find the skill and the money to develop her resources. And these have been scared away by Touré's politics.

How Communist is Guinea? From the atmosphere of the lobby of Conakry's plush Hotel de France, one would have to say that if the country isn't Communist, the Reds can't be blamed for not trying. Since most of Guinea's top political leaders, like their boss, came up through the ranks of the Communist-dominated labour movement, they had plenty of friends to call upon among the caviar-and-vodka set during Guinea's hour of need. Within a few months of Guinea's independence, enough shady characters poured into Conakry to provide the *dramatis personae* for several Grade D spy films. On almost any evening, men of a dozen nationalities could be found whispering in the corners of the de France while keeping an eye on groups presumably inimical to their interests: sallow Semites gawked belligerently at husky uncombed Russians in too-tight suits; tie-less East Germans stared unfraternally at the Poles whose government holds so much of what was once German territory; Bulgars with hands like Smithfield hams glanced suspiciously at city-slicker Czechs; in the centre of things, fellow-travelling Africans gesticulated madly and argued in exquisite French while a rotund American diplomat looked on with prim displeasure. The Toilers of the East on hand during our visit ate dinner at an appropriately peasant hour and there was little action at the bar, although vodka was stocked.

All of the de France's bedrooms face the sea and each evening men from both sides of the Iron Curtain risk a nasty fall by hanging over their balconies, the better to focus their field-glasses on the mysterious freighters sneaking in and out of the harbour at nightfall. When the visibility is reduced, everybody takes to his typewriter to pound out the day's report. The enthusiastic comrade in the room next to us, perhaps hoping to win an Order of Lenin, Third Class, started pecking away at three o'clock one morning and not even the most terrible reactionary oaths could deter him from his path. A few hours after he had finished, we staged our own White Terror when Kitty unlimbered *our* machine to the background music of my caterwauling from the shower.

But these, like the fellow-travelling French who have stayed on in Guinea, are birds of passage. Touré and his underlings all maintain that they are neutralists, not Communists, although one would be inclined to say that they are neutral in favour of the Communist bloc. Certain top P.D.G. leaders—including Minister of the Interior Fodeba Keita, who organized the *Ballets Africains* which enjoyed such a success in its sixteen-week American tour, Minister of Public Works and Communications Ismael Touré, the premier's brother, and Saifoulaye Diallo, the slender Foulah who negotiated the 1959 Russian loan and is Guinea's Number Two politician—come rather close to being Communists. Others, like Sekou Touré, have been influenced by the Reds, are not ill-disposed towards them, but are far from being party members.

Much of Guinea's welcome-brother attitude towards Communist agents may be attributed to pique at the manner in which France left Guinea and the tardiness of the United States and other Western nations to fill the economic vacuum left by France's departure. Guinea needed trade, aid and loans and she found the Communists willing to supply all three at bargain-basement prices. And there was also this factor: Guinea was not displeased at having an opportunity to hurt France. She reacted like a sullen teen-ager forbidden by strict parents to date an unkempt teddy boy. When parental control was relaxed, she encouraged him because it would annoy her former guardians even though she realized that she did so at the risk of her virtue.

The United States bid for Touré's allegiance in late 1959 when President Eisenhower invited the West African leader to make an official visit to America. In New York Touré was somewhat taken aback to find that Ghanaian flags mistakenly had been raised in his honour. He attended ceremonies in various parts of the country, including a multi-racial dinner held by North Carolina's Governor Luther Hodges. In Washington Touré was greeted with 'Bienvenu' banners strung across his route into town, received a promise of 150 scholarships for Guinean students but no development money was forthcoming. Nor did a subsequent visit to Britain produce anything substantial.

A few months later Touré demonstrated both his own diplomatic ineptness and the amount of Communist infiltration by becoming the first non-Communist nation to recognize East Germany. Dr. Adenauer had already been angered by the Guinean president's allegations, made in a letter to the United Nations, that the Federal Republic had assisted financially and technically in the development of the French atomic bomb and that members of the *Bundeswehr* were serving in the Foreign Legion, statements which had their inspiration from East Germany and which were described by West Germany as 'a monstrous slander'. Touré's actions did seem a bit ungrateful since West Germany had been one of the first nations to recognize Guinea and had accorded him full honours during a visit to Bonn at a time when Guinea's relations with France and England were strained. In addition, West Germany had already given Guinea £160,000 in technical assistance and an economic mission contemplating further aid was due to leave for Conakry.

There followed a comedy of errors in which the Guinean ambassador in Bonn said that he knew only that press reports stated that Dr. Seydou Conte had presented his credentials to East German President, Wilhelm Pieck. Touré was asked by the West German ambassador in Conakry if he would deny that relations had been established and, with unattractive evasiveness, replied the announcement had not come from him and that therefore he was not the one to issue a denial. In the end, it was denied that Guinea had recognized East Germany, with whom she now does £2·8 million worth of trade every year.

In recent months Red influence in Guinea has grown more profound and the country's economic position has further deteriorated. East Germans, Poles, Hungarians and Czechs have a finger in every pot from physical training to economic planning. Western goods have disappeared from the shops. Russian and Czechoslovakian cargo planes, their contents unloaded secretly and under guard, have made frequent appearances at Conakry's airport which, like the harbour, is run by Czech technicians. Czech-made Praga and Skoda motor-cars are seen on the streets and Communist money is building a printing plant and a radio station. Red China has opened its first embassy in Africa and its technicians have arrived with advice on rice cultivation and offers of technical and economic assistance. But despite all this and the Russian loan, Guinea is discovering that she could have obtained better prices for her bananas in the Western market, the state-owned trading agency is deeply in debt, Guinea's treasury is bare and heavy taxes have been imposed on foreign oil companies in an attempt to keep the country solvent. When even these draconian measures failed him, Touré took the portentous step of cutting his ties with the French franc. Guinea now uses its own francs (printed in Communist Czechoslovakia) which, by the terms of Touré's decree, have no value in foreign trade.˜He has also made it mandatory for firms doing business in Guinea to establish subsidiary (and more susceptible to local political pressure) companies in Conakry. As a result of these measures, several important firms are considering leaving Guinea, and the economic future, although Touré has announced that Guinea will spend £6 million for development between 1960 and 1963, looks bleak indeed. From the West's point of view, political prospects are not entirely pleasing.

The totalitarian nature of Touré's Guinea has become more apparent in recent months. In the spring of 1960 Red-trained secret police arrested hundreds of 'Gaullist enemies of the state' accused of seeking to oust Touré in the cause of 'French colonialism and its black lackeys'. Leader of the plot, according to Guinean sources, was an intellectual former civil servant named Ibrahim Diallo who had asked Touré's permission (not granted) to form an opposition party. According to unconfirmed reports, at least five of the arrested men were tortured to death at Alpha Yaya military barracks and their bodies sent home in sealed coffins which were buried under police supervision. It was alleged that Diallo's teeth were knocked out and his fingernails extracted to gain information about the plot. Forty of the accused were brought to 'trial' before a 'People's Court' (no defence attorneys were present) and nineteen of them, including Diallo, were sentenced to death. The rest, including four white men, were handed long jail sentences. Later it was disclosed that one of the Frenchmen had died already . . . of a 'heart attack'. So much for freedom.

Touré likes to talk in Communist jargon and he has made full use of Red organizational techniques, which happen to suit his political requirements. But Guinea, although it appears to be a police state, is not yet a Communist satellite. What the left wing of the P.D.G. has done is to create a favourable climate for Communist infiltration. If the Communists can gain control of Guinea, it will give them their first firm hold in Africa south of the Sahara. By utilization of the Ghana–Guinea *entente* and UGTAN, whose influence Touré spread to British Africa by naming Ghana labour leader John Tettegah as the union's vice-president, Communism stands a good chance of working its way into Ghana where it will be able to seize control of the Pan-

African movement to an even greater degree than it already has. A Red Guinea can be the cancer to poison the body politic of all Africa.

And that is why it is so important for the United States to understand Sekou Touré, this young, tough and intelligent leader. Touré is unquestionably a brilliant organizer, a spellbinding orator and a hardworking administrator. He has a buoyant faith in himself and a mystical sense of his and Africa's destiny which brooks no opposition and is not above brutality. He is going to be around a long time and we are going to have to learn to work with him or face the consequences of seeing 200 million black Africans lose their Western orientation.

The important thing is to convince Touré that the West wants and is capable of giving him the friendship and assistance he needs. If we cannot do that, the extremists in his party will force him further down the path to Communism. No diplomatic task is more challenging; in none are the stakes higher.

Chapter 13

*

WOMB OF EMPIRES

'The people of this region,' wrote Leo Africanus concerning the inhabitants of Mali, 'excel all other negroes in wit, civility, and industry.'

Leo, known to the folks around Granada (where he was born) and Fez (where he grew up) as el-Hassan ibn Wezaz, was no mean judge of African character. When Christian corsairs captured the young Arab on the Mediterranean, he had travelled extensively in that wide belt of scrub savannah between the Sahara and the rain-forest, which is known as the Sudan.

Although only in his early twenties, Leo at the time of his capture was looking for a publisher: he had with him a rough draft in Arabic of his monumental *History and Description of Africa*. The Christians who fettered Leo were probably illiterate and certainly impressed because they carried the young scribe to Rome and presented him to Pope Leo X, rather than peddling him in one of the great slave markets of Pisa or Genoa. Leo X was a Medici—the son of Lorenzo the Magnificent—and he had a lot of time for artists and intellectuals. He freed the young Moor, put him on the papal payroll, saw to it that he became a Christian and gave him his own name of Giovanni Leone, although history was to know this great traveller only as Leo Africanus.

Leo's book, published in Italian in 1526, was to remain almost the sole source of European knowledge of central Africa for two centuries.

The great kingdom of Mali (the name is a variant of the word 'Mandingo'), which Leo saw tumble before the resurgent might of Songhai, stretched at its apogee from the Atlantic to the middle Niger, from the sands of the Sahara to the forests of the Ivory Coast, a vast military empire of more than half a million square miles, bigger than Texas, California and Colorado combined.

Mali was the successor to the earlier empire of Ghana, the remnants of which it absorbed in the thirteenth century and which had extended over roughly the same area. The Arab historians tell us that Ghana, which had no connection with the present state of the same name,

312

waxed great from its trade in gold and slaves at the time that Norman William was preparing to invade England. The king of Ghana, draped in jewels and wearing a golden head-dress, held court at Kumbi, now nothing but a ruined hamlet. Behind his throne stood ten pages bearing shields and gold-hilted swords. Ten horses in golden trappings stood beside the pavilion where the king sat and his personal charger was tethered to a gold nugget which one historian tells us weighed thirty pounds.

The sons of vassal princes, with ornaments plaited into their hair, stood at the right hand of the pagan Negro ruler. His Muslim viziers squatted before him and dogs wearing collars of silver and gold snapped and growled at the king's feet. His subjects knelt before the monarch and poured dust over their heads while Muslim visitors clapped their hands softly as a demonstration of respect.

The Arab historian, el-Bekri, who saw all this, said that the king of Ghana could field an army of 200,000 men and that Kumbi was the largest market in the Sudan. This was the kingdom which the mystic-warrior Abu Bakr and his fanatical Almoravid Muslims (the same crowd who conquered Spain), overthrew and converted to Islam in 1076.

The personality of Abu Bakr was the driving force behind the Almoravid conquest and when he was killed eleven years later his warriors lost part of his kingdom to the Fulani military confederacy of Sosso and some of the tribes of Ghana reasserted their independence only to be crushed by their former vassal, the relatively unimportant Mandingo kingdom of Mali.

Relations among the tribes of the region had always been strained and, as insurance against any Malian adventurism, Sosso warriors had murdered eleven sons of Mali's king. The twelfth, named Sundiata, a sickly child, was allowed to live on the presumption that he would not long survive his brothers.

Sundiata not only survived but lived to conquer Almoravid-racked Ghana in 1235, the year in which the Mongols were making things hot for Europe in Poland and Hungary. Sundiata's armies fanned out over the Sudan and by the time his grandson Mansa Musa came to the throne (1307), Mali's fame had spread to Europe and the Middle East.

Mansa Musa enhanced his prestige by a lavish pilgrimage to Mecca in 1324. He apparently did not subscribe to the American Express Company's theory that one should never carry more than $50 in cash: he was preceded by 500 slaves, each carrying a four-pound staff of solid gold, while behind him toiled 100 camels, each laden with

300 pounds of gold. An Arab who visited Cairo twelve years after Mansa Musa's sojourn reported that the gold market was still depressed as the result of the prodigal charity of the big-spender from the West.

While Mansa Musa was paying homage to Allah, his generals were busy with the work-a-day business of conquering the neighbouring kingdoms. When the Malian king returned, he found himself master of an empire which, superimposed upon a map of Europe, would stretch from Brest to Warsaw.

Mansa Musa died in 1332 and, a century after his death, the kingdom of Songhai, which had never been completely pacified although his generals had captured Gao, its capital, rose and broke the back of Mali. Songhai's turn came in 1593 when Ahmed el-Mansur, Shereef of Fez, greedy to seize the gold mines which he believed to lie in the area, sent an *élite* camelry force of *European* mercenaries and Christian captives in a dash across the desert. More than half the army died on the waterless way but its commander, a blue-eyed Spanish eunuch named Judar, routed the Songhai army and captured Gao. In crushing Songhai, el-Mansur had defeated his own purpose: the gold came not from Songhai but from the Negro states to the south and the trade could only prosper in times of a peace which the Moroccan army was too small to enforce.

This gold was obtained through a system of 'dumb barter'. Caravans of as many as 20,000 camels trudged to Timbuktu loaded with salt and trade goods from the Arab north. These were taken by the Sudanic tribes and dumped at the edge of the forest or on the banks of a stream, the gold-seekers then withdrawing some distance. The forest Negroes came out, inspected the salt and the trade goods, and left what they considered to be a fair amount of gold. They then hid themselves and the first group returned. If the traders were satisfied, they took the gold and left the salt and trinkets; if not, they went away a short distance and the process continued until agreement was reached. From time to time the northern peoples captured a forest Negro and attempted by bribery or torture to discover from whence the gold came. Invariably they were unsuccessful: so pressing was the Negroes' need for salt (men can live without gold, after all, but not without salt) that the hostages without exception refused to speak. The two commodities were frequently bartered on a weight-for-weight basis.

Judar, who had been kidnapped from his native Granada as a child by a Moorish raiding party, found his efforts to trace the gold to its source fruitless. His successors (and there were 128 *pashas* in one ninety-year period) had even less luck in maintaining order than he, the gold trade dried up, Morocco lost interest and the territory controlled by the white invaders (many of these Christian troops had been captured at the battle of El Ksar el Kebir, which we infidels call 'Alcazar') gradually shrank. They intermarried with the Songhai women, sired a mulatto military class known as the *arma* which exists to this day, and, within a few centuries the descendants of the white conquistadors were indistinguishable from the rest of the population.

Other kingdoms arose—Tekrur, Kaarta, Segu, Macina, Wagadugu, to name a few—but none were strong enough to recapture the glory or match the power of Ghana, Mali or Songhai.

When René Caillie, after suffering many privations, reached Timbuktu in 1828, he found it 'nothing but a mass of ill-looking houses, built of earth'. Caillie, who made the trip disguised as an Arab and was the first white man to reach the fabled city and return alive, added with disappointment that 'I found it neither so large nor so populous as I had expected; its commerce is not so considerable as fame has reported'.

So exhausted was the Sudan by centuries of warfare that it fell like an over-ripe peach to French soldiers and administrators who followed Caillie. Louis Leon Cesar Faidherbe, 'the Colonial Napoleon', jumping off from his St. Louis base at the mouth of the Senegal River, easily subjugated the Sudan and added 400,000 square miles to the French empire between 1854 and 1865. As we have seen, French West Africa was administered as a single unit from 1895 to 1957 when the *loi cadre* gave each territory a separate personality. Out of the confusion arose a new but short-lived Mali whose boundaries coincided to a remarkable degree with those of the old empire of Mansa Musa.

Thus modern Mali, which broke up last year, was but the sixth of a line of great empires which have ruled this dusty land between the desert and the forest, heir to the glories of Ghana (eighth to thirteenth century), Mali (thirteenth and fourteenth centuries), Songhai (fourteenth to sixteenth century), Moroccan Pashalik (sixteenth and seventeenth centuries) and the French (nineteenth and twentieth centuries). Truly this land is the womb of African empires.

THE NEW MALI: WHAT IT IS

Modern Mali, which took shape in 1959, consisted of the former territories of Senegal and Soudan. It achieved full independence on June 20, 1960. Both states retained their local legislatures and capitals but there was a federal assembly and executive while Dakar, which is the capital of Senegal, also served as the federal capital. Modibo Keita, who was premier of Soudan, was also prime minister of Mali.

Mali was shaped roughly like a grinning man lying on his belly with his head to the west: Senegal was the head (and this simile is apt in more ways than one) and the Soudan the body. The Senegal River, which forms the boundary between Senegal and the Islamic Republic of Mauritania (another member of the Community), was the top of the head. Dakar, which juts out into the Atlantic towards Brazil, was the nose. The British enclave of Gambia, which consists only of both banks of the river of the same name, was the mouth. Casamance, the area of Senegal south of Gambia and north of Portuguese Guinea, was the chin. After being compressed into a narrow neck at the juncture of Senegal and Soudan, Mali bulged into a chest which pressed down between Guinea and the Voltaic Republic to touch Ivory Coast. Then the country swung away in a great curve to the north. Thus Mali was bordered to the east by Niger and Algeria, to the north by the latter and Mauritania, to the west by the Atlantic and Gambia, and to the south by Portuguese Guinea, Guinea, Ivory Coast and Volta.

Mali measured 1,500 miles from east to west but was no more than 150 miles from north to south at one point and portions of the country were closer to Madrid than they are to Dakar. Six million people lived in Mali's 540,000 square miles ($2\frac{1}{2}$ times the size of France) and they are divided among at least thirty-four different tribes. The three principal tribes, each of which have about 900,000 members, are the Wollofs of Senegal, the Bambaras of Soudan and the Sereres, who are bisected by the Senegal–Soudan border.

Economically and socially there were vast disparities between the two states of Mali. Senegal, the earliest point of French penetration, is—for Africa—heavily industrialized; Soudan (now called Mali) has no industries. Senegal has not only the magnificent city of Dakar but three other towns with populations of more than 40,000; Bamako, the capital, is the only Soudanese town of comparable size. Senegal has vast phosphate deposits and considerable reserves of titanium; Soudan has no mineral wealth. Senegal has hundreds of miles of paved roads and railways; Soudan has few of either. Senegal has a small but influential Catholic population; Soudan is almost solidly Muslim. Senegal has 50,000 whites; Soudan has about 7,000. In common they shared only the groundnut, which is the basic cash crop of both states, and the desire to create a vast Franco-African federation, independent of and equal with France. And now let us take a closer look at the two territories which before the break-up of the federation last year constituted Mali.

SENEGAL

The French established their first West African post at the mouth of the Senegal in the 1630's and built their headquarters on the island of St. Louis, in the river's mouth, 301 years ago.

By 1800, a year in which Pittsburgh had a population of less than 500, St. Louis had more than 7,000 inhabitants and had enjoyed municipal status for twenty years. In 1833, a century before the first rumbles of African nationalism, all the inhabitants of St. Louis (and of the other three of the so-called *Quatre Communes*, Goree, Rufisque and Dakar) became French citizens entitled to elect representatives to sit in Paris.

Faidherbe became governor in 1854, laid out the city's symmetrical street plan, established Senegal's first schools and sired a flock of ginger-coloured piccaninnies, an example which was to be followed by many of his administrators and which was to make St. Louis—like Bathurst, Freetown, Monrovia and Libreville—a mulatto Athens peopled by a coloured *élite* intellectually tied to Europe.

St. Louis reached the height of its glory in 1878 when it became federal capital of French West Africa. Five years later the federal government moved to Dakar, which is more centrally located and has a better harbour. But for seventy-five years St. Louis was to have the unique status of capital of two territories, since the Senegalese government remained there and Mauritania was too poor and barren to afford one of its own.

Despite this distinction, St. Louis slowly withered and died in the desert heat as its brighter young men moved to Dakar where opportunities were greater. As the tradition-steeped cultural centre of Senegal, it was thought in the 1940's that St. Louis might be selected as the site for West Africa's new university but even this went to parvenu Dakar. The final blow came in 1958 when the governments of both Senegal and Mauritania moved out.

St. Louis—one of whose governors used to keep a half-tame lion on his roof—has no industries, few modern buildings, an excellent I.F.A.N. museum, a top-flight (and expensive) hotel and that sense of quiet, timeless decay which is at once serene and melancholy. It lives by the fish which its people pull from the sea and stack like cordwood into waiting trucks which deliver this much-desired protein in a slightly 'high' form to towns hundreds of miles in the interior. There is far more activity, in fact, on the beach than there is in the decaying business district. If most of its glories are past, St. Louis still has the Lycée Faidherbe, Gallic Africa's first school. The bridge which connects the island to the south bank of the river is also named after the redoubtable soldier-administrator.

The island-town of Gorée, which blocks the entrance to the harbour of Dakar, is even older than St. Louis, although its association with France is a little shorter. The island was discovered by the Portuguese explorer Dinis Diaz in 1444 and was held by Portugal for 150 years. The Dutch ousted the Portuguese in 1597 and were routed in turn eighty years later by the French. The island changed hands a number of times (as did St. Louis and all the other West African settlements) as France and Britain battled for supremacy in a series of world wars in which the American Revolution was no more than a minor skirmish. Finally, in 1817, France got Gorée, a tradition-steeped little dot visited by such globe-trotters as Bartholomew Diaz, Vasco da Gama and Christopher Columbus (St. Francis Xavier also Slept Here), for good.

Once France was firmly established on the mainland, Gorée's importance quickly declined. Dakar became the gateway to the interior and Gorée was relegated to the role of a suburb of the city. This town of fading pastel colours peeling in the sleepy sun, a well-mellowed ghostly place of hot sand streets lit by wrought-iron lamps, comes to life only on weekends when Dakar beauties with metallic red hair make the twenty-minute ferry trip to sport on the sheltered little beach and eat cold lobster at the rose-coloured Hostellerie du Chevalier de Boufflers. A few poor Negroes live in crumbling once-elegant homes and make a living fishing among rusting cannons (vintage 1859) spiked with concrete which litter the off-shore, a reminder of some forgotten raid.

Dakar is as burgeoning and buoyant as St. Louis and Gorée are decaying and sleepy. This ardently vertical city of 300,000 people, crammed on to the narrow Cap Vert peninsula, is brash, bright and bustling. It has 30,000 whites, skyscrapers and a cost-of-living index to match. Dakar in many ways is symbolic of the new Gallic Africa: it is Frenchy but not really French. The buildings are starkly modern yet the streets are littered with trash; there seem to be as many blind people groping their way across the traffic-happy Place Protet as there are bikini-clad French girls water-skiing in the harbour. The residential and administration suburb known as the Plateau is filled with canti-levered office buildings and luxurious homes, but the teeming squalor of the native quarter, the Medina, is not a quarter of a mile away. It is in a sense ironic that this most Europeanized city between Casablanca and Leopoldville is a centre of resurgent African nationalism.

The Genoese admiral Noli discovered the lava peninsula upon which the city sits and named it Cap Vert but it was the Wollofs who christened the settlement N'Dakarou, meaning 'the land of the Saviour'.

Dakar is one of the great air and sea relay stations of Africa, served by fourteen international airlines and hundreds of ships. In 1957, 13,900 planes landed at Yoff field which handled 287,984 passengers, 7,000 tons of freight and six tons of mail. In the same year, the busy port handled 4,936 ships totalling 15·2 million tons, figures which have fallen a bit because of the increasing uncertainty of the African political picture. Strategically, Dakar is vital to the West because it dominates the channel between the North and South Atlantics and is the nearest Eurafrican point to the New World. Dakar's fine natural harbour is a fortuitous exception to the rule in West Africa, a phenomenon caused by the existence of a chain of volcanic islands connected to the mainland by a sandy isthmus.

Parts of Dakar look like a French Miami. The city has a suburb named Hann and one called Fann, an Avenue Pasteur and a Boulevard de la République, an Etoile and a Rue Jules Ferry. Tall Mossi soldiers wearing red felt shakos, baggy trousers, boots and spurs, stand guard with drawn four-foot cavalry sabres outside the residence of the French High Commissioner, which faces the eleven-storey concrete-and-glass slab of the former Grand Council building, now used by the Senegalese government. Of equally stark modernity are the Assembly building, with its indirect lighting and delegates' desk of coral pink, and the Palace of Justice, with its rose-coloured marble pillars and doors padded with red leather. To the north of the city, past the military base of Ouakam and opposite the craggy Isle of Serpents, are flower-draped villas whose picture-windows look out upon the sea of Mediterranean blue.

Dakar seethes with life: extravagantly gowned Wollof women curse in strident tones as heavily-laden trucks force them against the walls of houses; men in flapping robes of every colour—blue-black, royal purple, coral, burnt-orange and just plain white—hawk kola nuts, mass-produced 'native' carvings and bundles of six safety matches tied neatly with a thread; African sailors, wearing tight, brief shorts, matching white knee-socks and sneakers, off some Portuguese corvette bound from Lisbon for Bissau, jostle hard-eyed Moors who appraise them like livestock with the inveterate slaver's eye. Colours and sounds are harsh and bright, smells are pungent and emetic. All is motion and light and clamour.

This capital of Senegal (and former capital of Mali) has 4,000 active tuberculosis cases (and 100 T.B. beds in its hospital), twin hills which the French can and do call nothing but *Les Mamelles*, a luxurious cinema dramatically dubbed *Marche Indigène*, two out of every five private cars and a third of the commercial vehicles registered in Gallic Africa, a groundnut industry which provides its own power by powdering the shells of the nuts and forcing this substance through jets into a furnace, and swimming clubs where you pay 75 African francs (2s. 4d.) to enjoy a dip in water as cold as a Maine lake, a painful sunburn and a closer look at the bikinis. At the multi-storeyed N'Gor hotel twelve miles from town, Dakarois swill Algerian wine from ice-filled tumblers or sip *tomate*, a mixture of grenadine and pernod, mutter about rising prices (a small apartment costs as much as £180 a month but wages are high and most *colons* manage, as only a Frenchman could, to save money). Sloops, Stars and Cat-boats with checked and striped sails chase an off-shore wind while native fishermen in canoes with fibre sails beach a catch of jade and indigo-coloured fish, some of which have beaks like parrots.

From November to April it is pullover weather, a time of brilliantly blue and cloudless skies. From July to October the city bakes in a dancing heat, the rich whites go home, the poor ones go mad, and the Africans consent to remove their balaclavas and overcoats. There are Indo-Chinese restaurants where you can guzzle birds'-nest soup and consume piquant portions of chicken and almonds basted in butter, chrome-and-glass eateries where you can get a hamburger and a reasonable imitation of a milk shake.

The government has made herculean efforts to clean up the Medina by bulldozing acres of shacks made from tin cans, grass, bits of wire and pieces of wood but, like the desert, the slums return to an area a week after it has been cleared and decent housing erected. But Africa would not be Africa without its Medinas for here you can buy a charm to kill your enemy, tantalize your lover or keep the smallpox away, purchase a baseball cap or a goat's horn from a cunning trader wearing the currently popular enormous (there seem to be no sizes smaller than 12) yellow leather slippers with the heels bent in which cost £2 a pair and come all the way from Morocco.

As it is the centre of Gallic African political, commercial and social activity so too is Dakar the intellectual centre and it boasts eight of the eleven republics' fourteen newspapers. These range politically from the P.F.A.'s *Condition Humaine*, which is Senghor's mouthpiece, to an American-baiting sheet which comes out with headlines not calculated to promote inter-racial understanding ('Africans! The Lebanese are your enemies!'), gives full coverage to Little Rocks and lynchings, and is much appreciated by the not inconsiderable extremist white element.

As a city Dakar has no rival anywhere in French Africa but there are other Senegalese cities such as flamboyant-edged Kaolack, the dusty groundnut port which sits on a shallow finger of water eighty miles from the coast; Thies, a regional farm centre on a fertile volcanic plain from which sprout trees with lemon-yellow whorls which give the town from a distance the appearance of being embedded in a bank of golden snow; and Ziguinchor, the groundnut centre of Casamance, known as 'the town of tears' because its entire population was once wiped out by a yellow fever epidemic.

GUÉYE VS. SENGHOR

Although the Four Communes had been represented in the French Assembly since 1848, it was not until 1914 that Senegal produced its first important black politician. This was Blaise Diagne, who espoused the cause of Dakar's *Lebous*, the expropriated landowners of Cap Vert. Diagne, who represented Senegal almost continuously until his death in 1934, won confirmation of the political rights of the Four Communes in exchange for his support in the recruitment of 181,000 Africans to fight for France on the Western Front during World War I.

Because Diagne seemed more interested in the rights of Gorée, Dakar, Rufisque and St. Louis than in political development of Senegal as a whole, his mulatto successor, Galandou Diouf, was given a mandate to work for the extension of political rights. Diouf died in 1945 and the Senegalese political story from that date until 1958, when they buried the hatchet, has been a tale of struggle between two great black politicians, Lamine Guéye and Leopold Sedar Senghor.

Tall, white-haired Lamine Guéye, now sixty-nine, got off to a fast start after the war by organizing the urban proletariat and using it as a springboard to the Senegalese and French assemblies, the Senate of the French Union (and now of the Community), the Grand Council of West Africa and the Dakar mayor's office, the most vital post in

Gallic Africa. Guéye, who is a Muslim lawyer, affiliated himself closely with the French Socialist Party, perhaps too closely to suit the conservative chiefs of Senegal, and this gave Senghor the chance in 1951 to build his own political machine.

This squat fifty-four-year-old Catholic, the son of wealthy Wollofs, was the first African to become a full professor at a French university, fought as an infantryman for France in World War II, and spent four years as a prisoner in Occupied France. Senghor, whose second wife is French (his first was a daughter of F.E.A.'s late, great Felix Eboué), is one of the most Gallicized of all Africans and his lyric poetry (*Hosties Noires*, *Chants d'Ombres*) has earned him a place among the intellectuals of the world.

Senghor—who has a mystic sense of Africa's destiny—felt that Guéye was moving too fast at the expense of much that was good in Africa's heritage. He countered the Dakar mayor's strength in urban areas by building up a political organization tied to Senegalese tribal and religious traditions. Senghor, who like Houphouet and Lisette has represented *France* at the United Nations, based his electoral programme on the elimination of economic and political inequalities while emphasizing the unity of France and Africa. So successful was this platform that, although Guéye's personal political stock remained high, Senghor's Democratic Senegalese Bloc (B.D.S.), an independent party, by 1957 controlled forty-seven of the sixty seats in the Senegalese Assembly. In the process, the little bespectacled professor became a French Secretary of State, four-term member of the National Assembly, mayor of Thies and, of course, the political leader of the majority Senegalese party.

The second rise to power of Houphouet's R.D.A. in 1956 set the stage for a rapprochement between Senghor and Guéye. Although he had firm control of Senegal, Senghor saw that he lacked the interterritorial organization necessary to combat the R.D.A., which was already beginning to organize in his own backyard. In addition, Senghor—who had originally been far more conservative than Houphouet—became convinced that the latter's policies would abort the flowering of the African unity which he felt to be so necessary. He resented, too, Houphouet's prestige in France (the Ivory Coast leader was largely responsible for the drafting of the *loi cadre*) and was determined to reassert his own right to speak for French Africa.

For his part, Guéye found himself in the twilight of his political career as only a minority leader in Senegal while his Socialist Party (M.S.A.)

was losing ground in the other African territories to the resurgent R.D.A. Guéye and Senghor merged their parties in 1958 to form the African Regroupment Party (P.R.A.), which the R.D.A. declined to join. This gave them solid control in Senegal, provided Senghor with the organization of the defunct Socialists to spread his political theories and brought Guéye back into the limelight.

Senghor was able to use Guéye's branches to detach Modibo Keita and the entire Soudan R.D.A. organization from Houphouet's camp and to come within an ace of bringing Volta and Dahomey into his then pet scheme, the Mali Federation. To push his federal thesis, Senghor dissolved the P.R.A., Keita dissolved the Soudan R.D.A. and the two merged in March 1959 to form the African Federalist Party (P.F.A.), which controlled Senegal and Soudan and had branches in Niger, Dahomey and Volta. When Senghor became president of the P.F.A. in 1959, it was the fourth political party he had headed within a decade, an example of the staying power of individuals and the ephemeral quality of political labels in Gallic Africa.

Many French Africans have been jealous and fearful of the political supremacy of the Senegalese and, to avoid this, Senghor stepped down (or rather sideways) into the role of political theorist and titular leader of Mali, pushed Guéye aside and handed the two vital roles of Mali premier and secretary-general (operational leader) of the P.F.A. to Soudan's able young premier, Modibo Keita. Guéye—who is married to a West Indian—received the mainly honorific job of president of the Senegalese assembly. The key post of premier of Senegal and vice-premier of Mali went to Mamadou Dia, a forty-nine-year-old school-teacher, mayor of Diurbel, member of the French and Senegalese assemblies, former senator.

Senghor and the other Senegalese leaders fought off a bid on the part of the Soudanese during independence negotiations to make Mali a unitary state with a strong, American-style presidency. Last year, however, the fundamental nature of the break was repeated when Senghor and Dia arrested Keita, announced that he and the Soudanese were planning a coup, deported the Soudanese officials and declared the federation to be at an end. Keita for his part declared an economic war on Senegal, renamed Soudan, Mali, and swore to oust Senghor and his confederates. So ended the federation of Mali, as far as Senghor is concerned; Senghor became president, Dia remained as Prime Minister, and Guéye became president of the Senegalese Assembly.

Although Lamine Guéye has slipped a lot in the last ten years, this grand old man of African politics is still the indispensable ward-boss. 'The Master', as the Senegalese call him, knows everyone, is familiar with every political trick in the book. Guéye's handshake has the duration of the veteran politician's, his smile is open, he guides you gently by an elbow into his plush office, punctuates his talk with jokes which he obviously enjoys, and touches you conspiratorially on the knee when making a point. Guéye, who may well be approaching his last hurrah, has mellowed with the years from the ardent radical he once was.

'Everything that has been done here,' he said, 'has been accomplished by France. In the end, it will be the language and the culture of France that will create a new and united Africa.'

Dia is a self-effacing man who, on slight acquaintance, appears to lack the charm of Guéye, the driving force of Keita or the mystical intellectualism of Senghor. Dia is basically an economist (publications: *New Studies and Problems of the African Economy*, *Reflections on the Economy of Black Africa*, *The Co-operative Movement in Black Africa*). He likes to wear flannel trousers and sports jacket to the office, is an enthusiastic taker of correspondence courses, lives unostentatiously in the Medina, has a reputation for being a good administrator. But some who know him well maintain that the Senegalese premier is easily influenced by those around him, a reflector of forces rather than a creator of them, a man who may ride history but will not make it.

Potentially more important that either Guéye or Dia are two more radical politicians now in secondary roles. These are Gabriel d'Arboussier and Valdiodio N'Diaye.

D'Arboussier we have met before: this pudgy fifty-two-year-old attorney is one of the ablest and most volatile (as Houphouet has discovered twice to his discomfiture) of Gallic Africa's politicians, an ebullient, balding will-o'-the-wisp who has been up and down the ladder of political fortune more frequently than a house painter.

D'Arboussier was educated in France and, at the age of twenty-two, joined the French colonial service. He later studied law and was posted to Ivory Coast in 1943. There he met Houphouet and the two planned the formation of the R.D.A. D'Arboussier left the colonial service in 1947 and was elected in the same year to represent Ivory Coast in the assembly of the French Union (although he has also held elective office in Niger and Mali, d'Arboussier has never represented his native Soudan).

As secretary-general of the R.D.A., d'Arboussier gave the party such a communistic tinge that he nearly deprived that organization of mass African support. After Houphouet, who viewed him as an opportunist devoured by personal ambition, gave the Soudanese attorney the boot, d'Arboussier regained the Ivory Coast leader's confidence, was readmitted to the R.D.A. and became premier of Niger and president of the Grand Council of French West Africa.

D'Arboussier relinquished his post in Niger to the young and able fellow-traveller, Djibo Bakary, and, as he spent more time in Dakar, drew away from Houphouet and towards Senghor. Although he went along with Houphouet on the matter of remaining within the Community, d'Arboussier broke with him for the second time over the issue of federalism, which he now favours in opposition to Ivory Coast's premier. Banned from Niger by the conservative régime of Hamani Diori, d'Arboussier is now small potatoes indeed for a man of his experience and energies.

An African home, like the man who owns it, is often not quite what it seems: I found d'Arboussier's home up a filthy alley, mounted a flight of stairs from the walls of which the paint was peeling, then entered an apartment furnished in the most modern and impeccable taste. D'Arboussier asked me to wait for a moment while he finished with a brace of darkly conspiratorial-looking characters, reappeared shortly thereafter accompanied by a wide grin and two highballs.

Unlike most French Africans, d'Arboussier speaks excellent English, and I asked him how he'd acquired it. 'My grandfather,' he said, 'was an Irishman.' Which may account to some extent for his political exuberance, although others lay it to the fact that d'Arboussier, whose father was a French administrator, is hypersensitive about his mulatto origin, jealous of the cultural and intellectual attainments of Houphouet, Senghor and Guéye.

It can be said in all fairness that if d'Arboussier was not an active Communist as late as 1955, he certainly talked like one. Yet so agile is this political chameleon that he recently was called upon to address a travelling party of the U.S. National War College, a feat which he performed with notable moderation and success. D'Arboussier was once ardently anti-American but a visit to the United States in 1959 has done much to dispel this and he now ranks as one of our best friends in Gallic Africa.

The second man, Valdiodio N'Diaye, is significant less for what he has accomplished than for what he is. N'Diaye, a thirty-six-year-old Wollof attorney, holds the vital portfolio of Senegalese Minister of the Interior and is responsible for the republic's public security. As such, he is the focal point for the left wing of the P.F.A., breathing hotly down the more mature and conservative necks of Senghor and Guéye.

We had a talk which got around, as such talks inevitably seem to do, to the subject of the United States. 'We admire the United States,' N'Diaye said, 'for your technological progress but, as a nation, you lack humanity. We feel roughly the same way about you as we do about the Russians.'

Opposed to the government is only a disorganized and improbable combination of extreme nationalists, Communists and reactionary religious fanatics now grouped under the R.D.A. label. The leader of these dissidents is Ibrahim Seydou N'Daw, a formidable man of sixty-nine, crippled eleven years ago in a motor-car accident. N'Daw led the attack against federalism from his wheel-chair but neither his personal prestige (he is a former president of the Senegalese assembly) nor the energies of his young and radical St. Louisian aide, Abdoulaye Ly, a neo-Communist who receives direct support from Guinea's Sekou Touré through the latter's UGTAN network, could offset the fact that the opposition party lacked both a popular programme and an effective organization. Although several influential *marabouts* (Muslim religious leaders) supported this patchwork crowd and managed to generate enough enthusiasm to result in one killed and more than a score wounded in fighting during the 1959 election (in which there were half a million abstentions), the R.D.A. affiliate polled only 16 per cent of the 700,000 votes cast (the remainder going to the P.F.A.), won not a single seat in the eighty-member Senegal assembly.

The country, despite the glamour of Dakar, is not wealthy. Senegal is twice the size of Bulgaria and has as many people (2·2 million) as Philadelphia. It lives almost exclusively from the sale of groundnuts (about 600,000 tons worth about £32·4 million), its only cash crop, and from revenue from its role as the third largest seaport in the French Community (after Marseille and Le Havre). There is a substantial trade deficit and Senegal's annual budget is about £17 million.

THE RICHARD-TOLL SCHEME

But groundnuts, a native-grown crop introduced to Senegal from Central America in 1820 and strongly promoted as a cash crop by Faidherbe, are viciously hard on the soil, which is rapidly becoming exhausted. The 1958 crop amounted to a record 808,000 tons and it is improbable that France, which guarantees import quotas and supports groundnuts sold in the Metropole at prices as much as 33 per cent above the world level, can absorb much greater amounts.

Despite these ill omens, more and more land has been put under groundnuts as the centre of gravity for production shifts from northern Senegal to Casamance.

As a result, Senegal every year finds itself in the position of having to import increasing quantities of food. To give Senegal an alternative cash crop, the French early hit on the scheme of developing a huge cotton-growing scheme in the Senegal valley, once a populous farming area now alternately devastated by floods or parched by drought.

As food imports mounted to 100,000 tons a year, it soon became obvious that Senegal needed rice rather than cotton and emphasis was shifted to this crop. In 1945, a government body called *La Mission pour l'Aménagement du Sénégal* (M.A.S.) began work on a large-scale, heavily mechanized rice-growing programme at Richard-Toll. In 1948 M.A.S. turned the management of Richard-Toll over to a private company and devoted itself to the larger problem of the over-all development of the Senegal. Technically, Richard-Toll has been a success: good rice yields have been obtained from land which was virtually useless. Financially, it has been a resounding flop: it has cost the French and Senegalese governments £5·7 million to build a small dam and put 15,000 acres into production. Like most projects in Africa engineered by enthusiasts from the far-away hills, Richard-Toll's planning was not all that it might have been although not even a soothsayer could have known, for instance, that millions of *queleas* birds would eat half of the 1952 crop.

And if the scheme has not been a roaring success, it must still be pursued: the Senegal River, if subjected to an intelligent and realistic plan, could become the rice bowl of West Africa. What M.A.S. would like to do is to build a dam on the Senegal at Gouina which would create a reservoir containing enough water to irrigate the middle valley for two consecutive waterless seasons and generate two billion kilowatt hours per year, enough to light half of Senegal, power a fertilizer industry to utilize the local phosphates and electrify the Dakar-Bamako railway. Progressive control of the Senegal would make available enormous quantities of hydro-electric power, facilitate river navigation and trade, and bring hundreds of thousands of acres now useless under the plough. Lacking is the money and experts say that it would take five years and at least £116 million merely to take the initial step of building the Gouina dam.

There are those who say that Senegal cannot afford such large-scale expenditures. But African nationalists maintain that the money is in the country but is being siphoned out by the three so-called *Grands Comptoirs*, the French trading companies which dominate the economies of Senegal and of all Gallic Africa. The senior member of this trio is the *Compagnie Française de l'Afrique Occidentale* (C.F.A.O.), a Marseille firm founded in 1887. C.F.A.O. exports Gallic Africa's produce, imports manufactured goods through its 154 outlets and, in a year termed 'difficult' in its annual report, managed to pay a 30 per cent dividend. The other giants are the *Société Commerciale de l'Ouest Africain* (S.C.O.A.) and the United Africa Company (a Unilever affiliate), which operates under a different name in each republic. The small retail trade is dominated by Syrians admitted when that state was a French colony (they are unpopular now with the French because of their country's politics and with the Africans because of their sharp trade practices) and by Mauritanians. The complaint about the *Grands Comptoirs* heard most frequently from the Africans is that the Big Three have encouraged Senegal's one-crop economy to facilitate their own operations, have tended to establish monopolies and fix prices, and have repatriated their profits and put nothing into the country. On the other hand, the *Grands Comptoirs* have encouraged hundreds of thousands of Africans to enter the cash economy, have paid generally fair prices, and have made sizable contributions to the state through taxes and voluntary contributions. It is difficult to see how Senegal could better her financial position by putting the bite on the trading companies.

What Senegal needs to finance schemes like M.A.S. and Richard-Toll is to find additional revenues without resorting to confiscatory taxation. Oil is one possibility and three firms are prospecting at the moment. Another source of revenue lies in the exploitation of Senegal's considerable deposits of phosphates and titanium. At the moment she produces about 150,000 tons of the former and 35,000 tons of the latter, and both figures are being increased considerably.

The political manœuvrings and the economic headaches, of course, are matters far removed from the lives of most Senegalese. For the women—or at least for those of the Wollof tribe—fashion is the only thing that counts. A Wollof woman sweeping into Dakar's teeming market-place resembles nothing so much as a gaily caparisoned ship in full sail. Part of her get-up—and she would not dream of leaving the house without it—is her wig. This is usually made of horsehair and plaited into a shape resembling a Dutch girl's cap or the horns of an ox. Since the women are almost invariably generously proportioned, the latter effect is most often achieved. For variety's sake, she may forswear the horns and instead weave threads of black silk into her hair and attach to these balls of dark velvet. To the front of her wig she attaches as many gold coins as possible, so that they hang down upon her brow. Gold amulets are then attached to the top of the wig, as many as a dozen gold ear-rings are inserted not only in the lobe but all along the outer edge of the ear. To this dazzling display are added finger and toe rings, bracelets and anklets.

Her dress is just as startling: the Wollof costume is based on the high-busted Empire line popular in France from 1795 to the end of the Napoleonic period. The style was introduced to St. Louis by an anonymous (and courageous) French lady, picked up by the mulatto St. Louisians, adopted and adapted by the Wollofs, who have made it their national dress and passed it on as far east as Nigeria.

Around her wig the Wollof woman ties a turban. But it is a turban unlike anything you have seen before. It is usually made of yards of muslin, light and stiff, which is wound, tied and counter-tied until a floppy creation which seems to defy all the laws of physics is realized. Turbans may be in vivid colours or in soft pastels, and the effect, when achieved by a talented courtesan, is equally striking.

The dress usually has a high waist-line but the neck has been dropped to reveal the magnificent breasts of which the Wollofs are justly proud. The sleeves are puffed and one of these has been allowed to fall over a shoulder. Over the entire ensemble, a cloak of stiff muslin, organdie or tulle, transparent and intricately designed, is thrown. This is usually allowed to trail in the lady's wake, despite the dust and the filth.

Having donned her wig, covered herself with gold, tied her turban, thrown on her dress and slipped into her cloak, her task is about half finished. She draws a thin blue line immediately under her eyelashes to make her eyes look larger, paints her lashes, the palms of her hands and bottoms of her feet black, puts on nail polish, inspects her gums to see that their blue tattoo is in good order, inserts a chewing stick of manioc root (the toothbrush of Africa) into her mouth and saunters out to face the evening.

The job of keeping these capricious ladies in the style to which they are or would like to become accustomed has blossomed into a multi-million dollar business and fashion's centre of gravity has slipped from St. Louis to Pierre Grosse's Dakar shop which is complete with mannequins, showrooms and style contests. The cost of acquiring and maintaining a Wollof woman (at least £140 per year) is way beyond what the average male can afford and the result is that Wollof men are increasingly seeking their wives from less fashion-conscious tribes. Fortunately the sexual proclivities of the African are such that the Wollof tribe is in no danger of ethnic suicide. A by-product of the situation is the increase in prostitution: if a Wollof woman cannot find a man to provide her with gold and clothes, she gets them as best she can and there are said to be more prostitutes in Dakar than there are in Paris. Although Dakar's cost of living is high, the competition mercifully keeps the price down and it is a buyer's market.

A group less spectacular than the Wollof women but equally interesting are the *griots*. This is not a tribe but a class of troubadours, minstrels, dancers, soothsayers, clowns, jesters and sages. The *griot* spins yarns, relates history, asks riddles and tells jokes of the most personal nature at your expense, to the amusement of everyone else. By the same token, this master teller of fairy tale, epic, satire, farce, fable and allegory will exalt your virtues to the heavens for a five-franc note. He neither reads nor recites but improvises and embroiders upon his story to suit his own whim and the nature of his audience. Almost every family has its *griot*, who sings its praises in return for his daily bread. Although a famous bard may be wealthy, the class is held in contempt and upon death the bodies of *griots* are stuffed into the hollow trunks of baobab trees.

MONOD THE "MAD"

The business of the baobabs was explained to us in Dakar by Theodore Monod, director of I.F.A.N., and one of the most remarkable of the white Africans. Monod came out to Africa twenty-seven years ago and literally immersed himself in the continent. Wandering across the Sahara regions of Mauritania, Algeria and Soudan, alone or accompanied only by a nomad family, he learned all that there is to know of every aspect of the life and history of this region. Many thought him mad and, in a sense, he is: his is the madness of René Caillie, of Mungo Park, of Savorgnan de Brazza, the madness which is total love of and preoccupation with Africa.

Monod has published more than 450 books and articles, is an acknowledged expert in the fields of geology, geography, archaeology, history, marine biology (he went down in the bathysphere with Piccard), ethnography, botany, zoology and languages. Coupled with this broad and intense mentality is a physical courage and indifference to suffering which has been characteristic of all the great whites in Africa's history. Had he lived 150 years ago, Theodore Monod would unquestionably have been one of the greatest of the continent's explorers.

As it is, this jockey-sized (he can't weigh more than nine stone) scientist with a face like a skull, who founded I.F.A.N. in 1938 and has directed it since then, has created in I.F.A.N.'s mosque-like Dakar building a fine library and collection of recorded African music, a good museum, and a research centre which has no equal on the continent.

The great hope of Monod and I.F.A.N. is not so much that European knowledge of Africa will be extended but that the Africans themselves may be encouraged to take a real and scientific interest in their own history and culture instead of aping, with frequently unfortunate results, the worst elements of Western culture. To date little success in this endeavour can be reported and few Africans have joined I.F.A.N.'s staff. It is a sad commentary on the African character that in explaining this situation Senghor has said that 'our students do not burn with the desire to devote themselves to so arid and unremunerative a career'. Until some Africans start burning along these lines, African culture will remain the sunglasses-and-suede-shoes affair it is today.

Monod finds himself increasingly tied to his desk but as recently as five years ago he found the time to wander 600 miles across a waterless waste never before seen by any white man. He did this at the age of fifty-two with four camels, two bedouins and his compelling curiosity for company. Their provisions for the forty-seven-day trek: a pint of water a day mixed with tea and sugar, one daily meal of rice.

'The bedouins are getting soft,' Monod told me. 'In the old days we took only water and dates. Now they will not stir without tea, sugar and rice.'

I.F.A.N. will soon be moving its headquarters to the campus of Dakar University where Monod's academic burden will be increased, despite the efforts of Raymond Mauny, his younger assistant and a man cut from the same cloth, to keep open the trail to the desert.

The university, which at the time of writing is the only institution of higher learning in all Gallic Africa, has had a checkered career. It grew out of the Dakar school for medical assistants, was broadened in 1948 by the addition of faculties of arts, science and law, and attained full university status in 1957.

It has only recently moved to its new campus where dormitory facilities are provided for 50 per cent of its 1,253 students, of whom nearly half are law students. The university has fine modernistic buildings and a library of 100,000 volumes. But it has had staffing problems in the past and, in addition, has too frequently received as students only the second-rate scholars. The reasons are obvious: although Dakar has glamour, no student will pass up a chance to study in France to attend the local university. The serious students want the opportunity to study under the really great French intellectuals, the smart boys with a penchant for the bright lights are unwilling to pass up the Folies Bergère.

Possession of the university has been one of the main bones of contention (the other being Radio Dakar) which has arisen out of the division of assets which became necessary after West Africa and the Mali federation broke up. Senegal had received almost 20 per cent (£50 million) of all the French funds invested in West Africa, mostly in projects such as the university, the radio station (range: 2,000 miles) and other public buildings designed to serve not just Senegal but all A.O.F.

When Guinea seceded from the Community, she expropriated all the federal property within her boundaries and relinquished all other claims. The pink marbled *Palais de Justice* in Dakar obviously could not be dismantled and the building stones distributed among the other seven former members of the federation. Many of the French maintained, with some logic, that Radio Inter (as the Dakar station is called), was Community property and should continue to be operated by the Community. Tempers became so heated that the Senegal government forced the station off the air for several weeks. In the end, it was agreed that each territory's past contribution to the federal budget would be weighed against the value of the federal property within its boundaries and that those with a positive balance would compensate those who had received least. The university, high schools and hospitals through French West Africa would remain open to all. In effect, this means that Senegal, which needs all the money it can get its hands on for economic and political purposes, will have to pay off the other seven territories. Ivory Coast's contribution to the federal budget was particularly heavy (almost 50 per cent of the total) and this means, ironically, that Senghor will have to make heavy payments to that republic which Houphouet can be expected to use to push a political programme diametrically opposed to that of the Senegalese leader.

During the same meeting at which these agreements were reached, the seven republics of French West Africa capitalized on the spirit of conciliation which prevailed to create a customs union providing uniform tariffs and internal free trade and to establish an inter-state health commission. It is probable that further protocols furthering common policies in the fields of justice, labour, public services and socio-economic planning will be reached. Both Houphouet and Keita favour such co-operation for opposed reasons: the former believes that successful common action at this level will demonstrate the super-fluity of political federation while the latter hopes that such action will inevitably lead to federation!

The intellectualism of Senghor, the bright lights of Dakar and the efficient planning of schemes like Richard-Toll sometimes obscure the fact that Senegal is still Africa, that underneath the skyscrapers and the production plans there is still something changeless and slow, difficult to define. Although Senegal has had the longest contact with France of any state of Gallic Africa and 77,000 students attend her 405 schools, resistance to Westernization is strong enough among the 75 per cent of the population which is Muslim to make it necessary for a Rufisque school not only to provide free room, board, uniforms and tuition for its girls but also to pay them to attend and dole out a bonus based on the number of years of attendance when the pupils leave!

Senegal—the name is from the Portuguese word for the mangrove swamps which block a portion of the coast—has 1,000 miles of paved roads and 465 miles of railway but in the Ferlo desert a few hours from Dakar, an immense tract of waterless waste, you can see ostriches standing under baobab trees that look like dropsical animals or gnarled hands clawing at the sky, and walk for days without meeting a human being. Most Senegalese are more interested in wrestling (each village champion decked out in amulets and charms designed to frustrate a half-nelson) than working, the youths of the Balante tribe must steal an ox to demonstrate their manhood, and the Floups of the Casamance still like to dine on their deceased kinsmen.

Senegal, for all its bustle and promise, like the rest of Africa is a study in contrasts, the old juxtaposed to the new in startling relief.

THE GALLIC GIANT

MALI

Mali (the former Soudan) is the largest of the French African states and, after Volta, the most populous. This vast, sun-baked plain, through which the Niger River cuts like a knife, is almost twice as large as Texas, has as many people as Chicago. In the entire country there is only one town, the capital city of Bamako, with a population of more than 40,000.

Mali has more than twice as many camels (40,000) as Christians (17,000) and only 7,000 of its 3·7 million people are whites. The French have only themselves to thank for the fact that 97 per cent of the republic's population is Muslim: although the Pax Gallica put an end to the forcible conversion of pagans to Allah, it facilitated the spread of Islam by improving communications, encouraging trade and giving preferential treatment to Muslim religious practices and tribal organization not extended to comparable pagan institutions. French anticlericalism at the same time discouraged the Christian missionary activity which might have acted as a counterbalance to the appeal of Islam.

Mali is sparsely inhabited by a conglomeration of diverse tribes remote from the sea and hindered by the paucity of the land's resources from adjusting to a money economy to the extent which has characterized the coastal tribes. The remembrance of the great Negro empires, the continued strong position of the chiefs and the conservative influence of Islam have combined with Mali's poverty (the annual budget is £8 million and French assistance since 1947 has amounted to £10 million) to prevent the state from becoming more than superficially Westernized.

This was strikingly revealed in 1946 when, with the abolition of forced labour, there was a wholesale exodus from the schools. Almost overnight, more than half of the student body simply melted away, leaving one with the impression that the Malian was overwhelmed not so much by a thirst for knowledge as by an ardent desire to escape the uplifting experience of wielding a shovel. Today some 45,000 children have been coaxed into the country's 267 schools.

This country twice the size of France has 200 miles of paved roads and it took twenty-four years to build the republic's single railway, a 320-mile line linking Bamako to Kayes and providing Mali with the means of exporting the 50,000 tons of groundnuts which are virtually its only cash crop. Although a third of the country is desert and most of the population is huddled on the life-giving banks of the Niger, Mali is Gallic Africa's biggest millet producer and proper control of the big river could turn the area into a major food exporter.

The entire countryside is a mass of red and browns and looks as if it came half-baked out of a potter's kiln. The Malians build millet grana- ries which resemble giant inverted egg-cups, drink a cranium-cracking beverage of fermented grain called *dolo*, and one tribe (the Songhai) makes exquisitely lovely 'jewellery' of tightly woven golden grass.

The republic contains Gao, Kumbi and Timbuktu, ancient capitals and famous market towns of the once-great Sudanese empires, the holy city of Djenne, and Mopti, an African Venice laced with canals on which Bambara tribesmen pole their 'gondolas' laden with freight and passengers.

Timbuktu, a city of flat-roofed, crumbling mud houses inhabited by 8,000 people, nomad tents surrounded by flocks of white camels hanging on its outskirts, is still difficult to reach by land. To the south and west of the city are the great Niger marshes, which extend for 300 miles and are as much as eighty miles wide. To the north is the ever-encroaching desert. Timbuktu is situated eight miles north of the Niger but was probably a river-port in the days when this part of Africa was wetter.

Most visitors will be as disappointed with the city as was René Caillie, for the only things of real interest are the ancient Sankore mosque built by Ibrahim el Saheli, the poet-architect who returned to the Sudan with Mansa Musa after the latter's fourteenth-century pilgrimage and introduced burnt-brick to the country, Caillie's house and that of Major Gordon Laing, the British explorer who reached Timbuktu before the Frenchman but was murdered before he could return.

Timbuktu's fate was sealed when the gold trade was disrupted by war and the mines were finally exhausted, when European intervention halted the slave trade, when imported salt became cheaper than salt from the pits of the Sahara. As trade patterns were reversed to funnel the area's exports and imports through the Atlantic ports rather than across the Sahara to North Africa, Timbuktu found herself in a position parallel to that of the proprietor who builds a plush restaurant only to find that the new super-highway constructed a mile behind him is diverting all the traffic and leaving him bankrupt. The city had no resources of its own and was wholly dependent upon its role as an entrepôt on the gold-salt-slave route. As the caravans slowed to a trickle, the oases dried up without the slaves to till their soil, the desert advanced and Timbuktu found itself at the end not only of a little-used road but of one no longer practicable.

Gao, which is 200 miles downstream from Timbuktu just below the point where the Niger bends to the south, was the capital city of the great Songhai empire and contains the tombs of its Askia princes. Songhai was founded by Sonni Ali, a cruel and vigorous soldier who made Gao one of the most important eleventh-century market towns of the Sudan. This small (7,500 inhabitants) mud town sits on the left bank of the Niger, its gum trees reflected in the river's placid waters. All that remains of its past glories are the marble and green schist pillars dating from the twelfth-century empire which have been set in the walls of the Dioula mosque. This, however, is more than Kumbi can boast, for the ancient capital of Ghana no longer exists as a town.

Caillie found Djenne to be more interesting than its more famous rivals and this remains true today. Djenne lies 200 miles to the south-west of Timbuktu and the Niger marshes form a shield which protected her from the thrusts of the desert raiders. The town was a commercial city famed as a centre of Koranic learning as early as the thirteenth century. Its location on an island enabled it to withstand ninety-nine sieges laid by the kings of Mali, although it finally fell to Sonni Ali's Songhai warriors in 1473.

Although Djenne is of little commercial importance today, this town of 7,000 people (mostly Songhai tribesmen whose ancestors stormed the city's walls) ranks with Nigeria's Sokoto as Islam's most holy West African city. The focal point of religious activity is Djenne's magnificent mosque, a Gothic hymn in the traditional Sudanic style designed, of all things, by an infidel *French* administrator, a man who must rank with Ibrahim el Saheli as premier architectural interpreter of the spirit of sub-Saharan Islam.

Near Djenne is the interesting Dogon village of Sangha. These pagan tribesmen live in two-storey mud huts shaped like quart milk containers on the tops of which perch—usually at rakish angles—grass roofs which look like nothing so much as straw boaters. Sangha is built at the foot of, in and at the top of a sheer cliff, a position which enabled its inhabitants to resist Islam until the advent of the Pax Gallica brought the inhabitants into the towns to work, where many of them succumbed to the call of the Prophet.

A more vibrant Soudanese town is Mopti (it is twice the size of

Timbuktu, Gao or Djenne), a hustling, bustling centre fifty miles north of Djenne which thrives on its dried-fish industry and boasts a marvellous mosque which glows in the African sun like a coin of burnished gold. Mopti's situation on three islands bursting with hibiscus, bougainvillaea and flamboyants makes it one of the more attractive towns of West Africa. The Moorish influence still discernible in the pottery, dress and diet of the people on the north bank of the Niger is more diluted for Judar's battalions held slight sway here.

Bamako, like the smaller town of Kayes, is a French creation, a city of dusty, winding streets with a new mosque and Soudanese assembly building constructed in the Islamic style which adapts so well to modern architectural techniques. Bamako, which has 2,000 whites, is the centre of medical research aimed at wiping out leprosy and trachoma, two of the great scourges of West Africa. Yet within sight of this generously air-conditioned city, on the slopes of Mount Koulouba, lie villages which live in a fashion unchanged since the days before the French came.

Although we have encountered them before, we cannot go on without saying something about the 176,000 Tuareg tribesmen who inhabit the north-eastern section of Soudan. The Tuareg (Tuareg is the plural form of Targui) are tall, slender, fair-skinned people with long faces and their children often have blond hair which. later turns dark. Their history is obscure and titillating and the Arabs call them *Muleththemin*, meaning 'the people of the veil', and sometimes refer to them as the Christians of the desert.

The Tuareg men are believed to have adopted the veil some time during the first millennium after Christ and there are those who say that this practice is a vestige of Mithras worship. More tantalizing is the question of why the Arabs call them the Christians of the desert, although they are followers of Mohammed. Were they once followers of Christ? Unlike other Muslims, the Tuareg are monogamous, you find names among them which Arabs seldom use such as Samuel, David and Saul, and the cross plays a prominent part in their heraldry. Their word for God is *mesi* (Messiah?), *andjelous* means angel. We know that Paul, Peter and Mark spread the Gospel into Asia Minor, Greece and Italy. What happened to the rest of the Apostles? Would it not have been logical for one or a group of them to have pushe¦ west along the fertile North African coast and thence south across the desert with one of the great salt caravans to Soudan? This parched old country holds more mysteries in its black bosom than there are faults in a

£5 suit, and the origin and religious history of the proud Tuareg is not the least of these.

THE POLITICAL STORY

Politics in the Soudan spells one name: Modibo Keita. But this was not always the case and the dynamic young leader is, in fact, a late-comer to the African limelight. The land-locked territory's first political party was formed after the war by Fily Dabo Sissoko, a canton chief and former teacher. It was basically a conservative grouping (Sissoko joined but almost immediately resigned from the R.D.A.) and the revolutionary, detribalized element soon found a spokesman in another ex-teacher, Mamadou Konate, who founded the local branch of the R.D.A.

For a decade Konate, representing the urbanized element, and Sissoko, who had the backing of the rural areas and tradition-bound classes of the city, fought inconclusively for political supremacy. Like the rest of the R.D.A. leaders, Konate slowly swung to the Right, making himself more acceptable to conservative Muslims.

At the same time, a new element was introduced into the picture by the rise of the brilliant young Socialist, Hamadoun Dicko, who quarrelled with Sissoko, his boss, over the question of the leadership of the party. At the crucial time in the political history of Gallic Africa (1956) when the Socialists were torn by internal struggle and the R.D.A. was gaining strength, Konate died and was succeeded by his young and more radical deputy, Modibo Keita.

In the *loi cadre* elections of 1957, the first in which he directed the R.D.A.'s fortunes, Keita's party swept to power by winning sixty of the seventy assembly seats (later increased to sixty-four by Socialist defections) and both Sissoko and Dicko lost their seats. Thus within a matter of six months, Keita, who had been nothing more than a second-stringer, became one of the most important West African political leaders.

Keita, who is forty-five but could pass for thirty-five, was born at Bamako and is a devout Muslim. The tall, powerfully-built Bambara did well in primary school, won a scholarship to William Ponty High School and, in 1936, became a secondary school principal. Keita and Konate played leading roles at the Bamako Conference of 1946 and the young teacher became a close friend of Houphouet. The French paid a high compliment to his abilities by jailing him immediately after the congress. Upon his release, he was elected to the Soudan's first territorial assembly but two years later the administration accused him of being 'an unrepentant Communist' (this was at the height of the R.D.A.'s collaboration with the French Communist Party and just before its break with that group) and short-circuited his political activities by posting him to a one-room school in the most desolate Saharan region of the Soudan. In 1952, a year in which the R.D.A. was in better grace with the authorities, Keita was allowed to return to Bamako to become vice-president of the assembly and a year later he was elected to the assembly of the French Union.

In 1953, Keita consolidated his domestic political position by being elected mayor of Bamako, three years later was sent to the French Assembly to replace Konate, his dead leader, as the representative of the Soudan. The next two years he was to spend mostly in Paris working with Houphouet on the drafting of the *loi cadre*. In the meantime, he became the first African deputy speaker of the *French* Assembly and did a tour as a French secretary of state. He also had time to visit Accra twice, there to make Dr. Nkrumah's acquaintance. As befits a man with federalist ambitions, Keita was the last president of the Grand Council of French West Africa, which was dissolved when the Fifth Republic came into existence.

A year in prison and two years in semi-exile helped to sour Keita's regard of the French just enough to bring about the break with Houphouet in 1959. Keita was willing to string along with the inscrutable little Baoule chief on the advisability of remaining within the Community (327,421 Soudanese said *oui* and 8,267 cast negative ballots) for the time being but he could not agree that the Community was an end in itself. Those who know the Ivory Coast leader best maintain that no defection hurt him more personally than that of Keita, who had been one of his fair-haired boys.

Keita joined forces with Senghor, Guéye and Dia, and threw himself energetically into the task of creating Mali. He directed the Bamako and Dakar federalist conferences and rammed a federalist constitution through in Soudan.

In the general election held in Soudan on March 6, 1959, to confirm Keita's leadership, his federalist party won 534,946 of the 703,032 votes cast (76 per cent) and secured all eighty seats in the assembly. The high abstention rate—there are 2·2 million registered voters in the Soudan—can be of little consolation to opposition leader Hamadoun Dicko who failed to receive a majority of the votes cast in his own county, district or home town. Impressed by the glitter of the young Soudanese premier's rising star, Senghor stepped aside and gave him the post of Mali's premier.

Keita, who some claim is a descendant of the kings who ruled ancient Mali (Africa has not yet reached the stage where it is politically profitable to have the equivalent of a log-cabin background), maintained as we talked in his plush Dakar office that the Community is 'not an end but a beginning: France and the African states must become a confederacy, along the lines of the British Commonwealth'.

This fundamental constitutional readjustment was made last summer when the sixth session of the Executive Council of the French Community met in St. Louis. At the inaugural congress of Keita's P.F.A., held the previous July in Dakar, a motion had been passed unanimously calling for Mali's independence, extension of the federation and transformation of the Community into a multi-national confederation. This, of course, was all diametrically opposed to the idea of the Community held by de Gaulle and Houphouet. But much had happened in the sixteen months of the Community's life and de Gaulle quickly conceded Mali's right not only to independence but, more important, to continued membership as an independent nation within the Community. De Gaulle, addressing the delegates, said France's new idea was that the Community should consist of 'organized friendship' and added that to make the new arrangement constitutional, the Community's 'institutions may, if necessary, be adapted'. On a poignant note, he concluded with a quotation from St. Luke: 'Abide with us, for it is towards evening, and the day is far spent.' Keita hailed de Gaulle as 'France's chance' and added that his liberalism had allowed a peaceful renewal of relations between France and the African states. 'France,' he said, 'is no longer alone.' Houphouet flew home to the Ivory Coast without comment, and later bitterly demanded (and received) immediate independence for the Union of Benin.

France would be well advised, Keita told me, to support Mali as a bulwark 'against *Anglo-Saxon* and Communist influences' in Africa. What Keita really fears is now that Nigeria's 35 million people are free, the appeal of membership in a powerful federal state with which they have strong racial and religious affinities will prove potent for republics like Niger and Chad, perhaps stronger than their attraction to Mali.

For the moment, Keita needs French financial help and he is directing his political energies into attempting to entice other Franco-African republics into Mali. Touré is a personal friend and he has hopes of getting the Guinea leader to bring his country into Mali now that conservative Senegal has left the federation. Like Guinea, Keita's country last year received a loan from Ghana, after which Nkrumah announced that the two republics would have a common parliament. Nothing has come of this, however. Other areas on which he is putting heavy pressure are Volta, which joined Mali and then backed out, and Mauritania, Mali's neighbour to the north.

Keita, who opposes France's use of the Sahara as a testing ground for her atomic bomb, has many economic troubles and groundnuts are almost his sole source of revenue. In an attempt to remedy this situation he is pressing for increased French assistance in the mammoth T.V.A.-like *Office du Niger* project.

Five hundred years ago there was a great fresh-water lake at the confluence of the Upper and Lower Niger Rivers and around this lived a heavy population of prosperous farmers. As the waters dried up, the region became depopulated and the French found only a few small tribes there cultivating rice and millet when they arrived in the late nineteenth century. Now all that remains of the great inland sea is a series of small lakes stretching from Debo to Timbuktu.

In 1932, the semi-autonomous *Office du Niger* was organized to carry out a grandiose plan which envisioned the irrigation of a million acres of cotton country and another million acres of rice cultivation, these to be farmed by 800,000 African peasants organized by the scheme's managers. The scheme ran into most of the troubles encountered by Richard-Toll and other similar projects: it became obvious that it would cost far more than had been anticipated, that the Africans had many reservations about becoming tenants, and that the cotton grown was of too poor a quality to stand the heavy transportation costs to the sea and then compete successfully even in a subsidized market.

But after many revisions, the scheme went ahead in 1934 with the laying of the foundations of the £7·5 million Sansanding dam. The dam, which has 500 sluice gates and is 884 yards long, was not completed until 1947. The dam and its embankment, which stretches for nearly two miles, raised the water level fourteen feet and made it possible to irrigate the plains to the north of the Niger through the Sahel and Macina canals. On top of the dam the French built a bridge—the Niger is spanned only three times in its 2,600-mile journey to the sea—with tracks to serve as a crossing for the non-existent trans-Saharan railway. In anticipation of greater days to come, the station-master's office is used as a storehouse.

To make the scheme more attractive to Africans used to a communal tribal organization. *Office du Niger* established Native Agricultural Associations which extend credit, facilitate communal cultivation, process part of the crop and market it. New colonists are given a hut, farm implements, some stock and twelve acres of ploughed land. Families are grouped in villages of from 200 to 400 people and fed until the first harvest. After paying rent for his land and contributing part of his crop to communal seed and food reserves, the individual may, if he wishes, market the remainder of his produce on his own. Families who farm their areas in the approved fashion may at the end of ten years obtain titles which are inheritable but not saleable.

At the moment, some 25,000 farmers are settled on more than 100,000 irrigated acres, now devoted almost exclusively to rice-growing, the *Office* is making a small profit and its tenants are receiving an income ten times higher than that of the average Malian peasant. All this has been accomplished, it should be noted, with the aid of Marshall Plan funds. It has cost more than £57 million, a sizable sum one would have to say, for putting 108,000 acres into production to grow rice which still cannot compete economically in coastal regions with imported rice. All the same, *Office du Niger* has been a limited technical, social and economic success and its enthusiasts at the Segou headquarters of the project are looking to the day when they will have 2·2 million acres under cultivation. Each year more than 30,000 square miles are inundated by the flood waters of the Niger and if this could be controlled it would create a fertile crescent stretching from Bamako to Timbuktu, capable of feeding all West Africa. The engineering would be facilitated by the fact that there is not much silting (which detracts, however, from the soil's fertility) but the big problem will be money.

Keita and his able Catholic deputy premier, Jean-Marie Kone, are in search of funds at the moment. One can hope that they will be offered an alternative to a low-interest Soviet loan.

Chapter 14

*

LAND OF THE MOORS

North of Senegal and Mali is Mauritania, one of the most fascinating and little-known territories in Africa, an eyeball-searing desert where nothing has changed for a thousand years, containing unknown sub-soil wealth which promises soon to make the republic's wild and woolly 650,000 inhabitants among the richest men on the continent.

Mauritania, which obtained its independence last year, has one high school, no hospital and not a single foot of railway or paved road. It is the only territory in Gallic Africa in which not an acre of land has been alienated for white settlement (the white population is less than 500) and is also the only one which has no missionaries or mission schools. If these seem negative virtues, let it be said that Mauritania, which is twice the size of France, has more camels (290,000) than male adults and there are more than eight sheep and goats (a total of five million) for every man, woman and child in the country. There is also a satisfactory supply of cattle and donkeys (950,000).

Mauritania was too poor until last year to afford its own capital so it is building one from scratch in the sand dunes six miles from the town of Nouakchott, which in 1959 had a population of exactly nineteen white people and 9,540 Africans. Accommodation for travellers is restricted to a two-room hotel 'avec tout confort' and a six-bed dormitory. Another town and the country's only seaport, Port Etienne, has 1,500 people most of whom live in concrete igloos collectively dubbed (as is Dakar's Terme Sud district which is built in the same fashion) Nichonville, or Breast Town. Scattered over the parched countryside are only 1·3 people to the square mile (vs. 25·9 in Senegal), the lowest population density in West Africa, and when well-diggers strike water there is as much jubilation in this thirsty land as if they'd found oil.

To get to Mauritania from the south, you take the three-car diesel 'train' (really more of a tram) called the Michelin. It runs on time, the trip takes four and a half hours, and once you are in St. Louis you have the problem of how to go on from there. When you cross the

Senegal, you are in camel country: although you can get camels to take you south of the Senegal-Niger line, it will cost you dearly, for the nomads know by experience that the animals will die within a few weeks after going south of this point. There is no problem, of course, heading north. Those contemplating using this mode of transportation must have strong spines, be impervious to motion-sickness and have some expert help in rental or purchase of their mounts. There is as much difference among camels as there is between a thoroughbred racehorse and a farm plug. If you keep your eyes peeled, you may be lucky enough to spot the Cadillac of the breed, the acorn-red *mehara* racing-camel whose long-distance lope devours the miles and for which a Moor will give his own eye or cut somebody else's throat. The *mehara* is recognizable from the angle at which his head is affixed to his neck (at a right angle rather than at a slope) and his gait is so smooth that you can read a book while you travel, once he gets into his pace.

Mauritania (and Senegal, for that matter) is a great autobahn-smooth plain with an average height of 600 feet above sea level, one of the largest uniformly level areas in Africa north of the equator. The name means 'Land of the Moors' and was once used as the designation for all north-western Africa.

The first thing to remember about Mauritania is that it is a *white* country. With the exception of the sedentary negro tribes which farm the banks of the Senegal, which forms the boundary between the Islamic Republic and Senegal, Mauritanians are no darker (and may be much lighter) than the average Portuguese, Spaniard or Italian. The Mauritanian is usually small in stature, has thin bones, light skin, grey or dark eyes, long straight hair, small hands and feet, a slightly hooked nose and a capacity for looking treacherous which belies his honest and courageous heart. His ancestors swept down into the desert from the North African littoral and he regards the Negroes of the Sudan with an attitude verging on that of Governor Faubus. The Mauritanian is a fighter, a sharp trader (Dakar's Moors are despised by the blacks because they control many urban water outlets and sell the water at an exorbitant price), a wanderer, a religious ascetic sure of his own values and contemptuous of those who do not happen to share them. The only way to impress a Mauritanian is to excel him at his own game; any other path to his heart is blocked by the enormous disdain with which he regards outsiders.

More than 90 per cent of Mauritania is desert and the population, including the Negro agriculturalists, is solidly Muslim. The early history of the state was marked by successive southward pushes of Arab and Berber tribes towards the water and grazing of the Senegal valley. The Berbers, who are members of the 'white' race, and have had an alphabet related to the scripts of the Aegean since the second century, were the original inhabitants. They were conquered and Islamized by the Arabs and the two, under the leadership of the Almoravids, routed the Negro empire of Ghana.

The Almoravids—the word means 'people of the hermitage', for the founders of this Muslim 'protestant revolution' went into seclusion on an island in the Senegal River to instruct their first apostles—faded away into the desert after the death of their great prophet, Abu Bakr, and the cleavage between Berber and Arab has been more typical than their rare fits of co-operation. Essentially this is in the nature of the people: the Arab to this day is basically a nomadic herdsman, prone to religious fanaticism and tightly bound to a feudal tribal system. The Berber, on the other hand, has become more of a town-dweller, a democrat, and (when he can) a tiller of the soil. Although the Berbers are famed for their Koranic scholarship, they are seldom moved to religious excess.

Europeans arrived in the fifteenth century (Portuguese, then Dutch, British and French) seeking to monopolize the gum trade on the north bank of the Senegal. France obtained a free hand in Mauritania from Britain in exchange for confirmation of the latter's rights on the Gambia and French military expeditions began to fan out over the country.

At first the French were not only unable to subjugate the Moors, who make up 85 per cent of Mauritania's population, but they were incapable even of protecting the Tucolors along the Senegal, who were their vassals, from pillaging Moorish raiders who swept south from the desert and disappeared again into the trackless sand dunes. Fortunately, the right man was in the right place.

His name was Xavier Coppolani. This French officer had sufficient knowledge of Moorish and Islamic customs to realize that the only way France could hope to pacify Mauritania was by capitalizing on internal disputes. In an age when most men looked with pride on their ignorance of African customs and organization, Coppolani was astute enough to see that he could drive a wedge into Mauritania by utilizing the resentment felt by the *maraboutic* Berbers for the Arab warrior tribes which had conquered them two centuries earlier.

Through the influence of the *marabouts*, Coppolani induced some important chiefs to place themselves under French protection in return for support against their rivals. Without firing a shot, losing a life or spending more than a few thousand dollars, Coppolani in three months of negotiations during 1905 was able to bring most of Mauritania within the French orbit. Before he could complete the job, he was assassinated at the age of thirty-nine.

Coppolani's task was completed by Colonel Gouraud in 1909. The immensity of Coppolani's achievement can be seen when it is appreciated that Mauritania is the only case on record in which Muslim religious leaders have voluntarily used their influence to bring their co-religionists under the political control of the infidel.

But if Mauritania was easily conquered, it was administered only with great difficulty. The highly mobile population, which still moves south towards the Senegal every dry season, was impossible to educate and difficult to tax. Trouble continually arose between the *hassane*, the warrior tribes, and the *zaouia*, the priestly clans of Berber stock. Restless too were the *haratines*, the Negro slaves attached to each nomad family. The French administration freed the tributary groups of their fears of the desert warriors, left the latter without a useful function to perform.

The French attempted to rule through the great emirs of Trarza, Brakna and Adrar. The Emir of Adrar soon demonstrated his dissatisfaction with this arrangement by killing a French officer and fleeing across the border into Spanish Rio de Oro, from which he continued to harass the government, as did his northern kinsman, the so-called Blue Sultan.

In retaliation, the French reduced the *horma*, the tribute owed to the chiefs by their vassals, thus creating further unrest which only the savage campaigns of the *goumiers*, hard-riding Arab partisans of the French, were able to suppress.

Although Mauritania shared in the extension of political freedom which occurred after World War II, the absence of large towns, the economic backwardness of the country (French aid in the decade ending in 1957 amounted to only £5·4 million), the strength of the chiefs and the influence of conservative Islam have all served to insulate the republic from radical politics. A subject upon which a book could be written but which we can only note in passing: north of the Sahara, Islam has become a radical political force; south of the desert, it is the most stable and conservative factor in the political situation.

More typical of Mauritania than the political conferences and labour disputes which characterize so much of the rest of Africa is the time of ripening dates, which comes to Chinguetti in July and August. In the fifteenth century, this central Mauritanian oasis boasted eleven mosques and was one of the seven great cities of Islam. Now it lies in ruins, only one square minaret still stands, and the population is: 'Europeans, 4; Africans, 600 to 4,000, depending on the season'.

In August, all 4,000 will be there, for the dates bring the nomads in for a month. It is a time of interminable cups of mint tea, talk of politics and love and war, a time to pray and a time to dance, a time to swell your belly with sweet dates, to fire your rifle for pure joy, to marry off your most eligible daughter, making sure first that the groom is prepared to include at least one *mehara* in the bride-price.

In the city, the lean, sun-bronzed Moors look out of place with their ground-consuming desert lope and their gaze fixed above the level of the crowd, as if scanning a horizon. Here they seem natural and in harmony with nature with their robes of blue or white tucked up between their legs to form baggy trousers, their loose turbans falling over their ears. Their women, who dye their lower lips in an attractive, washed-blue colour and are inordinately beautiful, tie their hair into braids which they loop together to create a bird-cage effect, over which a veil of blue or black is thrown. If the Moor looks a trifle cruel and wild with his dark, piercing eyes, narrow lips and thick fleece of shoulder-length black hair, he is nature's perfect response to his environment.

When the dates have all been eaten or bartered for gunpowder and salt, old friendships and animosities renewed with equal enthusiasm, the last camel traded and the last glass of mint tea consumed, the Moors fade away from Chinguetti for another year and you know that you have been privileged to see something magnificent.

BALLOTS AND BULLETS

The first Moor to sit in the French Assembly was Horma ould Babana, a government official and founder of the territory's first political party, *L'Entente Mauritanienne*. When Babana attempted to introduce a socialist programme to Mauritania, the conservative elders backed by young Muslim intellectuals combined to form an opposition party, the *Union Progressiste Mauritanienne* (U.P.M.), since renamed the *Parti du Regroupement Mauritanien* (P.R.M.).

The leader of the P.R.M., Sidi el Mokhtar, who is of mixed Moorish and Wollof extraction, defeated Babana in 1951 and his party captured twenty-two of the twenty-four seats in the territorial assembly the following year. Sidi el Mokhtar again defeated Babana in 1956 whereupon the latter set a pattern by fleeing to the court of the King of Morocco, whose claim to suzerainty over Mauritania he promptly acknowledged.

Babana's action, since emulated by other disappointed office-seekers and by the Sultan of Trarza, who has 50,000 rifles at his call, well illustrates Mauritania's basic political dilemma: it is a 'white' state and hence much more closely tied to Morocco and North Africa than to Senegal and the Black Africa with which it was associated throughout the last half-century for purely administrative reasons.

Babana's adventurism touched off a series of raids deep into Mauritania on the part of the so-called Moroccan Army of Liberation. It appeared for a few tense months in 1956 and 1957 that the Algerian struggle might well be extended to the desert but *goumiers* stiffened by battle-hardened French paratroopers flown in from Algeria got the situation in hand after a series of bloody battles. Mauritanian leaders, however, still periodically accuse Morocco's King Mohamed V of subversive meddling in their affairs.

Mauritania gave de Gaulle a loud *oui* for his Fifth Republic (113,897 for, 8,160 against), fought off pressure from Mali, christened itself the Islamic Republic of Mauritania and decided to remain in a direct relationship with Paris. An election held in May 1959 confirmed these moves when 90 per cent of the registered voters cast their ballots for the P.R.M., which won all forty of the assembly seats unopposed. A new party called *L'Union Nationale Mauritanienne* was formed too late to participate in the election but the low abstention rate suggests that had the U.N.M. been eligible its candidates would have got little more than exercise out of their run for office. Late last year Mauritania, like the other French republics became independent. The French thoughtfully flew in champagne, Corsican lobsters and peppermint sodas for the celebration.

In his dealings with Mali and Paris, Assembly president Sidi el Mokhtar, who is so popular that he doesn't have to campaign for election any more, has been greatly aided by the emergence of one of the ablest leaders in West Africa.

This is Mokhtar ould Daddah, Mauritania's premier and its only barrister. Ould Daddah, who is sometimes confused with Sidi el Mokhtar because of the similarity of their names (they are kinsmen), looks like something out of *The Desert Prince*. He has a strong, handsome face, frank black eyes, a well-trimmed fringe of beard around his jaw and a pencil-thin moustache. His hair, which he wears in something approaching a crew-cut, is raven-black except for a spot the size of a half-dollar on the top of his head which has turned to silver.

Ould Daddah is thirty-six (the average age of the Mauritanian assembly is thirty-four) and he is of a warrior tribe which has strong connections with the religious clans. The premier is the son of a sheikh. His father sent him to school in St. Louis and, after a tour as an interpreter in the French Army, he studied law at the Sorbonne, where he met his pretty French wife. Although Ould Daddah's official residence is a prefabricated house in Nouakchott and he buzzes back and forth to Dakar in a tiny Citroen, he likes nothing better than to doff his well-cut tweeds, slip into the robes of a desert warrior and wander off into the desert with his camels and his wild brethren to subsist for a few weeks on dried dates and camel's milk. In this he is something of an exception: one of the principal causes of unrest among the tribes ten years ago was that their leaders were becoming too fond of the fleshpots of Mauritania's St. Louis capital, giving in to a life of indolence, and returning to their people, often by aeroplane, only to collect tribute.

It was perhaps with this in mind that Sidi el Mokhtar and Ould Daddah in 1959 decided to move the republic's capital from St. Louis. St. Louis, of course, is in Senegal but the Mauritanians were spared the humiliation of having their capital in a 'foreign' territory by locating their headquarters on a sandbar on the north side of the river connected to the main town by a bridge. This spit of sand, fancifully dubbed 'The Tongue of Barbary', is Mauritanian territory.

Some of the more Westernized Moors wanted the capital to move upstream on the Senegal to Rosso, which would not be too far from the bright lights of St. Louis and Dakar. Mauritanian jingoes wanted Atar, a nomad camping-ground in the middle of the desert where there is nothing more distracting than the moon-drawn wails of the jackals. Instead, Sidi el Mokhtar and Ould Daddah chose a site in the sand dunes near Nouakchott and there the new capital will be built.

Five years ago Mauritania would have been too poor to build a camel stable, much less a new capital. It exported a couple of thousand tons of gum and dried fish, produced 10,000 tons of dates (most of which were consumed locally) from the country's half a million palm trees. Attempts to introduce new production techniques were not enthusiastically received.

The Imraguen fishermen who work the Senegal's mouth saw no virtue in the use of rollers to beach their heavy canoes, continued to rock their double-prowed craft up the beach like men moving a heavy wardrobe trunk. For this and other reasons their catch, which could amount to 200,000 tons a year, has never exceeded a tenth of that figure. Suggestions to the effect that a programme of planting and pruning might increase the date yield were rightfully rejected by pious Muslims who protested that they would not be so blasphemous as to try to improve upon the handiwork of Allah. The nomads devoted themselves with complete and understandable enthusiasm to the task of loving, fighting and peddling a few worn-out camels and spindly-shanked goats to their Moroccan cousins.

All this now stands to change dramatically. As early as 1934, the French knew that a jagged ridge of iron 1,500 feet high and twenty miles long rose out of the flat, stony desert in northern Mauritania. They maintained an outpost there—Fort Gouraud—to stave off slaving parties from Rio de Oro. The big problem was how to get the ore out of the ground, since the local citizenry considered it sporting to shoot prospectors, and how to get it to market through a countryside lacking in roads or railways. Consequently, it was not until 1951 that a joint Franco-British firm (MIFIRMA) could be found willing to undertake the exploitation of deposits estimated to total some 100 million tons of very high grade (66 per cent ore content) iron and one *billion* tons of 40 per cent ore content. But only in April 1959 was enough water found in underground pools twenty miles from Fort Gouraud both to serve the mines and to irrigate the few acres necessary to support a labour force.

Before operations could get beyond an experimental stage, the question of the railway had to be decided. A 230-mile line to the Spanish port of Villa Cisneros was one alternative; another was a 430-mile all-French route to the Mauritanian port of Port Etienne. In either case, the cost was thought to be prohibitive. At this crucial moment, further iron ore deposits were found near Port Etienne, which swung the balance in the favour of that route.

In the spring of 1960 the World Bank agreed to lend MIFIRMA, now bolstered by Italian and German investors, £23·5 million to build the railway and exploit the iron, a project which will involve a total expenditure of £57 million. Surveyors are at work on the mountain, in whose shadow an air-conditioned town (summer temperatures: 115 degrees) housing 10,000 is springing up. When production begins in 1964, two 10,000-ton trainloads of ore will leave for the coast every day. Four million tons will be exported that year, a figure which will rise later to six million tons. Under the concession agreement, 50 per cent of the profits will go to the Mauritanian government.

By the building of this railway, it will become possible to exploit the vast copper reserves discovered at Akjouit (1959 population: 25 whites, 2,300 Africans) in central Mauritania in 1934. Nobody really knows how much copper (or iron, for that matter) the country contains, but in the immediate vicinity of Akjouit there are thought to be at least 25 million tons, probably far more. The problem in regard to the copper was that it was of too poor a grade to be shipped economically unless it could be treated first on the spot, which required water, a commodity of which Mauritania has little. After extensive exploration, large underground pools were found near the mines. Seemingly Allah was rewarding his servants for not monkeying with the date palms.

All this adds up to the fact that, in contrast to much of the rest of Africa, Mauritania's economic future looks bright. Sidi el Mokhtar, who at first had opposed the operations of the French-run Common Organization for the Sahara Regions, has been quick to realize that co-operation with O.C.R.S. poses no threat to the political autonomy of his country and has now become an ardent advocate of mineral exploitation. Mauritania, once the poorest of the poor, may well soon have a higher *per capita* income than any other African state. It will take money and time, of course: to develop only the iron will cost £85·6 million and at least five years. It will probably cost another £35·6 million to get the copper into production. In addition to installing mining apparatus, the railway must be built and Port Etienne's facilities, which have never handled more than five ships a month or 15,000 tons of freight in a year, must be expanded and modernized.

But come it will and overnight Mauritania, which used to stagger along with an annual budget of £2·3 million, will be wrenched from biblical times into the industrial age. Although it is easy to become sentimental and mourn the passing of the country's primitive pastoral purity, the desert land desperately needs to exploit its mineral wealth, particularly to build a school system.

RECALCITRANT SCHOLARS

In the past, Mauritanian children and their parents have been so opposed to Western education that French administrators literally have had to send their armed *goumiers* off to raid the nomad camps for students, then mount guard on the schools to keep their wild charges from escaping to their beloved desert. It was never possible to keep more than a couple of thousand students in school and those who were corralled learned little: since there were no educated nomads, the only teachers available were Negroes, despised by the Mauritanians as an inferior people. In at least one instance a Negro schoolmaster was stoned by his pupils for attempting to assert his authority over them. Under these circumstances, few Negroes have been willing to undergo the occupational hazards attendant upon teaching in Mauritania. To those who have run the risk, Mauritania owes a great debt.

In an attempt to overcome the nomads' hatred of urban schooling, the French have made an interesting experiment in moving the mountain to Mohammed. Instead of requiring Mauritanians to leave their children in school, teachers have been assigned to wander across the deserts with the nomads, teaching in tents as they go. Since the Arabs seldom trek in large groups because of the limited supply of water and grazing for their flocks, this presents big problems and teachers have only been available for service with clans who have twenty or more school-age children.

Some of these nomad schools travel more than 600 miles a year and they have enjoyed a definite but limited success. Started in 1924 and earnestly encouraged by the French educator Marc Lenoble, most of Mauritania's present leaders first encountered the three R's in a goatskin tent warmed by the desert sun. The curriculum has been tailored to satisfy the religious requirements of the Moors and more and more of their own clansmen are becoming available to take over the teaching jobs. For this they are well suited: Mauritania for nine hundred years has been famed as a centre of Islamic learning and orthodoxy. Since 99 per cent of the country's population is Muslim, Mauritania has not a single mission school and is highly unlikely to acquire one. Hence these nomad schools fill the gap before its people are ready for sedentary education and public funds are available to provide it. In all, 5,500 Mauritanian students (3 per cent of the school-age population) attend seventy-one primary schools and the country's one high school manages to keep some three hundred itchy-footed pupils at their desks.

THE BRIDGE

I talked with Mokhtar ould Daddah about his country's political future, subjected as it is to strong pressure from the black states to the south and from Morocco in the north. The young leader, who looks like a youthful version of Haile Selassie, admitted that Mauritania's position is a delicate one.

'I should like to emphasize one point,' he said. 'We have strong ties with Morocco, that is true. But M. Babana and others who lose an election and then dash to Rabat to proclaim their fidelity to the King of Morocco demonstrate a lamentable ignorance of history. They seem to forget, as do the Moroccans, that the Almoravids came from our desert.' He gave a short laugh.

'In fact, on a historical basis, it is Morocco which belongs to us, not we to them. That, of course, is not our policy. We hope to enjoy the most cordial relations with Morocco for we enjoy strong common racial and religious affinities. As for the black states, we hope to be friends with them too. One should not disguise the fact, however, that there are strong racial feelings in my country which are not dispelled overnight. We have always been the white conquerors from the north bringing both civilization and religion to the Sudan. It is not natural that we should be expected now to submit ourselves to a Negro majority under a system of government which gives power to the majority. Nevertheless, we wish them well and hope that our two countries may enjoy a happy commercial relationship if, for the moment, any sort of political federation is out of the question.'

As we said our good-byes and Mokhtar ould Daddah invited us to come with him some day on a camel trip into the interior of his country (an invitation which I intend to hold him to one day), the young premier had a final thought:

'Perhaps the most important role which my country can play is to act as a bridge—politically, culturally and religiously—between the Arab North and the Negro South. This would be a task worth accomplishing.'

THE GALLIC GIANT: A FINAL WORD

For the last seven chapters we have attempted to touch upon the prospects and problems of a vast area the size of the United States peopled by 25 million inhabitants broken up into a multiplicity of tribes so various as to confound the imagination. Some trends have emerged which are worth restating, particularly to compare with those obtaining in Saxon West Africa.

The first of these is that the people of Equatoria—Gabon, Congo,

Central Africa and Chad—are in Western terms far less advanced than the former territories of French West Africa. Even in pre-European days, these states had none of the well-developed Negro and Muslim empires which characterized the Sudanic region. In some ways this might have been expected to bring them more quickly into the European cultural orbit, since they had less to forget. This might have been the case had not the great forest of Equatoria and the rapids on her rivers made access to the interior difficult, dangerous and expensive. These same conditions, with the possible exception of Gabon, have retarded the region's economic development and can be expected to do so for some years to come. This decade is likely to be one of prosperity for West Africa, as the Common Market brings German and Dutch capital to the aid of these under-developed republics; the next decade may belong to Equatoria.

On the political side, three important leaders have emerged. Ivory Coast's Felix Houphouet-Boigny clearly stands out as spokesman for the conservative forces south of the tenth degree of north latitude. He represents those republics—Niger, Dahomey, Volta and Ivory Coast—which feel that they can achieve their economic and political goals within the context of the French Community with an individual rather than a collective approach. They feel, in short, that their more pressing problems are economic rather than political.

Less conservative than this is the position adopted by Mali's Modibo Keita, who feels it is desirable to join all the republics into a powerful political federation. Keita recognizes the need for economic co-operation with France but feels that this can be achieved only on a basis of equality, which to him implies the creation of a large federal African state.

Guinea's Sekou Touré, on the other hand, takes the most radical view of all. He believes, as demonstrated by his actions, that all of Gallic Africa should secede from the Community, assert its 'African personality', work for union with Ghana, Nigeria and Liberia, then obtain financial assistance from either the non-Communist or Communist bloc, depending upon which offers the better terms.

The political history of Gallic Africa during the 1960's will be the story of the struggle for supremacy of the personalities and programmes of these three leaders. Houphouet's R.D.A. either controls or participates in the coalition governments of six of the eleven Gallic African states while Keita's P.F.A. controls only two but has branches in three other republics. The other three republics—Congo, Central Africa and

Mauritania—are governed by unaffiliated local parties. But the situation is not quite as simple as this. Even in two of the four states of the Union of Benin—Volta and Dahomey—adherence to Houphouet's bloc was more a response to economic imperatives than a declaration of ideological solidarity. In short, Houphouet's domination of the political scene is more apparent than real; only his own Ivory Coast and Niger are in total agreement with his political and economic programme.

We have stated the differences which divide the fourteen Gallic republics of this vast land mass. Binding them together to an extent unknown in the Saxon West (the four Afro-British states and Liberia) are the culture and language of France. To a large degree this implies no difference in the qualities or capacities of the inhabitants of either area. Rather it is to be explained by the differing national personalities of France and Britain and by their contrasting systems of administration and attitudes towards education.

The French, far more than the British, brought their culture with them to Africa. By the same token, they have always demonstrated a greater capacity to understand and appreciate African culture. The British came to Africa to bring British law, trade and religion to the heathen. The French came not to bring the African something but to make him part of them. The British have thought it advisable that the African become *like* them; the French have never doubted that the best thing that could happen to an African was for him to *become* a Frenchman. The distinction is important.

With this in mind, the French on the whole ignored African political groupings and administered directly. The British, on the other hand, applied Lord Lugard's thesis of indirect rule and governed through existing native institutions. The result was that French Africans more readily were brought to think in Western administrative terms while the British gave their support to the chieftaincy, an institution which for all its virtues is hardly suitable as the basis for a modern society.

In line with their programme of Gallicization, the French educational programme concentrated on and succeeded in producing an intellectual *élite*. This was done, of course, at the expense of basic education for the masses. French anti-clericalism removed the possibility that the mission schools might come into conflict with government policy in this regard. The British generally worked on the thesis that it was better to give many people some education than a few a great deal. As a result, the French have been able to create a class of people who *are* black Frenchmen, something that the British have never tried to do and certainly have not accomplished by accident.

The French policy of political assimilation has also tended to emphasize this feature. Most of the top leaders like Senghor and Houphouet have spent fifteen years serving in *French* parliamentary bodies, an experience that has sharpened their political wits, afforded them a greater insight into European thought-patterns and made them generally more sympathetic to the European way of life. Important, too, is the fact that these political leaders are the intellectuals of Gallic Africa. While a black intellectual *élite* does exist in Saxon Africa, it has never had the numbers or the backing to control the political situation and, with a few exceptions, it has retreated to the universities and left the business of government to a turbulent and not always well-prepared middle class.

The end result of all of this is to make, as Lamine Guéye said, French language and culture a unifying factor which has no similar counterpart in Saxon Africa. Hence it will be far more difficult than Dr. Nkrumah thinks to add the Gallic republics to his sphere of influence. Far more likely is it that French Africa will eventually coalesce into one or more blocs, and Saxon Africa into another, that these will maintain their separate identities for at least a decade and perhaps for ever.

This is no popular notion with African nationalists who prefer to discount the influence which the arbitrary division of Africa has or should have on their continent's destiny. But the fact remains that trade patterns, language barriers, currency blocs, cultural orientations and administrative usage are not matters which can be eliminated by legislation any more than they can be erased from the personalities of individuals within a single generation.

French Africans do think and act to some extent like Frenchmen; British Africans may not behave like Englishmen but they certainly do not resemble Frenchmen. These are matters that should be remembered.

On to Saxon Africa.

III

THE SAXON WEST

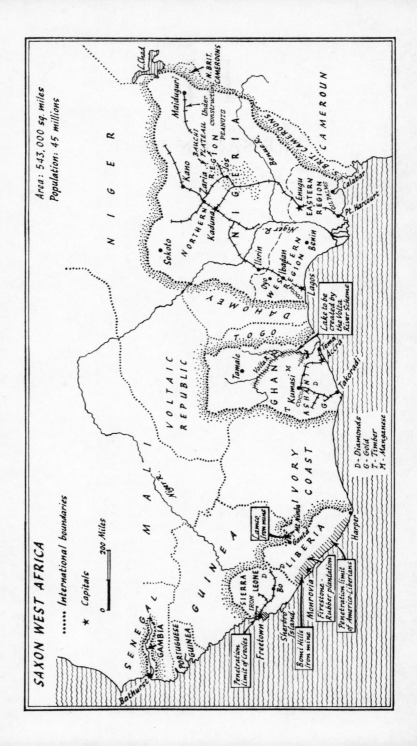

SAXON WEST AFRICA

Area: 543,000 sq. miles
Population: 45 millions

...... International boundaries
★ Capitals

0   200 Miles

D – Diamonds
G – Gold
T – Timber
M – Manganese

Penetration limit of Creoles

Bomi Hills iron mine

Firestone Rubber plantation

Penetration limit of America-Liberians

Lamco iron mine

Lake to be created by the Volta River Scheme

Under construction

PEANUTS

OIL PALMS

COCOA

N I G E R

M A L I

VOLTAIC REPUBLIC

S E N E G A L

GUINEA

PORTUGUESE GUINEA

GAMBIA

SIERRA LEONE

LIBERIA

IVORY COAST

GHANA

ASHANTI

TOGO

DAHOMEY

NIGERIA

NORTHERN REGION

WESTERN REGION

EASTERN REGION

CAMEROUN

S. CAMEROONS

N. BRIT. CAMEROONS

Bathurst

Freetown

Bo

Sherbro Island

Monrovia

Harper

Tamale

Kumasi

Tema Accra

Takoradi

Lagos

Benin

Ibadan

Oyo

Ilorin

Sokoto

Kaduna

Zaria

Kano

Jos

Maiduguri

BAUCHI PLATEAU

Enugu

Pt. Harcourt

Calabar

L. Chad

Benue R.

Niger R.

Volta R.

Ganta

Mt. Nimba

IRON

Bomi Hills

Chapter 15

*

THE RIVER STATE

Of all the nations and territories of the New Africa, Gambia is the most implausible. This oldest and smallest of Britain's West African possessions is bordered on the north, east and south by Senegal and on the west by the Atlantic Ocean, and it consists of little more than both banks of the river from which it takes its name. Thus Gambia, which is about the size of Jamaica, is a wriggle of a country often less than seven miles wide stretching 180 miles inland as a muscular crow might fly but 300 miles in river distance.

Gambia, which one eighteenth-century wanderer described as 'a country much talk'd of and little known', has no university, daily newspaper, radio station, industry or railway and the tax rate is the highest in British West Africa. The white population is less than 300 and there are fewer Negroes in the country (about 260,000) than there are in Washington, D.C. There are no towns with populations of more than 5,000 people with the exception of Bathurst, the capital, a sleepy Victorian hamlet on the coast. Groundnuts are the source (98 per cent) of the territory's revenue and Gambia can barely meet its current expenses in a good year, much less lay anything aside for development purposes. A recent government report states that 41 per cent of this geographical absurdity consists of 'undulating sand hills' and a good proportion of the rest is water or mangrove swamp. There are few cattle: Gambia lies within the tsetse belt.

This Gilbertian British colony 2,600 miles from England is the only African Commonwealth territory in which one drives on the right, testimony both to its position and shape (it looks like a hot dog inserted into a Senegalese roll) and to the Gallic abandon with which drivers from Senegal hurtled down its highways on the wrong side of the road before the switch was made in 1959.

There is no abundance of these thoroughfares. Gambia has exactly forty-two miles of paved highways and its dirt roads, the worst in Africa, are passable only from December to July, the year's four feet of rain falling in the remaining months. This works no terrible hardship on the majority of the population because Gambia boasts no more than 1,200 vehicles. One of these, a magnificent new German bus, is permanently marooned in Bathurst because its proud owner miscalculated the width of the new bridge joining the city to the south bank of the river. This paucity of conveyances is not completely to be deplored since the enthusiasm with which the African drives is often more marked than his skill. A Bathurst administrator told this story: he had gone out to give an African a driver's test in the man's truck, which the applicant promptly smashed into a brick wall; when asked if he thought a little more practice might not be in order, the African said that he thought he'd done rather well considering the fact that he'd only had enough money to hire the truck to take the examination and had never been behind the wheel of a car before. 'When he put it that way,' added the official, 'I rather had to agree with him.'

Gambians are renowned for their hospitality and Francis Moore, a trader writing in 1731, reports that 'the Girls would have People think they are very modest, especially when they are in Company; but take them by themselves, and they are very obliging; for if you will give them a little Coral or a Silk Handkerchief, you may take what Liberty you please with them.' A hunk of coral will not get you very far these days, however.

The country's army, the Gambia Field Force, is the smallest (three commissioned officers, two warrant officers and ninety-five enlisted men) independent military unit in the British Commonwealth and proudly bears its own colours. Veterans of this Lilliputian group fought gallantly against the Japanese at Frontier Hill and Mychaung and participated in the liberation of Rangoon.

To keep everybody from starving to death, the government in one six-year period slaughtered 180,000 baboons, 95,000 monkeys and 50,000 wild pigs. So poor is this minute enclave that it possesses only a dozen university graduates, one airport and not a single restaurant. There are three trade unions with a total membership of less than 500.

Yet men once felt that Gambia was destined to be the richest jewel of the Guinea Coast, a prize for which nations went to war and men died. The first Europeans to reach the river were a Venetian adventurer named Alvise de Cadamosto and his Genoese companion, Antonio Usodimare, both in the service of that great half-English (his mother was the daughter of John of Gaunt) Portuguese prince, Henry the Navigator. The pair sailed a short way up the river in search of gold in 1455 but were turned back by hostile natives.

Cadamosto, who describes himself as 'young, well fitted to sustain all hardships, desirous of seeing the world . . . to draw from it honour and profit,' returned the following year with three 'caravels of Portugallo . . . well furnished with every necessity', and cast anchor on a Sunday morning in the lee of an island 'shaped like a smoothing iron' a few miles upstream. There a sailor named Andrew, who had died of fever, was buried and, because the dead man had been well loved, Cadamosto named the island St. Andrew. For the next 300 years the history of the European occupation of Gambia was to be largely the story of a five-acre sandy lump named in memory of a popular salt.

Cadamosto was impressed by the fact that the Gambians clothed themselves while the people of the Senegal went naked and thought their baggy Muslim trousers to be 'the most comical things to be seen in the world'. The Gambians must have been equally diverted by his appearance—he wore clothes 'after the Spanish fashion, a doublet of black damask, with a short cloak of grey wool', hardly the sort of thing for the tropics—and amazed by his ship, which they said had portholes in its bow so that it could see where it was going.

Although Cadamosto found no sizable quantities of gold, Prince Henry was interested enough to send out a few colonists to hold what his explorers had discovered. Most of these unfortunate individuals, men 'of the basest behaviour', died of fever, drink or the arrows of the natives and those who survived interbred with the Africans with such enthusiasm that, in the course of time, it became difficult to distinguish them from the local citizenry. Still, they styled themselves Portuguese, affected European dress and names, professed Christianity and, as late as the 1750's, separate 'Portuguese' churches and communities maintained their identity.

In 1587, a Portuguese renegade, one Francisco Ferreira, piloted two English ships up the Gambia, which was then thought to be a mouth of the Nile, and brought them home again with a cargo of hides, ivory and spices. The following year Antonio, Prior of Crato, a claimant to the Portuguese throne seized seven years earlier by Philip II of Spain, found himself exiled in England and running short of cash. To raise a bit of ready money, he sold to certain merchants of London and Devon the right to trade between the Senegal and the Gambia rivers, an area previously reserved to Portugal by a Papal bull of 1481. Sailors in the service of these merchants attempted to enter the river but were thwarted by the Portuguese garrison and reported to their masters that the Gambia was 'a river of secret trade and riches, concealed by the Portingalls'.

In 1618, an expedition commanded by George Thompson made another try, this time with the intention of finding a route to fabled Timbuktu. Thompson left his ship and struck out overland, reaching a point almost 400 miles from the sea. When he returned, he found that the rascally 'Portingalls' had burned his ship. Some of his party were able to make their way to Cape Verde and thence to England. Thompson, who like most of the breed had plenty of courage, stayed on the Gambia with seven men, one of whom murdered him in a drunken quarrel. A relief expedition under Richard Jobson seized some Portuguese shipping in reprisal but was unable to show a profit and the patent-holders shifted their attention to the more promising Gold Coast.

In 1651, a group of Roundhead merchants made the mistake of accepting new letters patent from the dour Cromwell. They were made to see the error of their ways by dashing Prince Rupert, nephew of the beheaded English king, and a cavalier apparently as much at home on the poop deck as he was at the head of a squadron of light cavalry. Rupert, accompanied by Prince Maurice, his brother, sailed three Royalist vessels to the Gambia and cleared the river of Commonwealth shipping before setting sail for the West Indies.

In the same year, James, Duke of Courland, a godson of James I of England (who was Rupert's grandfather), obtained from the Gambia chiefs the cession of St. Andrew's Island. James had been given the island of Tobago by his royal godfather and this Baltic prince (Courland, which was later incorporated into Latvia and Lithuania, is now part of the Soviet Union) hoped to find both gold and slaves in the Gambia to work his West Indian plantations. The Courlanders erected a fort on the island and established smaller settlements up-river. This promising start received a severe blow when the Duke and all his family had the misfortune to be captured by the Swedes in a war between that country and Poland, whose vassal he was. During his two-year imprisonment his agents leased the islands to the Dutch who were promptly expelled by a French privateer in Swedish service, the Courlanders taking over again when the Duke was released from durance vile.

Meanwhile, back on the farm, Charles II was king in England, Cromwell's body had been exhumed, drawn and quartered amidst general Restoration jollity, and Prince Rupert (brother Maurice had been drowned during the pair's buccaneering tour of the West Indies) was the darling of the court. Rupert, spurred on by rumours of a mountain of gold at the headwaters of the Gambia (a legend still aired in Bathurst bars), urged his royal cousin to grant him leave to return to Africa. When this was refused, Rupert and the Duke of York got a royal charter and incorporated themselves as the Company of Royal Adventurers Trading to Africa.

Major Robert Holmes, an old pal of Rupert's and a member of the 1652 Gambia expedition, sailed to St. Andrew's Island and demanded the surrender of the garrison, now reduced to five men and two women. This was a bit hard on the Duke of Courland, who had contributed generously both in men and money to the Stuart cause, but his fever-racked garrison was hardly in a condition to argue the merits of the case with powder and shot. Holmes renamed the stronghold James Fort in honour of the Duke of York. The seizure and occupation of the fort on March 19, 1661, was the first permanent British settlement on the Guinea Coast.

Command of James Fort became a short-term duty assignment as the French captured the stronghold—which had no permanent water supply (the Gambia is brackish for several miles up-stream)—four times in one thirteen-year period. Although the French were unable to hold the fort for any appreciable length of time, they established their own post at Albreda on the north bank of the river and maintained it well into the nineteenth century.

In 1719, a buccaneer named Howel Davis captured James Fort and so impressed the locals with the joys of life under the Jolly Roger that, two years later, part of the garrison mutinied under Captain John Massey—who had served Marlborough 'with great applause'—appropriated the Company's ship and themselves turned pirate. Since profit margins in those days often reached 1,000 per cent, the stockholders hung on to enjoy twenty years of relative quiet and considerable prosperity.

Life for the garrison on this unhappy sun-parched sandbar was at its best never very good and one visitor in 1749 reported that the settlement was 'in a most miserable condition, the people in a melancholy situation for want of goods to carry on trade to support their garrison, not having had any supplies for upwards of five years'. Nothing was done to remedy this 'melancholy situation' and the following year the garrison was 'reduced by sickness from twenty-five or thirty men to five or eight and, the officers being all dead, a common soldier had succeeded to command.'

Finally Britain revoked the company's charter and, for the next eighteen years, Gambia formed part of the Crown Colony of Senegambia, whose capital was St. Louis, which the British had wrested from the French. As part of the general settlement of the world war during which Britain lost her American colonies, England handed back St. Louis and Gorée to France, and Senegambia ceased to exist.

Although a new charter was issued, nothing much was done on the Gambia with the exception of the purchase of Lemain (now MacCarthy) Island 200 miles up-stream for use as a penal colony. Fortunately for the jailbirds, this project lapsed and the intended residents were sent to the comparative spa of Botany Bay. The Gambia saw only lonely travellers like Major Houghton, Mungo Park and Major Grey, all of whom trooped through on their way to death and a bit of glory in search of the elusive Niger.

In 1816, Britain officially committed herself on the Gambia by sending Captain Alexander Grant to enter into treaties with 'the King of Kombo' and establish a permanent base. Grant decided against attempting to refortify miserable James Island, then nullified his wisdom by selecting the swampy island of Banjol off the south bank. This he renamed St. Mary's Island and on it he built a stockaded post which, being anxious to become major, he named Bathurst, after the then Secretary of State for the Colonies. An annual tribute of 103 bars of iron was to be paid for the cession of the site; it is believed that the King of Kombo collected at the end of the first year.

James Island was never reoccupied and today its cannons, still pointed bravely out to sea, rust quietly in the sun. The Gambia's annual floods have washed away at least half the island and the buildings which stood upon it; tree roots, sun and rain pull down the walls which still stand over the graves of long-forgotten governors. In the sandy thickets there still can be found rusted regimental buttons, an odd coin and thick pieces of green glass, remnants of the bottles of rum consumed by the forsaken garrison as they searched the shimmering horizon for the friendly sails which never appeared.

In 1821, Gambia was placed for twenty-two years under the jurisdiction of the governor of British Sierra Leone. To block the French, the British bought from the natives the so-called Ceded Mile, a twenty-four-mile long and one-mile wide stretch on the right bank of the river. When more land was obtained from the King of Kombo on the left bank, settlements of freed slaves, refugees and discharged

West Indian army veterans were established. These became the ancestors of Bathurst's proud Akus, 2,500 detribalized Negroes who speak no native tongue, profess Christianity and aspire to Western standards of living.

The connection with Sierra Leone proved mutually unprofitable and Gambia became a separate colony in 1843, then reverted to Sierra Leone from 1866 to 1888, when it once more adopted an individual identity. These experiments in federation were more a matter of economy than of choice: it was not so long ago that Gambian austerity was so severe that the government abolished the post of Health Officer.

This is the more striking in that the Gambia was and remains to a lesser extent today one of the unhealthiest spots in Africa. Out of one contingent of 199 British soldiers landed in 1825, 160 were dead within six months. One stalwart white woman set some sort of record by burying five husbands in three years and cholera wiped out nearly half the population of Bathurst in 1869. A post-World War II health survey revealed that 55 per cent of the population have malaria, 35 per cent have serious liver diseases, 8 per cent suffer from 'gross infective eye conditions', 4·4 per cent have sleeping sickness and 2·5 per cent are eaten by leprosy. Minor ailments such as malnutrition, skin diseases, yaws, filariasis and helminthiasis are described as 'prevalent'. Round-worms, hook-worms and tape-worms, according to a 1957 report, 'all flourish' and the infant mortality rate is about 50 per cent.

In an attempt to combat this appalling situation, the World Health Organization doles out dried milk and vitamin pills to Gambia children under six years of age, school children under ten, pregnant women and nursing mothers. Since the people did not care for the milk alone, the Gambian government made a free issue of sugar. In 1957 1·9 million daily rations (two ounces of milk and half an ounce of sugar) were distributed. This amounted to 106 tons of milk, 26½ tons of sugar and 261,000 vitamin pills. Distribution, however, was of necessity limited mostly to populous areas. Gambia has two hospitals with a total of 350 beds.

In the period of colonial expansion the French did such an efficient job of annexing Gambia's hinterland that the pestiferous colony was of little value to the British, who came close to following the recommendation of an 1864 parliamentary commission that England abandon all of her West African possessions with the exception of Sierra Leone, valued for its excellent and defensible harbour. The dynamic Faidherbe was the moving force behind the French efforts to obtain Gambia and twice during the 1870's negotiations to accomplish this were nearly completed. Each time the opposition of the mercantile groups (who one is inclined to believe were more interested in making a case for compensation than in arresting the transfer) of educated Gambians fearful that cession would negate their one economic asset, a knowledge of English, and of Protestant missionaries, who were afraid of religious domination by French Catholics, defeated the scheme. In 1902, Britain took both banks of the river for 300 miles upstream under her protection.

In contrast to the French, who ruled Africa directly, it has been British practice to administer through existing native institutions. In Gambia's case, this has meant that Bathurst, its adjoining peninsula of Kombo St. Mary's and a few other pinpoints where British contact has been long-standing and intense have been dubbed a colony and permitted to rule themselves under English law while the rest of Gambia, called the protectorate, has been administered through thirty-five chiefs, a set-up which has succeeded admirably in emphasizing the personal, political and economic cleavage between the detribalized Akus of the colony and their tribal brethren of the interior. As in Sierra Leone and Liberia, this rivalry has become the basic political fact of life in a country too small and poor to afford disunity.

CRICKET AND COCKTAILS

Bathurst today reflects all Gambia's problems and prospects, its charm and pettiness. This river town of 20,000 people was at a fever pitch (or as high a pitch as can be managed by a sleepy Victorian village) as we lurched over the bridge which joins the island to Kombo St. Mary's. White officials in smartly cut white shorts, open-necked shirts and knee-socks, Akus clad in rumpled tweed suits and sun-helmets, billowing Wollof women, long-striding Moors and effeminate-looking Mandingoes in flowing white robes were streaming towards the centre of the town. Only a few swarthy Lebanese traders in slacks and sports shirts stood languidly against the doors of their cavernous shops. Thinking there might be a fire, a riot or a political meeting—all popular outdoor sports in Africa—we followed the crowd.

In the middle of 'downtown' Bathurst was a vast meadow (its name is MacCarthy Square) around which the crowd was thronged. In the dancing heat I could see young men, both white and black, dressed in white flannels and wearing the little skullcaps one is forced to don in the early forms of private school, cavorting around the green.

'What's going on?' I asked a portly Negro wearing an overcoat despite the ninety-degree heat. 'Why, sar,' he said, 'this be Gambia–Sierra Leone test match. Cricket, you know.' Just then a young African wearing a bat-wing collar and the black cloth coat of a clerk exclaimed, 'Well caught! Well caught, indeed, Gambia!' The crowd gave vent to a round of restrained applause. The match lasted for five days, during which little business was transacted in Bathurst.

The wild excitement afforded by the occasional inter-territorial cricket match and the monthly arrival of a small steamer bound for England are major events, things to be clutched at and savoured until they are gone. This isolation does odd things to people. It makes them cordial yet backbiting, voluble yet prone to lose a thought and break off in mid-sentence to stare out of the window. It makes them cluster around the bar of the Atlantic Hotel—Bathurst had no hotel five years ago and the recent introduction of jets to the England–Africa service threatens to make this one as obsolete as a coach house after the introduction of the motor-car since Bathurst is no longer needed for refuelling—not so much to drink excessively (most British administrators of the new stamp have neither the money nor the inclination for this) as for company. 'The silence of the Gambia,' said one old-stager, 'is the terrible thing, old man. You come to the bar to lock out the silence.'

It was the opinion of Sir Richard Burton, who visited Gambia in 1863, that the site of Bathurst had been selected 'for proximity to mud, mangrove, miasma and malaria'. Although much of the white population lives twelve miles away in Fujara to escape these four inconveniences, this unflattering description is not completely true today. In the main, Bathurst has the slightly down-at-the-heels, sleepy charm of many small towns of the Southern States. Decaying wharves, their piles covered with clusters of oyster (which you eat at your mortal peril) reach out into the oily waters of the river, the paint peels from the walls of one-storey general merchandise stores and green lawns stretch away to bungalows raised on stilts against the flooding which Bathurst suffers at the end of each rainy season. Native homes are built by erecting a frame of rhun palm around which are fastened plaited bamboo strips called 'krinting'; this is covered with 'lasso', a local lime made from burnt and pulverized oyster shells, on goes a roof of corrugated iron and there you have your house.

The centre of the town is the playing field of MacCarthy Square, fringed with yellow-blossoming casuarina trees. At one end of this is the small brown church of St. Mary of Kombo with its flower-beds of honest English petunias, pinks, hollyhocks and daisies and its plaques in memory of innumerable young subalterns and midshipmen who lost their lives in the storming of a native stockade or expired 'from the miasma'. Nearby is the multi-racial and dilapidated Reform Club, faithfully attended by elderly and correct Akus who seem to have stepped out of the Victorian Age. Oddly enough, the pidgin spoken by the Akus has more of a nautical Georgian ring: an implement for cutting the grass is a 'cutlass', if you are perplexed or annoyed you are 'humbugged', and a small ship is a 'cutter'.

There are no public cinemas and few other forms of amusement in Bathurst so funerals are quite popular. The dead are deposited in an ancient graveyard in a palm grove facing the ocean. It is a pleasant spot and the hordes of people who attend funerals do not necessarily indicate any intimacy between the supporting cast and the character playing the title role. It is nice just to squiggle your bare toes in the sand, listen to the singing and watch the slow rollers breaking on the beach.

Although this is more the result of Gambia's unpromising economic position than of any large-scale demand for headstones, Bathurst's population, in strong contrast to almost all other African cities, declined more than 5 per cent between 1944 and 1951. Half of Bathurst's 20,000 people are Wollofs although the Mandingoes, with 105,000 people, are by far the largest tribe in the country. Since the town has no industries, the municipal council is hard put to find revenue. Its only direct tax, an impost on all palm wine which enters the town (of which there is a gratifying sufficiency), provides most of its revenue.

Bathurst weather is fine for two or three months of the year, hot and unpleasant for five months and ghastly during September and October, a time of sultry humidity when the air is laden with the odour of rotting vegetation and the sun beats down in sullen frenzy. Brief and sometimes vicious tornadoes often buffet the town and, in 1957, the ferry to the north shore capsized in midstream with the loss of fifty-two lives. This wheezing, one-car vessel is a World War II landing craft which, when working at top efficiency, can take five cars across the river in a day. You drive off at the Bathurst side through the surf and on to the beach. It is considered bad form to bellow 'Gung Ho!' when the ramp drops into the waves.

The physical remoteness and economic poverty of the colony have combined to give Gambia a reputation for racial liberality which it seldom deserves. It is too poor to afford many white officials (there are about 200) so many Africans hold top posts in the government and the white population is thus too small to be completely exclusive. Yet, although everyone knows everybody else, only a few blacks attend each social function.

At one such cocktail party at Fujara, the suburb facing the ocean outside Bathurst, we met a pleasant young African woman who is Gambia's first woman college graduate. We talked innocuously enough of local politics and the lady said that she hoped that some day Gambia would federate with Senegal, since the colony was too poor to support itself and the people of both regions have much in common. The race question never arose. When she left, our hostess asked me what I thought of her and I said I had found her to be attractive. 'She is *most* anti-white,' hissed the lady as she poured me a drink, 'but then you are an American and perhaps you didn't notice.'

In the mornings the wives of the administrators gather for coffee in Fujara or in the lounge of the Atlantic to dissect their friends of both races, an unendearing spectacle which leads one to wonder if the history of Africa might have been different if white women had been banned from the colonies. Certainly race relations were better in the days before the women came out. And yet many women have done a great deal of good in Africa.

'You see that woman,' said an administrator, indicating a lady in the middle of a description of her houseboy's latest *faux pas*. 'When her husband was a commissioner in the interior she was the only white woman for miles around. She went on trek with him, helped to organize clinics and adult education courses, took a real interest in the people. Here in Bathurst her only amusement is character assassination. There are other people to do the necessary jobs and the women are thrown back on each other. Soon they go sour.'

Indeed, there is little enough in Bathurst to occupy one who doesn't have a job to do or an interest in reading. There is one store in which to shop, a little swimming for the intrepid (sharks are not unknown), and the weekly film shown by the Bathurst Film Society at the Atlantic, to which all flocked dressed as if for an opera. The wonder is that there are no more drunks among the men and shrews among the women. It is a long-standing joke that peripatetic government V.I.P.s from Britain tour Nigeria for a month, allow a week for Ghana, spend the night in Sierra Leone . . . and have lunch in Gambia.

THE SAXON WEST

After a week of talk and cocktail parties—the visitor to Bathurst is not so much entertained as put on display—we were glad enough to elbow our way through the clamorous crowd pushing its way aboard the *Lady Wright*, the 540-ton 'groundnutter' which, along with her sister ship, the *Fulladu*, once a week lugs freight and passengers up to Basse. Beyond this town, which is 250 miles from the sea, vessels with a six-foot draught can go another fifty miles to Koina, on the Senegalese border.

This 1,100-mile-long river is only 175 yards wide at the eastern end of Gambia but as it approaches the sea it widens to a twenty-seven-mile funnel. The Gambia rises, like the Niger, in Guinea, and so light is its flow in the dry season that salt water backs up into the river for 100 miles. It is the longest deep-water indentation in the Guinea Coast. The source or meaning of its name—which has been written Gambra, Gambo, Gamboa and Gambea—is unknown. There are few islands in the river and those that exist are tidal affairs with names like Dog, Deer, Seahorse, Baboon, Elephant and Crab Island.

There was no gangway and, since the tide was running, *Lady Wright* tugged against her moorings leaving a gap of about three feet between the dock and her deck. Fat Wollof mammies hurdled over this chasm with a scream, colliding with those already jamming the deck and endangering those trying to leave the ship. Goats bleated, chickens clucked and the smell of sweat, excitement and rancid butter mingled with that of diesel fuel and cooking rice. The apple greens, electric blues, royal purples and burnished golds of the women's clothes made them look like bulky birds of paradise flitting about a nest of ants.

The ten-year-old riverboat heeled sharply to port as boxes of WHO dried milk, bedsteads, drums of kerosene, foot-lockers, sacks of flour, cases of Dutch beer in quart bottles, chicken coops, crates of whisky, baskets, motor-cycles, tables, two ploughs and a refrigerator were piled upon her martyred forecastle by sweating black stevedores naked save for loin cloths and the ubiquitous stocking cap of Norwegian wool, just the thing to keep off a chill. On top of this clambered deck passengers: Mandingo women wrapped in the rainbow-hued cloths called *pagnes*, Serahulis from up-river wearing diadems and bracelets of silver called *manillas* (once a form of currency in West Africa) and silk cloaks of extravagant colour, Jolas, the moneylenders of Gambia (despite Islam's prohibition of usury), going up-river to dun a debtor, Akus wearing panama hats and soiled cotton suits, barely able to conceal their distaste for the whole business of being among such uncivilized people, one or two aloof Mauritanians (in Gambia called Narrs), starting their long journey back to the desert after selling a herd of scrawny cattle in the Bathurst market, sailors in old-fashioned uniform caps and blue denim shorts, and minor officials too poor to rent a place in the crew's quarters but affluent enough to slip cookie a shilling for the right to brew a spicy stew on his galley stove.

A family of Syrians, the men sharp and alert, the women swathed in black and looking dumpy and pale, scrambled aboard and were followed by the Catholic bishop wearing a dirty white cassock, socks and a sash of purple. Finally a Land-Rover pulled up and out clambered a young police officer complete with sunburned knees, pipe and swagger cane. The bulky black captain, resplendent in white uniform and hat, leaned over the bridge and shouted something to one of the deckhands. He cast off the bow line as *Lady Wright*'s whistle blew a strident note which tore from the crowd a noise midway between a cheer and a moan. Half the people who had come aboard now fought to get back ashore and, in the process, a chicken fell overboard, submerged for a moment, then popped to the surface and slowly floated away in an upright position like a slightly bedraggled duck. An African stripped off his shirt and shorts and stepped up on to the rail; a sailor made a grab for an ankle but he dived overboard, retrieved the chicken, and climbed back up a line with the bird's legs held firmly between his teeth, its wings flapping feebly. The captain swore, a *griot* sang a song of praise from the dock, the whistle hooted again, and more portly Wollofs and slender Mandingoes tumbled across the widening gap from the ship to the dock. *Lady Wright's* engines turned over, the stern line was cast off, and slowly she edged out into the river, still heeling to port from her uneven load. The space between ship and shore grew greater and soon the shouted words of the people waving from the dock could no longer be heard and Bathurst's long, low line of waterfront buildings melted into the sand. And then the sun sank, staining the river scarlet, and the town was covered with mist and finally disappeared as *Lady Wright* set her course up-stream through the pressing hands of the mangrove swamps.

We stowed our kit under the lower bunk of the nine-by-three-foot cabin and went up to the small deck forward of the passengers' lounge where a *seyfu* (chief) in a peach-coloured gown and red fez was taking his ease in a deck chair behind which stood a squire holding the silver-headed staff of chiefly office and a *griot* plucking the horse-hair strings of a *susa* as he 'told the names' of the mighty man's ancestors and exalted the wisdom and bravery of his chief. The moon was climbing slowly and unrolling a carpet of silver across the quiet waters of the Gambia.

Aboard, in addition to the *seyfolu* and their women, were a trio of African clerks, an old white-thatched Syrian trader accompanied by his wife, their young son and pudgy daughter, the Catholic bishop and another cleric, a public works engineer, the policeman and one of the four up-river administrators.

The steward, a bullet-headed black who doffed his uniform in favour of a pair of white shorts and an undershirt as soon as we cleared Bathurst, had his own system of segregation with which one failed to comply at one's own peril. The clerics and the commissioner were assigned to a small table near the passageway where the breeze was good. The police officer and the public works engineer were given the next best table, which had five places. We were a puzzlement because we were not British and had no official status. The steward scratched his head for a moment and told us to sit with the elderly Syrian at the table with the policeman and the engineer. The rest of the Syrian's family and the *seyfolu* (plural of *seyfu*) were assigned to the third table. Although there were two extra places there, the three African clerks were told to eat later with the *seyfolu's* women. One clerk started to say something and then thought better of it. At the end of the first day's run, the commissioner disembarked, the police officer moved over to the bishop's table, the Syrian's son joined us. By the time we reached Basse three days later, the engineer was dining with the clerics, the Syrian's wife was with us, and the three African clerks had made it to the *seyfolu's* table.

For the first two days there is nothing to see because the banks are low and the mangroves cover them and stretch out their roots over the water like gnarled fingers, moving imperceptibly in on the river year by year, being torn out by storm and decay, then returning again to choke the throat of the stream with their sickly grey cloak.

'My place is not far from here,' said the old Syrian. The groundnut season was finished and the people had spent what money they had and used up as much credit as the Syrian would give and now he was going up-stream to close both his stores. He would inventory his stock and then move it all to storehouses on high ground safe from the floods and then go back to Bathurst to spend the next few months with his family. A few weeks before the groundnuts came in he would go up on the steamer again, take his goods down to the stores, clean out the mildew left by the flood waters, try to collect his debts, and sell what he could for cash. He and his son had moved £100,000 worth of merchandise in the past season but had been paid for only £57,000, so his profit margin must have been high to keep him in business. Goods on the shelves for more than two seasons, he added, are sold at auction and even then a small profit is possible.

'These are bad times,' he said. 'The price of groundnuts is way down and that means that the people can neither pay their debts nor buy new cloth for their wives.'

'What do you do then?' I asked.

'I eat less,' he said with a wry smile. 'Still, business is not too ba and I like the Gambia.' He had been here for thirty-six years.

'Is your home in Lebanon or in Syria?' I asked.

'It depends upon politics,' he said. 'These days it is better to be Lebanese than Syrian. So I am Lebanese.'

The mangroves thinned out and suddenly were gone and in their place were high banks of red clay and behind them the dusty savannah country, flat and brown and parched, stretching away into the distance, broken by groves of stunted trees and patches of tall grass with round tufts, called Lions' Tails. The horizon shimmered and the coarse grass, which in the early time of the rains is covered by a crimson carpet of puffs called Fireballs, drooped in the windless air. There was a small rise of ground near the river.

'That,' said the engineer, a fair-headed young man burned to the shade of a boiled lobster, 'is Arse Hill.'

'An unusual name,' I commented. He added that it was customary in the old days for white and black to expose their bottoms in the direction of the hill whenever they passed this point in the river. Otherwise, the natives said, one would surely die. We omitted this ceremony and suffered no ill effects.

Baboons could be seen scrambling on the banks of the river and sitting in lines in the branches of the trees: big dog-faced grandfathers, surly young bucks, and mothers with their infants clinging to their belly fur.

Twenty miles above MacCarthy Island on a small, flat-topped hill (there are no hills in Gambia higher than 300 feet) known as Monkey Court, baboons gather regular as clockwork every Friday for what purpose one is not advised. All the natives know is that they have been coming for years to this particular place.

As *Lady Wright* veered inshore to follow the winding channel, the bull baboons barked and shooed their females and the young off into the bush, after which they beat a leisurely and dignified retreat. In one recent season baboons ate a quarter of the food crop and now they are hunted mercilessly. There is a bounty of two shillings on a baboon tail and 30,000 are killed every year. The baboon plague, many people say, is the result of shooting the leopards, who prefer baboon over all other meat. One wonders what new curse will arise from the natural imbalance caused by the elimination of the baboons. Meanwhile, the bounty stimulates the creativeness of the Africans who split the tails in an attempt to gain a double award.

On one cool alabaster dawn, a hippo rose snorting from the depths of the river to protest at *Lady Wright*'s intrusion upon his privacy and crocodiles scuttled from a sandbank into the water with a splash. But most of the game is gone from Gambia although the river is still a bird-watcher's paradise. From the marshy creeks flutter herons, snowy chicken-breasted egrets, spur-wing geese, brown doves, scarlet cardinals and electric-blue kingfishers, scolding jays, swallows, swifts and storks, pompous pelicans and plump teal, orioles, pigeons and scavenging fish-eagles, gulls, terns and flamingoes. Among the acacias, silk-cottonwoods and baobabs scuttle guinea-fowl.

At Kuntaur you are 150 miles from Bathurst, the last stop for nineteen-foot-draught ocean-going vessels. Kuntaur handles much of Gambia's groundnut crop, hence its wharf is more substantial than the flimsy affairs at other river towns. Although there are supposed to be thirty-three 'wharf towns', at some there is no landing-stage: we stopped after dark in midstream at one of these and *Lady Wright*'s whistle gave one impatient toot. Slowly out of a small creek came a large rowing boat, nothing showing at first but its stern lantern glowing in the distance like a large firefly. After a while the voices of the Africans in the boat could be heard floating over the water, soft and melodic, and then you could see the boatman standing in the stern sculling. As she came alongside, *Lady Wright*'s bridge searchlight pinned her against the inky water and her laughing passengers reached out to the strong arms extended to them and swung aboard. A few chickens, a packet of mail (the ship has its own post office and mark, and is the only mail service to the interior), a protesting goat and several bicycles were loaded aboard in the same fashion and *Lady Wright*, with a blast on her whistle, left the boatman and his sputtering lantern lonely on the river.

The 'wharf towns' are bustling places during the groundnut season which lasts from October to April. Groundnut cutters built and rigged in a fashion copied from the Portuguese caravels which navigated the river three centuries ago bring dusty burlap sacks of nuts and farmers eager for the news into the centres where white rags float above the huts capable of receiving lodgers. To pass away the time until the buying agents arrive, the men hike themselves on to the *bantaba*, a platform of woven mats raised a couple of feet above the ground and shaded by a thatched roof or an ancient fig. There they tell stories, gossip, chew kola nuts imported from Sierra Leone and play a sort of African draughts with a board of wood or clay shaped like a muffin tin.

Each 'wharf town' has its individual personality and its own speciality, which is spread out on the river banks for the perusal of *Lady Wright*'s passengers: one village sells double-spouted pottery jugs, another features camp chairs of split bamboo, a third peddles krinting prayer rugs while, at a fourth, you are tempted by native toffee, the purchase price of which includes the bowl in which the stuff is made.

As we passed Georgetown, a pleasant little place with a building of stone which looked like a Norman church and turned out to be a warehouse, the Catholic bishop told us of the Druid-like stone circles which are found near MacCarthy Island. There are thirty-four concentric circles in all, the megaliths ranging in height from a few inches to ten feet. This Gambian Stonehenge stands in a grove of huge old trees and the local people know nothing of the origin of the circles, although they shun them. Skeletons have been found among the stones which are definitely of the pre-Islamic era and there are some who say that the stones were erected by the Carthaginian voyagers who are believed to have navigated the Gambia long before Christ.

But this is speculation; nobody knows who erected the stones, when they did it, or for what purpose. They are just there. Africa has been called a continent without history; it has a vast history but it also has the capacity for swallowing men and the works of men, digesting them and leaving those puzzled individuals who come later only a large question-mark. One wonders if, 2,000 years from now, there will be much to recall the brief moment of the white man upon these shores.

This is brought home again a few miles above Georgetown when *Lady Wright* passes close inshore to give the passengers a view of the memorial to Mungo Park, the Scottish surgeon who 'discovered' the

Niger in the sense that he reached the river and determined that it flowed not west but east, a fact which generations of geographers had been unwilling to accept. Park embarked on both his journeys from what was once the busy trading centre of Pisania, which boasted an English population of three in 1795 when Park stayed there. Today nothing remains of Pisania but the modest obelisk in memory of Park, who trudged off into history from here. Even now the bush has overgrown the monument and hippos browsing in the moonlight find it convenient to scratch their leathery hides against it.

Basse is the last port of call and beyond here only boats with shallow draught can go, and these push on as far as Barrakunda Falls in Senegalese territory. Like most Gambia River towns, Basse is two settlements in one, containing a low-water quarter and a high-water area on a slight rise a thousand yards from the river. This gives the settlement a ghost-town appearance because no more than half the buildings are occupied at any one time; the rest are shuttered and barred and the total effect is depressing.

The river rises as much as thirty feet and during flood time villagers often pole their canoes down the main streets of the low-water town to angle for the fish which lurk under the eaves of the buildings. Concrete structures seem to survive the annual inundation fairly well and, if a mud house collapses, it is easily rebuilt.

In the Basse market one can sometimes buy native musical instruments: *koras*, heavily-strung calabashes, the fiddle-like *susa*, the calabash xylophone called *balafo* and *kossi neio*, crude castanets played by the women. And it is the women who dominate the market, sharp-tongued wenches who haggle with their customers and unleash a stream of invective at their competitors. In the old days, Gambian women were kept in line by a 'devil' with the nice name of Mumbo Jumbo. From time to time Mumbo Jumbo, clad in leaves, appeared among them and whaled the daylights out of shrewish maidens and erring wives, to the particular amusement of those guilty ones who had escaped apprehension. This salutary custom, one regrets to report, has gone by the board.

Basse boasts both a Catholic girls' school and a resident district commissioner who, like his three colleagues, is furnished with a launch as well as a car, since much of his 'safariing' has to be done when parts of his district are several feet under water. It also has one of the few trans-Gambia ferries, there being no bridge across the river from its source to its mouth.

As soon as *Lady Wright* was well secured, the black wooden boxes covered with heavy official seals (the government payroll for several months) debarked and the goats, chickens, passengers, dried milk, ploughs and other impedimenta disgorged, the captain, who must have had a girl in each of the 'wharf towns', had his motor-cycle unloaded and disappeared into the night. All hands reappeared the next morning looking properly the worse for wear after their 'shore leave' and *Lady Wright* took on her freight and passengers, hooted imperiously, and loafed downstream with a following current past a solitary canoeist who looked up once, as his great-great-grandfather may have done at Mungo Park from the same dug-out, spat expressively and manœuvred his craft into a slow-flowing creek.

GROUNDNUTS . . . PERIOD

'That,' said George Peters, pointing to several crates of dust-covered dishes, glassware and kitchen utensils which littered his Bathurst office, 'represents Gambia's most recent failure in its struggle for solvency. I got the lot for five quid.'

Peters, a burly seventeen-year veteran of the territory, was accurately if over-dramatically pointing out that Gambia cannot hope for economic (or political) independence until she can find some source of revenue to augment her annual budget of £1·4 million, now wholly dependent upon the world's enthusiasm for groundnuts.

The crates whose contents Peters had purchased were the abandoned property of a bright hope, the Imperial Chemical Industries' ilmenite mining scheme. In 1953 prospectors found the mineral, which is related to titanium, in sufficient quantity to induce I.C.I., a major league firm, to obtain a concession. Mining operations began on the coast near Cape St. Mary in 1956 and by 1959 50,000 tons had been extracted. But the lode proved less extensive than had been believed and the costs of working with untrained local labour under poor conditions proved too high: I.C.I. closed down last year, wrote off an investment of £1 million and threw 650 Gambians (10 per cent of the country's salaried labour force) out of work. A ketchup factory also folded.

This is not the first time (nor possibly the last: oil prospecting is under way) that Gambia's high hopes have been dashed. A few years ago the Colonial Development Corporation, a semi-autonomous government organization, came to the conclusion that it would be a fine thing for Gambia to have a poultry industry which, its experts said, would sell

20 million eggs and a million dressed chickens to the English market every year. At a cost of nearly £1 million, C.D.C. built row upon row of concrete block asbestos-roofed hen-houses near Bathurst's airport (which bears the engaging name of Yundum), importing more than 300,000 fat hens. Chicken feed had to be imported when local feeding schemes collapsed, the refrigeration plant went on the blink, less than 39,000 eggs were produced in two years and all but ninety of the hens died of Newcastle's disease. The money was not completely wasted: the hen-houses, cleared of their perches, now serve as the dormitories of the country's one teacher training high school. 'A diploma from that school,' quipped one Bathurst wag, 'is something to crow about.'

The C.D.C. next turned its talents to the extraction of shark oil. Spurning a pilot scheme and taking little note of local conditions (how American it all sounds!), it proudly launched a factory ship called the *African Queen*, imported a large staff of experts and built shore installations to the tune of £500,000. The sharks were unco-operative and this money also went down the drain.

Bloody but unbowed, the C.D.C. embarked upon a project for growing rice under heavily mechanized conditions which, British taxpayers were assured, would put 23,000 acres under cultivation. Like its two predecessors, the Wallikunda rice scheme was a flop. It cost £800,000 to farm 200 acres which produced half a ton of rice to the acre, about what a native can do with a hand hoe. The scheme was abandoned as impractical, a real understatement since even if it had succeeded peasant farmers working with their usual tools could not have employed the lessons demonstrated.

It is easy to fault the C.D.C. but there are factors which make Africa the most unpredictable continent in the world on which to work. In most cases, the statistical material necessary to any large-scale operation simply is not available. Costs can only be estimated roughly and time schedules are meaningless. African labour, which is said to be cheap, is in reality among the most expensive because it is not dependable and is capable of wreaking real havoc on expensive machinery which must be imported from long distances. (Paraphrasing Winston Churchill, businessmen say of Africans: 'Give us the job and we will finish the tools.') If a top-drawer firm like I.C.I. can pull a boner, there is no reason why C.D.C. should be immune. There are two important differences, however: C.D.C. is working with public funds and its consistency in failure has been marked.

Nor has C.D.C. retired from the arena. At the bar of the Atlantic Hotel we encountered a young Scot brooding over a pink gin. With some reluctance he admitted that he was a C.D.C. man engaged in making a survey of the country to assess Gambia's economic prospects. The conversation, after touching lightly on the treacherous role played by the United States in the Suez adventure, inevitably got around to the subject of Gambia's poverty and the C.D.C.

'Speak not to me of hen's eggs,' intoned our new-found friend, 'neither offend my ears by chatter of rice and sharks. But you have an honest if uninspiring face and I will tell you a secret: Gambia may well become a notable producer of limes. Those, for your information, are the source of a juice which, when mixed with gin and water in sufficient quantities, produces that sense of blessed forgetfulness so sought after by those who have been engaged in previous C.D.C. ventures in this benighted country.'

Leaving our Scot muttering wildly about the beneficial properties of the lime, I called on an official in the Agriculture Department, a young and harassed gentleman who seemed to regret the day he abandoned his green Yorkshire acres.

'Certainly limes will grow here,' he admitted. 'So will melons, beans and papayas. Only last month I sent some of our experimental papayas to Amsterdam and they said they could use several tons a year at better than a guilder for each fruit.'

'In that case,' I inquired, 'why do you not litter the landscape with papayas?'

'There are three reasons,' he answered. 'First, we have a devil of a time getting shipping to call here on a regular basis. Second, we can't cultivate on an economic plantation basis because white settlement isn't allowed and the Africans are not keen on co-ops. And third, the Gambians don't want to grow papayas. They are a very conservative people. They have been growing groundnuts for years and making money out of it. It is an easy crop to cultivate and they see no reason to change. Each year Gambia ships to a grateful world 65,000 tons of nuts. The problem is that the price paid to the grower, which is subsidized above the world market level, has dropped over the last decade from £35 a ton to less than half of that. There is only about £175,000 left in the price stabilization fund and, when that is gone, the screams which you will hear from the interior will be those of my buying agents being run through the decorticating machines by an outraged yeomanry.'

'What's the solution?' I asked, as my agriculturalist gloomily poked at his pipe with a matchstick.

'Our salvation lies in two directions. All would be jolly if an ice-cap would descend on Western Europe, permanently wiping out cultivation of that despicable crop, the olive. You Americans tend to look upon these primarily as vehicles for what I believe you term martinis. It may not have occurred to you that the oil of the olive and of the groundnut, when completely refined, are identical both in colour and in taste, more accurately in lack of taste. When cold weather ruins the Spanish and Italian olive crops, our groundnut oil is featured both in the barber shops and in the salad dressings of those countries. When Latin skies are sunny, we must rely upon the greed of baseball fans and zoo animals and the enthusiasm of young Saxons for that disgusting spread known as peanut butter.'

'That eventuality seems remote. What is your other hope?' I asked.

'Increased production: prices go down, we produce more, the farmer gets the same amount of money, no decorticated agents. Simple, isn't it? Simple except for the fact that we can't get our Mandingo, Fulah, Wollof, Serahuli and Jola friends to take the necessary steps to increase production. Our research people have come up with a simple and inexpensive fertilizer which could more than double yields. We know because we've got 1,700 pounds of peanuts off an acre next to a farm where a native is getting 700 pounds. We're importing the fertilizer but the Syrians, who know their business, refuse to handle it because they say the Africans won't buy. We're going to distribute it ourselves through the department but I must confess that I have my doubts. The Africans will catch on in time, of course. Trouble is that with falling prices, decreasing funds available for stabilization and increasing erosion, time is getting short.'

Gambia's poverty limits the quantity and the quality of its social programmes. Take education:

On the primary level Gambia has 47 schools attended by 6,465 students, less than a third of whom are girls (although Islam was not entrenched solidly in Gambia until the eighteenth century, there has been sufficient time to crystallize opposition to female education). There are five high schools with 674 students, of whom 219 are girls, and two vocational schools with a total enrolment of 45. Despite the fact that 195 of Gambia's 266 teachers have less than a high school education, there is only one teacher-training high school with an enrolment of 73 pupils. Of the four territories of British West Africa, Gambia is the only one which lacks a university, although ninety-one Gambians are studying abroad, a third of them on government scholarships. Despite the fact that more than 90 per cent of the population lives in the protectorate, two-thirds of all students are colony children. In part this may be traced to Mohammedan opposition to education and to the general conservatism of the peasant class; but the fact remains that many Gambians are too poor to pay the one shilling monthly tuition at government schools or the ten shillings charged by mission institutions. Although expenditure on education has doubled during the past seven years (as have allocations to agriculture, police, prisons and public works), Gambia's revenue is so minute that she can afford to appropriate only 9 per cent of her slender budget to education at a time when 90 per cent of the school-age population gets little or no schooling. As a result, there are only about 10,000 literate people in the entire country. The real battle in Africa is the struggle to strengthen the economy enough to give the mass of the people the education and social services necessary to make independence something more than a tragic chimera.

But if Gambia has been unable to come up with an alternate source of revenue, important gains have been made in the growing of food crops. From the beginning of time until as recently as five years ago, Gambians suffered through an annual 'hungry season' from June to October when the previous year's rice crop was eaten and the groundnut money spent. At a time when energy was required for the planting of new crops, most people were lucky if they had one meal a day (Gambian food is largely a matter of cornmeal porridges and rice stews highly seasoned with pepper and onions and guaranteed to explode your eyeballs). Fatalities were not unknown and the bulk of the population lived a third of their lives in a state of semi-starvation.

After the costly 1953 C.D.C. mechanized rice-growing flop, Gambia's Agriculture Department picked up the pieces and instituted a programme of swamp rice growing. The successful cultivation of swamp rice brought three advantages: it relieved pressure on the erosion-seamed hills where highland rice was grown, made a food crop available during the 'hungry season' and, since swamp rice yields (1,000 to 1,400 pounds per acre) are twice as great as highland rice, increased the tonnage of food available.

Some gains were registered through mechanized cultivation of mangrove swamps by government tractors. But even more was achieved by the simple expedient of constructing access causeways into the swamps which made it possible for the people to cultivate them in the traditional fashion. In one of the few really brainy moves we saw in Africa, the Agriculture Department induced a British firm to manufacture improved versions of the four traditional tools used by Africans in the cultivation of rice. These cost only 6d. each more than the less efficient native implements and they last twice as long. No expensive machinery, no complicated plans, no maintenance problem. Just a better type of tool with which the African is familiar and is willing to use, good enough to increase production sufficiently to make the difference between a full belly and four months of hunger each year, something to put him to thinking about other ways of increasing his yields. This is the sort of simple horse-sense which too frequently escapes the experts.

What Africa needs to achieve stability is a gradual rise in income and living standards of the entire population. Extensive and heavily-mechanized schemes can, with proper planning, be made to work. But they can deal with only a minute section of the continent and touch the lives of only a small fraction of the people. What is needed in all fields—agriculture, health, education, housing, industry and commerce—is not so much the introduction of modern tools and methods as improvement of existing native implements and methods. An African emerging from the Stone Age cannot be expected to comprehend the intricacies of a combine. But he can and will recognize a better hoe when he sees one in use. Only by grafting simple technology to a frame of reference which can be understood can any appreciable and lasting gains be made.

As a result of limited use of machinery under strict supervision, the construction of access causeways and bunds, and the introduction of improved native implements, Gambian rice acreage has doubled since 1946 and yields have shown a substantial increase. Rice imports have fallen to less than 6,000 tons per year.

The 'hungry season' is now a thing of the past. The women, who once worked only in the highland rice fields while the men handled the groundnuts, can now give their husbands a hand with the cash crop. This obviates the need for the 10,000 'strange farmers', Senegalese share-croppers, who moved into Gambia every year to help with the groundnuts. These migrant labourers, although they performed an important service, not only consumed part of the badly-needed food crop but deprived Gambian cultivators of a share of the groundnut profits. If the Agriculture Department can now convince the Gambian farmer—and this will be far from easy—that he should give his wives a hand with the swamp rice, a better life is possible for the people of the river-state.

This will make Gambia a more contented colony but it will not, of course, do anything towards solving the problem of bringing in the additional revenues required if the country is to make political and social progress. Can tax revenues be increased? Not appreciably, says V. E. Davies, Gambia's rotund Financial Secretary:

'We can't impose high taxes on luxury items such as cigarettes and liquor because it's too easy to smuggle the stuff in from French territory and we'd lose what revenue we do accrue from this source. There is no industry to tax so all that's left is the poor old groundnut-grower. He is already paying a 20 per cent export impost, a yard (capitation) tax and duties on the imports he buys if he has any money left after that. Tax revenues already amount to 25 per cent of our gross national product. Yet our reserves are falling and we can only meet current expenses in a good year. In a way I dread the £1·4 million we are liable to get for development purposes over the next five years from the Colonial Development and Welfare Act. [Actually allocated: £1 million over the next three years to improve communications and the development of crops.] That means more schools and hospitals which are fine in themselves, of course. But where am I going to get the money to pay for the books, drugs, teachers and doctors to put into them? A country with an annual *per capita* income of £18 just cannot afford the maintenance costs of an extensive social programme. This is a job which should be Africanized: it would give the local politicians something to think about.'

Over the past fifteen years, Gambia has received £2·3 million in grants for development, a paltry sum but possibly the largest amount which the country is capable of absorbing. Uncertainty as to Gambia's political future coupled with the failures of two private and three government schemes has inhibited private investment (50 per cent of all salaried employees in Gambia are civil servants). Development loans in the commercial money market are out of the question because Gambia cannot afford to pay the interest. As the result of a seventeen-year adverse balance of trade, Gambia is getting deeper and deeper into a hole from which she cannot hope to climb until she varies her economy, and this she cannot do because funds are limited, her people backward.

Gambia in 1957 exported 49,000 tons of groundnuts worth £3·7 million and 1,112 tons of palm kernels, hides and beeswax worth £77,000; her imports in the same year cost £4·8 million, leaving her with a sizable deficit (Britain is by far Gambia's most important customer and supplier). Gambia exported a record 61,000 tons of groundnuts in 1958 but declining prices reduced the crop's value to £3·5 million. As a result, in 1959, when the Gambia Oil Seeds Purchasing Board was paying £18 a ton for groundnuts, the heavily subsidized French price was £32 and the shuffling noise heard the length of the river was the sound of Gambian farmers loping across the border to market as much of their crop as possible through their Senegalese cousins. Thus 1959 groundnut exports were worth only £2·3 million. Consequently it is almost impossible to make economic plans based on expected groundnut production when annual figures waver from 40,000 to 75,000 tons. And so it goes.

There have been a few isolated encouraging signs. Item: savings deposits have risen from a miniscule £5,000 before World War II to £300,000 today. But the Gambian government is not optimistic and it believes that 'during the next few years the provision of *essential* services is likely to be a most difficult problem'.

Unless oil is found, this country's economic problems seem insoluble. Britain, of course, will continue to make up such deficits as occur and to provide development funds as long as Gambia remains under her wing. But who, if anybody, has the responsibility of paying Gambia's way if she becomes independent? Is nationhood the inalienable right of every former colony no matter how ridiculous its geography, small its population and limited its resources? Do two banks of a river constitute a nation in Africa any more than they do in America? Can Africa afford its Monacos and Lichtensteins? Who's going to pick up the check?

THE POLITICAL ANSWERS

Both because of her poverty and the uncertainty as to her political future, less constitutional progress has been made in Gambia than in the other three British West African territories, despite the fact that she had a Legislative Council twenty years before Sierra Leone, nineteen years before Nigeria and seven years before Ghana.

At first all members were British officials. Later unofficial (non-government) members were appointed and, in 1945, Gambian unofficial members for the first time out-numbered officials. The following year saw the election of the first unofficial member. A 1954 constitution increased the number of elective seats to fourteen and gave unofficials a majority on the Executive Council. But of the fourteen elective seats, four were allocated to the Colony, which has a population of 28,000, and only seven to the Protectorate, which has 240,000 (the other three members were elected by these eleven from names submitted by local councils in the Colony, which further weighted matters in the Colony's favour).

The governor, Sir Edmund Windley, still has the final say in most matters, can veto legislation, dismiss the Legislative Council and rule by administrative fiat. Gambia has representative but not responsible government in that there is a majority of elected African members both in the Legislative Council and in the Executive Council, the latter being an embryo cabinet. But a vote of 'no confidence' in Legco or Exco, as they are invariably termed, cannot and does not cause the fall of the government as it would in Ghana or Great Britain. For this reason, some observers have called these institutions empty debating societies. However, they serve two important functions: they keep the governor informed on local opinion (and it is highly unlikely that he would impose any measure universally opposed by the elected members) and they provide a training ground for the men who one day will have to run the government.

We lunched with Sir Edward and Lady Windley at the yellow, rambling hulk of Government House, which sits on the Marina and faces the sea behind an ancient six-gun battery. The centre part of the house was built by Grant, the founder of Bathurst, and two wings were added at a later date. It stands in a tree-shaded garden brightened by flower cuttings brought by Lady Windley from Kenya, where her husband served for twenty-six years as an administrative officer. One striking peculiarity of the house is its porthole windows, cut to suit the taste of one of its sailor occupants.

Windley, a floridly handsome man, is, like his predecessor, a small-boat enthusiast. Until the régime of the last governor, no one swam or sailed off Bathurst for fear of the sharks. When the body of a fisherman was recovered after several hours in the water with nary a nibble taken, the governor dropped his centre-board and his minions somewhat timorously have followed his lead.

Said Sir Edward: 'Our primary political problem at the moment is the realignment of power not between ourselves and the Africans—we are willing and prepared to go as soon as we can do so without causing

385

undue hardship to the country—but between the people of the Colony and those of the Protectorate. It was in the nature of things here as elsewhere in Africa that the urban areas should progress more rapidly than the interior, where the bulk of the population lives. As a result, the 10 per cent of the population which lives in Bathurst and Kombo St. Mary's has had representative government for years while administration up-river has been through the chiefs. Now the time has come for the people of the interior to take their proper place in the national picture.'

The new constitution supplanting the 1954 document resolves this power struggle between the Akus and the tribal people in favour of the latter by giving the Protectorate twenty seats in the expanded thirty-four-member Legco to the former's seven. Three members are elected by Legco itself 'in the public interest' and at least three (but not more than six) Africans have ministerial rank. There are four official members. Of the twenty members elected from the Protectorate, eight are elected by the thirty-five chiefs, who because of their prestige also have considerable say in who fills the twelve 'common seats' from up-river. The most important change in the new constitution, which came into effect in 1960, is the introduction of universal adult suffrage. In the past, direct suffrage was limited to Bathurst and Kombo St. Mary's and only those over twenty-five could vote. Under the new arrangement, urban constituencies are still over-weighted: the Colony has one legislator for every 4,000 inhabitants while the Protectorate has only one for every 12,000. Nevertheless, political control has shifted from the intellectual *élite* of Bathurst to the people and conservative chiefs of the interior.

It should be noted, however, that although a few of the *seyfolu* belong to the old chiefly families of Gambia, more have been selected by the government for their brains, integrity and—perhaps—docility. A counter-weight to their authority is exercised on the local level by the so-called Native Authorities.

Under the old system, there were as many N.A.'s as there were *seyfolu* and each chief ran his little district with slight supervision from the white commissioner and no interference from other Africans. The thirty-five chieftaincies now have been merged into six N.A.'s responsible for local roads, water supplies, markets and the construction of access causeways into the fields of swamp rice. Although the *seyfolu* take part in the administration of the new-style N.A.'s, they are a minority in a team which includes local schoolmasters, traders and other prominent Africans. The obvious next step is to make membership on the Native Authorities elective and, when this comes to be, plebeian rural leaders are bound to arise who will challenge the national authority of the chiefs.

The two most prevalent African political issues do not obtain in Gambia: there has been no white settlement (hence no land problem and little serious racial friction) and Africanization of the civil service is highly advanced with blacks directing customs, medical services, the printing office, the veterinary service, treasury, post office, surveys, prisons and a host of other departments, holding (at March 1959) 53 of 113 senior government posts. In contrast to the situation in East Africa, Indians have never been admitted and all subordinate posts are held by Gambians.

Political parties for the moment are pretty well confined to the twenty square miles which constitute the Colony. What the leaders of these parties—there are four—have to do is to attempt to spread their power to the Protectorate's 4,000 square miles and, once one of them has become supreme, decide what should or can be done with the bauble of self-determination, which will probably come within five years.

It should be said for the Gambian leaders that they seem to realize that they are playing an Alice-in-Wonderland game with a low pot-limit imposed by the economic imperatives. There are five possibilities for Gambia, none of which the British would block if the politicians, chiefs and people could reach a reasonable consensus. These are:

1. Independence.
2. Union with an independent Sierra Leone.
3. Territorial and political integration with the United Kingdom along the lines once considered for Malta.
4. Internal self-government while remaining a British dependency.
5. Federation or integration with Senegal.

I. M. Garba-Jahumpa, one of Gambia's two political leaders with cabinet rank and leader of the sectarian Gambia Muslim Congress, states that his party seeks full internal self-government as soon as possible and eventual independence within the British Commonwealth. Garba-Jahumpa, who is a portly, bespectacled Rotarian type, adds that he would like to see closer integration of economic matters and research facilities between his country and Senegal. Political integration with Senegal, he said, is possible but will have to wait 'until we are independent and able to bargain for ourselves'. He opposes any links with Sierra Leone, with which Gambia has twice been integrated, on grounds that the two countries are 'too far apart geographically and politically'.

How, I asked, could Gambia afford independence?

'We hope to get more money from the Colonial Development and Welfare Act as more British colonies become independent and hence ineligible to receive these funds. We also feel that the United Kingdom should help us after independence (Garba-Jahumpa apparently saw no inconsistency here). We want aid without strings and would oppose integration with the United Kingdom along the lines once proposed for Malta.'

Although he seemed a trifle unsure as to how all this would come about, Garba-Jahumpa stoutly maintained that his party would be the one to make the final decisions. 'We Muslims,' he said, 'constitute 97 per cent of the population of this country and we will not be ruled by Christians.' What the Minister of Agriculture failed to mention was that his party, like the other three, has no strength up-river despite the fact that the people of the Protectorate are his co-religionists.

Garba-Jahumpa's opposite number, the Honourable *and* Reverend John C. Faye, Minister of Works and Communications, would contest his colleague's claim to speak for the people of the interior. Faye (rhymes with sigh), the fifty-three-year-old leader of the Gambia Democratic Party, was a teacher until 1947 when he was ordained a deacon in the Anglican Church. This bullet-headed politician, who has high cheekbones and sports a little Hitler moustache, did missionary work up-river for seven years and was appointed to represent a portion of the interior in Legco and named to the Executive Council. Since 1951, Faye has been an elected member from Bathurst.

The deacon—his political activities have 'delayed' his ordination as a priest—wears a crucifix outside his shirt but maintains that he has the support of 60 per cent of the Muslims of the interior. 'Gambians do not mix religion with politics,' he adds. Faye, like Garba-Jahumpa, is anxious for Gambia to get internal self-government but is a little more realistic than his colleague when he admits that he does not 'see how we can become independent if the present economic situation continues'.

On the Senegambia question Faye asserts that 'we are British and will remain British, although there is no reason why there should not be economic and cultural co-operation between the two countries'.

The deacon holds that if independence could be obtained through federation with Sierra Leone, this course should be 'favourably considered'. Such a merger, he argues, would create a pool of qualified personnel for service in either country and would reduce costs. He would not consider integration with the United Kingdom or maintenance of the status quo.

The four-year-old Gambia National Party is led by an energetic thirty-eight-year-old Wollof accountant named K. W. Foon. Foon, who is a Muslim and is married to an English girl, is less concerned now with what course Gambia will take in the future than he is with the country's present constitutional structure. 'It is pointless,' he said, 'to talk about Gambia's future until every member of the Legislative Council is directly elected by universal suffrage and a system of responsible government is instituted. When the chiefs have been eliminated and we have such a situation, there will be time enough to discuss Gambia's destiny. For the moment, I would not rule out independence, association with Sierra Leone or union with Senegal. But the constitution is the important thing now.'

King Mahoney, the Roman Catholic Aku who acts as secretary-general of the Gambia United Party, takes the gloomiest view of all in regard to Gambia's future. His opinion:

'Independence is a luxury which we cannot afford. All we can hope for is internal autonomy while retaining some tie with Britain. My party distrusts the idea of federation with Sierra Leone. It has been tried unsuccessfully under the British and we have no reason to believe that African governments can make it work. What voice could our 250,000 people have against Sierra Leone's 2·2 million? Senegambia? Again, we would be out-voted and there would be the further complication of the clash between the Franco-African and Anglo-African cultures. We might favour integration with the United Kingdom but I doubt if England would consider it.'

It should be pointed out that King Mahoney's party has the strongest Christian-Aku bias of the four and that almost any solution looks bad to him because inevitably it will mean political domination by the more populous Muslim tribal groups of the interior. The power of any of these parties is suspect because the up-river peoples as yet have neither organized themselves politically under the chiefs nor made their wishes known through other means.

In this murky political situation the most electric personality in the country is a lawyer in his late forties who maintains that he is not interested in politics although he is a member both of Legco and of Exco. This is Jacob L. Mahoney, King Mahoney's brother. The two are as much alike as beer and champagne: King is placid, formal, old-fashioned and polite; Jake is abrupt, nervous, provocative and has a mind as supple as his mobile face.

Jake, who read law at the Middle Temple, is one of Gambia's seven lawyers. He worked for the Colonial Office, married an English girl, practised privately in the United Kingdom, and visited India and Ceylon before starting business in Bathurst in 1946. In his London days he was a member of the group of young Africans who are making history: Kenyatta and Mathu of Kenya, Azikiwe and Awolowo of Nigeria, Nkrumah, Busia and Appiah of Ghana.

Jake maintains that he sits in Legco and Exco only 'as a civic duty' and he has never stood for public office (he was elected to Legco indirectly by the members of that body and appointed to Exco by the governor). But his views, in contrast to those of the other leaders, are clearly defined:

'There is only one possible solution for Gambia and that is integration with Senegal. Anything else is economic and ethnic lunacy. We are Africans, not British or French, and it's time we started thinking like Africans. Independence? Only an idiot could believe that sand dunes and a river make a nation! Anyway, as Foon says, it's all hot air now. When we have universal suffrage and direct elections, my interest in politics may intensify.'

On the facts of the case, it would seem obvious that independence can be achieved only at the cost of freezing the country's social services at a ridiculously low level. Federation with Sierra Leone would have few advantages and many drawbacks: apart from the geographical and ethnic differences between the two territories, Sierra Leone has its own financial problems and could give little help to Gambia. Nor has Sierra Leone evinced much interest in such a solution. The Malta plan would seem to be a dead duck: nobody in Gambia really wants it and if the British found Malta—which is small, strategic and European in culture—too unpalatable a pill to swallow, it is unlikely that they could digest the African state. Internal autonomy and continued links to Britain make sense but, with nationalism on a rising wind throughout Africa, this solution is too conservative for any political leader to espouse. In the end, as Jake Mahoney says, union with Senegal is the only sensible course of action.

The economic and ethnic arguments for such a union are solid. The

Gambia is navigable for 300 miles into the heart of Senegal's groundnut-growing region and is that country's natural highway to the sea. With customs barriers down, trade would flow down this stream to the obvious benefit both of Bathurst and of the 'wharf towns'. An integrated road system would facilitate communications and the consolidation of government departments would effect savings which could be used to provide more and better social services. Gambia at its broadest is only twenty miles wide and there is no ethnic barrier. The same tribes speaking the same languages sprawl across the present frontiers. Even now there is so much movement across the borders both ways that every Gambian has a cousin in Senegal. The problems created by the differences between the administrative methods and the cultures of the former colonial powers are real but not insuperable.

However, there are several important groups in Gambia opposed to such a solution. British reactionaries reject the idea of merger on grounds that it is an insult to England germinated in Paris. Most Gambian politicians are hesitant because they fear that their importance would diminish if they were lumped in with more populous Senegal. Gambia's chiefs are fearful because they are well aware that the chiefs of Senegal have been reduced to a powerless position. The same mercantile interests which fought the cession of Gambia ninety years ago reject it today and for the same reason: they want to make a case for compensation rather than actually preventing the transfer. Lastly, the scheme can have no sweetness for the Akus of Bathurst. These people, already outnumbered thirty to one by the Muslim population of Gambia, are not rapturous at the thought of integration with a Muslim giant completely lacking in sympathy for the language, religion and customs which they hold so dear.

One fisherman who has not yet cast his line into these troubled waters but can be expected to do so at any moment: Ghana's Kwame Nkrumah. With Modibo Keita seeking to re-establish his Mali Federation, giant Nigeria newly independent and Guinea drawing away from the Accra-Conakry axis, Nkrumah desperately needs a dramatic move to underline his claim to Pan-African pre-eminence. It is underestimating Nkrumah's astuteness not to expect a bid from him. If by an offer of development funds from his cocoa reserves Nkrumah could induce Gambia to federate with Ghana, his chances of obtaining a similar union with Sierra Leone and English-speaking Liberia would be considerably enhanced. To allow Gambia to join Senegal would be an admission that Nkrumah, despite his fast start on the Pan-African stage, is little more than a regional leader.

Sleepy, poverty-ridden Gambia is an important psychological prize which no politician with Pan-African pretensions can afford to spurn. My money is on Senegal and Jake Mahoney.

Chapter 16

*

MOUNTAINS OF THE LION

On a muggy March morning we reached the north bank of the river with the nice name of Great Scarcies, which marks the border between Guinea and the former British dependency of Sierra Leone, a saucer-shaped nation the size of Ireland, a Gaelicly green hot-box of steamy swamps, rust-coloured hills covered with stumpy secondary growth and acned with erosion, of sweeping golden beaches. It was hot, a prickly dusty heat, and the locusts were singing in the acacias while the Great Scarcies, here a limpid rock-strewn stream, bubbled happily down towards the sea.

It had not taken long to clear customs because it was a Sunday and the Creole official was so uninterested that he did not even leave his small cinder-block office to peer through the windows of our car. 'How are things in Freetown?' I asked. He gave a wry smile and shrugged his shoulders.

'I haven't been there for some time. But trade is bad and (he glanced at the black policeman filling out our forms and lowered his voice) politics is worse. Talk to Neale-Caulker in Freetown. He'll give you a story.' I nodded although I had no idea what he was talking about.

The ferry at the Great Scarcies is one of those hand-pulled, one-car affairs and it took fifteen minutes and considerable stamping of feet and much guttural chanting for the crew of eight to pull it across the twenty yards of water from the opposite bank. I gave the crew half a pack of cigarettes and we made better time on the return trip.

The road was rough and wound through flat, burned-out bush coated with ginger-coloured dust thrown up by the lorries. The series of small villages which lined the road were made of thatch and mud and few people were in sight. In one, an African was stretched out asleep in a hammock. He didn't stir as the dust from our tyres settled on him. Ahead a thicker column of dust masked the road and we knew that we were following a lorry. I speeded up and the dust thickened and then I could see the truck, a Freetown vehicle loaded with sacks on the top of which swayed two Africans.

393

I leaned on the horn and pulled out to pass. The truck veered into the middle of the road and small stones flew up from his tyres and bounced off my radiator. I was afraid that one would puncture it. It did not occur to me to think that one might break the windshield. I honked again and motioned to the Africans riding on top of the load to tell the driver I was trying to pass. They said something to each other and laughed. Each time I pulled out the truck driver edged over to cut me off. Finally I stayed right on his tail with my hand down hard on the horn, the dust billowing in through our vents.

'He doesn't want you to pass,' said Kitty.

'Bastard.'

It went on like this for twenty minutes and then we saw why: the driver shot over the crest of a low hill, signalled that he was slowing down, and stopped at the banks of a broad river. It was the Little Scarcies and he had wanted to beat me to the ferry. I jumped out of the car and ran up to the cab of the truck. The driver was picking his teeth with the rusty point of a fisherman's knife, the kind with a cork handle which will float if you drop it overboard.

'Why didn't you let me pass?' I bellowed.

'I didn't hear you.' He gazed out over the river.

'Then your ears must be dirty. I've been honking for ten miles and those men on the back of the truck saw me.'

'I didn't hear you.'

'In that case, why did you bother to signal when you stopped here?'

He looked at me slowly. 'Don't humbug me, bo. I didn't hear you.' I started to put my hand on the handle of the cab, remembered the knife and thought better of it. I wrote down his licence plate number and told him I intended to report him to the police in Port Loko.

'Sho, bo,' he said. I walked away in a rage as the ferry edged into the muddy landing ramp, where women were pounding the washing on rocks around which swam naked children. One of the passengers from the truck, a young African clad in neat knee-socks, shorts and open-necked shirt, all coated with orange dust, came over to our car.

'He heard you, sir,' he said.

'Don't tell me.'

'Is it your first visit to Sierra Leone?'

'Yes. And my last.'

'Please don't judge my country by him. He is a UPP man.'

'He's worse than that. What is UPP?'

'The Freetown Creole party. They are very bitter about white people since 1951.'

'And you?'

'I am a civil servant and am not allowed to belong to a political party. But I am from the Protectorate. I have no palaver with white people.'

'Where are you going?'

'Port Loko.'

'We're going that way. Get your stuff and come with us. Perhaps you can get your fare back from the driver.'

The Little Scarcies is much broader than the Great Scarcies and there was a lorry on the other side which had to be unloaded before it could be got on to the ferry. Then its load had to be manhandled on to the ferry. We had plenty of time to talk with our friend, who was a student agricultural officer.

It was nice of him to talk to us because it was Ramadan and he was a Muslim, like most Protectorate people, and had had nothing to drink since dawn. We went behind the truck to take a swig from the water-bottle.

'You don't have to do that,' he said. 'I don't mind.'

'It will be over soon, won't it?'

'Yes. It will be over in a week and then it will be Eid-el-Fitri.'

'It must be hard for you to work during Ramadan.' He laughed.

'It is not so bad except for the sleepiness. We eat and drink all night, which makes it possible for us to get through the day. But then we are very tired and, towards the end of Ramadan, men who work with machinery start having accidents.' He gave another clipped chuckle. 'Fortunately, we do not have much in the way of machinery in Sierra Leone.'

Finally the ferry came and we slithered the car down the greasy bank and up the ramp. 'We have too many ferries,' said our friend. 'The government is building bridges so there are now more lorries and more accidents.'

It took a long time to get across the river because the outboard motor choked in midstream and we had to be pulled across. 'If you give them cigarettes,' whispered the Protectorate man, 'they will start the motor.' I let them sweat and gave them no cigarettes.

We dropped our passenger at Port Loko, a sleepy administrative centre of whitewashed mud buildings with roofs of corrugated iron, cloaked in the white blossoms of the lophira trees, and pounded down the road and over the Rokel River, one of the country's ten major

395

rivers and one of the few that are bridged. The country was greener now, with a few trees, and the villages were larger. The people were still asleep. We stopped at a two-room shack for a bottle of warm beer. It had a sign out in front saying, 'Piccadilly Circus Hotel, accommodation, wine and beer'.

The paved road began and we could see the mountains of the peninsula upon which Freetown sits. They were rumpled and rocky and sloped down into the sea. The traffic got thicker as we passed through the brown and lumpy villages of Waterloo and Wellington and then there was Freetown, a mass of rickety red-roofed houses crammed on to a shelf between the mountains and the great estuary of the Rokel River, an anchorage large enough to take the whole British fleet. With green hills climbing above the blue bay, Freetown looked from a distance like Hong Kong or Gibraltar. At closer range, it was more a West Indian town. The houses were of crumbling wood and the sun-baked paint was faded and peeling. Their roofs were of rust-coloured tin and the houses had gingerbread fretwork in their eaves, broken in places. Along the sides of the streets were open drainage ditches two feet wide and four feet deep jammed with refuse. When the rains come—and Freetown is pelted with fifteen feet of rain a year— the ditches turn into raging torrents which shoot down to the bay carrying with them unwary chickens, dogs and the occasional child. Now they were dry and full of garbage, faeces and the odd bloated corpse of a cat. The heat sat on the town in a thick and humid haze and the whole place stank.

Double-decker green buses, which had served their time in London or Manchester, rumbled down streets shaded by yellow-blooming cassias and under a banner stretched across the avenue which read: 'SPEED KILL YOU QUICK COURTESY OF HASSAN SULAIMAN, TEXTILES & PRODUCE.' Above the unplanned tangle of Freetown's irregularly shaped blocks rose like a symbol of British solidity the ugly, yellow bulk of Government House. This singularly unattractive building, built on the ruins of Fort Horton, is a surprisingly comfortable place with an unexpected garden, tennis court and deer park raised a couple of hundred feet above Freetown's slums to a point where the air is more rarefied and the breezes constant.

Its occupant, Sir Maurice Dorman (our first visit to Sierra Leone took place before independence), is one of the energetic new breed of British governors which spends more time poring over development plans than shooting elephants. This forty-eight-year-old Cambridge-educated civil servant, a stocky man with blue eyes and curly hair going grey at the temples, has as broad a background as any governor in the Commonwealth: before coming to Sierra Leone he served successively in Tanganyika, Malta, Palestine, London, Ghana and Trinidad. He was the first governor of Sierra Leone ever to visit Liberia, although the two countries have existed side by side for more than a century. His is the ticklish job of mediating between Creole and countryman, of maintaining order and fostering trade, of bringing Sierra Leone to the point where independence is something more than a bad joke.

Freetown was the only town in Africa in which we saw African boys flying kites. It has eight of Sierra Leone's eleven newspapers (all but one of which look as if they are printed on old rags with a toy typewriter) and it handles 1,200 ships and two million tons of freight a year. With the building of the three-ship deep-water Queen Elizabeth II quay in 1954, at a cost of more than £2·5 million, Freetown also became one of the most modern ports in Africa. But ignoring all this, lateen-rigged native ships copied from a seventeenth century Portuguese vessel still bring fresh vegetables three days a week from the Bullom shore to the Portuguese Steps to be bought by house 'boys' and carted to the Freetown suburbs of Wilberforce, Signal Hill, Murray Town, King Tom, New England and Cline Town. In this city live half of the 150,000 people who inhabit the Colony's 260 square miles of rocky peninsula.

'CONTINENTAL CUISINE'

This year Freetown can boast a spanking new seventy-two-bed hotel, 70 per cent financed by the Colonial Development Corporation and built at the foot of Tower Hill near Government House. At the time of our visit there was no hostelry which would receive Good Housekeeping's Seal of Approval and so we followed the main road past the old mosque and up the steep climb to the government rest house. Two waiters in white trousers, tennis shoes and white coats were sitting in the lounge. 'Have you any room?' I asked.

'I don't know. I'm not the manager.'

'I really didn't think you were. Where is the manager?'

'Asleep.'

'Call him, please.'

'I can't. He's asleep and the phone is out of order. Try Miss Lucy Bishop's.'

'Where's that?'

'Congo Cross.'

We picked up a young African who said he knew where Congo Cross and Miss Lucy Bishop's were. He found Congo Cross but later admitted he had never heard of the lady in question. We paid him off and stopped a young Englishman who was driving down the street with a pair of bathing trunks and a towel beside him on the front seat.

'Place to stay? Well, there's the rest house but it's usually full and invariably stuffy. The food is good at Miss Lucy's—it's that yellow stucco house with no sign right behind you—but she only has six rooms, is expensive and is full anyway. There's the City but the bedbugs there have been known to charge when wounded.' He looked doubtfully at Kitty. 'You might try the Riviera, down by the railway tracks. It's a little rough but they usually have room.'

The Riviera was in the Syrian quarter and we found it easily by following the tracks, which ran within five feet of the general merchandise shop which occupied its ground floor, a cavernous and gloomy place with a counter down the middle and everything from caviar to cotton goods stacked in the back. There was a room. The proprietor, a sandy-haired young Englishman with a scruffy goatee and one eye, helped us carry our kit across the tracks, cheerfully advised us that everything in our car would be stolen during the night and probably the car itself unless we gave his night-watchman a 'dash' (bribe), introduced us to his other half-dozen guests who, it being a muggy day, were wearing their undershorts and clutching glasses of beer, and bought us a round of drinks which later appeared on our bill.

'Welcome to Freetown,' said our host. 'Just call me "Jeff the Beard"; everybody does.' Apart from the fact that Freetown was gripped in its perennial water shortage (which meant that the toilets wouldn't flush), the presence of a diverse and belligerent insect life, the penchant of the clientele for an Aussie ballad called 'The Pub with No Beer', and the predilection of the thirsty sailors who thronged the bar for chucking their empty beer bottles out of the window and on to the roof of our car (I must say that they made a very satisfactory tinkle), we found our stay at the Riviera both pleasant and instructive. There were those who maintained that 'Jeff the Beard' should be forced to add the word 'Dark' to his brochure advertising 'continental cuisine' and some sadists even implied that he should be made to eat it. But he was a good fellow and participated enthusiastically in the brawls which inevitably followed his announcement that the bar of his 'Freetown Hilton' was closing. In the mornings he was a bit startling to behold with his glass eye as clear as a bell while its mate was red and cloudy but we liked him and we wish him well.

The heat was bad even at night and we lay naked on our sticky beds and listened to the drumming from the native quarter of town and knew that the Muslims were stuffing their stomachs with food and drinking water by the quart against the hot and waterless day to follow. The servants of the Syrians live on the flat roofs of the houses which rise around the hotel and, when the first shafts of light came across the bay and it was just getting cool enough to sleep, we could see them silhouetted against the faint light as they knelt in that most graceful of all movements and kissed the ground, then rose to face the east and chanted their prayers.

'Are you awake?' I asked.

'Of course,' Kitty said.

'It's the last day.'

'Of what? Ramadan?'

'Yes. They'll be happy tonight.'

And they were happy. As dusk fell on Eid-el-Fitri (the Feast of the Candles), the streets filled with dusky forms who cavorted in shuffling dances, beat tom-toms and sang, the whole crowd swaying to the rhythm of the beat like a hypnotized snake a block long. The crowd wove slowly along the railway tracks and up the hill. They looked a little drunk.

'Jeff the Beard' was surveying the scene from the balcony of the bar. I asked him if there was no danger from the trains.

'Ha!' he snorted. 'This is the only train in the world from which you can negotiate for a bunch of bananas while it's going at full speed. The engine couldn't catch that crowd.'

'Where are they going?' I asked.

'To the Eastern Police Station. "H.E." will be there to give prizes for the best float. I wouldn't go if I were you. These crowds can get ugly when they're stoked up on booze.'

'But they're Muslims!'

'Doesn't mean a thing. Muslim, Christian, pagan. Muslims consult a witch-doctor when they're in trouble, Christians tie Koranic amulets to the arms of their children, pagans take what suits 'em from both religions. All of 'em drink when they're happy or sad or rich or mad. Right now they're happy. But they might get mad.' I noticed the police Land Rovers blocking the side-streets, channelling the crowd up the tracks towards the Eastern Police Station. We finished our beers and followed the crowd up the stinking, dimly-lit street. The crowd got thicker and finally it was wedged into a narrow street and could no longer dance; it just swayed and the people moaned a low chant.

A Land Rover appeared and the people in the middle of the street yelled and pressed back against those behind them to make room. Children screamed and a woman fell and it was too tight to pick her up. She lay on the ground screaming as the crowd stepped on her. The Land Rover edged its way forward and we swung in behind it and followed it all the way to the police station, in front of which was a big torch-lit square packed with people. Someone helped us up on to the porch where Sir Maurice Dorman was making a speech. An interpreter was repeating what he said, first in pidgin, then in Krio, which is the language of the Creoles and is quite distinct from pidgin. Nobody could hear what he was saying.

Up one street the floats could be seen inching their way towards the square. These are called *fenals*, from the Portuguese word for 'lighthouse', and are models of ships, aeroplanes, automobiles and public buildings made of sticks and coloured paper and lit from within by candles. Built by local clubs, some are thirty feet long and take as much as three months to build. In one ship model, proudly dubbed H.M.S. *Apapa*, after the Elder Dempster steamer which serves the West Coast, Africans dressed in travesties of naval uniforms stood proudly at salute. *Apapa* got a big hand.

'What is the significance of this?' I asked Davidson Nicol, a handsome Creole physician who was acting as one of the judges.

'We don't know,' he said. 'In Bathurst the Christians make *fenals* at Christmastime. Here we do it at the end of Ramadan. Nobody knows why.'

When the time came for announcing the prizes, there was something approaching silence. No applause, except from the sponsors of the winners, greeted the announcements. The crowd was silent for a moment when it was all over and then a drum began to beat and, in one motion, the crowd surged down the street and off in another direction. I asked Nicol where they were going.

'To King Jimmy's cottonwood tree on Pademba Road near the Law Courts, where the witches hang their capes. There they will dance and sing all night. Why don't you come with us to the Cape Club where most of the rest of the town will be doing the same thing.'

The Cape Club was jammed with young Creoles doing enthusiastic tangos, Syrians with their Creole mistresses, and non-government Britons, some with their wives and others with their girl friends. The party spread out on to the lawn where there was dancing on a concrete platform. Suddenly the wind began to blow hard, the sky, although it was some hours before dawn, took on the colour of brass, and the rain began. It came first in big, solitary drops which hit the powdery dust with a hiss and made it jump, someone broke a glass, a woman swore, and then the rain came down in a hard sheet and everybody ran for the building, kicking aside the chairs and tables as they ran. Inside there were too many people and it smelled bad from the rain and the drunks were more obvious and troublesome than they had been outside when it was always possible to drag them down to Lumley Beach and throw them in the surf. So we went home to bed.

MISCELLANY

Sierra Leone yields nothing to other African territories in the matter of paradox, contrast and eccentricity. It has a giant rat three feet long, a shorter but more vicious poisonous red centipede called a Mende Train; pencil-thin two-foot iron rods called 'Kissie pennies' were the medium of exchange until not so long ago. Sierra Leone, which is the only one of the four British West African states not surrounded by Gallic Africa (it is bounded on the north, east and south by the independent republics of Guinea and Liberia and pounded on the west by the Atlantic surf), imports far more beer than soap, always a sign of a highly Westernized country.

The country's prominent individuals have nice family names like Lightfoot-Boston, Redwood-Sawyerr and Boston-Mammah, and monkeys each year eat half of the cacao crop (14,791 of these pests were killed last year over a four-day period in a single district in a vain attempt to save the crop). The world's biggest alluvial diamond was found in Sierra Leone (its glass replica was promptly stolen from the Freetown Museum) and the population density is 66 to the square mile as compared to 753 in England and Wales. In 1957, Sierra Leone exported 4,500 tons of broom bristles and 1,626 monkeys and chimpanzees.

Sierra Leone has its own three-plane airline and a 311-mile narrow-gauge railway (completed in 1914) which manages to lose £2,000 a day, or more than £700,000 in 1958, a sum considerably in excess of the export value of many of the country's crops. There is a stop about every three miles on the route to the Protectorate centre of Bo (known to all as 'Black Man's London') and the express is said to reach a maximum speed of 18 m.p.h. going downhill, although this has not been confirmed. Despite the fact that the country is so poor that only 3,000 people or one-seventh of one per cent of its population of 2·3 million (including 2,000 non-Africans) paid income tax last year, African cabinet ministers are allowed to take up to four wives with them on annual vacations abroad. Sierra Leone has a 107-man navy and is now thinking of acquiring a ship.

Tribesmen of the interior respectfully call British administrators 'Pa' and before the land is sown it is customary to set traps of burned sticks to snare any witches who may be lurking about. A woman newly widowed smears herself with a mud pack made from the water used to wash her husband's corpse; when it falls off she is free of his influence and may marry again, unless the dead man's brother, nephew or uncle wants to take her on. The interior had no system of organized native administration until 1932 but its elected representatives now hold national power.

There is one international airfield and this is located at Lungi across the seven-square-mile harbour from Freetown, which was once capital not only of Sierra Leone but of Nigeria, Gold Coast and Gambia as well. The harbour is thirty feet deep and until recently there was a paw-paw tree growing out of the tower of Freetown's Anglican Cathedral. The city, which has always had a well-earned reputation for violence, suffered severe rioting in 1955 as the result of a labour dispute. Mobs of strikers attacking the dock area in an attempt to get at 'scabs' who had gone to work were dispersed with baton charges, tear-gas and gun-fire. The strikers cut off the city's water, fires and looting broke out and lasted for two days. The army had to be called in to restore order and the final toll was one white police officer killed and sixty-one police injured; seventeen rioters were killed and sixty wounded, pretty fair shooting for 175 rounds fired.

Although they have the ability to touch off disasters like the riots, Sierra Leone has only eleven trade unions with a paid-up membership of about 10,000 men out of a total salaried labour force of 80,000. The army has 1,500 men and there are three Sierra Leoneans holding the rank of captain or above. It costs £785,000 a year to maintain this small force, a sum which Sierra Leone can ill-afford. The waterfront, the mines and the government are the country's biggest employers. A little more than half the civil service jobs are held by Africans and almost all of these are Creoles, a source of some dissatisfaction to the country's political leaders, who are Protectorate men.

The Protectorate, as the interior of the country is termed, has not been without its share of violence. In 1955, the District Commissioners' unarmed Court Messenger force, which had in the past handled the infrequent troubles which occurred, was disbanded and the jurisdiction of the police was extended from the Colony to the Protectorate. This apparently was understood by the chiefs to mean that the Commissioners no longer held any power: some of them immediately began imposing illegal taxes with fanciful names such as 'shake-hands' and 'good-bye', instituting forced labour and generally running rough-shod over their people, some of whom reacted in a reasonable fashion and beat the stuffings out of their chiefs and burned their homes. In the hearings which followed the restoration of order, witnesses sworn on the Bible, the Koran and 'court medicine' (a piece of iron shaped like a crocodile's jaw and guaranteed to 'eat' any dishonest pagan witness) testified, among other things, that one man had been required to pay his dead brother's taxes for five years, that a lecherous chief had had some comely beauties stripped and their bodies searched by medicine men to see if they 'were possessed of a devil', that a man late with his taxes had had his face whitewashed and been tied inside a pepper sack. 'Pegging', it seemed, was a common practice: this is a system whereby a chief assigns to each village, in addition to its lawful taxpayers, a number of under-age or non-existent persons ('pegs') upon whom a tax has to be paid into the chief's pocket. Among those involved were a cabinet minister, a member of Legco and twelve other chiefs. Of the fourteen chiefs involved, ten were deposed, required to resign or suspended; four were exonerated.

Despite these high-jinks, one has the feeling that the chiefs are not what they were in the old days when some had as many as 300 wives. One methodical old rascal had each of his better halves sew a serial number into her garments so that he might not make the mistake of marrying her again should she catch his fancy. Chiefs a few years ago travelled by bush-cart, a rickety chair covered by a canopy and set between two wheels with six-foot diameters. This remarkable contraption was pushed along narrow country trails by his vassals, at considerable hazard to the rider. Now chiefs drive Fords.

The Protectorate also has its 'human leopard' society, the principal purpose of which is to procure the ingredients necessary for the manufacture of *borfima*. As everybody knows, to make this potent medicine you need the white of an egg, the blood of a cock, a few grains of rice, skin from a human hand, foot and forehead, part of a man's liver and a pinch of his genitals, the point of a needle, a piece of a chicken's oesophagus and a piece of cloth taken from a menstruating woman. Stir slowly and allow to simmer. A good dose of *borfima* will fix anything from a hostile jury to a troublesome hang-nail and is obviously worth the bother necessary to obtain its varied ingredients.

From time to time there is an outbreak of cannibalism but this sort of thing is now considered rather *infra dig*. After some well-chewed human remains were discovered in 1958, Freetown's leading newspaper observed with some disdain that 'these days are hardly the time for cannibalism'. After all, capitalists, who tend to be as plump as milk-fed Beltsville turkeys, would be understandably chary of visiting or investing in a country inhabited by such unorthodox consumers.

There are thirteen indigenous tribes in the interior, of which the two largest are the Mende and the Temne. Temnes, who have a reputation for being strong and stubborn, dominate the north and live in the shadow of Bintimani and Sankenbiriwa, the two highest peaks in Sierra Leone (both top 6,000 feet). The easy-going, astute Mendes live in the more forested south. And in between them you have the Loko, Limba, Susu, Yalunka, Sherbro, Mandingo, Bullom, Krim, Koranko, Kono, Vai and half a dozen non-indigenous tribes which have filtered into the country in the last two or three centuries.

Found in the river-beds of the interior are curious figures of men sculptured in soapstone. They apparently were carved by an earlier culture and are much coveted for their ability to ensure a good rice crop, after first being placed in the fields and whipped 'to make them work'. Bo, a characterless town of 20,000 people, is the only urban centre in the Protectorate and slavery of the domestic variety still persists in the countryside, although now the slaves are called 'servants' or 'cousins'.

Most of the men of the interior wear either the Muslim gown or a facsimile of Western clothes while the women dress themselves in a gaily-coloured wrap-around skirt called a *lappa* and a loose sort of blouse called a *booba*. The most renowned member of Sierra Leone's fair sex is Madame Ella Koblo Gulama, one of Sierra Leone's 148 chiefs and the only woman to sit in the House of Representatives. Madame Ella, a devastatingly attractive woman who dresses in the Wollof fashion, put Sierra Leone on the map in 1959 with her three-month tour of the United States. She visited New York, Atlanta, Dayton, Cleveland and Porto Rico, made several television appearances and came home convinced that the Sierra Leone government should send scholarship students to America (161 of the 173 university students studying abroad are in the United Kingdom).

There are 140 miles of paved roads (for an area nearly as large as Eire) and improvements on the network made the number of trucks in the country jump from 375 to nearly 3,000 in a four-year period. Automobile accidents increased eightfold in the same period, since most Africans learn to drive 'on the job'.

Diseases described as 'common' and 'endemic' by the health department include gastro-intestinal infections, respiratory illnesses, gonorrhoea, malaria, yaws, leprosy, sleeping sickness, schistosomiasis, elephantiasis and tuberculosis. Falls from palm trees are another important cause of hospitalization.

In one seventy-year period, five governors and seven acting-governors died in the saddle and the Anglican Church Missionary Society lost 109 missionaries in its first twenty-five years in Sierra Leone. Soldiers did little better and there are many plaques in Freetown's Cathedral of St. George like the one which pays tribute to a young subaltern who 'survived the Battle of Waterloo only to perish in this unhealthy clime . . .'

In 1957, UNICEF-WHO detected 50,000 cases of yaws in Sierra Leone's Northern Province alone and inoculated a quarter of the population against the disease. In the same year there were 4,700 cases of smallpox and the leprosy rate was estimated to be 5 per cent. A scrotum weighing 106 pounds has been amputated at Freetown's hospital and there are 1,511 beds and 75 doctors to care for a population of 2·2 million.

The Anglicans moved into Sierra Leone, their first West African toehold, in 1806 and even today, despite the far greater importance of Ghana and Nigeria, the Archbishop of West Africa has his seat in Freetown. But times are changing: in the old days, Muslims who asked permission to establish a mosque within this Christian citadel were laughed to scorn; today a quarter of the Creoles and most of the 'bushmen' of the Colony are Muslims. In 1959 Freetown Mayor Lucien Genet, a French-educated Catholic, became life-chairman of the city's new and ornate mosque. The whirring noise heard for weeks thereafter was occasioned by nineteenth-century Creoles revolving vigorously in their graves.

The Wesleyans, Baptists, Evangelical United Brethren and Seventh Day Adventists are fairly well established, although 28 per cent of the total population is Muslim and most of the rest are animists. The Mende (pronounced Mendee) people of the south, whom we in our arrogance call pagans, worship Ngewo, the Supreme Creator. Those Temne (rhymes with 'chimney') of the north who are not Muslims pay homage to a Supreme Being called Kurumasaba. These two tribes account for 60 per cent of the population of Sierra Leone and, until a few years ago, the head of a dead Temne chief was his successor's most cherished possession. This practice was discouraged after it was learned that some of these trophies were being removed while their owners were still in occupancy.

An interesting Muslim sect which does missionary work not only in Sierra Leone but in most of the world's countries is Ahmadiyya, founded by Hazrat Ahmad (peace be on him) 125 years ago in what is today Pakistan. Hazrat Ahmad, a bulky man with a flowing black beard, attended no schools, attempted and failed a legal examination before fortuitously receiving instructions from Mohammed that he was to be the Redeemer of his age. Hazrat Ahmad asserted that he had come to save not only Muslims but all the people of the world and maintained that he had private information that Jesus had not died upon the cross but had been taken down in a swoon and had travelled to India where he died a natural death some years later. His six Pakistani missionaries in Sierra Leone claim 5,000 converts, run six government-assisted schools and have three Sierra Leoneans in Pakistan on university scholarships.

THE PROVINCE OF FREEDOM

It was the desire to participate in the slave trade which brought Britain to Sierra Leone in the seventeenth century while the hope of suppressing the same traffic kept her there. But to put the country into better perspective, one must go back a bit further:

That far-ranging tourist, Hanno the Carthaginian, may have visited these shores in 500 B.C. If he did, none followed him until the Portuguese navigator Pedro da Cintra watered his galleons in the estuary of the Rokel River in 1460. Da Cintra gave the peninsula the name which was later applied to the whole country and means 'Mountains of the Lion'. There are three schools of thought as to the derivation of the name. Some say that there were lions in the mountains which partly ring this third largest harbour in the world (larger: Sydney, Rio). Apart from the fact that African lions usually don't live in mountains and none have been seen in the Colony and only one in the interior in the last two centuries, this is not too implausible. Another group maintains that the coastal mountains, when seen from the sea, have the profile of a crouching lion. This is possible for one of a poetic temperament: they also look like the south end of a herd of donkeys headed north. Others say that the constant rumble of thunder in the 3,000-foot mountains behind Freetown reminded da Cintra of the roar of lions. This could be, if his visit coincided with the beginning of the rains. Da Cintra was a careless fellow and he leaves us no clue as to his reasons.

The Portuguese established a small fort on Bunce Island in the estuary. They also built a slave baracoon and a church, seeing no paradox in this since they were always careful to baptize their black ivory before packing it off to the New World. For a hundred years their ships bound for the Indies stopped here to take on water and provisions.

John Hawkins, one of the Elizabethan 'sea hawks', embarked a cargo of slaves from Sierra Leone ('a plentiful watering place with abundance of fruit') in 1564, thus earning the dubious but profitable honour of being the first Englishman to engage in this trade. Elizabeth made pious protestations of horror . . . and knighted John Hawkins, whose coat of arms contains chained Negroes. Drake touched here also as did the Dutch admiral, de Ruyter, each destroying the trading posts of the other's nation. The Dutchman left a stone tablet enumerating his accomplishments which today is affixed to King Jimmy's Wharf.

The English merchants who threw up on Bunce Island a fort 'very handsomely built' soon realized that their post could not resist the attacks of hostile natives, pirates and rival European powers until it was stiffened with a permanent settlement. Colonists, they reasoned, would protect their warehouses from attack, provide a ready market for their merchandise and serve as a means of civilizing (i.e., making consumers of) the natives of the interior. They became increasingly anxious about the matter after the French sacked the fort in 1704 and made off with six thousand 'elephants' teeth . . . with an abundance of merchandise fit for the trade of the country'.

The mercantile interests found powerful and paradoxical allies among three groups: eighteenth-century Little Rock types, abolitionists and imperialists. In 1772, the abolitionists led by Granville Sharp obtained a court ruling to the effect that any slave touching English soil was free. Within fourteen years there were about 1,500 freed slaves in England, most of them poverty-stricken and miserable. The abolitionists in their kind *naïveté* suggested that these freedmen be settled on the coast of Sierra Leone in what Sharp liked to call 'The Province of Freedom'. English racialists were happy to be rid of these troublesome people and the mercantilists were delighted at the prospect of getting their colonists.

In 1787, 351 Negroes desperate or depraved enough to be willing to embark upon such a venture (or unlucky enough to be caught on the streets without a visible means of support) gathered at Plymouth. The colony's managers at the last moment discovered there were almost no women in the group. This seemed to militate against the chances of the settlement becoming a permanent one. This shortage was remedied in engaging eighteenth-century fashion: press gangs plucked sixty whores from the taverns and jails of Plymouth to become the Founding Mothers of Freetown. Their comments on British justice when they discovered their destination and their new mates have not, unfortunately, been recorded.

Some of the Negroes died aboard the brig *Miro* on the passage to Sierra Leone; the rest of the colonists were dumped ashore by Captain John Taylor with six months' provisions on twenty square miles of the rocky peninsula where Freetown stands today, purchased from King Tom, the Temne chief, for rum, muskets and an embroidered waistcoat. And then the ship sailed away. Ex-slaves and harlots do not always make good colonists (jailbirds are better): the pilgrims quarrelled among themselves, the crops failed and the natives scattered the tiny settlement. Within two years, only sixty remained alive.

Reinforcements arrived from Nova Scotia in 1792 in the form of a shipment of 1,131 ex-slaves who had run away from their American masters during the Revolutionary War. Some of these had borne arms and they were made of sterner stuff than the first group. Led by Lieutenant John Clarkson, Freetown's first governor, they rebuilt the town after the French burned it in 1794 and a new and equally vigorous injection of new blood came with the arrival of 'the Maroons', Barbados Negroes who had rebelled against their masters.

By 1808 it became apparent that neither the missionaries nor the mercantile interests had the strength to protect the struggling settlement, and Freetown and the peninsula which the natives call Romarong, meaning 'Place of the Mountain', an area of 200 square miles, became a Crown Colony. The previous year the British parliament had passed a law making the slave trade a prohibited occupation for Englishmen.

And if John Bull was to have no cakes and ale, were others to make merry? Since they were excluded from this lucrative trade, the British mercantile interests did their best to see that traders of no other nationalities prospered from it. Freetown became a major base for the British navy's anti-slavery operations and every year hundreds and sometimes thousands of slaves snatched from the holds of French, Spanish, Portuguese and American ships were unloaded at Freetown.

Few of these people knew where their homes were (most of them were probably from what is today Nigeria) and all of them lacked the means to return there. They had no common language, their tribal organization had been destroyed and they were alone in a strange land. From this unpromising raw material was to grow the Creole society of today.

They quickly adapted themselves at least to the outward form of Christianity, learned English and developed Krio, a patois which contains English, Portuguese, Yoruba and words of its own. One philologist has identified words from fourteen West African languages, several European tongues and various Caribbean dialects in the Krio vocabulary. Some people fallaciously confuse Krio with pidgin; the basic difference is that Krio is the native language of the Creoles while pidgin is not the mother tongue of any who speak it. Pidgin has a simple structure and a small vocabulary while Krio is relatively complex and has a large vocabulary, to which words are constantly being added. Many of the English words it employs are archaic, obsolete or regional in character. Few people outside Freetown's 25,000 hardcore Creoles can speak it well because there are tonal complications (the words for 'spice' and a 'white football player', for instance, are spelt the same). There is no good Krio grammar or dictionary but plays and poetry have been written in Krio by Freetown intellectuals and the language is rich in homely sayings called *paraibuls*.

The Creoles built Freetown into a bastion against the strange and savage tribes which lived beyond the mountains. By 1851, the city had a population of 18,000 people, most of them Christians and a few with a smattering of white blood.

Essential to the understanding of Creole society as it exists today is an appreciation of the Victorian Englishmen who conditioned the Creole mystique. The Victorians lacked our racial prejudices. There were no master races in those days, no genetic supermen. Charles Darwin was not too old to be spanked and the man who was to write *The Golden Bough* was still sucking his thumb. A few uncomfortable fossils were turning up but nothing serious enough to prevent any right-thinking man from believing that the world was created in six days 5,700 years ago.

The Negro was primitive and backward but it remained for a more enlightened age to suggest that he might be biologically inferior. What he lacked was the 'British Way of Life' (the best of all possible ways, of course). Wedge the Negro into a pair of trousers, send him to church regularly, teach him Latin and hand him a cricket bat, instruct him in the fine art of constructing a gimlet, transport him to the Middle Temple to read law and, presto!, out comes a black Englishman.

To a certain extent (nothing in Africa is ever an unqualified success) the Victorians were successful. Top hats and bustles blossomed in Freetown, each dusky family produced a triumphantly double-barrelled name, the Church became the centre of Creole life and education its shibboleth. Freetown was the first West African city to have a mayor and town council (1799), the first to have a railway station. Creole society produced the first black knight (Sir Samuel Lewis, an early mayor) and the first African bishop, Samuel Crowther.

On the negative side, the Church did nothing to discourage the Creoles' supercilious disdain of the people of the interior when it preached that the men of Freetown were a chosen people destined to spread the Gospels and civilization to the naked heathen. Government reinforced Creole pride by admitting its representatives to its councils while banning the people of the interior from the Legislative Council until 1951. Together Church and State admirably succeeded mainly in convincing the feckless and well-mannered Creoles that manual labour was beneath them, and here perhaps lies the key to Freetown's air of melancholy and decay.

In 1811 the first unofficial member was appointed to the Advisory Council (which became the Legislative Council in 1863 and the House of Representatives in 1957) by the governor 'from amongst the most considerable of the Protestant inhabitants residing in the Colony'; it was not, however, until 1924 that the first elective member took his seat. By 1827 Freetown had a university, the first West African institution of higher learning and the only one for more than a century, and it was possible for a visiting British educator to remark in 1868 (six years after the last cargo of slaves was landed on Freetown's wharf) that 'fair writing on slates, moderate reading of the Testament and passable spelling are not unusual accomplishments in Sierra Leone'. It should be remembered that at this time many Englishmen and Americans were illiterate. Educated Creoles fanned out over West Africa as missionaries, civil servants and traders.

Unfortunately the economic life of Freetown did not match its social splendour. The soil of the peninsula was poor and most of the Creoles had little knowledge of or interest in farming (Hebrew was taught for twenty years before Sierra Leone got an agricultural school). From the little towns which ring the peninsula and have English names like Gloucester, Charlotte, Kent, Sussex, York, Aberdeen and Allentown, the Creoles flowed into Freetown to get jobs as traders and clerks, most of all, to try to get education, the key to a top hat and a soft job.

In 1896, six years after Freetown had ceased to be the capital of British West Africa, Britain declared a protectorate over the interior and a few of the more enterprising Creoles went inland to make their fortunes in the 27,925 square miles open to them. The chiefs of the interior had no objection to coming under British protection. In the first place, they obviously did not understand the political implications and, in the second, they were pleased at the prospect of acquiring 'goodies' such as red flannel nightshirts, rum and mirrors. On the other hand, they took strong exception when advised that they were to desist from slaving and fighting tribal wars. The last straw was the imposition of a hut tax.

To demonstrate their feelings on the matter, the tribes rose in 1898 under the leadership of Chief Bai Bureh and massacred a few British officials, a cluster of fundamentalist American missionaries and about a thousand Creoles. There was a bit of shooting, some selective hangings (thirty-three chiefs), and peace and the realization that it is better to evade taxes than to refuse to pay them came to Sierra Leone. But most of the Creoles were scared out of the Protectorate and, as Syrians began to filter into the country from surrounding French territory, they gradually lost their place in the commerce not only of the interior but of Freetown itself for the simple reason that a Syrian can live at a standard little better than an African's, is a sharper businessman and is willing to work long hours for a small profit.

Their social and economic position received a further blow with the discovery that quinine could mitigate the effects of malaria. Regular use of the drug made it possible for more white men to come to the tropics and to live longer once they reached what had before been called 'the White Man's Grave'. The need for educated Creole teachers, missionaries and civil servants declined as more white men arrived. With them came, in increasing numbers, their wives and these in their old endearing fashion did much to widen the gap between Creole and white man.

England suddenly became aware of the potential wealth of Ghana and Nigeria. Missionaries shifted the emphasis of their work to populous Nigeria where Christianity had the chance to make millions of converts in a single tribe, as opposed to the difficulty and expense of working among the small and scattered tribes of Sierra Leone.

Freetown's British civil servants withdrew to the pristine purity of cool Hill Station, high above the sway-backed roofs of sweltering, brawling Freetown, descending each day by a miniature railway on which seats were strictly allocated by rank and seniority. The English developed a more seemly prejudice towards the darker people of the world and the Creole attempts to mimic the lives and mannerisms of the English, which once had been considered laudable, became laughable.

The Creoles began to realize that the rules had been changed on them in the middle of the game. The community, always plagued by a gnawing inferiority complex which its patronizing attitude towards the 'savages' of the interior inadequately concealed, withdrew into itself, shaken, hurt and embittered. Top hat society did not come to an end: church attendance (if not moral standards) remains gratifyingly high, antimacassars sit primly on the backs of over-stuffed chairs, young Creoles continue to read law with a vengeance and to quote Lucretius with facility. Still favoured in middle-class Freetown homes are stiff family portraits slightly over-exposed to make the skin look lighter, faded pastoral wallpaper and china figurines of the shooting-gallery genre.

The sons of prominent families continue to speak of England as 'home' and to shun the excellent Bo School deep in the heart of the Protectorate because, so a teacher told me, 'they know they will be eaten'. The Creole community still produces admirable men like the thirty-eight-year-old Cambridge-educated pathologist and poet, Davidson Nicol, whose library contains something more than the standard African nationalist's spread of Howard Fast, Karl Marx and the *Federalist Papers*, designed for display rather than enjoyment or use.

But Creoledom is losing force and it is losing it not because of British political treachery but because the philosophical and social conditions which made possible its rise and give it force and meaning no longer exist. When Christianity ceased to be a vital force in the lives of Western men and in the policies of their governments, when first we had doubts as to the veracity of the values of our civilization, then was sealed the fate of the Creoles who flattered us by imitation.

Already cracks are appearing in Creole social unity. In the old days, many Protectorate people adopted hyphenated names and donned toppers in an effort to pass as Creoles; today politically ambitious young Creoles are soft-pedalling their Freetown associations and 'discovering' tribal ancestors in the family tree. The religious differentiation between Creole and countryman is beginning to blur and the same people bellowing hymns of pious hope in St. George's on Easter morning sing Allah's praise at Eid-el-Fitri. Toppers and spats are being discarded by young Creoles in favour of 'Aloha' sports shirts worn outside the trousers. Creole girls more and more are beginning to marry, if not with people from the Protectorate, with the Kru and Bassa tribesmen from Liberia who had worked Freetown's waterfront for years and have a consistent record of good citizenship which sets them apart in a town where thievery is rampant.

This social disintegration has not been without its tragedies: juvenile delinquency has quadrupled in six years, family disputes reported to the government have risen by 40 per cent and there has been a steady increase in Freetown's general crime rate. Krio is beginning to lose its identity as more English, native and pidgin words filter into it. This community, which was never really wholly European or African, Christian or Muslim, is beginning to slip away into Africa's black maw.

The social decline and the collapse of old standards might have been borne were it not for the political disaster which has overtaken Sierra Leone's 30,000 Creoles: the Goths are within the gates.

The Creoles accepted their military defeat at the hands of the natives of the interior in 1898 with relatively good grace. The Protectorate has always seemed remote (it was not linked to Freetown by a road until 1940), savage and unimportant to them. They were satisfied with their own institutions and way of life in the Colony and many Creole families took in Protectorate children and gave them homes while the youngsters acquired the much sought after education.

In 1951 the British did the thing which causes Creole truck drivers to hog the road: they merged the two areas into one administrative unit represented in the Legislative Council, which for the first time was given an African majority. Before 1951 only the Colony had been represented in Legco, now there were twice as many seats allocated to the Protectorate as to the Freetown area. Since the Protectorate outnumbers the Colony by twenty-one to one and only about a third of the

Colony's population is Creole, this was the death knell of Creole political predominance.

'This place,' said one Creole lady, relating the injustice of it all to me, 'is worse than Russia!'

'Wasn't it inevitable,' I asked, 'that under a democratic system control should pass to the largest group?'

'We've fought Britain's wars,' she answered, 'and we're British subjects while the people of the interior are only British protected persons. It's not right to throw us in with them. When the white settlers howl in Kenya, Britain takes notice. When we complain, we're told we're being undemocratic. Let them have their government and we'll have ours.'

THE BROTHERS MARGAI

The 'savage' into whose hands Britain has delivered her embittered Creole stepchildren is hardly of the loin-cloth set. He is sixty-five-year-old Sir Milton Augustus Strieby Margai, a pipe-smoking wisp of a man who was the first 'bushman' to attend Fourah Bay College, the citadel of Creole learning, and the first to qualify as a medical practitioner.

Dr. Margai, who became the Protectorate's first knight in 1959, was born at Bonthe on Sherbro Island, a locale otherwise distinguished for the fact that it produces most of the world's piassava, the palm cuttings from which the bristles on street brooms are made. Sherbro is theoretically part of the Colony (the island was purchased by Britain in the nineteenth century from the Caulkers, a Creole family in whose veins flows the blood of English buccaneers; a Caulker was one of the three chiefs to remain loyal to the Crown in 1898), but Margai maintains that he is a Temne.

His father was a merchant prosperous enough to see that young Milton got a good education. He attended a mission school run by the Evangelical United Brethren, an American fundamentalist sect well respected in Sierra Leone, and Freetown's Albert Academy. After graduating from Fourah Bay College, Margai took his medical studies at the University of Durham, parent school of the Sierra Leonean institution. After two years of private practice, Margai entered the Government Health Service. By the time he retired in 1950, the white-haired physician had served in eleven of Sierra Leone's twelve districts, an experience which was to serve him well when he turned his hand to politics.

Too many educated Africans are interested in a job only for what they can get out of it; this, of course, is true of many white people, the difference being that Africa's educated class is so small that even failures are given positions of responsibility. But Margai was anything but a time-server. Shocked by Sierra Leone's terrible infant mortality rate, which in many areas exceeds 50 per cent, the doctor determined to devote his life to improving hygiene where it would count: with the women of the country.

Many white missionaries have tried to reduce infant mortality by attempting to ban female circumcision (excision of the clitoris). This curious rite has taken the lives of many women and children: the scar tissue which forms after the operation, performed in the girl's teens, frequently makes giving birth hazardous, particularly with the first child. But Margai understood as only an African could that the weight of tribal tradition was too strong to allow for the eradication of female circumcision. So he decided to use the Bundu Society, the women's secret group which performs the rite, to achieve his ends.

Since he frequently supported Bundu (the parallel boys' organization is called 'Poro') against its critics, Margai gained the confidence of the powerful crones who guide it. Rather than pressing the society to give up female circumcision, which he knew was useless, Margai convinced the women of the necessity of seeing that the operation was performed in as sanitary and safe a way as possible. Through Bundu he trained native midwives and introduced mothercraft and domestic science into the most tradition-yoked villages. By attempting only what was possible and devoting himself singleheartedly to this end, Margai saved the lives of countless hundreds of women and children.

The year after his retirement this vigorous Methodist was elected to the Legislative Council. He helped to found the Protectorate's first newspaper and welded two splinter groups into the Sierra Leone People's Party (S.L.P.P.), an organization devoted to furthering the political rights of Protectorate people. In 1953, when six Africans were appointed to the Executive Council, Margai became Minister of Health, Agriculture and Forests. The following year he became Chief Minister.

In 1957 the franchise was widened, the Protectorate's representation increased from fourteen to thirty-seven (twenty-five of these elected by the people and twelve elected from the 148 chiefs by district councils), while the Colony's total was raised from twelve to fourteen. There were to be four official members (since removed) and two non-voting members appointed by the governor in the general interest. In this last great political battle between the Creoles and the people of the interior,

Margai's S.L.P.P. (motto: 'One People, One Country') won all the Protectorate seats and eight of the fourteen in the Colony, including that held for twenty-one years by the great Creole leader, Herbert Christian Bankole-Bright, who died in 1959 at the age of seventy-five. Bankole-Bright, who had been leader of the Opposition, served in the Legislative Council and the House of Representatives (its successor) almost continuously from 1924 until his 1957 defeat.

In his moment of triumph Margai was faced with the greatest threat to his political career. This came not from the shattered United Progressive Party of the Creoles but from within the S.L.P.P. in the shape of a revolt led by his forty-nine-year-old brother Albert. Albert is so different from his elder brother that it is hard to believe that they are related. Sir Milton is a wizened little man who looks rather like Gandhi; Albert is beefy and broad-shouldered and has a paunch like that of a retired wrestler who has surrounded too many mashed potatoes; the doctor is contemplative and reserved; Albert, who is the first 'bushman' to earn a law degree, is expansive and out-going; the elder is politically conservative; the younger is an admirer of Sekou Touré.

Albert has more or less followed in his distinguished brother's footsteps. He received a high school education in Freetown, then served for thirteen years as a clerk in the medical department. With financial help from Sir Milton, Albert went to London to read law, returning to go into practice in Freetown in 1948. The following year he was elected to the now defunct Protectorate Assembly in which his brother was the guiding force. The two of them set up the S.L.P.P. and were elected together to Legco in 1951. Albert served as Minister of Local Government, Education and Welfare in his brother's cabinet and emerged as leader of the party's more radical wing.

After the S.L.P.P.'s 1957 victory there was a caucus to confirm the party leadership. Albert had been lobbying secretly to convince the forty-five newly-elected S.L.P.P. members of the House of Representatives that his radical policies could sooner win independence for Sierra Leone than his brother's more cautious programme which called for self-determination in 1961. In the secret balloting, Sir Milton failed by one ballot to get a vote of confidence from the party which he had led to victory at the polls; the way appeared clear for Albert to take over as premier.

The doctor then dealt with Albert with the skill he once reserved for an offending appendix: he requested all those who had voted for him to join him in a conference room to discuss his future course of action. Now it was one thing to vote against the old fox in a secret ballot and quite another to admit that you had done so by refusing to join him in the conference room. A compromise was reached whereby the doctor was to remain head of the party and premier but Albert and his followers were to receive important portfolios and to be consulted on policy matters.

Sir Milton then did a hasty job of mending his fences, offered Albert and his friends a lesser number of portfolios than they had expected and, when they complained about it, advised them to leave the party. Only twelve S.L.P.P. delegates were willing to follow Albert into the political wilderness to form the People's National Party. Sir Milton still had thirty-two members behind him while the United Progressive Party, then led by C. B. Rogers-Wright (Dr. Valesius B. Neale-Caulker is now at the helm), could muster only six seats.

Shortly thereafter Sir Milton took the precaution of having himself elected Life-President of the S.L.P.P., which should preclude the need for any more troublesome votes of confidence from within the party. For the moment, the doctor seems to have Albert, who repented and joined Sir Milton's cabinet in 1960, in the isolation ward; but the patient is resting anything but easily and can be expected to furnish some fireworks in the years to come.

The U.P.P. has pretty well had it. Their attempt to establish the illegality of the merger of the Protectorate and the Colony has failed; their suggestion of a federal solution has gained no currency; not only have they failed to stop the S.L.P.P. in the interior but have taken a whacking on their home grounds. We attended their 1959 annual convention held in a rickety old Freetown building and the keynote lay in the meeting's opening hymn bellowed lustily by dignified old Creoles:

> 'Trust on, trust on, believers,
> Though long the conflict be,
> Thou yet shalt prove victorious,
> Thy God shall fight for thee.'

Only Divine assistance stands to make the Creole's faltering U.P.P. of more than nuisance value in the future political struggle between Milton and Albert Margai, and the then party leader, C. B. Rogers-Wright, was so embittered by the course of events that he was reduced, in 1959, to protesting that the scheduled visit of the Queen to Sierra Leone was 'inopportune and unwanted'.

Early last March Sir Milton announced that his Sierra Leone People's Party had instructed him to request independence by April 1961 at the constitutional conference to be held in London in April 1960. Later the same month it was announced that all political parties would present a united front at the conference under his leadership and that the requested independence date would be moved forward to December 7 (Sir Milton's birthday), 1960.

The conference came off without a hitch and Sierra Leone became independent on April 27, 1961. Britain has promised a total of £7·5 million in loans, grants and technical assistance to help the country to absorb the initial financial shock of independence and a mutual defence agreement is to be negotiated. At the conclusion of the two-week conference, Sir Milton said that he was restrained from dancing for joy only by the presence of Iain Macleod, Secretary of State for the Colonies!

The frail political leader is approaching seventy and the question of a successor may arise. There is no heir apparent but two men are usually found at the doctor's side, and one of them would probably take over should he retire.

The first of these is burly Mohammed Sanusi Mustapha, the Minister of Finance. Mustapha, who seldom wears Western clothes, was born in Freetown and is sometimes called a Creole although he is of Temne blood and a devout Muslim. He is, in fact, representative of a new class of Protectorate people who have come to the Colony, become urbanized and are slowly bridging the social gap between Creole and countryman. Because he is the living embodiment of Protectorate intrusion upon Creoledom's closed preserve, Mustapha is the target of many darts from *Shekpendeh*, the Creole newspaper.

The fifty-seven-year-old politician attended Freetown schools, captained his high school cricket team, then went to work as a government clerk. Twenty years later he retired on medical grounds after a wartime stint as a corporal in the army. After that he read law at Lincoln's Inn, returned to Freetown to organize a profitable import-export business. In 1951 he defeated a bed-rock Creole for the Freetown East seat and became a minister in Margai's first cabinet. He was re-elected in 1957 and backed Sir Milton in his tussle with Brother Albert, coming out of the fracas as Sierra Leone's first African Minister of Finance, a vital portfolio in a country which has to sail close to the financial wind.

Mustapha has done a first-rate job under difficult circumstances:

ordinary revenue has grown from £3·2 million in 1951 to £10 million in 1959 and development loans totalling £3·9 million have been floated.

The second contender for the top job is a man so unusual in modern Africa that I would have had to say something about him even if his political future were not so bright. Like their white counterparts, very few African political leaders have any interests outside their own careers; most are cultural Dead End Kids.

This cannot be said of forty-five-year-old John Karefa-Smart, the Minister of Lands and Labour, who looks like a star forward in the Harlem Globetrotters. Karefa-Smart was born in Rotifunk and his father was a Protestant clergyman. He was educated at mission schools and entered Albert Academy a year after Dr. Margai started in practice. He took his B.A. at Freetowr's Fourah Bay College, then went to Otterbein College in Ohio for his B.S. From there he went to McGill in Montreal for his medical degree and thence to Harvard for further graduate study.

Then Dr. Karefa-Smart broke all the rules so rigidly adhered to by most African intellectuals. You can read 'Dr.' (honorary) Kwame Nkrumah's autobiography straight through without knowing that there was a world war going on while the Ghanaian was attending an American university. Most educated Africans, with some justification, felt that the war was a white man's quarrel. Only the very few like Karefa-Smart thought deeply enough to realize that freedom is everybody's business.

As it turned out, his war was not a rough one: he was commissioned as a medical officer and posted to Nassau for the duration. In 1946 he came home with his American bride, Hartford-born Rena Weller, a girl too pretty to hold two degrees from Yale. Karefa-Smart still felt that he had a debt to pay to his people and to the missionaries who educated him and he went back to Rotifunk for a two-year stint as a medical missionary. Given the educated African's distaste for rural life, this again puts the young doctor head and shoulders above most of his contemporaries. With that behind him, he became regional medical officer for West Africa for the World Health Organization, serving in this capacity in Monrovia, Lagos and Brazzaville. Karefa-Smart then taught at Nigeria's Ibadan University College Medical School, came home in 1957 to be elected unopposed to the House of Representatives from Tonkolili West (an appropriate constituency since it contains the bulk of the country's iron). Margai immediately named him to his new cabinet.

Despite his double-barrelled name, this father of three is no Creole. His family, which has been Christian and American-educated for three generations, is of mixed Temne-Mende origin. But of all the S.L.P.P. cabinet ministers, his strong Christian orientation and urbane sophistication make him most acceptable to the Creoles. It remains to be seen, however, if this is an asset or a political liability.

THE DIAMOND WAR

As Minister of Lands, Mines and Labour, Karefa-Smart has the ticklish job of defending the one political sore spot which could bring about the fall of Dr. Margai's government: his diamond policy.

Sierra Leone has always been poor. The climate is too catastrophic and the soil too infertile to attract plantation companies; the population is too small to provide enough of a market to encourage large-scale trading or light industry. A little ginger, some palm kernels, a few tons of coffee and a bit of piassava were exported and that was about it.

In 1930 diamonds were discovered near the Guinea–Liberia border and the Sierra Leone Selection Trust (an affiliate of the vast de Beers combine which taps South Africa's minerals) obtained a mining concession over the entire country. The diamonds, which range in quality from poor industrials to fine gem stones, are scattered over the 500-square-mile drainage system of the Sewa River in the remote Kono district of eastern Sierra Leone. The pipe has never been found and all diamonds won in Sierra Leone are alluvial stones which have been embedded in the banks of the streams for thousands of years.

The mining process is simple but expensive: gravel is dug out of streambeds with steam shovels, loaded into trucks, carried to washers and sloshed over a wax coating to which the diamonds stick, the waste washing away. One stone of 770 carats, probably the fifth largest in the world, was found in 1945.

Since the Selection Trust employed 2,600 Africans and paid out 45 per cent of its profits in taxes, relations between the company and the government were good. But trouble began in 1954 and is far from ended now. No one can say how it started or why it did not begin at an earlier date. It was apparently due to a number of factors including a bad crop year, an increasing desire for consumer goods among the people of the Protectorate, and the general feeling of restlessness and defiance of authority which raged through Africa with the end of World War II and the outbreak of nationalism.

Some 30,000 Sierra Leoneans and 'strange' Africans from as far away as Nigeria and Senegal in numbers estimated at 50,000 poured into the diamond areas and began illicit mining. Brawling, disease-breeding shanty towns rose among piles of empty brandy bottles and skeletons of wrecked automobiles which the few lucky diggers bought and then abandoned when they ran out of fuel. For most of the wild-catters, however, it was hard work and £1 a carat, with most of the big money going to dishonest chiefs and Syrian middlemen. As they worked out their evil-smelling pits—called 'Burma' by the army veterans who remembered the shell-pocked landscape of the war—the diggers grouped themselves in bands of fifty or a hundred men and invaded the area where the Selection Trust was working.

The only law enforcement officers in the Protectorate were the District Commissioners' unarmed Court Messengers and the diamond company's small force of security guards; the police were not then allowed to operate outside the Colony. The Court Messengers, some of whom doffed their uniforms to do a little digging themselves, soon proved totally incapable of handling the bands of armed diggers. All the diamonds won by the diggers were turned over by them to illicit buyers (African 'big men', Syrians and—one is inclined to believe—one or two unscrupulous Britons) who smuggled them out through Liberia or Guinea. Most of these smuggled stones are thought to go to Israel for cutting by Dutch Jews. The bulk of the industrial diamonds are said to find their way to Russia.

The Selection Trust, which had a ninety-nine-year concession over all of Sierra Leone, gave an understandable howl and the government repealed legislation forbidding police action in the Protectorate and rushed in large numbers of men. More than fair play was at stake: Sierra Leone's able governor, Sir Maurice Dorman, pointed out that the illicit diggers and buyers were depriving African children of the chance to go to school by defrauding the country of more than £5 million a year in royalties and taxes. Even more serious than this was the realization that news to the effect that Sierra Leone could not maintain law and order would scare off much-needed foreign investment and possibly result in a delay in the granting of independence.

Still the situation worsened, additional police and finally the army were thrown into the battle. It became obvious that, if the government was not to lose control of the situation, the 'strange' Africans would have to be deported. In 1955 Sierra Leone expelled between 40,000 and 50,000 aliens (thus doing a very good job of spreading the smallpox epidemic which had riddled 'Burma') and sat down with the Selection Trust to negotiate a new agreement, since the government realized it was unable to live up to the old one. The diamond company agreed to give up its concession over all lands except those which it was working (about 500 square miles), to shorten its concession by forty-five years and to increase its tax rate from 45 per cent to 60 per cent of net profits. In return it received about £1·5 million compensation for the loss of the national concession and the government's promise that it would do everything in its power to protect the new arrangement.

Some Sierra Leoneans held that the Selection Trust had given up only worthless territory and should have been compelled to close down completely. Dr. Margai quickly quashed this by pointing out that any court of arbitration might order as much as £30 million compensation for the company and that this was clearly beyond the country's means even if it wished to close down the Selection Trust.

In an attempt to control the situation while furnishing an escape valve for the indigenous diggers, Sierra Leone began issuing alluvial licences to Africans which permitted them to dig outside the Selection Trust area. Additional legislation was passed giving the government the right to admit no one to the diamond districts without a permit and to expel trouble-makers without a trial.

A depression immediately set in: although they had paid no taxes or royalties, the illicit miners had spent the money paid to them by illegal buyers, promoted business, and most of the profits earned by Syrian smugglers had come back into the country in the form of trade goods on which the government obtained import duty. In the four years since the new arrangement has been in effect, roughly £14 million worth of alluvial diamonds have been legally mined and exported by Africans. But the wild lawlessness has only increased.

'There is good reason to believe,' Dorman told me over a cup of tea at Government House, 'that the value of diamonds produced by licensed diggers and legally marketed has been far less than that of diamonds smuggled out of the country.' In 1959, as illicit diggers again invaded the shrunken Selection Trust concession in force, it appeared possible that the firm might have to close its doors, a move which would cost Sierra Leone £1·4 million a year in taxes and wages. In response to what the Governor termed 'something very near armed rebellion', hundreds of extra police, air reconnaissance units and again the army were thrown into battle against hordes of diggers armed with slings and cutlasses. More than 2,500 arrests were made in a single ten-week period despite tougher legislation hustled through the House of Representatives by Karefa-Smart which makes a year in jail mandatory for contraventions of the diamond ordinances, including possession of mining tools in a diamond area, a rather difficult regulation to enforce since all one needs to go after alluvial diamonds is a shovel, a pan and a strong back.

In 1959 at least a third of Sierra Leone's 2,000-man police force was tied down in the diamond area, new detention camps had to be built and wardens hired to handle the influx of arrested persons, and hiring of extra police and prison guards alone was costing £260,000 a year.

The issue of about 5,000 licences a year to alluvial diggers and the step-up in security measures has cut down to some extent on the amount of illicit mining (although smuggled exports during 1959 were estimated at between £8·5 million and £9 million as compared to legal exports valued at £5·8 million). The big problem now is how to get the gems won by licensed diggers into the Selection Trust's Yengema headquarters for purchase rather than into the hands of illicit diamond buyers. But even assuming that no diamonds get into the hands of dishonest persons (20,962 small stones worth £125,000 were recovered from illicit diggers and buyers in 1957), the situation leaves much to be desired on grounds of simple efficiency: Selection Trust's workers produce an annual average of 133 carats while the average of licensed diggers is only 50 carats a year. In addition, the tax structure is such that although the alluvial diggers out-produced the Selection Trust by 465,000 carats to 400,000 carats, the company paid nearly £350,000 more than the diggers in taxes the same year. In other words it is more to the advantage of the country as a whole for the Selection Trust to win diamonds than it is for the diggers to do so.

The effects of the diamond rush have extended far beyond the mining sphere: before the trouble began, Sierra Leone was an exporter of rice, groundnuts, palm oil and beniseed. Now she can barely meet her own needs and in some cases must import these commodities. In addition, exports of bananas and ginger, although they have not stopped, have slowed to a trickle. When word came that there were diamonds to be had, only the women, the old people and the cripples were left to tend the land; the rest trooped off to the diggings.

Even without the diamond rush Sierra Leone's agricultural economy was headed for trouble. Most of the rain drums down in a ninety-day period, leaching the nutrients from the soil. Wind and sun do the rest. In the past there has been enough room to allow for a system of shifting agriculture in which the land is cultivated for a year or two, after which yields fall sharply, and then allowed to lie fallow for seven or eight years. As long as there were tribal wars, famines and plagues to keep the population down, this worked pretty well. Britain brought police, doctors and agricultural officers, and the natural controls on the population level were removed. As the people multiplied, the pressure on the land increased, plots were farmed longer and yielded poorer crops. The natural response was to clear more land, until today only 5 per cent of Sierra Leone is forested. This geometric progression is a fact all over Africa today and the effects are bound to be severe within this century.

The answer, of course, is to plant higher-yielding strains and to cultivate the land more scientifically. Sierra Leone has made an attempt to do this with palm products which comprise more than 50 per cent by value of all agricultural exports, over £2 million worth in 1957. More than one million improved seedlings which when mature will yield twice as much oil as the wild variety have been given away over the last ten years. But, despite a bonus paid to the farmers for each free seedling which survives their heavy-handed care, more than two-thirds have died.

In another attempt to get the natives interested in high-yielding varieties, the Sierra Leone government established nine mills to express the oil of the fruit. This is what S. M. Taylor, chairman of the Sierra Leone Produce Marketing Board, had to say about this project:

'Apart from the one mill supplied by a plantation, there was practically no active interest among producers in supplying palm fruits to the mills. These mills cannot be a success . . . if the farmers would plant the free improved seedlings on a plantation basis we could pay them a higher price and operate the mills at a profit. As it is, we're losing £35,000 a year and the mills will have to be closed.'

In an effort to salvage part of its investment in the oil mills, the government, in co-operation with the Colonial Development Corporation, this year established two 1,000-acre palm plantations. (A total of six plantations will be developed under the supervision of the Produce Marketing Board at a cost of £1 million.) One cannot be too sanguine about this venture since the United Africa Company, which has the strongest possible profit motivation, declined an invitation to participate in the scheme. An earlier government fisheries project, like the one in Gambia, failed completely.

Another sorry spectacle is the rice situation. No Sierra Leonean considers that he has eaten unless the meal contains rice. And not in Lyons' portions: T. S. Jones, deputy director of agriculture, reports that he has seen two natives finish off a four-gallon bucket of rice at a single sitting without a burp. Most of Sierra Leone's rice is of the upland variety and enough was produced before the diamond rush (more than 200,000 tons a year) to feed the local population. The paddies were abandoned by the men, consumption levels rose as the result of the injection of illicit diamond profits into the economy and the arrival of the 'strange' Africans amounted to 50,000 extra mouths to feed. As a result, Sierra Leone now imports 20,000 tons of rice a year at a cost of almost £1·5 million.

Here again the solution is close at hand: Jones estimates that if the people would agree to cultivate swamp rice, Sierra Leone could grow enough to feed twice her present population. At least 330,000 acres of *boli*, as the fresh-water swamps are called, are available to grow a rice which yields five times as much as the upland variety. But still the farmers are not interested: the lowland rice is not sweet, the climate is too bad, the gods do not favour it.

By dint of herculean effort, the government managed to reduce upland rice acreage in the most heavily eroded areas by about 20 per cent and, by 1957, to get 12,000 acres of swamp rice under mechanical cultivation. But although the yields were as high as promised, the farmers refused to pay the £3 an acre fee to have their paddies ploughed by tractors, many of which had to be landed in inaccessible areas by assault landing-craft. Swamp acreage fell in 1959 to 7,000 acres.

The government's principal agricultural research station at Njala, set amidst rolling hills in a bend of the River Taia, experiments manfully on possible new crops for the country such as 'Webb's Wonderful' lettuce, 'Hundredweight' cabbage, 'Money Maker' tomatoes and 'Louisiana Green Velvet' okra. One learns that American 'Tendersweet' carrots are highly thought of and that Sierra Leone, which already produces ginger, could sell many more tons if the growers would maintain the quality specified by London confectioners. Cinnamon is another possible export, but the Agriculture Department is reluctant to introduce the trees other than experimentally because they believe that the local Africans are too lazy to learn to roll the spice in the fashion of the Indian growers, which is the way buyers want it. Fortunately for the country's cultivators of piassava, the lower part of the leaf stalks of the raphia palm used in making street-broom bristles, Sierra Leone for once sets the standard which the rest of the world must follow: 'Prime Sherbro', named after the island on which it grows, is the best you can get and 'Sulima', another variety, is also highly regarded.

To try to get more protein into the African diet, the Agriculture Department imported eggs of improved strains which were sold to the farmers for hatching. It was discovered that in one recent year, 40,000 of the 45,000 eggs sold for this purpose ended up keeping company with a rasher of bacon on Sierra Leone's breakfast tables. The department itself has pulled a couple of boners such as the establishment of a piggery in a predominantly Muslim country. In one area where hogs were in demand, of seventy-eight improved boars sold by a 'research' station all but four were slaughtered by their new owners. Collectively, all this means that production of twelve of Sierra Leone's fourteen crops has declined at a time when her population is doubling itself every twenty-five years. (Perhaps it is no coincidence that the two crops which have improved, coffee and piassava, are not handled by the government purchasing board.) You don't have to be much of a mathematician to understand the implications of this.

About the only aspect of the country's economy which looks bright at present is iron mining. From the earliest days it had been known that Sierra Leone contained iron and in 1926 a survey team discovered two large hills of solid ore rising out of a bushy plain in the central part of the country near the fifty-five-hut village of Lunsar. To exploit the find, the British government made a £500,000 loan (since repaid) to a group of Scots who put up the same amount to form the Sierra Leone Development Company. Before a ton of ore could be exported, a port and a fifty-two-mile railway had to be constructed.

In 1933 the port of Pepel, up-river from Freetown on the Rokel River, was finished and a standard-gauge railway completed. The timing was opportune: when Hitler cut England off from Swedish iron, Sierra Leone's Marampa mine was able to supply 40 per cent of the United Kingdom's ore imports.

You drive west down the valley of the Rokel from Makeni, the capital of Northern Province, to reach the mine. It is a hot and dusty trip through country which could be anywhere in Africa: a parched brown landscape dotted with a few scraggly thorn trees festooned with the spherical nests of orange and black weaver birds, here and there a big cottonwood, villages of thatched huts, with goats, skinny chickens and naked brown children rolling in the dust. Off on the left appears the truncated cone of Masaboin, the larger of the two hills, its height lowered 100 feet by a quarter of a century of 'mining'. But this is a mine only in the sense that it produces a mineral: tremendous earth-movers (their size may be gauged by the fact that a single tyre costs £900) rumble up a steeply banked road, sweep up a couple of tons of grey dust and dump it into a conveyor belt which carries the stuff down to the mill at the base of the hill where it is refined and railed to the coast. Near the mill—which with the railway and the port installations represents a capital investment of more than £10 million—are the pleasant cottages of the white professional staff, the ubiquitous club and swimming pool and, on the other side of the hill, the not-so-nice labour lines grouped in tribal hamlets of about forty cottages each.

In comparison to the Congolese and Rhodesian mines, Marampa— which works three eight-hour shifts a day—is not over-generous with its employees. The only free food provided is two cups of rice per day (more is available, however, at a heavily subsidized price). Housing is not free, although workers pay only two shillings a month for a room. And free schooling is provided for only at primary level. There is a small community centre which shows one free movie a week, a pension set-up and medical services are free. The company makes available only four scholarships to mission schools but, reasoning that mechanics are just as important as lawyers, has its own five-year course for apprentices, who are not required to remain in the service of the company. There is very little of the spoon-feeding of workers which you find in more labour-hungry areas of Africa.

A mining engineer explained this to me quite simply: 'Our business is to mine iron. We are not in the health-education-welfare profession. We pay heavy taxes to enable the government to handle that. We do what we can to give our miners a decent life and if it's not enough, they can go elsewhere.' The fact that turnover is small is commentary both on the lack of other paid employment in Sierra Leone and on the ability of Scots to handle men (a book could be written on the contribution of Scotsmen to the development of Africa: these hard-working realists, lacking in the standoffishness of the English, have brought to everything from mining to missionary work an earnest self-discipline and an unsentimental yet human approach to the African which has made them usually liked and universally respected by Negroes all across the continent). Marampa has not had a strike in eight years, despite the fact that the exhaustion of the outer core of 65 per cent pure red hematite last year resulted in the lay-off of two-thirds of the 3,000 African mineworkers (there are sixty whites). The inner core, a soft grey powder, is less rich and must be refined on the spot but almost the whole operation can be handled mechanically. Annual production now runs about 1·5 million tons (a figure which could probably be doubled by further mechanization and expansion) worth £3·5 million.

Most of the force laid off at Marampa has been absorbed in the development by the company of the vast new iron deposits at Tonkolili, to the east of Marampa. Here there are three 'pimples' of iron ore, called Simbili, Numbara and Marapon. Simbili is 3,000 feet high, the largest of the three, and will be worked first. Its 90 million tons of red ore lie in a crescent 200 feet deep and a mile long. The smaller mountains contain less important deposits of a lower grade. Work has begun on a seventy-mile railway extension which will give work to 4,000 men and run through a mile-long tunnel to link Tonkolili with the Marampa railhead. A town for 2,000 people will spring from the bush by the time the mine opens in 1965. Production is expected to reach 3·5 million tons annually and reserves are estimated at more than 200 million tons. Capital expenditure will be about £25 million.

The Development Company, whose production of ore has averaged about a million tons for each of the twenty-seven years it has been in business, pays £1·5 million annually in direct taxes alone (the Selection Trust pays more than £1 million) and spends another £5·5 million within Sierra Leone in most years.

In 1957, all Sierra Leone's exports were worth £15 million. Of this, more than £13 million came from the sale of 863,202 carats of diamonds, 1·4 million tons of iron ore and 53,000 tons of palm kernels. All other products (coffee, cacao, piassava, chrome ore, kola nuts and ginger, in that order) brought in the balance. In the same year, the country imported £28 million worth of cotton goods, beer, tobacco, rice, motor vehicles and motor fuel, leaving a trade deficit of £13 million. In 1958, the value of exports climbed to £16·5 million and the trade deficit was reduced to £3·3 million, as the government clamped down on illicit mining and credit tightened on over-stocked merchants. Estimated 1959–1960 revenue is £12 million, leaving a small surplus over estimated expenditures.

A disturbing aspect of Sierra Leone's economy concealed by her relatively high (for Africa) trade figures is the fact that the increasing value of her exports does not reflect the efforts of her peasant farmers as is the case in Nigeria (palm oil, groundnuts, cacao), Ghana (cacao) and Gambia (groundnuts) but is the result of European exploitation of mineral wealth which will be exhausted within fifty years. As a result, individual incomes are lower in Sierra Leone than anywhere else in British West Africa.

Since the end of World War II, Sierra Leone has received £5·7 million in British aid and has floated loans on its own account for another £7 million. The country hopes to get something like £14 million in aid from Britain over the next five years and 30 per cent of this year's budget of £10·4 million will be used for capital works.

IGNORANCE FOR ALL

The re-establishment of law and order in the diamond fields and the rejuvenation of her agriculture are no more serious problems than the reorganization of Sierra Leone's educational system. Paradoxical as it is, the first country in British Africa to have a university today has one of the largest expatriate (as Britons are called here) groups in West Africa in its civil service, purely because adequately trained Africans are not available. In 1957, for instance, 75 per cent of the 800 young men who took the Civil Service Examination failed, despite the pass level being a knee-high 40 per cent. Several months later 1,200 candidates attempted the examination and exactly seventy-four passed. If you have ever had dealings with a junior government clerk, you cannot believe that the examinations require too high a standard.

The focal point of Sierra Leonean education since its founding in 1827 has been Fourah Bay College which perches on the lofty slopes of Mount Aureol, high above Freetown. One is impressed to learn that in 1876, the year in which the college entered into a much-cherished relationship which remains today with England's Durham University, Fourah Bay's curriculum included Latin, Greek, Hebrew, Arabic, French, German, Political Economy, Philosophy, Logic, Mathematics, Natural Science and Music. One is less impressed to hear that there were only seventeen students in the college in 1944. By 1900 little progress had been made in Sierra Leone's educational development; by 1920 there was a definite decline; by the end of World War II the great universities of Nigeria and Ghana were on the drawing boards and Fourah Bay's sun was eclipsed.

Sierra Leone now is making frantic efforts aimed not so much at recapturing its past position of intellectual predominance (it is too late for that) as at providing an adequate educational standard for an independent country. It is appropriate that a member of the community which produced the first flowering of education on this coast should be leading the drive. He is forty-four-year-old H. E. B. John, squat son of an Anglican bishop and a Creole.

John was educated at Fourah Bay and went on to Durham to get an honours degree in Modern History. He taught and did administrative work in Freetown high schools, helped found and became general secretary of the S.L.P.P. When the portfolios were handed out, John was the natural choice for Minister of Education and Social Welfare.

Although Sierra Leone still has a long way to go, important educational progress has been made. Government expenditures on schooling have increased from a paltry £70,000 in 1947 (5 per cent of the budget) to £1·5 million in 1959 (17 per cent of the budget). Between 1950 and 1958, the number of primary schools increased from 277 to 521 and the number of primary students soared from 34,520 to 67,805. Secondary school attendance climbed from 2,792 to 5,924.

Although the Protectorate has long lagged behind the Colony (where 80 per cent of all children get some schooling) and continues to do so, the educational gap between the two is less striking than it used to be. In 1935, only 5 per cent of the school-age children got any education in Southern Province while in the Muslim north the percentage was less than 1 per cent. A veteran American missionary whose work in the interior earned her an M.B.E. can well remember paying a northerner a £4 bonus to send his four sons to a free school. Today the lowest percentage in any of the provinces is 6 per cent, a modest but real gain, and attendance over all of Sierra Leone is 14 per cent. The Development Plan of 1954 hoped to provide primary education for half of the school-age children by 1964, a goal unrelated to the facts of Sierra Leone's financial life. John has lengthened the primary course by one year (a total of seven) and hopes within five years to double the number of primary places, which still will provide for less than 30 per cent of the children.

John maintains that his long-term aim is to introduce universal, free and compulsory primary education to Sierra Leone. This looks very much like a pipe dream. To realize this goal, an additional 370,000 pupils would have to be accommodated. This would mean at least 3,000 more schools and a minimum of 10,000 additional teachers (almost half of the country's 2,200 teachers are untrained) at a time when Sierra Leone's six teacher-training high schools can barely produce enough graduates to take the places of the instructors who die, retire and leave every year. A start is being made by increasing the number of annual graduates of existing teacher-training institutes from 187 to 320 and by establishing two new colleges. The total yearly output of teachers by 1964 should amount to about 550. The entire expansion scheme would require a capital expenditure of at least £9 million and would involve a current expenditure of £3·6 million per year, more than 35 per cent of this year's budget.

Unquestionably a major effort needs to be made in the area of primary education. In 1958 Sierra Leone spent twice as much on secondary and higher education as she did on primary schooling, although 90 per cent of those who do get to school never reach those exalted levels and more than half drop out after the third grade.

An important aspect of John's programme is the revitalization of Fourah Bay, which took 112 years to produce its first woman graduate. At the end of the war the college came close to being converted to a technical school. By the slimmest of margins Sierra Leone convinced Britain that the college was worth keeping and wangled a £350,000 grant which enabled it to move from its ancient buildings on the seafront to an eagle's eyrie of a site perched a thousand feet up on the slopes of Mount Aureol. The approach to the college, which sits upon the ruins of a seventeenth-century Jesuit mission, is calculated to curl one's hair: up, up, up you go on a corkscrew road too narrow for two cars to pass, innocent of guard rails, past women washing in the bubbling mountain streams and the wrecks of cars jamming the gullies, the roofs of Freetown shimmering in the heat below you. One is somewhat relieved to hear, when the summit has been attained, that there are few accidents on the road because it is so dangerous that even the Africans drive carefully. The wrecks, one is told, have been pushed over the precipice for insurance purposes.

The college site was occupied by a wartime hospital and Fourah Bay moved right into the abandoned buildings: wards became class-rooms and dormitories, the old operating room was converted into a physics laboratory and the hospital concert hall became the college assembly room. The total effect, of course, is reminiscent neither of Cambridge nor Princeton. 'But we do not feel,' manfully maintains Davidson Nicol, the Creole principal, 'that cinder-block walls preclude high thinking' (although a library of only 19,000 volumes must inhibit research projects). Fortunately, however, a programme to rehouse the college, which has an annual budget of £300,000 (to which the missions which founded the school contribute only about 1 per cent, the rest coming from fees and from the government) is under way.

431

This is a ticklish business because there is so little space on the shelf upon which the college stands that each building must remain in use practically until the roof comes off. Then the students are crammed in elsewhere while a new edifice with wide eaves, louvred windows and concrete walls goes up on the old site. This type of construction is lacking in grace but lasts well and is suitable for Sierra Leone's climate and its budget. The job is about half done and has cost about £700,000. The total cost may go as high as £1·8 million because new plans include facilities for 950 students.

All but a handful of the college's present enrolment of 410 students are studying on government or mission scholarships and are 'bonded' to work for the organization which pays their way for a certain number of years after graduation (at full salary, of course). Although this does not seem unreasonable, resentful Africans maintain that it constitutes 'intellectual peonage' and admittedly the system does serve to produce some monumentally square pegs in round holes. Even a private scholar in Africa is like a mutual fund: his family, clansmen, distant relations and friends invest money in his education and expect him in return to contribute to their support for as long as he lives. Consequently, it is often impossible not only for an educated man to accumulate capital but even to live up to the standard to which his training and associations have accustomed him. For the educated office-holder, corruption is virtually his only path to anything approaching financial independence. In this context, corruption becomes not so much a vice as a necessity and, in some cases, a positive virtue.

It is something of a paradox that, after all the effort to rejuvenate Fourah Bay, which in 1960 achieved university college status, there are not nearly enough Sierra Leoneans to fill it. The present student body instructed by fourteen African and forty-six expatriate professors is one-third Nigerian. Why? The blame seems to lie in Sierra Leone's faulty primary and secondary school organization. In 1956, for instance, only 70 per cent of the high school graduates attempted their final qualifying examination and 44 per cent of those who did so failed, a standard well below that achieved in Northern Nigeria, long considered an educational backwater. By trying to do too much, Sierra Leone has accomplished virtually nothing.

The problem of education, of course, is immensely more complicated in Africa than it is in England or America. Nowhere in the world is there an atmosphere so inimical to scholarship as that which prevails in the average African home: there is a constant hubbub, lighting is either poor or non-existent, food is sketchy, regular study periods and bed-times are unknown. To this untutored mind, it seems virtually impossible to achieve a decent educational standard in Africa until the entire system is placed on a boarding-school basis. This is borne out by the experience of the Protectorate's famous Bo Government School, a 350-student boarding high school founded in 1906 to educate the sons of chiefs, where thirty-one of thirty-seven students passed the same examination in 1956 flunked by 44 per cent of Sierra Leone's graduating students. At the much smaller Holy Ghost secondary school at Bo, an institution with both boarders and day-students, of the eight students who took the examination, five boarders passed and three day pupils failed.

An all-boarding system has two weaknesses: it is expensive and it runs the risk of isolating too thoroughly the boys who are to become the country's educated class from their less fortunate brethren (for this reason until a few years ago Bo students were not allowed to wear shoes on school grounds). Neither objection is insuperable and it is at least arguable that even Sierra Leone could afford to educate 25,000 primary pupils, 5,000 high school students and 750 university scholars each year on an all-boarding basis. The present arrangement is clearly inadequate for the country's needs and unsuitable to its economic position.

The political battle of Sierra Leone is over now with the tribes of the interior under Margai's leadership reclaiming the heritage which King Tom bartered for an embroidered waistcoat. The greater challenge which must be met by both Creole and countryman is to bring Sierra Leone's economic and educational standing to such a level that independence will be more than a charade.

This is no easy task.

Chapter 17

*

LOVE OF LIBERTY

To the south of Sierra Leone and Guinea lies Liberia, a republic the size of Iceland which alone among the territories and nations of Africa has never been ruled by a European power, a state at once as progressive and backward as any on the continent.

Liberia's forty-mile-deep coastal plain, which has an Atlanta-heat-wave climate, rises slowly through forested green hills until, 220 miles from the ocean, it erupts in rock-studded mountains. To the south, through dripping jungles peopled by Stone Age tribesmen and pygmy hippopotami, lies Ivory Coast and there the coast swings eastward from the bulge of Africa so sharply that every West African seaport from Abidjan to Port Harcourt faces due south to the Antarctic.

Liberia is the oldest republic in Africa and, until recent years, was one of the world's worst governed. Its mere existence was one of the best arguments for colonialism and even Negroes looked on it with scorn. In 1929 the expenditure for brass bands was greater than that for public health. Liberia had to borrow money to stay alive and the interest on its debts at one stage in its chequered career absorbed 67 per cent of the national revenue.

Liberia, like Sierra Leone, was founded as a refuge for freed slaves. This did not deter its ruling class, former slaves called Americo-Liberians, from enslaving the people of the interior, with whom they fought a series of bloody wars. So disreputable was the country that many Americans maintained that Liberia should be forced to change the name of its capital, Monrovia, which honours the fifth president of the United States, during whose second term Liberia was settled by freed American Negroes. For a short time, missionary-founded Monrovia was called Christopolis.

The first motor-car did not reach Monrovia until 1916 when one was unloaded by mistake. It was just as well because the highway network as recently as 1948 consisted of one and a quarter miles of paved roads. Well-to-do Liberians, when they dared, swayed around the interior in hammocks carried by 'pawns', or domestic slaves. Just plain folks still travel by what is euphemistically termed 'the ankle express'.

Monrovia until a few years ago had no port facilities, telephones, lights, sewerage or paved streets; and it took less time to get a message from the Firestone rubber plantation, then the country's only industry, to Akron, Ohio, with which it had a radio-telephone connection, than to Monrovia forty miles away. World War II saw the construction of Liberia's first airfield and there is still not a foot of passenger railway in the country.

Only in recent years has Liberia produced its first doctor and Lord Hailey, a political scientist not given to verbal excesses, has described the country as 'a permanent reservoir' of disease. Today it is estimated that the incidence of malaria among Liberia's probable population of 1·5 million (there has never been a census) is 100 per cent and the infant mortality rate hovers around 70 per cent.

Although corruption is so rampant that the President must initial any expenditure of £36 or more, Liberians are prodigious churchgoers and it is customary to address anybody who owns a necktie as 'Honourable'. So addicted are the people of Liberia to this title that it is applied to institutions, the Senate, for instance, being referred to in official documents as 'the Honourable Senate'.

This penchant for formality carries over into matters of dress and, until a few years ago, it was not unknown for a distinguished personage to be buried wearing a topper. The top hat is seen less frequently on the streets today but woe betide the white man who is 'disrespectful' enough to enter a government office without coat and tie even though the thermometers have burst. As a result, the average Monrovian businessman looks as if he has just finished a half-mile run and is dissolving on the spot. So sensitive are Liberians that an individual or a firm which does anything which can be construed as reflecting racial bias is fined heavily in the first instance and deported in the second.

Liberia must surely be unique in that an estimated three-fourths of the population do not understand the official language, which is English. Only about 11 per cent of the school-age population attends school and most of these are Americo-Liberians or coastal people long exposed to the 'civilizing influence' of the original settlers. There has been a university of sorts in Monrovia since 1862 but one president of this institution appropriated the entire budget of the education department to send his daughters to school in Italy. For years this 'university' had no laboratories, scientific equipment or library. In modern Liberia there is exactly one public library with 3,000 volumes on its shelves.

Burglars called 'rogues' abound in Monrovia, particularly during the rains when their footsteps are muffled, and it was the only town in Africa in which our car was broken into. White foreigners are fair game and it is not unknown, I was told, for a white man who has fought and captured a rogue in his own house to be charged with assault and battery. One missionary awoke one morning to find that his entire garage had been dismantled and carried off during the night. Going before a Liberian court is no joke and one observer of the Liberian scene declared that 'perjury, discrimination, unmitigated harshness emphasized by pomp and deceit—these are the cornerstones of a legal system which makes the most corrupt court in the United States seem like a tribunal of wisdom and mercy by comparison'. Until recent years, prisoners went hungry unless their relatives provided them with food.

Liberia has always had a special relationship with the United States which cannot be found in the lexicon of political science. The U.S. Government has never exercised a protectorate over the West African state but often has supported its ruling class not only against European imperialism but against the not unnatural revolts staged by the natives of the interior.

In an unfriendly world, the United States has been Liberia's prop, and the African republic declared war against Germany during the First World War as soon as the United States became involved. Monrovia was then shelled by a German submarine but it is untrue that the Government considered surrendering. Liberia discreetly waited until 1944 to declare war on Nazi Germany, a year in which Teutonic fortunes were not at their highest point.

This American stepchild, larger than the three Benelux nations combined, has its Greenville, its Lexington, its Philadelphia and its Hartford, and there is a county named Maryland. A small force of American Negro army officers and N.C.O.s trains the Frontier Force and has in times past led it in action against the tribes. American, British, French and German customs receivers were used once in an attempt to curb Government corruption.

Liberian politics are colourful, to say the least, and one presidential candidate performed the remarkable electoral feat of extracting 243,000 votes from an electorate of 15,000 people. In 1943, a dressed-up monkey cast his ballot and a small village of a dozen huts delivered 5,100 votes for the government party and seven for the opposition.

Criticism of the Government or the passing of unfavourable information to foreign diplomats is punishable by imprisonment and the law requires that the Liberian president's photograph hang on the wall of every shop and office in the land.

This hot, green and humid republic has a national handshake (the middle fingers of the right hand are snapped together at the conclusion of the grip) and all the door-to-door traders in Monrovia are known as 'Charlies'. In 1953 it rained hard enough to break the capital's meteorological instruments and the dripping soil bursts with dark blue violets, moonflowers and hibiscus. Although the soil was Liberia's only source of wealth until the exploitation of iron in the last decade, there was no department of agriculture until the late 1940's. As recently as six years ago, 80 per cent of the country's teachers had less than elementary education. The postal service is slow: letters, packages and periodicals are frequently not delivered at all; when they are, they often appear to have been read not only by the clerk concerned but by all of his family and most of his friends. Stamps are frequently removed from the envelopes of outgoing letters.

Liberia used to be called the Grain Coast, deriving its name from the peppers which grew there. It has never had a drought, a hurricane, a tornado or an earthquake and it is 1,600 miles from Brazil. Liberia lost its membership in the International Boy Scouts in 1934 when it was discovered that the Liberian branch was functioning as a juvenile wing of the militia. Dishes called dumboy, fufu, palaver sauce and bitter leaf are local delicacies and 93 per cent of the country has received an aerial survey, or about twice as high a percentage as in the United States.

Middle-class Liberians can be rude, lazy, incompetent and have exaggerated inferiority complexes. The Westernized upper class are high livers and conspicuous consumers. Although most of the upper class is Christian, many consult witch-doctors called 'zos' in times of trouble and others belong to human-sacrifice groups like the Leopard Society or the Snake People. Like Hollywood stars, Liberians tend to be vertical polygamists. One curious custom is to leave rugs in the plastic sheaths in which they come from the factory, thus giving the impression of a new purchase.

The Constitution states that the purpose of Liberia is 'to provide a home for the dispersed and oppressed Children of Africa, and to regenerate and enlighten this benighted Continent'. Perhaps with this in mind, only those with Negro blood may become citizens, only citizens may own property, and only property holders may vote or hold office. Hence political control is vested firmly in a Negro oligarchy. Despite this discriminatory legislation there were more than 4,600 whites living in Liberia in 1959, a quarter of whom were Americans. Thirty-four nationalities are represented among the foreigners, including three perspiring Finns, a lonely Japanese, a solitary Mexican and eleven stateless persons.

Like Sierra Leone, Liberia was the child of a curious marriage between philanthropists and reactionaries. In the last years of the eighteenth century and the first years of the century which followed, many American slave-owners, Washington and Jefferson among them, either freed some of their slaves or provided in their wills for manumission of loyal servants. Others allowed industrious slaves to purchase their own freedom.

As the number of freedmen grew (there were 31,000 in the Northern states alone in 1790), liberal circles looked with increasing concern on the economic plight of these unfortunate people, many of whom were unable to fend for themselves. During the first two decades of the nineteenth century, slave rebellions broke out in various parts of the South. Since the leaders of these rebellions were proved or thought to be ex-slaves, the planters of the South soon demonstrated a strong interest in the repatriation of this 'seditious' element. The Virginia Legislature, among others, recommended that Negroes 'obnoxious to the laws and dangerous to the peace' be resettled in Africa or South America.

From this synthesis of fear and charity grew the American Colonization Society. Its first president was Bushrod Washington (nephew of George) and numbered among its members were Andrew Jackson of Tennessee and Henry Clay of Kentucky. My own state of Maryland, whose population was 35 per cent Negro, regarded the American Colonization Society's resettlement programme as too slow and formed its own group aimed at the rapid and complete repatriation of her 8,000 former slaves. Congress appropriated £36,000 to resettle with the colonists of the two societies the cargoes of slave ships seized on the high seas by the navy.

The initial attempt in 1820 to establish eighty-eight freedmen in West Africa failed, but the following year the agent of the American Colonization Society, Dr. Eli Ayres, landed from the sloop *Alligator* on Providence Island off Cape Mesurado, the site of present-day Monrovia. For bullets, powder, a box of beads, two hogsheads of tobacco, six pieces of blue cloth and assorted umbrellas, iron bars, hats, boxes of soap and kegs of rum (all worth £32), the wily doctor 'purchased' (as usual, the natives believed that they were bartering the use of their land, not the land itself, which by native custom may not be sold) a 130-mile stretch of coast forty miles deep.

The survivors of the previous settlement and a batch of new colonists who had braved the fifty-six-day voyage, 114 in all, came ashore in 1822. Sickness soon put a third of the settlers out of their misery and only the alertness of a formidable matron named Matilda Newport, who used the ashes from her pipe to fire a cannon during an attack, and the leadership of Jehudi Ashmun, a white Congregationalist missionary known as 'the Prophet', preserved Monrovia from extinction.

Meanwhile, 200 miles to the south, the schooner *Orion* landed thirty-one Baltimore Negroes ranging in age from two to 110 on a swampy patch of land at Cape Palmas which was to become known as Maryland-in-Liberia. Each of these stalwarts, after signing a statement that he or she would abstain from 'ardent spirits', had been furnished by the Maryland Colonization Society with £1 4s. 8d., shoes, seed, coffee, trade goods and farm implements. Like the larger settlement on Providence Island, Maryland-in-Liberia was a private venture supported only by a colonization society, not by the U.S. government. Its flag was Old Glory with a cross replacing the stars, and its first governors, like those of the northern settlement, were white Americans.

Maryland-in-Liberia named its capital Harper, after an early advocate of colonization, and in Southern fashion established 'good clean cotton' at 8d. a pound as its currency. Later it issued its own banknotes bearing reproductions of goats, ducks, tobacco leaves and chickens.

As if hostile tribesmen, a killing climate, indolence and poverty were not trouble enough, both settlements found their existence challenged by the merchants and governments of England and France who refused to recognize their rights as long as they remained the wards of private corporations. Since the United States was unwilling to embroil itself by declaring a protectorate, the American Colonization Society stepped aside in 1847 and the Monrovia settlement became the Republic of Liberia. The colonists' first non-white governor, the able Virginia octoroon Joseph Jenkins Roberts, became the infant state's first president. Maryland-in-Liberia became independent seven years later but, hard-pressed by the natives, gave up and joined Liberia in 1857. A Harvard law professor drew up a constitution modelled on that of the United States; a replica of the Stars and Stripes except that it has but a single star and eleven stripes (one for each signer of its declaration of independence) was sewn together by Matilda Newport and six other women, and the motto 'The Love of Liberty Brought Us Here' was adopted.

England and France quickly recognized the new republic. Paradoxically the United States, whose citizens had established the state and whose arms had sustained it, withheld recognition until 1862, a year in which Southern opinion held little force in the cloakrooms of Capitol Hill.

The new nation was a sickly child. Five times within the next fifty years only the timely arrival of American assistance prevented the overthrow of the republic by the tribesmen. With the end of the Civil War and the emancipation of America's slaves, the number of freedmen willing to return diminished. The end of the slave trade cut off that source of immigrants and Liberia was left with 15,000 freed American Negroes and 5,000 slaves rescued from the Middle Passage, upon which to build a nation. With the support of the colonization societies withdrawn and the United States unwilling to commit herself beyond the maintenance of the coastal settlements, Liberia lost hundreds of square miles to the neighbouring French and British colonies. Estimates as to the amount of territory lost range from 10 per cent to 60 per cent, with the first figure probably being closer to the mark. It should be remembered, however, that Liberian control outside gunshot of the coastal settlements was always tenuous and usually brutal. It is difficult to fault the colonial powers for removing primitive tribes from the administration (where it existed) of a government which offered them nothing but slavery and abuse. By the same token, one should recognize that it was to the advantage of the colonial powers to justify their policies by emphasizing that the Liberian Government was unfit to rule.

With no source of revenue and little knowledge of the workings of finance, Liberia's leaders floated at piratical interest rates a series of loans with private European investors. The money was invariably squandered, Liberia was unable to meet her debts and the republic on several occasions came close to being 'foreclosed' by its creditors. The greatest tribute which can be paid to the first two generations of settlers is that they survived and the country survived them.

After the weaklings had perished—and perish they must in any frontier situation—the tougher breed of Americo-Liberians, as the ex-slaves and their descendants were to be termed, rolled up their sleeves and got to work. For their children if not for themselves they laboured with hammer and plough to re-create the Old South, or what they remembered of the Old South: a black gentry based, like all good aristocracies, on the twin pillars of the land and the Church, a leisured society with themselves in the role of master and the indigenous people playing the same part the Americo-Liberians had played in the cotton country of the New World was their goal. That their descendants might read Greek and be called to the bar, they sweated in the fields, traded with all comers and reduced the tribesmen to a status of semi-slavery.

Unfortunately, they succeeded. Liberians who are old today were brought up to scorn labour and to love litigation. They sent their children off to Europe for education, sold the natives into peonage in the cacao fields of French Gabon and the Spanish island of Fernando Po, milked the government of such revenue as it had, affixed an 'Honourable' in front of their names, and let the businesses and plantations established by their more industrious ancestors go to seed.

The situation in regard to the oppression of the people of the interior came to a head in 1931 with the publication of a League of Nations report which revealed that high Liberian officials, including Vice-President Allen Yancy, were receiving £16 from the Spanish government for every native 'recruited' for service on Fernando Po. The League's commission of inquiry stated that natives were 'recruited under conditions of criminal compulsion scarcely distinguishable from slave raiding and slave trading' and added that 'intimidation has apparently been and is the keyword of the government's native policy'. This traffic had the support of 'the highest officials' and Yancy, said the commission, was the chief beneficiary. This should have come as no surprise: as early as 1920, a United States diplomat in Monrovia warned the State Department that American assistance to Liberia made it 'morally responsible for the perpetuation of a government notoriously inefficient, corrupt, and hostile to effective reforms'. In fact, the Government of Liberia in the past has been more concerned with protecting the position of privilege held by the ruling oligarchy than in the maintenance of Liberia's international integrity. There was talk of expelling Liberia from the League or of declaring the country to be an international protectorate. In the end, President Charles King and Vice-President Yancy resigned, Liberia promised reforms and, it is said, massacred hundreds of tribesmen who had testified to the League commission, and the crisis blew over. Significantly, nothing was said about expelling Spain from the League.

MADISON AVENUE AND CATFISH ROW

Of the three territories which border Liberia, only Guinea has a highway link to the republic, although it will soon be possible to reach Sierra Leone by road. After convincing the Guinean authorities with some difficulty that there was no reason why we should not be allowed to leave the country, we huffed up a steep hill and followed the red snake of the road as it slithered and twisted through broken hills before reaching the banks of an oily stream beside which stood the tin-roofed mud shacks of the Liberian border post.

Outside sat a fat Negro in American fatigue uniform who was in the process of looting the belongings of a truck-load of Africans. From one old Muslim he appropriated a pair of the ugly plastic sandals so much admired by West Africans; a second had only a carton of soft drinks and the official contented himself with removing a bottle of this; a third apparently carried nothing of value in his tin trunk so the inspector merely appropriated the lock. There were a number of Africans talking excitedly within the building. The cause of their dismay was a second uniformed but tie-less official who sat with his knees blocking the doorway and refused to let them out until each had given him a few francs or some American coins (Liberia, which has coinage but no paper money of its own, used the pound sterling until 1942, when it switched to the dollar).

The doorkeeper let me pass and I walked through this scene of confusion to a small office where a group of Muslims were sitting quietly while a wizened clerk scrutinized their papers. This took some time for one lens of his glasses was broken and he had to squint with one eye. He motioned to me to come up to the table and I handed him our passports with the pages opened to our Liberian visas.

He considered these for a moment or two and said something which sounded rather like 'weydeahyazgwantatuday?'.

'Pardon?'

'Don't you understand English?' he roared. 'I want to know where you're going!' The question seemed superfluous since Liberia's only road leads to Monrovia but I advised him that I was about to make good a long-cherished ambition to see his country's capital. He muttered and wrote something in my passport.

'Can you read?' he asked.

'I do fairly well,' I said.

'Read this [I was instructed to report to the Immigration Department within twenty-four hours upon pain of arrest] and see the Honourable in the next office.'

This Honourable was the customs man and he was a fat and cheery soul. His desk was littered with papers and piles of money, mostly small coins. He was disappointed when I told him that I had no money with me because my bank would be cabling me some in Monrovia. He made up for this by reading me the portion of my passport which admonishes me not to vote in any foreign elections or to serve in the armed forces of alien nations. I assured him that much as I admired the 2,000-man Liberian Frontier Force, I had no intention of enlisting and ventured that since President Tubman had been in office for sixteen years, it seemed unlikely that he would require my help to remain at the helm. This seemed to satisfy him and we parted good friends.

Outside a couple of Frontier Force troopers were giving the fender of my car an appraising kick or two, looking longingly at the contents in the back and admiring Kitty's knitting, an art unknown in these parts although knitted scarves and hats are worn. As I got behind the wheel, one of the troopers held up his hand and turned to the shack.

'He go?' he asked.

'Lettum go,' came the genial and welcome reply.

Ganta, the Liberian border settlement, is a drab and characterless town, one block thick on each side of the road, with the dark shops of the Syrians facing the street and the native huts grouped behind them. It is also the site of the American Methodist mission run by Dr. George Harley, a prominent physician and anthropologist, who hiked in from Monrovia some thirty-five years ago. As recently as 1947 Harley and his wife had to walk the middle third of the trip up from Monrovia before they could be met by an ancient Ford which the doctor assembled in northern Liberia after it had been carried up in head-loads.

At the end of the town was another police barrier and then an arch of branches drying over the road which showed that a dignitary from Monrovia had passed through within the last few months. Beyond this the road stretched out red and glistening in the light rain which began to fall, a smooth well-banked dirt highway built with American funds and some day to be paved.

In our travels in central and southern Africa, Kitty had been so disconcerted by the way that whites would pass Africans without any

443

indication that they saw them that she always waved when we passed natives and was usually greeted by a filed-tooth grin and a wave in return. But here the people were sullen and turned away when we passed, ignoring her waves. Perhaps they are too civilized to be courteous. Or have the road and cars meant nothing more to the people of the interior than an intensification of oppression from Monrovia?

There was another funny thing about the road: with the exception of the branch off to the then unfinished 'highway' to Sierra Leone, there were no access roads. Mile after mile the road cut like a red knife through the dripping green of the jungle; no roads and few paths joined; no towns of any size were linked by it, although one hamlet boasted a Pittsburgh Bar, Missouri Café, Maryland Restaurant and Dew Drop Inn . . . but no school. It seemed almost as if the road had a personality and a purpose of its own, so little concern had it with men. It just went on through the dripping emptiness.

Then there was a road block and a detour sign and we found ourselves driving through the ordered ranks of the biggest rubber grove in the world, Firestone's Harbel plantation. The road got better, the Africans waved back occasionally, and then the road swung out of Firestone and back on to the main route, which had become paved (in 1957, Liberia had forty-two miles of paved road). And then there was Monrovia.

The town, which has a population of about 35,000, was shabby and unkempt but infinitely smarter than what we had expected. Anything written prior to 1950 mentions unpaved streets studded with rocks, a wheezing electricity plant and the absence of hotels, telephones, taxicabs, sewers and modern buildings. All this was true at the time. But an economic boom of which we shall hear more later has changed the face of Monrovia, although it will never rank as the Paris or even the Pittsburgh of Africa.

On Mamba Point, the 800-foot-high hill which dominates the town, are the foreign embassies, a luxury hotel, a lighthouse, and a monument to J. J. Roberts, the republic's first president. Broad Street, which runs part-way up the side of Mamba Point only to peter out in a pile of rubble, is a wide paved avenue lit by fluorescent lamps and lined with three (count 'em) hotels, one Greek, one Liberian and one Spanish-owned. For £4 a day at the best one, you get a surly desk clerk, a decent double room with an air-conditioner which may work, a tiled bath, expensive but edible meals and two free tickets to the movie next door.

Down Broad Street and between it and Ashmun Street (named after an American governor, as are Johnson, Carey, Randall, Mechlin and Buchanan Streets), is the block-square 'Executive Mansion', a rotund white-painted affair guarded by sloppy Frontier Force troopers and set beside a garden nicely illuminated at its four corners by statues of a leopard, an elephant, a bushcow and a hippo, electric lights planted in their respective mouths. And then the town seems slowly to come to pieces: the paving ends, the new concrete office buildings become more infrequent, and the houses degenerate from slightly tatty old frame affairs into hideous shacks of rusted iron and scraps of wood. Here and there are half-finished buildings which obviously have not been worked on for some time. Monrovia looks like a small and unattractive city which has just suffered some major disaster; but ten years ago it looked like a pathetic slum too unprepossessing to warrant a disaster. The improvement has been immense.

Monrovia, which is the only town in the republic with a telephone system, gets 200 inches of rain each year, and palms, coconuts, mangoes and cashews give the capital a leafy charm and dull the harshness of the slums. But the city is not all slums by any means. Although many government buildings are sway-backed affairs apparently on the verge of collapse, a vigorous public works programme is replacing them at a rapid pace. An impressive example of this is the strikingly modern capital building at Camp Johnson, just outside the city. This rather startling edifice, designed and built by a German firm at a cost of nearly £1 million, looks more like a combination of an ultra-modern cinema, a missile launching pad and an airport control tower than a house of assembly: it consists of a large rotunda built with generous use of glass and flanked by two wings of offices elevated on concrete stilts. It contains two bars to cater to thirsty law-makers. In addition to government construction, many firms have modern office buildings and the city now can boast its first four-storey apartment house.

Rich Liberians (and there are more than a few of these) live in split-level ramblers on an opulent 'gold coast' along the seashore outside the city, although even here one may see Cadillacs parked beside thatched huts. But despite the wealth of the upper class, it is soon obvious that the standard of living of the mass of the people is far lower than in other parts of West Africa: it is difficult to buy a ball-point pen or a pair of shoe laces in Monrovia, items which are pressed upon the traveller by enterprising small traders from Dakar to Douala.

Monrovians like eighteenth-century quadrilles, reels and grand marches and are very clothes-conscious and well-dressed, most of the upper class buying their clothes in New York or Paris. In contrast, the cotton cloth worn by the people of the interior is cheap and colourless compared to the everyday material in British or French Africa. Monrovians are keen on King Kong films, fried chicken and fraternal societies such as the United Brothers of Friendship and the Sisters of the Mysterious Ten. Attendance at a movie theatre is a valuable if not a pleasant experience: although English is the official language, few understand it and those who can follow the dialogue interpret what is going on to their friends in loud voices. Since the dialogue is not understood by most, audiences tend to concentrate their enthusiasm on the action. The film which we saw was a musical and the audience's reaction seemed in direct proportion to the amount of female underwear displayed in the high-kicks of the dancers. 'This,' whispered a white woman sitting next to us, 'is like spending two hours in a darkened baboon cage.'

Illiteracy in the capital, which is home for half of the descendants of the Americo-Liberians and of the 60,000 'Westernized' coastal natives, is a matter of official record: a 1956 census revealed that Monrovia has a population of 41,000 of which little more than a quarter could write English (and this generally means the ability to write one's name) and less than 10 per cent had attended secondary school. The proportion of educated women, however, is probably higher here than anywhere else in West Africa and many upper-class women work full-time. Posts held by female Americo-Liberians include Assistant Secretary for Public Works, Commissioner of Writs, Director of the European Desk of the State Department, and Assistant Attorney General. There is also one female chief. Monrovia now has its own airport. Before this, passengers took a light plane from Robertsfield to a meadow near the city rather than brave the fifty-mile drive over a rock-studded road.

You drive easily down Water Street, the commercial centre of the Syrians, because the people are too poor to afford the bicycles which jam the streets of other West African cities, and across the bridge which spans Stockton Creek (named after the captain of the *Alligator*) and out on to Bushrod Island, where the Kru fishermen live. Here is the modern port and a new hotel, run by the brother of Liberia's Vice-President. If it is late enough in the day, you may hit some traffic, for despite the hellish weather Monrovia officials and businessmen come tardily to their offices. They make up for this, however, by leaving early.

LOVE OF LIBERTY

BOBOR SHAD

The history of Liberia can be divided into two periods—B.T. and A.T.—so potent and decisive has been the sixteen-year régime of the republic's eighteenth president, William Vacanarat Shadrach Tubman.

Tubman, who is sixty-four, was born at Harper, the old capital of Maryland-in-Liberia and his father was Speaker of the House of Representatives (the Number Three post in the country) and a fire-and-brimstone Methodist preacher. Both sides of the family emigrated from Georgia. His mother was one of the few Negroes to come to Liberia after the Civil War, arriving in 1872.

Shad, as his friends call him, went to the government primary school in Harper and then to a Methodist teacher-training school, finishing his formal education in 1913. While holding down a high school teaching job, Tubman taught himself law (and cricket!), later served as court recorder, revenue collector, and county attorney. After service with the Frontier Force as a subaltern during three campaigns against the tribes of the interior, Tubman became at twenty-eight the youngest senator in the country's history. He was involved in the slavery scandal of the 1930's to the extent that he was the legal adviser of Vice-President Yancy.

In a sense, the slavery episode helped Tubman's career: with the resignation of King and Yancy, Liberia's dictatorial Secretary of State, Edwin J. Barclay, Tubman's mentor and a kinsman of his present wife, became president. Barclay named Tubman to the five-member Supreme Court in 1937, nominated him six years later to be his successor. Tubman, whom Barclay backed on the premise that he would act as his stooge, soon proved himself to be the most forceful and able executive since Roberts.

Before Tubman, no Liberian president had desired or dared to go more than forty miles into the interior. Tubman had the sense to see that, with African nationalism on the rampage, the Americo-Liberian oligarchy could not hope to maintain control of the country without receiving at least token support from tribal elements. He was a sufficiently astute politician to realize that the tribes would pledge their loyalty to the president who opened to them the door of political freedom and patronage. Tubman, who is fond of Johnny Walker Red Label and outsized Havana cigars, criss-crossed the country on foot, mule, car and hammock, called on the coastal tribes in his sumptuous yacht, announced to astounded tribesmen, whose previous contact with the Monrovia government had meant only more taxes, or forced labour, that they were to be allowed to vote like anybody else which means that they can vote for the True Whig Party, which has completely dominated Liberian politics for the last ninety years. He also extended the franchise to women and arranged for the election of the country's-first and only female member of the House of Representatives, a venerable lady known as the Honourable Ellen Mills Scarborough, who holds a graduate degree from Columbia.

Perhaps more important than this theoretical emancipation of the native population (the same Monrovia gang selects the True Whig candidates) has been Tubman's practice of calling 'Executive Councils' in the interior. At these councils, which are attended by headmen, chiefs and government administrators, Tubman listens to complaints, exhorts the people to greater effort, promises government help, settles tribal disputes, preaches his 'Unification Doctrine', and occasionally fires a particularly oppressive government official.

The President from time to time wears tribal dress and men of tribal origin hold the posts of Secretary of State, Chief Justice, Director of Public Health, and Under-Secretary of the Interior. This absorption of the more progressive tribesmen into the central government serves the dual purpose of revitalizing the Americo-Liberian aristocracy and depriving the peoples of the interior of leaders who might otherwise adopt a revolutionary posture. Gradually Tubman hopes to extend civil law into the interior (where native law now prevails) and to grant fuller political representation to the tribal element. Their representation at the moment consists of eleven members in the thirty-seven-seat House and none in the Senate.

The degree of administrative control over each of the twenty-eight tribes of the interior varies. Close to the coast control is generally strong and Monrovia is able to nominate the chiefs and 'guide' their actions; in the interior, where some strong chiefs exist, the central government sometimes finds it more discreet to confirm a powerful chief in office rather than try to replace him with a Monrovia nominee. As in other parts of Africa, the tribes vary in their characteristics: Krus are industrious, Vais (who are the only Negro people to have a self-developed alphabet; the Amharas and Berbers, of course, are not Negroes) are intelligent, Gbundes are warlike. All of them will have something to add to the Liberian nation.

Tubman, who is a Mason, an Oddfellow and holds a dozen honorary degrees from American Negro colleges, comes down hard on anybody who refuses to co-operate on the unification programme and he recently warned the chiefs and people of one district that 'if you do not work voluntarily, Government will have to force you to plant farms'. Those are words which no white administrator would dare use to a colonial African. But then Bobor (Brother) Shad, as the people call him, has never been one to mince words and the unification programme, which aims at the eventual elimination of all distinctions between Americo-Liberians and 'aborigines' (as the people of Monrovia call tribesmen), is close to his heart. He put it this way at Harper in 1954:

'If any person, civilized or uncivilized, opposes the unification of this nation, he is an enemy of the State, a confirmed political lunatic and should not be followed.'

Although Tubman tolerates no open criticism of himself or of his régime, many older Americo-Liberians are bitterly opposed to unification, which they regard as cultural and political suicide, and Tubman, like Haile Selassie, is more liberal on many matters than his subordinates and the aristocracy. The reason that feeling of this sort is not as widespread in Liberia as in Sierra Leone is that the Americo-Liberians and 'civilized' tribesmen (the test of civilization in Liberia is the ability to read and write English) remain firmly in control of the political situation.

The chiefs and those people of the interior who know what is going on are, of course, delighted with Tubman's action. This somewhat pathetic but indicative statement was made by Central Province Paramount Chief Gbassee Kparngba in answer to a question about his feelings on the subject:

'President Tubman has really turned this country around. We tribesmen can now mix up with the civilized people freely and nobody is looking down on us. We can now eat at the same table, shake hands and dance with the civilized men and women. God will bless him to live long. We want him to be president until he dies.'

The fact of the unification programme, of course, is not as pretty as the theory. Too often it has meant only lavish entertaining of the chiefs, not betterment of the lot of the people. Although anyone who can show a receipt for his 14-shilling hut-tax can vote, the constituencies and organization of the True Whig Party are so rigged that tribal political influence is negligible. Social prejudice against the 'aborigines' remains and the bulk of civil service jobs still go to Americo-Liberians. But government officials at least are beginning to realize that Tubman expects them to do more than just oppress the people of the interior.

State schools and clinics, something never before seen in the bush, are being established and efforts are being made to give the tribesmen a voice in the government. These gains, modest as they are, would have been unthinkable twenty years ago.

Tubman's second great accomplishment has been the economic development of his country. Before he took office the only form of business activity in the country was Firestone's vast rubber plantation. Liberians, not without due cause, have always been fearful that foreign investment might mean foreign domination. Tubman was not slow to appreciate the fact that lack of foreign investment certainly meant national poverty. To avert the one, he was willing to risk the other. He moved quickly to announce an 'Open Door Policy' offering favourable conditions to any enterprise whose presence would help Liberia. This policy, which has made it possible for American investment in Liberia to swell from £1 million to more than £25 million in little more than a decade (and has resulted in an influx of Swedish, West German, Italian, Israeli and Spanish capital as well), has raised Liberia's national budget during his administration from a miserable £268,000 to its present level of more than £7·1 million. More of this later.

His third great contribution has been in the field of foreign affairs. At a time when Nkrumah, Touré and Keita are agitating for an often ill-conceived African unity which threatens through adventurism to destroy that which it ostensibly hopes to achieve, Tubman joins Houphouet in interjecting a conservative and realistic note.

The Liberian president advocates the creation of what he likes to call 'The Associated States of Africa', a grouping 'based on treaties and conventions . . . on the basis of mutual respect and equal consideration for all'. Tubman dubs Nkrumah's bid for Pan-African unity (under Nkrumah, of course) as 'unrealistic and utopian', and adds that 'any hasty or superficial semblance of unity in areas where conflicting issues are not carefully resolved may undermine the entire structure of any permanent political unity and retard real co-operative effort'.

Tubman has doubts that Nkrumah's ill-defined 'Pan-African Socialism' is adaptable to the African way of life and maintains that each African state 'should be left free to work out the ideology best suited to its particular needs and its own will'. Taking another swipe at the Ghanaian, Tubman points out that Pan-African congresses which include individuals and groups rather than the representatives of nations 'are not competent to plan political strategy on the national or international level'. 'Communism,' states a Liberian Government publication, 'is considered as a *hypnotic* fantasy of suave, erroneous ideology.'

Tubman, who has been taking an ever more active role in Pan-African affairs since the African 'Big Three' (himself, Nkrumah and Touré) met at Saniquelle in Liberia last year, sees the Associated States as a loose federation providing for the peaceful solution of disputes between members. He favours a uniform reduction of tariffs to create a West African common market and the creation of regional authorities to promote health, research and culture.

The proclamations which came out of the Saniquelle conference were very close to this so apparently the Liberian has convinced his more radical neighbours. He is not putting all his eggs in one basket, however, and has recently concluded a treaty of defence with the United States, a fact which it did not suit him to reveal while the Saniquelle meeting was in session.

For presenting such a programme, Tubman has been pilloried by African extremists as an 'Uncle Tom' and described as 'a black tool of the imperialists'. Liberian delegations to the various Accra conferences have been virtually ostracized and their speeches boycotted. As a result, a few of the younger generation of Liberians have urged the President to conciliate Ghana and Guinea. This he has done to some extent but Tubman's basic position is still far closer to Houphouet's than to Nkrumah's or Touré's.

Tubman, a stocky, self-assured man of medium height, is fond of the ladies, convivial male companionship and yachting. He wears horn-rimmed glasses, is invariably accompanied by a cigar clamped precariously in a holder, and likes to have the squat towers of the Saturday Afternoon Club illuminated when he is regaling his friends with shaggy dog stories or working out policy decisions. He has visited the United States three times and has been lavishly received in Spain by Franco, a man whom he resembles in some ways. But he spends plenty of time at his souvenir-littered desk in the Executive Mansion and is easily the hardest working man in the country. Although he is a staunch advocate of rigorous protocol, Tubman can be a relaxed and informal host, likes to wear a sports shirt when showing visitors around his private zoo at his country estate.

His personality dominates Liberian life. To some extent this is in the nature of the political organization of the country. Liberia's constitution is similar to that of the United States in that there is an elective president and a vice-president serving terms of limited duration, there are two legislative bodies called the House of Representatives and the Senate, and there is a Supreme Court with a theoretical separation of the powers of the three branches. This similarity is more apparent than real, however, for one basic reason: Liberia is a unitary state rather than a federal one and there are no local elective offices. This means that Liberians vote for exactly forty-nine people: the president, the vice-president, the thirty-seven members of the House of Representatives and the ten members of the Senate. Everybody else—dog-catchers, diplomats, district commissioners, army officers, school superintendents, public health doctors and Supreme Court justices—are appointed by and serve at the pleasure of the president. This patronage weapon, which gives the president not only the power to reward loyalty but to punish disobedience, in effect makes Liberia a popular dictatorship. Under Tubman Liberia has experienced a wise and benevolent dictatorship, but the definition remains true.

The only possible challenge to Tubman or to any other Liberian president comes from within the True Whig party, which has held office in Liberia since 1870. Like Ghana and Mali (but unlike Guinea) political opposition is theoretically legal although certainly not encouraged. Last year, when Tubman received 530,566 votes to be re-elected to an unprecedented fourth term (his first was an eight-year term; succeeding ones are four-year), he was opposed by an elderly organist and former judge who described himself as 'not particularly opposed' to Tubman but running 'in response to the ardent desire of Dr. Tubman for fair and friendly competition'. The organist's sheep symbol (the symbol of the True Whig party is the elephant) received forty-one votes, including Tubman's. This was something of a moral victory for the opposition candidate, W. O. Davies-Bright, who in 1955 received only sixteen votes. Despite this feeble opposition, two policemen, an army officer and a civilian were killed during disorders at the polls in 1955.

But when as in 1951 there was a real threat from the Kru leader Didwo Twe, who had called the League of Nations' attention to the slavery situation, Tubman did not hesitate to drive his opponent into exile and to declare the opposing party illegal. In 1955 he used an alleged assassination attempt, which looked very much like a red herring, to jail several other Liberians not in accord with his policies.

Liberia is, then, in fact if not in theory, a one-party state. Tubman controls the central committee of the True Whig party which nominates the candidates who are to stand for assured election. This he manages by keeping loyal supporters in key posts and by the force of his own personality and the obvious benefits which Liberia has reaped from his administration. The True Whig party can never lack for funds since it thoughtfully deducts two weeks' salary from the annual wages of all civil servants and a month's pay during election years.

Like any wise leader, Tubman makes sure that no rival within the party accumulates power, prestige or popularity sufficient to challenge his authority. When one of his vice-presidents grew too ambitious, Tubman made him ambassador to England, and gradually pushed him down the ladder until the rival went into retirement. His present vice-president, a chubby little man with a moustache and sideburns, is primarily interested in the business ventures which occupy his time, while the Speaker of the House is a colourless man incapable of mounting opposition if he so desired.

The net result of all this is that Tubman's personality pervades every aspect of Liberian life. The new capitol building stands on Tubman Hill and a larger-than-life bronze statue (clutching a bronze cigar) gazes contemplatively over the grounds of the University of Liberia. There is a 'Bobor Shad' beer, a Tubman Bridge, an Antoinette Tubman stadium, and the President's slightly goitrous profile adorns everything from women's compacts to 'T' shirts in comic book colours worn by Broad Street cowboys. Government reports and the country's two subsidized newspapers refer to him only in capital letters and extravagant adjectives ('Our Honourable and Prophetic President').

In a country where the average wage is less than three shillings a day, Tubman's salary is £12,500 and his 'perks' are unlimited. He is not above spending £1 million of a £2·7 million loan on building himself a new official residence or blowing another £300,000 to replace his already opulent presidential yacht, the 463-ton *President Edward J. Royce*, as he did in 1959, a year in which 90 per cent of Liberia's school-age children got no education. The *Royce*, named after the first Liberian president of pure Negro stock, had accommodation for thirty-six passengers and maintenance costs absorbed 1 per cent of the national revenue. The new yacht, called *Liberian*, is a little larger but carries 'only' twenty-five guests and thirty-five crewmen. The President maintains that the yacht is required for national defence and perhaps he is right: it constitutes the Liberian navy.

Tubman owns about 4,000 acres of rubber and is supposed to be the third largest private planter in the country. He also owns a cacao farm and considerable real estate in Monrovia. A German manager runs his

Totota rubber estate and profits must be substantial as two of the President's sons (he has five children) attend an English boarding school and another has attended Harvard and Rutgers. The constitution was amended to allow Tubman to serve consecutive terms of office and a presidential inauguration can cost as much as £350,000.

Tubman's weaknesses are human ones and there is nothing mean about them. He is an engaging, hard-working, intelligent man possessed of a considerable social conscience, great human understanding and immense political ability. His accomplishments far exceed his failings and to regard Tubman as a comic-opera figure is to misunderstand him. Both for Liberia and for the West, Tubman has been and is the best man for the job.

THE BLACK BOOM

It was sunrise and pleasantly cool. The thin-trunked rubber trees, each about fifteen feet tall, stretched away in rank after rank to form ordered, leaf-roofed corridors down which swirled a light mist. Along the road, which was the colour of burnt cinnamon, came the tappers, the stainless steel buckets hanging at either end of the sticks which they carried across their shoulders making them look like hulking black milkmaids. They come early because the rubber coagulates in the afternoon and will not flow.

Each man went to a numbered tree, dumped the milky fluid (called 'scrap') from the small cup affixed to the bark of the tree into his bucket. Then he made a long diagonal slash parallel to and not more than the thickness of a page of paper from the old cuts which marked the bark like an off-centre griddle. He fixed the cup at the point of the cut closest to the ground, squirted a few drops of ammonia into the receptacle and walked on down the line of trees repeating the operation as he went. Each tree is tapped for twenty-three consecutive days, then allowed to rest for twenty-three days; they bear for about thirty years. By the time his six-hour work-day was finished, he would have tapped 300 trees (it takes one minute to tap a tree) and made about three shillings. So begins and ends every day at Firestone's vast (90,000-acre) Harbel plantation forty miles from Monrovia for tappers with pleasant names like Dinner Pail, Pay Day and Christmas (there are so many Josephs that they are numbered according to seniority).

History does not record if the late Harvey S. Firestone wore white plumes in his fedora when he came into Liberia's life in 1926. But he must have looked like a knight in shining armour to the West African republic. The Akron industrialist wanted a place outside the colonial writ in which he could grow rubber. By 1922, Britain controlled 75 per cent of the world's rubber plantations and was able by price-fixing to force the cost of a pound of rubber up from one shilling to nine shillings. This did not please Mr. Firestone and, after considering Mexico, Sarawak and the Philippines as possible sites, he settled on Liberia. The West African republic needed a loan to get its European creditors off its neck and it wanted the presence of a sizable American investment to increase U.S. interest in the country and thus forestall possible annexation by a colonial power. Firestone, one of the first American firms to invest in Africa south of the Sahara, obtained a ninety-nine-year concession to rent at 5d. an acre up to one million acres of fertile land centred on an abandoned British plantation at Mount Barclay, thirty miles from Monrovia. In return, the Ohio firm lent Liberia £900,000, 90 per cent of which went to pay off existing obligations. Rubber cuttings were imported from Brazil and by World War II Liberia was supplying 20 per cent of the United States' rubber requirements.

Firestone envisioned investing £36 million in his huge concession to produce 200,000 tons of rubber a year, giving jobs to 350,000 Liberians. The actuality fell far short of the dream (Firestone has invested about £7·2 million, annually produces 40,000 tons of rubber, employs 25,000) but within twenty years the company's production of rubber constituted 97 per cent of Liberia's exports by value. Although its relative importance as a revenue source is decreasing rapidly as iron mining moves towards a dominant position in the economy, rubber still pays Liberia's way (68 per cent of her exports by value in 1958). And rubber in Liberia, despite increasing activity on the part of the B.F. Goodrich Company (600,000-acre concession with 50,000 acres under cultivation on the Lofa River; no production until 1962) and individual Liberians, still spells Firestone.

Today Firestone cultivates twelve million rubber trees on 100,000 acres at Harbel and the smaller Cavalla plantation. On the two planta-tions are 10,000 houses, two modern hospitals, seven club houses, two excellent golf courses, sixteen schools and churches, 275 miles of the best roads in the country, a telephone system, a hydro-electric plant, a radio station, an airfield, the largest latex factory in the world, a brick-making plant and an eye-catchingly modern research centre.

It is not being chauvinistic to say that Firestone is one of the best equipped and most efficiently run firms operating in Africa today: only the mining companies of the Congo and South Africa can rival it in this respect. And the company's shadow spreads far beyond its grove of rubber trees: one of its subsidiaries is the largest export-import firm in the country—it imports rice for the general market at subsidized prices, it managed the country's first bank and it contributes to everything from the university to the building of roads.

Although it has in the main exercised its tremendous power with restraint, Firestone's relations with the government and people of Liberia have not always been cordial. Because of the pressure of events, Firestone obtained the initial concession at a ridiculously low tax rate and is under constant pressure to revise the agreement, a pressure to which the company has been wise enough to accede. Last year the company agreed to raise Liberia's tax on its profits from 25 per cent to 35 per cent and to allow the republic to tax the salaries of its foreign employees.

Many of Liberia's 'young turks' grumble that Liberia's share should be increased to 50 per cent and a few maintain that the concession should be terminated. But the 'big men' of Liberia have profited by the company's presence. Firestone has made it a practice to give seedlings and technical assistance to Liberians who want to become rubber planters and to buy all their production from them. In one recent year, £714,000 was paid out to 1,200 Liberian planters for ten million pounds of rubber and more than 7·5 million seedlings have been given away. The full significance of this programme becomes more apparent when one learns that £606,000 of the total went to twelve planters, all of whom are big wheels in the True Whig party. Of the Big Twelve, who own most of the 50,000 acres under Liberian cultivation, one made £70,000, two received more than £53,000 and two others made more than £35,000.

Although the men who run Liberia are disinclined to slay a goose which so agreeably lays golden eggs in the proper nests, this does not prevent them from attacking the company's record on racial matters. During our visit in 1959, exactly two of the company's executive, professional and managerial staff of about 180 were Liberians. Firestone maintains that it is more than willing to hire qualified Liberian personnel when such are available. There is some justice in the inference that such men are not available but Liberians maintain that if this is so, it is a serious indictment of the company's thirty-year-old training and scholarship programme, although the firm offers twenty-five university scholarships a year to employees and their children.

Apparently there was enough discrimination to cause the passage in the Liberian House of Assembly of an anti-discrimination bill so loosely drawn that any employer who shows racialist tendencies, not necessarily actions, either by word or deed, will be fined for the first offence and expelled for the second. No matter how warranted anti-discrimination legislation may have been, the present law is a dangerous and neurotic one which makes it virtually impossible for any firm to fire a Liberian no matter how incompetent or insubordinate he may be.

These are quarrels which involve only the ruling class and the government of Liberia. The common man has only two complaints against Firestone. One is that in 1957, when Liberia enjoyed an alluvial diamond rush similar to that of Sierra Leone, Firestone lost so large a proportion of its labour force that it complained to the government. The hated Frontier Force was ordered into the diamond country, the diggers were cleared out and the fields were temporarily closed.

There is also some evidence that tribal chiefs use their influence to 'persuade' their young men to work for Firestone. The chiefs have more than a passing concern with the economic welfare of their people: they are allowed to retain a percentage of the taxes which they are able to collect and (like the district commissioner) receive a not inconsiderable number of hampers of rice from each farmer. They may also be required to furnish a certain number of labourers to work on the farms of prominent politicians. Labour is short because in the past many natives unable to pay their taxes and justly fearful of the consequences of delinquency, fled to neighbouring Sierra Leone and Guinea, never to return. To compensate the chiefs for the loss of the services of their young men, Firestone pays ten shillings to a chief for every one of his people who works on the plantation for a year. In addition to this, there is 'a regular scale of non-monetary gifts'.

It should be said, however, that Firestone treats its labour well and in recent years has experienced only one strike. Firestone pays top wages (2s. 4d. a day) for common labour and far more than anybody else for semi-skilled and skilled workers. The common labour rate is 2d. a day above the minimum wage required by law and there are indications that Firestone would pay more except for the opposition of Liberian planters, who are unwilling or unable to pay their 8,500 employees at the present level. The company also provides its employees and their families with free housing, medical treatment (spending half as much for health each year as does the Liberian government), and educational facilities (only 10 per cent take advantage of the company's free schools) and it pays their taxes. Food and clothing are available at heavily subsidized prices. Workers stay as long or as briefly as they please (there are no contracts), may switch from one division of the plantation to another, and are infinitely better paid and treated than those 'employed' on the plantations of the private growers. Despite this, however, labour turnover is about 30 per cent each year.

For the obvious reasons, it appears unlikely that Firestone will attempt to increase the 210,000 acres now under lease. In 1957 it harvested almost £10 million worth of rubber and showed an average yield of 1,100 pounds per acre, nearly double the average attained either by East Indian plantations or by private Liberian growers. A newly-developed strain should increase the yield to 1,600 pounds, thus enabling the company to raise its production by more than 35 per cent without running the political risk of expanding its acreage. And remember that only half of the leased land is cultivated at present.

In the main Liberia has not been the loser through its relationship with Firestone. Unlike mining, rubber cultivation is not susceptible to mechanization, hence the company provides a permanent source of employment. The loan, since repaid in full well ahead of schedule, freed the country from its dependence on ruinous European loans. Firestone's presence prevented the annexation of the republic and the company's prosperity helped Liberia to get on its financial feet. Most important of all, Firestone's success triggered the boom which brought more than thirty American firms into Liberia and raised U.S. investment in the country from £1 million to more than £60 million in little more than a decade.

The boom, although initiated by Firestone's success, goes far beyond the rubber industry: Liberia, whose name has been synonymous with rubber, bids fair to become one of the major iron producers of the world within this decade.

In the forest-clad Bomi Hills north-west of Monrovia geologists located a fabulously rich (69 per cent ore content) lode of iron believed to total 350 million tons. This makes it the world's purest ore (20 per cent richer than the Lake Superior variety) and it can be used almost like scrap. The Liberia Mining Company, in which Republic Steel holds a majority interest, built a forty-seven-mile freight railway to the capital and began production on its eighty-year concession in 1951 with a modest 186,000 tons. Annual production now is in the order of 2·5 million tons and more than 1,100 shiploads totalling better than 13 million tons have been exported. In 1957 the company put into operation a £2·8 million beneficiation plant, a thingamajig which removes most of the impurities before shipment, and iron exports now exceed £3·2 million a year, or more than 20 per cent of the total value of all Liberia's products. Like Firestone, the Liberia Mining Company runs a model industry complete with all fringe benefits including a £44,000 hospital and three-way segregation of housing among American, European and African employees. Most of its operation is mechanized so its labour problems are less severe, and its relations with the government are good.

This is only the beginning of the iron story: Mount Nimba, a 4,000-foot eminence near the Guinea border, has been found to be a mound of almost solid iron ore and a company financed 60 per cent by Swedish capital and 40 per cent by American investors is sinking £71 million into the exploitation of reserves which may hit the one billion ton mark. To begin the first phase of the operation, which will give work to 25,000 Liberians, the firm (called LAMCO) had to head-load ninety tons of material up eight miles of mountain trails through dripping forests of giant ferns which have undergone no botanical change since the Stone Age. The lode is 65 per cent ore but to get it to the sea LAMCO will have to build a 200-mile railway and construct a modern port at the sleepy hamlet of Buchanan on the St. John River. The port will accommodate ore ships of 80,000 tons and will be larger than Monrovia's Free Port. The railway, unlike the Bomi Hills line, will be of standard gauge and will carry passengers and miscellaneous freight.

In return for a seventy-year concession over 500 square miles, which includes not only Mount Nimba but a smaller deposit in the Bassa Hills said to amount to fifty million tons, LAMCO has given the Liberian government 50 per cent of the company's stock. Since Liberia will thus be taking half the profits, there will be no additional corporate taxes. Production will begin in 1962 and LAMCO President Johnson Avery estimates that it will reach an annual figure of ten million tons by 1965.

A third group, National Iron Ore Co. (15 per cent owned by Liberia Mining Co. and the remainder by the Liberian government and private Liberian investors) is launching a £7·1 million operation with production expected to reach five million tons next year. And a German firm is initiating a £32 million iron ore project in the Bong Hills. At prevailing prices, the LAMCO and NIOC projects alone will more than double the value of Liberia's exports by 1965.

Another source of revenue snared by Tubman's Open Door comes from Liberia's position as a 'sea-power': the little West African republic boasts the third largest commercial fleet in the world and is first in tanker tonnage. The ships, of course, are only registered in Liberia, not owned by Liberian nationals (about 53 per cent are Greek-owned while another 40 per cent are American in origin). Liberia, like Panama, attracts shipowners to its flag because its registration fees are low and conditions of work comparatively unregulated.

This does not mean, however, that the 6·9 million tons of shipping which flies the Liberian flag is a tin-can fleet. Of the new large-capacity tankers (over 35,000 tons), more than 50 per cent have Liberian registry. Less than 4 per cent of the entire fleet is of pre-World War II vintage.

American and British trade unionists attack these so-called flag-of-convenience registries but the International Trust Co., Liberia's maritime agent, maintains that putting Liberia out of business would not, as some labour leaders say, provide more and better jobs for seamen. I.T.C. claims that the owners could not afford to keep the fleet at sea under any other arrangement and that salaries and labour conditions, while not on a par with those offered in England and America, are higher than those many countries. From the strategic point of view, it seems no bad thing for the United States to have these ships afloat and under the flag of a friendly state (registry can be transferred within twenty-four hours); for its part, Liberia is very happy indeed to have £590,000 coming in every year from registrations and renewals.

A source of Liberian wealth still virtually untapped is her great forests, the largest stretch of virgin wood in West Africa, which cover 37 per cent of the country (8·7 million acres) and contain 235 species of timber, at least 104 of which are now in commercial use. Not a foot of timber was exported in 1957 but it is estimated that three billion board feet of Liberia's total of 140 billion board feet could be exported each year without danger of undue depletion (it is believed that local farmers waste 750 million board feet worth £17·9 million each year in clearing for cultivation). Two companies (German and American) have negotiated concessions of 250,000 acres each and

Liberia seems destined to become one of the world's major suppliers of tropical timber with an annual cut greater than all U.S. timber production east of the Mississippi.

After rubber and iron ore (£10·8 million and £2·9 million respectively out of total exports worth £15·9 million in 1956), diamonds, which were worth £856,000 in the same year, are the country's most important export. Estimates as to Liberia's diamond wealth vary widely but the country may well be as rich as Sierra Leone. The difficulty of evaluating the fields, which lie around the Lofa River, is the number of diamonds smuggled into Liberia from Sierra Leone for re-export. It is believed that smuggled diamonds were worth £3·6 million in 1956 and half that much the following year. The Liberian tax on diamonds is 15 per cent and the evaluation is nominal, since each of the companies has Liberian stockholders who one may presume enjoy some political influence. A Liberian diamond rush in the spring of 1957 brought 30,000 wild-catters to the fields and stripped the rubber plantations of labour. Some 1,600 prospecting licences have been issued but the government has balked at European attempts to obtain mining concessions. Palm kernels worth £357,000 are the fourth most important export and all others (piassava, cacao, the inferior Liberica coffee) were worth £1 million in 1956. Imports in the same year, including £1·4 million worth of food, totalled £9·8 million, leaving the country with a healthy and favourable balance of trade.

Tubman's 'Open Door', which means no limit on earnings which may be taken from the country (in 1957 private investors put £6·4 million into the country, took out £12·5 million), recovery of initial investment, 35 per cent corporate income tax (although this increasingly is being replaced by 50 per cent Liberian government stock participation), and in the case of American investors, no convertibility problem, has produced a stream of foreign investors: Americans grow rubber, cacao and palm kernels and mine iron; Italians run cold storage plants, bakeries, plumbing concerns and construction firms; Israelis are building a £714,000 luxury hotel and constructing the new executive mansion, hospital and Treasury building; Germans grow oil palms, coffee and bananas, and build roads; Spaniards run hotels, brick factories, cinemas, petrol stations and saw-mills. And Liberian capital is becoming active on a small scale.

As a result, Liberian revenues have increased every year since 1940 with the exception of 1952 and the budget has been balanced since 1935. Between 1946 and 1958 national revenue climbed from

£266,000 to £7·1 million, foreign trade increased from £4·6 million to £25 million, and foreign investment zoomed from £1 million to £42·7 million. The same problem exists here, however, that we found in Sierra Leone: the statistics measure the intensity and success of foreign investors exploiting wasting assets; they do not reflect the endeavour or prosperity of the mass of Liberians. Nor has heavy foreign investment meant as much employment as might have been expected. In 1956, Liberia's ten largest companies employed 48,532 Africans and 30,000 of these were Firestone workers. The Big Ten paid out £3 million in salaries or an annual *per capita* native wage of £65. Since heavy investment over the next five years will be in mining, an industry susceptible to mechanization, comparatively few more jobs will be made available. When Goodrich comes into production and the timber industry expands, however, this situation should improve.

Although the gross domestic product rose between 1942 and 1958 from £17·5 million to £44 million and is expected to reach £107 million by 1966, Liberian *per capita* income lags below the £35 level as opposed to £70 behind the Iron Curtain and £892 in the United States. Since Liberia has no post-auditing process, it is impossible to see just how much of Liberia's current £26 million development programme is filtering down to the average citizen in the form of social services and public works. Despite the fact that standards of public morality are rising, one is inclined to believe that a bit of the cheese is being nibbled as it passes and too much of the budget goes into administration (40 per cent in 1957). At least 80 per cent of the people still derive their living from the soil and the obvious disparities in wealth are disconcerting to those interested both in fair play and in the political stability of the republic.

Although most foreign firms have a good record in this regard, the Liberian labour code is wide-open to abuse. An official government publication boasts that Liberia has no legislation 'relating to the minimum age of employees in any category, to workers in hazardous and fatiguing occupations, or to the employment of women or children'. This Dickensian document adds apologetically that an eight-hour day and forty-eight-hour week are obligatory but consoles prospective employers with the news that there are no provisions relating to rest or lunch hours and confides that the minimum wage for unskilled labour is 3d. an hour. It continues with the glad tidings that the labour code makes no mention of 'safety standards, unemployment insurance, sanitary standards, sickness benefits . . . social security benefits, family and children's allowances, or guaranteed employment plans'.

Because of its intimate and peculiar relationship with the United States, Liberia throughout its history has received from America a certain amount of diplomatic, technical and military assistance. In 1879, for instance, when France offered to place Liberia under its 'protection', the United States advised the colonial powers that it felt 'a peculiar interest' in the independence of the republic and France backed off. To a large extent, however, this aid has been limited and sporadic and it was not until after America entered World War II that much was attempted. Nor has any president before Tubman expressed the desire to receive such assistance.

In 1942 the United States built Liberia's first airport, the 25,000-acre Robertsfield. This base, which has two 7,000-foot runways, acted as a relay station for 600 bombers a month ferried to the Middle East and the installations were guarded by 5,000 American Negro troops. At the conclusion of the war, the field was handed over to Liberia and the United States agreed to finance the construction of a modern £7·9 million port at Monrovia, with the stipulation that it should function as a free port and that revenues accruing from such use would be applied to repay the United States.

The free port, which went into operation in 1948, has facilities for three large cargo ships and in its 507-acre zone merchandise may be 'brought, unloaded, stored, mixed, repacked, blended, processed, manufactured and reshipped' without payment of duty. The idea was that it would serve as a collecting point for those territories of West Africa lacking in deep-water facilities. Although it handles 2·3 million tons of freight each year (two million of it iron ore), the free port has not been a tremendous success for two reasons: British and French development schemes have provided deep-water facilities for most of their territories and, despite the political realignment going on in Africa, colonial trade patterns remain largely intact. There is little question, however, but that the American-managed free port will prove of immense value to Liberia as her own trade expands. For the moment many Liberians regard it as a white elephant and bitterly object to having to pay for the port—which has 750 acres of protected water, a 2,000-foot wharf and storage facilities for 6·6 million gallons of fuel—which they say was promised as a gift for Liberia's services during the war.

A regular technical assistance programme was inaugurated in 1951. In nine years of operation this programme has ploughed £5·5 million into Liberia while the republic has contributed a slightly larger amount from its revenues. In 1960 the U.S. contribution was increased to £856,000 and the Liberian government has agreed to set aside 20 per cent of its revenues for development purposes. The older generation of Liberians is suspicious of U.S. assistance while the generation about to seize political control of the country regards it as totally inadequate. They reason, as do the Ethiopians, who apparently are shifting from a pro-Western to a neutralist posture as the result of Haile Selassie's loan-bagging tour last year through Russia and the Communist bloc, that America is niggardly towards her friends and generous towards her potential enemies.

This younger generation overlooks the fact that on a *per capita* basis the U.S. contribution to Liberia is larger than that of any colonial power to its territories. It is arguable, of course, that Liberia needs funds more desperately than Nigeria or Ivory Coast precisely because she has never enjoyed the benefits of colonialism: almost every colonial territory comes to independence with at least a basic communications and education system created by its 'oppressors'; Liberia is trying to do now things which were accomplished a generation ago in the most backward West African colony. However, it is by no means certain that Liberia at her present stage of development could readily digest more money with profit to anybody other than top government officials. Nor are American aid programmes as presently constituted well-tailored to fit Liberia's needs.

One International Co-operation Administration official put it this way:

'In Liberia we are trying to apply to a pre-technical, pre-literate society the same sort of programme utilized in Western Europe and the more advanced areas of South-East Asia. Even in remote parts of Asia, an illiterate man is a member of and participates in a society which has a religious and cultural base. Here the people have nothing. The *per capita* income is low, there is an overall planning body in name only; roads, electricity, water power, tools, domestic capital and credit facilities, and labour are rudimentary and scattered where they exist at all. Less than 15 per cent of the population participates in the money economy. Infant mortality is high, there is not enough food even of a low-protein type, and there is no agricultural extension service. Schooling is sparse and poor and the literacy rate is less than 10 per cent. The public debt is rising too fast and most of the politicians are on the take. A counterpart programme in which we train a man to match each of our technicians isn't valid because so few people have enough education even to be considered. Where would you suggest that we begin?'

I.C.A. itself is not blameless and it would seem that too much of its funds (47 per cent in 1960) is going to pay the salaries of American technicians. My informant said that it cost £6,000 to keep an American (including his family) in the field for a year, a figure which would not be so bad if the people were top calibre. Unfortunately, Liberia's reputation is bad enough to preclude this possibility, despite a 25 per cent hardship pay differential.

More than 36 per cent of U.S. assistance goes to educational projects, 18 per cent to agriculture and 15 per cent to transportation and ninety-one Liberians have been trained and seventy-seven other, are either in the United States or scheduled to go this year. Some of the money spent undoubtedly does a great deal of good. But one of the 101 U.S. technicians serving in the country in 1960 had this to say about the thirteen-year-old Suacoco agricultural research station jointly run by the United States and the Liberian governments:

'The politicians are interested in this station, which is the only one of its kind in Liberia, for what they can get out of it. We can always tell when there's going to be a big party in Monrovia: a government truck pulls up, one of the cows from our experimental herd is slaughtered and our vegetable gardens are systematically looted. More than £85,000 a year is being spent each year to run this place as a catering establishment.'

This is not to suggest that the U.S. aid programme should be curtailed. Nowhere is it more desperately needed. But it certainly needs to be reorganized and the Liberian government encouraged to institute a post-auditing system so that it is possible to see how funds allocated for development purposes actually have been spent.

One of the greatest areas in which assistance is needed is in the field of education. In the past, Liberians had little confidence in their school system. Although education has been 'compulsory' since 1912, the total national appropriation thirteen years later, which was supposed to cover the university as well, was less than £7,000! The politically powerful and the well-to-do (the two groups are almost synonymous in the republic) sent their children to America or England for schooling, often even in the primary grades and usually at government expense. In 1959, the government revealed (and put an end to the practice) that more than £25,000 was being expended annually to educate abroad elementary school students, most of whom came from wealthy families.

Today Liberia has something like 637 elementary schools, 365 run by the government and the rest by missions. There are about 50,000 school children taught by 1,758 elementary teachers. There are 22 high schools staffed by 217 instructors teaching 2,509 students. So say the statistics. How reliable they are is anybody's guess. Secretary of Public Instruction Nathaniel V. Massaquoi admits that 'some of the schools registered this year (1958) at the Department of Public Instruction did not exist'. There were no records at all for the western third of the country in the same year 'due to the death of the Supervisor', who apparently did not bother to keep any files. There are shadow teachers as well as shadow schools: one enterprising employee was discharged when it was discovered that he was all four people listed on the school's payroll!

A young Liberian has a fighting chance to get a decent education only if he is geographically lucky. If he is fortunate enough to live in Montserrado County, which includes the area around Monrovia, 19 per cent of his teachers will have college degrees while 'only' 41 per cent will have failed to progress beyond the elementary school. If his parents have the bad taste to live in Sinoe County, only 5 per cent of his instructors will have degrees and 76 per cent will have called it quits before reaching high school.

To raise standards appreciably, Liberia needs 24,000 trained teachers. Most qualified instructors are utilized at the high school level or above, which means that elementary students who can barely read and write are advanced, and high school instructors either lecture well above their students' heads or have to go back over all the ground supposedly covered in primary school. The net result is that by the time a Liberian reaches the lofty heights of the University of Liberia he is barely performing on the high school level. By dint of tremendous effort, the government has been able to replace half of the teachers with less than a complete elementary education.

The curriculum, despite the fact that less than 1 per cent of all students go on to college, is still highly academic and boys who should be learning how to handle a wrench spend their years conjugating

Latin verbs. Although Booker T. Washington, the country's one vocational school (463 students), has been modernized and expanded with the assistance of twenty-three refugees from something called Prarie View A. and M. College, little has been done to reorient or consolidate the other twenty-one weak high schools. Even in their chosen academic curriculum, the high schools are woefully inadequate in most fields and it is possible for a graduate to possess credits in physics and chemistry without having scorched his eyebrows on a Bunsen burner: there just aren't any laboratories.

The picture at the university level is only slightly better. In 1848, an American named Joseph Tracy wrote that 'a few gentlemen of Monrovia have under consideration the establishment of a well-endowed College or University in Liberia'. Liberia College got under way in 1862 with J. J. Roberts, the former Chief Executive, as its first principal. Its beginnings were humble and progress since then has been slight.

It has been a very simple story: untrained and poorly-paid professors teaching unqualified students in rickety and ill-equipped buildings. The curriculum was lopsided in favour of the classics, the children of politicians received degrees even if they failed all their classes and honorary doctorates were doled out like ham-hocks to the True Whig faithful. The rottenness of the university was reflected when its graduates went abroad for further study and found themselves relegated to freshman and sophomore classes. Mercifully the college produced only fourteen graduates in the first thirty-eight years of its existence.

There are signs that the college, which was elevated by statute to the rank of University of Liberia in 1950, is headed for better days. Its teaching staff has been bolstered through the addition of UNESCO instructors and Firestone has contributed heavily to the construction of a new science building. In thirty-six-year-old Rocheforte Weeks, a lawyer trained at Washington's Howard University and at Cornell, the University has its first Liberian president (his predecessors were usually American Negroes) and one who has sworn to be tough enough to raise standards and stick to them. He will have a rough task: crammed on to the university's minute (fifteen-acre) campus are 250 college students and 500 high school and non-degree pupils 'studying' everything from sewing to chemistry in an atmosphere of total confusion. To straighten out the situation Weeks has a fairly adequate £77,000 annual allocation from the government.

A better institution, although it receives only £3,300 a year in government subsidies, is Cuttington College and Divinity School at Suacoco in northern Liberia. The college, which is run by the American Episcopal Church with assistance from the Methodists and Lutherans, was established on the coast in 1888. It expired during the Depression and was reopened in the interior in 1949. We got to know Cuttington pretty well during a ten-day enforced visit: somebody had padlocked a chain across the bridge at the Guinea border and walked off with the key in his pocket.

Cuttington, which offers four-year B.A. and B.S. courses and a three-year graduate course in theology, has to work with the same miserable raw material as the University of Liberia: when students arrive, their English is almost unintelligible, their scientific training nil, their study habits erratic and their egos overblown. Because it has a dedicated and well-qualified staff (fifteen Americans and three Liberians) and has all its students as boarders (all U. of L. students are day pupils), Cuttington's 107 students absorb more and no graduate of the college has ever failed a post-graduate course in the United States although a government report states that 29 per cent of all Liberian students in the United States are failing. There is a sizable group of Tanganyikans in the student body, their tuition paid by that East African British dependency's premier political party, and the students, each of whom costs the Episcopal Church £300 a year to educate (annual fees are £53, *per capita* costs are about £357) went on strike while we were there because they were not offered transportation to a free picnic. Our Lady of Fatima College, a new Catholic institution at Harper in Maryland County, with about fifty students, completes the picture of higher education in Liberia.

With the possible exception of Cuttington students, there is little doubt but that Liberians trained abroad (33 per cent are girls) get a better university education than they would at home. But the annual cost is high (£700 per student) and failures (aptitude tests for govern-ment 'scholars' were not initiated until 1959 and there still is no means test) are frequent. In addition, once a Liberian gets abroad it is often difficult to get him home again. The attractions of student life are so strong that, although the number of students abroad increased 63 per cent to 480 between 1955 and 1958, only 6 per cent of Liberia's overseas scholars returned to the country in 1958. Thus Liberia, which badly needs trained personnel in all fields, is slow in obtaining a return on its annual investment of £300,000 in overseas education, a sum larger than the national budget a decade ago.

The United States has helped the situation by handing out government scholarships but Senator Theodore Green of Rhode Island revealed in 1957 that such students were receiving £2,250, or almost twice as much as they could expect to make when they returned to Liberia as graduates, a situation not calculated to encourage students to curtail their academic careers.

Despite all its weaknesses, education in Liberia is improving: fifteen years ago there were 200 schools, 13,000 students, and 200 instructors; now there are almost 600 schools, nearly 60,000 students and 2,000 teachers. Current expenditure on education has jumped from a few thousand dollars to £714,000, 10 per cent of the national budget. The missions, ICA, UNESCO and the Liberian government are putting an equal amount into capital improvements. Although the situation is still desperate, it is improving.

Some strides, too, have been made in public health, which in the past was deplorable. Most Liberians are under-nourished and a National Planning Association study published in 1956 states that 'although all manner of rodents, reptiles, and insects are avidly eaten by the tribal people, this protein source is too small and uncertain to make up much of the deficiency'. The report adds, by the way, that forced labour and debtor servitude ('pawning') have not been 'completely extinguished'.

Liberia had no public health service until 1931. Today the republic claims it spends 10 per cent of the national budget or £357,000 on health. This, it alleges, is 'a greater proportion of the national income allocated to health than any other nation apart from Sweden'. There are six general hospitals, two of which are well-equipped, and about 100 clinics. In the entire country there were fifty-seven doctors in 1955, half of them government physicians. Of the remainder, nineteen were missionaries or company doctors and ten were private practitioners.

THE NEW MEN

One of these days (when he is ready and not before) Bobor Shad is going to step down and a new generation of Liberians is going to take over this country. These young men, who are spread throughout all walks of life, are as different from their parents and their grandparents as Swedes are from Spaniards. I have spun the old tale of Liberian stupidity and corruption not because it pleases me to do so but because it is a fact without which the country cannot be understood; I can also say that no group of young men in West Africa impressed me more than the young executives of Liberia.

Most of them are Americo-Liberian boys and many of them were educated at Monrovia's excellent 121-year-old Methodist High School. Three out of four of them went to college in the United States or Canada, although this percentage fell to 54 per cent in 1958 with a marked preference being shown for British universities. Some of them had scholarship help but a surprisingly large percentage of them either worked their way through school or worked in the summers to make ends meet. Many attended Southern institutions and few reported having any racial problems. To a large degree this seems to be attributable to the fact that Liberians, because of their country's long-standing tie with the United States and their own contacts with American missionaries and businessmen, know what the score is in the United States and do not expose themselves unnecessarily to red-neck abuse. In addition, their Americo-Liberian culture makes them easily assimilable into American coloured society while 'black' Africans with tribal backgrounds find this more difficult.

You find this group everywhere in positions of secondary authority: thirty-seven-year-old Romeo Horton, cigar-chewing founder and president of the first Liberian bank and the first local insurance company, a graduate of Morehouse College and the Wharton School of Finance; jockey-sized forty-one-year-old Reggie Townsend, director of the Liberian Information Service, who attended American University and Michigan State; Howard- and Cornell-trained Rocheforte Weeks, president of the University of Liberia; dapper thirty-two-year-old attorney Pohlman Bracewell, educated at South Carolina State, Western Reserve and Harvard; the brilliant thirty-one-year-old diplomat Ernest Eastman, who guides the Liberian State Department's African Affairs Desk, a graduate of Oberlin and Columbia; at the top of the heap is Charles Sherman, Liberia's handsome, hulking Secretary of the Treasury, president of the World Council of the Y.M.C.A., and the man believed down for Tubman's job when the old man steps down, a dynamo of a man in his early forties who likes to describe himself as 'an intellectual capitalist'.

These young Liberians differ from their predecessors in several important respects. In the first place, they are the first generation to think of themselves as Africans rather than as Negroes or Americo-Liberians. Although not insensitive to the studied rebuffs dealt them by radical African nationalists, they favour some form of African unity and want Liberia to play a more dynamic role in achieving this goal. Like the first couple of generations of Liberians but unlike their fathers and grandfathers (and equally unlike most British- and French-trained Africans) they are not ashamed to work for what they want. Commerce and industry occupy the place of honour once reserved for law and politics. They have a better and more sympathetic understanding of the United States than their fathers had but are not inclined to be as servilely pro-American. Being better balanced men, they are slower to take offence during discussion of racial matters but not afraid to speak up without bitterness in their own defence.

This generation owes much to Tubman and to some extent is fashioned in his image. Although they sometimes grow impatient with his conservative approach, the New Men understand and appreciate his ability. Like all young men they are not afraid to acknowledge their debt or slow to say that, when their time comes, they will do things differently and better. Most of them favour the development of a two-party political system. This generation is going to be more interesting to watch and easier to understand than the old one. It is also going to be more difficult to deal with. These boys learned more in America than how to wear a button-down shirt.

It is more important than most Americans realize that the United States should improve its relations with Liberia and reach an understanding based on mutual respect with these New Men. In the first place, Liberia is the only country in Africa which is giving free enterprise a fair chance. In French and British Africa everything from the railways to the palm nuts is socialized. If we have any interest in the success of modern capitalism in Africa, we must be sure that it succeeds in Liberia.

More important is the fact that Liberia is incorrectly regarded by Africans and colonials alike as an American 'colony'. This supposition is not so unnatural when you recall America's historic relationship with the republic and note the fact that 78 per cent of Liberia's exports go to the United States and it provides 63 per cent of her imports. It would be unnatural if America were not blamed for everything wrong about Liberia. It does not follow, of course, that she will get any credit for what goes right. But it does follow that the United States should in her own defence see to it that things go as well as possible not only for the Americo-Liberians but for the people of the interior. It would be a tremendous blow to American prestige in Africa if the one black country with which the United States has had the longest and most intimate of associations should turn her back. And this, of course, is just what Communist agents in neighbouring Guinea are working to encourage.

Liberia, with all its past faults and present weaknesses, is the one spot in Africa where the United States cannot afford to fail.

Chapter 18

---
*

SATURDAY'S CHILD

No territory in emergent Africa has received a greater share of plaudits and brickbats than Ghana, the former British colony led to independence in 1957 by American-trained Kwame Nkrumah. This West African republic, which lies between Ivory Coast and Togo at the approaches to the infamous Bight of Benin, is about the size of the United Kingdom, has a population of under five million, and is the richest territory south of the Sahara apart from the Union of South Africa. Tales of its mineral wealth (it was said to be the source of the Moorish gold caravans) led seven European nations to battle for supremacy on its shores and to christen it the Gold Coast. But although Ghana's gold brings her more than £10 million a year, ranking her as the fourth largest producer in the Commonwealth, it is cacao which is her wealth: Nkrumah's country is the world's largest producer of cacao, which makes up five-sevenths of her exports by value, six times as much as that earned by gold. Ghana's 500 million cacao trees, her gold, diamonds and manganese, give the country's twenty tribes a *per capita* domestic product of more than £70, three times higher than that of any other tropical African Commonwealth territory.

Wealth has meant progress and sophistication for Ghana: more than 50 per cent of her children receive some education, her capital city of Accra is the best laid-out and cleanest city in British West Africa, and a diarist records that Africans were playing cricket in Ghana as early as 1861. But the old Africa is still very much in evidence. At least 60 per cent of the population is illiterate and, as recently as 1959, a Ghanaian was arrested and charged with trying to sell a five-year-old boy in Accra for £40. Tema, a new port still under construction, is the only town in the country with sewerage and the average wage is 6s. 6d. a day. Enormous snails are found in Ghana and are said to contribute more protein to the African diet than any other source; this is not hard to believe when one learns that, based on cattle slaughterings, the average Ghanaian gets only eight pounds of meat per year. She cannot feed herself and £18 million worth of food is imported annually, more in proportion to her population than any other West African country.

One out of every four Ghanaian children dies before it is a year old and tropical diseases such as malaria, leprosy, tuberculosis, yaws, trypanosomiasis and onchocerciasis are 'rampant'. In 1958, Ghana had 226 doctors (one to every 23,000 people), 18 dentists and 2,031 registered nurses and there were 54 government, mission and mining company hospitals with less than 5,000 beds.

Ghana is famous for a high-voltage liquor called *akpeteshi*, known locally as 'Kiss Me, Darling', 'Make Me Hot', or 'Blue Train', which was illicit before independence (which did nothing to discourage either its production or consumption) but is now the subject of a government research study with the object of establishing a local distilling industry on a commercial basis. Famed also are Ghana's 'Jaguar Girls', young and highly talented prostitutes who cater mostly to Europeans and Lebanese and to Africans of ministerial rank (their mothers were more prosaically known as 'Bungalow girls' in colonial days). Ghana also has goblins called *mmoatia*, who come in three colours (red, white and black), communicate by whistling, are twelve inches tall and have their feet facing the wrong way. As everybody knows, the black ones are quite harmless but the others cause people to break their pots at the well and make them late for appointments. There is also a hairy monster with blood-shot eyes which sits in a tree with his legs dangling over a branch and strangles the unwary with his feet.

In the northern part of the country, which was not closely administered until 1931, there are less than 100 high school graduates (Tamale's 'Education Ridge' has one teacher-training institute, a high school and trade school to cater for an area larger than several American states) and, in some districts, only about one in a thousand children goes to school at all. The women wear leaves fore and aft and the more advanced southerners are shamefacedly but energetically attempting to insert them in clothes donated by generous Americans. This will satisfy the national pride but create something of a health problem since there is little enough water to drink in the North, much less any in which to wash clothes. It is a social offence in the northern grasslands to tread upon someone's shadow or to pass behind him while he is eating. From the North you can ride round-trip to Mecca for £30, running the risk, of course, of being sold into slavery while on pilgrimage. More than half of Ghana's population is animist, about a quarter are Christians and the rest are Muslims. In the entire country there are less than 12,000 whites and white settlement is forbidden by law. Ghana has only one lake, at the bottom of a volcanic crater in the middle of the country, and it is inhabited by a potent fetish which forbids fishing with nets, canoes, paddles or metal hooks, which makes it rather hard to angle, since you must lie on a log, propel yourself with your hands and feet, and land your quarry with a wooden hook or spear.

In addition to its six major tribal languages and sixty-five dialects, Ghana has its own brand of English and when you are invited to a 'drinks party with small chop and cloth ladies' you will know that cocktails and hors d'œuvres will be served and that Ghanaian women in native costume will attend. Ghana's parliament, however, like a dutiful child of Westminster, has its out-sized ceremonial mace and its question period, during which black politicians clad in the multi-coloured togas which are the national costume debate with heavy Oxford accents. A road not too far from parliament splits to avoid a ju-ju stone, which could, of course, be moved only at great peril. There are twenty-one newspapers in the country, five of them dailies.

Ghana is a flat country with hills up to 3,000 feet only in the extreme eastern area and the Volta is its only river of consequence. The only towns of any size are Accra (150,000), Kumasi (85,000), Sekondi-Takoradi (60,000) and Cape Coast (28,000). All but Kumasi, which is the capital of the ancient kingdom of Ashanti, are ports which have grown out of three of the forty-two forts built along the 350-mile coast by early European traders. Eighteen of these 'castles' are still in use, seven of them as rest-houses. The rains drum down from March until June and from September to November (although Accra gets only about 28 inches and is the driest city on the African bulge), and Ghana bakes for the rest of the year.

Ghana has a two-ship navy, a miniscule commercial fleet and the only railway in Africa that can show a profit, mostly because it has short hauls (there are only 500 miles of track) through country rich in minerals, timber and cacao. The railway's headquarters are in Takoradi, Ghana's bustling port, which has a population of 1,000 whites and twice as many prostitutes. There is no connection, however, between the two figures. The northern two-thirds of the country has no railway at all.

Most of Ghana's important tribes stretch into adjoining territories and the country thus has neither ethnic nor geographic unity. The national consciousness which has swept this land during the last decade is primarily the result of the labours, for good or for evil, of one man.

Many men made the Gold Coast; but the stamp of one man is deeply etched on the face of the nation which the Gold Coast became.

'SHOW-BOY'

When it came time for him to find a title for his autobiography, Kwame Nkrumah called his book *Ghana*. Although the thick-lipped West African nationalist is not renowned for his modesty (he is pictured in fifty-three of the sixty illustrations in the book), the linking of his own name with that of the new African nation was not inaccurate: Ghana is his personal real estate.

Francis Nwia Kofie Nkrumah was born at Nkroful in the Nzima country, which backs up against Ivory Coast, on September 18, 1909. Every Akan child is known by the day of the week upon which he or she is born; Nkrumah was born on a Saturday and hence has always been known as Kwame. Had he been a girl, he would have been called Ama, the name given to female children born on Saturday. While Kwame was still an infant, his mother took him to live on the French border in a fishing village dubbed Half Assini by some whimsical district commissioner (there is a town of Assini in Ivory Coast). Kwame's father was a goldsmith, a well-to-do man with several wives. The boy was his mother's only child and she spoiled him rotten. Nkrumah recalls that she never allowed his father to strike him and beat him herself only once, when he spat into a kettle of stew being prepared for the family dinner.

Although his mother was illiterate, she insisted that young Kwame go to school and saw to it that he was baptized into the Catholic faith (he now calls himself a non-denominational Marxian Christian, whatever that means). At first young Nkrumah resented the authority of his teachers but was soon peddling chickens to help pay his school fees. After eight years of school, a German Catholic priest named George Fischer helped Nkrumah get a job as a pupil-teacher and the boy did well enough to be sent on to a teacher-training high school in Accra. There he came under the influence of Dr. Kwegyir Aggrey, the great Gold Coast educator and philosopher. Nkrumah remembers that it was Aggrey, an exponent of racial co-operation, who first aroused his nationalism and inspired him to go to America to study.

Nkrumah ran in track events but failed to excel at team games and today he has no hobbies, indulges in no sports. He went in heavily for dramatics, an art form at which he is still a master. He also joined the local debating society and was named a prefect. When he finished the course, he joined the staff of a Roman Catholic primary school at Elmina, the point of original European penetration into the Gold Coast, as Ghana was called before it became independent in 1957. Nkrumah took and failed the London matriculation (high school level) examination in Latin and mathematics, moved on to teach at a Roman Catholic seminary. His new environment stimulated his religious fervour to such a degree that the idea of becoming a Jesuit lingered with him 'for a whole year'.

But Nkrumah had bigger fish to fry and, in the autumn of 1935, he found himself at the gates of Pennsylvania's Lincoln University with £40, a second-class teacher's certificate and a letter of introduction from an African nationalist in his pocket. He was admitted on a probationary basis and, since he was fairly bright and had neither money nor prospects, was awarded a fellowship. To earn pocket money, he worked as a library assistant and wrote book-reports for fellow students at seven shillings a throw. He won second place in an oratorical contest, was initiated into a Negro fraternity, joined the Masons and was voted the most interesting member of the class of 1939. Since he was unable to get his degree because he owed money to the university, Nkrumah returned to Lincoln the following autumn as a philosophy assistant. Tussling with Kant, Hegel, Schopenhauer and Co. led him to enrol in Lincoln's Theological Seminary. At the same time, he worked on his Master's degree in education at the University of Pennsylvania. By 1942, a year in which most men Nkrumah's age were heavily committed elsewhere, the West African had added Bachelor of Theology, Master of Arts and Master of Science to his B.A. in economics and sociology.

During all this period Nkrumah held a number of odd jobs: nightshift counter in a Chester shipyard, Harlem fish hawker, labourer in a soap factory, pot-walloper, waiter and bell-hop on a New York–Vera Cruz ship. It certainly never occurred to Nkrumah to enlist in the allied forces (he never mentions either of the World Wars in his book) and he apparently found life at sea unpleasant during wartime, for he made his last cruise in 1939. When he was broke during stays in New York, Nkrumah rode in the subway between Harlem and Brooklyn all night, and became a follower of Father Divine when he discovered that the Faithful could get 50-cent chicken dinners and dime haircuts. He preached in Negro churches and was insulted in Baltimore. Nkrumah was not too busy to study politics and he admits that all he knows about organizing underground movements he learned from the

Communists and Trotskyites. He joined or participated in enough leftist organizations to raise any Republican Attorney-General's blood pressure by several points, read and was impressed by the lives of Napoleon, Lenin, Gandhi, Mussolini and Hitler; Marcus Garvey's racialist back-to-Africa movement gripped him. In May 1945, Nkrumah's ten-year stay in America came to a close and he took a ship for England.

Waiting for him on a London railway platform was the late George Padmore, an ex-Communist West Indian journalist who first planted in Nkrumah's mind the dream of a great pan-African union. Nkrumah enrolled at Gray's Inn to read law and attended lectures at the London School of Economics. But the academic life was small beer for the bullet-headed nationalist and he quickly turned to the headier wine of political intrigue. Before long he met British Communists Emil Burns, Palme Dutt and the late Harry Pollitt. He joined the left-leaning West African Students' Union and, at the hardly collegiate age of thirty-six, became its vice-president. With Padmore and a small group of leftists, he threw himself into the task of organizing the Fifth Pan-African Congress, held in Manchester in October 1945.

Previous congresses had been in the main organized and attended by American and West Indian Negroes. Although the Congress was chaired by Dr. W. E. B. DuBois, an American Negro Communist sympathizer, the focal point for the first time was the African continent. As Nkrumah puts it, the Congress's 'ideology became African nationalism and it adopted Marxist socialism as its philosophy'. To implement its resolutions, the Congress established a secretariat at 94 Gray's Inn Road with Nkrumah in charge. Staff members scavenged the streets of fuel-short London for lumps of coal and gathered nightly over the weak blaze produced by their efforts to air grievances and dream great dreams.

What were these dreams? The Watson Commission of Inquiry, sent to Ghana by the British government to investigate the causes of disturbances there in 1948 stated that 'he (Nkrumah) appears while in Britain to have had Communist affiliations and to have become imbued with Communist ideology which only political expedience has blurred. ... Nkrumah has not really departed one jot from his avowed aim for a Union of West African Soviet Socialist Republics and has not abandoned his foreign affiliations connected with these aims.'

Whatever his dreams may have been, Nkrumah showed that he was a capable political in-fighter. He gave up his studies and became a full-time plotter, not only for African freedom but for the dominance within the nationalist movement of Kwame Nkrumah. Finding the West African National Secretariat a bit bourgeois, he organized a vanguard group called the Circle, whose members pledged personal loyalty to him. The Circle declared war on 'demagogues, quislings, traitors, cowards, and self-seekers' and swore to oust from Africa 'foreign, despotic, and imperialist governments'. 'Members of the Circle,' Nkrumah recalls in his autobiography, 'began to train themselves in order to be able to commence revolutionary work in any part of the African continent.'

At this time, a letter came from Dr. J. B. Danquah, leader of the Gold Coast's anti-Communist United Gold Coast Convention, asking him to return to the Gold Coast as the nationalist organization's general secretary. Nkrumah's reaction to this offer gives some insight into his character: he states that, at the time he received the offer, he felt that the philosophy of the U.G.C.C. was 'contrary to the political aspirations of the people of the Gold Coast'. He felt that it was 'quite useless to associate myself with a movement backed almost entirely by reactionaries, middle-class lawyers, and merchants'. Despite this, he accepted the post, and demanded and received £100 from the U.G.C.C. for his passage from England.

Nkrumah returned to the Gold Coast in December 1947. He had been gone twelve years and his mother at first did not recognize him: he was born with a gap between his two front teeth, which caused him to lisp; false teeth had remedied this oratorical impediment. Within six months Nkrumah organized more than 500 U.G.C.C. branches, issued thousands of membership cards and raised funds. Nor did he neglect to build up the personal power and popularity of Kwame Nkrumah at the expense of his more conservative employers.

Shortly after Nkrumah's return, rioting in which twenty-nine were killed and 237 injured broke out in Accra. It is by no means certain that either Nkrumah or the rest of the U.G.C.C. leadership were behind the rioting. In the event, the U.G.C.C. was blamed and Nkrumah, who was found with an unsigned Communist Party membership card in his possession, was arrested, as were Dr. Danquah and four other U.G.C.C. leaders. They were imprisoned in the remote northern section of the country for two months.

After his release it became apparent to Nkrumah that the U.G.C.C. was becoming a bit apprehensive about its choice of general secretaries. The stocky leader moved quickly to form the Committee of Youth

Organization, ostensibly a youth wing of the U.G.C.C. but in reality the personal political machine of Kwame Nkrumah. To spread his fame to non-party members, Nkrumah took his first flier into journalism with the establishment of the Accra *Evening News*, a periodical not distinguished for its ethical or intellectual standards but one able to present Nkrumah to the people in the image of their liberator. 'Day by day,' Nkrumah recalls in his autobiography, 'in its pages the people were reminded of their struggle for freedom, of the decaying colonial system, and of the grim horrors of imperialism.' By the summer of 1949, when Danquah finally got around to expelling him from the U.G.C.C., Nkrumah was ready to announce to a chanting, cheering crowd of 60,000 at the mining centre of Tarkwa that it was his own organization, the new Convention People's Party, which would lead them all to independence and prosperity. As an answer to the U.G.C.C.'s demand for 'full self-government within the shortest possible time', he promised 'self-government now'. The hymn, 'Lead, Kindly Light', now a C.P.P. battle cry, was sung and Nkrumah was on his way to power.

The red, white and green banner of the C.P.P. (motto: 'Forward Ever, Backward Never') went up in every hamlet and Nkrumah, who badly needed financial support, rallied to his cause the rich and powerful market women who not had only money but physically controlled the markets, the political centres of the country (he rewarded them in 1961 by establishing in the National Assembly ten additional seats reserved for women). Political meetings, once merely polite debating societies, took on the combined flavour of a Harlem fish fry, a jazz concert, Ringling Brothers circus and a middling riot, with a dash of oratory of the Fourth of July type for seasoning.

Danquah and the other Gold Coast intellectuals, the products of stiffly Victorian families, Brahmins who had isolated themselves from the main stream of their country's people, drew back aghast at the antics of Nkrumah's 'veranda boys (so-called because many of them were homeless city proletarians who slept where they could), hooligans, and Communists', who with equal alacrity would play a saxophone solo or beat up an oppressive sub-chief for the sake of a vote or two. Danquah stressed the moral right of the people to self-determination; Nkrumah promised that the buses would be free when he came to power, added that 'when the gates of paradise are opened by Peter, we shall sit in heaven and see our children driving their aeroplanes, commanding their own armies'.

Nkrumah soon had the chance to test his new power. A government commission had recommended sweeping constitutional reforms but had failed to set the date for the self-government which the nationalist leader demanded. Nkrumah countered by calling for a constituent assembly and a general election, threatened a general strike if he did not get his way. His demand was refused and he immediately called a public meeting at which he threatened the chiefs, who regarded him then as they do now as a parvenu, and called for 'positive action' and a general strike. The government acted quickly, arrested Nkrumah, padlocked his newspapers and declared a state of emergency. But the country was calm and Nkrumah's conviction on four charges ranging from sedition to inciting an illegal strike provoked no serious disorders. The C.P.P. leader drew three one-year sentences, to be served consecutively, and settled down in Accra's James Fort, a seventeenth-century trading post now used as a prison.

Nkrumah, who has taken to carrying a cane but never wears a hat, groused about his treatment by 'undisciplined warders', the food ('scanty and poor'), and the sanitary arrangements ('embarrassing and most degrading') but he knew that the British had given him the greatest gift any emergent nationalist could hope for: the cloak of political martyrdom. He and his ten cell-mates, all C.P.P. big-wigs, were put to work mending fish nets and cleaning cane for use in basket weaving, while C.P.P. members keened outside the walls to the tune of 'The Battle Hymn of the Republic':

> 'Kwame Nkrumah's body lies a-mouldering in the jail,
> But his soul goes marching out.'

And Nkrumah's soul was not all that was going out: to keep his finger on events and maintain his name before the people, Nkrumah smuggled pronouncements scribbled on pieces of toilet paper to the C.P.P. faithful. After fourteen months of these salutary exercises, Nkrumah got his chance; a general election (Ghana's first with universal suffrage) was called for February 8, 1951. From his cell Nkrumah stood for election and in his Accra constituency the C.P.P.'s red cockerel symbol received 22,780 of the 23,122 ballots cast.

Four days later Nkrumah was released from Cell 9 by the British to allow him to take his seat in the Gold Coast parliament (the Director of Prisons resigned). He was met by K. A. Gbedemah, regent in his absence, and by a howling mob who escorted him to an outdoor arena. There Kwame Nkrumah, sometime aspirant to membership of the

Society of Jesus, B.A., B.T., M.A., M.S., and Member of Parliament, stepped barefooted seven times in the blood of a sacrificed sheep. He was cleansed.

The C.P.P. had won thirty-four out of thirty-eight elective seats and the Governor of the Gold Coast had no choice other than to ask Nkrumah to form a government. His programme: bribery and corruption, 'part and parcel of the colonial set-up', were to be stamped out; the C.P.P. was to extend its sway over the common people; amendments were to be made to the law of sedition, which was 'aimed at hindering the progress of the people'; there was to be no fraternization between C.P.P. men and white officials; no C.P.P. ministers were to accept the rent-free bungalows supplied by the government; C.P.P. assemblymen, like French Communist parliamentarians, were to surrender their salaries to the party and draw for their needs from C.P.P. funds (a system which has the double advantage of keeping the party solvent and ensuring parliamentary discipline).

Nkrumah, who usually averaged about four hours' sleep a night during this period, had more surprises for the British. He stated that he would like to 'clear out from the civil service all its old leaders' and replace them with loyal party members. He got assistance in this from the white civil servants, 223 of whom resigned out of a total of around 800. Nkrumah's distrust of an impartial civil service, which is the basis of Western democracy, was soon apparent. When the government machine began to wheeze and cough a bit with the introduction of incompetent Africans, Nkrumah offered attractive terms to keep expatriate officials in harness and there were more serving in Ghana in 1959 than there were before independence. Although the government has stated its intention to Africanize completely the permanent cadre of the civil service by 1964, whites are still being recruited and eleven of fourteen government departments in 1960 were headed by Europeans.

Nkrumah also reversed himself on the cocoa question. This crop, which is the basis of the country's economy, has been under attack in recent years by a blight called swollen shoot. There is no way to cure the disease and only vigorous cutting out of blighted trees can prevent its spread. Since the pods continue to bear for two or three years after becoming infected, farmers were reluctant to cut down diseased trees. Nkrumah had made big political capital out of the situation by charging that the agriculture department's attempt to weed out diseased trees was an imperialistic plot to suppress the African. In office now, the question was dumped in his lap: take the political risk of cutting diseased trees or watch the Gold Coast's economic future go down the drain. To his credit, Nkrumah imposed heavy fines on farmers who refused to cut blighted trees.

In local government elections which took place in 1952, the C.P.P. made further gains and won control of most local councils outside Ashanti, the centre of the cocoa-growing country. Between Gold Coast whistle-stopping, Nkrumah found time to get to America to accept an honorary doctorate from Lincoln (and has called himself nothing but 'Doctor' ever since) and to make a state visit to Liberia.

In the 1954 general election, the C.P.P. won 72 out of 104 seats in the Assembly and Nkrumah demanded full independence for what he proposed to call Ghana (it was his former boss and bitter enemy, Dr. Danquah, however, who originally suggested that the Gold Coast should adopt the name of the once-great Sudanic empire as its own). The going was not entirely smooth, however: opposition crystallized in Ashanti, the home of a warrior people and the centre of the cocoa, timber, gold and diamonds which are Ghana's wealth. Led by Danquah and by K. A. Busia, the Ashantis demanded a federal form of government which would give them local political autonomy and greater control over the revenues derived from their lands. Rioting broke out in Ashanti and neither Nkrumah nor any other C.P.P. minister dared to speak in Kumasi.

Despite Opposition efforts in Ashanti and the admission of an African cabinet minister that he had taken a bribe from a contractor, the C.P.P., which polled 398,000 votes to the Opposition's 299,000 (only 50 per cent of the electorate cast their ballots), was able to win 71 of 104 seats in the 1956 election and, on March 6, 1957, the 113th anniversary of the signing of the first treaty between Britain and the Gold Coast chiefs, Gold Coast became Ghana, an independent member of the British Commonwealth. Nkrumah gave a hint of what was to come in his book, which was published on the day of independence, when he stated that 'even a system based on social justice and a democratic constitution may need backing up, during the period following independence, by emergency measures of a totalitarian kind'. More of this later.

Since independence, Nkrumah has done everything possible to personify himself to Ghana and to Africa as the George Washington of his country and the Napoleon of his continent. His image replaces that of the Queen on Ghanaian coinage (complete with an inscription modestly describing him as 'Founder of the State'), a more than life-sized £40,000 statue of him giving the 'freedom salute' (a sort of sloppy 'Heil, Hitler') graces the lawn in front of the National Assembly, he appears with Abraham Lincoln on postage stamps, and streets, schools and clinics are named after him; his birthday is a national holiday. For sale in the Accra market are postcards which bear quotations from the Bible and show Nkrumah and Jesus, apparently consumed with mutual admiration. The President is, in fact, worshipped as a messiah and 'Nkrumahism' was described to me by one Ghanaian as 'a great new philosophy which will soon replace Christianity'. The C.P.P.-owned Accra *Evening News*, which has received substantial government loans, generally manages to run at least one picture of Nkrumah in every edition and describes him as Katamanto (Man Whose Word is Irrevocable), Uyeadieyie (Man of Deeds), Kukuduruni (Man of Courage), Nufenu (Strongest of All), Osuodumgya (Fire Extinguisher) or Kasapreko (Man Whose Word is Final). When at a loss for words, the *Evening News* just identifies him as Osageyfo (Great Man). In the unlikely event that the C.P.P. should ever get out of hand (he is its life chairman and C.P.P. general secretary Tawia Admafio refers to him as 'our superman, master and God'), Nkrumah has organized a 10,000-man Builders' Brigade made up of uniformed thugs who owe him personal allegiance for the four shillings a day, free bed and food which they receive. To build an international image of himself acceptable to other African states, the fifty-one-year-old politician has called conference after conference in Accra, and at each has laid claim to the leadership not only of Ghana but of all Africa.

Although in 1959 he became the first African to be named a Privy Councillor (and the first to stay as an overnight guest at Balmoral), Nkrumah has made Ghana the Commonwealth's third republic. This means that the West African nation, like India (which became a republic in 1950) and Pakistan (which followed six years later) no longer regards Elizabeth II as Queen of Ghana but only as the head of the Commonwealth, of which Ghana is still a member.

There is no obvious advantage to Ghana in its new status. But it is a fact that in the non-white areas of the Commonwealth, as opposed to the old Dominions, the Crown is regarded not as a reminder of a common political and emotional bond but as a symbol of former servitude. In the particular case of the African, his is a relatively simple mind when it comes to dealing with Western concepts and his leaders have been worried that he might miss the fine distinction between one who reigns and one who rules. In other words, African leaders are jealous for political reasons of any loyalty afforded the Crown, believing that it may act as a detriment to their personal popularity and to the achievement of their pan-African dreams.

Nkrumah announced in January of 1960 that he would hold a referendum on the republic, which would be combined with the election of the first president, the following July. The United Party immediately stated its objections—it would have preferred an elective monarchy with regional paramount chiefs acting as chief of state in rotation—but nominated its elder statesman, J. B. Danquah, to oppose Nkrumah. The referendum took place in April and the electorate voted overwhelmingly for a republic with Nkrumah as its president. Danquah asserted that balloting had taken place during 'a general reign of terror imposed upon the country by certain leaders and members of the party in power'. Nkrumah took office on July 1.

The republican constitution, which the U.P. has called 'worse than the crudest colonial constitution of the nineteenth century', places even more power in Nkrumah's hands than he held before. The president now exercises the powers which once were split between the prime minister and the governor-general, the Queen's representative. He chooses his own cabinet, is commander-in-chief of the armed forces (he has the right to dismiss or suspend any member of the services), has control over the civil service and the right to appoint judges. He has a veto over legislation (he is entitled to veto part of a bill without refusing the whole of it) and can dissolve Parliament, but must resign himself if he does so. The presidential term is for five years and in future elections the president will be chosen not by the people but by the majority party's legislators. When a candidate stands for the National Assembly he must state which presidential hopeful he intends to support (after first gaining the presidential candidate's approval) and the decision is irrevocable. The president is not a member of the National Assembly but has the right to address it.

The life of the assembly, which is a 114-seat house, is for five years unless dissolved by the president. The present assembly is due to be dissolved by July 1961 but it is likely that Nkrumah will regard the referendum as a general election and prolong the life of the house, in which his C.P.P. has an overwhelming majority, until 1965. Appeals from the courts to the Privy Council are no longer possible and the constitution gives the legislature the power to surrender 'the whole or any part of the sovereignty of Ghana' to permit the creation of a union of African states.

Nkrumah has left very little to chance. The new constitution borrows a little from the British, French and American systems and contains just a dash of totalitarianism. It is similar to the U.S. constitution except that it lacks its system of checks and balances. Many British and American liberals were shocked by the document, yet it only formalizes a situation which has existed in Ghana for some time: all real power is concentrated in the person of one man.

The President's personal life is opaque. Nkrumah, who neither smokes nor drinks and seldom eats meat, admits that he has never outgrown a deep-seated fear of women, although in 1957 he married Fathia Ritzk, a pretty University of Cairo student (she is Egyptian) who has given him a son and a daughter. They had not met before the marriage and Mrs. Nkrumah is seldom seen in public. Nkrumah, who has melancholy eyes that can flash with humour, has been described as everything from a eunuch to a satyr. He describes himself as 'a very normal man with probably more than average self-discipline'.

The one vice of this man of average height (his hands and feet are exceptionally small) is the love of power and acclaim. He is a brilliant, exuberant actor who believes wholeheartedly both in the play and in his part in it. He is a fine speaker in that he can play expertly upon the primitive minds and passions with which he is confronted. By absolute standards, his speeches are banal and repetitious but he delivers them with a flamboyance which delights the Africans. This is why they call him 'Show-Boy'; this is why he has no peer in the field of African politics.

Despite his apparent academic qualifications, Nkrumah is no intellectual. The questions which might arise about the qualitative value of the Lincoln degrees are reinforced by the speed with which Nkrumah pasted the honorary doctorate on to the front of his name. Like too many Africans—and like too many Americans, for that matter—Nkrumah appears to be more interested in the prestige of graduate degrees than in knowledge itself. By no stretch of the imagination is Nkrumah either a philosopher or a deep thinker, political or otherwise, although he likes to think of himself and have others think of him in these terms. With all the trappings cut away, Nkrumah is an able political organizer with a streak of determination in his character, a brilliant politician but not the great statesman which Africa so desperately needs, a man with a few set ideas and no great flexibility or depth of vision. What Nkrumah yearns for, like all vain men, is political success in his own lifetime and a favourable judgement from history. It is still possible that he may get both. It should be said, of course, for those who do not know it, that Nkrumah did not 'win' independence for Ghana. Before Nkrumah returned to his country, the Burns constitution had given Ghana a considerable African majority in the assembly and set its feet upon the path from which there is no turning, that to independence.

Nkrumah, a man of sophisticated, boyish charm, hurried back in time to pull Danquah out of the saddle and ride his country to independence. He showed skill as a jockey but his mount was a winner from the time the starting gates opened. And they opened long before Kwame Nkrumah was born. Another question that should be dealt with before the facts become too obscured by the legends which are already growing up is that of Nkrumah's Communist affiliation. Was Nkrumah a Communist? Possibly. He was certainly well indoctrinated in America and England. Never having been involved in African colonialism, Russia has a particular allure for African nationalists. Or Nkrumah may have accepted membership in the Party as a necessary and cheap price to pay for access to the secrets of political organization. It is extremely doubtful if Nkrumah understood then or does now what Communism really means because he has a blind side to his intellect which seems to characterize most African leaders at this stage in history: he neither knows nor cares about the rest of the world except in so far as it directly, immediately and obviously affects Africa. A slight in a Baltimore restaurant can mean more to such a man than a dozen Budapests or Tibets. There are a few diehards who maintain that even now Nkrumah, who has a 525-ton luxury yacht and a mansion outside Accra, is a dedicated Communist still nursing his goal of a vast Soviet Socialist Republic in Africa. Nothing could be further from the truth. Communism, even in its most warped and rudimentary form, requires a degree of self-discipline and sacrifice which does not appear in Nkrumah's make-up. He worships at his own shrine and there is no room there for any ideology which might diminish his personal stature by one jot. When Ghanaian policy appears at times to be duplicating the party-line, this is only because Nkrumah happens to feel at the moment that it is the right policy for himself, for Ghana, for Africa. In that order.

HOW IT GOT THAT WAY

We have been talking at some length about Kwame Nkrumah because to a great degree he is both typical of his people and, at the same time, responsible for the direction in which Ghana is heading, politically, culturally and economically. But although Africa's history seems to have begun only yesterday, in fact it stretches back into time. And if one is to understand the problems of modern Ghana, which we will be exploring a little later, one must have some knowledge of men and events before Nkrumah.

It has been pretty well established that Ghana, which is bounded on the west by Ivory Coast, on the north by the Voltaic Republic, on the east by newly-independent Togo and on the south by the Atlantic Ocean, was virtually uninhabited until the sixteenth century. The consensus is that the tribes now living in the West African state migrated from the north-east during that century and the one which followed. Some African writers, who tend to be better nationalists than historians, now claim that the tribes of Ghana are the descendants of that segment of the population of the ancient kingdom of the same name, which stood about 300 miles to the west of Timbuktu, which moved south to avoid the imposition of Islam by their eleventh-century conquerors.

W. E. F. Ward, the most responsible historian of the area, rules out this theory and postulates that, by the time the ancient kingdom of Ghana fell, the Akan tribes who were the ancestors of modern Ghanaians were already settled well south of the Niger. He reckons that they moved into what is today Ghana about A.D. 1400 as the result of local disturbances and states categorically that, since the Portuguese reached the Gold Coast in 1471, 'there is no nation now dwelling in the Gold Coast which has been in the country much longer than the Europeans'. The ties between the two Ghanas are those of emotion rather than fact.

The early Portuguese voyagers found so much gold in the hands of the natives that they gave the name of the metal to the coast and Portugal determined to establish permanent trading stations. Don Diogo de Azambuja, accompanied certainly by Diaz and possibly by Columbus, landed to the west of present-day Accra with 500 soldiers, 100 artisans and quantities of dressed stone and cut timbers to build what must have been one of the first prefabs, the castle of Sao Jorge da Mina. It still stands today and performs the more prosaic role of police academy.

The Portuguese built smaller forts at Axim, Shama and Accra and hoped to monopolize the lucrative trade in ivory, slaves and gold. For some years during the sixteenth century, traders annually sent back to Portugal an amount of gold equal to a tenth of the world's supply at that time. From the first, this monopoly was challenged by Spanish, English and French freebooters. The Portuguese excluded the Spanish by diplomacy, organized a convoy system for their twice-yearly gold fleets and hanged any foreigners they found trading on the coast. But new voyages of discovery opened up to Portugal the riches of the Indies and Brazil, and her interest in the Gold Coast waned. As it did, the forays of interlopers intensified and, between 1500 and 1531, 300 Portuguese caravels were captured off the Gold Coast by French corsairs. In 1580 Philip II of Spain annexed Portugal and the Portuguese possessions thus became fair game for Philip's rebellious Dutch subjects. In 1595 the Hollanders made their first voyage to the Gold Coast and bracketed the castle of Sao Jorge at Elmina with four forts of their own. Meanwhile, the establishment of large-scale plantations in the New World had created a strong demand for slaves and English interest in the coast revived. The struggle for mastery of the Gold Coast was joined between England and Holland with the Portuguese and newcomers to the coast such as the Swedes, Danes, French and Prussians, all of whom established fortified posts, rather uncomfortably in the middle.

On a sweltering June day in 1637, Count Maurice of Nassau stormed Elmina with 800 troops and 160 years of Portuguese rule came to an end. The Danes ousted the Swedes and natives sacked the single French post. The Prussians abandoned their forts in 1708. Forts were built, abandoned, bartered, sold and sacked. It seemed to make little difference to the Africans who held the forts, although local animosities and rivalries did arise. In the main, Fanti and Accra middlemen, who acquired slaves from the warlike Ashanti of the interior, sold their black ivory to the highest bidder and left the forts alone, as long as the occupants honoured their 'Note' for rent. The 'Note' for Elmina was two ounces of gold per month, an ounce of gold then being valued at £4. Apart from an occasional skirmish with the natives, life on the coast was pretty much a matter of drink, disease and boredom. A man could get rich, if he lived. The odds against this prospect are illustrated by the fact that the Danes had twenty-four governors in fifty years and twenty of these died in harness.

While the European nations were battling for supremacy on the coast, events were taking place in the interior which were to cause Kwame Nkrumah considerable trouble three centuries later: the Ashanti confederacy was in the process of being born. Like the Iroquois and the

Hellenes, the Ashanti were a number of small, quarrelsome tribes inhabiting the broken forest country behind the coastal plain. They had in common a language, certain rituals and many enemies. If an alliance was to be anything more than a temporary military grouping, some strong unifying force was required. This force was supplied by two great men: an Ashanti chieftain named Osie Tutu and the wizard Okomfu Anokye.

This black Merlin called together all chiefs of the Ashanti at Kumasi, Osie Tutu's town. The wizard harangued the chiefs, produced darkness and thunder and great clouds of white dust. Down through these clouds floated a Golden Stool which landed on the knees of Osie Tutu. Anokye, speaking on a hillock which now boasts a multi-million-dollar hospital, proclaimed Tutu as chief of all the Ashanti, stated that the Golden Stool contained the soul of the Ashanti nation and that while the stool remained safe, Ashanti would grow great. Then the wizard drove an iron sword into the ground and promised that until someone drew the sword from the ground, Ashanti would remain united. The builders of the hospital carefully laid their plans so as not to disturb the sword and it is there today. In the Golden Stool, Anokye gave the Ashanti an outward and visible sign of their inward and spiritual unity. Henceforth and to this day, Ashanti was a nation one and indivisible, linked by a common national consciousness and a mystical bond. The immediate result was the launching of Ashanti imperialism; the secondary result and the one which more immediately concerns us, has been that the Ashanti people, unified under their king (called the Asantehene) and linked by the Golden Stool, have been the only force cohesive enough to offer any real opposition to Nkrumah's drive to power. More of this later.

Ashanti war parties struck out in every direction and usually with success. The Ashanti were not only terrible warriors but good psychologists: conquered nations became Ashanti provinces with much local autonomy. Their rulers were given places on the Ashanti council of state and their princesses were numbered among the Asantehene's customary complement of 3,333 wives. To the Asantehene these satraps owed a feudal allegiance which was, of course, a two-way street: although the Asantehene's power was tremendous, it was limited by custom and by religion.

In the northern part of what is today Ghana, society was less stable and more primitive. The people there had lived for centuries in totemic clans under priest-kings. From the fifteenth century small bands of better-armed strangers familiar with a rudimentary form of Islam descended on the local tribes to impose a territorial and secular leadership. The priest-kings became land-priests, known as *ten'dama*. The people owed secular allegiance to the strangers; but the land and rights and ceremonies pertaining to it remained the province of the *ten'dama*. The North was and is arid and poor. To purchase guns, salt and kola nuts, the North had only one 'export crop': slaves. So while the coastal tribes were assimilating some European influences from the white traders and the people of the interior were being welded into a cohesive Ashanti federation, the North remained in a state of uproar as rival chiefs raided each other's territory for slaves. The traditional split loyalty of the northern tribes, drawn on the one hand to the *ten'dama* and on the other to the secular chief, has its results today in the lack of political punch of the North; the primitive conditions caused by the slave raids and the isolation of their position far from the coast have left the northern tribes far behind those of the coast and Ashanti in matters such as education and economic development and have made them easy prey to the more advanced southerners, whom they hate and distrust. Thus it can be seen that it has been the pattern of events set hundreds of years ago which makes Ghanaian politics what they are today. Back now to Ashanti for a moment.

In 1805 the Ashantis, seeking new conquests among the coastal tribes, became involved in the first of seven wars against the British which were to be the principal feature of nineteenth-century Gold Coast history and eventually were to result in the secular eclipse of the Ashanti state. These Ashanti invasions coupled with the 1807 British interdict against the slave trade completely reversed the political situation on the coast. Raids before had been desirable since they provided the raw material of the slave trade. Now the white traders could only prosper in the traffic of palm oil, timber and gold, and this trade could go on only where peace and order prevailed. In 1821, in an attempt to achieve this, the British revoked the charters of the companies and took over the forts in the name of the Crown. It is worth noting here that, as has happened in our own time, high idealism unbacked by hard thinking can cause more suffering than it alleviates: one of the immediate results of the outlawing of the slave trade was to give a terrific impetus to the practice of large-scale human sacrifice, a custom not unknown to the Ashanti. The blood-bath which followed the end of the slave trade was in part an appeal to the old gods for success against the enemies of the Ashanti; it was also a logical means of relieving society of unwanted mouths to feed which, in the days of the slave trade, had had a commercial value. Slaves and prisoners were sacrificed by the Ashanti on any public occasion and, at the death of one Asantehene, 2,600 were slaughtered. When the British finally took Kumasi in 1873, they found a brass bowl five feet in diameter which had been used to collect the human blood necessary to wash the stools of dead kings. In any case, the closing of the coastal market for slaves meant only that more were destined to make the killing trek across the Sahara to the harsher servitude of Asia Minor, many of them after undergoing castration, which increased their commercial value. By outlawing the European slave trade before first being in a position to police the religious customs of Africa and to cut the Arab slave routes, the Western nations relieved their own consciences and condemned thousands of Africans either to ritual murder, death in the desert or lives of misery in the Arab world.

The first governor, Sir Charles Macarthy, soon found himself embroiled in an Ashanti war. Through a series of blunders he managed to get himself cut off from his base by the main Ashanti army at the village of Nsamankow. When his ammunition ran short, Macarthy sent an officer back for reserve supplies. This gentleman arrived at the eleventh hour with four kegs, which were eagerly opened. Three were found to contain macaroni. This not being very lethal stuff unless consumed in quantity, the Ashanti cut up the British column, wounded Macarthy (who committed suicide to avoid capture), and returned to Ashanti bearing the governor's head, which is said to be nicely pickled and a big ju-ju around Kumasi to this day.

The Ashanti came down again in 1826 under the personal leadership of the Asantehene and at Akantamasu a battle was fought which decided the fate of the Gold Coast. At a crucial moment the British fired a barrage of rockets which completely unmanned the Ashanti. The Asantehene, wounded seven times and depressed by the news that the Golden Stool had been captured, was seating himself on a keg of gunpowder preparatory to giving himself the kind of send-off which such a military disgrace required when news came that the Golden Stool had been recaptured and spirited away. The Asantehene consented to live, paid the British an indemnity of 4,000 ounces of gold and gave hostages.

Weary of its unprofitable responsibility, the British government withdrew from the Gold Coast leaving administration in the hands of the merchants. As their governor the merchants chose a man little known today, although he must rank with Warren Hastings and Cecil Rhodes as one of the great men of the Age of Imperialism. George Maclean, who came to the coast in 1828 and remained there until his death nineteen years later, did more to make possible the Ghana of today than any other man. Armed with little money but much patience, without recourse to arms he virtually ended the slave trade, eradicated human sacrifice and gradually grafted Western culture on to the lives of the people. When the British government returned a few years before his death, Maclean stepped aside and accepted the lesser post of Judicial Adviser. He followed the path of honesty and understanding and when he died, the natives, who are no mean judges of human nature, gave him the funeral of an African king.

In 1844 the British formalized their position in the Gold Coast by signing a Bond with the chiefs, who acknowledged their jurisdiction. Six years later they bought from Denmark her five remaining forts and, in 1872, 274 years of Dutch rule ended with the sale of Holland's remaining posts to Britain. From that date until 1957 Britain was the boss.

In 1896 another Ashanti war broke out, Kumasi was captured and the British demanded an impossibly high indemnity of £357,000 in gold. When this was not paid, the Asantehene, the Queen Mother and other important chiefs were accommodated in the Seychelles (as was Archbishop Makarios, at a later date), the palace was looted, and the sacred trees and altars dynamited. Not content with this, Sir Frederick Hodgson, the new governor, in 1900 demanded the surrender of the Golden Stool so that he might sit on it. This was an unimaginable sacrilege. Not even the Asantehene himself may sit upon the stool, which contains the soul of the nation, and always rests on its side atop a stool of its own. The Ashanti could no more have allowed Hodgson to sit on the stool than a Polish bishop today could permit Khrushchev to feast off the communion plate at the high altar of a cathedral. For his stupidity Hodgson was besieged in Kumasi for two months before the Ashanti were finally subdued, more chiefs were deported to the Seychelles and the warriors were disarmed. It was the last Ashanti war and the kingdom was formally annexed. In 1924 the Asantehene was allowed to return from exile.

With peace and a solid economy firmly based on cocoa, diamonds, gold, manganese and timber, the Gold Coast made advances in all fields during the first half of this century. When it became obvious at the end of World War II that colonialism was a dead-duck, the Gold

Coast was the obvious place for the British to begin their 'creative abdication' in Africa. In 1946 the Legislative Council, established as early as 1850, was reconstituted and the Gold Coast became the first territory in British Africa with a black majority in its political institutions. Things were moving along in this direction smoothly enough until the return of Kwame Nkrumah, who has made a great deal of noise but changed little of the pattern of history in this nation of five million people. Kegs allegedly full of gunpowder still show up stuffed with macaroni in this part of the world.

THE WEALTH OF GHANA

The story of cocoa is the story of Ghana. No roads could have been built, no children educated without this tree; only the money which Ghanaian cocoa earns has made possible Nkrumah's political adventurism. The first crop, exported in 1891, amounted to exactly eighty pounds. Last year's bumper crop of 321,000 tons, about 10 per cent above the average for the last decade, earned about £62 million for Ghana, much of it in hard currency, thus accounting for nearly 60 per cent of the country's £114 million worth of exports. Her cocoa, 40 per cent of which goes to Common Market countries which will soon raise a tariff against it, provides more than a third of Ghana's revenues or twice the combined amount spent on agriculture, education, public works and medical services. The Cocoa Marketing Board, a public agency, buys the whole crop at a fixed price and retains a percentage for price stabilization, research, scholarships and donations in the public interest. Its reserves have been as high as £107 million and it has lent more than £40 million to the government for development projects, given more than £5 million in grants to the university and to research projects, paid out almost £14 million in compensation to farmers whose diseased trees were cut down, and spent, in one recent year, £6 million to stabilize the cocoa price above the world market level. Ghana's cocoa, a third of the world's supply, more than half of which is grown in Ashanti, is sold to a score of countries with the United States being her best customer.

Cocoa was introduced to Ghana from Fernando Po seventy years ago by an Accra blacksmith and today it is still a peasant crop grown by some 300,000 farmers on plots averaging about three acres. Although this fact helps to give Ghana a robust economy because so many of her people are directly occupied in and share the profits of her wealth, there is little chance for Ghana to increase her earnings from this source. Most of the suitable land is already in production and capital and labour are in short supply. Where Ghana could add to her cocoa tonnage is by increasing yields. There are now about four million acres in cocoa; Ghana's farmers are getting only about 150 pounds of cocoa per acre while any farmer worth his Sears mail-order catalogue should be able to get three or four times that amount. The problem is that small-scale peasant production is uneconomic, but cocoa is too much of a political football to be tampered with. The very mention of cocoa plantations is enough to raise Ashanti ire. In an effort to convince the Africans that they should operate on a big scale, American advisers have dropped that word from their dictionary and now speak of 'orchard' cocoa, not 'plantation'. But nothing has come of it yet and, although Nkrumah took the risk of enforcing Draconian measures which involved the cutting of 68 million cocoa trees to eradicate swollen shoot, he has not yet been willing to suggest any form of compulsory collectivization. If financial circumstances should force him to do this, you can look for big trouble in Ghana.

Nkrumah planted some seeds in the summer of 1959 which may reap him a harvest of political trouble in the future. In difficulty to find the funds to finance his grandiose £343 million Second Five Year Development Plan (Ghana actually had available at most only about £90 million), Nkrumah announced that the United Ghana Farmers' Council had 'volunteered' to accept a five-year cut in the producers' price of cocoa from 72 shillings to 60 shillings a load (60 lbs.), which would contribute an extra £25 million to the Plan. This means that the growers will receive £112 for a ton of cocoa which the government will sell for £210 (£560 in 1954). One wondered just how 'voluntary' the decision had been when it was announced shortly thereafter that the government was putting out of bounds to cocoa carriers twenty-seven roads and rivers leading to Ivory Coast and Togo, where the price is considerably higher. Sceptics were fortified in their doubts when the Ghana Co-operative Movement, representing more than 51,000 cocoa growers, announced that its members did not support the price cut. Chickens like these may come home to roost when and if Nkrumah holds his next general election, now scheduled for late 1961.

The entire Second Five Year Development Plan is an exercise in wishful and sloppy thinking. It is predicated on the assumption that Ghana will be able to borrow £228 million from foreign sources which, for a number of reasons, is highly unlikely. Even if Nkrumah were able to obtain loans, Ghana lacks the ability to spend such amounts profitably and the recurrent charges would exceed the available revenue.

Not that Ghana is wholly dependent on cocoa. Right behind cocoa are timber, gold, manganese and diamonds, which together bring in more than £38 million per year. Ghana, which had sterling reserves of £182 million at the end of 1958, is the Commonwealth's fourth largest gold producer (after South Africa, Canada and Australia) and she exports 750,000 ounces a year, some of it dug from mines 4,000 feet deep. Her 1958 production, which gave work to 21,000 Africans, was worth £10·6 million and since she first was called the golden coast, Ghana has exported more than £200 million worth. The West African state exports three million carats of diamonds worth £9 million every year, half won by 9,000 wild-cat black diggers. Although her diamonds are almost entirely small industrial stones, Ghana's production is exceeded in volume only by the former Belgian Congo. Ghana is, after Russia, the world's second largest producer of manganese (the United States buys 60 per cent of Ghana's manganese, 40 per cent of her timber, 30 per cent of her cocoa). Timber exports, however, have probably reached their peak and a belated reafforestation programme cannot be expected to forestall a decline in the value and volume of production.

There are signs, in fact, that none of these four exports are capable of much greater production levels than those already achieved. And foreign investors have been understandably chary of putting money into Ghana until her future political course is charted more clearly. This situation has got Nkrumah up a political tree: he has made a lot of pie-in-the-sky promises over the last eight years and produced nothing but stale jelly-roll. The nationalist leader has built the little man into an effective political force and he well knows the power of the mob. If the urban proletariat, caught between a spiralling cost of living and increasing unemployment, ever turns on him, Nkrumah is finished. To prevent this most unpleasant eventuality, Nkrumah has followed two courses of action: he has embarked on a series of external adventures which he calls Pan-Africanism to distract the attention of Ghana from its domestic problems and he is pushing ahead on the grandiose Volta River project.

The Volta River project is nothing new. For years everyone has known that Ghana contains deposits of bauxite estimated at 220 million tons and exports of this red dirt have doubled to 200,000 tons since 1948. What Nkrumah wants to do is to harness the Volta and use the electricity to produce aluminium and power a score of other industries. The scheme as originally planned called for a 350-foot high dam at Ajena, a spur railway to the bauxite deposits 200 miles from the dam site and a new port at Tema, nineteen miles east of Accra. The aluminium complex, Nkrumah claims, would give employment, income and training to at least 10,000 Ghanaians for two centuries. Formed by the dam, seventy miles from the Volta's mouth, would be a lake 3,500 square miles in area (about 4 per cent of the total land surface of Ghana) and 230 miles long. The lake would provide fishing grounds, cheap transportation and irrigation for the arid Accra plains. Spokesmen for the project maintain that the lake could produce 18,000 tons of fish annually worth more than £1 million. Since Ghana imports more than £2 million worth of smoked and canned fish each year, a valuable currency saving would thus be effected. Initial production of aluminium would be in the neighbourhood of 100,000 tons with eventual expansion to more than twice that figure. And the planners say that this would increase the value of Ghana's exports from £114 million to £130 million, giving the country a larger income per head of population than any other enterprise. Says Nkrumah: 'It could be the beginning of our industrial age.' And this is a prospect very near and dear to the heart of every African nationalist.

The project was originally proposed in 1951 by the colonial government and met with immediate approval as a means whereby Gold Coast's economy could be diversified while at the same time providing Britain with a source of aluminium outside the dollar zone. By the time final plans were presented in 1956, most of Britain's enthusiasm had evaporated: world aluminium production was greater than demand, political uncertainties had arisen in the shape of Ghana's impending independence, and the cost of the project, already huge, appeared to be increasing daily (in 1956, it was estimated that the project would cost £300 million; by 1959, conservative estimates had been raised to £356 million). But Nkrumah had decided early in the game that he was going to have his project and by 1953 he had authorized construction of the port of Tema and of the bridge over the Volta below Ajena, both essential parts of the scheme. When no capital for the project was forthcoming from the sterling area, Nkrumah hinted darkly that he would go behind the Iron Curtain if necessary; but first he paid a call on President Eisenhower. The upshot of Nkrumah's 1958 talk with the American president was that the United States agreed to bear half of the cost of the reassessment of the project by the Kaiser Corporation of California; if Kaiser reported favourably, it was intimated, the United States would do what it could to provide the funds or find them elsewhere. In February 1959, Kaiser returned a favourable report on a modification of the scheme which would move the site of the dam and the smelter, thus effecting a considerable financial saving. Work began on the initial stages of the modified scheme in 1959.

The scheme now under way is estimated to cost £110 million, is included in the Second Development Plan and will be built in three stages. The first stage will involve the construction of a dam and generating plant with an installed capacity of 768,000 kilowatts at Kosombo. This could be in operation by 1966. Two smaller dams and a transmission network to bring electricity to Kumasi, Accra and Takoradi would be built as the money became available, as would eighty-three miles of railway to the bauxite deposits. The electricity produced would be 100 times that now available in Ghana. Not included in this modified plan is a smelter, which will be built by a consortium of American, British and Canadian aluminium interests if adequate financing can be found. Assuming that the Volta Aluminium Company (as the consortium is called) is successful, the World Bank will lend Ghana £14·3 million, the U.S. will advance £10·7 million and the British government will provide £5 million. Ghana will supply the remaining £30 million necessary to get the project under way.

At the moment, the harbour and city of Tema, the first phase of which will cost more than £17 million, is being built from scratch at the site of a tiny fishing village. Already in operation are four deep-water berths with another four under construction (eventually there will be eighteen berths). The coast of Ghana, like much of West Africa's, has no natural harbours and until the construction of the modern artificial harbour at Takoradi, everything brought into the country had to be transhipped in whale boats paddled by muscular Kru tribesmen. Tema is linked to Accra by rail and its 500 acres of 36-foot-deep closed water will do much to ease the load on Accra importers, whether or not the Volta project is ever completed. Behind the port is the entirely new town of Tema, a city planner's delight, complete with schools, churches, jails and shopping areas. At the time of our first visit in 1959 work was going slowly because of a shortage of technicians. Built were 319 houses, each with electricity, piped water and sewerage, accommodating 4,483 people in homes ranging from modest workers' apartments to substantial middle-class homes. A sixty-six-bed hospital was waiting for its first patient and two primary schools were open. Two thousand homes a year is the schedule set by Tema's planners and they hope to have by 1970 a city of 80,000 people living on a standard higher than that of any other African urban dwellers. Everybody is happy about this except those Tema people who believe it is taboo for water to touch metal (and hence refuse to use the piped water) and the original inhabitants, whose pleasant little fishing village has been moved down the beach to make room for all this progress.

Also at Tema (although not part of the Volta Scheme) is the £1·5 million naval base for Ghana's infant navy—two inshore minesweepers —and Radio Ghana's four short-wave radio transmitters. The four 100-kilowatt transmitters, as powerful as any in Africa including Radio Cairo, were installed by a British firm at a cost of £830,000, can be heard all over Africa and in parts of Europe, India and America. A staff of about a thousand, including a dozen whites, broadcasts in English, French, Swahili, Arabic and Hausa.

There is this about Tema and the whole Volta project: it will be either a tremendous success, in which case Nkrumah will be in political clover, or it will be the biggest white elephant seen in these parts since Romain Gary was a vice-consul. In which case Ghana will be in for some unhappy days.

In the past, Ghana has been able to pay her own way: of the £106 million which she spent for development purposes between 1951 and 1958, only about 4 per cent was aid from Britain. Most of that was spent on giving Ghana what is probably the best internal communications in West Africa, including a good diesel railway and 2,000 miles of paved roads. Since independence, she has received loans from foreign sources but little in the way of outright grants; she has technical assistance agreements with the United Nations, the United States, Russia (a £14·5 million loan), Britain and Israel. From this posture Ghana is vaulting into a position where she apparently intends to put herself, if she can find takers, deeply in debt. That is the only implication which can be drawn from the £343 million Five Year Development Plan published in 1959. From her annual revenue of about £53 million, Ghana can barely manage to pay for her current capital investment of about £18 million a year. Liberia could tell her that political freedom and economic dependence on foreign powers are not a happy combination. That troublesome business of the fellow who pays the piper wanting to call the tune is bound to arise.

THE SAXON WEST

FREEDOM ARCH

None of this is readily apparent to the wanderer entering Ghana from the east. After passing through Ghanaian customs at the Togo border and being 'invited' by a policeman to give one of his friends a ride to Accra, you lurch over some really horrible roads which indicate that you are passing through part of the anti-C.P.P. portion of Trans-Volta Togoland, the former United Nations trusteeship territory which voted three to two in 1956 to join Ghana when she became independent (not to be confused with French-administered Togoland which became independent in 1960). The bridge across the Volta is too high up the river to do you any good and, as a result, you find yourself perspiring behind a long line of trucks waiting to cross on the ferry. With luck you may get over in an hour (or you may have to wait a day if traffic is heavy) and then you are skimming along over a good paved road which cuts its way across the Accra plains, bare, dusty and golden in the winter sun.

The entry into Accra is not imposing. The road swings over to the coast, pounded by the Atlantic breakers, and passes through a slum section of town which gives way suddenly to a cleared area in which stands the monolithic Freedom Arch, built to commemorate Ghana's independence. One's first thought on seeing this marble edifice, on which is inscribed 'Freedom and Justice, A.D. 1957' (U.P. wags maintain that 'Rest in Peace' should be added to the scroll), is how many cases of yaws could have been cured for the price of its erection. On the left is the glistening white pile of Christiansborg Castle, built by the Danes three centuries ago from Danish stone brought as ballast in slave ships. Christiansborg, complete with leaning palm trees and crenellated battlements, is a maze of corridors, arcades and courtyards, in one of which is buried a Portuguese governor, over whose body a melted cannon was poured. The castle sits on a pile of rocks overlooking a small cape and buses marked 'Xborg' queue up on its landward side. Christiansborg, which must be damp from the Atlantic spray, was once the home of Britain's governors; now it is Nkrumah's guest house. Turning to the right, you drive past the striking American Embassy, a modernistic structure built on struts which the Ghanaians don't like (although the Ghanaian government is purchasing the building from the U.S.) because it is an interpretation of a type of house built by the palm-oil ruffians in the days of imperialism. Next to it stand the government office buildings, a series of airy, tile-roofed buildings

500

where C.P.P. ministers hold forth and British civil servants manfully keep upper lips stiff under well-trimmed moustaches. And then there is Ghana's pride and joy, the five-storeyed, 100-room Ambassador Hotel, built at government expense (£1 million) and designed (for those who can afford £5 a day for a room) to prove that everything is up to date in Kansas City. The handsome House of Assembly with Nkrumah's statue in front (advising one to 'Seek ye the political kingdom and all other things shall be opened unto you'), Christiansborg Castle, embassy row, the Ambassador, Freedom Arch—this is one Accra; the other Accra, the one where the people live and hope and fornicate is down by James Fort, where Nkrumah once spent his time, and now the residence of his political opponents. There is a great dusty square where the evangelists come, bringing their clapping, singing flocks by the truckload to revival meetings. There the young Nkrumahs, yet unknown, exhort their constituents to greater efforts in building a new Ghana and promise them great rewards for so doing. There is a little Greek-run hotel near the lighthouse on High Street with five bedrooms built around a court and a second-floor veranda open on both sides with a bar in the middle which provides a vantage spot for viewing the life of Accra. Over the top of James Fort one could see the lighters, paddled by ten muscular blacks holding paddles whose blades were carved in the shape of hands, scurrying like water bugs in the blinding sunlight between the ships which lay at anchor off the city and the beach, where they dumped crates marked 'Fragile' with a most satisfactory crunch on to the concrete apron of the warehouses. In the evenings, when they had finished perhaps two dozen trips (one to two tons of freight per trip) to and from the ships, the 2,000 of them were paid off and some came to get drunk at the native bar on the corner, and then rested against the cool wall of the hotel and sang and laughed far into the hot night. On Tuesdays their cousins, the Ga, will not fish, for it was on a Tuesday in 1660 that the Ashanti defeated their ancestors in a great battle near Accra.

It was hot until long after midnight in the high-ceilinged, fanless room with its outsized furniture and creaking bed, and from the clusters of grass huts and from the mud-walled buildings with their corrugated iron roofs rusted to the colour of cinnamon came a constant rumble which sounded halfway between a great sigh and thunder heard at a great distance. It was all Accra panting, for there was drought and most of the city had had no water for days. The people danced and drummed to make the rains come and the women slept in the streets beside the pumps in the hope that there might be water in the morning. When the pumps remained dry, they fought each other for a chance to get at the nozzle of the tank-truck which brought water to our humble tavern. It was interesting to discover that there was still enough water for toilets and showers at the Ambassador Hotel, where an international conference was under way. Beer sales went up and those who could not afford beer bought water for a penny a quart. One wondered what those who had no pennies did. And all the while Dr. Nkrumah was saying that he would have his Volta River Project if he had to sacrifice every other public works project in the country.

For a West African city Accra is relatively clean. The downtown section is a hodge-podge of modern buildings, corrugated iron shacks, old government offices of the neo-Grecian school, grass huts, rambling and cool Syrian shops jammed with enamelware from Japan, Lancashire cottons, dried fish from Scandinavia and grey cloth from Hong Kong, sway-backed mission churches, and squares packed with humanity, half of them pumping furiously on sewing machines and the other half bargaining in the loudest possible voice for a pinch of salt, a pile of kola nuts or a packet of matches. The main streets are broad and paved but in the dusty alleys behind them emaciated chickens scratch for grubs, short-legged goats (all of whom seem to be on the verge of giving birth) tug at piles of refuse, old men lie fast asleep on the ground, naked piccaninnies are scrubbed vigorously by slightly older and more clothed brothers and sisters, and women plait each other's hair into tight ringlets or pound yams in wooden mortars. Although the women are not as flamboyantly well-dressed nor as regal in bearing as the Wollofs further up the coast, they hold the purse strings of Ghana through their control of the retail and transport trades. Many have thousands of pounds of credit with the big trading companies and could buy and sell most of the white guests at the Ambassador. Double-entry book-keeping is unknown to them yet credits, debits, the day-to-day price changes of commodities and, of course, net worth are tabulated in the heads of the market 'mammies', available for instantaneous recall.

Accra's most famous 'mammy' is Dedei Aryetey, a generously proportioned woman better known as 'Mrs. Flour' (she sells it). Mrs. Flour started her commercial life in a stall called 'Why Worry?' and, indeed, she has small cause to do so. She owns a rambling, relative-jammed house adorned with C.P.P. symbols and is head of the party's women's section. She backed Nkrumah in the days when he owned only one shirt and, although she is barely literate, is one of the most potent figures in the party.

For entertainment the people jam themselves into Accra's open-air cinemas to shout themselves hoarse at six-gun operas or ogle in disbelief at the antics of 'primitive' natives in Hollywood's latest series of 'Africans'. For the more sedate, there is the jazzy Community Centre, built in 1951 at a cost of £350,000 by the United Africa Company and designed by British architect Maxwell Fry (who also did the government ministry buildings), complete with, of all things, a reproduction of Salvador Dali's *Crucifixion*. The Community Centre offers magazines, lectures of the 'Mysticism of Thomas Mann' variety and, occasionally, boxing, a sport of which Ghanaians are particularly fond. There is also the racecourse (conveniently located just behind the ministries; thirty-five racing days a year) and a clutch of nightclubs named 'Weekend in Havana', 'Paradise', 'Tip Toe in the Gardens' (managed by an American Negro who once ran a Harlem juke joint), 'Weekend in Kalamazoo' and 'Kalamazoo Shake-Your-Head', a rather stuffy place where the clientele are forbidden to fire 'toy guns or Christmas crackers'. 'Coconut Grove', run by a member of the Accra aristocracy, is the Stork Club of the circuit and charges an annual membership fee of twelve guineas. When it was opened, Minister of Economic Affairs Kojo Botsio said it would fill 'a long-felt need'. The café society of Kumasi, Ghana's second city, is not to be outdone and it has, among others, 'Sentimental Saloon', 'Old Folks', 'As Usual', 'The Way Fairies Inn' and, my favourite, 'The Decency Bar'.

In Accra a quarter of the male population seems to drive taxis, which you hail by stepping out into the street, clapping your hands and bellowing 'Service!', and another quarter rides in the front seat and relieves the driver at the wheel when he becomes weary. The third quarter drives trucks with fanciful names such as 'Poor Boy, No Friends', 'King Kong Special', 'I love You, Baby', or 'Money is My Friend' which have no brakes, half their springs gone, and are invariably overloaded either with shuffling dancers who like to jitterbug in the bed of the truck while it is in motion, or with oil drums, crates of beer, sacks of wheat or other paraphernalia. The fourth quarter can be found sitting behind expansive desks in the ministries with expressions on their faces varying from bored to frustrated to confused. In the main, the top level civil servant is competent and courteous. The problem is to reach him through the mob of underlings on the government payroll. So formidable a task is this that one often does better to call on the Honourable Minister at home or catch him on a Saturday night when, with the rest of Accra, he will be letting his passions go with a bit of 'High Life' dancing at the Greek hotel, which resounds with blaring saxophones until well into the early hours of the morning, when everybody goes out to Labadi Beach for a moonlight swim.

The exuberance of the off-duty politician and the average man in the street at any hour is matched only by the proper reserve demonstrated by the students at Ghana's twelve-year-old university college, which next year will assume full university status. The University College, which is located a few miles outside Accra on Legon Hill (Legon means 'mountain of wisdom') has been built almost entirely by Ghanaian funds (£6 million at this writing) and it is something to see. The college stretches along both sides of a wide, palm-lined avenue in a series of two-storey residence halls (four for men and one for women) built around courtyards and each with its own chapel, library (there is also a university library with 140,000 volumes), auditorium and lecture rooms, panelled dining hall with sedate high table. At the end of the avenue, up ninety-six steps, is the Senate House and its 130-foot-high Independence Tower. With its graceful Spanish-style architecture, red tile roofs and its bubbling fountains set in shady nooks, the university looks like nothing so much as a well-endowed California junior college. Each of its 600 students (eventual capacity: 5,000), of whom forty-one are women, wears an indigo academic gown, has a private room with a balcony, and lives a life well isolated from the turmoil of Accra (another 515 students attend Kumasi's College of Technology, Ghana's other institution of higher learning, and 1,300 are studying abroad).

Eighteen of the 153 members of the university's senior faculty are Africans, fees are £100 a year per student (costs per student are close to £2,600), a quarter of the money has come from the Cocoa Marketing Board, the faculty bar has sterling beer mugs and the School of Agriculture's pig sties are air-conditioned. The university has a School of Engineering and may soon get a medical school. The Law School, however, has been established in Accra (Nkrumah has had too much trouble with lawyers not to keep fledgling attorneys under his thumb). Although British traditions are aped in almost every other form, most students are too sedate to ride bicycles, which are the form of locomotion of the lower classes. Almost every student is on a full scholarship, although about a hundred are well enough off to have cars. The college, like its sister institutions in Nigeria, Uganda and Rhodesia, enjoys a special relationship with the University of London, which means that each of the 439 graduates of its nineteen teaching departments holds a degree from the University of London, which passes on his qualifications and sees to it that standards are kept up to scratch. Although there have been some slight modifications to the curriculum, Ghanaian students must still struggle through the Lake poets and learn their Imperial History. Most do well, surprisingly well when one considers the type of school from which many of them came. One such 'institution' existed right outside the window of our hotel room. It consisted of a sheet of corrugated iron supported by four six-foot posts. There were no books and a single blackboard. Some thirty children clad in ragged khaki and ranging in age from about four to ten sat on wooden benches with slates in their hands and occasionally repeated the words of an older child, presumably doing the lesson. The 'teacher', a husky young man in his twenties who probably had little more education than his charges, was armed with a large stick and a copy of 'Ebony'. The first he applied vigorously to various sections of the anatomies of those within his reach when the noise unduly distracted his attention from the second.

In 1958 634,011 Ghanaian children (a third of them girls) were attending 5,062 schools. Although primary school theoretically is free and compulsory and junior high school will soon become so, only about half the children in the country go to school. An estimated 60 per cent of the primary teachers and 25 per cent of the junior high school teachers are untrained. Much of the funds allocated to the Ministry of Education under the Second Five-Year Development Plan, which got under way last year, will be employed in expanding the secondary system from thirty-nine schools with 11,000 students to sixty-five schools capable of accepting 6,000 new students per year. The number of primary and junior high schools in 1959, which will be slightly increased under the plan, was 3,400 and 1,100 respectively. In 1951 there were only 218,000 students enrolled in schools of all types. Ghana has come a long way but she still has far to go.

THE OPPOSITION

Although Nkrumah has by no means neglected his country's educational needs, the university is one of the focal points of opposition

to his administration. This is not difficult to understand: since his
accession to power Nkrumah's government has shown little regard
for the fundamental principles of Western democracy. Despite constitutional safeguards specifically designed to prevent it, the central
government has taken to itself more and more power and has
increasingly abrogated the liberties of the people both in theory and
in fact. Among its more obvious actions, the C.P.P. government has
enacted new and stringent treason and sedition laws, given the police
increased powers of investigation, instituted imprisonment without
trial on the basis of mere suspicion rather than on acts, suspended many
chiefs, abrogated the powers of the regional assemblies and then
eliminated the assemblies themselves, gagged the local press, deported
foreign journalists and opposition politicians. Ashanti, which was the
centre of resistance, has had its western lands taken from it to form a
sixth region of the country called Brong-Ahafo. The trade union movement has been placed under direct control of the government (and its
members told it is 'ideological heresy' to vote non-C.P.P. members into
union offices). The posts of district and regional commissioners, which
once were civil service jobs, have become political appointments. To
ensure political conformity of toddlers, Nkrumah has created a 'Young
Pioneers' organization for those too young (under eighteen) to don the
green trousers, yellow shirts and red caps of the Builders' Brigade. The
Union of Printers and Newspaper Workers has called on the C.P.P. to
amend legislation 'to ensure that the Press becomes an instrument for
the defence of the State' and to create a registry which would restrict the
profession to those with the proper ideological backgrounds. Ghanaians
can now be sentenced to fifteen years in jail for making false statements
'likely to injure the credit or the reputation of Ghana or of the Government of Ghana' even if the individual is unaware that the statement is
false. The government has given itself the right to 'supervise' the activities of persons whose deportation may be impractical, supervision to
include specification of residence and restriction of activities. Judicial
appointments have been transferred from an impartial commission to
the prime minister's office and the Legislative Assembly has voted itself
additional authority to discipline its members. The government has
announced that it will increase the police force from 6,000 to 9,000
men and double the size of the army.

All this has been done in the name of law and order and there is
little question but that, in a newly independent state in which the mass
of the people are at best only semi-civilized, such actions may be

necessary to prevent chaos. Dr. Nkrumah, of course, did not point out this when he was seeking independence and asserting that his country-men were in every way capable of governing themselves. But disquieting as are the acts themselves, the manner and direction in which they have been applied is even more so. Upon even a cursory examination, it becomes obvious that there is one set of laws applying to the Opposition and one to the C.P.P.

When you consider that the C.P.P. has had ten years (four of them without the restraining factor of the British presence) in which to cement its hold on the civil service and the police, to dispense patronage, to deport and jail political opponents, the wonder is that the United Party has been able to keep the fifteen seats (the rest being C.P.P.) in the 114-member Legislative Assembly which it now holds. That the position of the Opposition is becomingly increasingly difficult is illus-trated by the fact that it held thirty-two seats when independence was granted in 1957, more than half its strength having been whittled away from it by the steps which the C.P.P. has taken in the past three years. Opposition was and still is centred in the North and Ashanti, where the traditional chiefs backed up by Ghana's intellectual aristocracy regard Nkrumah as a dangerous demagogue. It is interesting to note what has happened to the great chiefs who opposed Nkrumah: with the exception of the Asantehene, whose person is still too sacred for Nkrumah to touch, every important anti-government chief has either abdicated or been deposed and his place taken by a more supple individual. Even the Asantehene has been stripped of his closest court officials and forced to adopt an officially neutral line. States where opposition was strongest have been dismembered and unfriendly councils have had their books and actions scrutinized with a thoroughness which neither they nor their pro-government counterparts can stand. The leader of the Opposition, Dr. K. A. Busia, has fled into exile in Holland 'because of fear of arrest'. Although the leader of the United Party (symbol: cocoa tree) is a quiet-spoken northern chief named S. D. Dombo, assisted by Joe Appiah, son-in-law of the late Sir Stafford Cripps, the existence of the Opposition is to a large measure a token of the abilities of four other individuals.

The first of these is Dr. Joseph Kwame Kyeretwie Boakye Danquah, a sixty-four-year-old white-haired Accra attorney whose friends call him J.B. Danquah, who was defeated by Nkrumah in Ghana's first presidential election, is an aristocrat, being both a third generation intellectual and a kinsman of Ofori Atta, a powerful chief who ruled

500,000 tribesmen until recently deposed. Danquah earned his B.A. at London University, later read law at the Inner Temple, returning to the Gold Coast to establish the country's first newspaper. When Nkrumah was failing high school Latin, the portly attorney was agitating (in modulated tones) for greater African participation in Gold Coast affairs. Danquah founded the United Gold Coast Convention and was elected to the Legislative Council in 1947. The story of his hiring of Nkrumah and of the latter's assumption of political power we already know.

After Nkrumah's advent to power Danquah twice unsuccessfully stood for election. But although he holds no seat in the Assembly, Danquah is high in the councils of the United Party and his law practice is busy if not lucrative: most of his time is spent in defending U.P. members in court, obtaining writs to prevent their deportation, or filing *habeas corpus* proceedings to get them out of jail and into court. In between all this, Danquah has found time for a visit to the United States and the publication of works ranging from monographs of Akan customs to rather esoteric poetry (he was the recipient of the first United Nations Bryant Mumford Writing Fellowship).

After I had wangled my way through a host of bodyguards and hangers-on, Danquah received me in the prim upstairs parlour of his Accra home. On the walls hung his various degrees, pictures of the many delegations on which he has served, a portrait of his second wife, and a faded mezzotint of himself draped in a Roman toga and leaning against a piece of vaguely Grecian stage scenery. While I nursed a scotch, the stubby politician chain-smoked State Express 555s and gave his impressions of Nkrumah and of Ghana's political future. The president he regards as a brilliant, shallow man. As long as Europeans lead the army and the police (here we have whites in Africa reverting to their traditional role of mercenaries), he sees no chance of a coup and would not favour one under any circumstances. Charges of planning a coup lodged against two U.P. parliamentarians which resulted in their imprisonment in 1959 he regards as trumped-up. 'A coup,' he added, 'is no solution to anything; it can only be followed by another coup.' But he believes that a spontaneous revulsion against Nkrumah's government, either within the C.P.P. or in the country at large, could bring the U.P. to power. He went on:

'People are hungry. The women in the North have to walk ten miles to get a bucket of water and Dr. Nkrumah gives £10 million to Guinea. The people of Ghana are not idiots. Soon they will realize that

Nkrumah is only using them to further his own wild dreams of making a Pan-African hero of himself. When they have had enough, they will leave him.'

You come away from Danquah with the impression that he is a highly intelligent, pleasant, cunning, reasonably honest and very disappointed man (and one is always a little wary of the statements of disappointed men). It seems almost too much for him to bear that, in addition to snatching the plum of national leadership from him, Nkrumah has changed Dr. Danquah's home address from 34 Station Road to 34 Kwame Nkrumah Avenue. The lawyer gets all his mail at the office.

Equally charming and intelligent is K. A. Busia, the forty-six-year-old self-exiled leader of the Opposition. Busia lacks Danquah's personal bitterness because he never pictured himself as an occupant of Christiansborg Castle. Teaching was and is his one great love and he went into politics only because friends urged him to do so for the national good.

Busia was born at Wenchi in Ashanti country and his family were chiefs and cocoa farmers (Nkrumah recently had Busia's brother removed from the Wenchi stool and himself took the title of Yeferihene, or head of the Wenchi royal family). He attended Methodist mission schools and took his B.A. at Achimota College. He then went on to Oxford to get a high 'second' in Modern Greats, completing the three-year course in two years. It is worth noting that no African has yet got a 'first' at Oxford. Returning to Wenchi in 1941, he became one of the first two Africans to be appointed district commissioners in the Gold Coast. After four years as an administrator, he went back to Oxford to get his doctorate in Social Anthropology. After more graduate work and a Carnegie research fellowship, he joined the staff of Ghana's University College in 1951 as a lecturer in African Studies. In the same year he was elected to the Legislative Assembly. He has held visiting professorships at North Western, Waleningen (Holland) and Oxford.

Busia, who is a slight, gnarled little man, is married and has four children. He neither smokes nor drinks anything stronger than water (no coffee, tea, milk or soft drinks) but has, one is relieved to discover, a sense of humour. Although he is a diabetic, Busia plays a smart game of tennis and in his youth was a shin-cracking hockey player. He reads voraciously (mostly heavy stuff), likes to listen to Handel and Mozart.

In 1956 Busia went on leave from the university to become leader of the Opposition. When his two-year leave expired, pressure was put on him (it was a State university) either to give up his chair or quit politics. He elected to remain leader of the Opposition. In 1959, needing care which could only be obtained in Europe for his diabetic condition, Busia applied for and was refused leave from the Legislative Assembly. His wife and children left by ship from Takoradi. Busia, who in Holland later told me that he had information that the government planned to lift his passport and place him under arrest while he was going through customs, slipped secretly into Ivory Coast and flew from Abidjan to Freetown, where he met his family. The government declared his parliamentary seat vacant and steam-rollered a C.P.P. candidate into office. Busia is now professor of African sociology and culture at Leyden State University in Holland but still holds the position of leader of the United Party.

He describes himself as a Liberal, at the same time admitting that European party labels have little validity in African politics. 'Socialism,' Busia pointed out when we talked in Accra, 'is silly for Africa. We have never had enough capitalism here to warrant socialization. We favour small-scale development which touches directly the lives of the common people, rather than grandiose, expensive and impractical schemes like the Volta River project.'

Busia is enough of a realist to realize that the C.P.P. has the political deck stacked against him (he stated in Holland that he would be arrested if he returned to Ghana) and against his party. But he still feels that the seeds of Nkrumah's collapse are already sown: 'People who thought of independence in completely materialistic terms are becoming disillusioned. The C.P.P. can't give everybody a job. Farm incomes are down and every summer we have a severe water shortage. More and more Nkrumah must rely on dictatorial methods, which indicates to me that he is worried. Every time he employs these methods, he makes hundreds of enemies.'

Did he plan on returning to Ghana, I asked him in his quiet Dutch study. 'I will return when my presence in Ghana is required. For the moment, there is little that I could accomplish by allowing myself to be imprisoned. One thing we have no shortage of is political martyrs.'

Far to the north of the Accra homes of Danquah and Busia is Kumasi, the ancient capital of Ashanti, tucked away in hot, green hills rich in cocoa, gold and timber. The city is one of the great trade centres of Africa and its market and lorry park are a constant hub-bub of screeching tyres, yelling men and bleating animals, some trucks pulling out for the North and the French territories, others bringing their improbable freight, animate and inanimate, to the New Jerusalem of Accra. Kumasi has a hotel called de Kingsway with a palm tree growing out of the floor of the lobby and there were boxing matches in the lounge on occasions. While we were there, 'Kid Benin' was tangling with 'Sugar' Onahoro and a jazz band played between rounds. The city also has a magnificent 500-bed hospital complete with six-corpse mortuary where the customers are kept on ice in sliding trays, like a file cabinet. The hospital, which has tiled floors, air-conditioning and windows which admit light but not heat, trains 300 nurses a year and cost £3 million. It is a talisman of progress but is too foreign to the lives of most Africans and we were told that not more than 60 per cent of its beds have ever been full.

Kumasi is the centre of two traditional crafts, stool-making and the weaving of *kente* cloth. The stools, which are ornately carved and shaped in the contour of a parabola, are chipped out by hand and the head of each family of substance owns at least one. The *kente* cloth is hand woven on primitive looms in long, narrow strips and these are then sewn together to make the toga-like gowns which may cost as much as £115. There are sixty-three patterns and each has a meaning. Some, like Scottish tartans, are the property of particular families. In the old days (*kente* has been made for four hundred years), only royal families wore *kente*. But Nkrumah has changed all that and no young nationalist worth his manifesto would dream of going abroad without his toga.

The top man in Kumasi is still the Asantehene, or King of Ashanti. He is a golf-playing Methodist in his fifties and was a storekeeper before he was selected to succeed his uncle, the king deported to the Seychelles. His name (among others) is Prempeh II (which means 'Tubby') but he is addressed as 'Nana', or 'grandfather'. The Asantehene is allowed a hundred wives but only has three and his salary is about £18,000 a year. To be considered for the job (it will go not to his son, an English-trained dental surgeon named G. O. Prempeh, but to a nephew) a man must be whole and without blemish. He has a corps of strong-arm men called the Zongo Volunteers who patrol the foreigners' sector of the city, and pictures of de Gaulle and Churchill stand on his bookshelves.

The Ashanti are still a proud and warlike people more inclined to rely on shillelaghs than syllogisms to solve their political problems. More than once since independence the Ashanti have broken C.P.P.

skulls. Only one of their own, maverick Ashanti Krobo Edusei, has been able to pacify the hills with his own unsubtle brand of persuasion.

Although Ashanti is comparatively quiet now, opposition still smoulders in Kumasi's jumbled market. Puffing hard on the embers of the tribesmen's discontent are J. W. Tsiboe and his wife, Nancy. The Tsiboes publish the *Ashanti Pioneer*, Ghana's most erudite newspaper, run a fleet of trucks, own a nice chunk of real estate and are generally in the chips. Both are sworn and active foes of the C.P.P.

Tsiboe is fifty-ish, a short, balding Methodist who scuffs around his Progress House office in shirt sleeves and braces. He writes most of the editorials and likes to set a stick of type. In a country where almost all news, political or economic, originates with the Government, his staff have a tough time getting information. News, he said, is inevitably leaked to the two C.P.P. papers, the *Ghana Times* and the *Morning News*, and they frequently have full texts of important speeches far in advance. Tsiboe maintains that government lawyers scan every issue of his paper in an attempt to find libellous material. 'I tell my staff,' he says, 'to report anything that's true. And that,' he adds, with a tight smile, 'gives us a lot of latitude.' Tsiboe claims that he has won almost every libel case brought against him but has difficulty collecting damages from the government even after obtaining court orders. 'But in the few cases which I have lost,' he said, 'I've been required to pay immediately or have the *Pioneer* padlocked.' Other financial pressure is brought to bear on Tsiboe by turning the *Pioneer* down for government loans to buy new presses while the C.P.P. papers, which have received government loans, are equipped with the most modern German presses. One of them has a staff larger than that of any Washington daily paper.

Despite all this, the *Pioneer* has managed to keep its paid circulation above 40,000, which makes it the second largest paper in the country behind the British-owned independent sheet, the *Daily Graphic*. Tsiboe does well because both C.P.P. papers are loaded with party hacks who don't know a participle from a paragraph. The *Pioneer* comes off its creaking flat-bed presses looking as if it was made-up by a tipsy copy boy. But there is usually something in it worth reading.

Nancy Tsiboe is a plump, motherly woman whose charm belies her toughness and organizational ability. She is one of Ghana's few women magistrates and national treasurer of the United Party. Her pet project is a school which attempts with considerable success to turn homeless delinquent girls into good housewives. This school the C.P.P.-controlled

Kumasi Municipal Council chose to demolish on thirty-minutes' notice when an alleged flaw was found in its building permit (Mrs. Tsiboe was awarded £7,000 damages by a court, which ruled the demolition unlawful, but as yet has not been able to collect). Mrs. Tsiboe works hard organizing the Ashanti women against the C.P.P. and sees to it that the U.P. stays solvent. Like many other African women, she has more drive and is more articulate than her husband.

'We worked for Ghana's freedom for years,' she points out, 'and all we have won is a greater tyranny.'

Although Dombo and Appiah are both able, these four people are the heart of the United Party. It is difficult to determine just how effective the Opposition is. Man for man their leaders come from better social backgrounds and are better educated than their opposite numbers in the C.P.P. Partly for this reason the U.P. works under the same political liability as the Republicans in the United States: rightly or wrongly, the U.P. has been tagged as a reactionary grouping of 'the rich, the well-born, and the able'. And although the U.P. leaders are distinguished lawyers, erudite professors and skilled physicians, it is less sure if they are good politicians.

On the surface the U.P. would seem to have little chance of pulling off an electoral victory against Nkrumah. But there are other factors which should be noted which strengthen the Opposition's position and could lead under the proper circumstances to a victory at the polls. Or to a successful coup. The Ghanaian civil service, which ranks with that of the Sudan as the best in emergent Africa, is almost solidly anti-C.P.P. To the civil service over the years have gravitated the best minds in Ghana, the third generation types to whom the British way of life with all its shibboleths and taboos (including a deep regard for democratic principles) is something deeply ingrained and important. Their resentment at what they consider to be Nkrumah's betrayal of the democratic system is guarded but real. It is worth noting that when Nkrumah needed a legal brain to draw up the acts which give Ghana its totalitarian tinge, he turned not to a Ghanaian but to gap-toothed Geoffrey Bing, an Englishman. In addition to their opposition to the government on idealistic grounds, the civil service has been under heavy fire for attempting to maintain impartial standards. This apparently does not fit in with the C.P.P.'s idea of the African personality.

As might be expected, the judiciary is also a centre of hidden opposition to the government. Again, Ghanaian judges have been weaned from birth on the British principle of the supremacy and impartiality of the bench. To their great credit, it is still possible to get a fair trial in Ghana . . . if you can get to court. With Bing as Attorney-General, the tendency has been to by-pass the courts where possible, to negate their rulings when necessary, and, by taking the appointment of judges out of the hands of a commission and handing it to Dr. Nkrumah, to pack the judiciary with tractable C.P.P. judges.

Less easy to evaluate than the opposition of either the civil service or the judiciary is that of the students and the military. Although there have been no important student strikes in Ghana as yet, we found in the institutions of higher learning a growing concern with the government's policies. Universities and colleges have always been in the vanguard of those who value freedom (and perhaps do not totally understand the need for order) and it is therefore not unnatural that this should be so. The government, however, has a strong hold over Ghana's young intellectuals by the fact that virtually every student is on a full scholarship paid by the government which can be withdrawn at any time. And there are increasing signs that the government is ready and willing to take the necessary steps to police the political thought of Legon Hill, as it has that of the press (publication of news 'contrary to the public interest' is punishable by two years in jail).

Last year when he formally opened the new £100,000 headquarters of the C.P.P. in Accra, Nkrumah said that the government was 'merely the agent of' his party, which he described as 'the living embodiment of the whole glory of our people and the moral mainstay of our lives'. Taking dead aim at the university, he stated that there were 'some persons, both staff and students, who mistakenly believed that the words "academic freedom" carried with them a spirit of hostility to the party and the government'. He warned that the C.P.P. could not allow this and in the future would attach the greatest importance to the ideological education of youth. So much for freedom of speech and thought.

The situation with the military is also obscure. As in many other under-developed countries (one learns that this now has come to be a term of opprobrium to sensitive nationalists and one is advised by the U.S. State Department to refer to such states as 'developing nations'), the officer cadre is made up of men deeply steeped in Western traditions and impatient not so much with unconstitutional acts as with the corruption and inefficiency of which these acts are so often an indication. Nkrumah has had the foresight to retain British officers in key positions of command, and enlisted ranks, although they are mainly recruited from anti-C.P.P. areas of Ashanti and the North, are well-disciplined and will do as they are told. But the fact that there is unrest among the military was borne out in 1959 when the government court-martialled, dismissed from the army and placed under preventive detention a Ghanaian major, for failing to report an alleged attempt to organize a coup and assassinate Nkrumah.

The opposition of the chieftaincy, as we have noted, has been important, open and so far unsuccessful. In the building of a political machine based on mass support, Nkrumah inevitably came into conflict with these leaders of the old régime. Nkrumah's vigorous attack on the chieftaincy has led many, like the Asantehene, to switch their allegiance and others, like Ofori Atta, to be deposed. Nor is there much doubt but that the chieftaincy was much in need of reform. Corruption and malpractice did exist and this feudal structure was unlikely in its existing form to add much to the development of a modern state. But by the selection of its victims, the C.P.P. has demonstrated that it is attacking the chiefs not so much because of the state of their morals but because they represent a rival pole of opposition to Nkrumah. Tractable chiefs have been left in power and intractable ones replaced. Unfortunately, little has been done by Nkrumah to bring the chieftaincy, which represents a stabilizing force in the lives of most Ghanaians, into step with modern times. As a result, he has succeeded only in driving underground many of his opponents, as we found when we talked with one northern chief.

It was twilight when we reached his village, a dusty hamlet near a town with the nice name of Tamale. The air was laced with the smoke of burning grass and there was a bite in the desert-blown air which made it seem like autumn in Virginia. The chief was seated on a pile of rugs heaped on a great raised dais which had a roof of thatch. Around him squatted the elders of the tribe, men with pock-marked faces wise with years, clothed in short, shapeless smocks and stocking caps. Our African interpreter took off his shoes and stepped on to the dais. Behind the chief's shoulder a drummer pounded out a rapid staccato. After an exchange of words accompanied by brief interludes of drumming which apparently interpreted what had been said, the chief, a handsome clean-featured man in his early forties, motioned to us to come up on to the dais. I had assumed, since the chief was a member of the Legislative Assembly and had been a school teacher before becoming chief, that he would speak English. I explained through my interpreter why I had come and the chief welcomed us in the local dialect and asked us to sit down.

'So that the elders may know why you have come,' he explained in perfect English, 'I speak first in my own language. Now we can speak English.' The chief explained his recent shift from the U.P. to the C.P.P. this way:

'My people looked around them. They saw that the tribes ruled by C.P.P. chiefs got roads and bore-holes. There is famine in the land now and the C.P.P. tribes were given more of the maize which your country kindly sent us than we. The rains failed and my people were thirsty and hungry. The elders said that my political views were making it difficult for my people. That is why I crossed the carpet. But I have not changed,' he said, tapping his chest, 'here.' The real problem in the North, as in much of Africa, is not politics but survival: the people would far rather have an extra inch of rain than a ringing political manifesto. But the political loyalty of such 'supporters' is obviously more than suspect.

This is not to say that Nkrumah's government will fall tomorrow, either through constitutional means or by a coup, or to imply that it would necessarily be a good thing either for Ghana or the West if it did so. Although the U.P. leaders are honest men and make pious protestations, one is disinclined to believe that, were they in power, their rule would be much different from that of the C.P.P. The basic and inescapable fact is that the people of Ghana were no more ready to rule themselves in Western democratic fashion than those of any other African nation. The choice for Nkrumah lay between totalitarianism and anarchy. The choice is not a happy one.

AFTER NKRUMAH

Kwame Nkrumah will be fifty-two next year and Africa is a continent where old age is the exception rather than the rule. Despite the fact that, with the exception of a bout with pneumonia during his student days in the United States, Nkrumah has been in excellent health, there was pressure on him, in the days before the republic, from within the C.P.P. to name a deputy prime minister, who would become his political heir apparent. This Nkrumah refused to do, probably because he had no wish to build up an alternative leader in his own lifetime or to alienate those who consider themselves in the running for the job.

The type of man who succeeds Nkrumah will, of course, go a long way towards determining Ghana's future course in domestic and international affairs. If the C.P.P. remains in power, he will be a close confidant of Nkrumah: to win the confidence of the C.P.P. hierarchy and of Ghana's street mobs, the new man will have to glow with a good deal of 'Show-Boy's' reflected light. The two top candidates have to be Minister of Finance K. A. Gbedemah and Minister of Economic Planning Kojo Botsio, with Minister of Transport and Communications Krobo Edusei pressing hard upon this pair.

Gbedemah (the 'G' is silent) is far and away the smoothest and probably the most capable of Nkrumah's ministers. One comes away from an interview with many African politicians with the impression that you have been chatting with your gardener. Gbedemah, who is forty-seven, is well-tailored, incisive and articulate. He was born in Nigeria where his father, an Ewe trader, was established in business. His family's home, however, is in that portion of former German Togo now part of Ghana. When the time came for Togo to choose its future, Gbedemah was instrumental in obtaining a favourable vote for *anschluss* with Ghana. And one may presume that Gbedemah is master-minding Nkrumah's ill-concealed drive to force Olympio's little republic into some form of union with Ghana.

Like many other Ghanaian leaders, Gbedemah was educated at Achimota and there he met Nkrumah. Komla Gbedemah had hoped to be a physician but failed to win a scholarship and his family could not afford a university education for him. The balding economist set himself up as a sweet manufacturer in Accra and taught high school science for £9 a month. Later he became a timber contractor. In Dr. Danquah's salad days, Gbedemah was one of the now-defunct U.G.C.C.'s bright-eyed boys. When Nkrumah returned from England in 1947, the Ewe leader was astute enough to see which way the wind was blowing: he lined up with Nkrumah against the Old Guard and the two since have been inseparable.

The ex-candy merchant had the business experience which most of Nkrumah's 'veranda boys' lacked. Gbedemah, who was one of the founders of the C.P.P. and organizer of the party's powerful youth wing, soon became the C.P.P.'s treasurer and first editor of Nkrumah's Accra *Morning News*. His editing in 1949 earned him eye-strain (he wears glasses) and a six-month sentence for 'publishing false news'. This not only entitled him to wear the C.P.P.'s honoured 'P.G.' (prison graduate) cap, a gimmick which he thought up, but enabled him to cement his position within the party: just as Gbedemah was released from prison, Nkrumah and the other C.P.P. top brass were locked up for staging their 'positive action' campaign. For the fourteen months that Nkrumah was in prison, Gbedemah led the C.P.P. In this period he might well have usurped the position of his chief, as Nkrumah stole Danquah's laurels; instead the Ewe kept Nkrumah's name before the people, assured his leader's election to the Assembly, which made possible Nkrumah's release from prison twenty-two months before his sentence was due to expire. Nkrumah appointed him to his first cabinet and Gbedemah and Botsio are the only survivors of the 1951 group. In addition to the Finance portfolio, he has served on different occasions as Minister of Health, Labour, Trade, Commerce and Industry.

Gbedemah, who usually wears Western clothes and has little of the ham about him, has the habit of cracking his knuckles when concentrating, and works at a breakneck speed which keeps his five office telephones humming. As Minister of Finance, he is the man on the spot to find the money to finance the Volta River Project and to attract foreign capital to Ghana. Ghana's sterling reserves have dropped sharply and foreign investment in Ghana has slowed to a trickle since independence. Little of this is his fault, of course: Ghana's reserves have fallen because she has been utilizing 'capital' rather than 'income' for development; foreign investment has fallen off because of adverse political publicity and economic conditions over which Gbedemah has no control. Gbedemah's position in regard to the Volta scheme is reasoned and refreshing: "We want this project very much. But it would be unwise to go against the advice of a committee of experts like the Kaiser people. Talk that we can get the money from Russia if the United States turns us down is irresponsible. Why should the Soviets dash us £285 million? There is bound to be a *quid pro quo*. We are a responsible government and I want to see us behave in this affair in a responsible fashion.' One leaves Gbedemah with the feeling that he could fill Nkrumah's shoes very well, that his brand of realistic thinking is just what Ghana needs in a period when there is an obvious need to rethink many of the country's problems *sans* rose-hued spectacles. And that applies to more than just the economy.

Gbedemah's principal competition for the top post comes from a man who has been closer to Nkrumah for an even longer period than he. Kojo ('Monday') Botsio, four years younger than the Finance Minister, was, like Gbedemah, educated at Achimota. Later he went on to Freetown's Fourah Bay, completing his B.A. in Education at Brasenose College, Oxford. Botsio, who was strikingly handsome before independence but has gained about thirty pounds on the strength of a cabinet minister's salary and opportunities, knew Nkrumah slightly in high school. When the future prime minister arrived in England from the United States in 1945, Botsio was on hand to welcome him. In the cheap restaurants of Camden Town and Tottenham Court Road, the pair drank weak tea, ate stale buns and talked of the day when Ghana would be free. When Nkrumah became boss of the West African National Secretariat, old pal Kojo became treasurer. Botsio, who is a Catholic, urged Nkrumah to accept Danquah's offer to help with the U.G.C.C. and the two sailed for Ghana on the same ship, Kojo to become a high school principal, a job which he soon gave up to follow Nkrumah's political star. Botsio became the C.P.P.'s first general secretary (he is also its 'director of ideological studies'), which meant that he and Gbedemah, who was treasurer, were acknowledged by Nkrumah to be his top lieutenants. Botsio also found time to edit one of Nkrumah's newspapers and was jailed in 1950 for his part in the 'positive action' campaign. Like Nkrumah, he was elected to the Legislative Assembly from prison in 1941, and was named Minister of Education and Social Welfare. He has been a member of every cabinet, held the portfolio of External Affairs, and is now Minister of Economic Planning with special responsibilities to implement the Second Five-Year Development Plan and to stimulate other investment and industrialization.

Botsio did not impress many people with his handling of Ghana's foreign affairs. The Ghana-Guinea 'union' has certainly proved abortive, relations with Togo have been more than strained, France has been completely alienated by Ghana's recognition of the F.L.N. 'régime' in Algeria and her reaction to the A-bomb tests in the Sahara (freezing of French assets and recall of Ghana's ambassador to Paris), while both of Ghana's important African neighbours, Ivory Coast and Nigeria, have remained unconvinced of Nkrumah's role as Africa's self-styled leader. His chief asset as a prime ministerial hopeful is his record of unswerving loyalty to Nkrumah, which might lead the Prime Minister to favour him over Gbedemah, of whom Nkrumah is said to be more than a little jealous. Botsio has considerable mass support and is not unpopular with the party hierarchy.

If Nkrumah should elect to give his personal support to neither man, a stand-off might well take place which could hand the job to one of the more engaging politicians on this continent or any other.

Krobo ('The Crowbar') Edusei is a squat (five feet four inches, 170 pounds), gravel-throated Ashanti pug with a minimum of education and a maximum of physical courage of the back-alley type. After a few years of elementary school, he gave up the unequal battle and launched his career as a debt collector for Tsiboe's *Ashanti Pioneer*. 'In those days,' Tsiboe recalled when we chatted in Kumasi, 'Krobo used a piece of newsprint as a handkerchief and earned £7 a month, which was considerably more than he was worth. Now his salary is £3,500 a year.'

Whatever his moral and intellectual failings, 'The Crowbar' has guts. Ashanti has always been the centre of opposition to Nkrumah and Edusei's own sister in 1955 was shot during rioting in Kumasi. Against this background, Edusei left his job at the *Pioneer* to become regional propaganda secretary for the C.P.P. in Ashanti. What Edusei has been unable to accomplish by pure logic or moral suasion he often can bring about through less orthodox means.

When Nkrumah went to jail in 1950, Krobo went with him. He stepped out fourteen months later as a member of the Legislative Assembly, Government Chief Whip and ministerial secretary in the Justice Department, an appointment which must have occasioned a good deal of shaking of bewigged heads on the bench. In 1954, Edusei was re-elected to the Legislative Assembly and named propaganda secretary of the C.P.P. In 1956, he was re-elected for a third term and became Minister without Portfolio in the first post-independence cabinet. In 1958 Nkrumah made him Minister of the Interior and Edusei finally got the opportunity to display where his talents lay.

Krobo endeared himself to howling C.P.P. mobs by promising them the homes of white businessmen who failed to hang Nkrumah's picture on their walls and warned that 'anybody who gives a speech to the discredit of the government will be jailed'. Crowed Krobo: 'I love power and I am going to use it sternly and strongly.' 'Heah, heah!' bellowed the approving citizenry. 'The job of the politician,' commented theorist Edusei, 'is to uproot his enemies.' In a playful mood in 1959, Krobo personally led a crowd of 3,000 to demonstrate in front of the French Embassy in protest against atomic testing in the Sahara.

In 1958 Krobo, who never does things by halves, jailed the entire central committee of the Accra branch of the United Party. Dr. Nkrumah, he declared, was a born leader and would be prime minister for ever. When a judge ruled Krobo in contempt of court for deporting four anti-C.P.P. men, Edusei had an act rushed through the Assembly in twenty-four hours exonerating him completely and, in effect, ending the rule of law in Ghana. In the same year, Krobo boasted that he was going to withdraw the passports of the entire Opposition and added that he had thousands of secret police watching every non-C.P.P. man's every move. This provoked such a storm of criticism abroad that the Government hastily stated that 'it had not yet decided' to lift the passports (it did not deny that it had considered such an action or was still considering it) and Nkrumah moved Krobo over to the portfolio of Transport and Communications.

I asked Edusei about charges that he had been just a shade heavy-handed in the discharge of his duties. His reply was disingenuous: 'Sure, I bust 'em,' he retorted, 'and I'll bust 'em every time. I've been all over the world: Abidjan, Lomé, Lagos. You think they got roads like we got? You think the Opposition in England or America allowed to talk nonsense like we let these U.P. men? I bust 'em every time!' It may seem incredible to think that a man like 'The Crowbar' has a chance of becoming prime minister. But that's the way it is. He has always been loyal to Nkrumah. He has plenty of physical courage and a native cunning. Most of all, the mob loves him. If there should be a deadlock between Gbedemah and Botsio, power-loving Krobo Edusei could think of no better compromise candidate than himself, and a lot of Ghanaians would say 'heah, heah!' to that.

GHANA'S FUTURE

Prime Minister Kwame Nkrumah spends a good deal of his time attacking the Union of South Africa. Yet paradoxically one discovers that Ghana is embroiled in the same red-herring treason trials, the same deportations, the same imprisonments without trial which characterize the Union. There is the same inability to see any right in one's opponent's case, the same parochialism, the same strident and rather ludicrous nationalism which exists south of the Limpopo. Those friendly to African nationalism mutter about 'growing pains' and 'inevitable periods of adjustment'.

There is some justice in this. Nkrumah did everything he could before 1951 to bring government into disrepute and some of it has rubbed off on him. Nor should it be forgotten that it was the colonial government which taught Nkrumah the autocratic art of maintaining order by denying the right of opposition. As a result, he has had to get tough to prevent civil war. One of the depressing aspects of the situation is the facility with which many Britons have adapted themselves to a régime which would have made Lugard shudder. The usual attitude of the white official in the Ghana government to questions as to corruption and misuse of authority is this:

'Of course I know there's funny business going on. But not in my department. Besides, why should I stick my neck out? It's the Africans' country, let them run it the way they please, is what I say. Anyway, I'm going home when my contract's up.'

Nkrumah himself maintains that Africans should not be judged by an absolute standard (although they demand absolute equality). 'You must consider,' he says, 'the depths from which a man has risen as well as the heights which he has reached.' The unfortunate thing is that the 'African personality' seems to embody not the best features of African and Western culture but the worst. Ghana has gone straight from tribalism to Tammany Hall.

Nkrumah's problem in keeping the country together is that the one great unifying force, opposition to colonialism, disappeared when the black-starred tricolour went up in 1957. As soon as Ghana became independent, the struggle was joined between Nkrumah, the C.P.P. and modernism against the old order, the chiefs and the old gods. Nkrumah is winning this battle and its results may have more far-reaching consequences than the mere fact of political independence. In effect, Nkrumah has released five million Ghanaians, many of them in a relatively primitive state of social development, from the restraints of custom and traditional authority. For these restraints he is attempting to substitute the fetish of nationalism. It will be interesting to see what will happen when the new fetish does not produce all that was promised of it.

This much may and should be said in Nkrumah's favour:

Ghana has survived four years of independence without civil war and without large-scale repressions, although the apparent growth of Russian influence in recent months certainly bodes ill for the future. The jails house perhaps sixty political prisoners but Ghana has not reached yet the concentration camp stage. Few people have lost their lives as the result of opposition to Nkrumah. The *Ashanti Pioneer* still appears and Opposition politicians still sit in the Legislative Assembly. And they still dare to speak. Their passports have not been withdrawn. Foreign journalists are allowed into the country and may write what they think, although they stand a chance of being deported if they do so. Although there has been considerable misuse of public funds, this practice has not yet reached the level of proficiency seen in some Asian and South American countries . . . or in some American cities. Elections, although not always impartial, have so far been held at regular intervals.

These are real achievements. Nkrumah and Ghana have not yet failed. But this should not disguise the fact that both the man and the nation have disappointed many of the high hopes held for them, hopes perhaps never warranted by the facts. Ghana's status not only in Africa but in the world ultimately will depend on the manner and the degree in which she solves her domestic problems. Should Nkrumah turn his considerable talents from international buccaneering, a subject which we will discuss in the concluding chapter, to the reform of his party and the development of his country along solid democratic lines, Ghana could recover much of her lost prestige. What is needed is a demonstration to the world that a black nation can rule itself with intelligence, moderation, respect for law and concern for the well-being of minorities.

And now on to Nigeria, the giant of Africa.

Chapter 19

*

BIRTH OF A NATION

Had I only a month to spend in Africa and one country to spend it in, Nigeria would be my choice. No other nation or colony on the continent can match this brawling giant for colour, zest, humour, accomplishment or potential. From the great Muslim market centres of the thirsty North to the history-laden creeks of the East, where white men came to trade for slaves, Nigeria bubbles with exuberance and flashes with colour.

This new nation—in October of 1960 it gained its independence without a drop of blood spilled and with hardly a harsh word spoken—is destined to play a major role certainly in Africa and possibly in the world. One out of every three citizens of the New Africa is Nigerian and its population of 35 million (25,000 whites) dwarfs that of every other country on the continent. It has seven times as many people as Ghana, or a population 50 per cent greater than that of the eleven republics of Gallic Africa combined. Put another way, Nigeria has more people than Canada, Australia and New Zealand together and one million new Nigerians are born every eighteen months, a 2 per cent annual increase. Apart from the tiny Belgian trust territory of Ruanda-Urundi, Nigeria is the most densely populated country in Africa. Even including Mediterranean Africa and the great multi-racial states south of the Congo, one out of every seven Africans—black, white and brown—is Nigerian.

Its size matches its population: within Nigeria's borders France, Belgium, Holland, Luxembourg, West Germany and Ireland would fit most comfortably. The new nation is the world's thirteenth largest country, bigger than any European state except Russia. In American terms, it is half again as large as Texas, if that is possible.

Nigeria used to be described as 'halfway between Purgatory and Hell'. More precisely, it lies in the crook of Africa's arm, where the coast falls away due south towards Antarctica, and it stretches inland from the Bights of Benin and Biafra nearly 700 miles to the shimmering shores of Lake Chad. Like Ghana and Sierra Leone, it is surrounded on its three landward sides by Gallic Africa: the Cameroun Republic (and slices of British Cameroons) lies to the east; to the north is the great sandy waste of Niger; to the west is tiny, palm-fringed Dahomey. As in the rest of the New Africa, its boundaries are artificial and arbitrary. The Hausa-speaking peoples of Northern Nigeria, who constitute the federation's largest ethnic bloc, spread well over into the neighbouring Gallic republics and Hausa, the most important indigenous language of the continent (and one which had been reduced to written forms before the advent of the white man), is understood from Dakar to Brazzaville.

To celebrate its independence, Nigeria has a spanking new coinage embossed with the double triangles of Solomon's seal (the national emblem), palm fronds, cocoa pods, and groundnut vines, these being the country's three principal crops. Currencies used in the past have included slaves, gin, cowries, manillas, brass rods and copper wire. The manillas were not all redeemed until 1949, when millions were bought at a favourable price and either dumped into the sea or sold as scrap in Europe. Nigerians are intensely interested in money and bribery is rampant. This has given rise to a worthy organization called the League of Bribe Scorners, whose members wear badges saying 'Fight Bribery and Corruption'. They come into the limelight occasionally—as did League Member Johnson Omopariola in 1958—when sentenced to jail . . . for demanding a bribe.

Nigerians have nice but unpronounceable names (which they like to change with alarming frequency) but none to match those of their forefathers. The treaty signed between Great Britain and the city-state of Opobo in 1884 bears the signatures of the following: JaJa, Cookey Gam, Prince Saturday JaJa, Finebourne, John Africa, How Strongface, Black Foubrah, Shoo Peterside and 'Duke of Norfolk'. Many of these native chiefs had great wealth: in 1894 when the British stormed Brohemie, the stronghold of the Jekri chief Nana, they captured 106 cannon, a machine-gun, 2,000 muskets, 14 tons of gunpowder, thousands of rounds of ammunition, 5,000 slaves and 8,300 cases of gin. Gin was a good investment because its value increased with the years as import taxes on spirits—once the source of more than 50 per cent of the Nigerian government's revenues—increased.

Nigeria is well-stocked with contrast and paradox: although it is the first country in the world to carry all mail by air without additional charge, child-stealing for slavery or human sacrifice is a popular sport (in 1958 the British Colonial Secretary reported that there was 'a slight increase' in the practice). In a society which can boast 697 lawyers (156 in Lagos itself) and 623 doctors (but only 34 dentists, or one for every one million people), it was possible in 1958 for an Eastern Region legislator to be arrested and charged with leading a ritual murder group. There is a constant pressure, I was told, upon Nigerian medical students, who perform 700 post-mortems a year at the University Teaching Hospital in Ibadan, to supply their less evolved friends and relatives with human organs which are much in demand for ensuring good crops, winning fair ladies and punishing one's enemies. Nigerians drink six million gallons of beer per year, buy four million pairs of shoes, purchase enough textiles (three million square yards, almost half of it from Japan) to cover Lagos three times and are enthusiastic boxers (both Hogan Bassey and Dick Tiger are Nigerians). Their government officials, who work only from 8 a.m. to 2 p.m., are entitled to more than one hundred working days annual leave. These officials are dead keen on state secrets and Macmillan's 1960 visit to Nigeria was still on the secret list in Lagos four days after it had been announced in London.

Although only 4 per cent of the federal budget is allocated to public health (the regional governments spend more, of course), a horrifyingly high 2 per cent of the population suffer from blindness and more than 500,000 are lepers. More than half of all registered deaths in 1957 were of children under five years of age. The people of the North, who live on grain, millet and groundnuts, get adequate calories and proteins but their diet is deficient in some vitamins. Southerners (as the inhabitants of the Eastern and Western regions are called) live almost exclusively on root crops such as cassava and yams and their intake of calories and proteins is regarded by health experts as being 20 per cent below a satisfactory level. An ancient 'cure' for dysentery (half the population suffers from amoebic infection) was iron rust burned in brandy and mixed with cold arrowroot spiced with chalk.

As far as education is concerned, Nigeria has two universities (and more than 3,000 students studying abroad), three technical institutes, 17 trade schools, 289 teacher-training colleges, 522 secondary schools and 16,000 primary schools, with 2·6 million students (another 3·7 million Nigerian children do not attend school) and 85,000 teachers. These are impressive figures for Africa, yet it is estimated that only about 25 per cent of the population over seven years of age is literate. Education in the early years was the province of the missionary (called by the Yoruba *Onibuku*, or 'possessor of the book'). Their lack of success in the predominantly Muslim Northern Region accounts for the low percentage of literacy. An estimated 7·3 million Nigerians profess Christianity while 15·5 million are Muslims and 12·2 million are animists.

British financial aid to Nigeria has been extensive (£34·3 million since 1945, not counting £27 million in loans made during 1959 and 1960) and, as a result, Nigeria has a larger railway network (2,000 miles of track) than any other nation in the New Africa, 35,000 miles of roads, nearly 4,000 miles of which are paved. It also has fifty cinemas (half of them in Lagos, the federal capital). One million pounds was spent on the independence celebrations—most of it on street decorations —and 3,693 entries from sixteen countries were received in the £1,000 contest to provide the music for the new national anthem written by an English stenographer (she received £100). As the prize was about to be awarded to a Nigerian 'composer', embarrassed officials discovered that his entry was a copyrighted British military tune! The award finally went to a London cabinet-maker's wife, who spent ten minutes on the composition and 'made it simple for people who cannot play the piano very well'.

The march to Nigerian freedom has been accomplished at the cost of much ink and sweat, if not blood: in the last decade, there have been no less than six major constitutional conferences to work out the blueprint of nationhood. Nigeria was not administered as a single unit until 1914. In 1954, a sharp constitutional corner was turned when Nigeria became a federation, rather than a unitary state (regional assemblies had been established in 1947 and their powers extended in 1951). Self-government came to the Western and Eastern regions in 1957 and the North (which declined it in 1957) became self-governing in 1959. Although both white and black maintain that there is little racial friction in Nigeria, a poll of 1,500 'expatriate' (white) federal civil servants in March 1959 revealed that only 10 per cent had definitely decided to stay on after independence if they were asked. Forty per cent said they would not stay and 50 per cent were undecided.

Conditioning the life, the politics and the history of Nigeria is the sweep of the great, slow-moving river from which the country takes its name. Niger, it should be said, has nothing to do with the Latin word for black; it comes from a pre-Roman indigenous term meaning 'great river', from the same root as Nile (ancient cartographers called the Niger 'the Nile of the Negroes'). Nigerians sometimes call the Niger the Joliba, the Kworra, or the Fari'n Rua. Although most of the

Niger's 2,600 miles lie in Gallic Africa, 800 miles of it flows through the centre of Nigeria, where it is joined by its major tributary, the Benue (sometimes called the Chadda, Shari, or Baki'n Rua). After the juncture of the two rivers, the Niger—which is the world's ninth and Africa's third longest stream—flows almost due south to fan out near the coast into a great and confusing 14,000-square-mile delta larger than that of the Nile. This orderly, majestic giant drains a basin of 500,000 square miles, one-sixth the size of the continental United States.

The coastal zone is hot, low-lying and cloaked in grey-green mangrove swamps which hinder land travel and impair navigation of the river system. Fifty or sixty miles inland this gives way to a forest zone which thins out gradually into orchard bush as the Niger is approached. Finally, in the far north, there are the slowly southward-moving sands of the Sahara and the 4,000-foot-high Bauchi plateau.

Nigeria's racial diversity is as pronounced as her topography. No less than two hundred tribes, some of which are as similar to each other as Eskimos are to Spaniards, inhabit its 350,000 square miles. There are as many languages as there are tribes (forty principal tongues) and one Western Nigerian 'language' is spoken by exactly thirty people. As elsewhere in Africa, the one cohesive force linking these diverse people is English language, tradition and administration. With this common tie weakened with the withdrawal of the last of these, centrifugal forces have been unleashed which could wreck the federation.

Of this confusing ethnic welter, there are six major tribes. Living in the vast Northern Region, which embraces two-thirds of the total area of Nigeria, are six million Hausa, 3·5 million Fulani and 1·5 million Kanuri, sedate Muslims to whom Islam is a way of life, not just a religion. In the creek-wrinkled palm forests of the Eastern Region (and these regions are administrative districts, not geographical areas) are the Ibo people, 5·5 million individualistic, hard-working black Scots. Here fetish and cross replace Islam's crescent. Among the steamy cocoa forests of the West dwell the Yoruba, five million strong, a proud, devious and intelligent people heavily influenced both by Christianity and by Islam.

In each of Nigeria's three regions (Lagos, the federal capital, forms a fourth administrative unit) these tribes form the political and cultural majority. But in each case, roughly 40 per cent of the population does not belong to the dominant tribe. The real and imagined fears of these minorities constitute a delicate problem for Nigeria's new rulers.

Nigeria is unique in the New Africa in that her peoples, with the exception of the Ibos, have lived for generations in towns of considerable size. Ibadan, for instance, the capital of the Western Region, has nearly half a million inhabitants and is the largest black metropolis in the world, the most populous city between Cairo and Johannesburg. In the Western Region alone there are no less than six cities with more than 100,000 inhabitants while thirty-five Nigerian centres top the 30,000 mark and there are 343 towns with more than 5,000 inhabitants. More than 20 per cent of Nigeria's people are city-dwellers, urban concentration being heaviest (50 per cent) in the West and lightest (9 per cent) in the North, while the figure for the East is 15 per cent. Paradoxically this does not mean that the majority of Nigerians are salaried people or small businessmen, although the percentage of urban workers is higher (15 per cent) than elsewhere in Africa: like Calabrian peasants, Nigerians prefer to live in cities but they trek miles into the countryside to till their fields. An estimated 75 per cent of the population is engaged in agriculture (which produces 50 per cent of the national income and accounts for 85 per cent of all exports) and the town-dwelling habit is thought to have developed as a means of mutual protection against warrior tribes and marauding slavers. Population density is heaviest in the East (269 people to the square mile) and lightest in the North (67). The West has 148 people per square mile and the national average comes to 93.

Although Nigeria is not wealthy by European or American standards, it possesses a sound economy based on varied foundations. Its national income, estimated in 1958 at £812 million, is larger than those of the copper-rich Central African Federation and the three British East African territories combined, although its *per capita* income of £30 falls well below Ghana's £56 per head. Nigeria's sterling reserves, built up during the war and now diminishing as development programmes are financed, are in excess of £200 million.

There are three main props to the Nigerian economy and, fortuitously, these are divided among the three regions. The premier export of Nigeria is palm products (oil and kernels) grown mainly in the East and, to a lesser extent, in the West. Exports usually total more than 600,000 tons worth about £33·4 million. Groundnuts, grown almost entirely in the North, hold second place with an average export crop of 507,000 tons worth £30·3 million. Cocoa, 113,000 tons of which are exported, mostly from the West, brings in £25·6 million. Behind this big three are cotton—71,000 tons worth £8 million, almost all of it from the North—and rubber, 40,000 tons worth £7 million, most of it from the West. These five crops account for 96 per cent of agricultural exports.

Of lesser importance are tin (11,500 tons worth £6·3 million), timber (15 million cubic feet worth £5·2 million), hides and skins (8,000 tons worth £3·1 million) and columbite (1,500 tons worth £1 million). Timber is primarily a product of the Western Region while the other three come from the North. Exports of groundnuts, cocoa, cotton and rubber are expected to increase substantially by 1965, by which time the Eastern Region's petroleum may be worth as much as £5 million per year. Total exports are worth £136 million.

Nigeria imports £167 million worth of goods, of which the most important are textiles (£26·1 million), motor vehicles and machinery (£18·6 million) and Scandinavian stock-fish (worth £7·7 million). Other imports include corrugated iron sheets, petrol, cement, liquor, bicycles, tobacco, flour, salt, sugar, electrical appliances and medicines. A worrisome factor in the trade picture is that £40·7 million or 31 per cent of Nigeria's exports go to Common Market countries, which are expected to raise tariffs against these goods.

In all, the Nigerian economy appears to be growing more muscular every year. Over the last decade, exports have doubled in both volume and value while imports have quadrupled in both respects (Nigeria's best customers are the United Kingdom, Holland and West Germany while Japan displaces Holland and joins the other two in the ranks of her three most important suppliers). Two reliable indices of development are motor vehicles and telephones: the number of the former has increased from 14,200 in 1950 to 42,050 in 1958 (a quarter of them in Lagos). In 1946, 350,000 telephone calls were made with 5,800 instruments over 60 exchanges; in 1958, 2·3 million calls were made with 31,000 instruments over 111 exchanges. By 1962, there will be 48,000 telephones on 144 exchanges, 75 per cent of them automatic. Foreign investment in 1958 totalled £20 million.

Industrial expansion is slow (now less than 5 per cent of the gross domestic product is made up of manufactured goods) but steady, and has averaged £2·5 million per year since 1950. Important enterprises include cement, textile, cigarette, plastics and metal factories and half a million Nigerians are employed by 4,000 concerns which pay an annual wage bill of £5·2 million, split fairly evenly among the three regions. But 75 per cent of the people still derive their living from the land and it has been estimated that a capital investment of £90 million is required to provide employment for 1 per cent of the adult male labour force. As industrial assets, however, Nigeria possesses numerous raw materials, adequate labour, coal, hydro-electric potential and a large domestic market. When industry comes to the New Africa, it will come first to Nigeria.

In an effort to hasten industrialization and to provide improved social services, the federal and three regional governments between 1955 and 1962 will spend a total of £339 million for development, 78 per cent of these funds from Nigerian sources. External debt in 1958 stood at only £21 million.

Here, then, is a nation born to be great. Too often in the New Africa we have seen splinters of territory unendowed with natural or human resources in which the bombast of petty political leaders has made only a grim charade of the nationhood of which they boast. Nigeria is a nation on the American scale: it has wide horizons, great cities, rich resources, and a numerous and vigorous people. This, if anything, must be the cornerstone of a great Pan-African confederation.

PRIESTS, BLACKBIRDERS AND PALM OIL RUFFIANS

It was in the musty mangrove swamps along the coast that white men first made contact with what is today Nigeria and, as it was in so many parts of Africa, the Portuguese took the first tentative steps into the unknown. Their high-pooped caravels had coursed the Bight of Benin by the middle of the fifteenth century and, in 1485, Joao d'Aviero, accompanied by a few soldiers, hacked his way through the forest to the fabled city of Benin. He was well received by the *oba*, or king, and was allowed to leave only after promising to return. Columbus' exploits diverted Lisbon's attention to the New World and two decades were to pass before d'Aviero saw the Oba's court again. When he left Benin for the second time, d'Aviero took with him a son of the king and the command to return with priests.

The priests came, bringing with them coral beads and an umbrella of proportions and colour to delight the heart of any ruler. Today, the umbrella is still the symbol of chiefly office. Churches were built and the Oba and his court learned to read, write and speak Portuguese. The priests accompanied the Binis (the people of Benin are also called Edos) on their raids into neighbouring kingdoms. One wily Bini chief, when called upon by the priests to give up polygamy, retorted that he would do so only if his spouse could be a white woman, a condition which he may have thought the priests could not or would not meet.

But they set off post haste for St. Tomé, persuaded a pious peasant girl that it was her duty as a Christian to save Africa for Christ, and presented the chief with what must have been a more than skittish bride.

Gradually Portugal's international position declined and she found herself less and less able to support her far-flung islands of empire. Wearied by the climate and appalled by the heavy loss of life incurred by the fever of that malodorous coast, the priests handed over the churches to black deacons and, accompanied by the few Portuguese traders who had established themselves in Benin, set off for home.

Ecclesiastical inspectors returned periodically but gradually the visits grew less frequent. The last Portuguese priest called at Benin in 1688, the year that James II fled to France. Native priests carried on for a time but ultimately reverted to the old fetishism. Christianity was shunted to the Bini subconscious, coming to the surface only in the horribly distorted forms of human sacrifice and a curious fixation on crosses. White settlement in Nigeria was finished for two hundred years.

But trade continued. In 1553, Thomas Wyndam, the first Englishman to visit these treacherous coasts, sailed with the ships *Primrose* and *Lion* accompanied by the pinnace *Moon*. Wyndam's log states that his crews were 'men of the lustiest sort'. They had to be. Wyndam reached Benin but found his crews so rotted with fever that he had to scuttle one ship and maroon some of his men at the oba's court. The expedition lost 100 of the 140 men who sailed but the survivors returned with 150 pounds of gold dust. When a ship reached Benin the following year, there was no sign of the abandoned mariners. Presumably they died of fever, were sacrificed at the oba's ju-ju altar or were killed while attempting to reach the coast.

An expedition under John Lok in 1554 realized a handsome profit of 1,000 per cent while James Welsh, in 1559, brought back 'pepper and Elephants' teeth, oyle of palm, cloth made of Cotton wool very curiously woven, and cloth made of the barke of palm trees'. An even more lucrative trade was soon to be developed as blackbirders of all nations swooped down on the coast to procure slaves for the cotton fields of America and the cane brakes of the West Indies. English interest in Nigeria received a tremendous boost in 1712 when the Treaty of Utrecht gave Britain a thirty-year monopoly on the slave trade to the Spanish colonies. By 1788, 100,000 slaves were being shipped out of West Africa each year. No one can say what proportion of this human loot came from Nigeria; but the great depopulated stretches of Nigeria's so-called Middle Belt, cruelly caught between the coastal raiders and the Muslim slavers of the north, indicate that the percentage was not inconsiderable.

But still there was no settlement. In part this was due to Nigeria's unhealthy reputation. So many white men lost their lives on the coast that the classic refrain arose:

> Beware and take heed of the Bight of Benin
> For few come out though many go in.

A perhaps more important factor was that, in contrast to much of West Africa, Eastern Nigeria possessed safe harbours. There were competent middlemen in the persons of the coastal tribes to do the slave-catching. As a result, the usual procedure was for a ship to make her way up the Cross River, anchor off Calabar, step her masts and raise awnings of thatch over her decks, and wait for the war chiefs to fill her hatches with black bodies. Some of these Calabar gentry were wealthy and efficient businessmen, and a few could write and keep accounts in an age when the average Englishman was illiterate. This was particularly true among the Efik traders, one of whom, Antera Duke by name, kept a diary in pidgin English for the years 1785–1788. This fascinating document chronicles his comings and goings and those of his friends Little Otto, Egbo Young, Eyo Willy Honesty, Egbosherry Sam Ambo, Coffee Duke, Cameroon Backsider Bakassey, King Tom Salt, Willy Tom Robin, George Old Town, Otto Ditto Tom, and Duke Sam Jack Esin, ancestors of present-day Calabar's Top People.

Antera Duke tells of the high old times when they cut off the heads of fifty slaves to add spice to a beer party, caroused with the English captains over spicy palm oil chop (a sort of stew) and gallons of trade gin. The flavour of that day when a man owned as much as he could defend and death was never far away seeps through the faded pages and garbled words of Antera Duke's diary when he tells us on June 7, 1787, that 'wee see Robin Tom King John and Otto Ditto Tom. King John send them to com for mak play to Duke & my father and Egbo young mother so the cut one woman head of to Duke and 7 Barr Room men to be cutt for my father so the play all night.'

In 1807 Britain abolished the slave trade, which was soon to be followed, however, by the traffic in palm oil. Europe had little knowledge of the interior, which was guarded by fever and by the coastal tribes, which sought to maintain their lucrative position as middlemen by confining the white man to his ships. It was known that there was a great river, along whose banks powerful native states flourished, but no white man knew where it began, where it ended, or which way it flowed. Ibn Battuta, the great Arab geographer, in 1350 wrote correctly that the Niger flowed east; but Leo Africanus, in an inexplicable error (he had seen the river himself) stated in 1513 that it went to the west. To add to this confusion, one geographer in 1829 proclaimed that the river flowed north under the Sahara and emptied into the Mediterranean. A young Scottish doctor named Mungo Park was to solve this mystery and usher in, over his body, a new age for Nigeria.

Park, the son of a yeoman of Ettrick Forest, was born in 1771. He was the seventh of thirteen children and was intended for the Kirk. Instead, he chose the medical profession. Park attended lectures at Edinburgh University and studied botany in his spare time. In 1792 he obtained an appointment as assistant surgeon on the *Worcester*, East Indiaman sailing for Sumatra. There he collected eighteen varieties of fish and attracted mild attention with the publication of his findings. History does not take place in a vacuum and were it not for the grumblings of American political firebrands and the Teutonic stubbornness of a half-German English monarch, Mungo Park might well have spent his life as a vaguely dissatisfied ship's doctor, collecting his fish, writing scholarly but dull papers for the Linnaean Society, dozing over a glass of port in thin-blooded retirement, another half-pay pensioner longing for the tropics.

In the event, America left the Empire in 1783 and the lords of the Industrial Revolution frantically sought new markets for the rising output of British goods. On their own, the merchants were too weak to commit Britain to the interior of West Africa. But important elements of the government saw in Africa the essential gap in the strategic Britain–India imperial axis, with its extension to Australia and the Far East. Although Britain was reluctant to commit herself in Africa, the activities of France made it necessary to act in defence of her interests. Important support, as we have seen, was found among Abolitionists anxious to crush the slave trade at its source.

The pressure of these various groups resulted, in 1788, in the formation of the Africa Association. The first choice of the Association to solve the riddle of the Niger was, oddly enough, an American named John Ledyard. Ledyard, a friend of Thomas Jefferson, had once tramped halfway across Siberia before being arrested by Catherine the Great's cossacks for lack of a visa. For one who had dreams of walking around the world, the Niger quest was a natural. But Ledyard died before he could leave Cairo. The Association's second choice turned back without accomplishing much and the third explorer was murdered near the Niger.

Park's turn came in 1795. The twenty-three-year-old Scot spent several months on the Gambia learning Mandingo, then struck off into the interior accompanied by a servant and a boy. He suffered incredible hardship, was stripped, plundered, beaten, starved, half crippled with fever and finally enslaved. He drank with the steers at the cattle trough of his African captors. But Park's Calvinist faith coupled with the grim determination which characterized all the great explorers of Africa enabled him to rise above pain and despair until the day came when he 'saw with infinite pleasure the great object of my mission: the long sought for, majestic Niger, glittering in the morning sun, as broad as the Thames at Westminster, and flowing slowly to the eastward'.

Park gave his captors the slip and made his way back to England. He married and set up a medical practice but Africa had left her mark on Park, as she has on so many others who thought to escape from her blinding sun to the more prosaic shadows of a comfortable life. His friend Walter Scott noted that the explorer was moody and Park confided that he would rather brave Africa and all its horrors than wear out his life as a drudge in Scotland.

In 1805 he was back leading an expedition of forty-five white men with instructions to follow the Niger to the sea and discover its estuary (many believed it flowed into Lake Chad). By the time Park reached the Niger, only four of his companions, one of them insane, were left alive. They set off down stream, were attacked by natives at Bussa, and died in the rapids. There were no survivors and it is said that Park's ring is big ju-ju around Bussa, as it should be (Park's son never gave up hope that his father was alive; in 1827 he struck off into the interior from Accra, presumably was murdered by Ashanti).

The Napoleonic Wars turned Europe's attention from Africa until the Denham-Clapperton expedition in 1820 crossed the Sahara from the north and discovered Lake Chad. Clapperton, the thirty-two-year-old son of a surgeon and, like Park, a Lowland Scot, had gone to sea at an early age, entered the navy via the press-gang route, and served during the War of 1812 in the Great Lakes, where he formed a romantic attachment for a Huron princess. Arrayed in full naval uniform, he became the first white man to reach the great caravan centre of Kano.

Five years later Clapperton returned to Kano and pushed on to Sokoto. There he died and to the forefront of history stepped that most extraordinary of all the great explorers, Richard Lemon Lander, Clapperton's valet. Lander was the twenty-one-year-old son of a Cornish innkeeper. An itchy foot had made him the servant of travellers and he had eagerly entered Clapperton's service when he heard that the naval officer was returning to West Africa. Now valets, according to the code of the nineteenth century, were expected to keep a chap in batwing collars, see to it that his socks matched and maintain a crease in his trousers. They were not supposed to go boffing all over the countryside discovering river mouths and things like that. Just not done.

With true Jeevesean aplomb, Lander pushed through to the coast, survived an ordeal by poison in Badagry, and later returned with his brother commissioned to trace the Niger to its estuary. For performing this major feat of exploration Lander was to receive £200. His brother was to get nothing. The brothers had an uneventful trip until they passed the confluence of the Niger and the Benue. Here they were seized by an Ibo war party but managed to persuade a character named King Boy of Brass to buy them from the Ibos and sell them to a British brig which providentially was standing off the delta (Lander was killed in 1834 while leading another expedition up the Niger).

With the riddle of the Niger solved, Nigerian history slowly assumed a new character. Now it was possible to push expeditions up the river and trade directly with the tribes of the interior, thus short-circuiting the coastal middlemen. This caused ill-feeling among the coastal tribes which was in no way ameliorated by British edicts against the profitable slave trade. Britain became involved in Yoruba politics because of the presence of British traders and missionaries and, as a result, was forced to annex Lagos in 1851.

The Industrial Revolution, which was probably more important in killing the slave trade than all the pious protestations of the Abolitionists, gave with one hand what it took with the other: the burgeoning factories of England demanded lubricants just as the plantations had required slaves. And the new urban proletariat employed in the factories, as their standard of living rose, called for edible fats and soap. So the same blackbirding ships came to Calabar and to Bonny, to Brass and Oron. The same florid-faced captains brought salt, beads, cotton goods, gin and guns to the same coastal chiefs. But now they came back with palm oil and kernels, not slaves.

Meanwhile, trade and exploration continued on the Niger. The

Liverpool merchant Macgregor Laird, an enthusiastic supporter of steam, managed to get two iron ships to Nigeria, the first to make an ocean voyage. Steamers continued to push up the river but fever always stopped them. On one expedition, forty-eight of 145 whites died.

Little was known of the nature of malaria and, as the word indicates, it was thought that sickness resulted from exposure to the night air. Conscientious captains battened down the hatches at night, which did nothing to make life on the coast more pleasant. The history of West Africa was altered profoundly in 1854 when Dr. William Baikie, born in the Orkneys and the son of a naval officer, proved that quinine could give protection against malaria (he did not, however, establish that malaria is carried by the anopheles mosquito; that honour belongs to Sir Ronald Ross, who made the discovery several years later).

Heinrich Barth, a German in British service, rounded out the classical age of Nigerian exploration when he returned to England in 1855 after wandering for six years through the northern part of the country. Baikie's medical discovery and Barth's travels, building on the foundation laid by the early wanderers, opened Nigeria for pacification and administration.

The embodiment of the new age was John Beecroft who in 1849 became British Consul for the Bights of Benin and Biafra, with instructions to 'regulate the legal trade between the ports of Benin, Brass, New and Old Calabar, Bonny, Bimbia and the Cameroons'. Beecroft, who had been a merchant seaman and had spent nine years as a prisoner of the French, ran the brawling coast from Fernando Po, ostensibly a Spanish possession but used by the British as an anti-slavery naval station. Beecroft, the first 'official' Briton to serve in Nigeria, established within a few years the basis of the administration which a few months ago led Nigeria to freedom.

But Beecroft's efforts were confined only to Lagos and the river areas near Calabar. In the Yoruba country a few missionaries operated —by 1859 Anglican missionaries had been among the Yorubas for thirteen years and were publishing Nigeria's first newspaper, *Iwe Irohin* (Book of News)—while in the Niger valley a clutch of small traders maintained isolated posts. The traders were weak and disorganized; the government was reluctant to act. The French, on the contrary, knew exactly what they wanted and were moving into the Niger watershed with speed and determination. Their goal: to link up their African possessions from Senegal to Somaliland on an east-west axis, thus crushing Rhodes' dream of a Cape-to-Cairo empire and isolating British India from Europe. Nigeria might well have become French had not, as so often has been the case in British history, the man strong enough to alter the course of events appeared upon the scene.

This man was George Goldie (his real surname was Taubman but he dropped it when he was knighted). Goldie, a Manxman born in 1846, was the fourth son of an officer in the Scots Guards and was himself intended for a military career. Commissioned into the engineers, he soon grew bored with military life. His first visit to Africa came in 1877 and he was immediately struck by the need to consolidate British economic interests in the Niger valley. He bought out two French firms trading in the valley and brought the small British traders into the firm today known as the United Africa Company. Within six years Goldie was able to lay before the Congress of Berlin a firm British claim to the Niger–Benue basin.

Goldie has never received his due as one of the great empire-builders for the very good reason that he destroyed most of his papers, swore his employees to silence and threatened to haunt his children if they consented to the writing of his biography or assisted it in any way. Unlike Rhodes, he refused to allow the new nation to whose foundation he contributed so much to be named after him (it had been suggested that the new territory should be called 'Goldesia').

The contrast between the two men is interesting. Rhodes was big and sprawling. Goldie was small, compact and lean as a terrier. He had a large head, a pronounced nose and the arrogant, mocking look of a man who has his own ideas about human nature. Like Rhodes, he was a visionary and had a mind sufficiently practical to allow him to achieve his goals. His intellect was probably sharper than Rhodes' and he was a better judge of his lieutenants.

The greatest of these was the man he chose to cement his hold on Northern Nigeria. Frederick (later Lord) Lugard was born in 1858. He took up an army career and fought in Afghanistan, the Sudan and Burma. In India he had an unfortunate love affair which he sought to forget in the classical manner by a big-game safari in East Africa (he later married Flora Shaw, a brilliant and influential writer on African affairs).

Unlike most of the makers of Africa, Lugard's influence was not confined to one area of the continent, although it was Nigeria in which he was to spend the bulk of his career and upon which he was to leave his most indelible impression.

Lugard, who had piercing brown eyes, high cheekbones, a receding hairline and a handlebar moustache which drooped almost to his collarbones, fought Arab slavers in Nyasaland, checkmated the French in Uganda and extended British interests in Bechuanaland before Goldie called him to Nigeria. Complacent Whitehall officials who distrusted him because of his fiery nature and his capacity for stirring up (or recognizing) trouble, made him wait until middle life before giving him an official role to play in Africa. Everything which he accomplished in East and Central Africa and much of what he did in Nigeria was done as a private citizen in the employ of chartered companies.

In a series of lightning campaigns, during which he had a piece of his skull chipped out by a poisoned arrow (he continued the fight and then marched thirteen miles), Lugard firmly established Nigeria's western boundary and pacified the tribes with a mixture of firmness and fairness.

In 1900 the charter of Goldie's company (then known as the Royal Niger Company) was revoked and Britain assumed responsibility for the administration of Northern Nigeria. Lugard stayed on as British High Commissioner and directed military operations against the northern emirs which resulted, in 1903, in the capitulation of Kano and Sokoto.

With the fighting over, Lugard demonstrated that the impetuous soldier was also a brilliant administrator. He became the high priest of the system of indirect rule whereby the British governed areas such as Northern Nigeria, which had a well-established history of indigenous government, through native rulers and institutions. It should be said, however, that there are those who have made too much virtue of Lugard's necessity: he lacked both the men and the money to administer the North directly and some whopping boners have resulted from attempts to apply his thesis of indirect rule to areas of Africa where comparable native tradition did not exist. It is arguable, too, that had direct rule been imposed, the North, today Nigeria's least evolved region, might have been better prepared to face the problems with which independence has presented it. Feudalism, for all its charm and virtues (it has many), is not always the best school for an emergent state.

Lugard also made sure that Islam would be protected against the activities of the Christian missions and that white settlement would never be permitted in Nigeria. In the case of the latter, he unquestionably saved Nigeria from many tensions. As for the former, the exclusion of the missions meant that the North was destined to lag far behind the other regions in educational matters, a gap which has not yet been closed and which continues to retard the development of the Muslim areas.

Lugard held the personal title later in his career of Governor-General (revived with the last colonial holder, Sir James Robertson), served on the League of Nations mandate commission, was created a peer and a Privy Councillor, and in 1945, in a world alien to him and disapproving of imperialists, went to his grave full of honours.

The Nigerian nationalist movement gave its first signs of life between the wars. The governor, Sir Hugh Clifford, commented that this 'loose and gaseous talk' emanated from 'a self-selected and self-appointed congregation of African gentlemen, a handful of men born and bred in British-administered towns, who in the safety of British protection, have peacefully pursued their studies under British teachers in British schools . . . men whose eyes are fixed not upon their own tribal obligations and the duties to their Natural rulers which immemorial custom should impose upon them, but upon political theories evolved by Europeans to fit wholly different circumstances'. There are those in Africa today who would say 'hear! hear!' to that.

But Sir Hugh's bark was worse than his bite and in 1922 he created a Nigerian Legislative Council which, for the first time, had a number of elected members. This was to be the only constitutional advance until after World War II.

In 1947 came the first of a spate of Nigerian constitutions. Their total effect was to hand over an increasing amount of political control while vesting this control not in the central government but in the three regions: the Hausa-Fulani North, the Ibo East, and the Yoruba West. The East and West achieved regional self-rule in 1957 while the North followed two years later. On October 1, 1960, Nigeria became an independent member of the Commonwealth.

We have gone into the history of Nigeria in some detail, a necessary task if one is to understand the problems with which the new nation is faced. It should be noted that African-British contact in the three regions has varied both in duration and in intensity. The Efik and Ibibio peoples of Eastern Nigeria have been in contact with Western civilization (although they may have seen some pretty poor examples of it) for 400 years. But these tribes barred the way to the interior and there are many in Eastern Nigeria who had never seen a white man thirty years ago.

BIRTH OF A NATION

Lagos has had intensive European contacts for more than a century. Yet Obafemi Awolowo, premier of the West, recalled that it was not until 1921 that he knew that there were more than six white men in the world. Lastly, many a Northerner is alive today who fought against Lugard at Sokoto. Here, again, the mass of the people of Nigeria have been required to make the full circle from savagery to independence in a modern and complex world during the lifetimes of living men.

A second important point is that the very immensity of the land and the varieties of its peoples are ready-made for a constrictive and antagonistic regionalism. It has been usual in Africa for the force of nationalism to overcome tribal differences to a greater or lesser extent. But the 1947 constitution, a pivotal document, gave legal and political form to centrifugal forces which are today the greatest threat to Nigeria's power and even to her national existence. And now for a closer look at the country and the people.

LAGOS: THE EXUBERANT BOIL

Lagos, the federal capital of Nigeria, is vividly, overwhelmingly alive. Ramshackle mammy wagons (we spotted SEA NEVER RUN DRY, WHO KNOWS MY DESTINY, NO SWEAT–NO SUGAR and GOD LOVES ME—WHY?) career through the twisting, crowded streets, their horns blaring, the door on the driver's side tied open to facilitate rapid evacuation should the situation become too desperate. Naked children, foraging chickens, blind Hausa beggars from the North in white smocks and skull caps, Yorubas wearing brightly coloured gown-like *agbadas* and pyjama bottoms contest with a host of bicyclists and hand-carts called *omulankes* for the narrow space between the lorries' path and the open drainage ditches from which climbs an odour composed of equal parts rotting meat, urine, decaying orange peel, excrement and stagnant rain water. Mixing with the braying of the automobile horns are the angry shouts of imperilled pedestrians, the high-pitched tinkle of bicyclists' bells, the strident quarrelling of the mammy traders and the bleating of goats being dragged unceremoniously to market by an ear or a leg.

Lagos' 400,000 people are crammed on to a small island (the population density is 1,500 to the square mile) and the congestion is such that the very buildings seem to quiver with the concentration of life. Ramshackle shops pieced together with mud, bits of wire, packing-cases and flattened tin cans surge into the streets and channel the noise

541

of this black Bombay (it also resembles a Negro Venice) until it rolls through the town like the booming of surf. Out on the Marina, the road which stretches the length of the lagoon, are the great shops of the Europeans, and here things are a bit more quiet and orderly. African school children, barefoot and dressed in clean khaki, gather in the most pretentious of these stores to ride the escalator, despite the forays of a Hausa store guard armed with a large stick. Across the bay are the puffing cranes and busy dockyards of Apapa, for Lagos is the federation's largest port, handling 2·6 million tons a year, or 55 per cent of the total exports and imports.

The city, which the local people call Eko, is one of the few in the world centred on a racecourse (the American Embassy has a nice position at one of the turns). The races are reputed to be the most crooked in West Africa and, in fact, Lagosians enjoy a remarkable reputation for dishonesty. The Jankara Market is devoted exclusively to the sale of smuggled goods, despite the heroic efforts of the Lagos Special Constabulary, a 500-man unpaid auxiliary force which does yeoman work in backing up the regular police. Ragged guards called 'watchnights' patrol many private homes after dark. The air of gay corruption seeps into public life and the town council was dissolved in 1952 when rampant irregularities were discovered. Although the city was founded in the fifteenth century by Yoruba refugees and later infiltrated by Binis, another western tribe, industrious and far-travelling Ibos from the East have surged into Lagos in recent years and in 1959 they ended the control of the Action Group, the dominant political party of the West, on the now revived city council by winning twenty-two out of forty-two seats for the Ibo-dominated National Council of Nigeria and the Cameroons. Although it is the most cosmopolitan city in Saxon Africa, witch-smellers of the Itiuka cult from Dahomey are much in demand in Lagos and the taxi-drivers' union regularly and with a notable lack of success make sacrifices to Ogun, god of iron, in an attempt to cut the accident rate. In the old days, a man was regularly killed and cast into the lagoon to propitiate the god of the sea and bodies still wash up on the foreshore with unpleasant regularity. It was not until 1914 that an odd form of slavery was eradicated in Lagos and other areas of the south: no member of a 'House' (clan) could be employed without the permission of the head of the House and runaways had to be restored to the House. Market stalls tended by Yoruba women wearing head-ties of colourful cloth knotted to look like huge butterflies offer just the thing for the visitor: super worm expeller, fertility lozenges and brain pills in addition to the usual ju-ju pharmacopoeia such as maggoty monkey skulls, dried mice, snakes' fangs, shrivelled birds and assorted bones, feathers and other mysterious commodities.

As we have seen, the British captured Lagos in 1851 in an attempt to choke off the slave trade, which was in the hands of Brazilian slavers, blacks who had earned their freedom from Portuguese masters (with whom they sometimes interbred) in Brazil and returned to enslave others. Around Tinubu Square, the Piccadilly of Lagos, named after a famous mammy slave trader, the crumbling houses of the Brazilians may still be seen and da Souzas, Ferrieras and Gomezes jam the tumbled cemetery where foot-long *agama* lizards with bright orange heads scuttle between the brilliant sunlight and the cool shade of collapsed graves. It was fifteenth-century Portuguese who gave Lagos its name. They called the lagoon *Lago de Kuramo*, or Lake Kuramo, and there is still a small village nearby which perpetuates the latter half of the name.

A traveller named John Whitford visited Lagos—the only break for hundreds of miles in the West African sandbar—two years after the British occupation and described it succinctly as 'a filthy, disgustingly savage place'. These were the days when male dogs were fetish in Lagos and were spitted in front of every house. Even today one sees mostly bitches in the native town. The British opened a consulate in Lagos and Burton termed this structure 'an iron coffin, containing a dead Consul once a year'. Burton agreed with Whitford and wrote that 'the site of the town is detestable'.

The native custom of burying their dead in shallow graves beneath their homes did nothing to add to the fragrance of the city. Dysentery and malaria bred in the oily lagoons took a fearful toll and, as late as 1896, one out of six of the white population died during a single year. A test of the town's 203 wells at the turn of the century revealed that 201 were polluted. In one three-year period, the Anglican church buried three bishops. Progress came slowly and it was not until 1916 that Lagos got piped water. Several years after the outbreak of bubonic plague in 1924, the first septic tank was dug. Oddly enough, Lagos enjoyed electricity by 1898, a year in which the streets of most English towns glimmered with gas lights.

In an effort to quarantine themselves from the rampaging diseases of the native quarter, the Europeans built the cool suburb of Ikoyi. On an island where nearly 400,000 are jammed into a few thousand acres, a golf course acts as a *cordon sanitaire* between Ikoyi and Lagos. Well-padded nannies push prams down paved streets fringing immaculately shaven lawns and one could as easily be in Wiltshire as in Nigeria. The original reason for this genteel seclusion, as has been suggested, was health. But long after the need has disappeared (although smallpox and rabies still break out with monotonous regularity), racial exclusiveness has given permanence to the arrangement. It has caused a good deal of ill-will and Africans feeling poorly quip that they are moving to Ikoyi, the only circumstances in which they would be able to live there being as inhabitants of the cemetery. Now that independence has come, of course, many African civil servants live in Ikoyi, but the bulk of the suburban population, which includes commercial people, is still white.

Lagos is making stern efforts to clear its worst slums and the city's Executive Development Board will spend £20 million between 1955 and 1965. The Board condemns an entire area, buys out the landowners and moves them to new housing developments on the mainland. The condemned area is levelled with bulldozers, four-lane streets are cut, water, electricity and sewerage are laid on, the area is redivided into larger plots (sixteen to the acre) and, where possible, resold to some of the former owners at the confiscation price plus 20 per cent for development. Purchasers are told the type and extent of the buildings which they may erect and a strenuous effort is made to keep people from flocking back into the cleared area. 'The job,' said one inspector, 'is much like scooping a hole out of the mud: no matter how hard you try, the edges crumble and the water seeps back.' Nearly 20,000 people have been moved from the seventy-acre pilot zone in the heart of the city.

Across Five Cowrie Creek at Magazine Point is Victoria Beach where the Atlantic rollers come crashing in with such force and tail-spin that drownings are the rule rather than the exception. On the seafront the seven-storeyed, 165-room Victoria Beach Hotel has been erected at a cost of £1 million and plots laid out for the residencies and chancelleries of the diplomatic corps accredited to the new nation. As part of the 1,500-acre scheme, Nigeria's new House of Representatives will be built here. But despite the low-cost public housing across Carter Bridge at Yaba and the plush vision of Victoria Beach, Lagos remains essentially what it has always been and what one suspects it will be when the city planners are dust: a vibrant, exuberant boil on the face of Nigeria.

Even at night Lagos is colourful and noisy. Mud houses lighted by little fires glow like enormous pumpkins, brightly lighted ships fill the harbour, now that the bar has been dredged, and oil lamps twinkle and glimmer like a host of fireflies to mark the stands of the mammy traders, many of whom remain open all night on the off-hand chance of selling a lump of sugar, a single cigarette or an inch of soap. The great trading companies could not exist without these small-scale retailers who alone can sell in quantities which can be afforded and which can be consumed before the mould of Lagos or the white ants destroy.

After midnight, when the town has had a chance to cool, suave Lagosian playboys gather at a score of explosive, amateurish open-air 'night-clubs' to dance the jubilantly sexual 'High-Life' with their lady friends. White men come with their black mistresses and not a few mixed marriages are represented.

Our guide and mentor on a visit to the popular 'West End' was a young radio executive whose great-grandfather signed the treaty which ceded Lagos to Britain, a polished young man with perfect manners except for the habit so prevalent among Africans of speaking to those of an inferior status in a manner which no gentleman should. He drove us down a dark street and parked the car. Out of the shadows materialized small boys who offered to guard the car for a sixpence.

'Who are they guarding it against?' I asked.

'Themselves,' he said. 'If I don't pay them they will let the air out of my tyres if I'm lucky, slash them if I'm not.'

The 'West End', which was merely a hole in a mud wall opening into an open inner court around which rickety tables are set up, sometimes extracts a shilling cover charge ('To keep out the riff-raff,' I was told) but tonight was a free night and most of Lagos seemed to be jammed into an area the size of a tennis court. Ben Enwonwu was there, the goateed Ibo sculptor who has a craze for collecting 'Dinky Toys' and turns out bronzes of exquisite grace. Cyprian Ekwenzi, whose novel *People of the City* is the first by an African to give an insight into the urban life of the New Africa, was gyrating crazily with women who seemed counterparts of the jazzy characters from his book. Amos Tutuola, the Yoruba writer whose books have done so much to recapture the demonic spirit of the Old Africa, was down from Ibadan and brooding sullenly over a large jug of palm wine, the milky, head-rending national drink. Slim Felix Idubor, the Edo who carries on the great tradition of the Benin sculptors, was celebrating the award of a German fellowship. Black architects, lawyers, politicians and administrators, clad like peacocks in the flowing gown, matching cotton trousers and skull caps which are worn by most Nigerians, whirled and twisted around the floor after their partners, who seemed to be composed in equal parts of jiggling buttocks and thrusting breasts. The orchestra blew until their lungs almost burst, caressed their instruments like living things and occasionally took them out on to the floor to dance a step or two with a comely maiden. Towards the end of the evening, when the sky was getting just a shade paler in the east, a man lurched over to our table and began making a nuisance of himself. He was the only obnoxious drunk in the place. He was also a white man.

Here, for a moment, one caught the feeling of what the New Africa might be. Here, for the first time, we encountered a complete society with its conservative businessmen and its bohemian artists. All shared one quality: a contagious joy which raised them above the level of the slums of their city and made them men with whom it was a pleasure to spend an evening. Africa may yet teach us how to laugh again.

And speaking of laughter, there is no tonic for hardening of the humour glands quite like a morning spent with a West African newspaper (about thirty are published in Nigeria). In Lagos they reach their highest level of development. The African press likes to speak of 'blood-sucking imperialists' and to call America 'a giant with a newt's head', but it also produces some startling and amusing twists with headlines such as 'Nightsoilmen to Appeal to Privy Council' and notes to emergent ladies of which the following is a sample:

'When at socials, don't try to be greedy, or make much puff when asked for a dance. Avoid spitting in public, for it is a very bad habit. When men come to propose love to you, don't feel too big. Rather, try to be courteous and polite, whatever your answer may be, whether "yes" or "no".'

And here is a typical obituary:

'Like all public men, the late Mbonu Ojike possessed a marked love of virtues and an abhorrence of vice. But among vices, there is none which he abhorred as much as obstinacy. Ojike believed that obstinacy is certainly a great vice, and in the changeful state of public affairs, it frequently leads to mischief. Ojike was very much concerned with the poor. No sooner had he established the Africa Development Corporation than he started selling some of his merchandise on hire purchase basis and this gave some young men beginning life the opportunity of possessing iron beds, radiograms, and other necessaries of life. This act showed how philanthropic he was.'

An indignant sportswriter in October 1959 told his readers that he had seen a visiting Ghanaian football team making ju-ju (drinking out of red and black skulls and making dolls representative of the Nigerian side to torment when the going got bad) before an international match. Ghana won. And a spate of letters to the editor demanded an end to 'the stupid and irresponsible attitude of some fans, players and club officials who take pride in beating up referees' when their team loses.

Accuracy has never been one of the strong points of the Lagos press and one distinguished leader writer identified the first Colonial Secretary ('under him we groaned under the Richards Constitution') rs 'Mr. Cordell Hull, an ex-miner'!

The Lagos press in turn lambasts and praises Alhaji Sir Abubakar Tafawa Balewa, prime minister of the Federation of Nigeria and Lagos' most distinguished citizen (although this proud Muslim might shudder to hear himself described in these terms).

Balewa, a tall, unassuming forty-eight-year-old Northerner of Hausa-Fulani extraction, was born in Bauchi province of the Northern Region. He is, of course, a staunch Muslim but does not belong, like other Northern leaders, to the aristocracy. Balewa completed his high school education in the North and then had two years at London University's Institute of Education.

On his return to Nigeria in 1946, Balewa—who has the impeccable Oxford accent of Katsina (no pidgin is spoken there)—taught for several years, was elected president of the Northern Teachers' Association and began his political career as a member of the Bauchi Native Authority Council (he was elected to the Northern House of Assembly in 1947). It is said that Balewa's personal incorruptibility, his intense desire for reform and his administrative ability soon made him unpopular with the Northern emirs. Perhaps as a means of ridding the North of a dangerous man whose talents were too great to be overlooked (his oratorical skill earned him the sobriquet of 'The Golden Voice of the North'), Balewa was induced to run in 1951 for the federal House of Representatives. He won and was named Minister of Works, later served with distinction as Minister of Transport and, in 1957, became first federal prime minister. When the Northern People's Congress won the 1959 elections, Balewa, who is shrewd, tactful and has a dry sense of humour, was selected by his party to become first prime minister of independent Nigeria. The fact that he is regarded as a conservative in Lagos and as a radical in Kaduna explains a good deal about regional Nigerian political ideas.

It is said in some quarters that Balewa is the stooge of the Sardauna of Sokoto, who is premier of the North and head of the N.P.C. Rumour has it that the Prime Minister, who is a keen cricket player and an honorary citizen of New Orleans (he visited the United States to study Mississippi Valley waterways), grovels before the Sardauna and cannot make a move in Lagos without first checking with Kaduna, the Northern capital.

Personally, I am not inclined to believe this. It is true that the Sardauna could have the federal prime ministership for the asking, if he wanted it. It is true that Balewa, as a commoner from a feudal area, is placed in a rather awkward position in that his party chief is of the bluest blood of the North. But Alhaji Abubakar is a man of too much character and intelligence to be any man's stooge; by the same token, the Sardauna, of whom we shall hear more later, is far too wise to attempt to impose such a relationship upon the Prime Minister. The Sardauna is clever enough to respect Balewa's qualities and to understand that he alone of all the Northern Muslims is acceptable as a leader to the people of southern Nigeria. The Sardauna controls the party and thus could unseat Balewa if he desired; but he fully under-stands that the Prime Minister—who gets up at 5 a.m. for prayers, frequently skips breakfast to get to his desk by 6.30 a.m.—is repre-sentative of the best in a new Northern generation. Balewa's high office gives hope to a Northern peasantry sometimes restive under the emirs, a class which might turn to the North's political opponents if Balewa were not there to command their loyalties.

For the moment, then, Balewa *is* the Sardauna's viceroy in Lagos. But he is a viceroy with considerable freedom of action (he accepted Israel's technical assistance over the violent objections of the Sardauna) and a not inconsequential personal following. Nothing that he has done in his eight years as a federal minister has diminished by one jot the re-spect with which the Prime Minister is regarded by white and black, Northerner and Southerner. If the Nigerian federation succeeds, its success will be largely due to the efforts of soft-spoken Alhaji Abubakar Tafawa Balewa.

His federal government is responsible for foreign affairs, defence, aviation, external borrowing, customs and immigration, currency and banking, shipping, railways, posts and telegraphs, and minerals. The regions control public health (except in Lagos), education and agriculture. Concurrent jurisdiction extends over public order, labour relations, higher education, social welfare, research, electricity, gas and water power. When a conflict occurs, federal law prevails; but residual powers lie with the regions.

Despite strong centrifugal tendencies, control of these federal powers (and of the federal budget, which runs about £85 million annually; the three regions together spend about the same amount) is a juicy plum and the battle for control of the 312-member House of Representatives and the 44-member Senate is vigorous. Seats in the House are allocated proportionally on a rough basis of one seat to every 100,000 people. Each of the three regions gets twelve seats in the Senate (which has similar powers to the House but cannot initiate or delay money bills; on other bills it has a six-month delaying power), Lagos gets four and four are appointed by the governor-general.

The present federal Parliament was elected in late 1959 and will sit for five years. The electoral battle was conducted with all the accoutrements of an American polling: Dr. Azikiwe's N.C.N.C. distributed to bare-bottomed children whistles that produced a shrill 'Zeee-eeek!' and balloons which deflated with the noise of a crowing cock, the party symbol; Awolowo sent skywriters up to etch palm trees, the Action Group's symbol, in a blistering December sky, popped down himself in a helicopter to harangue amazed tribesmen; the Sardauna of Sokoto, leader of the Northern People's Congress, kept his party's hoe symbol before the people by making 150 speeches in six weeks. There was the usual amount of fiddling—twelve busloads of would-be voters from Ghana were turned back at the border, four chiefs were arrested for trying to register 500 children under ten years of age, an entire Lagos high school tried to register *en masse*—but there were no disorders (21,000 police were standing by, just in case) as 80 per cent of the electorate of more than nine million cast their ballots for 1,000 candidates.

The distribution of seats (174 in the populous North, 73 in the East, 62 in the West and 3 in Lagos), despite vigorous opposition from the Action Group and dissident Hausa and the Middle Belt splinter parties, made it virtually certain that the Sardauna's N.P.C. would obtain a plurality. In the event, the N.P.C. won 141 Northern seats and one in the East; the N.C.N.C. and its allies took 58 in the East, 21 in the West, 8 in the North and 2 in Lagos; while the Action Group and its associated parties grabbed 33 in the West, 25 in the North, 14 in the East and 1 in Lagos. The other 8 seats, all in the West, went to independents. That left the N.P.C. with 142 seats, the N.C.N.C. with

89 and the Action Group with 73, none with enough to form a government. On the basis of a pre-election pact, the N.P.C. and the N.C.N.C. formed a coalition (as they had in the previous government) and Balewa again became prime minister, with Azikiwe becoming president of the Senate (he has since given up the Senate post to become Governor-General of Nigeria) and Awolowo the leader of the Opposition. Of the seventeen portfolios, ten, including that of prime minister, went to the N.P.C. and seven to the N.C.N.C.

For the next five years, then, control of the federal government and all which that implies rests with the politicians of the Hausa North and the Ibo East. Camel and lorry, alhaji and infidel, they make a strange pair.

Before leaving Lagos we lunched with His Excellency Sir James Robertson, G.C.M.G., G.C.V.O., K.B.E., a chunky Scot with a bristle of a moustache, a shock of iron-grey hair and a mischievous twinkle in his eye. Over steak and kidney pie on the wide and cool veranda of Government House, Sir James gave a new and humorous twist to an old saying about Africa: 'If all the Nigerians were to leave this country tomorrow, the British civil servants in the North, East and West would fall to fighting among themselves.' Although he was half-joking, there is little doubt but that, as many Nigerians claim, some British civil servants have become so gripped in the mystique of the regions in which they have spent their lives that they have done little to overcome tribalism and, in some cases, have intensified a narrow regional outlook.

On the other hand, as one English official pointed out, the British have been accused on the one hand of promoting regionalism and on the other of callously riding rough-shod over tribal and ethnic groupings in their effort to create a new nation. Both cannot be true.

THE WEST: AWO AND AKINTOLA

The Western Region, a territory the size of Cuba (45,376 square miles) with some 7·1 million inhabitants, is the least populous of Nigeria's three regions. It is also the richest on a *per capita* basis and has one of the most progressive governments in all of the New Africa. Among the 'firsts' that can be claimed by the West are free primary education, free medical treatment for those under eighteen and Africa's first television system.

The Yorubas are the dominant tribe of the West, constituting some

65 per cent of the population (14·4 per cent of the national population). Many regard the Yorubas as treacherous and degenerate but I met no tribe in Africa which as a whole I liked and respected more. If they are devious, they are certainly interesting and intelligent, which is demonstrated by the fact that more than three-fifths of all Nigerians studying at overseas universities come from the West.

Like so many of the great tribes, the origin of the Yoruba is obscure. They say that their town of Ile Ife is the spot where God created man, both black and white. Oduduwa ('The Great One who creates Existence') was sent down from above by Aramfe ('God Almighty') to make land, the earth then being covered with water. He freed a magical bird, which scattered pieces of dirt from a snail's shell, thus creating the continents. The Yoruba, whom some have equated with the Phoenicians or the ancient Egyptians, believe that their homeland was Mecca and that they were expelled for idolatry. The Nile Valley, however, is a more likely area and it is thought that they reached Nigeria, probably in two waves, about the eleventh century.

Yoruba is a generic term which once was applicable only to the people of Oyo, whose alafin (king) ruled from Accra to the Niger. The alafin, who is a direct descendant of Shango, the god of thunder, was expected to eat the heart and tongue of his predecessor, that he might inherit the dead man's courage and wisdom. To check a tendency towards parricide, the alafin's eldest son was required to commit suicide on the death of his father. Kings seldom appeared in public and, when they did, wore a veil of beads to hide themselves from the gaze of the unwashed.

Suicide was required also of Yoruba generals who failed in their mission. This provided an easy way for the alafin to rid his court of powerful rivals: he sent them with inadequate forces against a powerful foe. Occasionally leaders so condemned refused to follow their instructions and established new Yoruba kingdoms, thus accomplishing the dual end of freeing Oyo of trouble-makers and extending at least the nominal suzerainty of the alafin. But if an alafin became too tyrannical, a council of elders sent him a covered bowl containing parrots' eggs, the Black Spot of Yorubaland: he either committed suicide, which the Yoruba regard as an honourable death, or was strangled by his relatives.

The city-state of Oyo, which is in the northern part of Yorubaland, reached its greatest heights by the middle of the eighteenth century and broke up in the early part of the following century under the

onslaught of Hausa and Fulani raiders from the North coupled with
internal demoralization caused by the slave trade. Dissident princelings
took advantage of the situation to declare their independence of Oyo
and now the alafin is only *primus inter pares* of the five great Yoruba
princes, the Oni of Ife, the Alake of Abeokuta, the Awujale of Ijebu-Ode
and the Oba of Benin. The last of these, although his people are not of
Yoruba stock, is a descendant of the fourth son of Oduduwa.

In addition to his secular position, the Oni of Ife, a portly gentleman
who was once a railway clerk and is now Governor of the Western
Region, is the spiritual head of the Yoruba nation. The Yoruba worship a pantheon of 401 deities, including Shango, god of thunder,
Sopona, god of smallpox, Yemoja, god of rivers, Orisha Oko, god of
agriculture, Ogun, god of iron, Eshun, god of stone and Olokon, god of
the sea. They believe both in a future life and in the transmigration of
souls. The owner of a house struck by lightning has to pay the priests
of Shango, and the relatives of a smallpox victim shell out to Sopona's
priests, who are said to do a bit of pump priming by spreading the
disease. In recent years both Christianity and Islam have made heavy
inroads among the Yoruba and today about a third of the Western
Region is Christian, a third Muslim and a third animist, thus extending
the Yoruba tradition of disunity into the religious sphere. The features
of these quarrelsome people vary tremendously among individuals
because the Yoruba conquerors intermarried with the original inhabitants, but many have the thin lips and narrow noses which may indicate
a remote Caucasian ancestry.

Apart from its role as a holy city, Ife is famous as the site of an
exquisite and mysterious art of unknown origin. In 1910, the German
Leo Frobenius (who linked the Yoruba with the Etruscans) found
near Ife several terracotta heads and some brass masks and heads
of remarkable beauty. The brass heads are naturalistic works of a high
standard, quite un-African in treatment. It is not known exactly when
they were cast or if they were made by one artist. They so closely
resemble each other that it is unlikely that they were made over a long
period of time. Hamitic and Semitic faces are represented among some
of more Negroid types. Who are the people portrayed and who was
the artist? No one knows.

Because of their own warlike nature and the aggressiveness of the
Hausa in the North and the Dahomey people on their western flank,
the Yoruba have always tended to concentrate in towns. No less than
six of the eight Nigerian cities with populations of more than 100,000

lie in the Western Region (the others are Kano and Lagos). Ibadan, the capital of the West, was a strongpoint to shield the Yoruba from the Hausa while Abeokuta, which lies between it and the sea, was the sworn foe of Dahomey. When the Yoruba were not fighting the Hausa or the amazons of Dahomey, they raided for slaves among themselves and the ancestors of many American Negroes were shipped out through Lagos or Badagry to the New World.

When the British came, the Yoruba were exhausted by generations of warfare, Yorubaland soon submitted to British protection and Yoruba troops helped Lugard to pacify the North. Because of the long history of enmity between them, rekindled now through political policy, Northerners hate Southerners; nor is there much love lost between the Ibo and the Yoruba. More of this later.

The drive from Lagos to Ibadan was the most totally frightening experience we encountered in Africa. The average life of a lorry in Western Nigeria is six months and it was easy to see why. Down the twisting ribbon of pavement, encased within the green walls of the high forest, hurtled lorry after lorry, their drivers apparently intent upon suicide. Neither curves nor bridges nor blind entrances slowed them down: with horns blaring, passengers and freight tossing in abandon in the back, vehicle after vehicle shot down the road as if in quest of the Holy Grail. Before we reached Abeokuta, where we were to lunch with Dr. and Mrs. Thomas Lambo, we were greatly in need of our host's services: he is Africa's first psychiatrist.

Lambo, a tall Yoruba, comforted us with a couple of gins, and his wife, a pretty and gracious English girl, employed a good lunch to get us on our feet again. Dr. Lambo said that the range of mental disorders in Nigeria seemed to be about the same as in Europe, although the emphasis was sometimes a little different. He did not feel that urbanization so much led to mental disorders as made it possible to detect the symptoms. Traditionally Africans have employed their own form of shock treatment (beating) to exorcize mental devils. Lambo had just completed a study of mental disorders among young Nigerians studying in England. Some of his conclusions: financial trouble was a primary cause of much unhappiness while real or imagined racial discrimination ranked second. Inability to cope with academic work was not an important factor, although most students tended to work too hard rather than participating in sports or entering into social activities. In his day (universities of Birmingham and London) there were few African students in England, hence they tended to be absorbed more fully into the community. 'Many boys now,' he said, 'live, eat, study and have such social life as they do with other Nigerians; hence they never get fully integrated into the English pattern and their trouble, when it comes, tends to be more serious.' African students, he added, regard the Irish as the most potent white witches.

Abeokuta is dominated by a large cliff and the name of the city means 'under the rock'. It was founded by battle-weary refugees and then grew itself into a powerful warrior state. Abeokuta gets only forty-five inches of rain and is one of the driest places in the region. Today it is a bustling city of 100,000 people and its traditional ruler, the Alake, Sir Ladapo Ademola II, boasts a collection of ninety beaded crowns. Beaded crowns, sceptres and slippers are the symbol of royalty among the Yoruba, while the Binis of the eastern part of the region prefer necklaces and crowns of coral, most of which is imported from Italy. Coral was in short supply during the war and prices rose to astronomical heights.

The main street of Abeokuta was one of the most nerve-shaking pieces of road we encountered in a country famed for the same. The narrow strip of tar was lined on each side with steel telephone posts, each showing signs of battle with one or more lorries, followed by a wide and deep concrete ditch. The market lay on either side of the road and the constant ebb and flow of humanity and livestock across the road did nothing to add to the sense of well-being of the terrified motorist. Once through the city, however, we were in comparatively quiet cocoa country.

Cocoa is the wealth of the West. The little bean provides the free schooling and medical care, pays for the partially state-owned television and finances the campaigns of the region's political leaders. The tree was introduced to Nigeria only forty years ago but there are now 180,000 growers cultivating one million acres. Nigeria annually exports about 105,000 tons (1959 was a bumper year of 140,000 tons) and 90 per cent of this comes from the West. Four out of every five trees are past their producing peak, however, and during the past two years the regional government has distributed 20 million cheap and high-producing seedlings in an attempt to raise the average annual production to 130,000 tons by 1965. Although it is not as important a producer as Ghana, the West's cocoa exports are the third largest in the world and account for 20 per cent of the total supply.

In all, cocoa provides about 86 per cent of the region's current revenues and finances a budget which this year will spend almost

£15 million each on capital and recurrent expenses. Cocoa exports are worth £23 million per year, as much as the West's palm products, rubber and timber combined. Cocoa makes possible the region's five shilling daily minimum wage, one of the highest in Africa, and pays for the forty cinema vans and six barges which bring the outside world to the most remote Western villages. Revenue has climbed from £5·4 million in 1952 to £18·5 million in 1960 and the West now spends £5 per head of population, more than twice the East's *per capita* expenditure and almost five times that of the North.

As night fell we successfully negotiated a road which resembled nothing so much as a paved roller coaster and lurched into Ibadan. The name means 'by the side of the field' and, in fact, Ibadan does lie on the verge of the forest. The city has five sacred crocodiles and the Temple of Shango stands next door to a Methodist chapel. There is a 'Blessed Battery-Changing Co.', a 'Who You?' bar and a ten-storey bank building which looks like a gigantic radiator grille. Like Addis Ababa, which it resembles in many ways, Ibadan has the appearance of a Tartar camp which might be broken on an hour's notice: for miles, with the exception of a few modern buildings, there is nothing but the dull glow of mud and corrugated iron, the smoke of 10,000 cooking fires. Unlike most Yoruba towns, Ibadan has no king but like them its narrow streets are thronged with chattering people (there is a large Ibo, Nupe and Hausa population and the Yoruba-oriented Action Group frequently fails to win local political elections), buses, taxis, lorries and private cars, all packed to the brim and seemingly bent on mutual destruction. Cyclists proudly pedal bikes whose frames are wrapped conspicuously with the brown paper which identifies a factory-fresh purchase (there has grown up a thriving business in wrapping old frames to please the status-conscious). The shops are jammed with hand mirrors, soap, combs, patent medicines, exercise books, cigarette lighters, singlets and the pill-box velvet hats which are Czechoslovakia's principal export to Nigeria. And at night there is something in Ibadan which will soon become a feature of West African life: we saw a crowd gathering by a corrugated iron fence, peered over to see some twenty berobed Yorubas gathered in a backyard watching a custard-pie television comedy on WNTV, 'first in Africa', as the announcer boasted. Television came to Ibadan, Lagos and Abeokuta in October 1959. It cost £500,000 to install and the Western government has purchased 1,000 sets for schools (WNTV shows three hours of entertainment and one hour of educational films daily) and hospitals.

The 17-inch set, which tottered on a window sill, had cost £65 but its proud owner was not worried about the price: he was charging a shilling admission to his backyard cinema and reckoned he'd more than make up his investment within three months! Although there are said to be no more than 40,000 electricity consumers in the area now served, about 7,000 sets have been sold (government servants may buy on hire purchase) and the figure is expected to reach 15,000 with half a million viewers by early 1961, when Western viewers will also be served by a federal network. An African announcer flashed on to the screen with the news that Mobil Oil is good for your car and it seemed hard to believe that ritual murder could still be a problem. Or will the 'Big Eye' demand its own sacrifices? Perhaps.

Proud is Ibadan of its television and prouder still is it of the most modern teaching hospital in Africa and of Nigeria's national university. The seven-storeyed 500-bed hospital, which is associated with the university's medical school and contains its own nursing school, was completed in 1957 at a cost of £4·3 million. Its staff of sixty-one doctors (thirty-nine of them Nigerians) hatched their first batch of graduates last year and they hope soon to be producing fifty doctors and eighty nurses annually. The hospital looks rather like a Miami Beach hotel and Lagos politicians like to spend a rest cure in its luxurious suites. But, since medical treatment for children and teenagers is free in the West, the region's 15,000 beds in 175 hospitals are in great demand.

The university stands on a 1,600-acre wooded plot just outside Ibadan and has more than 1,200 students housed in modernistic buildings designed by British architects Maxwell Fry and Jane Drew. The five dormitories are light and airy, somewhat Brazilian in tone with fretted balconies and bands of vivid red, blue or yellow running their length. Some interesting tricks have been done with light, by cutting holes into the walls in shapes which make it look as if a giant had attacked the place with a pastry cutter. But they *are* tricks and I did not much like the buildings, with the exception of the Protestant and Catholic chapels which have simple and true lines. It was all a bit flashy and, unlike Ghana's Legon Hill, doesn't look as if it will age well.

The first students moved into temporary buildings in 1948 and construction began three years later. There are twenty laboratories, an arts theatre, two lecture blocks and a library capable of holding a quarter of a million volumes (it has over 100,000). The university has twenty-two academic departments divided among faculties of Arts,

Science, Medicine, Agriculture and Veterinary Science. The capital cost was over £3 million and the recurrent budget is nearly £1 million. Science is the most popular faculty, I was told, followed by Arts, Medicine and Agriculture. Of the academic staff of 208, in 1960 there were 61 Nigerians and 147 expatriates, including several South African Cape Coloureds driven by *apartheid* from their native land. It is hoped that there will be 1,500 students by 1965 and no doubt they will gather in Trenchard Hall, an assembly building donated by the United Africa Company, to debate the evils of colonialism.

We had a talk with Dr. J. H. Parry, the principal (he has since departed—to become principal of the University College of Swansea—to make room for Ibadan's first African head) and he said that about 90 per cent of the places were equally divided between the East and West, the remainder going to the more backward North and other West Africans. Only 6 per cent of the students, he said, were women. The boys were intelligent but discipline was always a problem in an Africa which has learned to boycott and strike but not to conciate and concede. Both the hospital and the university are federal affairs and have nothing to do with the West except for the fact that they are located there, although the West has plans for a university of its own.

But the West concedes nothing to any African state in its enthusiasm for education. In 1954 it became the first black territory to provide six free primary years for its children and about a third of the regional budget goes for education. Since the introduction of the free grades, the West has spent more than £6 million on buildings (there are more than 7,000 schools) and enrolments have ballooned from 430,000 to 1·2 million. The number of secondary students has risen from 9,000 to 85,000. It is estimated that 95 per cent of all Western children receive some education, by far the highest percentage in Africa. The big test for the West comes this year as the number of primary graduates swells from 72,000 to 190,000 with discharge of the first batch of 'free' students. To meet this flood the West has evolved so-called secondary modern schools with a practical bias for those academically or financially unable to go on to five-year secondary grammar schools. There are now 363 secondary modern schools with 25,000 students taking the three-year course. It is hoped that these schools will be able to absorb 50 per cent of the primary graduates (which will mean quadrupling their enrolments) while 145 secondary grammar schools will absorb 10 per cent of the primary graduates. The other 40 per cent will just have to leave school. An additional 11,000 teachers are being trained to meet this horde. The East, which likes to belittle the Western Region's considerable achievements (it is worth noting that Ghana and Guinea between them have less than 100 secondary schools), maintains that the secondary moderns produce ignorant children at great cost. But it seems better to teach children to use their hands and support themselves than to give them an academic education which will enable them to starve genteelly in what is still basically a peasant society.

The main business of Ibadan, apart from trade, is government. And this is the bailiwick of a most remarkable African, Chief Obafemi Awolowo.

This fifty-one-year-old Yoruba attorney had a Dickensian childhood. He was born at Ikenne, a small village in the Ijebu country to the south of Ibadan. The Ijebus are said by the other Yoruba clans to be frugal, ambitious, painstaking, proud and egalitarian. Young Awolowo—who was christened Jeremiah but never uses the name now—has a bit of each of these qualities in his make-up.

His father was a Christian in the days when membership in such a scandalously radical cult was a fighting affair. His mother more respectably was dedicated to Oluweri, the river god. Awolowo's father was a sawyer and a man of some consequence. He was contemptuous of the village animists and went so far as to destroy a shrine of the smallpox god. Shortly thereafter he caught the disease and died. By Yoruba custom the dead man's goods went to his brothers and sisters. Awolowo's share of 'the estate' was a gown. He sold it nine years later to pay for a shorthand correspondence course.

The family broke up after his father's death and Awolowo drifted away to Abeokuta where he lived with and worked as a servant for— in return for part of his school fees—a chauffeur, a blind scribe, a photographer and a surveyor. For a time he adopted the name of Coker, which was the surveyor's name.

His schooling was, to say the least, erratic: in five years he attended schools run by the Anglicans, Methodists, Baptists and Salvation Army. He was sixteen before he finished primary school. To earn his fees he cut elephant grass for the potters of Abeokuta and sold drinking water at a farthing a gallon. At the end of his primary education, which was about as far as ninety-nine out of a hundred Nigerian boys got in those days, Awolowo vowed 'to forego the glory of a job as a shop attendant, junior clerk or pupil-teacher for the far-off goal of a lawyer's gown and wig'.

He worked for a while as a teacher at a salary of thirteen shillings per month, then heard of a scholarship competition being held at Ibadan. To pay his way to the examination he weeded a graveyard. Awolowo won the scholarship and has never looked back since. After finishing high school at Ibadan, he earned honours degrees in commerce and law at London University. Returning to Nigeria, he plunged into journalism and trade union activity under the tutelage of Nnamdi Azikiwe, the Eastern Nigerian leader.

In 1951 he broke with Zik and founded his own political party, the Action Group, an outgrowth of the *Egbe Omo Oduduwa* ('Union of the Sons of Oduduwa'), a Yoruba cultural organization which he had formed three years earlier. Awo, as his supporters call him, quickly showed his knack for political organization by making the Action Group supreme in the West, was soon elected to the federal House of Representatives. When the West got more regional power in 1954, Awo moved back to Ibadan to become premier.

Under his guidance the Action Group cemented its hold on the West and gained enough seats in alliance with splinter groups in the East to become the official Opposition in that region. Although Awo gained some supporters in the North through his support of the move for a separate Middle Belt state, Zik's Northern Elements Progressive Union allies gained the largest number of opposition seats.

In his own region, Awo was, of course, the moving force behind the implementation of the West's comprehensive social service programme. And it was he who, for better or worse, brought television to Africa. After six years as Western premier, Awo declared that his job there was done. He stepped down, stood for the federal House of Representatives and, since 1960, has headed the 73-member Action Group Opposition on the national level.

Awolowo is a small man, about five foot seven. He wears gold-rimmed spectacles and is beginning to grey at the temples. He is a non-smoking, teetotalling, practising Christian (Anglican) and is very much the *paterfamilias* when surrounded by his brood of three daughters. He seldom smiles and is regarded by many as a cold fish.

We met at his Ibadan home and Awo wore a gown of blue (the traditional Yoruba colour), a wristwatch but no rings. His hands are very small, like Haile Selassie's, whom he resembles in some ways, and he often gesticulates with them to emphasize a point. He creates an impression of studiousness and sincerity. Awo is proud of the role he played in Nigeria's march to independence.

'Zik,' he said, 'has called me a British stooge but I have shown that things can be accomplished by constructive and constitutional methods. It is enough to make yourself heard and then to demonstrate that you deserve independence.

'My move to the centre,' he continued, as a servant poured orange pop, 'was necessary to underline the nationhood of Nigeria. If the leaders of the country remain in Ibadan, Enugu and Kaduna, how can Nigeria become strong?'

He was not discouraged by the fact that his Action Group trailed well behind the N.P.C. and N.C.N.C. in the 1959 federal elections: 'The Action Group is giving the country a vigorous parliamentary Opposition, and that is of great importance if democracy is to survive here.' Awo's hopes for coming to power in the future rest on the 15 million Nigerians who belong to none of the three dominant tribal groupings (Hausa-Fulani, Ibo and Yoruba). The carrot which he holds out to them is the creation of new states—perhaps fifteen in all—based on tribal groupings, each with limited autonomy under the federation. His chances for achieving this we will discuss later.

Awo, who has visited the United States, is the best friend the West has in Africa and he told me that he regarded non-alignment as 'diplomatic prostitution'.

'The world is divided,' he explains, 'into two camps. Anyone who denies that the Communist bloc is the greater foe of human rights is either hypocritical or stupid. Russia is not completely evil nor is the West completely good. But if one must choose between the two—and I believe one must—then one must inevitably side with the West. Of course we want economic aid but we choose the West not in the hope of dollars but because we believe in freedom. It is as simple as that.'

In foreign policy, as in domestic programme, Awo is at loggerheads with Zik, who is an advocate of neutralism. In its favour the Action Group has wealth and an apparently limitless ability for organization (Awo employed helicopters, sound-trucks, campaign buttons, give-away matches and other American paraphernalia in the federal elections). Against him he has the Action Group's reputation as a tribal party with autocratic tendencies. His battle is a difficult one.

Politics in the Western Region is fluid and volatile. Because the Action Group is associated with the chiefs (ten of fourteen regional cabinet ministers are chiefs), the middle class and the possession of wealth—all but one of the eighty-three members of the Western House of Chiefs are A.G. and one, the powerful Alafin of Oyo, was deposed in 1956 for meddling (anti-A.G. activity) in politics—the N.C.N.C. has been able to give Awolowo considerable trouble in his own back-yard. In 1954, for instance, the N.C.N.C. won twenty-three of the forty-two federal seats at stake in the West and polled 45 per cent of the popular vote in the regional elections two years later, most of its popularity being due to the fears of non-Yoruba tribes (the N.C.N.C. won sixteen seats to the A.G.'s four in non-Yoruba areas but only sixteen of sixty seats in Yorubaland).

The Action Group's political situation within the West has improved considerably since 1958 and the tragic death in a highway accident of Alhaji Adegoke Adelabu, the able leader of the Opposition in the Western House of Assembly. Adelabu, who was forty-three, had survived a score of what his supporters called 'political trials' and his Ibadan People's Party promptly blamed Yoruba ju-ju for his death and went on a rampage against those whose mourning appeared to lack verisimilitude. Houses and motor-cars were burned and twenty people were killed. The owners of the car which collided with the politician's were faced with suits from nine wives and seventeen children, all belonging to Adelabu.

As his regent in the West, Awolowo has left fifty-year-old Chief Samuel Ladoke Akintola. Akintola, who is regional premier, was born at Ogbomosho and is the son of a prominent Yoruba trader. He attended mission schools and worked as a railway clerk before winning a British Council fellowship to study public administration in England. Later Akintola (he is identified in the press as 'S.L.A.'), who is a handsome man with a small scar under his left eye, attended Oxford and earned a law degree at Lincoln's Inn. After whirls at teaching and journalism (he edited, successively, *The Nigeria Baptist* and Awo's *Daily Service*), he became legal adviser to the Action Group and deputy party leader. Awo sent him to the centre where he became federal Minister of Labour in 1951. After holding the Health portfolio for a year, he served as Leader of the Opposition in the House of Representatives from 1954 to 1957. In 1958 Akintola became federal Minister of Communications and, two years later, Awo called him back to Ibadan to become Western premier when he moved to the federal sphere to become Leader of the Opposition.

Akintola, who is a vigorous tennis player and occasionally gets out on the soccer field (he looks twenty years younger than he is), possesses a keen mind and is a good administrator. He is completely loyal to his chief and the change of premiers should result in no alteration in Western Region policy.

Of the same stamp is vast Frederick Rotimi Alade ('Timi' to everybody) Williams, a 300-pounder who towers well over six feet and is supposed to have the best legal brain in Nigeria. I met Chief Williams (his titles are Apesia of Itoku and Bobajaro of Lagos) as he dashed from his Western Region Attorney-General's office to the suite which he occupies as Minister of Justice. It was rather like encountering a large, unruly but jolly crowd.

Williams' personal history is not a story of victory over adversity. His father was a well-to-do Lagos lawyer and there was never any trouble in finding Timi's school fees. He proved himself to be a brilliant student, winning his Cambridge degree at the age of twenty-one (which is very young for an African) and being called to the bar at Gray's Inn a year later. Returning to Nigeria, he tried his hand at writing a regular column under the pseudonym of 'The Gentleman with the Duster'. It was one of the few really erudite and sprightly columns which have appeared in the West African press. He became active in the Nigerian Youth Movement, which he was instrumental in bringing under the Action Group's wing in 1951, the year in which he unsuccessfully contested a Lagos seat in the Western House of Assembly. So high was Awo's regard for his chubby lieutenant that he sent Timi to Australia and the United States to study their federal systems, which have been the basis for Nigeria's own form of government. He led the Action Group delegation to the All-Africa Peoples Conference in Accra where he distinguished himself by working hard to convince nationalist leaders that the incorporation of safeguards for human rights in their constitutions was more important than loose talk about the evils of imperialism. Williams is a brilliant debater (although he refuses to indulge in demagoguery) and was well respected by the British for the simple reason that he always did his ministerial homework rather than relying on bluff and evasion.

Williams holds his portfolio as a member of the upper house, the Western House of Chiefs, and—with the exception of two terms on the Lagos City Council—has never won an election. He is Nigeria's first Queen's Counsel and has resisted all attempts on Awolowo's part to bring him more fully into the political picture, perhaps because he has his sights set on a seat on the bench. But this amply-upholstered forty-year-old has considerable support among the younger Western intellectuals and his time will come.

Williams was tied up with the job of codification of the Western Region's laws (the first in Africa in which British law, English common law and customary law have been reduced to a single code) and he had little time to talk.

'But it's Christmas Eve,' he said cheerfully, 'and you don't want to spend it sitting around the rest house. I'm having a few people in for supper. Why not come along?' We came and what a party it was! Williams had doffed his *agbada* and was garbed in the two under-garments—which resembled a short-sleeved pyjama set of white eyelet lace. To the raucous jive of High-Life records, his great belly jumped and bobbled, his large white teeth flashed in a blinding smile as he shimmered and shook with his pretty wife, a lawyer's daughter and mother of three children. A champagne supper was served in the garden by barefoot servants clad in white gowns with red cummerbunds and fezes. But Rotimi Williams never ate. He danced on and on until the last lady was exhausted. Finally, he heaved his vast bulk into a chair, wiped his dripping forehead and asked how I was getting along. When I told him I had never been to a better party, he said, 'Stick around until New Year's Eve, then we really cut loose.' I wouldn't dare.

There were half a dozen mixed marriages at the party and I took the occasion to ask Chief Williams a question I'd had on my mind for some time: how did such liaisons work out in Nigeria? He said it depended a great deal on the individual couple. Many English girls came out with no knowledge of the African family system and were unable to accept the fact that their in-laws had a constant call on them for food, accommodation and money. Others, he said, didn't work out because the girls were low-class whites and Ibadan society quite rightly was not willing to accept them on an equal basis. But if the girls had a decent background and were willing to meet their husbands' families and society half-way, there was seldom any trouble. It all made sense.

ONI AND OBA

We motored out of Ibadan, somewhat red-eyed as the result of the hospitality of our heavyweight host, and headed for Ife, a city of acres of tin-roofed double-storeyed mud houses with elaborate carving and fretwork around the windows and doors. In the multi-storey yellow brick palace we were received by Sir Adesoji Aderemi I, K.B.E., C.M.G., the seventy-one-year-old Oni of Ife.

The Oni, who is tall for an African of these parts and chubby for an

African of any parts (we saw more rotund people in Western Nigeria than anywhere else on the continent), started life as a railway clerk, later became a trader. He has been the Yoruba 'pope' for thirty years, has participated in all the constitutional conferences, held a host of political offices, including federal Minister without Portfolio from 1951 to 1954 and president of the Western House of Chiefs. In 1953, he led the Nigerian delegation to the coronation of Elizabeth II and last year he was named Governor of the Western Region.

The Oni, who has a broad nose, a little moustache, and a quick smile, wore a brown *agbada*, yellow slippers scuffed down at the heels, a velvet cap shaped like a tired loaf of bread, and, for a spiritual leader, a very mortal undershirt in lieu of the matching blouse usually worn with the Yoruba gown. He settled comfortably into an over-stuffed, brown leather chair, removed his slippers and welcomed us to his home, which was liberally decorated with half a dozen pictures of himself with Sir Winston Churchill taken at an agricultural show in Kent several years ago. The only startling thing in the room was a silvered ju-ju shrine on a table in which a cut-out picture of the Oni appeared.

The Oni's career indicates the essentially democratic nature of the Yoruba chieftaincy. The traditional leader must be of the royal blood but need not be the eldest son or even in the direct line. The new chief is chosen by a council of elders. Hence all the royal pretenders have the incentive to work hard and, in most cases, the best man wins. His blood confirms his ability and, since most African families are tremendous, there are ample candidates for the job. The only drawback seems to be that it is impossible to predict who will succeed and thus to educate him for the job.

The Oni maintains that the indiscriminate award of chieftaincies— there are more than 10,000 chiefs in the Western Region alone—has reached the point where 'every third or fourth man' is a chief. The attraction, apart from the social distinction pertaining to titles, is that ambitious men hope to use the chieftaincy as a springboard to political power. A parallel situation exists in the East, which traditionally has not had a system of chiefs. In 1959 the East followed the other two regions in establishing a House of Chiefs as an upper chamber. Since then, in the words of R. O. Iwuagwu, Eastern Minister of State, there has been 'a mad rush to become chiefs and receive appointment to the upper house'. Although traditionalists may well decry the debasement of the institution, adaptation of the chieftaincy to modern political conditions would seem to be its one chance of survival. Awolowo is doing much to promote this by making it his policy to preserve and enhance the status of chiefs (while gradually reducing their power) and to encourage their association with local government institutions.

The Oni, who has five sons following various professions, was an old friend of Lugard's and he well remembers the skirmishing which preceded the arrival of the first white men to Ife. While the Oni talked on in excellent English and we surrounded large bottles of Danish beer, courtiers crawled in and out of the room on their hands and knees and conducted conversations with their spiritual lord from a prone position on the plum-coloured carpet. We finished our beer and the Oni took us out to see his new museum, which houses some of the famous Ife sculpture.

The brass heads, with their strange, enigmatic beauty, were pierced with small holes along the hairline and down the cheeks, presumably for attaching skin to emulate beards and hair. This was not so of a couple of figures which were smaller and may represent females. Most of the faces were marked with a longitudinal hatching which some say represents tribal markings; others maintain it was simply the artist's style. Some of the terracotta figures were of slaves with their arms bound behind them and their mouths gagged (when you execute some-one in Africa, it is said to be desirable to have the victim's mouth gagged or his tongue cut lest he speak a mighty curse). Other terracottas showed deformed limbs and a young Yoruba curator told us that his people had always been fascinated by the deformed. The African has an odd sense of humour and 'amused' might be closer to the point. Still, it was not so long ago that the courts of Europe kept their dwarfs. Some months later, on a blustery autumn morning, we visited Berlin's Volkerkunde Museum and saw there the largest collection of Ife brass and terracottas, and Benin bronzes in the world. They looked a bit forlorn so far from home.

We pushed on eastward towards the Niger and came at sundown to Benin. As we have seen, Benin was a powerful neo-Christian state in the fifteenth and sixteenth centuries. An early visitor described it as 'prodigious large' and said the city had wide streets two miles long. When the Portuguese left (Bini children still kill birds with miniature crossbows which are a Portuguese legacy), Benin went into a spiritual decline—from the Christian point of view—but its secular power, if anything, increased.

The Binis were among the first of the coastal tribes to trade with

Europeans. Their pepper, ivory, gold dust, palm oil and cloth enabled them to buy firearms. This, coupled with their well-established contact with white traders, assured Benin new prominence as the slave trade replaced legitimate traffic. By the first half of the nineteenth century, the Oba of Benin ranked as the most important monarch between Lagos and the Cross River. Benin's power declined with the end of the slave trade and the Oba's reaction was to close his country to all trade with the whites and, through human sacrifice, to conciliate the angry gods. When conditions failed to improve, the Oba devised more horrible forms of death for his slaves (who no longer had any economic value) and slaughtered them in greater numbers.

This did not sit well with the British and their consul visited Benin several times in an attempt to get the Oba to reform. It is also possible that Britain was not entranced by the idea of having a powerful and recalcitrant native state on the right bank of its Niger highway to the interior. Matters were brought to a head in 1896 when James Phillips, the acting consul-general, informed Oba Overami that he wished to visit him at Benin to discuss the questions of human sacrifice (the Binis added a nice twist to their beheadings: if the executioner failed to sever the head in one blow, he was beheaded by the new office holder, his *son*) and trade. Overami informed Phillips that he was celebrating 'the custom', or anniversary of his father's death, but would be happy to receive him in a few months. Since 'the custom' involved the beheading and crucifixion of hundreds, Overami was undoubtedly correct in assuming that the occasion was inappropriate for such discussions.

Against the advice of a loyal chief, Phillips set off for Benin with eight white men and 230 unarmed porters. In deference to the chief's entreaties, Phillips decided against taking the police band with him. Overami's warriors ambushed the party and only two of the white men and a few porters escaped. Captain Alan Boisragon, one of the two who slipped away into the forest, reports that Phillips' only order, given in the quiet tones of one exhorting an Oxford rugby club to play the game, was: 'No revolvers, gentlemen.'

Plenty of revolvers were to come, however. Within a matter of a few days a naval squadron and a punitive force of 1,200 marines, blue-jackets and native constabulary had been organized. As the expedition neared the walls of Benin, Overami decked himself out in full ceremonial regalia and ordered hundreds of slaves to be sacrificed in an eleventh-hour attempt to placate the angry gods. Then he fled, followed by his war-chiefs, his magicians and his favourite wives.

Boisragon, who accompanied the assault column, wrote that as he fought his way towards the city he found:

' . . . live women, gagged and pegged out on their backs, their abdominal wall being cut in the shape of a cross with the uninjured gut hanging out . . . as we neared the city, human beings were lying in all the paths . . . even in the king's compound—my God, the sight and stench of them was awful . . . the bush, too, was filled with dead bodies, their hands tied to their ankles so as to keep them in a sitting posture . . . all along the road decapitated bodies were found, blown out by the heat of the sun.'

Everywhere were scattered bones and bodies and each ju-ju tree bore its hideous fruit of crucified slaves in varying degrees of decomposition. Pits forty to fifty feet deep were found filled with dead and dying. On the ju-ju altars blood was caked so thickly that it could be dug out in chunks with a bayonet. The conquerors chopped down the ju-ju trees, filled the death pits, dynamited the shrines and (so it is said) gave a helping hand to a fire which destroyed the palace and much of the town. Overami, who surrendered, was exiled to Calabar and several of his priests and chiefs were executed.

Today, Overami's grandson, sixty-year-old Godfrey Edokparhogbuyunmwu Basimi Eweka, reigns—and to a certain extent, rules—in Benin. Fortunately he goes by the throne name of Akenzua II.

On the surface, Benin—where thirty-six different words mean 'good morning' depending on the clan of the well-wisher—looks much like any other Nigerian town of 65,000, a rambling, rather dirty place of mud walls and tin roofs. But despite the fact that the provincial education office with its pleasant, well-stocked reading room occupies the old site of the bloodstained altar of Ogiuwu, god of war and death, Benin is still, somehow, 'Ile-Ibenu', the 'Country of Hate'.

Akenzua's father three times was hauled into court (he now resides in the floor of the palace, his figure outlined in cowrie shells)—as recently as 1929—for making human sacrifice to his ju-ju shrine. There are few who would deny that human sacrifice still takes place in Benin, as it does in Lagos. Strangers avoid the city and the Ibo servants of white businessmen do not go out much at night. People disappear from time to time in Benin and the fact that such disappearances seem to be more prevalent at times when the ancient rites are performed gives the statistics a sinister air.

Akenzua, who is thin and rather tall, has a hard, bony face and long, delicate fingers. He usually wears a long white gown and a white biretta which, when he dons his steel-rimmed glasses, makes him look much like the late Pope Pius XII. He had a secondary school education and studied native administration in Abeokuta for two years before returning to Benin to act as his father's private secretary. He served for a time as a district magistrate and became oba on his father's death in 1933. A baby elephant was hacked to death in celebration of the occasion and Benin's livestock population was considerably diminished at the conclusion of the festivities. Dogs are much in demand as sacrifices because the Bini regard them as more nearly human than any other animal.

The first thing Akenzua did after his accession was to bury his mother. Not a moment too soon, either: the lady in question had been dead for seven years. Bini custom, it seems, forbids the burial of the mother of the senior prince until he takes the throne. The palace has more than two hundred rooms (each has a special use) and covers several acres so presumably she is shunted to an unused wing while awaiting her final resting place.

Before calling on the Oba, we paid a visit to the bronze-casters and wood-carvers and dropped in on a rubber factory. When the British sacked Benin they found a number of bronzes which compare favourably with those of Ife, from whose sculptors the Bini say they learned the art. The method is the same: a model is made in wax over a mud core which is then covered with several layers of mud; after this dries, the wax is melted out and replaced by molten metal; the mud is then knocked off, leaving the cast.

Although the technique is the same, the Benin bronzes struck me as looking decidedly different from those of Ife. The latter have tranquil Grecian appearance, while the former, with their foreshortening and distortion of the full figures, the ornate and intricately embellished devil-masks, could have been Siamese or Chinese. Chinese coins have been found scattered over the coasts of Africa and it is not inconceivable that junks reached these shores centuries ago. Certain tribes from the Cape Hottentots north have a decidedly oriental cast to their features, the tribes of Northern Nigeria wear the lamp-shade hats which every schoolboy associates with China, and many of the place-names of the North—Song, Pankshin, Jos, Shellen—have a Chinese ring to them.

The Portuguese unquestionably provided the Bini sculptors with new ideas and motifs and, in the Oba's little museum, bearded Portuguese soldiers performing feats of prodigious valour are represented in several of the ancient plaques. A few good pieces are still to be found at private ju-ju shrines (there are about 300 bronzes in the Oba's museum and another 1,800 are scattered around the world, mostly in Britain, the United States, Germany and Russia) but the Bini, although their artistic ability may have declined, are adept at giving new bronzes an aged appearance.

The Benin government has hired men from the clans famed for wood-carving and bronze-casting and put them to work producing objects with the traditional tools in the old style. Some of the work is good but one loses a bit of one's enthusiasm at the sight of a set of 'traditional' coasters for highball glasses.

At the Ikpoba rubber factory, which is run by the Western Region government, we found a harassed young British manager who said 'yes', we could have a look around but there really wasn't much to see. The plant had been built at a cost of close to £350,000 to make latex. The great cauldrons and the shallow aluminium pans were empty and cobwebs stretched across them. It seems that the Bini, too lazy to tap the rubber trees themselves, hire them out to Ibos. The Ibos not only slash the trees so badly that they die but add water and other un-mentionable impurities to achieve a larger saleable volume. Since the rubber tappers could not be induced to stop adulterating and it would cost too much to test each bucket, the plant had gone out of business. Now, in another part of the factory, rubber crepe, which is of less value than latex, was being made. The rubber was delivered in hard gobs which looked like sponges and ranged in size from an orange to a pumpkin.

'And don't they adulterate it in this form?' I asked.

'Have a look,' the manager advised. In a room as large as a tennis court was a tremendous hillock of rubber gobs. Each was split in two and the cross-sections contained wood chips, bark, stones and mango pips. Each hunk contained from 40 per cent to 80 per cent impurities. With colonialism no longer a factor in the New Africa, the big battle has yet to be won: the victory of the African over himself.

Rubber could be important to the West and the regional government is doing its utmost to improve the situation. A new and tough line made it possible for the factory to show a small profit last year and, since 1960, the regional government annually has distributed 2·5 million improved seedlings capable of yielding 60 per cent more latex than present trees. Nigeria now produces 2 per cent of the world's supply and 90 per cent of this comes from the West. The new scheme will add

10,000 acres a year to the present figure of 250,000 acres and production should be doubled within a decade.

The West is anxious to industrialize and the £2·5 million sawmill and plywood factory at Sapele, which is owned by the United Africa Company, is one of the largest and most modern of its kind. Another major venture is the £4 million cement factory (owned jointly by the regional government and British investors) at Ewekoro, forty miles north of Lagos, which produces 200,000 tons a year, all the West's requirements. Less fortunate has been the Lafia cannery outside Ibadan in which the government also has a heavy interest. The cannery can turn out 600,000 cans of pineapples, grapefruit, oranges and lemons per year but faulty planning has caused this £450,000 investment to stand idle for six months out of the year.

Leaving the rubber factory and its desperate manager, we drove back to the Oba's palace and had a look at the ju-ju shrine which stands at its entrance. It consisted of an almost life-sized clay figure of an oba clasping a sword in one hand and holding aloft the severed body of a man in the other. There were two mud 'muffins' about a foot high and three feet in diameter on which were bells, iron balls and a couple of dead birds. A roof of corrugated iron (the palace roof is of the same material) supported by four six-foot posts covered the shrine. I wondered when the last human life had ended here.

Slavery was declared illegal in Benin only in 1915 and the character who took my card in to the Oba did not have the appearance of the modern domestic servant: he was a husky lad in his twenties and his livery consisted of a pair of rather dirty undershorts of the brief type.

Akenzua received us in a long, gloomy room the walls of which were covered with yellowing photographs curling at the edges. Each portrayed Akenzua or his ancestors. There was a Hallicrafter radio in one corner and the usual clutter one finds in the homes of wealthy and recently evolved Africans: stacks of newspapers, ceremonial shields, ju-ju objects, more photographs, unopened packages, crates of soft drinks, a refrigerator. The Oba was accompanied by a wizened, barechested vizier who wore a white sarong, a necklace of coral beads and had the back half of his head shaved. Only a chief may cut his hair in this fashion and the coral beads are the symbol of nobility. To lose them or break the strand in the old days, even in battle, meant instant death. The vizier was followed by a couple of boys, naked save for the undershorts, who dispensed orange pop and English cigarettes from a brass tray.

The Oba, despite his rather forbidding appearance, is the most progressive ruler Benin has had. He is the first to have any formal education and the first to travel outside West Africa (he has visited England). When one of his daughters recently married (in the Catholic church) a university college professor, he made her a gift of £400 and a house worth £1,200; in the old days, the usual wedding gift for a princess was eighty slaves (he also gave the bride the traditional present of a brass fan, an old brass lamp, spoon and fork of brass, a cutlass, axe, knife and a pillow embroidered with coral beads). The Oba gets by with only eight wives (Grandpa Overami had 2,000 and Pa Eweka had several hundred), is a strong supporter of the Action Group and a minister in the Western government. For this reason, the Oba is not popular with all his people, many of whom support the N.C.N.C.

The Action Group is the party of the palace clique, the Ogboni Society, which favours a revival of Benin's old glories through the creation of a new state. The Action Group has agreed in principle to this and is, in fact, the only major party advocating the creation of additional states. But the situation is complicated by national political considerations and by the fact that many non-Edo-speaking people live in Benin and are not enthusiastic about the prospect of being turned over to the Oba. Memories of the old days are still green.

Ogboni, or its counterparts, exists in all areas of Nigeria and has many functions. Frobenius called it 'a decapitation company, limited' but human sacrifice apparently has ceased to play a major part in its policies. Members of the power *élite*—priests, merchants, politicians, lawyers, chiefs—buy their way into the societies and are assured of success by their membership: it is said that promotions both in government and in commercial firms go only to Ogboni men, that they get a break on their taxes, that they receive tips on land condemnations and the like. It is, in fact, a moot point as to who really runs Nigeria, the native rulers, the politicians, the people or Ogboni. Many would say Ogboni.

I asked Akenzua what he hoped independence would mean for Nigeria.

'Power politics,' he replied. 'We want to play power politics like Britain and America.' Benin could use a few prosaic things like hospitals, public housing, schools, electricity and sewers, one would think.

We had arrived in the middle of the week-long annual Igue ceremony devoted to the worship of the Oba's head and the Oba excused himself to don his ceremonial robes. The women of the Olokun cult, some young and sleek, their skin like burnished mahogany, others wrinkled crones with breasts like tobacco pouches, gathered on the left of a dais set up in front of the Oba's mud palace. The younger women had their hair pushed up into frizzy, towering pompadours. Their elders achieved the same effect by wigs of human hair built over mud moulds. Each festooned her coiffure with slivers of coral shaped like firecrackers, pieces of stone, leather amulets and Action Group buttons bearing Chief Awolowo's picture.

A single deep-throated drum began to throb from somewhere in the interior of the palace. Then the chiefs began to arrive, dancing. Their dance had no joy in it. It was gliding and stylized like sleepwalking. Some wore pleated armour of red felt and peaked Phrygian bonnets. Others were naked above the waist and wore layer on layer of sarongs, making them look big-bottomed, or like women in hoop-skirts. Still others wore a sort of cassock and short cloak, which must have been an adaptation from the habits of the fifteenth-century Portuguese priests. Before some walked half-naked boys carrying ceremonial execution swords shaped like canoe paddles. Others whirled their swords around their heads as they swayed from side to side. Behind each came a man carrying and twirling a massive and colourful umbrella, the symbol of chieftaincy. The crowd swelled and began to shuffle its feet in time with the dancing chiefs. More people poured in from the city until several thousand must have been packed into the courtyard in front of the palace and ju-ju shrine. The Oba's police cut at the bare legs of those in front with leather whips. The crowd howled as those in front fought to get out of range of the whips. Then it surged forward again. Someone held a naked, screaming child above the heads of the crowd and shook him several times, as if he were waving a banner. The beat and volume of the drumming from within the palace intensified and we pushed our way through the crowd to have a look.

One of the undershorts brigade stopped us at the door. This was for men only. Kitty went back to the dais and I pushed my way down the twisting corridor past a ju-ju altar laden with brass bells and bronze heads of obas. The artist's representation of the coral necklaces with which the obas were decked made them look as if they were wearing turtle-neck sweaters. Out of the top of each head, through a hole in the metal, rose an intricately carved elephant's tusk. I followed the drumming to an interior room. The drummers were old men but they were drumming hard and in perfect rhythm and beads of sweat glistened on their bony chests. The room had no windows but there was a hole in the roof and underneath it a catch-pool for rainwater, much like a Tuscan atrium. The sun shone wanly through the roof and cast a feeble light into the corners of the room. There, in eye-glazed immobility, sat the old war chiefs in recesses in the walls, their coral necklaces dangling to their hips. More people, clad in khaki shorts or flowing robes, their eyes rolling and their feet shuffling across the beaten mud floor, pushed their way into the room and it became difficult to breathe. The heat, the lack of air and the frenzied drumming within the confined space produced an anaesthetizing effect. Soon you knew that the drummers were beating a rhythm in time to the throb of your pulse, the humming of the blood in the veins of your head. I pushed my way outside and wondered for how many men that drumming had been the last sound they had heard.

It was mid-afternoon and the sun was hot. Suddenly more underwear types came bounding through the crowd to announce the coming of the Oba. He came swathed in what looked like a Navajo blanket bound around a hoop-skirt. On his left hip was a curious doll with a head of coral draped in cloth. The Oba's shirt and helmet was also of coral and his neck was imprisoned in great bands of the same substance. His arms, loaded with coral and brass, were supported by two courtiers. Akenzua hoisted himself wearily upon the dais, which was about a foot above the ground and covered with a canopy, and sat down upon a pouffe of white cloth. He was joined by sixteen of the royal children (he has about fifty) and by his wives, some squat, black and negroid in appearance, others thin-featured, light and hard-looking. Devil-masks of a protective nature, mounted on wooden sticks, were stuck in the ground in front of the dais to ward off any curses which might be headed in the Oba's direction.

Each chief danced slowly towards the Oba, stopped in front of the dais, raised his clenched fist in salute and cried 'Domo! Domo!', the greeting which must be used only to royalty. For four hours the chiefs danced in and out, slowly, rhythmically, whirling their swords in the air while a courtier sang their virtues from beside the dais. The drums beat on and the swaying crowd kept up its pressure against the cordon of police.

Then began the making of ju-ju which, if it works, will make the Oba live for ever. A priest came forward with a basket filled to the brim with roots and pieces of wood. One by one he held each piece aloft, intoned a chant describing its properties, then handed it to another magician who peeled some of it into a dish where a girl (was she a slave?) crushed it with a smooth stone until the mixture was the consistency of oatmeal. From time to time, the magician dipped a stick into the mixture and touched the Oba with it: forehead, eyes, shoulders, hands, stomach, knees and feet. The Honourable Akenzua II, C.M.G., sat staring out over the crowd, his eyes blank and unseeing, a few beads of moisture glistening above his upper lip. Night began to fall, the sudden, twilightless night of Africa, and a white cow, tethered in the nearby field and billed as the principal sacrifice, started to low plaintively. The chiefs came dancing in again, shaking their clenched fists at the Oba, worshipping his head.

We elbowed our way through the crowd of black bodies and rolling white eyeballs and walked away into the night. The drumming picked up, then stopped so suddenly that the silence seemed to howl. And then there came a great roar from the crowd as the white cow was led to its destiny. It has been a long time since an oba has had the traditional sacrifice of twelve humans, twelve dogs, twelve cows, twelve sheep, twelve goats, twelve chickens and one fish. It has been many years since blood ran in the streets of Benin and the stench of rotting bodies filled the air. But Benin, and for that matter much of Nigeria, is still very much in a twilight mood between the two worlds represented by Chief Awolowo and Akenzua II. It is possible, of course, that it may be dawn, not evening.

But perhaps that's what the fifteenth-century Portuguese said.

Chapter 20

*

BLACK GIANT

Across the broad sweep of the slow-moving Niger, still unbridged (a three-quarter-mile eight-span steel bridge will be completed in 1963 at a cost of £5·3 million), lies the Eastern Region, larger than the three Benelux nations combined and with more people (eight million) than Austria. This is a land of rain-drenched forest, of palm oil ruffians, of leopard murder and new universities. This is the home of the truculent, intelligent, hard-working Ibo people, of the river-dwelling Ijaws, of blasé Efiks, superstitious Ibibios and of a group of forest tribes so harried by slavers for generations that they now lie hidden deep in the jungle. It is a poor land, so poor that its people—who speak languages which are tonal like Chinese—have fanned out all over Nigeria in search of the El Dorado of Day-Glo neckties, Hercules bicycles and university educations for the kids.

The regional government calculates that 29 per cent of the population evades taxation and so prevalent is cannibalism in some areas that meat must be sold with part of the hide attached. More than 80 per cent of the region's income comes from the oil palm and 140 inches of rain drums down in the creek areas between May and October. In 1958 N.C.N.C. politicians hailed a government decision to pay £10 for the transfer of a ju-ju from a tree cut down by the highway department to another suitable leafy home as a victory for freedom of religion. The five largest cities in the region are Enugu, Port Harcourt, Onitsha, Aba and Calabar, and local government—since the Ibos are not lovers of chiefs—is on the English model, with seventeen county councils, eighty urban councils and hundreds of local ones. There are 6,620 primary schools with 1·2 million students and 32,000 teachers, 99 secondary schools with 17,000 students and 1,100 teachers, and 137 teacher-training institutes with 11,400 students and 700 teachers. A third of the regional budget is devoted to education. In one recent year, it was discovered that 70 per cent of the population of Nsukka division (where a new university has sprung up) was suffering from yaws and many Easterners prefer to consult a *dibia*, or witch-doctor, before going to a hospital. We saw this sign along one Eastern highway:

'Charms for quick Recovery. Regd. in Nigeria. For all kinds of charms and medicinal appliances call on IDADUNWANSHI, efficient and reliable ju-ju doctor. Charges are modest and yet effect of treatment is TREMENDOUS while efficacy of charms is TERRIFYING. TRY AND BE CONVINCED.'

The East has only 450 miles of paved road and so fond of litigation are the local gentry that it is estimated that every man, woman and child of one division spends at least one day a year in court. Schedules can become confused in the East because the Ibos have a four-day week while the Ibibio week is twice that long. The old dark face of Africa is never far away in the East: there have been 109 unsolved murders in the last couple of years and, in 1959, police reported that Onitsha had been 'invaded by slave dealers' and that 105 children had been reported stolen.

On the bright side, Easterners are famous for their dancing ability, from the vigorous male *atiliogwu* dances of the Onitsha Ibo to the slower, graceful *amaibi* handkerchief dance of the Ijaw women. There are special dances for both men and women (called *nmanwu* and *muanyi*) used exclusively at Ibo second burials, a curious custom which we will deal with later, and the *odi* may be danced only by men who have killed. Ibibio dancers wear beautifully carved masks of stylized female faces chalked snow-white. Musical instruments include the *oja*, a stubby pipe; *ubom*, conical wooden drums struck with sticks; and rattles of plaited fibre containing pebbles which are called *oyo*. The Ibo yam priest is supposed to be the clan's strongest man. In the old days if a man could kill the priest, the killer succeeded to office; if no one killed him, he was expected to commit suicide after seven years. The Ibos bury their dead inside their houses and sacrifices (formerly human but now animal) must be made in each room used by the dead person. The shade of the departed is said to wander in the forest, often for as long as a year, and during this period relatives must mourn continually and vociferously. The second burial ceremony which then takes place involves monumental eating, drinking and the detonation of as much gunpowder as can be obtained. The dead man's position in the afterlife depends upon the magnificence of this ceremony.

A less commendable celebration is the *otigbu anyinya*, the Ibo horse-killing ceremony. Worn-out animals are trekked down from the North to be sold for as much as £60 at a special market near Nsukka. Ibos proud of their material prosperity indulge in conspicuous consumption by buying these pitiable wrecks. The horse's throat is cut over a ju-ju altar, the tail is cut off (it is the symbol of the society), and the animal is beaten to death with clubs. Variations include breaking the beast's legs and throwing it alive on a fire or hanging the animal from a tree while it still lives. There are advanced degrees of this revolting freemasonry for men who kill more than one animal. None but the rich (who are presumably civilized) can afford such financial indulgence but all efforts to stamp out the practice have failed. Its origins are obscure but the ceremony may have grown out of a folk-memory of oppression from Northern cavalry.

Eastern Nigeria has long been thought of as an area barren of the type of civilizations which flowered in Ife and Benin but an important archaeological discovery made in 1960 may dispel this notion. Excavations made near the town of Awka yielded a collection of pottery, iron utensils, a large quantity of beads, and bronze vessels and ornaments of superior workmanship and unique design. The bronzes are fashioned with the technique of Benin but the style is utterly different. The hoard, believed to be the possessions of a priest-king, has not yet been authoritatively dated or evaluated. When a full report is available, some of the mystery which hangs like a veil over Eastern Nigeria's past may be lifted.

The Ibos, who are divided into more than 2,000 clans, are a mobile and industrious people who are no more popular with their neighbours than is to be expected with an energetic and expanding people. It was dislike and fear of the Ibos more than anything else which led British Cameroons to withdraw from the Nigerian federation. This same feeling may impel the United Nations trust territory to associate itself with the Cameroun Republic. As we shall see a bit later, many of the minority tribes of the Eastern Region share this attitude, which is particularly pronounced in the Calabar area. The Efik and Ibibio people of Calabar boast the highest literacy rate in Nigeria and it was the Efik language which was the language of instruction in the nation's early schools and into which the Bible was first translated. The Efiks controlled the *Ekpe* society, which maintained a secret rule over the neighbouring tribes, and their Ibibio cousins provided the manpower which the Efik lacked to become powerful. They built a great commercial empire based on Efik 'houses' and these black Hanseatics still dream of its revival. The N.C.N.C., however, blocks this separatist movement by controlling a solid bloc of thirty seats in the Ibo areas plus thirty-three others in the eighty-four-member regional House of Assembly. More of this later.

The East is the domain of Nnamdi Azikiwe, handsome, burly president of the National Council of Nigeria and the Cameroons, a man who can claim with justice to be Africa's premier nationalist.

Zik—as everyone calls him—was born in 1904 in Zungeru, a small village in Northern Nigeria where his father, an Ibo, was working as a railway clerk. He was educated at the Presbyterians' sixty-five-year-old Hope Waddell Training Institute at Calabar and later at a Methodist school in Lagos. With a record of top scholarship behind him, Zik in 1925 followed the trail of his idol, the eminent Gold Coast philosopher-educator James Aggrey, to America.

In the United States Zik bounced from Storer College to Howard University to Lincoln University to the University of Pennsylvania to Columbia University, ending up with something pretty close to an American accent, graduate degrees in both arts and science, and a drawer full of varsity letters for knocking people's blocks off, doing the 440-yard dash in under fifty seconds and demonstrating a bit of fancy footwork on the soccer field. He ran an elevator, washed dishes, boxed professionally and worked as a newspaper copyboy to support himself, and got insulted because of the colour of his skin. Oddly enough, Zik remembers that some of his worst racial experiences were with American Negro students at Howard who, in those pre-nationalist days, looked down on anyone darker than themselves.

While in America Zik toyed with Communism, as did most young African students, but dropped the Reds because they weren't black enough for him. He taught political science for three years before returning to Africa in 1934 to begin his long battle for African freedom.

Zik took his initial plunge into journalism in the Gold Coast, and quickly got himself deported to his native Nigeria. He landed on his feet in Lagos in 1937, gained the support of wealthy Ibos, and soon was editing the daily *West African Pilot*. Zik owns the *Pilot* today and has added four more papers to his string. In 1944 he made his political start with the founding of the National Council of Nigeria and the Cameroons, the country's first political party, of which he was life-president until his resignation last year, when he became Governor-General. Campaigning on a straight 'Independence Now' platform, Zik won election to the Legislative Council in 1948. In 1951 he resigned from the Central House, sought and won election not to the Eastern

House among his own Ibos, but to the Western House in Yorubaland. And that was rather like Averell Harriman going into the Alabama legislature.

What Zik hoped to do was to prove that he was a truly national leader rather than a regional politician, and to crush by the sheer force of his personality and prestige the Yoruba splinter movement which was to grow into the hated Action Group. Although Zik's presence unquestionably encouraged dissident Yorubas sufficiently to make the N.C.N.C. the official Opposition in the West, Awolowo was able to deny him a portfolio on the regional level.

Zik then found himself faced with a revolt from Eyo Ita, his satrap premier in Enugu, who refused to let Zik run the region by long-distance telephone from Ibadan. Zik resigned his seat in the Western assembly, flew back to Enugu and presented the rebels with typed letters of resignation. When they balked, Zik expelled Ita and his cohorts from the N.C.N.C. 'for life with ignominy' and himself took over as regional premier. Ita's rump, in alliance with the Action Group, now forms the Opposition in the East. Barely had the Eyo Ita business died down when Zik was faced with a rebellion staged by the N.C.N.C.'s two federal ministers, K. O. Mbadiwe and Chief Kolawole Balogun, who led a 'get Zik' movement when the Premier called for a change in the party's constitution to allow him to appoint all officers (all this is a good indication of Ibo individualism, one of the most striking characteristics of the tribe, which is in strong contrast to the respect given by Hausa and Yoruba alike to 'big men' and chiefs).

Zik won again, booted Mbadiwe and Balogun out of the party (Balogun has since been readmitted after apologizing to Zik), and forced them to resign their portfolios. Then came the African Continental Bank scandal.

Zik has ever been the astute businessman as well as the clever politician. He controls more than a dozen enterprises ranging from newspapers to trucking firms with an estimated net worth of more than £500,000. He set up the African Continental Bank ostensibly to compete with foreign (British) banks. A tribunal established by the British government to investigate alleged misconduct in the affairs of the African Continental Bank reported that Zik's 'conduct in the matter has fallen short of the expectations of honest, reasonable people'. While denying both the findings and the jurisdiction of the tribunal, Zik resigned and called a new election. He received an overwhelming number of votes, Eyo Ita alone of the nine regional and federal ministers who had opposed him was returned, and the N.C.N.C. gained a smashing victory.

In contrast to Awolowo, the exponent of regional autonomy and federalism, Zik, who holds honorary doctorates from several universities and has written four books on African affairs, believes strongly in a powerful unitary form of government over a number of small, weak states. At the head of such a government, of course, he sees no one but Zik. The enmity incurred among the Northern People's Congress, the governing group of the Muslim North, against Awolowo's campaign to break up the North into smaller states gave Zik his chance. Despite the fact that he was allied on the regional political level with the Northern Elements Progressive Union, the bitter foe of the N.P.C., Zik went into alliance with the N.P.C. on the national level to defeat Awolowo's Action Group in the 1959 federal elections, presumably hoping that the Sardauna of Sokoto might give him the nod over Balewa as federal prime minister. As the winner of the largest number of seats, the N.P.C. was invited to form a government. A coalition was arranged with the N.C.N.C. and Balewa again became prime minister. Zik had to satisfy himself with the largely honorific job of president of the forty-four-member Senate, the federal upper house, a post which he gave up last year to become the first black African Governor-General in the history of the British Commonwealth.

Azikiwe is a charming, magnetic and physically attractive man who still likes to referee a boxing match or play a vigorous game of table tennis. He has an explosive temper and in the old days was given to verbal excesses, such as calling Action Group supporters 'agents provocateurs, arch-tribalists, opportunists and careerists'. He has a massive, monolithic dignity and, although vain about his political accomplishments, lives a quiet and ascetic life. Unlike Awolowo, whose speeches are dull but whose planning capacity is practically unlimited, Zik is a brilliant demagogue but a bad organizer. The Ibo leader's fluency in Nigeria's three major languages and several of the dialects, in addition to his experience in two regional assemblies and the federal house, lends substance to his claim to be the only Nigerian leader of truly national stature.

Zik believes that Africa is entering into a period of economic reconstruction and cultural rebirth. After that he hopes that the free nations of the continent will make a political union and use their power to obtain civil rights for coloured minorities in other parts of the world, particularly in South Africa. Although he has strong ties with the

United States (he has a son at Harvard), Azikiwe maintains that Nigeria should follow a neutralist foreign policy (no regional public funds have been spent on French goods and services since the second atomic explosion in the Sahara) which would allow her freedom of action. As to his personal political future, Zik shrugs his shoulders: 'I've still got a few tricks left in my bag.' At fifty-six Azikiwe is at the height of his powers and one wonders if he will be content, after years of struggle, to find himself not only denied Pan-African leadership by Nkrumah but relegated to a position of strictly titular authority in his own country.

A six-car ferry huffed us across the Niger, past a sandbank bare except for the hut of a solitary naked fisherman. The current was gentle and the wind, freed from the tentacles of the forest, blew fresh and cool. A Volkswagen microbus belonging to a drug firm treated us to calypso music of a frenzied decibel rating and the captain came down off his bridge to dance a High-Life on the sun-warped deck with a generously proportioned mammy. Straw-roofed sampans slipped downstream with the current and dug-outs equipped with outboard motors taxied pedestrians across to the other side. Onitsha, the great Ibo town on the east bank, is a jostling, squalid, education-hungry town which boasts a new and extensive 3,000-stall market (built at a cost of £600,000) in which it is said one can buy anything from a cashmere sweater to a Spitfire landing gear. This mass of hovels contains no less than twelve secondary schools and it was the women of Onitsha who rioted most vigorously against Zik in 1957 when the Eastern government, which had followed the West's lead in instituting free primary education, had to reimpose fees or face bankruptcy.

Enugu, the regional capital, lies sixty miles to the east of Onitsha, over a tarred road which slithers through the forests like a black snake. The city is an artificial one, built around West Africa's only major coal mines, which began production in 1916. Reserves of the four producing Enugu mines total 72 million tons, enough to keep them going at the current rate of production for 100 years. Another 170 million tons in the Northern Region are not being exploited. Enugu produces more than 700,000 tons per year, of which 10 per cent is exported to Ghana. Of the remainder, the railways take half and the Electricity Corporation 20 per cent. One of the shafts is two miles long and the mines employ about 8,000 workers. There was serious labour trouble in 1949, nationalists fanned the embers for political reasons, and twenty-one were killed when the police opened fire on the strikers.

At a moment when diesel conversion of the railways threatens to ruin the mines, discovery of a new process promises new prosperity for the East. Although Nigeria contains large iron ore deposits (49 million tons near Enugu and 210 million tons near Lokoja in the Northern Region), the grade is too low (40 per cent) and the transportation difficulties too many to make export profitable. Nigerian coal does not coke, so there was no chance of developing the two resources locally. But recent German experiments indicate that, under a new method, Nigerian coal can be made to coke: if so, Nigeria may become the first African steel producer.

Enugu nestles in the heavily cultivated, erosion-scarred hills which produce the coal but the atmosphere of the ugly little concrete houses set amid green lawns and exuberant flowers (seventy-three inches of rain per year) is more governmental than industrial. Dominating this town of 80,000 both physically and symbolically is the Eastern House of Assembly and its attendant ministries. The House of Assembly, with its flat-topped bell tower and its roof of dull, metallic red, looks rather like an old-time battleship under full steam while the ministries, built around a central court, are 'Double-storeyed Imperial' with their high-ceilinged rooms, overhead fans, swinging doors of the bar-room variety, and over-sized desks draped with green baize. This will soon be a thing of the past: the Eastern government is erecting a twenty-storey ministerial block and a new House of Assembly as part of its £16·6 million four-year development plan. The Ibos can't stand having the Yorubas 'put one over on them' and they brought in free primary education and children's medical care (1959) and this year set up a television station. As the school debacle showed, the East just does not have the money to compete with the West (the Eastern budget for 1959–60 provided £12·4 million for recurrent expenses and £6·3 million for capital development). To bridge the gap they have evolved an energetic community development programme which finds villagers providing free labour to build roads, bridges, waterpoints, schools, hospitals, maternity centres, lorry parks, markets, fish ponds, literacy centres and plantations. One would have thought that the money being used on the grandiose ministerial skyscraper might have been better applied in such schemes.

In the old office block I caught porcine, hard-working M. I. Okpara, the man to whom Zik has entrusted the East. Mike Okpara, who at thirty-nine is the youngest major political figure in Nigeria, is a former medical officer whose hobby is photography. Okpara was born at

Bende and is an Owerri Ibo (the Ibos are divided between the Onitsha and the Owerri; they speak different dialects and there is little love lost between them). After several years as a government medical officer and a bit of private practice, Okpara went into politics and became Zik's Minister of Production.

Mike Okpara is one of the few Africans I've met who seems to have a clear idea of what an under-developed country has to do to get itself on its feet. Most African leaders say 'yes, we want foreign investment but we also want state control, staff guarantees and local participation'. Okpara, whose pleasant home on the outskirts of Enugu is overrun with children and hangers-on, describes himself as a Fabian Socialist but adds that 'socialism in Africa is just a dream'. 'We need capital,' he adds, 'and we can't wait for it to come to us. We're going to lay traps for it, the way Porto Rico has done. We'll give foreign investors every break in the world, including some freedom from taxation. Industries create a chain reaction and we'll make our money by taxing the secondary industries which grow up around the original investors. You can tell American businessmen this: name your terms and we'll work something out.' He has already succeeded in bringing a 200,000-ton capacity cement factory to the East.

The first American we met in Enugu, however, was not a businessman but red-haired Ernest Montgomery, the U.S.I.S. officer. We had heard about Montgomery in Monrovia, where he had the reputation for being one of the few white people the Liberians really liked. He had arrived in Liberia to find an atmosphere of racial distrust, but soon had an enthusiastic softball league going in which animosities of whites and blacks alike were redirected at the eternal scapegoat, the umpire (who was black). Monty had an infectious enthusiasm for Africa and Africans (he was a bachelor) and before we knew it we were hauled off to a party which he was throwing for the visiting American Negro songstress Camilla Williams. Miss Williams, who is a dish and knows how to get an audience on her side, did more for Ibo-American relations in half an hour than a flock of aid programmes.

At the party I met a man of whom more will be heard. He is thirty-year-old Michael E. Ogon, 'Shotgun' to his friends. Mike Ogon, who stands about five-five and weighs in above the 200 mark, has a quick, cherubic smile, an effervescent personality and hands like Smithfield hams, which he is said to employ on political opponents with a remarkable degree of success. In his official biography, Mike lists his pre-political occupation (he is Eastern government Chief Whip) as 'proprietor of schools'. His hobbies, he says, are 'shooting and reading of political literature'. Ogon has the rough equivalent of a high school education and although he is a strong N.C.N.C. man, is not an Ibo. He comes from Ogoja, the East's most remote and primitive district, which lies between the headwaters of the Cross River and the Cameroons highlands.

Another N.C.N.C. stalwart worthy of note is Chief Festus Okotie-Eboh, the forty-eight-year-old federal Minister of Finance. He has a remarkable background for an economist, being a chiropodist by profession. Chief Festus, who is tall, fat and jovial and likes to wear a straw boater complete with large ostrich feather, is a Westerner from Warri, in the Niger delta, and was educated at Baptist schools in Sapele. He is national treasurer of the N.C.N.C. and favours an *agbada* on which are emblazoned portraits of . . . Okotie-Eboh! He is a shrewd man and the crowd loves him, greeting him with cries which, when literally translated, mean 'Extravagant man!', an appellation which he well deserves. Okotie-Eboh's defeated opponent bitterly complained after the 1959 federal elections that Chief Festus had distributed sums of money, pieces of cloth, mosquito net, food, drinks and cigarettes to woo Benin River voters. If so, he was highly successful.

We got up to the dew-dipped cool which mercifully precedes the burning glare of the Nigerian mid-day and went to have a quick look at six-year-old Queen's School, the only government girls' secondary school in the region, and at the Enugu branch of the Nigerian College of Arts, Science and Technology.

Queen's School, whose white brick buildings sit on a slow rise above the town, can handle only about 150 students and the principal, a doughty lady with a firm jaw, said she had had 3,200 applications for the thirty places available for the coming year. The girls, she said, preferred to come to the government school rather than to the missionary institutions because fewer chores are expected of them here. One of the problems was to make sure that the girl admitted to the school was the same one who had passed the entrance examination since places were frequently bought and sold among the education-hungry Ibos. Zik's daughter is a student and, so we were told, a brilliant one.

The dormitories and classrooms of the Arts, Science and Technical College stand on the hills adjoining Queen's College. This is one of three branches (the others are at Ibadan and Zaria) and the aim is to provide post-secondary school instruction in fields as various as engineering and portrait painting. There are over 300 students at the Enugu branch, which specializes in estate management, town planning and land survey (Ibadan handles administration, pharmacy and accounting, while Zaria is responsible for engineering, architecture, education and fine arts), and, at the time of our visit, only one of the twenty-two members of the faculty was a Nigerian. Enugu is both the newest (none were in operation before 1954) and the smallest of the three branches. Like the others, it has suffered from its somewhat vague position on the educational ladder. Most Nigerians would sell their souls for a university education (the nation has about 2,000 graduates, about 25 per cent of them from American universities, and another 5,000 are now studying in England and the United States) and they are chary of substitutes. The three technical colleges, which have a combined enrolment of over 1,000, tend to get the failures and the students regard the colleges as a step towards Ibadan or an English education. As a result, the three branches have neither the staff nor the scholars to compare with Ibadan and they have been shot through with discipline problems.

Zik has long felt that Nigeria in general and the East in particular needs another university and now steps are being taken to create one on a 1,000-acre plot in a bowl of hills on the edge of a broad plain at Nsukka, forty miles north of Enugu. Zik, who owns a summer home there, envisages a university with 3,000 students, a quarter of them women. It will be patterned after American land grant universities, with emphasis on agriculture, engineering, science and business, in addition to a liberal arts programme. The university's curriculum will give special attention to problems created in the environment of Nigeria and Africa, and major fields of effort will be Nigerian history, African languages and the geography, economic history, literature and ethnography of the continent. The plans are drawn but just now Nsukka is mostly ant-hills and forests instead of 240-man residence halls.

Azikiwe says that he wants the university at Nsukka, which is the remote north-west of the region, because he hopes it will become a university not only for the East but for the entire country. It will be called, in fact, the University of Nigeria, although (unlike Ibadan which is a federal institution) it will be financed by the Eastern Region which will donate 25 per cent of its palm oil and copra profits; this should add up to £5 million by 1965. Two Michigan State College educators and the Vice-Chancellor of the University of Exeter have suggested that some forty Nigerians who already have advanced degrees should be sent abroad to train to become the nucleus of the new university's staff. Some £2 million is now available for the project and the university should be fully functioning by 1965. It will be a nice political feather in Zik's cap but will by no means solve all the region's educational problems.

As recently as 1956, 75 per cent of the East's primary teachers were untrained and, in one recent year, there were 10,000 candidates for 150 government secondary school places. Although school attendance has risen from the 1956 figure of 52 per cent, the knotty problem of how to provide free primary education for the masses remains. The East has reached the point where there are no fees for the first grade and reduced tuitions for Standard II to IV, but it does not have the revenue to pay out the £26 million which free primary education cost the West between 1955 and 1960.

OBONG AND NTOE

From Enugu we drove south towards Port Harcourt and Calabar, past bicyclists labouring into Onitsha, the frames of their vehicles laden with great gourds of palm wine, grass stuffed into the necks to act as a stopper. The bicyclists headed the other way had empty gourds and belted along at breakneck speed under the cool canopy of the forest. Port Harcourt is an artificial and ugly town of 75,000 (like Enugu, it did not exist before 1914), made up mostly of concrete government housing and four-storeyed piles of yellow cement which are the homes of prosperous African and Lebanese traders. Like Indian mansions on the East Coast, they are pretentious, gardenless and one home may house as many as fifty relatives and hangers-on.

Port Harcourt is Nigeria's second port, handling about 20 per cent (1·1 million tons) of the country's total trade, a percentage which will climb this year with the opening of three new berths built at a cost of £4 million. The port is forty-one miles from the sea on the Bonny River, it gets ninety-four inches of rain per year and is reputed to possess one prostitute for every ten inhabitants, which seems an equitable ratio. Completion of the 400-mile rail extension to Maiduguri in 1963 will bring more tonnage through Port Harcourt and expand the oil boom which it is now experiencing. Shell began its oil search in 1937 and spent £40 million before making a sizable strike in the delta area. Production began in 1958 with 230,000 tons worth £1 million. The company invested another £20 million in 1959 and this year's exports are expected to total 1·2 million tons worth £5·3 million. In 1959 Shell also struck oil 'in considerable quantity' at Ughelli in the Western Region, where Mobil is also prospecting. Further developments of these finds (production is expected to reach 10 million tons by 1970, putting Nigeria among the world's top ten oil producers) coupled with exploitation of natural gas pockets could mean a bright economic future for Nigeria.

And then we were off through Ibibio country to Calabar. The Ibibios are a curious people, practisers of ju-ju, believers in witches, a shadow-tribe living midway between Harvester tractors and human sacrifice in forest country where giant cobwebs hang in lacy mantillas among the telephone wires. Ibibioland appears to be sparsely populated because of the forest but trails lead off from the main road every hundred yards and suddenly there will be a clearing in the forest and a market jammed with women dressed in brightly coloured Dutch wax prints and head-ties, their skin hennaed to a seductive orange shade. There are small glades beside the road and here you find the life-sized statues which the Ibibio raise over the graves of their more distinguished ancestors. The carvings are rigid, stylized and the features of the statues appear more European than African. The persons represented are usually substantial citizens such as clerks, ministers of the gospel and railway engineers. Often behind the statues there will be a ju-ju shrine consisting of a screen of palm matting or an arch of leaves. Attached to this are fetishes: a human skull or hand, some feathers, an animal skin, a belt buckle, a calabash, a feather, some rags, an empty aspirin bottle. The ground in front of the shrine will be packed hard by generations of bare feet, cleanly swept, and sometimes the presence of a bit of dried blood and a few bones will indicate that the departed has recently had a chicken sacrificed to his memory.

The Ibibios and their cousins, the Efiks, who live east of the Cross River, have always had a penchant for ju-ju palaver. In 1906 after a lost medical officer was killed and eaten on the instructions of the so-called Long Ju-Ju of Aro-Chuko, the British launched an expedition which killed many of the fetish priests and destroyed hundreds of ju-ju shrines. But who is to say what goes on today in the noon-day twilight of these forest paths?

In 1946 the police established that there had been 157 murders by human-leopards directed by the Idiong Society. Some of the murders were committed to obtain human parts for medicine, others because it was felt that the local courts, either through corruption or ignorance, were allowing wrongdoers to escape punishment. The leopard men dress in skins and wear razor-sharp steel claws. After making a kill, they mutilate the body and leave leopard tracks around. Police became suspicious when they noticed that the tracks did not correspond to a real leopard's stride. Nor did they believe that a leopard, no matter how skilful, could remove a victim's shorts, excise some skin and flesh, cut off a man's head and wrap it neatly in a shirt. Seventy-seven were hanged. But that was seventeen years ago. Surely nothing like this happens any more: in 1956 an airliner crashed on the fringes of Ibibio country. Tribesmen were the first to reach the wreck and, when the police arrived, the bodies of six of the fifteen passengers were headless. In 1960 the police arrested twenty-seven tribesmen from Calabar on charges of killing and eating three of their neighbours. Nigeria is changing but the old ways die hard.

At Oron we managed to get our car aboard the Elder Dempster ferry which makes the three-hour run up the Cross River to Calabar. The Cross is one of the great highways into an interior of Africa and as you lean on the rail to catch the breeze of the ship's movement you wonder how many Africans, chanting their death songs, sailed down this river packed belly-to-back beneath a slaver's deck. How many bodies, white and black, lie rotting in the mud under the exposed bleached bones of the mangrove roots which line the shore?

Coming downstream with the tide are the hollowed log canoes of the Kalabari and Efik. They are covered with straw matting and some have simple sails. They are running goods to the Spanish island of Fernando Po. In the old days they took male slaves for the cocoa fields and girls for the brothels. What do they carry now? Nobody really knows but they come back with cases of Spanish brandy, green wine and English cigarettes which you can buy in Calabar at half the Lagos price. So their outgoing cargoes must be of some value. Perhaps a girl or two? It's quite possible because Kalabari and Efik women are famed for their beauty from Kano to Accra.

Although none of these Cross River tribes are known for their fighting ability they can be vicious as rattlers. In 1950 the Kalabari and the Okrika tribes clashed in a dispute over fishing rights in which more than a hundred were killed. The Kalabaris were required to pay a fine of £17,800 to the injured parties and the Okrika were so flush that not a sober breath was drawn on the Cross for weeks.

Calabar is announced by the flash of the sun off the tin roofs of the trading companies and then, off to port, lies Parrot Island where the Efik chiefs sacrificed albino slaves when trade with the Europeans was bad. Soon you can see reflected in the oily water the steeples of the Catholic Cathedral and the Presbyterian Church and make out the barrels of palm oil stacked on the beach. At Seven Fathom Point the steamer reverses her engines, snubs her hawsers, and there begins a general melée between those wishing to get off and the crowd on the jetty anxious to board.

Although a lively, almost gay sense of evil seems to pervade the place, all Calabar's past is not dark. In addition to characters like the palm oil ruffian who blinded one of his crew by painting him with whitewash while he lay ill, the Cross River is also Mary Slessor's country and generations will remember her name.

Ma—as the Efiks called her—was one of those no-nonsense characters with whom the Africans get on so well. She worked as a child-labourer in a Dundee jute factory, came out to the Cross River in 1876 at the age of twenty-eight as a Presbyterian missionary. She marched through ju-ju country in a hoop skirt and was not afraid to slap a cannibal chief when he talked sharply to her. Her mission in life was to save twins. In many parts of Africa twins were and to a certain extent still are regarded with abhorrence (although some tribes think twins are lucky). They reckon that a human can only have one child at a time, hence one of the twins is a devil, which means that the mother has slept with a devil. The usual remedy is to stuff twins head-first into a pot to die of suffocation and drive the mother into the bush to starve. Ma Slessor saved scores of twins and established them in a separate village. She learned to ride a bicycle at the age of fifty-six, climbed every tree around Calabar in an effort to work off the repressive atmosphere of the mission, worked in Nigeria for thirty-nine years, became an unofficial but highly respected magistrate of a native court and died in 1915 in the Cross River country which she loved. Her cure for dysentery: eat nothing but shortbread for a week.

The Efik tribe has controlled Calabar since the early eighteenth century when they split off from the Ibibios in a quarrel over an axe. One of the first Efik chiefs one meets when reading the old records is Tom Salt, famous for a cannibalistic sweet tooth which nothing but white men's flesh could satisfy. He was deposed by Duke Ephraim, who looms so large in Antera Duke's diary. The Duke's usual costume was a loin cloth and a round hat of gold lace but he sometimes donned a set of pink tights presented to him by a whimsical trader. He had 200 wives; and a skull mounted on a baton and carried by a small boy preceded him on his journeys. His slaves went docilely to their executions because he promised them they would be reincarnated as white men. The parties staged by the Efik chiefs for visiting captains, complete with beheadings, gallons of gin and nose-tingling palm oil chop or peanut stew (both still enjoyed in Lagos restaurants), went on all night and were as hard on health as the climate. James Grant, an English slaver who lived through an enforced residence at Calabar when the captain and entire crew of his ship died of fever, attributed his good health to 'abstinence from intoxicating liquor, and other excesses, as well as not sleeping in the dew during the night; which those who attended nightly dances on shore usually did, after being heated with spirits, and were consequently soon carried off.'

The Efiks had the nice trick of killing their victims by jamming chilli peppers up the nose, eyes, ears and anus. They also liked to stake them out at low tide and then leave them to be eaten by crocodiles as the water rose. Wives of a dead chief had their limbs broken and then were buried alive in the grave. The Efik chiefs charged the slavers and later (the slave trade was wiped out in Calabar by 1839) the traders a regular fee called 'comey' based either on the tonnage of the ship or the size and value of the cargo they picked up. The whites brought coral, copper bowls, glassware, beads from Rouen, French brandy, silk scarves, umbrellas, ox-horn drinking cups, pewter tankards, iron bars, copper wire, brass bells, cowrie shells, rings, scarlet cloth, cutlasses, firearms, thread, cloth caps, gin, shirts, sugar, salt, shoes and rugs. These they traded for slaves, gold dust, pepper, ivory, live monkeys, beeswax, gum arabic, palm oil, ostrich and parrot feathers, cotton cloth and mahogany.

Calabar has changed only superficially in the two hundred years since James Grant's time. There are many people of mixed blood to bear testimony to the lusty character of the old days and, when one sees the masts of steamers moving slowly above the trees which cloak these tropical fjords, it is easy to imagine sailors on the hidden decks raising roofs of thatch to shut out the killing sun. As we lay gasping for air under our mosquito nets, we could hear the throb of the drums from Duke Town at the bottom of the hill. They went on all night and more than one reveller must have ended up sleeping in the dew. Efik mothers still bathe their children in water containing an electric eel which, as everybody knows, prevents the youngster from being struck by lightning when the thunder grumbles over the green hills. Efik girls are still secluded and fattened before marriage and ordeal by poison, I was told, still takes place. You are in a bad way if a prominent Kalabari blows *egbo* (a magical dust) on you, for no self-respecting local will have anything to do with you until the quarrel is resolved.

We called on the local administrator, who lives in a corrugated iron box set on stilts, with an outside staircase and shutters hinged at the top. This is also the residence of the ghost of Sir Roger Casement who, after exposing the horrors of the Belgian rubber plantations in the Congo Free State, was posted to Calabar as consul. His ghost is a sad and gloomy spectre who gets along well with children but is hell on policemen. It is his commendable practice to seize any visiting law officer by the feet and drag him out of bed in the middle of the night.

Two chiefs rule in Calabar and one is Archibong V, Obong (king) of the Efiks. We found the royal palace in the depths of Duke Town, where there were windowless 'homes' too small to stand in. Archibong's palace was of mud, single-storeyed and the front door was so narrow that one had to turn sideways to enter, a good defensive arrangement. The Obong is in his nineties, which means he can remember the days when men were buried alive whenever a treaty was signed. Thus the signers knew that whoever broke the treaty first (it was apparently assumed that it would be broken) would be haunted by the dead men. Archibong was not looking his best. He wore a grey wool union suit and around his loins was a black and gold sarong. He sported argyle socks which were pulled up and gartered over the union suit. Sandals, a green shawl around his shoulders and a terry cloth towel over his head completed the regal attire. He said he was chilly, although the temperature and humidity were enough to dissolve an Egyptian. After an exchange of compliments we reached a conversational impasse and Archibong gave his old man's sigh. I asked him, through a young nephew attired in a purple suit who acted as interpreter, what he thought the chances were for the survival of the chieftaincy in an independent Nigeria. The old man mumbled for a few minutes. 'What did he say?' I asked the nephew. 'He says he thought you were somebody else.' I said my farewells and left Archibong moodily tugging at his shawl while his nephew thumbed through a tract by Dr. Azikiwe.

Ika Ika Oqua II, Ntoe of the Quas and Archibong's rival, is quite a different cup of tea. His house in Big Qua Town, on the north side of Calabar, was festooned with red, white and blue pennants and seemed on the verge of steaming down the river and out to sea. The double-storeyed structure had bay windows and was built of cement blocks painted to simulate bricks. The entrance was guarded by two small

591

brass cannon and a large drum. The pennants had been put up to welcome him home from the London constitutional conference of 1958 and he had liked them so much he left them hanging. The Quas were the original inhabitants of Calabar and they regard the Obong's Efiks in the same light as Boston's old families do the Irish.

Ika Ika has a few words of English and he wore a white short-sleeved shirt outside trousers of the same colour. No shoes. He quickly produced an album of pictures from London: Ika Ika talking with the Colonial Secretary, Ika Ika at a cocktail party, Ika Ika boarding a tube train. His performance at the conference was certainly well documented. His palace was chock full of finery: kewpie dolls of the type won at shooting galleries, mezzotints, china wash-basins, a bishop's throne, ceremonial swords, more photographs of Ika Ika at various high points in his career, a porcelain chamber pot with rosebuds rampant, at least a dozen clocks showing as many hours, carved cabinets and stools, a yellow silk dressing-gown, a car tyre, a birdcage (no occupant), a bicycle, a bedstead and a couple of spears.

The Ntoe broke out a couple of beers and showed me two chairs he had bought in London. They were vaguely oriental in design and inlaid with mother-of-pearl. The salesman, he said, had assured him that they once stood in Buckingham Palace. We talked a little politics and he complained that the times were changing too quickly. The young men no longer had any respect for their elders. I commiserated with him and told him we also had our Angry Young Men, a fact which seemed to surprise him. Then he posed for a photograph for the American supporters of the Qua faction.

Leaving Ika Ika surrounded by chamber pots, we drove out of Calabar to the habitat of *Elaeis Guineensis*. This is not another native monarch but the Latin tag for the oil palm, which provides 80 per cent of Eastern Nigeria's income. Nigeria turns out 50 per cent of the world's kernels, 30 per cent of its palm oil and is the largest exporter of the two commodities. Almost all of the oil and half of the kernels come from the East. The West, where prosperity has raised domestic consumption levels, provides the rest. The oil palm requires not less than sixty inches of rain spread over eight months and hence is an ideal crop for the dank forests of the south. Like coconut, groundnut, cottonseed, soya, sunflower, sesame and olive oil (and unlike the oils of linseed, castor, rapeseed and tung), palm oil is edible, although it must be high grade with a low free fatty acid content. Palm oil and coconut oil are the only dual purpose oils which can either be eaten or used industrially. Palm wine tapped from the tree decreases its yield but is rich in B complex vitamins.

Most people say that the oil palm is indigenous to Nigeria but one school of thought led by the eminent O. F. Cook, an American expert, insists that it was introduced from Brazil by the Portuguese. The O. F. Cooks of the world are the sort of people who tell children there is no Santa Claus. A pox on the O. F. Cooks. The Nigerians say that the oil palm is theirs and it is only good manners to agree.

The oil palm has a long, skinny trunk, a clump of fronds at the top and, in the middle of these, a spiny growth the size of a medicine ball. Clustered here are the acorn-sized red fruit which yield the oil to make candles, soap and margarine. The nuts are crushed locally but the kernels, which are the most valuable part, are shipped abroad for processing. The oil is either crushed out by hand in primitive hand-presses, by semi-mechanized methods at regional co-op mills or at the factories of big firms like Lever Brothers in Calabar. The hand system (foot would be more accurate: the nuts are placed in a canoe and the family climbs in and stamps) yields about 45 per cent of the oil, the hand-presses get about 60 per cent, the co-op mills about 85 per cent and modern factories can get 93 per cent. Of Nigeria's 125 co-op mills (there are 5,000 hand-presses), 100 are in the East. The women oppose use of the mills because they do the work under the traditional system and receive a large part of the profits. The mills are badly sited and are unable to get a regular and even supply of the fruit because native custom demands that all the cutting be done on one day of the month. Hence the mills stand idle for many days, then are swamped with heaps of fruit, much of it unripe, a large proportion of which spoils before it can be processed. Custom also forbids the cutting down and replacement of old and unproductive trees. Nigerians are loth to improve on God's work by setting up communal plantations, which is the only economic way to supply a factory. And they insist on adulterating the oil to such an extent that it gums up the soap manufacturers' machinery. This is not calculated to enhance the reputation of Nigerian palm oil and the regional government periodically makes impassioned pleas to the forest gentry to cease and desist. They recognize this as another N.C.N.C. plot to keep them poor and go right on their merry ways.

The Lever Brothers factory was surrounded by a beautifully laid-out plantation (only 7 per cent of Nigeria's palm exports come from plantations) with each section tagged for date of planting and yield.

The young man who showed us around had worked in Malaya. He said the Malays were more industrious, intelligent and troublesome; the Africans were generally good-humoured and, if supervised, did a slow but efficient job. He said that WAIFOR (West African Institute for Palm Oil Research) was engaged in research to produce a thinner-skinned and hence more valuable nut, and to develop a dwarf palm which would reduce the number of Nigerians who splatter themselves over the landscape in falls from trees. But nobody has figured out how to invent honesty.

Before leaving Calabar we paid a visit to Professor Eyo Ita's West African People's Institute. The school seemed on the verge of physical collapse but so keen is the Easterner's thirst for education that it has a capacity enrolment. In 1954 the Western Region made primary education free and Zik, who personally and politically can't stand having Awolowo ahead of him, followed suit in 1957, perhaps overlooking the fact that the West has the cocoa money to pay for such amenities. Primary school enrolment jumped from 775,000 to 1·2 million, 80 per cent of the school-age population, and Zik, who called the tune, found that he couldn't pay the piper, despite a tax increase and allocation of 40 per cent of the regional revenues to education. After one year, the six primary grades had to be put back on a fee basis (two sub-grades remained free), there were riots and a goodly number of cracked heads. In 1959 the East made a new start by eliminating fees for the first grade, at a cost of £450,000. Fees now are gradually being removed from the other grades at a cost of about £1,800,000.

Professor Ita, who is fifty-seven and a graduate of London and Columbia universities, was premier of the East until his break with Zik in 1953. As chief of the United National Independence Party, a group which wanted to divide the Eastern Region into two states, Ita was regional Opposition leader until 1957 when the Action Group's S. G. Inoku took over. Last year Ita made his peace with Zik, resigned from the U.N.I.P. and rejoined the N.C.N.C. The professor's educational theories are rather old-fashioned: he believes in character-training as well as academic learning, insists that his students do manual labour around the school. Outside, behind the school, the gentle little man showed us the rusting hulk of some paper-pulping machinery. He hoped to teach the boys to make their own paper but the machinery wouldn't work.

The nearby Hope Waddell School (the great Presbyterian outpost in West Africa), although austere, is in no danger of collapsing. Some of

Nigeria's most distinguished citizens (including both Zik and Eyo Ita) received their training here and each year the dour Scots who run it have to sift through 3,000 applications to select boys to fill their sixty vacancies. Hope Waddell has been in business for sixty-five years and, although some of the new government secondary schools are better equipped, it still has the knack of turning out good citizens as well as clever ones. It also has the best bookshop I saw between Dakar and Johannesburg.

Although the administration of Calabar is now in African hands, the European traders, whose predecessors were the first to come, are still very much in evidence. Leventis, John Holt, United Africa Company, Union Trading Company, Oil Rivers Company, all are still doing business. Even the jargon of the old days lingers on: cloth is measured in fathoms, palm oil in puncheons, time in bells; an office is a hulk, the kitchen is the galley, the floor is the deck (the Efik word for floor is *dek*), walls are bulkheads and the head of a firm is respectfully addressed as captain.

On our last night in Calabar we followed the strains of off-tune warbling to the corrugated iron shell of the Club, that little piece of space necessary to make an Englishman feel at home in the wilds. In contrast to every other British club in Africa, Calabar's, given over to commercials now that the English administration is ended, is loud, rollicking, almost a bit pathetic in its attempt to mimic the boisterous days of the dead past. In every other way it is typical of the hundreds of clubs which mark the white man's march across British Africa. It has its library, its billiard-room, its bar, its well-polished table covered with dog-eared six-months-old copies of *Tatler*, *Sphere* and *Illustrated London News*, its bound copies of *Punch*, the covers eaten by white ants. There are the silver cups recalling forgotten tennis tournaments and golf matches, the rattan chairs and the barefoot servants. The habitués listen to the seven o'clock Home News and swear about the weather. In the old days their lives were lusty; now they sit on bar stools carved to fit the bottoms of dead district commissioners (some monumental posteriors seem to have served on the Cross River), sip pink gins and sing about 'Ragtime Cowboy Joe' in cockney accents.

It is strange the attraction that Calabar and the Cross River have had for white men. The climate is miserable, the local people no more ingratiating than hundreds of other tribes. But come they did four hundred years ago and they're still coming. In the old days whites lived high and short lives, made and lost fortunes, stewed their brains in gin and, even when they had the chance to quit with money in the bank, most stayed on. One old palm-oil ruffian committed suicide rather than retire to England on a comfortable pension.

Perhaps it was the appeal of something so completely and totally evil that it exuded a strange and fascinating beauty of its own. Even the good deeds on this coast, like that Easter in 1884 when the native Christians celebrated their freedom from superstition by slaughtering all the once-sacred monitor lizards, have an evil and grotesque dimension. Despite Zik, free primary education and Moral Rearmament, there is a memory yet of the old Calabar which whispers on the quiet night wind. Africa does not forget so soon.

THE NORTH: SARDAUNA AND AMINU

As one drives north from Enugu, the forest slowly thins out into tsetse-ridden orchard bush, the sun gets brighter and the population thinner. In a few hours' time the dusty red road reaches the southern bank of the Benue, the Niger's largest tributary, and you know that you are well into the Northern Region.

Northern Nigeria, which stretches from the sands of the Sahara almost to the Niger delta, is as large as France and Germany combined and, with a population of 19 million (more people than Scandinavia), it is, with the exception of Egypt, the most populous territory in Africa. Three of its twelve provinces are as large as Ghana. As far as the Nigerian federation is concerned, the Northern Region comprises 75 per cent of the land mass and 55 per cent of the population.

Northerners are famous horsemen and wear quilted armour and chain mail, some of which is loot from the Crusades (the rest is imitation stuff made in the Sudan and in England). The North is great cattle country, because it is free of tsetse, and the beasts of the Lake Chad area have enormous horns honeycombed with air-pockets which serve the function of water-wings and enable them to swim as far as ten miles. The weather is blisteringly hot (120 degrees has been experienced) but lethal temperature variations of as much as 50 degrees within a few hours are not unknown and men have frozen to death at night after being fried during the day. Lake Chad, which is gradually drying up, has known frost, and hailstorms have been recorded. Northerners have been fighting men for hundreds of years and Hausa, Fulani, Kanuri, Tiv and Nupe tribesmen demonstrated during Wingate's second Chindit campaign in Burma, to the discomfiture of the Japanese, that this quality still remains. In Kano, the great commercial centre of the North, you are forbidden by law to pay more than £10 for a wife, although during the 1904 famine you could buy a child for two shillings. The region's coat of arms consists of a stallion and a rather dyspeptic camel holding a shield on which are embossed a cow, a goat and some maize stalks; an open Koran and a sword above the shield serve as warning to the infidel and the motto is 'Work and Worship'. Some Northern cities are a thousand years old and powerful kingdoms existed here before the Normans reached England. The North is virulently Muslim (844 destitute Northern pilgrims were repatriated from Mecca in one two-month period in 1959) and its people are, for the most part, Sudanic rather than Negroid. Their lines of trade, conquest and culture, before the British reversed these lines with an imposed unity, stretched not southward to the Atlantic but north across the Sahara to the Mediterranean and eastward to the Nile Valley.

But it would be a mistake to think of the North as a homogeneous whole. The dominant group are the Hausa, who number some six million. It is thought that they migrated slowly, perhaps from the Mediterranean to the Senegal and then on down the Niger valley, arriving in Nigeria about the thirteenth century. About a century later they became familiar with a rudimentary form of Islam but only fire and sword four centuries later were to make Islam what it is today in the North: not only a religion but a way of life. It is known that by 1452 there existed seven Hausa kingdoms (Biram, Zaria, Katsina, Kano, Rano, Gobir and Daura, called the *Hausa Bakwai*, or 'Hausa Seven') and seven kingdoms in which Hausa influence was important but not dominant. These were Zamfari, Kebbi, Nupe, Gwari, Ilorin, Borgu and Ghoorma, and they were called the *Banza Bakwai*, or the 'Bastard Seven'. Each of the *Hausa Bakwai* had a specific role to play: Biram, the senior state, was the political centre, Zaria handled the slave-catching, Katsina was the commercial hub, Kano and Rano were devoted to the industries, respectively, of dyeing and weaving, Gobir was the warrior state, and Daura was dedicated to trade. The Hausa language—which is probably of Berber origin—was reduced to writing at an early date but most records were destroyed in the Fulani uprising, an event which we will discuss later. The Hausa had, as has been mentioned, horses, chain mail and firearms; they also had walled cities, a well-organized fiscal system and a learned judiciary. It is this system of government, language and religious faith which have come to be characteristic of the Hausa people rather than any clear-cut ethnic differentiation from the surrounding tribes with whom they have heavily interbred.

The Hausa states were weakened by internal quarrelling and by successive invasions of Moors and Tuaregs from the west and north. They were also under more constant pressure in the east from the Kanem kingdom of Bornu, which for some years held the Hausa under a light yoke. The Kanuri, as the people of Bornu are called, are also devout Muslims and today they number some 1·5 million.

As Prince Henry of Portugal was laying his plans for the discovery of the world, a light-skinned people with long straight hair and thin noses entered the Hausa kingdoms as peaceful cattle nomads. These were the Fulani who, with three million people, are today the North's second most important tribe. No man knows whence they came. Some say that they are of the same Polynesian stock which colonized Madagascar; others maintain that they are descendants of the Zingari gypsies of Europe and trace their ultimate origin to India; a third school believes that they are one of the lost tribes of Israel while a fourth equates the Fulani to the Hyksos shepherd kings expelled from Egypt in 1630 B.C.

They entered Hausaland from the west, probably from the basin of the Senegal (where Fulani remnants live today) and, by the end of the sixteenth century, were spread from that river almost to the shores of Lake Chad. Two hundred years later every Hausa town had its Fulani quarter. Fulani religious leaders, who may have adopted Islam from their Hausa overlords, were famous throughout the land, and Fulani judges and generals were employed by the Hausa emirs. This happy state of affairs ended in 1802 when the pagan Hausa king of Gobir quarrelled with Othman dan Fodio, *shehu* or religious leader of the Fulani. Dan Fodio raised the standard of revolt and declared a *jihad* against pagan Hausa and those whose orthodoxy was not considered sufficient. This militant Muslim Luther gave flags to his fourteen chiefs (one had the nice name of Sambo) and, assuming the title of *Sarkin Mussulmi* (Commander of the Faithful), led the Fulani and the more orthodox Hausa into battle. What began as a religious reformist movement soon deteriorated into a scramble for slaves and loot as the Fulani hurled themselves against Bornu, whose Kanuri people had been Muslim since the eleventh century, when its borders stretched from the Nile to the Niger, from Fezzan to Lake Chad. The derivation of the name 'Bornu', it is interesting to note, may be from *Bahr Nuh* or 'Sea of Noah' and one wonders if this could be Lake Chad and if Ararat could be some lonely crag in the Tibesti Mountains. Bornu was once known as Kanem and its noble families, who still have Arab blood, were sending their sons to study in Cairo seven hundred years ago. Their ambassadors were known in Tripoli and the Bornu soldiery had firearms when many a European armoury was stacked with battle-axes and pikes.

It was a weak Bornu ruled by an indecisive emir which the Fulani attacked. But there arose in Bornu a leader as pious and resolute as dan Fodio. This was the Shehu Mohammed el Kanemi, a holy man born in Fezzan and educated in Egypt, who refused all titles save that of 'Servant of God'. The Shehu, a gentle person but one capable of ordering a mortal flogging of 400 strokes with a hippo-hide whip on suspicion of adultery during Ramadan, rallied Bornu and kept the Fulani at bay for twelve years until, on the death of dan Fodio in 1816, a truce was declared. Bornu was to be convulsed again, at the end of the nineteenth century, when Rabeh, foster-son of Zubeir Pasha, the great Sudanese slaver and friend of Chinese Gordon, occupied the country with a small but well-armed force of brigands. Rabeh held Bornu for seven years until he was defeated and killed by the French. Rabeh's son, Fad el Allah, held out for another year but the French caught up with him on a Friday. Since it was a holy day, Fad el Allah could not march; his piety cost him his life.

But if the Fulani were balked in Bornu, elsewhere they knew nothing but victories: by 1810 they had established on the ruins of all but one of the fourteen Hausa kingdoms new dynasties as powerful as the old (a holy man predicted at the outset of the rebellion that it would be successful and that the Fulani empire would last 100 years; the prophecy was wrong by seven months). The Fulani emirs owed an allegiance to the Sultan of Sokoto which was loose in secular matters, stronger in religious affairs. Dan Fodio returned to a life of contemplation and prayer, and split his kingdom between his brother and his son, Bello.

To Hausa, Kanuri and Fulani alike, the south of Nigeria was only a reserve of slaves, an area for loot and conquest. By the time the British arrived, their cavalry had pushed far south of the 'V' formed by the Niger and the Benue, and Fulani emirs, often supported by only a small band of retainers, ruled cities as close as sixty miles to the sea. Today the Northerners like to say that they would have dipped the Koran in the sea had the British not intervened. In point of fact, they had already extended themselves dangerously: their cavalry could neither live long nor operate effectively in the southern tsetse belt, the impetus of religious zeal was dissipated, and, as inevitably occurs with desert conquerors, the spoils of war and the vices of the city had dulled the fighting edge of the Fulani and their Hausa supporters.

The South, which with the exception of a few Yoruba states had no comparable culture of its own, accepted British occupation and Western ways fairly readily. Not so the North, whose people considered themselves to be vastly more civilized than the British. As late as 1901, the Sultan of Sokoto, *primus inter pares* of the Northern emirs, could write in reply to a friendly note from Lugard:

'From us to you. I do not consent that any one from you should ever dwell with us. I will never agree with you. I will have nothing ever to do with you. Between us and you there are no dealings except as between Mussulmans and Unbelievers, War, as God Almighty has enjoined on us. There is no power or strength save in God on high. This with salutations.'

A column of thirty-eight whites, seven hundred natives and four guns was able to smash Hausa-Fulani armies fifty times its size. Although the superiority of British weapons was unquestionably an important factor, such victories might not have been possible had the emirs had the unqualified support of their subjects. But their rule had grown both corrupt and harsh—punishments favoured in the North included tearing out fingernails with hot pincers, pounding limbs one by one in a mortar while the victim still lived, sealing men up alive within the city walls—and Hausa police had actually been in British service against their own kinsmen for forty years before the fall of Sokoto on March 15, 1903. One colourful diehard, the Emir of Kantagora, exhorted his followers to fight the British saying that they were fish (they came from the direction of the sea, advanced up the Niger and were colourless) and would die if they could be lured away from the river valleys. This warrior-prince, who later became a loyal servant of Britain, when asked by Lugard to give up slaving, replied: 'Can you stop a cat from mousing? When I die I shall be found with a slave between my teeth.' There is still a good deal of mousing going on today in Africa.

Fifty-six years to the day after the fall of Sokoto, the North became self-governing, while independence as a part of Nigeria came twenty months later. Today the Northerners, who 'rule out completely any idea of adopting a policy of neutrality in international affairs', are among the best friends the British have in the New Africa.

There are a number of reasons for this: Lugard, having defeated the emirs in battle, bolstered their authority through his policy of indirect rule, guaranteed their religion against Christian intrusion and trod softly on the slavery issue (slave-owners were not forced to give up their chattels unless the latter demanded their freedom, which usually was not the case). On the personal level, generations of British administrators (many remain today in the employ of the regional government) have got on better with the proud, courteous feudal barons of the North than with the sharper, more pushy peoples of the South. As we have mentioned before, this has had ill as well as good effects: as a result of indirect rule and the exclusion of the missions, democracy and education have come little and late to the North and the emirs recently awoke to the realization that, when the British left, Southerners would be the only Nigerians qualified to hold administrative posts not only on the federal level but in the North itself. It was largely at the insistence of Northern leaders that Britain saw to it that Nigeria developed as a federation rather than a unitary state, thus keeping the regional administration under Hausa-Fulani control.

Still, it is a noteworthy event in the New Africa when a black premier will say publicly as did Alhaji Sir Ahmadu Bello, the Sardauna of Sokoto, on the occasion of Northern autonomy, that 'for fifty-six years the British have been our instructors and our good friends; the people have been administered with honesty, justice and understanding'. Hell will freeze over before Zik comes out with a statement like that.

The Sardauna—his title is the rough equivalent of field marshal—is easily the most important Northern politician. He is a cheerful, hard-working giant of a man who sometimes drives his own DeSoto and has been known to work for seven years without taking a holiday. In bright green silk robe, red trousers, black and gold sleeves and twenty-four-foot white turban, he resembles some enormous and extravagantly plumed bird. Sir Ahmadu is a prince of the blood royal of Sokoto, a chief to whom the responsibilities of leadership come naturally. Although he does not suffer fools gladly and is every ebony inch an aristocrat, he has the reputation of being the most accessible of Nigeria's leaders. Sir Ahmadu is the great-great-grandson of Othman dan Fodio, the Fulani conqueror of the Hausa empire. The fifty-one-year-old leader was born in Sokoto, the Rome of the Fulani, and was educated there and at Katsina Training College (Katsina has an age-old reputation for being the intellectual centre of the North). This means that, in academic terms, he has had the equivalent of about a junior high school education. He has, of course, a vast store of the sort of knowledge one does not learn in a classroom.

It is said that when he was at school in Katsina, young Ahmadu travelled the three hundred miles from Sokoto on foot because the North had neither roads nor car. A more likely version is that he was carried on the shoulders of a slave.

After completing his education, he taught primary school for three years and served as a district headman for a time. In 1938 he was named Sardauna. He had been a strong candidate for the post of Sultan of Sokoto but, after a period of palace intrigue which so delights the Hausa heart, the job went to his aged uncle. Because he had been such a candidate it is said that for a while the Sardauna and his supporters went in fear of their lives. But the Sardauna prostrated himself barefoot before the Sultan, who is spiritual leader of all West African Muslims, and was accepted as his loyal vassal. The Sardauna became a member of the first Northern House of Representatives in 1952, was named premier of the North in 1954 and re-elected in 1956. He is, in addition, head of the Northern People's Congress which controls 112 of the 134 seats in the Northern House and is the senior partner in the coalition which runs the federal government.

Sir Ahmadu had never been outside Nigeria until he was thirty-nine but has travelled extensively since then. He has made three pilgrimages to Mecca and visited the U.S. and most of the countries of Europe and the Middle East. He represented the North at the various Nigerian constitutional conferences in London, where his contempt for the Southern politicians was barely concealed.

The Sardauna, who was a vigorous cricket and fives player in his youth, is a curious blend of old and new. While he remains essentially an aristocrat, his career in local government showed that he is also a shrewd and progressive administrator. He did much to improve conditions in local government (and for his efforts received the C.B.E.) and has always been active in charity work, particularly with the blind, who number some 200,000 Northerners (there are also 500,000 lepers in the region). His relations with the Christian missions, which are allowed to operate in pagan areas of the North (the region has about 13·8 million Muslims, 750,000 Christians and 4·5 million animists), have shown him to be broadminded as well as able.

Typical was an address which he made to the heads of Protestant missions at Jos in November 1958. The Premier stressed that differences of religion should not 'bar us from working together for the good of our people'. He said that 'the Christian holds a special place in the regard of Muslims throughout the world; if I add that in the past there have been occasions when we have sometimes felt that our regard was not reciprocated, I do so in the hope that you may understand that it is my fervent prayer that these differences can and will be overcome.' The Premier praised the missions for their educational efforts and described as 'baseless' complaints that the Northern government was retarding female education. He emphasized that 'our government is a government of Northerners, both Muslims and Christians', which is true: of the twenty members of the Executive Council at the time of the speech, four were Christians and seven were neither Hausa nor Fulani. 'We wish to allow all men to practise their religions as they wish,' he said, 'but we do not wish our young men to lose their respect for authority, whether that authority be their fathers, their village or district head or their chief.' In areas where a Muslim ruler found himself set above a Christian or animist population, the Sardauna said that the missionaries could play an important role by teaching their followers that differences in religion did not mean that they could flout secular authority.

Sir Ahmadu is just as level-headed when dealing with problems which have reduced other African political leaders to frothing at the mouth. When the Sudan expelled its British administrators, his government publicly invited expatriate officers to take up new careers in the North until such time as the region felt it had enough qualified people of its own. When independence came for Nigeria, he again asked Britons (he is particularly fond of Scots: 'In more than a geographical sense, they are the Northerners of Britain.') to stay at their jobs and there are more whites today in Northern Nigeria than in any other region. Unlike Nkrumah, who maintains that political freedom is the solution to all Africa's ills, the Sardauna has this to say about self-government: 'Let no one think that all our problems will disappear; they will still be with us and it is we who will have to solve them.'

The Sardauna has some reservations about democracy which the collapse of parliamentary government in the Sudan, with which the region has the closest of contacts, did nothing to dispel. This is easy to understand: Northerners have a sense of history; democracy is not to them the bright new plaything it is to the Southerners but an alien and imposed system which many believe to be inferior to their own system, which has the powerful advantage of being understood by both ruler and ruled, who combined to produce it. But the Sardauna is way 'left' of the regions' fifty-two emirs (twenty of these rulers are powerful enough to be termed 'first-class emirs'), although this is rather like saying he is 'left' of Metternich. He has a firm mental grip on what is possible in the North, however, as opposed to what is desirable. In another age he would have made a brilliant and benevolent despot. In this one, he must rank as one of the New Africa's most able statesmen, if only because he has kept his Northerners from leaping at the throats of the hated tribes of the South and, at the same time, has brought his own region along as quickly as possible in all spheres.

It may seem odd that the Sardauna, with his ability, interests, ambition and political power, has chosen to send Abubakar Tafawa Balewa to Lagos as federal prime minister rather than taking the post for himself, which he could easily do. But the Sardauna is too much of a Northern aristocrat to find pleasure in a self-imposed exile among unbelievers and even the post of premier of the North he regards apparently as just another public duty. The job he really wants is the one he missed before: Sultan of Sokoto. Now most of us have never heard of Sokoto, although it is twice the size of Holland and its sultan gets a larger salary (£6,000 plus a £3,000 establishment allowance) than either the regional premier or the federal prime minister, is the most important religious leader in the country and has secular authority over a vast area. To put it in Western terms, if you were an American Catholic would you rather be president or governor of California *and* Pope? The Sardauna is inclined towards the latter choice.

As the Sardauna is Northern Nigeria's Caesar, so would hollow-cheeked Aminu Kano be its Castro. Aminu Kano (most Northerners have only one name to which they, like Aminu, add the name of their birthplace, i.e., Joe Pittsburgh, Harry San Francisco; since many Northern towns are quite large, this results in a confusing multiplicity of 'surnames'), like the Sardauna, is a member of the Fulani aristocracy. Although he is not of noble blood, his clan (the Gyanawas) for centuries have been noted as Koranic scholars. The slight, fiery-eyed Fulani, who is forty, received his primary education in Kano and graduated from a Kaduna high school. After several years as a government education officer, he won a scholarship in 1946 to London University where he studied for a teacher's certificate. There he was 'made emphatically aware' of Northern Nigeria's political and social backwardness.

He came home in 1948 determined to do something about it. As a start he organized a teachers' trade union and agitated for higher standards and better pay. As Nigeria veered towards independence, Aminu Kano gave up his government job to found the Northern

Elements Progressive Union as a political alternative to the more autocratic N.P.C. Opposing the Sardauna at all was and still is a tricky business. But Aminu Kano's N.E.P.U. (sometimes called the Sawaba, of 'Freedom' Party) backed a programme which set even relatively liberal emirs to shaking their turbaned heads over cups of sweet tea. Wealthy Hausas learned with alarm that Aminu advocated a graduated income tax while the emirs (who like strong perfume and large rings, but are anything but effeminate) bristled when they heard that he demanded a lessening of their powers in favour of elected councils. He shocked conservative *muftis* by refusing to make his wife keep purdah and by advocating equal rights for women, who do not have a vote in the North. Shock turned to abhorrence as the young *mallam* (one learned in the Koran) pressed for land reform involving the dismemberment of feudal estates and the creation of peasants' cooperatives. Finally, in a move which brought down upon him the Sardauna's ire, Aminu Kano called for the break-up of the regions into small states in an attempt to discourage sectionalism and force the people of Nigeria to think of themselves as Nigerians, not as Northerners, Easterners or Westerners.

To N.E.P.U. flocked the North's disinherited (or those aware they were disinherited): the rabble of the cities, the more progressive women, some hard-pressed peasants and a few of the intellectual class. Aminu, who operates from the mud house in Kano in which he was born, now claims more than 100,000 members in some 2,000 branches, all in the North. In recent months, N.E.P.U. has shown signs of growing more powerful: it has gained and maintained control of seven big urban councils (including Kano's) and about a dozen rural councils; in alliance with Zik's N.C.N.C. it has won a few seats in both the Northern Assembly and the federal house.

It takes considerable courage to oppose the emirs on their home ground. Aminu Kano has been jailed twice and his followers (whom the contemptuous emirs call *yaniska*, which means 'sons of the wind', because many are rootless peasants) have been whipped through the streets of virtually every town in the North, usually on charges such as 'speaking disrespectfully of the emir', which is punishable by one hundred lashes and a year in jail. Said one British official staying on after independence: 'The emirs sometimes find it difficult to distinguish between the maintenance of law and order and the persecution of their political opponents.' But Aminu Kano is optimistic:

'We have tremendous hope for our future. Already, despite the persecution which we have suffered, our agitation has resulted in reforms within the emirates. We know that our work will be far from finished in ten years' time. We dream of a united Nigeria, democratic, powerful and proud. This is a worthy dream and, with God's help, we will make it so.'

What Aminu Kano is up against is an ultra-conservative Koranic society which neither understands nor believes in secular democracy. Working in his favour is the fact that the Hausa-Fulani people, who dominate the N.P.C., make up only about half of the population of the poor and backward Northern Region. The minorities, the smaller tribes who have been a helot class for generations, the Christians and the animists, are the raw materials on which a democratic movement can be based. Already it is these minority groups, most of which inhabit the Middle Belt area around the banks of the Niger and the Benue, who hold the bulk of the civil service posts in the North, since they are the only 'Northerners' with enough education to qualify. The real danger both to the aristocracy and to the North in general is not that Aminu Kano will succeed—he has been accused of being in the pay of Moscow, Washington and Cairo—but that he may fail utterly. Without the escape valve which N.E.P.U. provides for what for lack of a better term can be called the progressive members of the North's slowly stirring masses—an ugly situation, perhaps a peasant revolt, could take place. The political balance of the North is, to say the least, delicate. This is more understandable when one learns how short has been the North's political experience: until 1946 British governors 'legislated' by fiat in this immense area (of the region's twelve provinces, Bornu, the largest, is only a little smaller than England, and Katsina, the smallest, is six times the size of Northern Ireland). It was not until 1952 that the emirs, who had ruled alone, were compelled to consult (but not necessarily to abide by the advice of) Native Authority Councils. It was in these seventy-six N.A.s (there are also forty-one town councils and six hundred village councils) where the British first sought to bring democracy to the North by gradually introducing the elective principle. Now almost all councils have elected majorities and they control budgets ranging from a few thousand pounds to £2 million, run their own schools, water supplies, bus services and clinics, collect and appropriate their own revenues.

Regional political activity dates from 1951, when both the N.P.C. and N.E.P.U. were founded. The N.P.C. quickly demonstrated its power in 1956 by winning 109 of the 131 elective seats (four members were nominated) in the House of Assembly. Eleven went to the United Middle Belt Congress (largely a Christian-pagan organization), N.E.P.U. took six, one went to the Action Group and the rest to independents. The only real reversal suffered by the N.P.C. occurred in 1959 when Northern British Cameroons, which had been administered as an integral part of Bornu and Adamawa provinces, voted in a plebiscite to decide its political fate at a later date, rather than remaining with the North and Nigeria. In an unusual fit of pique, the Sardauna blamed the outcome of the plebiscite on British intrigue, a charge denied by United Nations observers. In a second plebiscite held in March of 1961, however, Northern British Cameroons reversed its earlier decision and voted for reintegration with Northern Nigeria, at the same time, Southern British Cameroons elected to join the Cameroun republic.

TIN AND PAGANS

At Makurdi the road to the North crosses the Benue on the railway bridge and the country slowly begins to rise. In a few hours' time the scrub thorn gives way to poplar and evergreens as you climb from 300 feet above sea level to the 4,000-foot Bauchi plateau, with green meadows, granite outcroppings and naked Birom pagans in G-strings guarding their scrawny flocks. These hill people—who once were head-hunters and are famed for the immensity of their alcoholic consumption—are smaller than the plainsmen, who raided them for slaves and pushed them up into these craggy highlands. Here the arrows of the pagans were effective, the horses of the Fulani were not and the battered tribes were able to keep their enemies at bay. Women go naked except for strategically placed bunches of leaves and the men wear penis-sheaths. These shy, simple people live in scattered villages surrounded by ramparts of cactus, know no chiefs and are organized on a kinship basis. They have few possessions, live on a millet porridge called *atcha*, and regard babies born feet first as unlucky. They are famed for their drummers who worship the moon and will not sell a drum because they believe the souls of dead drummers reside in their instruments. Now their plateau is the centre of the North's £7 million per year tin industry and the take-off point for the 400-mile railway extension which will tap the groundnut, cotton and cattle land of Bornu. The North contains six million of Nigeria's seven million cattle (the dwarf *muturu* are resistant to tsetse and can live in the South but they provide little meat and less milk), and fourteen million of its seventeen million sheep and goats. For lack of rail transport, cattle have had to be trekked south in the past, a gruelling journey in which weight losses of 100 pounds per steer have been recorded.

Because of the altitude, Jos, which is the commercial and mining centre of the plateau, has a magnificent climate which requires fires at night. The town is set in a circle of rocky, mimosa-covered hills and there are roses in the garden of Hill Station, where jaded administrators come to recoup from the muggy heat of the lowlands. There is an attractive little Anglican chapel (ourselves and the priest constituted the entire congregation at one vesper service) and a small but well-laid-out museum containing some fine examples of the Nok terracottas. These curious little figurines, named after the spot in Zaria province where they were discovered in 1931, are of high artistic merit and are quite unlike any other type of art in Africa. Their discovery indicates the existence of a Benue Valley civilization 2,500 years ago, which means that they are at least 1,000 years older than any other African art. This old continent still has some secrets to yield. We checked into the rest house (for some reason, they call cottages chalets all over Nigeria) and dropped down to the Plateau Club, which has everything but a swimming pool, which the shortage of water forbids. The faces of those of the five hundred members which we saw were glowing a bit at the news that Nigeria's tin production allocation had been raised. Because of world over-production, the sixty-two Jos mines—which have been in operation for fifty years—in 1958 were forced to cut their production almost in half, from 9,535 tons to 5,204 tons but an agreement reached in 1959 now allows them to produce at 80 per cent of capacity. Nigeria is the world's seventh largest tin producer (5 per cent of the total) but the mineral is a wasting asset and known reserves are sufficient for only ten more years of mining.

We drove out with a bearded South African miner to have a look at one of the mines on the edge of town. The red tin-bearing soil is cut from the surface with massive draglines and blasted under water pressure through a series of sluices. Being heavier, the tin ore sinks to the bottom while the mud is washed away. The process scoops out whole hillsides and makes a general mess of the landscape. But the companies pay the native owners compensation for the land they appropriate and, when it is mined out, are required by law to replace at least 75 per cent of the soil. They grade the land and sometimes sow grass or a crop before turning it back to its original owners. As in the

Sierra Leone mines, labour works here without a contract but the turnover is slight. The tin is shipped out in seventy-pound bags and theft is a big problem. Some small and unscrupulous firms find it more economical to buy stolen tin and then pass it off as production from their own virtually idle mines. Columbite, the ore of niobium, a by-product of tin mining, has also created some problems here. Columbite is highly heat-resistant and is valuable in the production of jet engines. Nigeria has 75 per cent of the world's supply and the United States stock-piled it from 1952 to 1955, paying a 100 per cent bonus on deliveries. As a result, expensive machinery was moved in, efforts were pressed to mine columbite at the expense of tin, and exports of the former rose to 3,000 tons per year. Because of the bonus, little columbite was available on the general market so manufacturers either stayed with the alloys they were using or developed other substitutes. When the United States stopped stock-piling, Nigeria was unable to find an economic market for its columbite and production fell to 737 tons in 1958. And much machinery stands idle. There is plenty of iron ore on the Bauchi plateau but it has not as yet proved economic to develop it.

From Jos we slipped down off the plateau at its north-western edge and drove across flat, open country to Kaduna (a Hausa word meaning 'crocodiles'), the capital of the Northern Region, a clean, sterile, artificial town which owes its existence to its central location. Zungeru, Azikiwe's home town, was the North's first capital (1900–1917). Lugard intended Kaduna, which lies on a grass savannah 2,116 feet above sea level, to be the capital of all Nigeria but the plan was dropped during World War I. It is an important railway junction (the North contains 80 per cent of the nation's track mileage) and has a population of 55,000. There is a large polo field (the father of the present Emir of Katsina introduced the sport to the horsemen of Nigeria) and be-turbaned cabinet ministers zoom around town in block-long Pontiacs and Oldsmobiles of pastel shades which usually seem to clash with their colourful gowns. Kaduna has its British Council, which seeks to inculcate the locals with a love for Shakespeare and the rule of law, and its U.S.I.S., which battles manfully to sell something more nebulous called The American Way of Life. The two indulge in a generally good-natured rivalry and, the first night of our arrival, their respective champions were to discuss British and American government for the benefit of a presumably avid audience at the Sabon Gari (strangers' quarter) Community Centre. Somebody had forgotten to put up the announcements and only about a dozen Nigerians, mostly Southerners, were on hand (the British Council had drawn a full house the previous week; lecture subject: British marriage customs). They had heard there was to be a dance but politely sat through the forthcoming harangue. The one Northerner present pointed out that the U.S.I.S. spokesman had neglected to explain how the nobles fitted into the American scheme.

Kaduna has a school for the blind which does good work in teaching them to make baskets. But most of the afflicted stay away because, in a Muslim country, begging is a profitable occupation since charity is a duty which helps the faithful to reach Paradise. Kitty was asked to tea by some wives of African government officials after visiting the school and reported that they were surprised to hear about the number of Negroes (300,000) living in Washington. They inquired about racial tension in Kenya and asked if it was true that blacks in the Union of South Africa had to walk on separate streets from whites.

The Sardauna hopes that Kaduna will become the industrial centre of the North, which now has only a dozen large cotton ginneries, a few groundnut mills, a boat-building factory at Makurdi and a dairy on the Bauchi plateau. The city is on the Kaduna River, which provides water and electricity, and a proposed dam will make both more abundant and cheaper. A start was made in 1956 with the construction of a £1·1 million textile factory jointly owned by the regional government and British investors. Its air-conditioned main building covers 4·5 acres and is claimed to be the largest in Africa. Three hundred automatic looms with 14,000 spindles run by 500 Nigerians turn out 12 million yards of grey baft each year (the North consumes 33 million yards) and a £400,000 estension raised 1960 production to 15 million yards.

We paid a visit to the West African Institute for Trypanosomiasis Research (blessedly contracted to WAITR), established in 1951 at a cost of £450,000, where British and American scientists are engaged in important tsetse fly research. The flies, which can be distinguished by the scissor-like position of their wings when at rest, are kept in cheese-cloth cages inside locked strongrooms. They are fed on a special flock of goats kept by WAITR and, to a lesser extent, on rats and guinea-pigs. The goats are used for one week, then rested for two; otherwise, their sides become bruised and the tsetses die of starvation because the flow of blood is hindered. Male tsetses must be a week old before undertaking familial duties while females are most willing to be fertilized at an age of three days. The female's breeding ability slows drastically after a hundred days. From this study of the love-life and habits of the fly, scientists hope to find a drug which will confer immunity for a year.

Only the malaria-bearing mosquito has played a more important role in banning the white man from Africa. If an effective immunization for men and cattle could be developed, it would open up literally thousands of square miles which today lie waste in Africa. And it would have another less pleasant effect: wild game, which is immune to the fly, would be eradicated as men and domestic animals moved into their last refuges. My heart was only half with the scientists of WAITR.

Zaria, an old walled city to the north of Kaduna, is the new educational centre of the North, as Katsina was the old one. Education in the North today is far advanced over what it used to be but in 1959 only 250,000 children were in school and most of these drop out after three or four years. In a country four times the size of Britain with a population double that of Australia, there are only thirty-one secondary schools. There was no provision at all for girls' education until 1928. The North has less than 10,000 teachers (there are 4,000 in training) and only 4,000 secondary school students. Less than fifty Northerners have university degrees—but 782 have now been awarded university scholarships by the regional government—and there are said to be only 500 Northern secondary school graduates. No more than 10 per cent of the school-age population is at school and the literacy rate hovers around the same figure. In an effort to change all this, the regional government between 1955 and 1960 spent £17 million of its £89 million budget (other major items: roads, £10 million; agriculture, £9·7 million; health, £9·6 million) on education. Of this year's £14·9 million recurrent budget (£9·1 million was appropriated for capital works), £2·3 million, or about 15 per cent, is allocated to education.

But the thirst for education among Northerners is not nearly as compelling as it is in the South. Said one British education officer: 'A Southerner will spend 80 per cent of his income to educate his children but a Northerner won't give you tuppence. We have to drive them to school and even then less than 10 per cent of the school-age children attend. Lack of funds and personnel makes it impossible for us to do more than keep pace with the natural increase in the population. Female education? Not on. We're aiming at a 2–1 ratio of boys to girls but the best we can do now is 10–1. The Sardauna and a few others say they're in favour but there's really bedrock opposition to it in any way, manner or form. There is a government girls' secondary school but most of the students are Christians. Some politicians seem to look on this school as a convenient place to inspect possible candidates for their harems. We have no Northern teachers with university degrees. In the past we took a likely looking boy with a couple of years of school, gave him a hunk of chalk and told him to get on with the job. It was all we could do. Now the North is paying for it.' Lugard's chickens, it seems, are coming home to roost.

At one stage it was thought that an adult literacy programme might help to solve the North's problem. A scheme was launched in 1948 with a goal of 25 per cent literacy throughout the region. To date more than one million people have gone through ten thousand *Yaki da Jahilci* (Fight against Ignorance) centres at a cost in excess of £1 million. Nobody really knows how effective it has been and another education officer described the programme as 'a farce, a solid mass of corruption' in which unlettered tutors sold literacy certificates at a shilling a time. In an attempt to encourage literacy, the regional government in 1954 formed the Gaskiya Corporation. Gaskiya is the Hausa word for 'truth' and the Hausa publication is called *Gaskiya Ta Fi Kwobo* or 'Truth is Worth More than a Penny', which is the price of the paper. Another twice-weekly publication of the corporation is the English-language *Nigerian Citizen*. The circulation of neither is more than 20,000.

At the root of the problem is the fact that Northerners, leaders and commoners alike, neither understand Western education nor are sure they want it. Most leaders realize that they need educated men to compete with the South; they also realize that, as surely as night follows day, an educated proletariat, as has happened elsewhere in the world, will rip the traditional fabric of Islamic society. One member of the regional House of Assembly has suggested, as a means of remedying the North's lack of secondary schools, that all primary schools be designated secondary schools. He was lustily applauded by Honourable Members. Money, of course, is a big problem. The North spends less than £1 *per capita* each year on all government expenditures and you don't get many schools out of that. In contrast, the East spends two and a half times as much and the West five times as much *per capita*. The North just doesn't have the money to spend.

In addition to an excellent secondary school and an agricultural institute neither of which we had time to see, Zaria has three schools worth telling about. The Institute of Administration is something worth duplicating on a continent in the process of taking control of its own destiny. The school, called Kongo because troops from the Belgian Congo were stationed during the war on the hill outside Zaria where it stands, offers courses in Hausa and English designed for everybody from emirs to apprentice clerks. Standards are high and, between its founding in 1954 and 1959, 69 emirs and chiefs, 73 local councillors, 308 district scribes and 221 local officials have struggled through courses in everything from how to write a business letter to the proper way to build a road. In addition, more than 2,000 other officials have taken extension courses. On a lower level—but an important one if the North is ever to have its own civil service—more than 1,300 clerks have been trained. In 1960 the Institute opened a law school whose graduates may be admitted to the bar, depending on the attitude of the Inns of Court (there are only five Northern lawyers, two doctors).

But the apple of the eye of M. J. Bennion, who directs Kongo, is the Administrative Course. This programme is designed to train young Northerners to step into the shoes of the white administrators who for years singlehandedly ran areas the size of Scotland. Being a district commissioner requires some qualities which are not always evident in Africans: he must be able to turn his hand to anything from running a court to repairing a recalcitrant generator, he must be physically tough, mentally sharp and morally incorruptible, he must be stern but fair; most of all, he must be capable of understanding and appreciating an alien people. And a Kanuri is no less alien to a Nupe than is an Englishman.

Candidates must have at least a high school education and university graduates are preferred. Courses taken range from comparative religion and public finance to first-aid. After they finish their academic course, student officers are shipped down to Man O' War Bay in the Cameroons for a physical conditioning and leadership course which approximates Marine Corps boot camp. There they shed their dapper city clothes and are issued khaki shorts and a pair of tackies. They row out to sea in small boats, build bridges, climb Mount Cameroon. Four have died in the process but graduates of Man O' War come out with something worthwhile—the realization that a man must face his own weakness and conquer it.

When the first ten-month course was established in 1957, Bennion had 450 applicants. He accepted sixteen and all but three of these passed out to become assistant district officers with the same pay, privileges and responsibilities as their English colleagues. If institutes like Kongo can succeed, African independence can have real meaning, for these are the men who will be entrusted with the lives of their fellow-countrymen. If they are of a high standard, all will be well; if they fail, nationhood becomes meaningless. Bennion, who says that his students are 'bulging with enthusiasm and as keen as mustard', thinks they can do it.

The Institute is small, pleasant, clean, practical and without frills. Students are housed in three triple-storey hostels, each with seventy-five single rooms. There are forty-nine staff houses, sixteen houses for senior 'students' such as emirs, three classroom blocks, a mosque and a chapel.

On the other side of Zaria is the Northern branch of the Nigerian College of Arts, Science and Technology. This is the largest of the three branches (nearly 400 students) and its buildings are modern and impressive. The emphasis in Zaria is on engineering and architecture and there are several hundred students who, when they are not being expelled *en masse* for discipline problems (as happened during our visit), learn how to build skyscrapers and construct super-highways. Although the college is important to the North, which contains no university, I somehow had the feeling that the curriculum offered was a bit too removed from actual conditions in the North. Mechanics, bricklayers and masons, it would seem, are more necessary at this stage of the game than high-level technicians who are difficult and expensive to train. A school linked closely indeed to the life of the North is Kano's School of Arabic Studies, headed by bearded Sheikh Awad, a grizzled Sudanese. This twenty-five-year-old institute teaches Arabic, Islamic law, history and literature to aspiring Koranic teachers, scribes, emirs' staff assistants, and Islamic magistrates. Tuition is free, the staff is composed of three Sudanese, three Britons and nine Nigerians, and there is a small but scholarly library. It is this traditionalist school which is to serve as the core of the North's future university. Shortly after independence, the Sardauna laid the cornerstone in Kano of what will be known as Ahmadu Bello College. The School of Arabic Studies will be absorbed into it and some time in the future it will become the University of Northern Nigeria.

At the lines of the Royal Nigerian Regiment I met Captain Zahariya Mailamari, a lean, tough Kanuri with a British accent so broad you could drive two Cadillacs abreast across it. Mailamari, who is in his early thirties, is Nigeria's first pro, its first graduate of Sandhurst. He is not the senior African officer of the federal army (sixty-seven Nigerians hold commissions and more will qualify this year)—there is a major and four other captains are senior to him—but he has the country's most important military job: he commands the Boys' Company, which is the training school for future Nigerian officers. Sons of soldiers and other boys with good qualifications enter at the age of fourteen and receive a five-year training course leading to a high school diploma. Outstanding graduates are sent on for more schooling and become officers while those not up to this standard are commissioned as warrant officers. All must serve for at least three years after graduation and, in the event, almost all stay on to become professionals. In addition to their academic instruction, the boys study strategy and tactics, weapons, army organization and undergo leadership tests. At the time of our visit, they were tackling with considerable gusto the problem of how four of them were to get a bucket of sand over a ten-foot wall with the aid of a single rope without boys or bucket landing in a 'mined' area.

It will be a long time before Nigeria's 6,400-man army (Nigeria also has a two-ship navy with 25 officers and 240 men), which now has 200 British officers and non-coms, can be fully officered by Nigerians. But men like Mailamari are working hard to make sure that, when the day does come, there will be no lowering of standards. In countries in which the trappings of democracy are sometimes more in evidence than the essence, the army can—as happened in the Sudan—become the last bulwark of real liberty as opposed to political licence. Nobody hopes that this will happen in Nigeria. But should it ever come to that, a Nigerian officer corps of intelligence and integrity would become a real national asset. Mailamari's boys will be those officers.

Under a desert sun which made the air come off the road in quivering waves and manufactured a genuine mirage of the lake variety on the baked hills, we came to Kano, which is to Northern Nigeria what Lagos is to the South. The city, the capital of a province whose population exceeds that of Wales, cannot have changed much since the British captured it and, in fact, Christ would find little here to surprise him except the bicycles, on which men in flowing robes are fond of stunting, as if they were Arab chargers. The walls of the city, which were built in the fifteenth century and have a circumference of eleven miles, have crumbled into dust heaps where the goats forage but little else has changed. The thirteen city gates still stand and the Cow-Fulani—called Boroje—olive-skinned desert nomads with hair as straight as spaghetti, still drive their white cattle in from the plains to barter for kola nuts, antimony, bits of glass and cloth. The Cow-Fulani have kept themselves racially pure while the Gidda, as their town cousins are called, have interbred with the darker Hausa and their slaves from the South and have lost most of their distinguishing characteristics. A Cow-Fulani wanders all his life with his herds, living in huts of poles and leaves like Indian wigwams, and he literally can speak the language of his cattle. Each beast answers to his name, like a dog, and it is said that the Fulani once used their bulls in war as a panzer force to break enemy ranks. They certainly used them in 1959 to disrupt meetings held by Action Group candidates. Many a district officer has recorded his inability to collect the *jangali*, a head tax on cattle: at the first signs of a pesky revenue officer, the Fulani herdsman simply whistles and his cows thunder off into the bush and will not stop until he calls them. The men are as straight as lances and the women are of such extravagant beauty that many an Englishman has taken them to his bed and thought no more of his broad-beamed sweetheart waiting at home. The Fulani are a very reserved people and demonstration of great sorrow, joy, interest or excitement is considered bad form. Before young men may marry, they must undergo an ordeal to prove their courage: while they laugh or pretend to groom their hair in a hand mirror as a sign of their contempt for pain, they are beaten until the blood flows. A Fulani aristocrat true to the old ways will eat neither in public nor with his wives and children.

Settlement of Kano dates from A.D. 999 when a group of smiths occupied Dalla, a precipitous hill in the northern part of the city, although there are those who say that the original inhabitant was a giant who killed elephants with a club and carried them home over his shoulder for dinner. In the old days the trek from Tripoli to Kano took as long as eleven months; now you fly it in five hours and are greeted at the Kano airport by a Hausa riding a camel who raises his clenched fist, gives the salute ('Sannu!'), then blows an ear-splitting blast on his eight-foot trumpet. But the caravans still come to the *Fagge*, the old camping spot outside the walls, and blue-veiled Tuareg rub elbows with Shuwa Arabs from Lake Chad, who speak a type of classical Arabic no longer used in the rest of the Islamic world, under the scrutiny of the Emir's *dogari*, mounted police who wear robes of red and green, red turbans and carry lances at the ready. Fulani chiefs, perhaps forgetting that their supremacy was based on the bow and that they adopted the horse from the defeated Hausa, ride through the teeming streets leading saddled but riderless horses as a sign of wealth.

Kano is nothing if not substantial. Its earth walls once were fifty feet high and eighty feet wide at the base. Additional protection was afforded by a moat filled with thorns which circled the 7·5 square miles of the city (today there are another ten square miles outside the crumbling ramparts). Of the new construction the most impressive edifice is the new mosque of glittering white with its two minarets like elongated chessmen and its dome of shining green. From the top of one of these you see the great open spaces left within the walls to provide grazing and room for crops in the event of siege. The mosque was built by the Public Works Department, which in one stroke of beauty almost wipes out the memory of the thousands of ugly edifices it has built. The Emir's palace, a low mud structure, covers twenty acres and is said to shelter five hundred people. Kano smells of dust, grease, curing leather, spices and excrement. And it is hot, so hot that the principal hotel serves breakfast from 4.30 a.m. for those who cannot sleep and want to get to their offices to work before the heat becomes unbearable. Government office hours are from seven to two with an hour out for breakfast and Kano sleeps in the afternoon.

The city for centuries has been famed for its dye pits. These are narrow, evil-smelling holes as much as twenty feet deep filled to the brim with an indigo solution. Kano cloth, made on hand-and-foot looms in six-inch strips and then sewn together, is dipped in this and, depending on the length of the immersion, comes out in shades from light blue to midnight black. More interesting to me were the cloth beaters: while we were at the dye pits, I heard rhythmical drumming of an odd resonance which I followed to a small hut. There, in the darkness, six men sat cross-legged on either side of a large log. Across the log lay a piece of blue cloth. With one hand the men, who had huge chests and biceps but were under-developed below the waist, as if they had been at it for years, threw specks on to the cloth which they beat into the material with enormous mallets held in the other. They beat butter, indigo, gum arabic and mica into the very fabric of the cloth, which comes out glossy, heavy and stiff, like the finest satin. The cloth is never washed and is prized from Tunis to the Congo. Other craftsmen of the city include the metalworkers, who cut boxes from scraps of tin, oil drums and discarded car fenders, and the saddlemakers, who build ornate, high-pommelled creations festooned with bits of metal, bright cording and colourful bits of cloth. A curious industry is the manufacture of Spanish fly from the cantharides beetles, green iridescent monsters who visit Kano only in September. They can spit a blister-raising juice for six feet.

Like all Hausa towns, Kano is a maze of red mud walls. Each man's compound has its ramparts, and narrow passages through which only one man at a time can pass link large areas of the city. Deep in the city where the sun never reaches, Kano exudes an atmosphere of ageless mystery, of stark poverty, of riches beyond counting, of the saintliness of Old Testament holy men, and of an oriental sin refined to a degree of voluptuousness too rich for men of the cold and misty forests of northern Europe. History is very close to you. Many an old greybeard dozing under a cloud of flies fought Lugard through the streets fifty-seven years ago. And any old man may legally be a slave, for only those born after April 1, 1901, have been proclaimed free as their birthright. Kano is one of the great trading centres of the world. To it the camel caravans bring, as they have always done, potash from Lake Chad, salt from the Sudan, antimony in shining heaps, hand hoes, ju-ju bells, cotton, brown native sugar, mirrors, rifles, yams, cassava the size of logs, spices, millet, python skins and gold dust. Less exotic commodities brought more prosaically by the railway, which reached Kano in 1911, include trinkets from Birmingham, blankets and skull caps from Czechoslovakia, watches from Switzerland, and sewing machines from Scotland and Japan. The caravans take away on their swaying frames indigo, cloth hand-woven, dyed and beaten with gum until it glistens stiffly, hand-worked leather goods ('Morocco' leather is made in Nigeria from the skin of the red Sokoto goat), embossed saddles, cruel-looking bits, coral. And perhaps a slave or two. The market 'bank' interested me most. In a cool, dark stall in the market sat old men with every currency in the world spread out before them. One ancient 'teller', sipping a cup of soup made from the leaves of the baobab tree, had clutched between his toes, as he sat cross-legged, American dollars, Belgian francs, Italian lire, *East* German marks and English pounds. Spread out before him in heaps were the silver and copper pieces of as many currencies, including Maria Theresa dollars. In addition to its traditional role as a caravan crossroad, Kano has become a major air stop and you can buy a ticket here for New Delhi or New York, Johannesburg or Edinburgh. So great has become the flow of travellers that Kano has become cynical and ragged little boys follow white men through the streets shouting 'Baturi! Baturi!', meaning foreigner, and all the prices go up. The little girls, who when they marry at fourteen or fifteen will go into purdah and spend the rest of their lives in seclusion, paint their faces shamelessly with antimony and rouge, waggle their bottoms as an earnest of their approaching womanhood.

Vultures squat upon every building, between strangely phallic out-croppings called *zanko*, 'dogs' ears', which originally were designed to keep rain from seeping in corners but now are largely decorative. The vultures join the goats in performing the vital function of keeping Kano clean, for there is no plumbing. The walls of some houses are covered with geometric designs which are sketched into the mud before it dries. Building material is dug from the great borrow pits which dot the city, forming lakes which gradually dry up towards the end of the dry season. Walls often crumble during the rains and are later rebuilt from the same mud. So no building in Kano is either new or old. All are ageless, eternal and linked with the earth so closely that they seem almost like caves. Inside the walls live 100,000 people. Outside in the Sabon Gari, which has a population of 40,000, live the hated Southerners. The Sabon Gari is more modern than the city and life here has the jump and energy of the South, and lacks the ageless dignity of the old city. Here are ramshackle printing shops, tiny native book-shops, restaurants, separatist churches, open-air cinemas and petrol stations open all night when, because of the heat, most journeys are made. Here a man may walk out with his women and get drunk if he wants to. The penalty for public drunkenness in the city is still forty lashes. Here it was that Akintola dared to make a political speech in 1953, the first made by a Southern leader in the North: 36 were killed and 214 injured.

Next to the Sabon Gari is the Nasarawa, the 'Conquerors' Quarter', a relatively shady section where the Europeans live and trade, splash in the swimming-pool of the Kano Club and worship in their pint-sized church. The Nasarawa is so cut up by railway spurs that one has the feeling of living on a siding. The streets are jammed with sweating blacks pushing great trucks loaded with groundnuts through the streets, for Kano is the centre of the growing area of this crop, which provides 65 per cent of the North's revenues.

Until a few years ago, one of the sights of the city was 'the pyramids of Kano', great piles of groundnuts covered with green tarpaulins which sometimes had to wait months before there were railway cars to move them to the coast. New diesel locomotives and additional rolling stock have made the pyramids a thing of the past.

Of the £54 million earned by Northern agricultural products in any given year—and nineteen out of every twenty Northerners live off the soil—£40 million comes from groundnuts. All the North's products, like those of the other regions, are bought, exported and sold through a regional marketing board, whose prime motives are to provide a stable price for the farmer, improve grades and increase production. Since the boards were regionalized in 1949 (before that each crop had its marketing board on an all-Nigeria basis), groundnut exports from the two million acres under production have zoomed from 175,000 to 700,000 tons per year, making Nigeria the world's largest producer, accounting for 35 per cent of the total. Although production fell in 1959 to 532,000 tons, completion of the Bornu rail extension is expected to raise the average annual export crop to 750,000 tons by 1965. Despite the fact that world groundnut prices have been falling in recent years, the Northern Region Marketing Board, digging into heavy wartime profits, has kept the price to the Nigerian grower well above the world level. Now the kitty is almost empty and prices are going to have to drop to a more realistic level. That means less income for the farmer, a smaller tax revenue for the region, and fewer schools and hospitals for Northerners.

I asked a marketing board executive if the Northern cabinet ministers, who control the board, fully understand the situation. His answer: 'When I told one of them that the world market was low, he told me "you must find us another world market". Judge for yourself.'

As has been noted, groundnuts account for £40 million and tin for £7 million of the North's £61 million worth of exports. The third important money-earner is cotton. In 1958 Nigeria exported 241,000 400-pound bales worth £7·3 million, 98 per cent of it from the North. Hampering the development of a more prosperous region are the primitive methods of the cotton cultivators: experiments indicate that use of good seed, application of manure and utilization of insecticides could increase yields from 250 pounds per acre (worth £6) to 2,200 pounds (worth £54), thus paying costs and leaving a large profit.

So the North, although it has political control of Nigeria, has many problems to face before its people will reach the level of Southern Nigerians. It needs more money, more schools, more hospitals. But if its leaders are not the greatest democrats in the world, they possess a sound and balanced character which augurs well for the stable development of the region. On the occasion of the achievement of self-government, the Sardauna told his people that 'self-government does not mean that anyone may scramble for what he wants for himself; it does not mean that anyone may cast off all restraint and behave in an irresponsible manner; it does not mean that those in authority need not be heeded; it does not mean that the laws need not be obeyed.

It does mean that we must all work harder, that we must bear more responsibility, that we must all show tolerance towards each other.' Those are wise words and they have been said too seldom in Africa. Now it is to be hoped that the Sardauna, taking a leaf from Aminu Kano's book, will give the people of the North what they are entitled to as free men: a greater share in their own government, a larger economic hope for their children and, most important of all, the fundamental freedom of political dissent.

NIGERIA TOMORROW

Nigeria's political power will depend to a large degree, as it does with other nations, on its economic position. Its basic condition is sound: it has an adequate and expanding rail system and, by African standards, a decent highway system; it possesses an ample labour force, an increasing number of qualified technicians and a reasonable standard of living; with its resources of cocoa, palm oil, groundnuts, cotton, tin, columbite, coal and oil it boasts one of the most diversified economies in the New Africa. Production of each of these could unquestionably be expanded (the value of exports rose by £27 million in 1959) and there are a number of new possibilities, such as a steel industry based on Eastern coal and Northern iron. The two principal limiting factors at the moment are lack of sufficient hydro-electric power to industrialize and the fact that, good as it is, the communications system as it now stands is unable to handle much more tonnage.

Both of these deterrents may be removed in a scheme which will dwarf any other development project in the New Africa. What the Nigerian government hopes to do is to make good the age-old dream of Mungo Park and MacGregor Laird, of George Goldie and Frederick Lugard, to turn the mighty Niger into a mammoth highway down which the products not only of Nigeria but of much of Gallic Africa can float in heavy volume and at low cost. No other similar project since the St. Lawrence Seaway so excites the imagination.

At the moment, the Niger handles little of the nation's traffic. The railways carry 2·8 million tons of freight (and eight million passengers), which is 58 per cent of the total. The highways bear 32 per cent and inland waterways account for only 10 per cent. As recently as 1955 the railways were unable to cope with the groundnut crop, which was stored at Kano. The new £19 million Bornu railway extension, financed in part by a £10 million World Bank loan (Nigeria's first) got under way in 1958 and will be completed in 1963, by which time the government will have spent £29 million on railway improvements over a four-year period. The new line, built with second-hand rails, will open up an area with a population of nearly five million. But the genial giant of the Niger, part of a 4,200-mile inland waterway system, remains the key to Nigeria's development.

There are many problems. Variations in rainfall, evaporation and run-off produce disparate depths in the river and discharge rates at its mouths, where silting is heavy. Tricky sandbars forbid night navigation and, as a result, the present river fleet is in operation only 30 per cent of the time. Hence charges are high, almost as great as rail fees, whereas in most countries water transport is only about 30 per cent the cost of rail freight.

The principal Niger exit, the Escravos estuary, which fifty years ago was accessible to vessels of 20-foot draught, has silted up to the point where vessels drawing more than thirteen feet cannot cross the bar. As a first step to opening up this great highway to the interior, the federal government is dredging the bar to twenty feet, building moles and modernizing the dying river ports of Burutu and Warri. This part of the project will cost £8 million, will be completed by 1964 and should treble the tonnage handled by the river ports (625,000 tons in 1959), as well as cutting costs considerably. On a year-round basis, the Niger is not navigable beyond Onitsha, 232 miles from the sea. Between Onitsha and Lokoja, where the Benue joins the Niger, only small vessels may operate during April and May, and only schooners can get beyond this point to Baro during these months and June. At Jebba, the highest point on the Niger accessible to steamers, the river is closed between March and July to everything but canoes. The situation on the Benue is even worse: navigation is possible to Makurdi only between June and November while Yola, near the Cameroon border and 850 miles from the sea, is open only from July to October. Garua, 100 miles further up the river, in the Cameroon Republic, is accessible only two months out of the year.

What Nigeria hopes to do—and the cost will be at least £200 million —is first to dam the Niger at Kurwasa, sixty miles upstream from Jebba (which would open the Niger to Niamey for nine months of the year), and then follow with additional barrages at Yola and Makurdi on the Benue and at the Shiroro Gorge of the Kaduna River, thus adding a third major route to the sea to the Lagos and Port Harcourt railways. In addition, the dams would provide enough power to light most of Nigeria, create an important fishing industry, make industrialization feasible, and water could be pumped at low cost to irrigate the great valleys of the Niger and Benue.

The federal government has allocated £121·5 million to the first phase of the project, construction of the Kurwasa and Shiroro dams. Unlike the Volta River project, the scheme does not depend for its economic success upon the development of a specific industrial complex but upon conservative estimates of the increase in demand for electricity, up from 77 million units in 1953 to 280 million units in 1960. After an initial borrowing of £40·5 million, the scheme would be self-supporting.

Transportation experts say that one barge-train operating over the improved system could carry the same amount of freight (20,000 tons) as fifty Nigerian railway freight trains. This would cut costs tremendously and make possible larger exports of bulk crops. But the scheme will provide no electricity before 1966 and its full effect will not be felt until 1970. This is a project which, unlike the Volta River scheme, could touch the lives of millions and raise Nigeria's revenues and the standard of living of her peoples to heights unknown in Africa. If she can pull off the Niger River Project—and Nigeria's international credit is so good there is little doubt that funds will be found—there will be no stopping this black giant.

The one cloud on Nigeria's future is a political one and it is basic not only to her position in Africa but to her very existence: is the new mystique of nationalism strong enough to overcome the centrifugal force of sectionalism and tribal animosity, to link together in a modern state feudal, traditional and Westernized societies? Like the Tudor kings, the federal government is faced with the problem of building up a central authority on the backs of truculent regional leaders. The antagonism which exists among Hausa, Ibo and Yoruba is as real as it is deplorable. And there is another dimension to this knotty problem: within each region are minority groups who fear that they will be 'swamped' politically and culturally by the dominant tribe.

The existence of these fears is enshrined in the third and last verse of the Nigerian national anthem, which implores:

'O God of all creation
Grant this our one request
Help us to build a nation
Where no man is oppressed.'

In the Western Region, the Bini people, who number almost a million, fear the dominance of five million Yorubas. In Benin, the kings are divine and succession is in the direct line. Among the Yorubas, as we have seen, rulers are selected from royal clans and their powers are circumscribed. Although Benin had early contact with the Europeans, it did not come strongly under Western influence until at least a generation after the Yorubas, who are more advanced and contemptuously call the Binis and the other minority tribes near the river 'kobokobo', meaning those whose speech is unintelligible. A commission which studied the problem in 1958 reported that 'the Binis are at least as different from the Yorubas as French are from Germans'. And what these black Frenchman fear is that the Yoruba-dominated Action Group, with permanent control of political power within the region, will control boards, corporations and judiciary, and with Teutonic thoroughness obliterate all that is not Yoruba.

Chief Awolowo is willing to allow the division of the West into two regions. But that raises the problem of the big Ibo population on the western bank of the Niger and of the 70,000 Ijaws who inhabit the delta. Although many of them are unhappy with their present condition, few would exchange it for a minority position under the Oba of Benin. In addition, cutting across the tribal groups is the religious division which finds the West's seven million people split almost equally among Christians, Muslims (although Yoruba Muslims neither observe purdah nor follow Sharia law), and animists, while the government of the West is basically Christian, thus adding an additional irritant.

Advocates of a Mid-West state based on the ancient kingdom of Benin have expressed themselves as unwilling to see such a state stripped of its outlying, non-Edo-speaking peoples. In other words, although they themselves are unwilling to be a minority, they are perfectly agreeable to dominating the tribes smaller than themselves.

The minority area of the Eastern Region is shaped like a reversed 'L' with its short axis touching the Niger. Here live 250,000 Ijaws. The two bars of the reversed 'L' meet at the Cross River, the home of 747,000 Ibibios and 71,000 Efiks. Up the long axis are a welter of primitive non-Ibo tribes. Many of the people who inhabit this minority region fear and dislike the five million Ibos who live in the crotch of the reversed 'L'. As is the case in the West, much of this fear focuses on the dominant political party, in this case the Ibo-oriented N.C.N.C. Cowboy-costumed members of the Zikist National Vanguard, the militant wing of the party, have been known to terrorize minority group voters, who have their own strong-arm outfit. In addition, the total population of the East is evenly divided between Christians and animists (there are very few Muslims), although the government is predominantly Christian.

Dr. Azikiwe's position is that he has no objection to the creation of additional states provided that such states are created in the other two regions and that no state is created which is not ethnically homogeneous, geographically contiguous and economically viable. In other words, he would agree to the formation of an Ijaw and an Ibibio-Efik state but not to a state which would include the Ijaws, the Ibibios, the Efiks and the smaller tribes which live on the Cameroonian border. Again, the smaller tribes not only fear the Ibos but mistrust each other.

The situation is most serious in the Northern Region where Hausa-Fulani raiders of the Muslim faith have imposed their rule on peoples who differ from them in race, religion and way of life. The situation in Ilorin province is a case in point. There a small number of Fulani, taking full advantage of their superior arms and the ambitions of the different Yoruba factions, was able to seize control of the government early in the last century and has held it ever since. In Ilorin, then, there is a very small Fulani aristocracy ruling a population which is 91 per cent Yoruba (but only 8 per cent Christian). Although the bulk of the population, like their masters, follows Islam, it was in many cases an imposed allegiance. In any case, Yoruba Mohammedanism is to the Islam of the Fulani as the American Baptist Church is to the Russian Orthodox. In adjoining Kabba province, which is 97 per cent Yoruba and 62 per cent Christian, the situation is even more explosive. Chief Awolowo maintains that these areas should be returned to the Western Region and this is a delicate situation which could explode at any time into tribal war.

Elsewhere in the North the situation is roughly similar. Although the borders of the Hausa-Fulani-dominated Northern Region extend well south of the confluence of the Niger and the Benue, in only a few districts south of the rivers does either tribe constitute more than 25 per cent of the population. And in the extreme north-east lies the Kanuri-dominated state of Bornu, which neither Hausa nor Fulani were able to conquer.

There are two tribes in the North, apart from Hausa, Fulani and Kanuri, which deserve mention. These are the Nupe, who number 360,000 and live on both sides of the Niger halfway between the

Dahomey border and the river's confluence with the Benue, and 750,000 Tiv, who occupy a similar position on the Benue. Both have a strong military tradition and each was active in the slave trade. The other minority tribes fear these two tribes as much as or more than they do the Hausa, the Fulani or the Kanuri. Yet each is the logical core of any new states which might be created in the Middle Belt of the North.

The United Middle Belt Congress, which would like to see all the Northern minority tribes lumped together in a Middle Belt State, has, in alliance with the Action Group, won some seats in both the federal and the regional houses. The Sardauna and the N.P.C. are virulently opposed to any Balkanization of the North—the N.P.C.'s motto is 'One North, One People'—and have received some support from both the N.C.N.C. and N.E.P.U. in this battle. To make life more tolerable for the 5·2 million Northerners who are either Christians or animists, the N.P.C. has instituted reforms of the legal code which should go a long way towards allaying the fears of minorities. In the past, for instance, Christian or animist offenders were liable for trial in Muslim courts where they were denied counsel and in which their testimony did not receive the same weight as that of a male Believer. A male Muslim could swear on the Koran that he was innocent, in which case he was released (and left to Allah's judgment if he had lied), an alternative not open to non-Muslims. In addition, compensation paid to the relatives of the deceased in a homicide case involving a Christian was set at 50 per cent of that applicable when the dead man was a Muslim, while relatives of a pagan victim received only 14 per cent.

The new code, which replaces Nigerian, native and Muslim law, provides a criminal code based on that of the Sudan, which is based on Indian law, which in turn stems from the English code. It contains nothing offensive to Islam and is acceptable to non-Muslims.

Although Awolowo and his minority group allies campaigned hard for the creation of new states *before* independence—an index of their faith in British impartiality and distrust of the N.P.C.-controlled federal government—they lost their fight and it is now virtually impossible for new states to be created, although Awolowo has now carried the battle to the federal legislature. A two-thirds majority is required in both federal houses, acquiescence of both houses of at least two regional governments, including the one from which the state would be created, and a plebiscite with at least 60 per cent favourable in the area concerned. The federal government must then prepare the appropriate legislation which must be approved again by the governments of at least two regions. Since the North will never allow the excision of a Middle Belt state from its territory and Zik has said that he opposes new states unless other regions agree, the only place where such a state might be created is among the Bini people of the Western Region. Paradoxically, there is less demand for this state than for any other.

The constitutional machinery for the creation of states is cumbersome and it is meant to be. This creates the danger, however, that legitimate aspirations may be frustrated and that separatist leaders may be driven to seek unconstitutional solutions. But proponents of the *status quo* maintain that the creation of new states would only manufacture new minorities, that unity has as good a chance of solving the problem as separatism, that the voting strength of the minorities, which constitute 42·5 per cent of the total population, is their greatest guarantee against oppression. This argument assumes, of course, that Nigeria will remain a democratic state and there are those who would contest the odds on that.

It is to be hoped that the dominant group in each region will, as the North has done, legislate to alleviate the fears of minorities within their boundaries. This is the way to a strong and unified Nigeria. Without such measures, minority peoples blocked from their hopes of separate states could erupt in a blood-bath which would ruin Nigeria.

Nobody wants this to happen. For as the Nigerian giant goes, so goes the New Africa.

Chapter 21

*

CONTINENT ON THE MOVE

The drive for independence is over in the New Africa for all practical purposes. In 1955, this vast area held only two independent nations—Liberia and Ethiopia—with a total area of 438,000 square miles and a population of 19 million. In five years since then, an almost inconceivably brief period, nineteen new nations have been born. These have an area of 4·8 million square miles and a population of 81 million. Only in the four minute and sparsely populated enclaves of British Gambia, Portuguese Guinea, French Somaliland and Spanish Rio Muni has political emancipation lagged. To the great credit of both the colonial powers and the people of Africa, these new states have been spawned with less blood let than the annual death toll from traffic accidents in the United States. This is a very real and important achievement.

Having gained independence (although nationalist leaders dearly like to say it, it is inaccurate to say that they 'fought' for it), the leaders of the New Africa are faced with the problem of what to do with the bauble of freedom. There has been a natural desire on their part to keep the political pot bubbling, born both of a genuine desire to aid in the emancipation of their still 'enslaved' brothers and by a less laudable but no less understandable urge to distract their electorates' attentions from domestic problems which were supposed to evaporate with political freedom. This desire has found expression in the philosophy and politics of Pan-Africanism.

The roots of Pan-Africanism run deep. They have their source in an amorphous black nationalism (which is quite another thing) which has been experienced for as long as four hundred years by the Negroes scattered over the New World by slave ships. This can only be defined as a feeling of being outside the society into which they were thrown, of belonging to another and alien culture tied in the dim past to Africa. Representations of this could be seen many years ago in the Dahomey-based voodoo of Haiti, in the few Yoruba words remaining in the West Indian and the American Negro vocabularies, in the terminology of countless 'Abyssinian Baptist' and 'African Methodist Episcopal' churches, in the longing when times were bad for return to this Black Zion.

The grandfather of Pan-Africanism was W. E. B. DuBois, a ninety-two-year-old American Negro educator. DuBois organized the first four Pan-African conferences, which met in Europe between 1919 and 1939 and were largely dominated by New World Negroes. Although his writings inspired some African nationalists, DuBois essentially represents the first phase, in which the important factor was 'blackness', not 'Africanness'. Another individual worthy of note in this period was Marcus Garvey, a fat Jamaican with a penchant for wearing uniforms of his own design and large plumed hats. He called for a return from the New World to Africa, swindled his supporters out of large sums of 'passage money', and ended his days in jail.

DuBois' heir was another West Indian, George Padmore, who died last year in London at the age of fifty-six. Padmore was born in Trinidad and was the grandson of slaves. He was educated at America's Fisk and Howard universities and was one of the few Negroes to join the Communist Party during the 1920's. His intelligence was quickly appreciated and he was whisked off to Russia where he joined the faculty of a red-brick institution called the University of the Toilers of the East. In addition to serving up Red-peppered lectures on the horrors of colonialism, slight, bespectacled George Padmore became chairman of Profintern, the international labour branch of the Comintern. His ability and loyalty gained him additional posts as executive secretary of the Communist-dominated International Trade Union Committee and editor of the black Communist's bible, *The Negro Worker*. The party sent him to Germany for a three-year (1930–1933) stint of writing and agitation. He took part in street-fighting between Communists and Nazis, for which he drew a six-month jail sentence.

In 1934 Russia joined the League of Nations and Padmore left the party in disgust over such bourgeois action. It was then, he told me a few months before his death, that he finally realized that 'Russia wanted to use Africa for her own purposes'. Padmore spent the next twenty years in London writing for various left-wing publications. There Nkrumah met him on the Ghanaian's return from America in 1945.

Padmore, who loved his pipe and his cricket, fired Nkrumah's imagination with his talk of a vast union of free African states and the pair were joint organizers of the Fifth Pan-African Congress which met at the Manchester town hall in October 1945. As the result of their efforts, Nkrumah was able to note with satisfaction that the congress lacked the taint of 'middle-class intellectuals and bourgeois Negro reformists' which he felt had characterized previous meetings. Here, then, was the turning point in Pan-Africanism: although Padmore continued to exert great influence on Nkrumah (he served from 1947 until his death as the Ghanaian leader's adviser on African affairs), leadership of the movement shifted from the New World to Africa and the back-to-Africa drive was dropped in favour of emphasis on the emancipation of colonial territories and their amalgamation into a large state, presumably under Nkrumah's leadership.

The first two conferences to be held on African soil took place in Accra during 1958. The first one was fairly innocuous. It had to be: in attendance were delegates from eight independent African states (South Africa did not attend) with widely divergent views of the world, of Africa's present and future in it, and of the role which Kwame Nkrumah was to play. The 'white' states of the Mediterranean littoral—Egypt, Libya, Tunisia and Morocco—divided by religion, history and race from Liberia and Ghana, could hardly be expected to dance to Nkrumah's tune. Pan-Arabism, in fact, is more of a competitor than an ally of Pan-Africanism. Nor could oligarchic states such as Ethiopia, Libya and Liberia be expected to find much in common with those nations organized on a more egalitarian basis. The only real point shared by all the nations participating was the fact of their geographic location on the same continent. The conference contented itself with coming out in favour of diplomatic non-alignment in the cold war, freedom for Algeria and economic co-operation. It condemned racialism in South Africa, the Rhodesias and Kenya.

Perhaps in an attempt to circumvent the reluctance of other African governments to accept his leadership, Nkrumah convened another conference in December of 1958 which was both polyglot and pliable, a conference not of governments but of organizations. To it was invited practically anybody who wanted to come: delegations from political parties, trade unionists, fellow-travelling journalists, leaders of youth organizations, educators, Mrs. Paul Robeson, Fenner Brockway, somebody identified only as 'Goodhart', the American Society of African Culture, Algerian rebels. Fraternal observers included three Russians listed cryptically as 'Potenkin, Jo Aginov and Azimov', 'Dambia Jack' from French Soudan, and an American Negro congressman. This was an instrument upon which Nkrumah could play and the tune he chose to compose is revealing.

CONTINENT ON THE MOVE

Despite a momentary setback afforded by the expulsion of Cissé Zakaria, 'Crown Prince of Mauritania and General of the Liberation Army', whom an alert clerk spotted as a dead-beat who had skipped out on an £80 hotel bill on a previous visit to Accra, the First All-African People's Conference got off to a fast start. In his opening speech, Nkrumah lashed out at the 'yoke of foreign imperialist domination', maintained that 'we are not bound, like slavish imitators' to accept all aspects of Western democracy, called for the unity of a free Africa, and warned that 'Colonialism and Imperialism may come to us yet in a different guise, not necessarily from Europe', a thrust which can be interpreted, depending on where you sit, at Washington, Cairo or Moscow. Conference chairman Tom Mboya of Kenya contented himself with a ninety-second speech the operative phrase of which was 'Scram from Africa'. The colonial imperialist bourgeois oppressors, that is.

The major address was that of DuBois, which was delivered by his wife, he being ill in Moscow. DuBois left little doubt about where he stands when he made his big pitch to the emergent African states to stay clear of Western financial assistance:

'You cannot choose between Socialism and Private Capitalism because Private Capitalism is doomed . . . American socialism is held at bay by sixty great groups of corporations who control individual capitalists and the Trade Union leaders . . . the African tribe, whence all of you sprang, was communistic in its very beginnings . . . for four hundred years Europe and North America have built their civilizations and comfort on theft of coloured labour and of the land and materials which rightly belong to those colonial peoples . . . the capital offered you at high price by the colonial powers like France, Britain, Holland, Belgium and the United States will prolong fatal colonial imperialism . . . you can starve a while longer rather than sell your great heritage for a mess of Western capitalistic pottage . . . you can compare the offers of the monopolized Western private capitalists with those of socialist countries like the Soviet Union and China, which with infinite sacrifice and pouring out of blood and tears, are at last able to offer weak nations needed capital on better terms than the West . . . its acceptance involves no bonds which a free Africa may not safely assume . . . it certainly does not involve slavery and colonial control which the West has demanded and still demands . . . local private capitalists, even if they are black, can never free Africa; they will simply sell it into new slavery to old masters overseas.'

631

Having described the evils of the Western nations and of capitalism and made his plea on behalf of the economic programmes of the great Communistic democracies, DuBois switched into the political sphere and asked Africans to 'give up individual rights for the needs of Mother Africa'. He concluded: 'Your nearest friends and neighbours are the coloured people of China and India . . . your bond with the white world is closest to those who support and defend China and help India and not those who exploit the Middle East and South America . . . Africa, awake, put on the beautiful robes of Pan-African Socialism!'

The two hundred and fifty delegates from twenty-eight nations cheered their approval and Chairman Mboya ordered an offending Nationalist Chinese flag to be removed after Red Chinese fraternal delegate Yang Shuo lodged a complaint. DuBois' speech might have passed as the rantings of a sick and embittered man had not the conference resolutions been of a hue scarcely less rosy.

The resolutions attacked 'the reactionary character of the institution of the chieftaincy and its sordid support for colonialism' and condemned 'racialism of alarming proportions' in South Africa, the Rhodesias, Nyasaland, South West Africa and Kenya. Although one might have had more respect if delegates had seen fit to qualify these charges, there was certainly some truth in their allegations. However, they then extended their condemnation to Angola, Mozambique, the Belgian Congo, Cameroun and Basutoland. There is as little colour bar in Portuguese Africa as there is economic opportunity or political freedom for white or black. The Congo, which became free in 1960, never under the Belgians had any form of *apartheid*. The attacks on Cameroun and Basutoland were even less comprehensible: at the time, Cameroun had full internal autonomy and was scheduled for early independence; Basutoland is ruled by a couple of hundred British administrators and white settlement is forbidden. The Basutos have internal autonomy and the last thing they want is for the British to leave: their country is a South African enclave and would quickly be absorbed by the Union.

The conference went on to characterize as 'territories where indigenous Africans are dominated by foreigners' the then autonomous republics of ex-French Equatorial and West Africa (this came as something of a shock to French African delegates who—with the exception of those from Guinea—were effectively isolated throughout the conference and kept in the dark by the language difficulty, all business being conducted in English), Sierra Leone, which was about to negotiate for its independence, Nigeria, which had been self-governing for more than a year, and the other two British protectorates in South Africa, Bechuanaland and Swaziland, which would share Basutoland's fate if British protection were withdrawn.

The conference called for the formation of 'an African Legion consisting of volunteers who will be ready to protect the freedom of African peoples' and the break-up of the Central African Federation. It rejected Portugal's claim that Angola and Mozambique are integral parts of the Metropole, and demanded the release of Kenya's Mau Mau leaders and the transfer of the white settlers' lands to the African people. It condemned the 'use of African soldiers in a nefarious global game against their brethren' in Cameroun (an insurrection against a lawfully constituted *black* government), in the Ivory Coast (to break up riots between natives of the autonomous republic and alien blacks from Dahomey), and 'in the Suez Canal invasion'. It lashed out at imperialist military and economic pacts 'such as NATO, European Common Market, Free Trade Area, Organization for European Economic Co-operation, Common Organization in Sahara'.

Kenya's Mboya closed the conference by stating that the South African situation demanded action rather than resolutions and that ways and means would be studied of giving Africans there 'material aid'. The four million Angolans, he added, 'will receive our material and other support'. He stated that 'we believe in non-violence' but added that violence should not be ruled out.

Pour me a double manhattan and call me Senator McCarthy but I had the impression when this conference was finished that the Pan-African movement, upon which so many hopes rest and which could be doing so much good, was directed either by Communists or fools, possibly both. In recent months, however, conferences held in Monrovia, Tunis and Addis Ababa indicate that the movement, with an infusion of new leadership, is becoming both more reasonable and more effective. This cannot be said for the second Afro-Asian Solidarity Conference held at Conakry in April 1960. Like its predecessor held at Bandung in 1955, the Conakry meeting, attended by three hundred delegates from seventy organizations in fifty Afro-Asian countries, contributed little more than a rephrasing of the same monotonous, Communist-inspired clichés.

The Ghana-Guinea axis, which we have discussed at some length earlier in this book, has, as critics like Chief Awolowo predicted, proved premature, hasty and ill-planned. This does not mean that the desire for some form of African unity is not real. It does mean that the early leadership of the movement gave way to the temptation of demagoguery rather than providing real and constructive direction.

In conferences held at Monrovia and Sanniquelle in 1959, 'Shad' Tubman proved to his doubters that he is an able diplomat and a statesman of some substance. At the Accra People's Conference, his True Whig delegates received rough treatment for suggesting that African union should take the form of an association of independent states. A year later, the Liberian president was able to convince Nkrumah, Touré and other African leaders that this is the proper way.

Almost all African leaders believe that the newly-independent states should co-operate in economic, cultural, health and educational matters. But even in this they have not been consistent: first Ghana and now Nigeria have given up both the currency and the airline which was shared by all four British West African territories. Nkrumah has nationalized the former West African Cocoa Research Institute and the two countries have established rival shipping lines. Here was a chance to show real Pan-African co-operation and it was missed.

On the political level, each nationalist leader has his own ideas about what sort of association is desirable and who should lead it. The four leaders most enthusiastic are Nkrumah, Keita, Touré and Azikiwe. The rest change from lukewarm (Margai, Awolowo) to uninterested (Balewa, Haile Selassie) to violently opposed (Houphouet). Rival power centres have developed in Dakar, Accra, Conakry, Lagos and Monrovia. The net result has been to diminish both Nkrumah's power and his prestige. And this was inevitable: Ghana is just not muscular enough to take Nkrumah where he wants to go.

And, as also was inevitable, the shadow of black imperialism is falling across the New Africa: Ethiopia and the Somali Republic enjoy an uneasy peace while Nkrumah has stated that the border between his country and independent Togo is an artificial barrier which 'can only be removed by the total integration of Togo with Ghana' (a solution which Togolese prime minister Sylvanus Olympio sharply rejects); the Ghanaian prime minister, by aiding and abetting dissident Ivory Coasters, has provoked Felix Houphouet-Boigny into warning him that 'not a foot of Ivory Coast territory' may be annexed by Ghana; relations are strained between Senegal and Mali.

This is not to say that there are no common grounds for agreement between the African states. There are. All object—and many made their objections public—to the use of Africa by France as an atomic testing ground (Nigerian leaders equated the explosion to 'a desire to wipe out the black race'). Ghana's action in freezing French assets of £5 million after the 1960 blast was acclaimed in most quarters, although many French Africans shared a secret pride with white Gauls on France's achievement. Most African states have now recognized the F.L.N. and called for an end to the fighting in Algeria. All condemn racialism in general and South Africa's brand of *apartheid* in particular. On these questions most African states are willing to use every weapon at their disposal, including radio propaganda (which is becoming intense), financial aid to their fellow-nationalists, economic boycott and pressure in the United Nations general assembly.

But any form of political unity, apart from general co-operation along broad lines, seems at least a decade away. When it comes—and it probably will—it is most likely that no more centralized form than regional confederations will be adopted. African leaders have done too good a job of whipping up nationalistic feeling to persuade their people to give up the nationhood which has been the great prize for so many years. The chances for confederation or even federation seem much greater in Gallic Africa than in Saxon Africa. The British territories are isolated from each other, and strong personal antagonisms exist between Nkrumah and most of the Nigerian leaders except Azikiwe. The Americo-Liberian orientation of Tubman's nation would make Liberia an uneasy partner with ex-British Africa, although the possibility of a federation between that state and Sierra Leone, with which it shares a common boundary, is not out of the realm of possibility. Gambia is too far away from the rest of Saxon Africa and too poor to enable anything but continuance of colonial rule or integration with Senegal to work.

The situation in Gallic Africa is quite different. Sekou Touré of Guinea may well join Mali, and there are strong federalist elements in the Voltaic Republic, Niger and Dahomey. To head off Mali, Houphouet has had to bury his objections to political federations and lead one himself. In either case, the Gallic African republics have a much better chance of making federation work for two reasons: they constitute a contiguous land mass and the cultural impact of the French language and culture has been great enough (in contrast to the situation in Saxon Africa) to overcome many centrifugal forces. By the same token, the highly centralized French administrative system has accustomed French Africans to think of themselves as a single group. When unity comes, it will come here first.

As for the Eastern Horn, there can be no federation between Christian Ethiopia and the Muslim Sudanese and Somali republics. Union between Somalia and British Somaliland took place in the summer of 1960. But this has no bearing on problems of federation elsewhere in Africa: the peoples of the two states are homogeneous racially, religiously and economically and this was a matter not of bringing together dissimilar peoples but of reuniting the members of the same tribe. If the nations of the New Africa were not so chauvinistic, they might follow the Somali solution to its logical conclusion and agree to some boundary readjustment along tribal lines among themselves. The boundaries of Africa *are* artificial and the chances of conflict produced by minority groups might well be reduced by such a process.

For the moment, each state is pretty much on its own and is subjected to a variety of influences. Britain and France, of course, will and should continue to play a major role in African affairs for some time to come. Culturally and financially both have made tremendous contributions to the personalities and physiques of the new nations. Although the New Africa will make its own decisions, it will inevitably be influenced by the attitudes of its former masters and present friends. Nor should the influence of lines of trade, credit and currency blocs be underestimated. The United States, as well, has a role to play here. The fact that leaders like Nkrumah and Azikiwe received their education in the United States is important. So too is America's position as a non-colonial power, although African leaders would prefer it if we were 'anti' as well as 'non'. It was inevitable that in so many years of British administration many British Africans should adopt some of the attitudes of their mentors towards the United States. Some regard our educational, cultural and moral standards as less lofty than those of Britain. But in all of British Africa there is a general fund of goodwill towards America which, in the interest both of the United States and of Britain, must not be squandered. These British African states—and Liberia, of course—all want and need American financial and technical assistance. They also expect a stronger United States position on the Algerian rebellion and on the racial situation in South Africa. If we can provide these, American influence in Saxon Africa will not be unsubstantial. The position in Gallic Africa is quite different. The French government has always been deeply suspicious—perhaps with some justification—of American intentions in her colonial areas. In addition, there has been considerably more white settlement in Gallic

Africa than in the Saxon West, and the settler population tends, as it does elsewhere in Africa, to be politically conservative, if not reactionary. As a result, French Africans have had it pounded into them for years both by government and by private individuals that America seeks to impose upon them a new and nefarious form of colonialism, that economic aid from the United States cannot be accepted without payment of a political price. And as we have noted, French African leaders have become relatively deeply imbued with French culture, a culture which has never had any doubts about its own superiority. The United States—and other nations, for that matter—will have more of a job here to convince Africans that its primary interest is the development of a sound economy and body politic. But French Africans are no fools and many realize that France has had her own reasons—and very good ones they are from her point of view—for painting the rest of the world as grasping, unprincipled and inferior.

Russian influence is growing in Africa. This, too, was inevitable, if only because such influence was totally absent five years ago. In 1955 the Soviets had only one diplomatic post (Addis Ababa) in the New Africa; now there are nearly a dozen. The economic reconstruction of Africa is going to be a tremendous job, one which may well be beyond the financial means of the Western powers. Given the precept that such reconstruction is necessary if these new nations are not to dissolve into anarchy and assuming that chaos is undesirable, it is better that such help should come from the Russians than that it should not come at all. Russian interest in Africa is no new thing (the first book about Africa was published in Russia in 1786 and a hundred new titles have been added since World War II) and it is unrealistic to expect the New Africa to exclude Soviet diplomats and to turn its back on the possibility of Russian economic assistance. The establishment of a Russian embassy in Dakar does not imply that Leopold Senghor is a Communist any more than the Soviet presence on Sixteenth Street means that the American president takes his orders from the Kremlin. The fact that an African NATO is no longer possible (the American State Department apparently is now willing to accept the neutralization of the New Africa) is tribute more to the Africans' feeling of an identity separate from that of Europe or American than to the skill of Soviet ambassadors. It is psychologically necessary for these new states to assert their complete freedom of action, their total self-reliance, before taking sides in the cold war. Two other Communist powers are showing an interest in African affairs (although many maintain diplomatic posts). These are Red China and Yugoslavia. The Chinese, who have the political advantage of being 'coloured', have launched diplomatic missions in Guinea, Sudan and Ethiopia and were active at the 1958 All-African People's Conference in Accra. Africans are intensely interested in China's industrialization programme and Peking may well turn out to be more of a political threat in Africa than Moscow. Although Yugoslavia maintains several diplomatic posts south of the Sahara, she has been most active in Ethiopia. Haile Selassie has made several visits to the Balkans and is on excellent terms with Marshal Tito, who owns a villa at Addis Ababa.

On the other side of the curtain, India, as a 'coloured' nation which has thrown off colonialism and is a member of the Commonwealth, holds a special place in African hearts. As in the case of China, many Africans feel, with some degree of logic, that they have more to learn about the technique of converting a peasant economy to an industrial one from India than they have from the United States and Britain, which are so far beyond that stage that they have forgotten many of its problems. Egypt, which made a strong bid during the 1950's to assume a position of leadership in Africa, has met with a remarkable lack of success. This failure rests on two factors: Nasser has as much difficulty masquerading as an African as Lyndon Johnson does as a Westerner; secondly, Islam south of the Sahara, because it is intertwined with a feudal way of life, tends to be a conservative rather than a revolutionary force. Muslims of the Sudanic belt regard the lax religious practices of the Egyptians with abhorrence. The Israelis, of all people, have performed the most brilliant job of diplomacy among the nations of the New Africa. Israel has given aeroplanes to Tubman and Nkrumah, and sent technical missions to most of the states of the Saxon West. Since it is a small nation, Africans feel that they can accept assistance from Israel without prejudice to their political freedom. A measure of Israeli success is that, despite Nkrumah's marriage to an Egyptian and his close relations with Nasser, Ghana and the other African nations until a few months ago steered clear of the Israeli-Arab quarrel; but recent conference resolutions have tended to put Africa in the Arab camp. In the last two or three years both West Germany and Japan have emerged as vigorous economic competitors in the African market and it is not unlikely that this may result in their enhanced political influence in the area.

In general, the New Africa can be expected to follow a policy of political non-alignment although patterns of trade and the need for financial assistance will tie it more closely to the West than to the East;

none the less, China, Russia and other Communist nations will make an effort to reverse this trend.

The type of political system or systems which will emerge among the newly-independent nations is still obscure. The level of parliamentary debate and deportment is low and shows small appreciation for the niceties of procedure. But before being over-critical, it should be remembered that the political correspondent of the New York *Herald* was able to write as follows about the American Congress on January 20, 1860, seventy-seven years after we had won our independence:

'The House has concluded its theatrical performance for this week, having taken but one ballot. The proceedings today were characterized by language of the most vulgar Billingsgate, by appeals to the wildest passions, by propositions and denunciations unparliamentary, discourteous, and disgraceful. The galleries are daily appealed to in general terms by inflammatory arguments, and often in language direct. Today so loosely was the business of the House conducted that members themselves presented more the appearance of a disorganized mob in a low pothouse than of the greatest deliberative body in the world. Unless those who profess to represent the people can give better evidence than they have done thus far, they had better not attempt to govern others.'

Africa's parliamentary trappings may be largely slapstick but they are not unique in this respect. There is, however, real doubt that Africans regard the essence of Western democracy with any real respect. In the first place, most of the present leaders of Africa are agitators, not statesmen. The man capable of employing demagoguery and intimidation to rally the broad popular support necessary to wrench constitutional change and eventual independence from a colonial power is seldom a man with respect for democratic procedure: he has used the democratic apparatus too long and cynically to regard it as anything but a technique to obtain and retain power, not as an end in itself. And, even if African political leaders wished it so, the application of democratic institutions to a primitive, superstitious and illiterate society would be almost impossible. In most Western countries, the mass of the people were experienced in the organization of democracy through trade unions and advisory urban and rural councils long before they obtained the franchise; in the New Africa, the granting of the franchise has preceded any such experience. In effect, the Industrial, Agricultural and French revolutions, the Magna Carta, Bill of Rights and the U.N. Charter, the Russian Revolution, the rise of fascism and the H-bomb, all these have been compressed into an emetic mass and forced in *one generation* down the throats of a society no more advanced than the German tribes of Tacitus' day. It is small wonder if the New Africa has political indigestion. One of the things the Africans have not been able to hold down is the role of the Opposition: in African thought the concept is foreign and the nearest translation is 'enemy!' This idea was reinforced in the days of agitation for independence when the breaking of the common front was considered reprehensible, if not treasonable. This concept has carried over after independence and, in some cases, opposition groups have done little to change the electorate's mind as to their function.

Parliamentary democracy has collapsed in the Sudan. It never existed in Ethiopia, although the Emperor has now given public opinion constitutional channels, if not an effective voice in government. The Somali Republic is heading towards a one-party system. There is no Opposition in Senegal or Mali. There is one-party rule in Guinea and Liberia and virtually that in Togo. Half of Cameroun is governed by martial law. Opposition members in Ghana are intimidated and imprisoned. Only in Nigeria, buttressed by a strong federal system, is the Opposition anything like effective. And without a vigorous parliamentary Opposition, democracy has little chance in Africa. With the ink barely dry on their constitutions, many leaders of the New Africa are talking today of 'guided democracy', 'people's democracy', and 'democratic centralism'. Nobody has bothered to define these concepts any more than they have defined 'the African Personality' or 'Pan-African Socialism' ('the African Personality,' seems to be an African way of doing things which is invoked when Western practice and theory breaks down; most Africans have no clear idea of socialism except that they feel it is somehow opposed to colonialism, hence their devotion to 'Pan-African Socialism', which seems to be not an economic system but an emotional posture). All that can be said at this juncture is that Western democracy is *not* going to work in Africa. Nor is government going to revert to a tribal framework. A new synthesis is in the making and something new in political organization is about to emerge, an 'Afrocratic' system which utilizes the form but not the substance of democracy and draws much of its inspiration from indigenous institutions. This implies limited freedom of speech, irregular and semi-free elections, a one-party system and rule of a popular dictator. Western democracy evolved from a given set of circumstances to fit the needs and aspirations of a small portion of the world's population at a given point in time. This is not the time in Africa and parallel circumstances, needs and aspirations do not exist among the peoples and nations.

The Africans themselves seem less concerned over the collapse of Western democracy than British and American observers, perhaps because they never understood or liked the system in the first place. Africa is intoxicated with the wine of self-government and she no more cares whether her governments are democratic or autocratic than an ageing father cares whether his only child is a boy or a girl. The miracle of the birth is the important thing. Africa wants not democracy but the right to rule or misrule herself, not an efficient civil service but a black one, not ballot boxes but the essential self-respect of political freedom, even at the cost of personal liberty. The slave-trade and the colonial period have left Africans with a massive group inferiority complex; what they want is to be recognized as *men*, not democrats.

This much may be said for the New Africa: it may be naïve, immature, bombastic and sometimes slightly ludicrous; it may be going off in all directions at once, often to its own detriment; it may be going in entirely the wrong direction; but it is *alive*, not stagnant. Great forces have been unleashed—within five years the Afro-Asian bloc will hold at least fifty of one hundred and four seats in the United Nations General Assembly—and Africa is a continent on the move. We may not understand her but we ignore the New Africa at our peril.

SOME SUGGESTED READING

Africa has a vast literature and this does not pretend to be a comprehensive bibliography. It is a list of books which I found interesting and helpful and which others may find so.

In any listing of general works on Africa, one must inevitably begin with Lord Hailey's monumental *African Survey*. Revised in 1956, it contains a wealth of detail although the sections on politics and administration are now out of date. John Gunther's *Inside Africa* is compelling reading but there are many small inaccuracies and it, too, is dated. A book in the same vein which preceded it but received little publicity is Oden Meeker's *Report on Africa*. Also dated but well-written is Vernon Bartlett's small book, *Struggle for Africa*. Walter Fitzgerald's *Africa* is the standard work on the continent's physical and social geography. J. D. Fage's *Atlas of African History* is invaluable.

There is no better way to get a feeling for the old Africa than to go to the journals of the early explorers, most of which are well-written, interesting, difficult to obtain and expensive. As an introduction, try *African Discovery*, by Margery Perham and Jack Simmons, which contains excerpts from these works tied together with an understandable narrative thread.

There has not been a great deal worth reading on the Horn of Africa. As far as the Sudan is concerned, I most enjoyed J. S. R. Duncan's *The Sudan, a Record of Achievement* and *The Sudan's Path to Independence*. There are other more scholarly works but Duncan, who served in the Sudan for many years, has 'a feel' for the country. There have been some recent books on Ethiopia but none to match Margery Perham's *Government of Ethiopia*, a fair and exhaustive study which should be revised and reissued. Eritrea is dealt with in S. H. Longrigg's *Short History of Eritrea*. I know of no good book on Somalia but believe that Dr. A. A. Castagno, of Columbia University, has a volume in preparation.

I could find nothing in English on the four states of ex-French

Equatorial Africa with the exception of a chapter in Alexander Campbell's *Heart of Africa* and a few pages in Gunther and in Stuart Cloete's *African Giant*. In most cases, only Brazzaville is covered.

Two small books which give a good general introduction to West Africa are F. J. Pedler's *West Africa* and Fage's *Introduction to the History of West Africa*. Very little has been published in English on French West Africa, although most general works include a chapter or two devoted to this immense area. Of great value, although its political sections are dated and its statistics are of less value now that French West Africa has broken up, is *French West Africa* by Virginia Thompson and Richard Adloff. Michael Crowder's more recent *Pagans and Politicians* helps to fill this gap. Elspeth Huxley, in her *Four Guineas*, has a good feeling for British West Africa. *The Golden Trade of the Moors*, by E. W. Bovrill, gives a vivid and authoritative picture of the pre-European African states of the Sudan.

Lady Southorn's *The Gambia* presents an adequate picture of that geographical absurdity. Moving down the coast, Roy Lewis' *Sierra Leone* is well-written and contains a wealth of material.

Liberia has not been kindly dealt with by most writers and so much has happened there in the past five years that books published prior to 1955 are no longer of much use. Charles M. Wilson's *Liberia* and Raymond L. Buell's *Liberia: A Century of Survival* are helpful on the pre-Tubman era.

Ghana is well-documented and the best place to start is with W. E. F. Ward's standard work, *A History of the Gold Coast*. Kwame Nkrumah's modestly titled autobiography, *Ghana*, describes the technique of nationalism, and J. G. Amamoo's *New Ghana* is of interest.

Nigeria has the richest store of literature of any of the nations of the New Africa. Sir Alan Burns' *History of Nigeria* is excellent while C. R. Niven's *Short History of Nigeria*, written as a text for African secondary students, deals exhaustively with history from the African point of view. Miss Perham's *Lugard* contains some excellent material on the conquest and early commercial activity of the country. Ellen Thorp's *Ladder of Bones* is an evocative treatment of early days in the South. The novels of Joyce Carey, Amos Tutuola, Chinua Achebe and Cyprian Ekwenze are all helpful in getting the feeling of this black giant.

Elspeth Huxley wrote to me in 1959 that 'trying to write a book about Africa nowadays is like attempting to photograph a horse race with an ancient camera: the subject is moving so fast that you are lucky if your film shows more than a blurred shape'. No truer words were ever written. But that is one of the fascinations of the New Africa.

INDEX

Aba Island, 26, 47

Abbas, Mekki, 33

Abboud, Ibrahim, 31–4, 37–8, 42, 45–6, 51, 54, 57–8

Abdallahi, Khalifa of the Sudan, 26–8

Abeokuta, 271, 275, 553–5, 558, 568

Abidjan, 241, 243, 247, 252–4, 256–8, 264–5, 276, 287, 434, 510

Abomey, 271, 274

Abyssinia. *See* Ethiopia

Accra, 230, 232–3, 298, 339, 473, 475, 488, 498, 500–4, 551, 588, 631, 634

Accra Conferences, 260, 301; of 1958, 36, 114, 299, 630–4

Achimota, 517–18

Action Group, Nigeria, 542, 549–50, 559–62, 571, 579–80, 594, 624, 626

Addis Ababa, 60, 63, 65–9, 75, 82, 86, 99–101, 105, 108, 113, 116, 126, 128, 131, 133, 555; Conference in, 633

Addis Ababa, University College of, 105–6

Adelabu, Alhaji Adegoke, 561

Ademola, Sir Ladapo II, Alake of Abeokuta, 554

Aden, 62

Aderemi, Sir Adesoji I, Oni of Ife, 552, 563–5

Adja tribe, 225

Adowa, Battle of, 75, 99

Aedesius, 70

Africa Association, 534

African Continental Bank, 579

African Democratic Rally (R.D.A.), 189–90, 248–52, 258–60, 263–5, 269–270, 278–80, 290–1, 303, 322–6, 338–9, 354

African Federalist Party (P.F.A.), 250–1, 265, 280, 321, 323, 326, 354

African Regroupment Party (P.R.A.), 323

Africanus, Leo, 312, 534

Agaja, King, 271

Aggrey, James, 476, 578

Agriculture: in Cameroun, 199, 210, 217, 218; in Ethiopia, 103–4; in ex-French Equatorial Africa, 183, 188; in ex-French West Africa, 247; in Gambia, 379, 381–2; in Ghana, 473–4; in Liberia, 465; in Nigeria, 620; in Sierra Leone, 420–6; in Somalia, 136, 148, 155; in Sudan, 41–4, 49

Ahmadiyya Muslims, 406

Ahidjo, Amadou, 204–14, 221, 223

Ahmed, Mohammed, Mahdi of the Sudan, 26–7, 30–2, 34–5

Ahomadegbe, Justin, 278–80

Ahoulan tribe, 225

Air Mountains, 268

Akan tribe, 488

Akebo tribe, 225

Akhito, Mohammed Omar, 87

Akintola, Samuel Ladoke, 561–2, 619

Akposso tribe, 225

Akus, 365–6, 368, 371, 386, 389, 391

Akwa, King, 198–9

Al Azhar University, 150

al-Azhari, Ismail, 30–1, 33–4, 36

Alake of Abeokuta (Sir Ladapo Ademola II), 554

Albreda, 363

Algeria, 244, 246, 266–7, 316, 348, 519, 635–6

Ali, Mohammed, 25

All-Africa Peoples' Conference (1958), 36, 114, 299, 562, 638. *See also* Pan-Africanism

Allah, Fad el, 598

Almoravid Muslims, 313, 345, 353

ALUCAM (*Compagnie Camerounaise d'Aluminium*), 195–6

Alumina, 196, 305–6

Aluminium, 183, 195–6, 305–6, 496–7

Aluminium Ltd. of Canada, 306

Amazons, 271–2, 274, 553

American Colonization Society, 438–9

Americo-Liberians, 435, 440–1, 446–7, 449, 471, 635

647

INDEX

Amharas, 64–5, 100, 121
Amharic, 65, 77, 112, 284
Ana tribe, 225
Anglican Church Missionary Society, 404, 537, 558
Angola, 186
Animals, wild, 62, 117, 129, 177, 288, 434; control of, 360, 373, 401
Animists, 52, 95, 165, 195, 208, 254, 264, 288, 313, 334, 355, 399, 406, 437, 474, 552, 558, 576, 602, 607, 624–5
Anis, Ibrahim, 32
Anokye, Okomfu, 490
Ansar, 27–8, 33–6, 47
A.O.F. *See* French West Africa
Apithy, Serou Mignan, 240, 248, 251, 278–80
Appiah, Joseph M., 390, 407, 513
Arabic, 53, 86, 151, 286, 499
Arabic Studies, School of (Kano), 614
Arabs, 139–40, 143, 158, 175, 184, 246, 293, 337, 345, 492, 599, 616
Archibong V, Obong of the Efiks, 591–2
Art, 192, 565, 568–9, 577, 587, 608
Asantehene of Ashanti, 490, 492–3, 507, 511, 515
Ashanti, 483, 490–1, 494–5, 501, 506–7, 509–14, 519–20
Ashanti Confederation, 271, 475, 489, 510
Ashanti Pioneer, 512, 520, 522
Asmara, 82, 84–5, 88, 90–1
Assab, 84, 87, 103, 113
Assale, Charles, 207, 212
Assembly of the French Union, 172, 186, 189, 206, 228–9, 270, 278–9, 290, 321, 324, 339
Assini, 244, 476
Associated States of Africa, 450–451
Aswan High Dam, 45–6
Atomic bomb, 309; tests in Sahara of, 341, 519–20, 581, 634
Aupiais, Father, 278
Awash River, 106–7, 116
Awolowo, Obafemi, 390, 541, 549–50, 558–62, 565, 572, 574, 580, 594, 624–5, 633–4
Ayres, Eli, 438–9
Axum, 70, 83, 108
Azambuja, Diogo de, 488
Azikiwe, Nnamdi, 219, 390, 549–50, 559–60, 578–86, 591, 594–6, 605, 609, 625, 634, 636

Ba, Ousman, 263
Babana, Horma ould, 347–8, 353
Baga tribe, 288
Baggara tribe, 51
Baguirmi, 188
Bahr Dar, 113–14
Baikie, William, 537
Bakary, Djibo, 248–9, 268–70, 291, 325
Baker, Sir Samuel, 26, 83
Bakongo tribe, 175
Bakr, Abu, 313, 345
Balente tribe, 333
Balewa, Alhaji Sir Abubakar Tafawa, 547–8, 550, 580, 604, 634
Bali language, 219
Balogun, Kolawole, 579
Bamako, 248, 251, 278, 316, 334, 337–9, 342
Bambara tribe, 335, 338
Bamenda tribe, 221
Bamileke tribe, 195, 203, 207, 210–11, 223
Bananas, 146–8, 195, 200, 210, 217–18, 247, 253, 261–2, 295–7, 309, 423
Bangui, 185–6
Bankole-Bright, Herbert Christian, 416
Baoule tribe, 224, 253, 258, 265, 339
Baptists, 216–17, 405, 558, 584
Barclay, Edwin J., 447
Barth, Heinrich, 537
Bassa tribe, 201, 203–4, 207, 210, 413
Basse, 376
Bathurst, 359–60, 363–71, 373–4, 377–8, 385–6, 388, 391, 400
Battuta, Ibn, 534
Bauchi Plateau, 607
Bauxite, 196, 286, 295, 305–6, 496–8. *See also* Aluminium
Bauxite du Midi Co., 306
Beecroft, John, 437
Behanzin, King, 273
Beja tribe, 94
Belgium, 112, 296, 631
Bell, King, 198
Bello, Alhaji Sir Ahmadu, Sardauna of Sokoto, 548–9, 580, 601–4, 607, 610–11, 620–1, 626
Benadir Youth Union, 143
Benin, 531–2, 537, 577, 621; history of, 565–7; bronzes, 568; Oba of, 531, 566–74, 624
Benin, Union of, 239, 243, 279–81, 355; economy of, 247, 252; formation of, 247–52, 263, 267, 270, 279; history of,

648

INDEX

INDEX

Graziani, Marshal, 78

Great Ardra, 271

Great Britain: aid and loans to Africa, 57, 157, 498, 631, 636; and Cameroons, 199–200, 203, 215–17, 223–4; and Dahomey, 273; early exploration and settlement, 244, 286, 345, 361–6, 489; and Ethiopia, 68, 74–5, 83, 85, 89, 97, 100–1, 114; and Gambia, 383–4, 387–391; and Ghana, 491–4, 497–9, 513–514; and Guinea, 296, 205, 308–9; and Liberia, 436, 439–40; and Nigeria, 527, 530, 532–6, 543, 553, 566–7, 570, 579, 599–601, 603, 606; and Sierra Leone, 407–8, 411–12, 414, 418, 426, 429, 431; and Somalia, 137, 141, 155–159; in the Sudan, 19, 22–3, 26–9, 53, 57; and Togo, 226–7

Great Scarcies River, 393

Greater Somalia, 112, 114–15, 152–4, 156–60

Greeks, 22, 24, 68, 198, 236

Grenard, André, 180

Griots, 330, 371–2

Groundnuts. *See* Peanuts

Grunitzky, Nicolas, 228, 232

Gruppo Misto, 143

Gudje tribe, 120–1

Guerze tribe, 288

Gueye, Lamine, 248–50, 321–4, 339, 356

Guinea, 214, 244, 282–8, 316, 326, 341, 370, 391, 393, 401, 420–1, 434, 442, 451–2, 457, 459, 472, 632, 635, 640; economy of, 247, 286–8, 291, 293, 295–302, 305–10; education in, 287, 291, 301–2, 308, 558; and Ghana, 234, 253, 298–302, 310, 508, 519, 633, 638; health in, 282, 286–7; history of, 246; politics in, 249, 260, 289–93, 303–4; relations with Iron Curtain countries, 292, 296, 300, 307–11

Gulama, Madame Ella Koblo, 404

Gwari, 597

Hadendowa tribe, 37

Hailey, Lord, 435

Hakims, 105

Hamar tribe, 51

Harar, Duke of, 110

Harbi, Mahmoud, 158

Hargeisa, 155

Harley, George, 443

Hassan, Ahmed, 156

Hassan, Mohammed bin Abdullah, 75, 141, 145, 153

Haud, 114, 154, 156, 159

Hausa language and tribe, 257, 267–8, 274, 499, 525, 528, 541–2, 547, 549, 552–3, 555, 560, 579, 596–603, 605–6, 609, 613, 616, 618, 623, 625–6

Hawkins, John, 407

Health, in Cameroun, 214, 218–19; in Ethiopia, 63, 104–5; in ex-French Equatorial Africa, 165; in ex-French West Africa, 247, 282, 286, 320, 337, 343; in Gambia, 365, 367; in Ghana, 474, 498, 510; in Liberia, 435, 469; in Nigeria, 526, 533, 575–6, 582; in Sierra Leone, 405; in Somalia, 136, 154; in the Sudan, 23

Henry the Navigator, 360–1, 598

Hides and skins, 146–7, 155, 218, 266, 297, 384

Hisbia Dighil Mirifle, 143–4

History and Description of Africa (Africanus), 312

Ho, 226, 230

Hodgson, Sir Frederick, 493

Holmes, Robert, 363

Hope Waddell Training Institute, 578, 594–5

Horton, Romeo. 470

Houphouet-Boigny, Félix, 234, 243, 248–53, 258–61, 263–6, 269–70, 280, 289–91, 303, 322, 324–5, 333, 338–40, 354–6, 450–1, 634–5

Howard University, 578, 629

Hungary, 58, 309

Hussein, Haji Muhammad, 146, 150

Human sacrifice, 272–4, 403–4, 437, 491–2, 525–6, 532, 565–7, 571, 587, 590

Hydro-electric power, 107, 113, 159, 179, 182–3, 185, 195–6, 227, 247, 257, 305, 327, 497–8, 531, 610, 621–3

Ibadan, 256, 529, 553, 555–61, 570, 579, 586; Ibadan People's Party, 561; University of, 419, 556–7, 585

Ibibio tribe, 575–7, 587–9, 624–5

Ibo tribe, 219–20, 223–4, 529, 536, 542, 545, 553, 555, 560, 567, 569, 576–8, 580–4, 623–4

Idubor, Felix, 545

I.F.A.N. (*Institut Français d'Afrique Noire*), 258, 274, 317, 330–1

654

INDEX

656

INDEX

Point Four Programme, 103–5
Pointe Noire, 181, 183–4
Poland, 296–7, 307, 309
Political parties: in Ethiopia, 158; in ex-French Equatorial Africa, 181–2, 186, 189; in ex-French West Africa, 202, 206–7, 229–32, 234–5, 248–50, 269–70, 278–80, 338, 347–8; in Gambia, 487–9; in Ghana, 479–80; in Guinea, 290–1; in Liberia, 452; in Nigeria, 559, 578, 594, 602, 605; in Senegal, 321–4, 326; in Sierra Leone, 487–9; in Somalia, 142–6, 150, 156, 158; in the Sudan, 30–1, 37, 42–3
Pollitt, Harry, 478
Port Etienne, 343, 350–1
Port Gentil, 179
Port Harcourt, 434, 575, 586
Port Loko, 394–5
Port Sudan, 19
Porto Novo, 271, 275–7
Porto Rico, 404, 583
Portuguese, 112, 229; exploration and settlement by, 72, 140, 246, 272–3, 318, 345, 360–2, 374, 397, 400, 406–7, 488–9, 500, 531–2, 543, 565, 568–9, 572, 593; language, 232, 409
Portuguese Guinea, 285, 316, 628
Poto-Poto, 192
P.R.D. (Dahomey Republic Party), 278–80
Presbyterians, 201, 578, 589, 594
Prester John, 60, 72
Priso, Paul Soppo, 207
Progressive League of Somalia, 143
Protestants, 203, 208
Pygmies, 185–6
Pysama, Stanislaus, 37

Qua tribe, 591–2
Quatchi tribe, 225

Rabeh, Pasha, 598
Radio Brazzaville, 170, 183
Railways. *See* Communication and transportation
Ramadan, 395, 399–400, 599
Ramadier, Jean, 206–7
Rano, 597
R.D.A. (African Democratic Rally), 189–90, 248–52, 258–60, 263–5, 269–270, 278–80, 290–1, 303, 322–6, 338–339, 354

R.D.D. (Dahomey Democratic Rally), 278–9
Red China, 24, 36, 51, 209, 265, 309, 631–2, 637–9
Referendum of September, 1958, 232, 247–9, 259, 265, 270, 292–3
Relapsing fever, 23
Republic Steel Company, 458
Republican Union Party (French Somaliland), 158
Rhodes, Cecil, 537–8
Rice, 183, 296–7, 327, 341–2, 378, 381–3, 423, 424–5
Richard-Toll Scheme, 327, 333, 341
Rio Muni, 176, 194, 200, 628
Roberts, Joseph J., 439, 444, 447, 467
Robertsfield, 446, 463
Robertson, Sir James, 540, 550
Rogers-Wright, C. B., 417
Rokel River, 396–7, 406, 426
Roman Catholics and Catholicism, 37, 53, 61, 165, 186, 195, 203, 207–8, 211, 222, 259, 276, 281, 316, 322, 366, 468, 476–7, 531, 589
Ross, Sir Ronald, 537
Rubber, 195, 218, 454–8, 461, 529–30, 555, 569–70
Rufisque, 317, 321, 333
Rumania, 58
Rupert, Prince, 362–3
Russia and Russians, 421, 639; and Cameroun, 209; and Ethiopia, 68, 85, 108, 112–14, 158; and Ghana, 499; and Guinea, 296–7, 299–301, 306–9; and Pan-Africanism, 487, 629–31, 637; and Somalia, 149, 157; and Sudan, 33, 43. *See also* Communism
Rutile, 196

Sacker, Alfred, 216–17
St. Andrews Island (James Fort), 361–4
St. John the Baptist, Fort of, 272
St. Louis (Senegal and Mauritania), 244, 317–18, 321, 329–30, 340, 343, 349, 364
Salt, 63, 314, 335, 337, 347
Salvation Army, 558
SAM (Sayed Sir Ali El Mirghani), 30–1, 34–5
Samory, Almamy, 285–6, 289
San Francisco Conference of 1945, 227
Sanaga River, 195
Sanaga-Maritime, 201

INDEX

INDEX

662

INDEX